THE LIFE AND LETTERS OF
DAVID,
EARL BEATTY
Admiral of the Fleet

'*History shows no instance of sea supremacy
once yielded being regained.*'

DAVID BEATTY
(*at Edinburgh University, 28th October,* 1920).

Crayon portrait of David Beatty
by John Sargent, R.A., 1919

THE LIFE AND LETTERS OF
DAVID,
EARL BEATTY

*Admiral of the Fleet, Viscount Borodale of Wexford
Baron Beatty of the North Sea and of Brooksby*

P.C. G.C.B. O.M. G.C.V.O. D.S.O. D.C.L. LL.D.

by Rear-Admiral
W. S. CHALMERS
C.B.E. D.S.C.

London
HODDER AND STOUGHTON

First Printed 1951

MADE AND PRINTED IN GREAT BRITAIN FOR
HODDER AND STOUGHTON LTD., LONDON, BY
HAZELL, WATSON AND VINEY LTD., AYLESBURY AND LONDON

PREFACE

THIS book, written at the request of the second Earl Beatty, is largely based on letters, journals, and papers preserved by his father, the late Admiral of the Fleet.

The Admiral wrote nothing about himself for publication; on the other hand, he wrote almost daily to his wife when his duties caused them to be apart, or when she was abroad. She carefully kept all his letters. Extracts from them, quoted as they were written, have been used to tell the story of his life, and when they appear in sequence become the Admiral's own autobiography for the period under review.

It is too near his lifetime to reveal all that he wrote, and his letters alone would fill several volumes. The day may come, however, when the historian will be glad to make full use of them; for it is certain that future generations will want to know more about the man who was not only Britain's greatest fighting admiral in the World War of 1914–18, but also the most effective First Sea Lord who ever stood up before the Cabinet as the champion of British sea-power.

W. S. CHALMERS

ACKNOWLEDGMENTS

I TAKE this opportunity to express my thanks to all the friends and shipmates of Admiral of the Fleet Earl Beatty who have so kindly provided me with personal recollections of him, and also to the Lords Commissioners of the Admiralty for access to Admiralty records. I am especially grateful to:

Commander the Rt. Hon. Earl Beatty, D.S.C., R.N., and members of his family for their wholehearted co-operation.

Admiral of the Fleet the Rt. Hon. Lord Chatfield, P.C., G.C.B., O.M., K.C.M.G., C.V.O., Admiral the Hon. Sir Reginald Plunkett-Ernle-Erle-Drax, K.C.B., D.S.O., and Captain (S.) Sir Frank Spickernell, K.B.E., C.B., D.S.O., R.N., for providing recollections and confirming the accuracy of events as seen from the bridge of H.M.S. *Lion*.

Rear-Admiral R. M. Bellairs, C.B., C.M.G., for his factual contributions and helpful guidance.

Commodore G. R. G. Allen, C.B.E., D.S.O., R.N., for his valuable criticism and advice.

Commander J. H. Lhoyd-Owen, R.N., for his careful scrutiny of all the text and for useful amendments.

Sir Shane Leslie, Bart., for his researches into family antecedents and correspondence.

I am also grateful to the undermentioned authors and publishers for allowing me to quote from their works:

The Story of my Life, Marie of Rumania, Cassell. *The River War*, Winston S. Churchill, Eyre & Spottiswoode. *Earl Beatty, Admiral of the Fleet*, Geoffrey Rawson, Jarrolds. *Memories of Forty-eight Years' Service*, Sir H. Smith-Dorrien, John Murray. *The Life of Earl Jellicoe*, Sir R. Bacon, Cassell. *World Crisis*, 1911–1915, Winston S. Churchill, Eyre & Spottiswoode. *Naval Memoirs*, Sir R. Keyes, Eyre & Spottiswoode. *Adventures Ashore and Afloat*, Sir R. Keyes, Harrap. *German Official*

DAVID BEATTY

Account of the Battle of Jutland (Admiralty Translation), H.M. Stationery Office. *Official History of Naval Operations*, Corbett and Newbold, Longmans, Green. *Kiel and Jutland*, von Hase, Skeffington. *The Fighting at Jutland*, Fawcett and Hooper, Hutchinson. *Admiral von Hipper*, von Waldeyer Hartz, Rich & Cowan. *The Navy and Defence*, Lord Chatfield, Heinemann. *Yarns of a Kentucky Admiral*, H. Rodman, Martin & Hopkinson. *The Victory at Sea*, W. S. Sims, John Murray. *The Navy from Within*, K. G. B. Dewar, Gollancz. *New Light on Jutland*, J. L. Pastfield, Heinemann.

W. S. CHALMERS

CONTENTS

INTRODUCTION *by C. S. Forester*   PAGE XVII

CHAPTER I   1871–1895   PAGE I
Early Years

CHAPTER II   1896–1898   PAGE 18
The Nile

CHAPTER III   1899–1900   PAGE 43
China

CHAPTER IV   1900–1901   PAGE 75
Marriage

CHAPTER V   1902–1910   PAGE 85
Youngest Captain to Youngest Admiral

CHAPTER VI   1911–1914   PAGE 107
The Great Opportunity

CHAPTER VII   1914   PAGE 134
The Battle of the Heligoland Bight

CHAPTER VIII   1914   PAGE 156
The Scarborough Raid

CHAPTER IX   1915   PAGE 181
The Battle of the Dogger Bank

[ix]

CHAPTER X   1915–1916   PAGE 195
Days of Tension

CHAPTER XI   1916   PAGE 220
The Battle of Jutland—I

CHAPTER XII   1916   PAGE 240
The Battle of Jutland—II

CHAPTER XIII   1916–1917   PAGE 265
Thoughts on Jutland

CHAPTER XIV   1917–1918   PAGE 293
Commander-in-Chief, Grand Fleet

CHAPTER XV   1918   PAGE 328
Victory

CHAPTER XVI   1919–1927   PAGE 350
The Fight for Sea Power

CHAPTER XVII   1919–1927   PAGE 385
Letters to Lady Beatty

CHAPTER XVIII   1927–1936   PAGE 415
'Home is the Sailor'

★

APPENDIX I   *Tribute from the British People*   PAGE 430

APPENDIX II   *Chronological Record of Services*   PAGE 434

APPENDIX III   *Rewards and Distinctions*   PAGE 436

APPENDIX IV   *The Rosyth Force*   PAGE 437

APPENDIX V   *The Last Operation*   PAGE 440

[x]

CONTENTS

APPENDIX VI   *Typical Letters to the*   PAGE 446
First Lord of the Admiralty, 1917–1918

APPENDIX VII   *Selected Speeches*   PAGE 452
1 Tribute to the United States Battle Squadron, 1918
2 Farewell to the *Queen Elizabeth,* 1919
3 Edinburgh University, Lord Rector's Address, 1920
4 Guildhall, 1923
5 Guildhall, 1925

APPENDIX VIII *Memorandum by Prime Minister*   PAGE 474
inaugurating the Committee of Chiefs of Staff, 1926

LIST OF ILLUSTRATIONS

Crayon Portrait of David Beatty by John Sargent, R.A., 1919   *Frontispiece*

FACING PAGE

Captain David Longfield Beatty, Admiral Beatty's father, from the cartoon in 'Vanity Fair,' March 1898   4

Mrs. David Longfield Beatty, Admiral Beatty's mother, from a water-colour portrait   13

David Beatty as a boy   32

Admirals Colville, Tyrwhitt, and Beatty when young officers in the Royal Yacht at Cowes, 1892   49

Lieutenant David Beatty, D.S.O., R.N., 1898   64

Gun-boats in action on the Nile, 1896. Drawing by Montbard from a sketch by H. C. Seppings Wright   81

Portrait of David Beatty by Philip de Laszlo, July 1911   97

Portrait of Ethel Beatty by Philip de Laszlo, December 1911   112

The Home Fleet moving off from Spithead, summer 1914. Photograph lent by Dr. Oscar Parkes, O.B.E.   128

'The Wounded Lion' by W. E. Wylie, R.A.   145

The Battle of Jutland by W. E. Wylie, R.A.   225

(Top Picture): The Battle of the Dogger Bank: 'Seydlitz on Fire.' Photograph lent by Dr. Oscar Parkes, O.B.E.   240

(Below): The Battle of Jutland: 'Seydlitz badly damaged'   240

FACING PAGE

Facsimile of personal message from Admiral Beatty to his old flagship, the Lion   283

'The Surrender of the German Fleet, Admiral Beatty reading out the terms. Fore Cabin H.M.S. *Queen Elizabeth, Rosyth, November* 16, 1918.*' Painted by Sir John Lavery, A.R.A.*   320

'The Day of Surrender': Admiral Beatty acknowledging the cheers of the men of the Grand Fleet   337

King George V *and the Prince of Wales with Admiral Beatty, Rear-Admiral Hugh Rodman, U.S.N., and Vice-Admiral W. S. Sims, U.S.N., on the quarter-deck of the American flagship* New York, 1918   352

Admiral of the Fleet Sir David Beatty on the quarter-deck of the Queen Elizabeth   369

(Top Picture): H.M.S. Alexandra, *Flagship of Admiral H.R.H. Duke of Edinburgh, Admiral Beatty's first ship,* 1886. *Photograph lent by Dr. Oscar Parkes, O.B.E.*   385

(Below): H.M.S. Queen Elizabeth, *wearing the Union Flag, Admiral Beatty's last ship,* 1919   385

Admiral Beatty's famous horse 'Gold Bridge.' Portrait by Nina Colmore   400

The bust of Admiral Beatty by Feridah Forbes   429

DIAGRAMS

SKETCH MAP	*The Nile to Khartoum*	PAGE 21
SKETCH MAP	*Operations around Tientsin*	47
DIAGRAM I	*The Battle of the Heligoland Bight*	147
DIAGRAM II	*The Scarborough Raid*	172
DIAGRAM III	*The Battle of the Dogger Bank situation at 9.25 a.m.*	187
DIAGRAM IV	*The Battle of the Dogger Bank situation at 11.4 a.m.*	189
DIAGRAM V	*The Battle of Jutland situation at noon*	224
DIAGRAM VI	*The Battle of Jutland situation at 2.30 p.m.*	226
DIAGRAM VII	*The Battle of Jutland situation at 4.48 p.m.*	238
DIAGRAM VIII	*The Battle of Jutland situation at 6 p.m.*	244
DIAGRAM IX	*The Battle of Jutland situation at 8.17–8.35 p.m.*	256
DIAGRAM X	*The Battle of Jutland situation at 11 p.m.*	260
DIAGRAM XI	*Grand Fleet escorting High Seas Fleet*	346

[xv]

INTRODUCTION

By C. S. Forester

IT all seems too fantastic ever to have happened, except that it did happen. If it were written as fiction and reviewed by someone ignorant of history, the reviewer would dismiss the book with a tolerant smile, as making too much demand upon the credulity of the reader; and yet the reviewer would be dissuaded from attacking the book too vigorously because he could not fail to be struck by the author's feeling for the drama of a situation, and the reviewer would be struck, too, by the author's sense of irony. Only an expert tragedian could have devised these intertwined series of events, or could have been ingenious enough to plot out the development of the action so that deeds performed conscientiously for one purpose should so frequently produce an effect exactly opposite. It would be a daring novelist who would presume to trace how a trifling coincidence in the life of a junior naval officer should, twenty years later, have the profoundest effect upon the history of the world, so that to this day men and women all over the world, from Eskimos to Central Africans, are affected in their daily lives by the results of that coincidence. And it could only be a novelist with the keenest feeling for irony and of vast artistic intrepidity who would venture to depict this man (whose decisions had been so important and whose resolution and courage had been so lofty) writing pathetically to his ailing wife to beg her not to make him unhappy with her complaints and jealousies.

Coincidence must play a large part in the life of every commander-in-chief: Alexander the Great was born the son of a king and Wellington was the brother of a Governor General of India; Napoleon made the acquaintance of Josephine at precisely the right moment and Nelson made the acquaintance of Lady Hamilton at precisely the wrong one—but if chance had sent Nelson at the opening of the French War to the Channel Fleet instead of to the Mediterranean he might never have become distinguished enough to attract Lady Hamilton's attention. Wolfe owed his command to the chance that attracted the notice of Pitt, and Marlborough owed his to the influence of his wife over the Queen. The one man who attains eventually the coveted command where a thousand others fail to do so must owe something to good fortune, however much else he owes to his own talents and personality. Even when bullets are flying he needs that good fortune; there were officers who were killed at Tientsin when Beatty was only wounded—the *Queen Mary* blew up at Jutland when the *Lion* survived.

In 1895 there was need for a new lieutenant to be appointed to the *Trafalgar*; it was the sort of routine appointment made a hundred, or a thousand, times every year. The *Trafalgar* was an undistinguished battleship of the Mediterranean Fleet, and an undistinguished lieutenant was sent to her after completing his two years of watchkeeping duty in another battleship, the *Camperdown*. The lieutenant was Beatty, but it might have been any one of a hundred other lieutenants, and Beatty might have received any one of a hundred other appointments. It happened that the commander of the *Trafalgar* was Stanley Colville, and ten years earlier Colville as a young lieutenant had been employed on the Nile with Wolseley's army attempting to relieve Khartoum. Now, ten years later, Kitchener was assembling on the Nile the army that was eventually to terminate the bloody tyranny of the Khalifa. Kitchener needed a gunboat flotilla; Colville, as a result of his earlier experience, was selected to command it. Colville had to choose subordinates, and he chose—among others—David Beatty. That was a tribute to Beatty's professional competence, and it was a tribute to his personality as well. Colville (his professional future hinging on the behaviour of the captains of his gunboats) had to guess how his selections would behave under fire and in emergency, and he believed that Beatty would behave well. That is a proof of the excellence of the impression that Beatty had made upon him, and of the high estimate Colville had made of Beatty's competence; Colville must have been personally acquainted with scores of lieutenants R.N. of suitable seniority, and his selections were limited to a mere half-dozen. But the good fortune lay in the blind chance that had transferred Beatty to the *Trafalgar* six months earlier and so made the two better acquainted. The unknown Admiralty clerk—forgotten by now in his grave these many years—who made the transfer, settled, in that five minutes' work, the course of the naval war which decided the fate of England twenty years later.

For during the prolonged peace whose surface was hardly ruffled by colonial squabbles, opportunities to obtain distinction and (more important) promotion out of routine were very rare indeed. Not one naval officer in a hundred had heard shots fired in action; even the generation that had taken part in the bombardment of Alexandria was passing. Colville's half-dozen lieutenants were the only officers out of thousands to be set on the path to glory. Nor was that all, for during the ceaseless skirmishing that went on up and down the river, Beatty received only a bullet through his sun helmet, while Colville had one through his arm, so that Beatty at the age of twenty-five found himself by the fluke of seniority the naval officer in command in action. He made every use of his opportunity and when the campaign ended he was a marked man with a mention in despatches and a D.S.O.—there were captains, and even admirals, without a single ribbon on their chests in that unbemedalled age. And of course when Kitchener gathered his strength for the final advance, Beatty's services were called for again, and he was in command of a gunboat at the victories of the Atbara and Omdurman.

He distinguished himself; that goes almost without saying, and his deeds are to be read about in a professional work. Bravery, skill, dash, energy; men had come to expect these of him. But there was another factor almost as important. For riding in the ranks of the 21st Lancers when they charged at Omdurman was a young Hussar officer, a blue-blooded young man, the grandson of a duke, the son of a Cabinet minister, who had with incredible ingenuity and by unabashed effrontery managed to attach himself to the expeditionary force in the vaguely mixed capacity of newspaper correspondent and supernumerary. This dashing young cavalry subaltern was dreaming at this time of military distinction, possibly of commanding in the years to come a British army in the field and rivalling the military fame of the Duke of Marlborough who was his great-great-great-grandfather. It was only later that he entered politics and attained to power and responsibility, and made the name of Winston Churchill famous. But it was Beatty's good fortune—and the chances against the possibility can only be compared with those against an astral collision—that when Beatty took the *Fateh* up to assist the 21st Lancers with her fire, the prowess of the 'white gunboat' should be noted gratefully by a future First Lord of the Admiralty in the heart of Africa.

But it was to be many years before that particular piece of good fortune should bear fruit; Beatty was to enjoy another at once. A step in rank was the certain immediate reward of his services, for he already had the D.S.O. He was promoted to commander over the heads of four hundred of his seniors. And as an example of how double-edged may be the gifts of fortune, it is worth noting that the other lieutenant promoted to commander at that time was a young man called Hood. His promotion helped him to flag rank, and as admiral he met his death when the *Invincible* blew up at Jutland.

It cannot be called good fortune that Beatty received immediate employment in his new rank, for the captain of the battleship *Barfleur* (who must necessarily have been consulted as to who should be his new executive officer) was Colville, who already knew him. Beatty could only owe this appointment (and to be commander in a battleship, and moreover a flagship, was a most desirable appointment) to his own talents and to the reputation he had acquired. But it was good fortune that sent the *Barfleur* and Beatty to the China Station at the very time when nationalism in China was about to burst into flame, so that less than two years after being in action against Dervishes in Africa he found himself in action against Chinese in Asia. There were some four hundred commanders in the Royal Navy at that time. Perhaps as many as six were engaged in active service in South Africa; another half-dozen fought in China. The mathematical odds against Beatty having a chance to distinguish himself and to gain further promotion, were some thirty or more to one—smaller odds and more calculable than those previously discussed, but thirty to one all the same. And when he plunged into action there were bullets that hit him, passing through his left arm. The wounds he received only left him in hospital for three days, thanks to his volcanic energy, but they left him with two permanently crippled fingers. And if some Chinese soldier across the Pei-Ho had held his rifle a little straighter, or if a bullet had diverged half an inch to touch the brachial artery, the battles of Heligoland, of the Dogger Bank and of Jutland might have been fought differently.

On this occasion, as before, any account of Beatty's military achievements lies outside the scope of this essay. It is sufficient to note that his bravery and energy were conspicuous, and that he won the respect or the admiration or the devotion of all those with whom he came into contact. His achievements had to be rewarded; no doubt about that. Nor was it a question of a mere *quid pro quo*, and neither was it the more important matter of rewarding dash and bravery so as to encourage other officers to be dashing and brave in the future. It is the duty of the admirals of today to make the best possible selection of the admirals of tomorrow. To give Beatty further promotion at this moment was to make it as nearly certain as anything could be that he would be an admiral later on. And he received that promotion; he was given the vitally important step and became captain. He was twenty-nine, thirteen years younger than the average age of newly promoted captains. With average luck in the matter of health, with even less than average luck in the matter of professional appointments, he could hardly fail (should peace continue) to end his career as the senior flag officer of the Royal Navy—thanks, in the ultimate analysis, to the chance which sent Colville and the *Barfleur* to China.

And now the German Navy began its prodigious expansion and the Royal Navy had to expand to meet the challenge. There could not be a better moment to be promoted captain than in 1900, at the time of the passage of the German Navy Law. Ships—whole fleets—had to be built; captains had to be found for the ships and admirals for the fleets. Beatty's promotion in November 1900 put him ahead of the many captains who owed their promotion to the vast naval expansion of the nineteen hundreds, so that with the numerous promotions to

[xxi]

flag rank he passed rapidly up the list during this period of transition. In a large navy or in a small navy promotion tends to flow at a steady rate; it is only while the small navy is growing large that the pace is accelerated—and the greatest acceleration is felt by those towards the top. He had been fortunate again in his moment, so fortunate that before he was forty he found himself a rear-admiral, and could read in *The Times* that newspaper's pontifical comments on his promotion.

Then he proceeded to imperil the whole safe future that his promotion opened to him. It is not easy to analyse the motives that impelled him. If he was gambling, it was a wild gamble, reckless to the last degree. If it was pique, ennui, disillusionment, then never in history has chance brought larger rewards to any sufferer from them. In either case it was prodigious good fortune, the final and most magnificent gift of all those which he owed to coincidence. He had refused the appointment which, in the ordinary course of routine, the Admiralty offered to him. Viewed as a matter of routine, the Admiralty was absolutely right. There had to be rear-admirals in a fleet, obedient to the commander-in-chief, and following in his wake. To be such a rear-admiral might be a little tedious, might even be a little galling, especially after experiencing the activity and responsibility of being captain of a battleship. An active and restless man might well feel that he was a mere fifth wheel to a coach in such a situation. The point of view of the Admiralty was that every well-equipped vehicle should carry a spare wheel. Not only that; the junior flag officers in a fleet could relieve the commander-in-chief of much desk and routine work, and if the junior flag officers found that unpleasant they could comfort themselves with the thought that in course of time they would cease to be juniors. Furthermore, while at sea they could learn something of the art of being an admiral. And there was always the possibility that the fleet might have to act in fractions, and there must always be available officers of rank and experience to take command of those fractions. So, as has been already noted, junior flag officers were a necessity in a fleet, and rear-admirals who declined such appointments were nuisances. It was all very well for an ambitious young officer to aspire to an independent command, but independent commands were rare, and while there was less attractive work to be done it was the junior officers' duty as well as their destiny to do it. If they should be tempted to refuse, it might be as well for them to remember that even in this expanded navy there were more admirals on the list than appointments available for them, and by the rules of the service unemployment ended in retirement. Lastly, there was an imponderable factor. A man might be suspected of what was called (oddly enough) 'side'—which meant that besides having a good opinion of himself he was sufficiently careless of convention to allow it to be apparent to others that he held that good opinion of himself. The man who violated that convention was suspect, as he would be if he violated any other convention, even though if the Navy read Nelson's letters (and presumably the Navy did) they could not fail to observe that Nelson had a high opinion of his own abilities and did not care who knew it. If the Navy thought about it at all, they must have decided that the man who had won the battle of the Nile was justified in 'putting on side' (although it was to be deplored), while the man who had fought at Omdurman and Tientsin was not—with his steam yacht and his wife's millions. So that with his refusal of the appointment of Second in Command of the Atlantic Fleet Beatty had, as far as most intelligent people could see, terminated his naval career. For all practical purposes it was already ended; there was the mere formality to be gone through of the necessary period of half pay, and then would come retirement.

Beatty had refused the appointment in the spring of 1911, when Mr. McKenna was First Lord of the Admiralty, and when Mr. Winston Churchill was Home Secretary. It is hardly credible that Beatty guessed that six months later those two men would exchange their Cabinet positions. Beatty was moving in good society, and he might have been in touch with Churchill, but to predict a Cabinet reshuffle six months in advance would be too remarkable a fact to be seriously considered. Churchill may have made his promises of when and if, but clearly he could not fulfil them without the consent and the co-operation of the rest of the Cabinet, and there was the electorate to be considered (this was 1911!) and the Irish Party—two major unpredictables. In any case once more the coincidences fell into place before the time-limit had elapsed. Mr. Churchill was First Lord of the Admiralty, and Beatty was Naval Secretary, and in less than two years he was in command of the battle cruisers and holding the most coveted appointment open to a man of his rank. One more chance at the longest possible odds had materialised, the last of a long series of chances, all leading up to this appointment; the naval historian can make an attempt at estimating its effect upon history, but even an actuary would hardly attempt to sum the odds against it over the previous twenty years.

For all the chances against it have not yet been considered. Beatty had long before this deliberately imperilled his career, by his own voluntary act. This had nothing to do with his professional qualifications at all, but that did not diminish the risk that he ran. He married a divorced woman. This was in 1901, at the close of the reign of Queen Victoria, but although the Queen was dead, the rigid standards she had set lingered on for many years—both before and after 1914 army officers of the highest talents found their careers wrecked by being divorced, or by marrying divorced women. There were reasons for the prejudice, even if there were not excuses. The holder of a commission might, even should, be presented to the King, and necessarily his wife might also be presented. And no divorced person could be presented at Court; that was final, incontrovertible. The Queen had made up her mind about it. So an officer when he became involved in a divorce one way or the other, had no alternative but to resign his commission. Incidentally, society still tended to frown upon divorce and to refuse to receive a divorced woman, and as half the policy of England was settled at dinner parties and social gatherings it could be inconvenient, to say the least, if a policy-maker, actual or potential, was barred from such meetings.

Beatty avoided these consequences by good luck and good management, as usual. He had been deeply in love with Mrs. Tree since 1898 when he returned to England from the Nile. But his duty took him almost immediately to the China Station, and when he came back to England he was a long time recovering from his wounds. Scandal did not link his name with hers; even when he was fit and well he was careful not to be seen alone in her company. He had the self-denial and resolution to carry on the affair only by letter. Mr. Tree was not vindictive, and the laws of the State of Illinois allowed divorce on the grounds of desertion of two years' duration. On 12th May the divorce was granted. On 22nd May, as soon as the fastest mail steamer then in service could bear the necessary papers across the Atlantic, they were married—a registry office marriage, naturally. So discreet had everyone been, so careful had Beatty been, that the newspapers missed the most succulent piece of society gossip of the year—the marriage of the youngest captain in the navy to a divorced woman, a woman who had actually lost the custody of her child on account of her desertion of her husband. The danger of disclosure and scandal diminished with the passage of time, and fortunately there was another label that could conveniently be affixed to Mrs. Beatty. She was known as a Marshall Field heiress, a very wealthy woman. And she was beautiful, and she rode to hounds, and she was a prominent hostess—with all these things known about her, gossip did not attempt to pry more deeply. And when necessary, hairs could be split to reconcile the consciences of those few people in Court circles who were aware of the facts. There must have been some close shaves as Beatty went up the ladder of professional recognition, when he became naval aide-de-camp to the King, when he received the membership of Royal Victorian Order for his personal services, and finally when he was knighted and Mrs. Beatty, the divorced American woman, became Lady Beatty. But by the time the marriage was a dozen years old, with the Beattys accepted everywhere, the danger must have been practically over. Beatty had taken a desperate chance, with his eyes open, and chance had decided once more in his favour. And the knowledge that his wife enjoyed a handsome income from the Field millions must have been a comfort to him when he was making the vital decision to refuse the appointment of Second in Command of the Atlantic Fleet.

It is a dramatic piece of irony that Beatty had taken the risks he had taken, had laboured so hard and so perseveringly, merely to involve himself in a personal tragedy. He was deeply in love with his wife, and he remained deeply in love; and the deeper his love, the more desperately his wife was able to hurt him. Sometimes she consciously made use of her power (if it can be said to be consciously), but more often she hurt him involuntarily or even unwillingly. They made each other ultimately terribly unhappy, and the irony of the situation is accentuated by the fact that neither of them could be blamed. Beatty to the end remained tender and loving and attentive—during all the long years of martyrdom he hardly allowed himself a moment's vent to his exasperation—and Lady Beatty's health was such that she could not be blamed either. As time passed her personal troubles grew and grew, according to her own disordered judgment, until at the tragic end they overwhelmed her. And it was perhaps symptomatic that she should attribute the majority of her troubles to the man she loved. In the beginning her unreasonableness wounded him continually, and when he came eventually to realise the true state of affairs he was no less wounded by the realisation. His professional distinction and his honours were of no worth to him weighed against the unhappiness he experienced.

For that matter they made it worse. The end of the war did not put an end to the demand for Beatty's professional services. Beatty sincerely believed that it was essential to his country's welfare that he should remain in harness, so that it was his duty to devote his enormous prestige to forwarding British interests in the manner that he thought best. He laboured for his country for eight years, and it was inevitable that by this time his wife should accuse him of deliberate neglect; it was inevitable that what he thought was his duty she should come to believe was merely an excuse to thwart her desire for his whole attention. The letters he wrote to her excite our pity to this day. He exerted all his ingenuity to placate her; his patience was inexhaustible. There can be no doubt that even during those dark hours his love for her was still tender and constant, and that he would have done anything whatever for her except to go against his conscience. It may have been as his *princesse lointaine* that he loved her, but the love was sincere—it was that which made his situation so frightful. And he bore the burden without complaint. No one save his few intimates knew of his troubles. Not one of the people who trembled before the frown of the First Sea Lord guessed that the First Sea Lord was himself waiting with apprehension for the next letter. There were the strains and stresses of the international conferences and of the Cabinet meetings; at the same time there were the harassing worries as to whether consultant or quack could bring a little repose to the tortured mind of his wife.

The Jutland controversy—the virulent Jellicoe–Beatty arguments—raged round him; there were questions of the most urgent naval policy to be decided, but he had still sufficient left of his funds of patience and understanding on which to draw on behalf of his wife. It is a very significant indication of his character that during this period he continued to learn; that he broadened his knowledge of men and affairs, and that even his literary style acquired some facility and polish. This introduction is not the place to discuss the acuteness of his judgment or his political sense, any more than it is the place to discuss the merits of the decisions he took at Jutland. But with regard to these last it is well worth noting that although he held strong opinions regarding how that battle should have been fought, he never once made public those opinions; it is only now, with this publication of his letters to his wife, that we can be sure what they were. He scorned to enter into the controversy. Yet along with his scorn, and despite the fact that he had been, and was, idolised by many of his fellow men, and despite the lofty position that he held and the adulation he received, it is pleasant to note the hint of humility in his letters. He had been one of the most fortunate men of his generation, but he never thought of himself as other than human.

CHAPTER ONE

1871–1895
EARLY YEARS

The family · Home life · Midshipman's days at Malta
Princess Marie · Royal Yacht · Mediterranean Fleet

DAVID BEATTY, the youngest British Admiral since Nelson, came from an old Irish family, well known in the county of Wexford for the past two hundred years. On the male side they were sportsmen and warriors. His great-grandfather fought at Waterloo, and another ancestor raised a troop of cavalry at his own expense, known as the Heathfield Horse, which served with distinction under Wellington in the Peninsular War.

There is a legend that the Admiral's great-grandmother, when believed to have died, was buried alive, and the entry of her name twice in the funeral register gives credence to this tale. The story goes that she was buried wearing a diamond ring. Shortly afterwards, the family butler entered the mausoleum and tried to cut away the ring, whereupon the corpse revived, and later joined her husband at dinner.

The Admiral's grandfather, David Beatty of Borodale, born in the year of Waterloo, was the fourth of his recorded line. He was Master of the Wexford Foxhounds for over forty years and hunted them at his own expense. He married Mary Longfield of Cork, also of old Irish stock, who, being an only child, inherited the family estates. Their home was at Borodale, in the Enniscorthy district: a fairly large sporting estate on the River Boro, where it joins that famous salmon river the Slaney.

They had two sons and one daughter. The eldest, David Longfield Beatty, born in 1841, was the Admiral's father. At the age of seventeen he went to Heidelberg University and, as a member of the Westphalian duelling corps, he spoilt the features of numerous young students with his schlager; three of his sons were destined to meet the Germans at a sterner game later on. He was a handsome man, six feet four inches tall, a hard rider, and devoted to horses all his life. He served as a subaltern in the 4th Hussars in India, where he excelled at polo and pigsticking, but left the Army early in his career and married Kathleen Edith, the lovely daughter of Nicholas Sadleir, of Dunboyne Castle, County Meath. After marriage they settled in Cheshire and for a time lived at Howbeck Lodge, Stapeley, near Nantwich. On 17th January, 1871, in this pleasant little country-house in the heart of a sportsman's paradise, David Beatty, the future admiral, was born, and although he was the second son, he was given the Christian name of his forbears. His parents were a distinguished-looking couple, and in the hunting field were always mounted on magnificent Irish hunters. These horses had been sent over from the family place at Borodale, and the Admiral's father, although comfortably off, soon found that he could do good business selling them to other sportsmen. The Admiral's friend and contemporary, Walter Cowan,[1] writes: 'The first full-sized horse I ever went hunting on, my father bought for my mother from old David. Later the Beattys came down to live in Rugby, and old David generally had a good horse to sell.'

In course of time 'old David' established quite a reputation for himself, not only as a judge of a horse, but also as a first-rate sportsman, and on several occasions he was chosen by Queen Victoria to pilot members of the Royal Family when they went hunting with the Warwickshire. A good description of him in later years is given in *Vanity Fair*, 1898, in the series 'Men of the Day'.

'. . . He was born to sport; began to hunt before he was ten; and has not yet ceased doing so. . . . Learning, on the authority of his Medicine Man, that he would never ride again [the result of a hunting accident], he sold his hunting-box [in Cheshire] and his horses; after which he mended and retired to Rugby, where he has since lived and entertained and hunted. He has always owned excellent hunters, but only within the last few years has he begun to train chasers; in which business, aided and abetted by his eldest son "Charlie" (who has already

---

[1] Later Admiral Sir W. H. Cowan, Bart., K.C.B., D.S.O., M.V.O.

won a name between the flags, across-country, and at polo), he has met with much success. . . .

'. . . "Captain David" [the father] has always been in front as a sportsman, yet he is not abroad in a drawing-room. He is always ready to lend a helping hand to the young sportsman, and his house "The Moat", at Rugby, is the resort of sportsmen and sportswomen who hunt in the neighbourhood; for all such he welcomes. Yet with all his hostility to vermin, he is very fond of a tame fox, which is quite at home under his arm. He is proud of his family, of his legs, and of his breeches; and he is distinguished by his remarkable hat.'[1]

Edith, his wife, was exceptionally beautiful, remembered for her glorious golden hair and her charm and dignity. She was deeply religious and adored by her children, who, being Irish and unruly, required firm but gentle handling.

The eldest was Charles, born in 1870. He became a well-known steeplechase rider and gentleman jockey, on one occasion riding second in the Grand National. In the South African War, while serving with the Warwickshire Militia, he was recommended for the Victoria Cross, and was eventually awarded the D.S.O. He died in 1918 of wounds received while fighting in Flanders with the Canadian Division.

Next came David, born in 1871, about whom this book is written.

Then followed William Vandeleur (Vandy), born in 1872. He is well known as an owner and trainer at Newmarket. He holds the Royal Humane Society's bronze life-saving medal, and served in the South African War and First World War.

Ten years later, in 1882, the fourth son George was born. He also became a soldier, and lived up to the family reputation as a steeplechase rider and polo player. He died in India in 1915 while serving in the famous cavalry regiment, Jacob's Horse.

The youngest, Kathleen, the only daughter, better known as 'Trot', was a close friend of her brother David, who in later years told her all his troubles. She was a typical wild Irish girl,

---

[1] In later years the Admiral was also well known for his 'remarkable' naval cap. It had a very large peak, and was always worn at a particular angle to suit the structure of his head.

taking part in all sports and riding with the best. She married Lieut.-Colonel Miles Fergusson Courage, of Preston House, Hampshire.

It was in 1885 that the family moved to Rugby, which in those days was an old-fashioned town with its markets and cattle fairs, and a social centre for hunting folk. A good shot and a good rider could always be sure of an invitation to one of the country-houses in the district, where in the evenings he could spend his idle moments in company grave or gay according to his tastes. Many of the old Victorian homes, with their pleasant gardens and green lawns, have been swept away and replaced by factories. The sport of hunting is still popular around Rugby, and quite a number of young people employed in industry get their pleasure and recreation by keeping a hunter for a day with the hounds at the week-end.

The Beattys were no exception to their times; they led the normal carefree country life of the last century, when every family depended on the horse for getting about; but they excelled in horsemanship, and rode more recklessly than their neighbours. The children would lay out their own point-to-point lines and race each other across-country. Their father had wisely taught them to ride bareback from childhood, and while at the Moat, he bought them a pack of draghounds. As they grew up they made their name as hard and fearless riders, hunting mostly with the Warwickshire and Pytchley.

They were a happy family, and sport was their paramount interest. In the shire papers and racing calendars of the '90s and early part of the present century, there are constant references to one or other of the brothers, especially Charles. Here is a typical extract: 'Captain Beatty's stable has been in wondrous form since his son, Mr. Charles Beatty, quickly shaking off the effects of a smashed collar-bone and generally ugly fall, returned to the saddle. A little time ago I observed that that daring yet cool young amateur had won five of the six chases he had contested since resuming sport.'

Young David's name appears occasionally in the list of entries when his brief spells of leave gave him an opportunity to ride. In one race at Worcester his horse ran away with him, which was not surprising, as he had only just returned from

Captain David Longfield Beatty,
Admiral Beatty's father, from the cartoon in *Vanity Fair*, March 1898

the Boxer Campaign in China, suffering from a badly wounded arm. His father and his three brothers all had serious accidents in the hunting field and on the race-course, and in later years the Admiral had more than his share. But these things were of little account to the Beatty family, for the habit of taking risks was in the blood.

They thought in terms of hunting, and the Admiral, writing to his sister (Mrs. R. F. Courage) after Jutland, described the battle as if it had been a hunt: 'I describe the battle to you thus, because only this way would you understand it!' Naval officers who are hunting enthusiasts will realise what he meant. The light cruisers are the hounds, it is their business to 'find', so that the huntsman may 'view' and the hunt can follow to the 'kill'.

Mrs. Courage and her brother, Major V. Beatty, in recalling childhood days both agree that David was their mother's favourite, and that she had said more than once that 'England would ring with his name'.

Away from sport David was different from the others. He was more intellectual and had a more vivid imagination. The sea and ships fascinated him, and his mother encouraged him in the idea that he might go into the Navy. Young David could not resist the call of the sea, so after a spell at a private school at Rhyll in Wales, he was sent, at the age of twelve, to Burney's Naval Academy at Gosport.

The entrance examination for the Navy in those days corresponded to 'Fifth Form' standard at the public schools, and only about thirty per cent. of the total number of candidates were selected: a stiff test for small boys. It was the custom, therefore, to send boys who hoped to become naval officers to a 'crammer', whose business it was to drive the required knowledge into their heads, by force if need be. 'Burney's' was a school of this type, and although it had a fine record for getting boys into the Navy, it is doubtful if the methods employed provided much of an educational grounding.

David's only concern, however, was to get into the Navy, and on 15th January, 1884, at the age of thirteen, he passed into the training establishment of H.M.S. *Britannia*, tenth in order of merit, out of a total of ninety-nine candidates. This was a creditable achievement, and the first indication, perhaps, of that strength of character and determination which he displayed so often throughout his career. Out of the thirty-two successful candidates who joined the *Britannia* with David, seven, including himself, reached Flag rank, and of these, Beatty and J. D. Kelly became Admirals of the Fleet.

The *Britannia* consisted of two old ships of the line, the *Hindustan*, a two-decker, and astern of her the *Britannia*, a three-decker. They were connected by a bridge, and moored in the River Dart just below the site of the present Royal Naval College. Countless small craft were available for taking the cadets to sea and providing instruction in sail drill, marine engines, boat-sailing and rowing. No boy who loved the sea could ask for a pleasanter introduction to the Navy than by way of the old *Britannia*.

David was just above the average as a scholar, and although not very strong and of slight build, he was a resolute Rugby football player and a good boxer. He had an exceptionally deep voice for a small boy and was often chaffed about it.

He was punished at Dartmouth nineteen times, mostly for 'skylarking', and there is a notation in 1885 that he was 'troublesome when under punishment'. The Commanding Officer in his report on the other future Admiral of the Fleet, J. D. Kelly, under the heading 'whether likely to be of use to the Service' gives the answer as 'Doubtful'![1]

Beatty appears in the photograph of his term-group standing at the top of a ladder in an extremely nonchalant manner. As he was smaller than the other boys, he probably chose this position deliberately.

One letter to his mother from Dartmouth, dated 29th November, 1885, has been preserved.

I hope you and all at home are well, and that Father is better and able to hunt again. It is a long time since I have heard from you, nearly a month, so I don't know anything about you, so please write soon and tell me. I suppose everybody is busy now working for the Election. They were electing down here yesterday, but I don't know which has got in yet. I don't think there was much of a row. I went on leave to Paignton yesterday to Mrs. Patrick: she is very nice and kind and blows you out like anything. It has been very wet down here lately. We have not been

[1] H.M.S. *Britannia* official records.

able to get out at all to-day, it having rained all the time. The term was photographed the other day: thirty-two cadets ought to have been, but owing to illness and being expelled, there were only twenty-nine cadets, I being among them. Our class want to give our Instructor a present, so will you please send me ten shillings to subscribe to it, and then I will get some photographs with it as well. Work is going on as usual: last Wednesday was our essay exam. We had three hours writing as hard as we could, after which my fingers were awfully stiff, then as Wednesday was wet I worked the whole afternoon as well. Have you had any good runs lately or does the frost stop you much? Only four weeks more, it will soon be over. With best love to all at home I remain

Your loving son,

DAVID BEATTY.

David's mother exerted her influence on his career in the material as well as the moral sense. On leaving the *Britannia*, he was appointed to China, which he took as a matter of course and was keen to go. His mother, however, thought differently, for when she heard of this she took the train to London on the pretext of shopping, and went straight to Lord Charles Beresford[1] with the request that her son might be sent to the 'best ship in the Navy'. Lord Charles, succumbing to her charm, immediately arranged with the Admiralty for young Beatty to be appointed to the *Alexandra*, the flagship of the Commander-in-Chief, Mediterranean Fleet, who was H.R.H. the Duke of Edinburgh, the second son of Queen Victoria.

David joined the *Alexandra* on 15th January, 1886, at a time when the Navy was passing from masts and yards to heavy armour and steam. The flagship was such a compromise; she was fully ship-rigged and had side armour of malleable iron. Her guns were ten-inch muzzle-loaders arranged in broadsides on two decks in a central citadel, and her seamen were trained to be handy with the cutlass and boarding pike. She was one of the last ships to be armed with muzzle-loaders, but paradoxically enough she was the first battleship to carry torpedoes. There were twelve of these, designed by their inventor, Mr. Whitehead, to carry a 30-lb. gun-cotton charge and to be fired through a square port by air impulse.

She was painted white, not merely for beauty, but to ward

[1] Afterwards Admiral Lord Charles Beresford, G.C.B., G.C.V.O.

off the sun's rays from her iron hull and so lessen the heat on her crowded mess-decks.

Although sails were rapidly disappearing, the art of seamanship still played a vital part in the training of officers and men. No officer was fit to handle a modern warship unless he understood the vagaries of wind and tide, no seaman was much use unless he could handle a boat, and no technician could ever aspire to commanding one of H.M. ships unless he had been fully tested as a seaman. The Navy has reason to be grateful to the old seamen of the past for their insistence that seamanship should form the basis of a young officer's training, thus creating an attitude of mind that made ship handling in fog and bad weather a matter of second nature to them in later years. There was a tendency, however, in those days to forget that the art and skill of both the seaman and technician were but a means to an end, for there were few naval history books to remind them that the real business of the Navy was to win battles. Victorian sailors were content to rest on the laurels of their predecessors; war at sea seemed to them very remote, and many worthy admirals passed away without ever having seen a shot fired in anger.

As Beatty grew up with the new order he became dimly conscious of the need for thought on war problems, and was always more interested in the use of the weapon than its maintenance. He was a keen student of war, and, ever looking forward, he tried to work out for himself the best way to fight the ship, how to use to advantage the torpedo and other new devices which appealed to him in the sense that they were designed to damage or destroy the enemy. He had a healthy respect for seamanship, especially where it provided opportunities to fight the elements, and he was always the first to volunteer for any service where he could, even for a brief spell, live dangerously.

He served practically the whole of his three years' time as a midshipman in the *Alexandra*. He was socially popular, and soon attracted attention by his horsemanship on the racecourse and polo grounds of Malta. Good looking and always well mannered, he became friendly with the Commander-in-Chief's family, being often included in their picnic parties to the picturesque little coves and bathing-pools for which Malta is famous. Princess Marie, the Duke of Edinburgh's elder daughter, later to become Queen of Rumania, was a particular friend. The Duke's residence was San Antonio, the Governor's summer palace, and it was here that his children, according to Queen Marie, spent the happiest days of their lives. 'Oh, the sweetness, the beauty, the enchantment! And still all these gardens beyond, beckoning to you from behind high walls, stepping through small openings from one to another . . . everywhere flowers, fragrance, sunshine, and the buzzing of a myriad wings.'[1]

The Duke's only son, Prince Alfred, was in Germany completing his education, and the rest of the family, living at San Antonio with the Duchess, consisted of Princess Marie, aged eleven, Princess Victoria, aged ten, Princess Alexandra, aged eight, and the baby, Princess Beatrice, aged three. The three elder girls were high spirited and devoted to riding. Their mother, who encouraged their liberty, gave them each a Barbary Arab, a breed of horse popular in Malta. Their play-mates were the midshipmen of the Flagship. Queen Marie recalls: 'Saturday was picnic day, and great riding parties were organised to some distant corner of the island. The start for these picnics was exciting to a degree, and full of clatter and noise. Our horses were fresh, prancing, ready to be off, difficult to hold. We in our fearlessness enjoyed their pranks . . . and our first gallop, which was always down the walled-in avenue by the courtyard, was a most unruly proceeding. We were more like a group of swooping Red Indians than civilised little girls. Our horses being stallions were all too ready with their teeth, and would often get a good grip of each other's tails, and thus, one behind the other, we would dash down that hard avenue, our naval friends pounding after us, whilst our horses were doing their best to buck us off. Our friends had horses as unruly as ours, although most of them rode with more science and decorum . . . Beatty was my special friend, and was already in those days a splendid rider and polo player. He has since said that I brought him luck . . . And those cooking parties on the *Alexandra*, when we fried eggs and bacon for tea, where we

[1] *The Story of My Life*, by Marie of Rumania.

washed our hands at the midshipmen's chests, each in the basin
of her own special friend, Beatty being my elected favourite . . .
And those wild games of follow-my-leader through the San
Antonio gardens, or all over the different levels of the great
house's roofs.'

Happy days indeed, filled with innocent, healthy amusement
in an environment of the highest social distinction, setting for
Midshipman Beatty a standard of self-confidence and easy
good manners which became one of the most attractive features
of his character, enabling him to hold his own in any company.
Princess Marie followed his career throughout her life and
wrote to him quite regularly. Here is a typical letter written at
the age of sixteen, when she was on a visit to London while
Beatty was a sub-lieutenant at Portsmouth.

> Clarence House,
> St. James', S.W.
> *27th June*, 1891

MY DEAR BEATTY,

I was so much pleased at receiving your letter. You must come up at
once and see us. We remain till after the 6th of July.

How nice it must be that all the old 'Alexandras' are down at Portsmouth. I have not seen them for a very long time—not one of them. Poor
Mr. Allenby! I quite imagine that he is not very pleased to go to China, it
must be a dreadful change. We played yesterday croquet and I thought of
your beautiful playing. We do not ride here because it is not worth while.
We have seen the naval exhibition which was very interesting. But now I
will say good-bye. I hope to see you once if it is possible for you to come up
to London.

> Many messages from us all,
> MARIE

And another letter from Coburg:

If you do go up the Baltic, be sure and come to Coburg. It would be
delightful, but it is rather far from Coburg.

Ruby, my dear Ruby will soon come now. How nice to gallop about
on him again. But we won't ride so wildly here as in Malta. You must
write to me soon, Beatty.

With my best love,

> Yours affectionately,
> MARIE

Ruby, the Maltese pony of happy memory, could not stand the cold climate:

My darling Ruby has not been well lately. . . . There is nothing going on here like there was at Malta, so we are all very quiet and sedate.

Then a little later:

I must tell you the most terrible news. My dearest Ruby has been sold. Isn't it terrible? My poor dear Pony !!!

MARIE

Destiny had a part for each to play in the war which was to come. She as Queen of Rumania and he as Commander-in-Chief of the British Grand Fleet. Throughout those grim years he kept her letters and cherished the memory of his boyhood romance.

The *Alexandra* was notable for the high percentage of her officers who reached Flag rank. H.M. King George V served in her as a lieutenant in 1888. The Flag-Lieutenant was Colin Keppel, afterwards Admiral Sir Colin Keppel, who was Serjeant-at-Arms to the House of Commons for twenty years. The First Lieutenant, F. S. Inglefield, and the Torpedo Lieutenant, F. T. Hamilton, both became Sea Lords. Of the watchkeeping lieutenants, James Startin and Stanley Colville,[1] later held important commands, and Charles Cust became the King's Equerry. In the gunroom with Beatty were Walter Cowan, Richard Phillimore, Reginald Tyrwhitt, A. W. Craig, and A. T. Powlett, all of whom served under Beatty in the North Sea in the 1914–18 War, and reached Flag rank, also Richard Webb,[2] who later commanded the Royal Naval War College, and for many years was the indefatigable editor of the *Naval Review*. The Chaplain of the ship, the Rev. C. J. Corfe, became a Bishop.

Richard Webb, writing of Beatty in *Alexandra* days, says: 'As always very quiet in the gunroom and certainly not in the least of a ragging disposition. His whole interest, outside the Service, centred of course in riding, and he was always in great demand as a jockey for the ponies of the officers of the Flagship

[1] Afterwards Admiral the Hon. Sir Stanley Colville, G.C.B., G.C.M.G., G.C.V.O.
[2] Later Admiral Sir Richard Webb, K.C.M.G., C.B.

—chiefly Stanley Colville. He was, I think, generally admitted to be one of the best light-weight jockeys in Malta.'

It was customary in those days for each watchkeeping lieutenant to have under him the same watchkeeping midshipman throughout the commission, and in this capacity David worked under Lieut. Colville. So began a long-standing friendship between the two, which lasted a lifetime, and had a profound influence on Beatty's career. Colville was a man of high principle and a lovable character. He was mad keen on the Navy, and one can imagine the two of them on the bridge in the night watches as the ship ploughed her way through the placid waters of the Mediterranean, exchanging views, over a cup of cocoa brewed by David, on life in general and the Navy in particular: Colville, with his sense of responsibility, fully aware of his influence on the younger man; David filled with admiration and a desire to learn, hanging on his words. Then inevitably the scene would change. A gale— an emergency, and 'Jump to it, you young blighter'.

We get another glimpse of Beatty from his friend, Walter Cowan: 'David was a good boxer as a midshipman. The boatswain, George South, used to teach us both in his cabin and sometimes a fair wreck we made of it. The only way to discompose South was a feint at his head, because he always wore a red wig!'

After leaving the *Alexandra*, Beatty was appointed, in September 1889, to the *Ruby*, a masted corvette (sail and steam), for intensive seamanship training. Having passed successfully through this a year later, he spent the next eighteen months ashore doing other training courses—including a spell at the Royal Naval College, Greenwich, where the young sub-lieutenants were taught mathematics, applied mechanics, physics, chemistry, nautical astronomy, navigation, surveying, meteorology, naval architecture, and foreign languages. A formidable syllabus, mainly academic, but too rushed to be of much educational value. In consequence, the cramming system prevailed, and those young officers who wished to gain the few months' seniority allowed for a first-class certificate could improve their chances by swotting up the various subjects by the light of the midnight oil. David was not one of these, and

Mrs. David Longfield Beatty, Admiral Beatty's mother,
from a water-colour portrait

most evenings found him in London (so temptingly close) enjoying the social round, or more often in company with the 'ladies of the stage'. A contemporary says, 'His cabin in Greenwich was full of photographs of actresses, some of which were signed in the most endearing terms.'

Shortage of cash probably limited his pleasures in those days. His friend, Walter Cowan, relates: 'Always impecunious, every now and then we journeyed to London in search of adventure; once we found ourselves with but 9*d.* between us and a long time to go before we had to return. Very hungry, we decided we would walk the length of Piccadilly and back in the hope of meeting someone we knew well enough perhaps to feed us, and I so well remember our mutual delight when the tall and unmistakably hatted figure of "Old David" (Beatty's father) loomed up, and away he swept us to the Cavalry Club, with the result that two well-nourished sub-lieutenants returned to Greenwich in complete contentment.' The attractions of London, however, never prevented young David from visiting his home and taking to the saddle when leave permitted.

The course at Greenwich was not altogether approved of in the Navy of those days. One senior officer remarked: 'He [the sub-lieutenant] is sent off to College to be run through a groove of higher mathematics, the use of which is rarely seen in his after life. . . . The sea is the only place where the seaman can learn the duties of his trying and arduous profession.' Young Beatty's views on this subject are not recorded. All we do know is that he got a third-class certificate in navigation, and we can assume that what he lost in theoretical education, he gained in knowledge of the world.

He had a good brain, and if he had really worked hard during his courses he might possibly have obtained a first class in each of the five subjects, and so have been promoted to lieutenant six months after becoming a sub-lieutenant. As it happened he only managed to collect a first class in torpedo, a second in seamanship, gunnery, and pilotage, and a third in theoretical navigation—a moderate achievement which brought no reward of seniority and compelled him to serve twenty-seven months as a sub-lieutenant. During this period quite a number of his contemporaries and juniors with better examination records achieved greater seniority, but they did not hold their lead over Beatty for long.

He served for a short time as a sub-lieutenant in the battle-ship *Nile*, and then had the honour to be selected for the Royal Yacht *Victoria and Albert* for her summer cruise with the Royal Family in July 1892. Queen Victoria described him as a nice-mannered boy. He was promoted to lieutenant in August, and appointed again to the *Ruby*, this time as a watchkeeper.

The *Ruby* was a rough ship, and life in her was very different from the pomp of the Mediterranean Flagship and the luxury of the Royal Yacht. Here is an extract from the diary of the Hon. L. J. Lambart, who served as a midshipman under Beatty in the *Ruby*: 'Our captain was W. A. Piggott, a hard-bitten old sea dog. His uniform was green from salt water and his trousers were very tight, all in wrinkles. On ceremonial occasions, when he had to put on his frock coat, that was in wrinkles too. He loved farming, and reared wonderful ducks in the Vale of Aylesbury. He was a consummate seaman, but very seldom interfered in evolutions, and I only once heard his voice raised during the whole cruise, and then it was raised to good purpose when the ship was nearly on her beam ends.

'I can hear his splendid voice now giving the order to shorten sail to topsails, from studding sails both sides; like this: "Fore and main clew-garnets and buntlines, topgallant and royal clew lines flying jib downhaul. Lower stun'sail tripping line, top-mast and topgallant stun'sail downhauls—Haul taut!—Trip up the lower stun'sail, lower away, haul down, clew up, shorten sail!" all in one order.

'He had two black poodles on board, they were nice dogs, but had the unfortunate habit of visiting in the early morning the topsail halyards or topgallant mast rope neatly coiled on the deck, which occasioned the most unprintable remarks when these ropes had subsequently to be used in a hurry.

'I had Mr. Beatty as officer of the watch for the whole trip, nineteen days under sail, from St. Vincent to Trinidad. Lieut. Beatty did not consider that his duty consisted only of teaching me more seamanship and urging me to call his relief: he had the knack, which is very rare, of turning a middle watch at sea from an irksome duty into a spell of companionship, during which he not only fed me, but put some ideas of life in general into my head which I have never forgotten.

'In the South Atlantic, when the Squadron was dispersed by bad weather, Beatty would hold on to the principal sails as long as anybody or longer, and as we were homeward bound, this was greatly to the liking of everyone, especially Captain Piggott, who I really think used to love the *Ruby* best when she was half-submerged like a good swimmer doing the crawl stroke. We broke the middle watch into periods which made time go very quickly, tea and caviare sandwiches at 1.45 a.m. and whisky and water and biscuits at 3.10 a.m. and talk in between of seamanship and hunting and leave and polo and every sort of subject.

'Then at the end I would go aft and read the patent log, whirring around, every turn nearer home, the ship laying her course East Magnetic, the Lizard light getting nearer and nearer with every turn. No more thoughts of the Diplomatic Service, it is time to put a little weight of one's own in the collar.'

From Lambart's remarks we get a true picture of Beatty at this time, and an insight into his professional ability, tenacity, and courage. From the *Ruby*, Beatty went to the *Camperdown* for two years and then to the *Trafalgar*—both battleships in the Mediterranean Fleet. He found that the character of the Fleet had totally changed since the peaceful days in the *Alexandra*. Masts and yards had disappeared, and the old ships had been replaced by heavily armoured battleships, armed with turret guns and designed wholly for fighting. They had very low freeboard, to reduce their silhouette, and had been developed from the Monitor design, which proved so successful in the American Civil War. The Admirals of the period, notably Sir George Tryon and Sir Michael Culme-Seymour, were endeavouring to find, by a system of trial and error, the best means of handling such a fleet in battle. These manœuvres were known as 'steam tactics'. They were carried out with mathematical precision in close order, and were not unlike the ceremonial movements of bodies of troops on a parade-ground.

They had their value, however, in giving Captains confidence in handling their ships with the Fleet, and as more experience was gained, greater risks were taken. In one manœuvre, owing to a miscalculation by Admiral Tryon and blind obedience to orders on the part of his second in command Vice-Admiral Markham, the *Camperdown* rammed and sank the *Victoria* with heavy loss of life.

Beatty joined the *Camperdown* a few months after this disaster, when Admiral Culme-Seymour, the new Commander-in-Chief, was busily engaged in restoring confidence by constantly exercising the Fleet in close-order manœuvres, which, at first, differed little from the exercises carried out by his predecessor. The command being wholly centralised in the Commander-in-Chief, subordinate commanders had little opportunity to exercise initiative, but fleets at that time were small, and could be conveniently manœuvred by a single authority. Seymour, however, was a good tactician, and kept firmly in view the destruction of the enemy as his main object. Assisted by Captain A. K. Wilson, V.C.,[1] he worked out schemes for locating the enemy by cruiser search, and introduced the masthead semaphore for long-distance signalling.

In October 1895, after two years of watchkeeping duty in the *Camperdown*, Beatty was appointed to the *Trafalgar*, another Mediterranean battleship of similar type, in which his old friend Stanley Colville was serving as Commander.

We get a characteristic glimpse of Beatty from a midshipman, who served with him in this ship:'. . . He [Beatty] is remembered by his dress immaculate, and specially his cap! . . . Bowles, Ingham, and I once ventured to drive a tandem to St. Paul's Bay. . . . Driving back, we came to grief, and half of the dog-cart was on the low wall, the leader in a field, and the wheeler still in the shafts. Lieut. Beatty rescued us and put us all together again in the twinkling of an eye.'

Other young officers who served directly under Beatty speak well of his devotion to duty, professional ability, and the encouragement he gave them. Although there was much to think about in this dawning era of modern naval tactics and

[1] Later Admiral of the Fleet Sir A. K. Wilson, V.C., G.C.B., O.M., G.C.V.O., First Sea Lord.

weapons, the dull monotony of three years of battleship routine had its effect on Beatty. There was none of the danger and excitement of the old sailing days in the *Ruby*, and his keenness for the Service was waning. He craved for action, and as if in answer to a prayer, his first opportunity came.

CHAPTER TWO

1896–1898

THE NILE

*The River War · Beatty's journal · Dongola, Atbara,
Omdurman, Fashoda · D.S.O. and promotion*

THERE was trouble in Egypt, and an expedition was being organised to drive out of the Dongola province a fanatical Arab army commanded by the Khalifa, and known as Dervishes.

The desert lines of communication of the combined British and Egyptian forces were long and difficult, so the Sirdar (Lord Kitchener) asked for a small flotilla of gunboats to operate on the Nile in support of his army. Colville, the Commander of the *Trafalgar*, was selected to command, and as might be expected, he chose Beatty to go with him.

Commander Hope Robinson, R.N., who was experienced in hydrographic surveying, was also appointed for the important duty of surveying the Nile cataracts. These appointments were made at the request of the Secretary of State for Foreign Affairs, and the officers were loaned by the Admiralty to the Egyptian Government, who undertook responsibility for their pay and administration.

Colville had previously served on the Nile with the relief expedition to Khartoum in 1885, and knew what was required. Periodical surveys of the most suitable passages were carried out. The vagaries of the current were closely watched, and means were devised to lighten the ships to the shallowest draught, so that the passage could be undertaken at the earliest moment possible. In this work of planning and preparation, Beatty, as Colville's trusted lieutenant, naturally bore heavy responsibility.

In addition to some small river steamers, there were already four gunboats on the Nile, *Tamai, El Teb, Metemmeh*, and *Abu*

Klea, normally employed on river patrol duties. The gunboats were shallow-draught stern-wheel steamers, lightly protected, and armed with light quick-firing Nordenfelts. At the same time three more gunboats of modern design were being shipped out in sections from England.

The strength of the current and depth of water in the Nile cataracts varied according to the season of the year, and the ascent of these swirling waters, through rocks and shoals, was a tricky piece of navigation. Colville's first duty, therefore, was to see that Beatty and the other officers selected to command the gunboats were thoroughly competent to undertake this dangerous task.

By the end of July 1896, the existing Nile flotilla had been assembled below the second cataract, and a fortnight later there was just enough water to allow the gunboats to make the ascent. Mr. Winston Churchill describes the passage of the gunboat *Metemmeh* thus: 'The boat had been carefully prepared for the ordeal. Her freeboard had been raised, guns and ammunition removed, a wire strop passed round the hull and the fires drawn. Five hawsers were employed, on which 2,000 men were set to pull, yet such was the extraordinary force of the current that, although the actual distance in which these great efforts were necessary was scarcely one hundred yards, the passage of each steamer occupied an hour and a half, and required the most strenuous exertion of the soldiers. No accident, however, occurred, and the six other vessels accomplished the ascent on successive days. Within a week the whole flotilla steamed safely into the open waters of the upper reach, and on 23rd August all seven steamers arrived in a stately procession opposite the camp at Kosheh.'[1]

This vivid picture by an eye-witness gives a good idea of the hard work and careful preparation which must have been put in by Colville and his men to achieve such a result.

Meanwhile, the desert railway had been pushed on as far as Kosheh, and the little town found itself humming with activity as the advanced base and naval dockyard for the entire expedition. The first freight to arrive by rail from Cairo included the sections and fittings of the new gunboats *Zafir*, *Fateh*, and

[1] *The River War*, by Winston Churchill.

Nasir, which were specially designed for the work, and were armed with 12-pounder and 6-pounder guns, howitzers, and maxims. They were 140 feet long, and although equipped with ammunition hoists, searchlights, and steam winches, they drew only 39 inches of water. The little ships were put together and launched at Kosheh by Messrs. Yarrow.

As there was no time to wait for the new gunboats to be completed, the Sirdar, on the 13th September, decided to advance with the old flotilla. The *El Teb* (Commander Hope Robinson, R.N.) unfortunately struck a rock during the passage of the Third Cataract, but Colville in the *Tamai* pressed on against the strong current with the *Abu Klea* (Beatty) and *Metemmeh* (Captain H. Oldfield, R.M.A.), followed by three small steamers.

The enemy, having some artillery, made a determined stand behind fortified positions at Hafir just above the cataract, but in spite of the current, the gunboats closed in to point-blank range. The Dervishes stood their ground. The *Abu Klea* was hit by a shell, which lodged in the magazine but did not explode. Beatty, realising the danger to his ship, picked it up and threw it overboard. The decks of all the gunboats were raked with heavy rifle fire. Beatty got a bullet through his helmet, Colville was severely wounded in the arm. The *Tamai* and *Metemmeh* were forced out of action by the current, but Beatty held his position, and the other two gunboats soon returned to his support. After two hours' continuous fighting Colville was compelled by his wound to turn over the command to Beatty, who immediately decided to attempt the daring manœuvre of leading the flotilla upstream beyond the Arab position. He was assisted in this by the army, which, thanks to the gallant fight of the gunboats, had now been able to establish artillery and infantry within close range of the enemy. Beatty had 35 miles to go before he could reach Dongola; his speed was painfully slow on account of the current, and he had to pass within 300 yards of the fortified enemy positions. Nevertheless, he pressed doggedly on with the other two gunboats in company, and reached Dongola late in the afternoon. The Arabs, seeing that their line of retreat was threatened, evacuated Hafir, and were racing along the river-bank trying to keep ahead of Beatty.

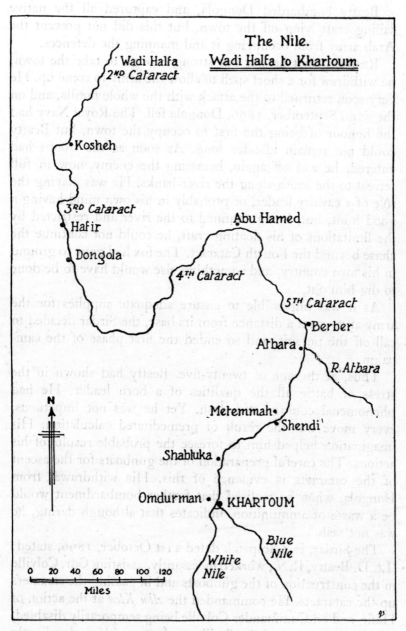

The Nile.
Wadi Halfa to Khartoum.

Wadi Halfa
2ⁿᵈ Cataract

Kosheh

3ᴿᴰ Cataract
Hafir
Dongola

4ᵀᴴ Cataract

Abu Hamed

5ᵀᴴ Cataract

Berber

Atbara

R. Atbara

Metemmah

Shendi

Shabluka

Omdurman   KHARTOUM

Blue
Nile

White
Nile

N

0   20   40   60   80   100   120
Miles

The Nile to Khartoum.

Beatty bombarded Dongola, and captured all the native sailing craft lying off the town, but this did not prevent the Arab army from occupying it and manning the defences.

Realising that he was not strong enough to take the town, he withdrew for a short spell to allow the army to come up. He very soon returned to the attack with the whole flotilla, and on the 22nd September, 1896, Dongola fell. The Royal Navy had the honour of being the first to occupy the town, but Beatty could not remain idle for long. As soon as the troops had entered, he was off again, harassing the enemy, now in full retreat to the south along the river-banks. He was playing the rôle of a cavalry leader, or probably in his own mind having a good hunt, but, being confined to the river and restricted by the limitations of his floating craft, he could not continue the chase beyond the Fourth Cataract. The fox had gone to ground in his own country, and something else would have to be done to dig him out.

As it was impossible to ensure adequate supplies for the army at so great a distance from its base, the Sirdar decided to call off the pursuit, and so ended the first phase of the campaign.

Thus, at the age of twenty-five, Beatty had shown in the stress of battle all the qualities of a born leader. He had phenomenal courage and dash. Yet he was not impetuous, every move was the result of premeditated calculation. His imagination helped him to foresee the probable results of his actions. The careful preparation of the gunboats for the ascent of the cataracts is evidence of this. His withdrawal from Dongola, when he realised that further bombardment would be a waste of ammunition, indicates that although daring, he was not rash.

The Sirdar, in a despatch dated 21st October, 1896, stated: 'Lt. D. Beatty, R.N., worked incessantly, assisting Cdr. Colville in the construction of the gunboats and in passing the steamers up the cataracts. He commanded the *Abu Klea* at the action of Hafir, and on Commander Colville being temporarily disabled, he took command of the flotilla, and most ably and gallantly led the way past the enemy's batteries. I cannot speak too highly of this officer's behaviour.' As a result of this, Beatty was awarded the D.S.O., and the First Lord of the Admiralty directed that his name should be noted for early promotion.[1]

There is evidence, in a letter which his father wrote to Henry Tollemache, that Beatty came near to winning the V.C.

I feel very grateful to you for the interest you take in my sailor boy. . . . The story of the shell incident was told me by Sudley of the Blues. 'Said that he was hero of the Nile and that both soldiers and sailors were indignant that he had not got the V.C.' I asked him what for? and he then told me that the Dervishes had hopped a shell into his boat. It had gone between decks, and my boy went after it, brought it up and chucked it overboard, thus saving boat and crew. Of course, the boy could not send his own name in for the V.C. . . .

Beatty had not mentioned this incident even in his family circle, and was not at all pleased when he learnt that the story had got about. He strongly deprecated the idea that some of his father's well-meaning friends should bring it to the notice of authority. 'The Sirdar', he wrote, 'was very jealous of that sort of thing.'

Beatty's well-earned leave at home came in the hunting season, but it was a sad homecoming, for his mother had died while he was in the thick of the fighting in Egypt, leaving an irreparable gap in his life.

His mother had laid the foundations of his career, and he well knew that the good fortune which had come his way was indirectly due to her encouragement and the care she had taken to see that his feet were set on the right road. He was denied the supreme pleasure of thrilling her with the story of how he had lived up to her expectations and showing her his D.S.O., the emblem of Her Majesty's approval of his deeds.

He sought distraction in hunting, and having had experience of land warfare, he took the opportunity while enjoying the sport to cultivate an eye for country, to imagine himself in the position of the quarry, and to dash in with determination for the kill, always, we hope, with due regard to the Master's conduct of the hunt. In his hunting activities there was no sign of caution, for he had only himself and his horse to consider. His personal safety meant nothing to him.

[1] Admiralty record.

In July 1897, Beatty, at the special request of the Sirdar, was again lent to the Egyptian Government for further operations on the Nile. He kept a careful diary of this campaign entitled 'Rough Record of Proceeding—Nile Expedition 2nd Phase'.

The flotilla had been reinforced by the new gunboats recently completed at Kosheh. Commander Colin Keppel, who had served on the Nile in a previous expedition, had relieved Colville in the Command, and Lieutenants Horace Hood[1] and Walter Cowan, two of Beatty's most trusted commanders at Jutland, were also in the force. The other officers commanding gunboats were Lieutenants J. B. Sparks, R.N., H. F. G. Talbot, R.N., C. M. Staveley, R.N., Major W. S. Gordon, R.E., Lieut. A. G. Stevenson, R.E., and Lieut. R. U. A. Newcombe, R.E. The machinery and ship repair work were in charge of Engineer E. E. Bond, R.N., assisted by Engineer Poole, R.N. They were a happy band, inspired by the deeds of their predecessors in the earlier campaign and the high prestige which the Navy had so justly earned with the Army.

Only a few days after Beatty had arrived on the scene the Sirdar ordered an immediate advance. The waters of the Nile were low, the current was running fast, and the Fourth Cataract had to be passed before the flotilla could move freely. Owing to the urgency of the situation, there was no time for the elaborate preparation which marked the success of the passage of the Second Cataract in the previous campaign. No one was more aware of this than Beatty, who remarks in his diary: 'On looking round before starting, found boats anything but ready. No material for stopping holes, no carpenters, no engineers' stores, and loaded heavily; protested, but to no purpose, as it was too late.' Early on 5th August, Hood in the *Tamai* tried the ascent, but was soon swept round, and after a narrow escape from capsizing was carried swiftly downstream. In the afternoon Beatty in the *El Teb* attempted the passage and, according to Churchill, this is what happened: 'Her fortunes were far worse than those of the *Tamai*. Owing to lack of co-operation and discipline among the tribesmen, and the want of proper supervision, the hauling power was again too weak.

[1] Later Rear-Admiral the Honble. Sir Horace Hood, K.C.B., M.V.O., D.S.O. Killed at Jutland.

Again the bows of the steamer were swept round, and as the hawsers held, a great rush of water poured over the bulwarks. In ten seconds the *El Teb* heeled over and turned bottom upwards. The hawsers parted under their new strain, and she was swept downstream with only her keel showing. Lieut. Beatty and most of the crew were thrown or glad to jump into the foaming water of the cataract, and being carried down the river were picked up below the rapids by the *Tamai*, which was luckily under steam.'

Another eye-witness states that Beatty was 'as good as new' an hour afterwards, and immediately took over the command of the *Fateh*.

Here is Beatty's own account from his diary:

'*August 5th*. Started with the *El Teb* at 2.30. Four hundred natives having turned up, considerably strengthened our hauling power, but were unfortunately another source of danger, as they were entirely undisciplined . . . caused the boat to forge out into midstream where there was an exceedingly strong fall of water in very rough water. . . . In less than 10 seconds she turned completely over and everybody and everything were thrown into the water and swept away in different directions. We lost three men drowned out of the fifteen on board, and it must have been a near thing for us all. Personally, clad as I was in heavy boots, tight trousers and belt, I was nearly water-logged, and was sucked under six times by the undertow which was very strong. The last time I thought it was all up, but hit a pole under water, to which I clung like a limpet and which pulled me up again, which I shortly after vacated in view of a box which was close and I thought would be better, but it took me five minutes to get that box, which were the longest five minutes I ever spent. Luckily the *Tamai* was all ready and came to the rescue and picked us all up.

'Then our attentions were turned to trying to pick up the *El Teb*, which was being whirled round and round bottom up in the large pool. Time after time we laid hold of her . . . she eventually disappeared down a small cataract surrounded by a regular litter of boxes of all descriptions, and eventually fetched up on a rock about five miles down in the middle of a lot of rough water where it was very hard to get at her.

'Of course, every mortal thing was lost with her, a terrible piece of luck, and left me stranded with only what I stood up in to commence a long and tedious campaign in, and no opportunity of being able to replace it for many a long day, but I must be thankful I still remained above water myself.'

After this accident the cataract was carefully surveyed, better passages were found, and a 'press-gang' was sent out on camels to scour the villages for more native labour to work the hawsers. By the 13th August the Nile waters had risen considerably and the *Metemmeh* passed through without incident, followed later by the *Tamai* and the three new vessels, *Fateh* (Beatty), *Nasir*, and *Zafir*. Describing the passage of the cataract, Walter Cowan says: 'All the haulage was done from one bank. . . . The din was terrific: what with the roar of the water and the howls of the natives, and of those trying to control them . . . . by far the most nerve-stretching business I have ever taken on.' Of Beatty at this time Cowan remarks: 'I used so to admire his never-failing efficiency and the way he was taken for granted and relied upon by everyone from Lord Kitchener downwards, and the pick of the whole British Army was there.'

Six days later the whole force was concentrated at Abu Hamed, the new railhead, in readiness for the advance to Berber, the Sirdar's next objective. As the railway could not be brought forward quickly enough, the work of transporting the whole of the army with their supplies and ammunition during the advance to Berber had to be done by the gunboats and steamers. Although these were filled to capacity, they could only accommodate a small proportion of the troops and stores, so the bulk had to be towed alongside in barges and native craft.

The mobility conferred upon the army by this means so accelerated the advance and surprised the enemy that the Khalifa's general, Mahmud, made no attempt to hold Berber, and fell back some 60 miles. The Sirdar's army followed cautiously, and by November had established a forward post at Fort Atbara, at the confluence of the Nile and Atbara Rivers. He relied on the gunboats working as far ahead as possible to cover his main concentration at Berber, and to keep the enemy on tenterhooks: accordingly, the gunboats penetrated deep into the Dervish country, harassing their supply lines, and at the same time providing the Sirdar with information of enemy movements, otherwise unobtainable.

The effectiveness of this armed reconnaissance was not limited by gun range, for each ship carried, in addition to her crew, a detachment of Soudanese troops which could be landed at will, either to support the advance patrols of the army or to raid enemy depots and strong-points.

In Cowan's words: 'Life up and down that river was full of incident and spectacle, and never a day not filled up to the brim with achievement of some sort; Lord Kitchener supplying the driving force and requiring the utmost from everyone. . . . A handful of black Soudanese soldiers with a British officer would be tossed into your steamer, and away you would go directed by the shortest verbal orders from Kitchener, to attack or reconnoitre some Dervish fort or concentration.' The enemy naturally did everything in his power to frustrate the efforts of the gunboats, and quite frequently they were under heavy fire. Beatty's ship was hit three times by shell.

Describing a meeting with Beatty, Cowan says: 'It gave me the greatest thrill to see my old friend on the deck of the *Fateh* with her funnel riddled with shot and holes in her side where shell had hit her. He looked serenely happy against this battle-scarred background. . . . Even at that age (twenty-six) and with that splendid lot of soldiers, he was with no show of arrogance a natural king of his company.'

At night the long fingers of the warships' searchlights swept the desert, disclosing any attempt by the enemy to mass for attack under cover of darkness, and at the same time terrorising the credulous natives with the idea of some supernatural power for ever watching. This was of immense value to the Sirdar, as darkness was an ally which the enemy might well have used to bring off a surprise attack with overwhelming numbers.

Beatty's diary gives a good first-hand account of life in the gunboats during these operations.

'*Sept.* 12*th* (1897). Started at 5.30 with the *Zapi* to see if we could lay our hands on the Nuggars[1] and get a shot at the enemy. . . . Observed a good-sized force on the ridge distant

[1] Native boats.

about 3,000 yds. We gave them the benefit of a couple of shells, but could not see the result.

'*Sept.* 14*th.* Sirdar arrived in the *Tamai* in the forenoon, and was received with a flourish of trumpets, guards, etc. The Sirdar inspected the town and the gunboats in the afternoon. Dined with the Sirdar, who was in great form and made many playful allusions to the *El Teb* disaster, which might well have been left unsaid.

'*Sept.* 15*th.* Left to patrol to protect the natives from raiding parties. All the islands are crowded with people who are starving and homeless without clothes.

'*Oct.* 6*th.* We proceeded with General Hunter[1] for the South, taking Wortley[2] for the good of his health, Fitton[3] for goodness knows what, more mysteriously important than ever.

'*Oct.* 7*th.* Several shots, from left bank; one fell on the deck between Ferguson and self, a narrow squeak. We turned round and sighted a force under some Dome Palms which we shelled, killing one man and one horse.

'*Oct.* 10*th.* Came up with them at Hassaia. We fired several shrapnels and killed three men and a horse. . . . The army made an excellent ambush. After half an hour's waiting, an advance party came slap at the ambush. They gave them a volley, and I am damned if they did not miss the lot clean. The Dervishes were so astonished that they merely stopped, swung round their spears, and gave them time to get in another volley, when they again missed. I never saw such a thing in my life, and never swore so lustily . . . pulled themselves together and knocked over two men at 400 yards.

'*Oct.* 16*th.* Sighted Metemmeh [town]. Distinguished the Forts, of which there were nine, but we soon found they only had one gun in each. . . . The Dervish army collected on the top of the ridge to view the situation. Baggaras[4] hovered round each Fort; object I have no doubt was to keep the Egyptian gunners in the Fort up to the mark, but we had the satisfaction of wiping out a couple of those sportsmen during the day's entertainment. As we approached, the fire became general with

[1] Major-General Sir Archibald Hunter.
[2] Major the Hon. E. Stuart-Wortley.
[3] Capt. H. G. Fitton, D.S.O., Royal Berks.   [4] Khalifa's guard.

all the ships and Forts, and soon the noise was terrific as we steamed slowly past. We made excellent shooting, hitting the Forts every time, but they were very thick, and I do not think did them much harm. We steamed past all the Forts and then turned round and steamed back, shelling the town and the ridge as well as the Forts. The magnificent array on the top of the hill dwindled away rapidly before several well-placed shrapnel.

'*Oct.* 17*th*. We started again at 4 a.m. . . . . It was a very pretty sight to see the boats steaming past keeping up a strong fire, which was answered by a much better fire than the previous day. Each flash showed up vividly against the fading darkness, while on the ridge behind the town the rising sun shone on the spears of the Dervish Army, who were again watching the proceedings, but who again disappeared on receipt of a shrapnel shell. . . . The fire of the Forts became more vigorous as we retired, while the army again appeared, a great host waving many banners, led by a man, on a white horse and wearing a white gibba, who was surrounded by clouds of horsemen. I am sure they considered they had gained a great victory.

'*Oct.* 18*th*. Reported our proceedings to the Sirdar, who was much interested and seemed very pleased on the whole.

'*Oct.* 24*th*. Great event: the correspondents arrived, Wortley in pursuit.

'*Oct.* 26*th*. I was sent up with the correspondents to give them a run. Wortley came, and very thankful I was, as he fairly held the floor. I am sure they ought to look upon Metemmeh reconnaissance as second only to Trafalgar! I gave them a very heavy lunch, and stuffed them as full as they would hold of stories.

'*Nov.* 4*th*. We passed the Forts again. The shooting was much better on both sides. We really made some beautiful shooting, getting into the embrasure time after time and they were very close to us.

'*Nov.* 12*th*. Landed the artillery and searched village. Result, one Dervish, two donkeys loaded with grain, and two camels.

'*Nov.* 18*th*. We received orders that the boats are to go to the southward of the cataract, which means isolation for at least eight months. . . . I have bought Wortley's pony with the idea of Polo, which they have started and is in full swing now three days a week.

'*Nov. 26th.* Commenced building stables for the ponies and house for the syces.

'*Nov. 28th.* We went round the cataract in a Felucca, poling all the likely places, found a general depth of 6 feet, now and then an isolated rock.

'*Dec. 4th.* Was informed Hunter had ordered another patrol to within sight of Metemmeh, to learn if possible the following abstruse points:

1. The number and disposition of the enemy.
2. The state of the food supply.
3. If there were any Nuggars (native boats).

Questions which appear to present some difficulty.

'*Dec. 5th.* I started off at daylight, picking up eleven scally-wags armed with rifles as scouts. Started off again by the moon, arriving at our old hiding-place, and sent out the scally-wags to occupy Omdega. . . .

'*Dec. 6th.* Remained all day. Was watched with great interest by a lot of Dervish horsemen on the left bank, who truly thought we were off our heads.

'*Dec. 8th.* Arrived off Shendy, having sighted and fired at a good many Dervishes *en route.* . . . In another moment we were out of range and right on the top of four Forts on the sand-banks in front of Metemmeh. As we passed we opened on them a terrible fire of everything we could get to bear. They only hit the *Zafir* once. . . . They still kept one Fort going on the mainland and one under the clump of trees and four to the southward. As we passed the Fort at Shendy we opened a very heavy fire, getting one shell right inside which caused an explosion and, as they never fired again, it is supposed we blew up some loose charges inside.

'*Dec. 10th.* The cricket things having arrived, we opened the D.C.C. with great éclat, but I fear the talent is not great, so play hockey instead every other day.

'*Dec. 18th.* Received orders to make an immediate survey of the Um Tiwe Cataract. . . . Reported that *Tamai* class could proceed up with Nuggars and down without Nuggars for another month.

'*Xmas Day*. Heard through a deserter that the Khalifa had stated that he was coming with all his force to wipe out the Turks. (As they call the Westerns.)

'*Dec. 26th*. Proceeded south and approached Shendy. They fired one shot at us, and we knocked away the corner of the Fort . . . proceeding north captured 2 Blacks, 1 Lady and 1 Baggara. One Baggara shot, trying to escape, also collared 2 donkeys and a quantity of Hashish.'

A critical situation arose towards the end of the year: the waters of the Nile had fallen so low that the Fifth Cataract ceased to be navigable, so the flotilla, working above the cataract, found itself cut off from its base at Abu Hamed. The Sirdar immediately decided to reinforce his advanced post at Fort Atbara and strengthen its defence, so that it could be used as a base for the repair and maintenance of his naval forces. Although the railway had now reached Berber, he was still faced with the problem of getting adequate supplies farther forward to Fort Atbara by other means. The enemy were known to be concentrating in force at Shendi, with the intention of advancing to the River Atbara, and there was grave danger that the forward British and Egyptian forces might be cut off. The flotilla at this stage was vital to him, so he used all his available resources in making sure that the Navy had a defended port from which they could operate.

The gunboats were thus enabled to roam the upper reaches of the Nile, seizing all Arab craft they came across and turning them to their own use. In March 1898, while Beatty in the *Fateh* was engaged on these operations, a large force of 1,000 Dervishes was reported to have occupied Shebaliya Island. Beatty closed the island, and landed Major Sitwell, with forty Egyptian troops, who were immediately attacked. Sitwell took up a defensive position in a ditch, and was himself wounded. Beatty, on seeing that a serious situation was developing, also landed, and took charge of the Egyptian force. After a while, Sitwell, who was lying in the ditch, unable to move, asked Beatty how the fight was going. 'It's all right, we're doing 'em proper' came the reassuring reply, quickly followed by the news that the enemy were in full flight.

Meanwhile, the desert railway was being brought slowly

and relentlessly forward with ever-increasing carrying power, until Fort Atbara itself became the main concentration area for the Sirdar's Army and a dockyard for his Navy. Newer and larger shipbuilding yards were erected on the Atbara. Gunboats, steamers, barges, and sailing craft were put in thorough order, native artisans toiling day and night under Engineers Bond and McHaig. 'The clang of hammermen, riveters, carpenters, and caulkers resounded along the river front. . . . An immense depot stuffed full of grain, provisions, ammunition boxes, ropes, wires, iron, medical stores and other material—like one of the great London docks.'[1]

In these operations the Army, while building up its own strength for a major offensive, carried out its traditional rôle of holding a base to enable the Navy to operate. Even in this campaign, trivial perhaps when reviewed in the light of two world wars, we see how the long arm of sea power demoralised the enemy and left him in no state to attack at a time when his prospects of success were brightest.

Beatty was fully occupied, and was learning, as Nelson learnt, the art of war by actual experience. Being a thinker and a student of war, this elementary lesson in true British strategy probably did not escape him.

In the middle of March, Keppel observed that Mahmud's Dervish army was advancing across the desert to take up a position on the River Atbara, having left behind a small garrison to protect their base at Shendi. Seeing his opportunity, Keppel fell upon this depot with a force of Egyptian infantry supported by three gunboats, including Beatty's *Fateh*. The garrison, being completely surprised, offered little resistance, and the stores and equipment were quickly captured. Kitchener meanwhile closed the main Dervish army, and on 8th April, 1898, he attacked and routed them at the Battle of Atbara. The gunboats took no part in the battle, except to 'hold the ring', but this did not prevent Beatty from landing with a rocket detachment and accompanying the troops into action. He describes the part he took in the battle:

'*April* 8*th* [1898]. Halted and waited for day to break, when we found ourselves formed into line, the British Brigade being

Khartoum Campaign, Bennet Burleigh.

David Beatty as a boy
(*Webster & Son, Chester*)

on the left, the Sirdar on their right, with his numerous and brilliant staff. . . . The night march had been a wonderful success and most extraordinarily well carried out. Throughout the night, whether marching or at the halt, not a sound was to be heard other than that of men on the march. . . . Once there was an alarm, each Brigade rose solidly up like a wall without a sound being heard or an order being given and in two minutes solidly lay down again. . . . At 6 a.m. the Artillery moved out to the front of the line and commenced a tremendous fire on their position, and enveloped the whole place in a shower of shot and shell. Every single part of the camp seemed to be under fire at the same time. I with the Rocket tube first occupied a position on the left of the Artillery, but the distance was too great and the ground unsuitable, so I moved off to the right of the line, where I was able to get within 300 yards but was ordered back to 400 yards. Here we did a certain amount of execution, firing the village in four places. . . .

'At 7.30 the Sirdar ordered a general advance to take place immediately. All the bands of the Anglo-Egyptian Battalions played up, also the Pipes of the Highlanders and drums and bugles of Warwicks and Lincolns, to which accompaniment the whole line advanced. It was a fine sight. They went to the crest of the hill and poured in a tremendous fire at 300 yards into the trenches for about ten minutes and were answered by an equally heavy fire from the enemy, luckily most of which went high. Up to this the Rocket party had advanced with the line, running out with the Rocket tube and firing in front of the line of Infantry. We had then expended the Rockets, so, after dropping the party to the rear and bringing up the camels, I left a guard, and with the remainder joined in the firing-line, who were advancing with a rush the last short distance, yelling for all they were worth which, in conjunction with the bands and pipes, made an astonishing noise. The British Brigade went in magnificently, rather slower, but as if on parade. It was during the last 100 yards that most of our casualties occurred, and they fell pretty thick, the enemy holding out until we got within 20 yards of them, but then left hurriedly. Very few got far before being shot or bayoneted. As soon as we were inside it was practically all over. The men went right through and out the other side, shooting the last of the fugitives as they crossed the bed of the Atbara. The Sirdar then appeared and said something to the British Brigade, who cheered him like blazes and everyone marched and formed up outside.... The Butcher's Bill was of fair size. . . . The enemy lost very heavily, the trenches being full of them and in places three or four deep. Mahmud taken prisoner, all the Emirs except Osman Digna and Zaki killed, and 2,000 men killed in the camp, besides Drums and Banners galore.... We marched back to Omdelia, everybody very tired but delighted.

'The Sirdar was in great spirits, and exceedingly pleased at the way everything had gone, and he had every right to be, as it was a triumph of organisation and rapidity.

'*April* 19*th*. We steamed up opposite to Metemmeh, landed, and paid the place a visit. We first examined the Forts, where several skeletons were left where they had been killed by the gunboat fire in our passages past the Forts at different times. . . . Inside the Fort was a great heap of dead men in the different degrees of decay from skeletons up. There were three great heaps of them. It was a horribly gruesome sight, a veritable City of the dead.

'Mahmud and the Dervishes constructed a straw hut or town to the rear of the old town. On the crest of one of the surrounding hills was his gibbet, where were stacked numbers of the skulls of his victims. The whole place was loathsome to a degree: nothing but dead wherever you went—horses, camels, donkeys, goats, sheep, men and women and children—carcases everywhere. There must have been 2,000 human bodies lying about without any attempt at disposing of them, apparently just as they fell.'

The victory at Atbara opened the way to Khartoum, so the Sirdar lost no time in continuing the advance. The distance to be covered, however, was some 180 miles, and the river was the quickest way to get along. As a first step a base was established below the Shabluka cataract about 70 miles short of the final objective; thus the whole army was brought forward, and then by stages to a position 11 miles below Omdurman. This process was not completed until the end of August, and during all the summer months the gunboats, in addition to carrying out reconnaissance duty, plied backwards and forwards, towing barges and transporting troops. The Sirdar insisted that every steamer, boat, gyasse, and anything that would float should carry three times their normal capacity. Fortunately, the river was high, and no great navigational difficulties were experienced.

The diary goes on:

'*August 7th.* The last fortnight has been a regular nightmare, dashing up and down the river carrying troops, Egyptian, Soudanese and British; and for the most troublesome beggars, give me the latter. They are a terror, want everything done for them, grumble. With one load I had 24 Officers and another (both British) 30, as tight a fit and as uncomfortable a lot as can be seen in a month's march. I first trotted up the Warwicks and then the Lancashire Fusiliers, the latter a most meritorious crew—didn't care a damn for anyone. Little Talbot[1] turned up. It was a real pleasure seeing him again, just the same, with a heart as big as his body.'

It was ticklish work for the gunboat commanders, handling their overcrowded ships in a tideway with overladen barges tied to their sides, while the brown waters of the Nile lapped upon the decks. Three new twin-screw gunboats, *Sultan*, *Sheikh*, and *Melik*, had joined the flotilla by this time. Although specially designed by the Admiralty for the work, they were not as satisfactory as the stern-wheelers. They were not as fast as had been expected, and required all their power for steaming, with none to spare for driving the dynamos to work the searchlights and circular saws. The gunboats and steamers were self-supporting for fuel. They all burnt wood, which could be got on board at night alongside the banks, every available man being used to cut down trees from the belt fringing the river.

On the 1st September the army crossed the Kerreri hills in close formation, and came within sight of Omdurman, the cavalry reporting that the Khalifa's troops were visible in large numbers on the plain outside the city. In the early morning of the same day Keppel and his gunboats, together with a new howitzer battery firing 50-lb. shells, started an intensive bom-

[1] Lieut. H. F. G. Talbot, R.N.

[35]

bardment of the forts and town of Omdurman. They continued firing throughout the day, causing very severe damage. The walls were breached in several places, and the enemy fire was quickly silenced. In Smith-Dorrien's view[1] it was this action, or the fear of it, which caused the Khalifa to evacuate the city and mass his troops in the open.

During the day the Dervish hordes, estimated by the cavalry to be 30,000 strong (actually 80,000), were seen to be advancing northward as if to attack. Kitchener, maintaining his close formation, took up a line of defence in a semi-circle, with the flanks resting on the river-bank. Three gunboats, *Sultan* (Keppel), *Abu Klea*, and *Melik*, covered the northern flank, and another group of four, *Fateh* (Beatty), *Sheikh*, *Hafir*, and *Metemmeh*, protected the southern flank. They did not remain static, but followed every tactical movement, giving artillery support where it was necessary. The two remaining gunboats, *Nasir* and *Tamai*, lay off Omdurman in support of the howitzer battery, which continued to shell the city.

At nightfall the cavalry were seen to be falling back, bringing a report that the enemy had encamped for the night some 3 miles south-west of the British position. It was thought that a night attack was certain, as this would enable the Khalifa to use his overwhelming superiority in numbers to the best advantage. The gunboats swept no-man's land with their searchlights, while the British troops put up a zariba of thorn bushes, and dug trenches. Nothing happened during the night, but at dawn the cavalry reported that the enemy were moving to the attack. Smith-Dorrien says[1]: 'We could hardly believe the news. We could not have selected a better place. . . . There was a huge open plain, without an inch of cover for an attacking enemy. . . . Their columns moved steadily down on our entrenchments. . . . Our gunboats, with their high fighting decks and bridges giving a command of 35 feet above the already high Nile, were able to bring their quick-firing guns and maxims to bear with deadly effect on the advancing masses. On the north side they played a most important part, as there some 10,000 Dervishes had cut off the Egyptian cavalry, Horse Artillery, and Camel Corps from our position,

[1] *Memories of Forty-eight Years' Service,* by General Sir Horace Smith-Dorrien.

and it was due to the gunboats that these mounted troops were able to join our right.'

This first onslaught of the enemy was beaten off with enormous losses: 'The endless columns of warriors led by mounted Emirs moving steadily on . . . it was a pitiable sight to see the awful effect of our fire all along the line. . . . They were simply mown down, and in very few parts of the line did they approach nearer than 600 yards.'

The impetus of the Dervish attack carried them northward across the British front, leaving open the way to Omdurman. Kitchener immediately seized his opportunity and re-formed his brigades for an advance on the city hinging on his left flank which rested on the river. He could well afford to take this risk, being happy in the knowledge that Keppel's flotilla would look after his communications and cover his flank. He had his anxious moments, however: Macdonald's brigade, left somewhat in the air to the north, found itself attacked by a mass of Dervishes who had been waiting in reserve behind Surgham Hill. The Sirdar was able, however, to send two brigades to extricate Macdonald, while at the same time cutting off the enemy from their capital. The gunboats kept up a heavy fire on the Dervish column, thus easing the pressure on Macdonald. The British and Egyptian force reached the city during the afternoon. Opposition was expected from the last enemy stronghold surrounding the Mahdi's tomb, but this was quickly overcome, and the troops poured in through the breaches in the walls, taking the Forts in reverse.

The fall of Omdurman meant that Khartoum across the river was again in our hands, and the power of the Mahdi finally broken. The total strength of the Dervish force which took part in the battle was estimated at 80,000, of whom 10,883 were killed in the course of a few hours. This indeed was sheer slaughter, but in view of the colossal superiority in numbers possessed by the enemy and their fanatical courage, credit must be given to Kitchener for his masterly generalship. It was a military necessity to make a quick job of it, and a single slip on his part might have caused disaster.

A few days after the battle the greater part of the British Army turned for home, but there was to be no rest for Beatty.

The Sirdar had received intelligence that a French force under Major Marchand had established itself at Fashoda, some 500 miles up the White Nile from Khartoum. The international situation was delicate, and the presence of a foreign white force on the Nile required investigation, so on the 10th September, 1898, Kitchener headed for Fashoda with a strong company of Cameron Highlanders, two Soudanese Battalions, and a mountain battery. The Sirdar took passage in Keppel's ship, the *Sultan*, while Smith-Dorrien, who commanded the troops, accompanied his friend Beatty in the *Fateh*. The other vessels selected for this mission were the gunboats *Nasir* and *Abu Klea*, and the steamer *Dal*. The troops were distributed as usual throughout the flotilla, and in barges under tow.

On the 15th September a Dervish force was encountered on the east bank of the river encamped in zariba, close to their one remaining steamer, the *Saffiyeh*, which had come into their hands after the fall of Khartoum in 1885. The gunboats steamed in close and opened fire with all guns. The fire was returned, but resistance was quickly overcome, and the enemy made off into open country. The *Saffiyeh* was too badly damaged by shell to be of any value to the Sirdar, who remarked to one of the naval officers, 'You damned sailors can never see anything afloat without wishing to destroy it'. On the 17th the expedition reached the village of Kaka, and from here the Sirdar sent a runner some 50 miles to Fashoda, with a letter to warn the French Commander of his approach. The information about the strength and intention of the French was vague: were they likely to be pugnacious or were they not? It was of the highest importance to avoid an 'incident', so the Sirdar proceeded south slowly, and on the 19th halted at some distance from Fashoda to give the French plenty of time to digest his note. Whatever happened Kitchener, in his capacity of Governor-General of the Soudan, would insist on Marchand recognising the Egyptian flag. He left nothing to chance. If Marchand should prove to be amenable, Smith-Dorrien was to land all troops and salute the French flag; transport would then be offered to take the whole French force to Cairo. If, however, Marchand was argumentative, the troops were to be landed far enough away from the French position to avoid a clash, but the troops and gunboats were also to be disposed as a blockading force to cut off French supplies and prevent their retreat.

On 19th September, when the flotilla was in sight of Fashoda Fort, a small boat flying a huge French flag was seen approaching the Sirdar's steamer the *Dal*. A French officer boarded her, and after a few words with the Sirdar the *Dal* moved to the river-bank, where Marchand and another French officer stepped on board. Smith-Dorrien and Beatty were watching the scene through field-glasses from the deck of the *Fateh*, 200 yards away. In Smith-Dorrien's words: 'After much bowing and scraping and saluting, what I supposed to be a map was spread on the table, then followed much gesticulation and angry conversation. Distinct signs of hostility on both sides. I was beginning to think there would only be one end to such forcible discussions, and that I should see negotiations broken off, when up the ladder moved a native, bearing a tray of bottles and glasses, and these full of golden liquid were soon being clinked together by the two central figures, who until that moment I had believed engaged in a deadly dispute.' Shortly afterwards the Sirdar returned Marchand's call. Smith-Dorrien landed his troops. The Egyptian flag was hoisted, and a salute of twenty-one guns was fired.

Marchand's force turned out to be pitiably small: only seven Europeans and 120 blacks. The Sirdar showed consideration, however, in permitting them to fly the French flag over the fort until they evacuated Fashoda.

Beatty now had orders to proceed down-river, salvaging the damaged *Saffiyeh* on his way. Shortly before leaving, Marchand asked Beatty to carry a letter for him. This Beatty refused to do, which pleased the Sirdar, who had previously stated officially that Marchand had sent no communication to his Government. When Beatty got back to Omdurman he learnt that Kitchener had been made a peer, and also that the French Government regarded Marchand's force merely as an exploring party. Beatty's action in refusing to take Marchand's letter probably saved considerable embarrassment all round.

The Sirdar's despatch of 30th September, 1898, contained the following reference to the work of the gunboats: 'The excellent service performed by the gunboats under Commander Keppel and his subordinate officers of the Royal Navy is deserving of special mention. These gunboats have been for a long time past almost constantly under fire; they have made bold reconnaissances past the enemy's forts and rifle pits, and on the 1st and 2nd September, in conjunction with the Irregular Levies under Major Stuart-Wortley, and the Howitzer Battery, they materially aided in the capture of all the forts on both banks of the Nile, and in making the fortifications of Omdurman untenable. In bringing to notice the readiness of resource, daring, and ability of Commander Keppel and his officers, I wish also to add my appreciation of the services rendered by Engineer E. Bond, Royal Navy, and the engineering staff, as well as of the detachments of the Royal Marine Artillery, and the gun crews, who have gained the hearty praise of their commanders. . . .

'The names of the following officers, non-commissioned officers, and men have been brought to my notice for good service:

'GUNBOATS

Lieutenant the Hon. H. L. A. Hood, R.N.
Lieutenant David Beatty, R.N.
Lieutenant Walter Cowan, R.N.
Lieutenant I. B. Sparks, R.N.
Lieutenant H. F. G. Talbot, R.N.
Lieutenant C. M. Staveley, R.N.
Major W. S. Gordon, R.E.
Major Prince Christian Victor of Schleswig-Holstein, K.R.R.C.
Lieutenant A. G. Stevenson, R.E.
Mr. Poole, Engineer.'

As a result of these recommendations, the following announcement appeared in the *London Gazette* of 15th November, 1898:

*'Honours for Egypt and the Sudan (including the Battles
of Atbara and Khartoum)*
C.B.: Commander Colin Keppel, D.S.O., R.N.
D.S.O.: Engineer Edmund Edward Bond, R.N., and
Lieutenant Walter Henry Cowan, R.N.

Admiralty Notice, 14th November, 1898

Promotions to take effect from the 15th November, 1898:

Lieutenants the Hon. Horace Lambert Alexander Hood and David Beatty, D.S.O., to be Commanders.

The following will also be promoted for services during the operations:

Commander Colin Richard Keppel, D.S.O., to be Captain on completing the necessary sea time to qualify him for that rank.

Engineer Edmund Edward Bond to Chief Engineer on completing eight years' seniority in the former rank.'

Thus Beatty became a Commander when he was twenty-seven years of age, having served as a lieutenant for only six years. The average time spent in lieutenant's rank was $12\frac{1}{2}$ years, so Beatty's step took him over the heads of 395 lieutenants and opened the way to high command. This promotion was the forerunner to other special promotions which Beatty gained at each stage in advancement as his naval career progressed. It came from no lucky chance, but from the considered opinion of Lord Kitchener, a stern judge of character, and better qualified than anybody to pick out a future leader. We can now consider briefly how Beatty's experience in the Nile campaigns would be likely to affect his mind and character at this impressionable age.

The actual fighting he took in his stride. Whenever there were opportunities for action afloat or ashore, he sought them deliberately, and delighted in the danger, thus establishing for himself a reputation for audacity and courage.

The navigation of the Nile was not always easy, but Beatty handled his ship skilfully, and with consummate coolness under fire. He gained valuable experience in many aspects of the seaman's art, such as manœuvring in a tideway, towage, salvage, and handling heavy equipment. He also learnt by experience that the surest way to arrive at a correct decision in war is to have visualised the situation beforehand, and so avoid, if possible, being caught by the unknown.

He learnt the ways of the soldier and appreciated his difficulties with sympathetic understanding. 'Beatty and the

[41]

Fateh' had a reputation in army circles for good fellowship and hard fighting.

On the higher plane of strategy he saw in practice how to employ a naval force to gain a military objective in co-operation with an army in the field. It was the responsibility of the gunboats to see that the army was transported to the right spot at the right time, and that their lines of supply by water were secure. They also had to bring pressure on the enemy by cutting off his supplies and destroying everything that was his in the Nile zone. When the army was engaged in battle, the flotilla was there with its artillery support. None of these basic lessons was lost on Beatty, but above all he enjoyed the advantage of serving under Lord Kitchener, whose conduct of the campaign was a model of leadership. Beatty, like everyone else in the expedition, could not fail to realise how the influence of a single personality can permeate a fighting force from top to bottom. Later on, in the First World War, there was no better exponent of the art of leadership than Beatty himself.

He also learnt that the responsibilities of a military commander do not end on the battlefield, and that even in the first flush of victory he may suddenly be called upon to undertake diplomatic negotiations involving the honour of his country.

Although the Nile campaign may be regarded as 'a bit of a picnic' from a naval point of view, it can be truly said that no experience of greater value could have been found for a young man destined to command the Grand Fleet in war, and to lead the British Navy in the difficult peace which followed.

CHAPTER THREE

1899–1900
CHINA

More active service · Beatty's personal journal · Promotion to Captain

WHEN Beatty got home from Egypt in the autumn of 1898, he found that he had become quite a popular figure, especially in the Midlands, where his family were well known on account of their reputation as horsemen. The exploits of a small naval force, operating with the army 2,000 miles from the sea, had naturally caught the public imagination, and there were few Press reports of the activities of the gunboats which did not contain some reference to Beatty. Furthermore, Beatty was the only naval officer who had been through both of Kitchener's Nile campaigns, and his conduct as a fighting leader had been as exemplary in the second, when he was specially promoted to Commander, as it had been in the first, when he got his D.S.O. This coveted honour was not awarded indiscriminately, particularly to Lieutenants R.N., who in those days, through no fault of their own, had few opportunities to earn it. In a maritime country the prestige of the Navy always remains high, even when the Army holds the limelight, so it was only natural that a Commander R.N., aged twenty-seven, with a D.S.O., should arouse interest. Social functions were organised in his honour and he was often the guest of hunting farmers whose country he knew so well. Municipal authorities made reference to him in their speeches, and the local Press embellished his deeds.

Beatty, from his own point of view, was not interested in public opinion. Having done his utmost for his country, and incidentally thoroughly enjoyed the doing of it, he was out to make the best of a few months' glorious leave, which as a naval officer he knew too well came so rarely. He hunted, raced, visited the old home in Ireland, danced, and flirted. Amongst the many women he met was Ethel Tree, the beautiful wife of Arthur M. Tree, and daughter of Mr. Marshall Field, the Chicago millionaire and pioneer of the chain-store system. The Trees lived at Compton Verney, near Warwick, and although both American, they were devoted to English country life. They hunted with the best packs, and she in particular was well known as a first-class rider to hounds. They had been married for some years and had one son. Their marriage was not a happy one, and they separated in about mid-March 1899. She and Beatty met out hunting, and were immediately attracted to one another. They had much in common, and it is possible that there may have been an understanding between them. Beatty certainly had declared his love, and they wrote to each other after he had gone back to sea, but the correspondence was short-lived.

On the 20th April, 1899, after four happy months, Beatty was appointed to the small battleship *Barfleur* as Commander. She was the Flagship of Rear-Admiral James Bruce, the second in command of the China station, and her Captain was the Hon. Stanley Colville. The post of commander of a battleship carries with it high responsibility, and is regarded in the Navy as the greatest test of an officer's executive and seamanship ability. The Commander is, in fact, responsible to the Captain for the management of the entire ship's company, her cleanliness, and general efficiency. Beatty had the knack of getting the best out of his subordinates, and in consequence, the *Barfleur* was well ordered and happy. Frederick Field,[1] who was the torpedo lieutenant of the ship at that time, says of him: 'No one could serve with Beatty, even in the early part of his career, without realising his high characteristics as a leader. He was always full of energy and self-confidence and always ready to take the responsibility if any junior officer should fail him.'

Beatty had a wide circle of friends, not exclusively confined to the Navy. He always took a keen interest in the Merchant Service, and did his best throughout his life to improve their conditions and their relations with the Royal Navy.

[1] Later Admiral of the Fleet Sir Frederick L. Field, G.C.B., K.C.M.G. First Sea Lord 1930–1933.

Captain William West, the Master of the Fleet Transport S.S. *Penarth*, attending on the *Barfleur* in those days, writes: 'Beatty invited me in the *Barfleur* wardroom and visited my ship several times and enjoyed being in the company of my wife, young son of eleven, and baby daughter, who sailed with me in *Penarth*. He often used to invite me to join him when going for a bicycle run ashore, he always fell. He used to send a picket boat to fetch us to church service on board the *Barfleur*. I considered him to be a very kindly disposed gentleman as well as a very efficient naval officer, which subsequent history abundantly proved.'

After twelve months of normal naval duty, Beatty again found himself on active service.

A political body with strong nationalistic views had grown up in China calling themselves the 'Righteous Harmony Fists', popularly known as Boxers. Their object was the expulsion and extermination of foreigners, and the movement started in Shantung, spreading like a flame through the Northern and Central provinces. It was at first treated with contempt by Europeans resident in China, but a real danger became apparent when it was known that the Empress Dowager and her Manchu ministers, who were sympathetic to the movement, had taken practically no steps to prevent the murdering of missionaries and engineers working in lonely parts of the country. The European nations with interests in China were obliged, therefore, to take steps to protect their own nationals. The situation became acute towards the end of May 1900, when the British naval Commander-in-Chief, Sir Edward Seymour, received a telegram from Sir Claude Macdonald, the British Ambassador, requesting that guards should be sent to the legation at Pekin, as the Boxers were troublesome and the attitude of the Chinese Government was doubtful. Seymour complied immediately. The guards took over their posts on 31st May, but their coming failed to produce the expected quietening effect.

The revolt assumed alarming proportions, so Seymour, with some units of the China Squadron, including Beatty's ship the *Barfleur*, anchored off the Taku bar at the mouth of the Peiho River, the nearest point to Pekin. Here Seymour was joined by warships of the following nationalities: Russian, French, German, and United States, with Admirals in command; and Austrian, Italian, and Japanese. He sent Jellicoe,[1] his Flag Captain, to Tientsin for the latest information, and at the same time called a conference of Admirals and Captains from the international fleet. Seymour happened to be the senior officer present, and all agreed to serve under his command. In full accord they worked out a plan to send an allied landing party of about two thousand men to Pekin, and they also agreed that Seymour should command the expedition.

Shortly after Seymour had telegraphed his proposals to the Admiralty, Jellicoe returned from Tientsin with a message from Sir Claude Macdonald, received through the Consul, stating that unless help was immediately sent to Pekin it would be too late. All arrangements for this expedition having already been made, Seymour, without waiting for Government approval, made the signal for the allied force to land, and on 10th June, 1900, the whole expedition was well away on the railroad to Pekin. When they had accomplished about half the journey they came to a stop at Lang Fang station. The line had been destroyed for miles ahead of them and there was no water for the engines.

Attacks by strong forces of Boxers were repulsed with heavy losses, but it soon became evident that regular troops armed with modern quick-firing guns and machine-guns were operating against Seymour's force. Gallant attempts were made to repair the railway line ahead, but after five days, when reports came in that the line behind was also being systematically destroyed, Seymour realised that his position was hopeless, and that the only course open to him was to fight his way back to Tientsin and resume the advance by road and river later on. Their food was nearly gone, and they had to eke it out with stray donkeys and ponies. The water too was almost undrinkable, owing to pollution of the river. After heavy fighting they managed to reach Hsi-ku arsenal, which they took by assault, and they found inside everything that they needed.

Reconnaissance in the direction of Tientsin, about 6 miles distant, ascertained that the foreign settlements were in a state

---

[1] Later Admiral of the Fleet Earl Jellicoe, G.C.B., O.M., G.C.V.O.

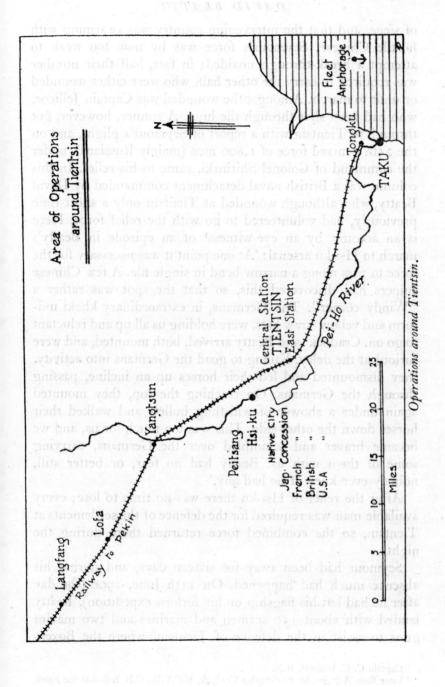

Area of Operations around Tientsin

Operations around Tientsin.

of siege, and that the intervening country was swarming with hostile Chinese. Seymour's force was by now too weak to attempt a break-through unaided; in fact, half their number was required to carry the other half, who were either wounded or unfit to march. Amongst the wounded was Captain Jellicoe, who had been shot through the lung. A runner, however, got through to Tientsin with a report of Seymour's plight, and on the 25th a mixed force of 1,800 men (mainly Russians), under the command of Colonel Shirinski, came to his relief. In this column was a British naval detachment commanded by David Beatty, who, although wounded at Tientsin only a short time previously, had volunteered to go with the relief force. Here is an account by an eye-witness[1] of an episode in Beatty's march to Hsi-ku arsenal: 'At one point it was necessary for the force to pass along a narrow bend in single file. A few Chinese snipers had discovered this, so that the spot was rather a "Windy corner". The Germans, in extraordinary khaki uniform and yellow straw hats, were holding us all up and reluctant to go on. Cradock[2] and Beatty arrived, both mounted, and were furious at the delay. Failing to goad the Germans into activity, they dismounted and led their horses up an incline, passing through the Germans. On reaching the top, they mounted again under a shower of whistling bullets and walked their horses down the other side. This was too much for us, and we became braver and scrambled over the Germans, carrying some of them with us. Beatty had no fear, or better still, nobody ever knew if he had any.'

After the relief of Hsi-ku there was no time to lose; every available man was required for the defence of the settlements at Tientsin, so the combined force returned there during the night.

Seymour had been away for sixteen days, and during his absence much had happened. On 11th June, 1900 (the day after he had left his flagship on his forlorn expedition), Beatty landed with about 150 seamen and marines and two maxim guns to assist in the defence of Tientsin, where the Boxers

[1] Captain C. C. Walcott, R.N.

[2] Later Rear-Admiral Sir Christopher Cradock, K.C.V.O., C.B. Killed at the Battle of Coronel.

Admirals Colville, Tyrwhitt and Beatty when young officers
in the Royal Yacht at Cowes, 1892

were being particularly troublesome. He got through without incident, but found the situation in the settlements very disquieting. The Native City across the river was in the hands of the Boxers, who were getting bolder every day, destroying railway communications, store-houses, and generally terrorising the countryside.

The Allied garrison had been sadly depleted to provide the Pekin relief force, there was practically no artillery, and no reinforcement from the fleet could be expected until the Taku forts at the mouth of the Pei-Ho River had been captured. A force of some 2,000 Russian troops, however, arrived from Port Arthur just in time to beat off a determined attack by the Boxers on the railway station, but failed to prevent them setting fire to the French settlement and destroying some valuable store-houses.

Inside the settlements was a mixed force of 2,400 men, with nine small field guns; outside were 15,000 Chinese regular troops, with plenty of modern quick-firing guns and unlimited ammunition, supported by a horde of Boxers who, although poorly equipped, were not lacking in enthusiasm.

The perimeter to be defended was about 5 miles in length. The defence was assisted over its most dangerous section by a mud wall and the river, but unfortunately the railway station, which had to be held, was on the other side. The Chinese kept up a continuous bombardment of the settlement, but their attacks were badly co-ordinated and easily repulsed. The garrison soon found that the most profitable form of fighting was to make incursions into the Chinese lines and establish strong-points to keep the enemy at a distance. This was work after Beatty's heart.

We know enough about the general situation to let Beatty tell his own story of the part he took in the defence of Tientsin. His personal journal covering the period June 9th–July 13th survives, so in this short autobiography we get, not only an account written fresh from the events, but also an insight into the character of the man, his modesty in the telling, the courage with which he ignored his wounds, and the initiative he displayed in seeking action where the fighting was heaviest.

He dedicates his journal to 'England' with a few lines of simple poetry scribbled on the fly-leaf:

'Land of chivalry and freedom
Land of all traditional fame:
May thy noble sons and daughters
Long uphold their honoured name.

Land where foreign foe ne'er venture
Land where tyrant never trod:
Land whose sons are ever foremost
Treading nobly Life's high road.

Land of simple-hearted kindness
Land of patriotic worth:
May your virtues ever flourish
Hardy clansmen of the North.

Land where rests in silent numbers
Ashes of our honoured sires:
May their memories long be cherished
Round our humble cottage fires.'

The journal begins:

'During the week ending the 9th June [1900], we in the *Barfleur* had been out doing our Prize Firing, [off Wei-hai-wei] both Heavy Gun and Light Gun. In the meantime rumours kept coming from the North of China, Pekin and Tientsin, of the depredations and increasing activity of Rebels called the Boxers, and in answer to the increasing demands for help, the Commander-in-Chief had ordered up all the Marines that could be spared to be sent to Taku in the *Algerine*, to be followed shortly after by the *Orlando*, and again by the *Centurion*, accompanied by the *Fame* and *Whiting*.

'*June 9th, Saturday*, we returned into harbour, and immediately prepared and embarked 40 of our Marines on board the *Humber* to protect the small watering-place of Peitaiho, N.E. of Taku. The same afternoon the *Aurora* sailed for Taku: so there we were, the sole ship left out of the hunt that apparently everybody expected, grumbling and growling at our bad luck.

'But our turn was to come, and I informed the men that night that if there was to be any serious trouble they could not do without the *Barfleur*.

'*June* 10*th, Sunday.* Directly after lunching with Rear-Admiral and Mrs. Bruce, a telegram arrived ordering us up to Taku at once to take command of the ships there and to prepare all men and guns ready for landing, so we immediately raised steam and prepared for sea, everything being hurry and bustle, but everybody glad at the opportunity they felt was coming. At 8 p.m. we sailed.

'*June* 11*th, Monday.* We arrived off Taku outer anchorage at 2.45 p.m., to find it crowded with men-of-war of every nationality, Russians in great force, Americans, French, Japanese, Austrians, Italians, Germans and ourselves, in fact, representing all the great powers of the world, with one Second-class Chinese cruiser anchored in their midst. Captain Burke of the *Orlando*, senior Naval Officer, immediately came on board and informed us that the C.-in-C. had that day started with a mixed force of 2,000 men to get to Pekin and withdraw the Legations from that hot-bed of revolt.

'Captain Burke also informed us that it was the C.-in-C.'s wish that we should land 100 seamen and what Marines we had left for the defence of Tientsin. And by 4 p.m. in one hour we were ready and had embarked in the tug in which we were to cross the Bar.

'The officers were—Self (in command), Luard (Gunnery Lieut.), Phillimore and Stirling (Company Officers), Gibbs, Brown, Donaldson and Guy (Company Midshipmen), Esdaile my A.D.C., Luke (Major R.M.L.I.) and Armstrong (Subaltern R.M.L.I.), with Wilson Assistant Paymaster and Smith Assistant Engineer.

'We left the ship at 4.30 p.m., just getting over the Bar very well pleased with ourselves and perfectly happy, but not in the least contemplating what we were in for, looking upon the business more in the light of a picnic.

'Well, we picked up a special train at 7 p.m., which was very comfortable and convenient and ran into Tientsin at 9 p.m. Here we found no one to meet us and had no idea of our geography, but with the assistance of a railway official we got

over the Bridge of Boats, which was guarded by a Russian seamen's guard, and which is kept open at night to prevent any
rush across. Little did we think, that night, as we wended our
way over the Bridge of Boats, that our next two months around
Tientsin would be filled with excitement, of the turmoils which
we were about to enter into, of the joys and wild delight, of
conflicts followed by the everlasting bitter regrets, of the heavy
losses we were about to sustain, and how in a short time we
should look upon this Bridge and Station as a veritable death-
trap, and of the devastating ruin and destruction which was
about to fall on the fine buildings, under which we now
marched. We passed first through the French Concession and
then into the British. I was directed to the Consulate, where I
found Captain Edward H. Bayly, Royal Navy, the Senior
Naval Officer in Tientsin, and to whom I reported myself. We
were soon billeted in Butterfield and Swire's Godowns, about
400 yards beyond the Consulate on the Bund, where we remained throughout our stay at Tientsin. We soon had the men
settled down with plenty of straw-matting, while the officers
were billeted at different private houses, the civilians being
exceedingly hospitable. We found in the Godowns 120 of
the *Aurora*'s men, all Bluejackets, under Lieut. Powell. There
were also in the settlement, in a Godown in Victoria Road,
a detachment of 100 men and 28 Marines under Lieut. Wright
of *Orlando*, which brought the British force in Tientsin up to
430 men and officers to defend the British settlement.

'*Tuesday, June 12th.* Having done fairly well for myself on
a sofa at the Chartered Bank, where I had put up for the night,
I was taken round to make the acquaintance of Mr. R. A.
Cousens, who was kind enough to say that he would put me up,
and made me free of the house. After establishing myself in
comfortable quarters, I returned to the business in hand:
taking over the defence from Wright of the British Settlement.
Employed the forenoon going round the line with Wright, who
explained the different points, accompanied by Luke and Luard.

'The position struck me immediately as ill-adapted for
defence with but 400 men, being a very extensive straggling
line with houses interspersed.

'The French Concession was to the end of the British, and

held by Russians and a few French sailors up to Victoria Road, the Americans prolonging us to the N.E. along Taku Road, while on the Meadows Road end we were jutting into the German Concession held by Jap, Italian, Austrian, and German.

'Round the walls of the Recreation Ground, Wool Mills, Chinese houses to the right, and the Cemetery on the inside, I had built up staging which enabled men to fire over the wall and be under good cover, giving them a fair position to fall back upon if too hard pressed. The salt-pans between the Mud Wall and Temperance Hall making excellent trenches, the mud wall itself being the 1st line of defence.

'The Bund I turned over to the *Aurora*'s men to provide sentries to continually patrol, and man a Nordenfelt gun which I placed on the Hong Kong and Shanghai Bank and a Maxim gun placed on the jetty opposite Barfleur Barracks, both of which commanded the rise both ways.

'The *Orlandos* provided Gun-crews for their two 9-pounders, one of which I placed on mud wall by Wool Mills and one at West Corner of Recreation Ground. The two Maxims I placed at Taku Road Temperance Hall, being the place most likely to be attacked. The Tientsin Volunteers I placed on the East End of the Bund, where they could do less harm than anywhere else. The mounted Volunteers I attached as Orderlies to different Commanding Officers and Positions, so that Communications could be kept up.

'Of Fatigues we had enough to keep us going morning, noon, and night, unloading trains from Taku, loading trains to be sent on to C.-in-C., building Barricades to all the Streets, digging trenches, throwing epaulments and making gun positions.

'This went on for the next four days uninterruptedly.

'*Wednesday, June* 13*th.* A Train arrived with the news that the Pekin Relief Column had been attacked by Boxers, of whom they had killed and wounded a large number, a few of the latter being sent down in the train and proving to be mostly youths of an irresponsible age.

'*Thursday, June* 14*th.* Communication with Pekin was cut off and we heard that the Imperial Troops, Marshal Nieh's men, had joined the Boxers and destroyed the Bridges.

'*Friday, June 15th.* A train with Captain Burke, who had tried to get to Loh Fa to take command and make a base for supplies and to get them on to C.-in-C., returned in the evening and reported that the line had been cut and the Bridges destroyed.

'During the day we could see the Boxers particularly busy passing backwards and forwards between the Arsenals and the City and Forts. They began burning all the villages surrounding the Settlement, all the outlying Missions and Churches and Chapels, including the French Cathedral. The Russians lined up their Artillery at the Station and fired two or three shells at the incendiaries, who massacred all the Native Converts and Christians they could find, wiping off old scores and debts. They did not work round to our position of the Settlement until 2 a.m., when they came in great strength, setting fire to all the Houses and outlying Villages they could, which in reality was doing us a good turn. They came on quite heedless of the Volleys we opened on them, never replying because the poor beggars had no arms to reply with, and coming up to within 300 and 400 yards armed with swords, spears, and torches. So there we squatted, knocking them over as they came along.

'In the meantime all was confusion in the Settlement. The gallant Tientsin Volunteers proceeded to gallop round the streets yelling and shouting, "The Boxers are on you!" and sounding their bugles, which was strictly against the order that on no account was any bugle to be sounded, as it would be taken as the "General Alarm". By some means they (the Volunteers) managed to get hold of the Bell Pull of the Church Bells and rang them vigorously, this being the signal for all the women and children to be taken to the Town Hall. Out of the Houses they poured in a dreadful state of excitement, anxiety and terror, some with nothing on but nightshirts and pyjamas, every woman and child in the place being in the streets at the same time, and it was difficult to reassure and persuade them to return to their Houses. At 6 a.m. everything had quieted down and we were able to withdraw the men back to barracks.

'*Saturday, June 16th.* The whole force had been out all night and had a bad time. Nevertheless, we had to buckle to and unload the train (from the coast) which ran in filled with much-needed stores. We also despatched two trains of 400 Russians, 40 British, and 50 French to clear the line. One train was under the command of Field, the other a Russian. They returned with both trains in the evening reporting all clear and everything quiet. Only a very few of the oldest and some of the Christian Chinese Boys remained. There was a large number of Refugees and Chinese Converts, who had come in from distant Mission-Houses up the line, and also those belonging to the Missions of Tientsin, who had collected in the Compound of Messrs. Jardine and Mathieson.

'In the meantime I had been sent for by Captain Burke, who told me that we were in for much more than was ever thought, and that he had information that the Imperial Troops had assisted the Boxers in tearing up the railway and that many had discarded their own uniforms and adopted the Boxer uniform. This was serious indeed, as at any moment our Communications might be cut, and there we were with rations for only three days and a small quantity of ammunition, having sent all that could be spared to the C.-in-C. As we were talking we heard that the telegraphic communication was cut between us and Taku. So I immediately went to the Taku Tug and Lighter Company, where they have a telephone to Taku, and after clearing every Chinaman who was within 100 yards out of the way, I telephoned them to send up from *Algerine* all the ·303 and 6-pounder ammunition they had. This luckily got through, and the *Algerine*, acting immediately, sent up by Tug and Lighter all they had. Keyes,[1] who had come up to see how matters were, went down on an engine and impressed upon the Rear-Admiral the straits we were likely to be in if all communication was cut, and the necessity of sending up provisions and ammunition, also the desirability of immediately taking the Taku forts.

[The Taku forts were bombarded by allied warships and captured by their crews on that same night as a military necessity to keep open communications between the fleet and Tientsin. They were defended by government troops, and the

---

[1] Later Admiral of the Fleet Lord Keyes, G.C.B., K.C.V.O., C.M.G., D.S.O.

allied action could have no other meaning from a Chinese point of view than a declaration of war. In consequence, Chinese regular troops in the district joined the Boxers in their attempt to dislodge the foreigner from the settlement in Tientsin.]

'*Sunday, June* 17*th.* During the early morning hours we heard the sound of distant gunfire, and knew that the attack on Taku Forts had begun, and after it ceased we were anxious to know how it fared with the Allied Forces. Luckily, there were large quantities of rice and flour in the Godowns, so we should never starve. It took a good deal to instil into the minds of many that we really were cut off both from the C.-in-C. and from Taku, and if the attack on the Forts failed, there was no knowing what we were to go through in the next month.

'All the forenoon at Tientsin there was an ominous silence, nothing doing on either side, each waiting for the other to play the next card, neither knowing the result of the attack at Taku, and yet both sides knowing that now we were committed to a war, if not with China itself, with Northern China and the Manchu Dynasty.

'Mr. Oswald, an Englishman, who had been an instructor in the Chinese Military College, showed the point where the British and German Concessions were across the river, so that it appeared to me to be absolutely necessary to seize them immediately, as they were in a position to dominate the whole of the Foreign Settlements.

'So after getting Captain Bayly's sanction at 12.30, we got hold of a mixed force of British Marines, Germans, Austrian, Italian, and French under Major Luke about 200 strong. At 1 p.m. the first gun of the Siege was fired from the Chinese Fort, pitching in the river, as if they had been informed of our plans and were going to forestall them. We started our mixed force across the river in sampans and two steamboats, and saw them get into the grounds without opposition. It was a marked contrast to see our Marines going over the Wall as if out for a paper-chase (each man lifting the other up). The Foreigners were dodging round the Gate.

'We heard heavy rifle-firing, and the result was seen in two dead Germans and a wounded Austrian. Twenty minutes after, out poured all the Foreigners, having destroyed the four guns that were there. They all came across with the exception of our Marines and some German sailors whom I stopped, and told to wait until they saw our Marines off the premises.

'Still the firing went on, and as the Germans could or would not give me any information, I got up a company of *Barfleur* sailors and went across to see what was going on. When I got there I found the Major and his Marines entirely unsupported driving the Chinese out of the Buildings which they were holding in the most stubborn manner.

'After a short time we had them all out, and on examination we found that we had accounted for some 50 Chinese killed, and then after burning the buildings we retired in our boats and recrossed the river. This was our first brush with the enemy and was entirely successful, with a loss of 5 men killed and 9 wounded, British being 1 Marine killed and 3 wounded. During the afternoon I sent small parties over the river to fire all the houses opposite and so clear our front, and very soon we had the whole river-front in a blaze, which showed the Chinese that we were as good at making bonfires as they were.

'Colonel Wogack, who was the Russian diplomatic representative in Tientsin, was very anxious about the Russian and French Guard that were at the Chiang Kiang Bridge and whose presence was now urgently required in Tientsin.

'Colonel Wogack was a most delightful man with charming manners, who spoke English like an Englishman and, in fact, was more English than any Englishman, but who nevertheless was diplomatically a thorough Russian who could lie scientifically and candidly, a trait which made it very necessary to believe what one saw only.

'*Monday, June* 18*th.* The Chinese seemed to spring into life, and then began one of the toughest days we have had. At 6 a.m. their attack developed at three places, their best men along the Taku Road driving the Americans out of their Mission Barracks across the open by the Wool Mills. The Russians held the Station and French Concession, and right well they bore themselves throughout the day.

'At 8 a.m. it became apparent that the Chinese objective was the Station, and they made great endeavours to drive us out, but it had to be held at all costs by us, the Train with 600 men having just departed to bring in the other 400 holding the Bridge. So I went up to reinforce them with 2 Companies, one *Barfleur*, one *Orlando*, at the request of Colonel Wogack, the Senior Russian Officer. They had sent up 50 French and 50 Japanese Sailors, so it made our force up to roughly 650 men to hold the position against at the least 5,000 Chinese and a heavy Artillery Fire. The Station Buildings made a magnificent target, and undoubtedly the Chinese made beautiful practice. The safest place we soon found was along and under the Station platform. Time after time the Chinese advanced under cover of tremendous Artillery Fire, the whole place being alive with shells and fragments of shells flying about, and a hail of bullets, so that anyone rising to fire at the advancing Chinese was immediately struck down.

'The Russians worked their guns like men, scorning to build up protection with the bales of goods that were there and which we utilised for our riflemen. After the Horses had been killed and wounded, Colonel Schirinsky decided to remove his guns, as he was afraid of their being captured in case we had to retire. Nothing that I could say would induce him to keep them, although I promised to have them dragged by the Blue-jackets. So there was nothing but to get up one of our 9-pounders which turned up in the nick of time, as the enemy was getting round our flank. When it arrived, the Russian Colonel was delighted, taking his hat off and cheering for all he was worth. I had a place built up for it on the platform of Bales of goods, making very good cover and so the shells took effect, driving the Chinese on our left flank out. But so heavy was the rifle fire that in ten minutes there were only two men left at the gun, Lieut. Wright and one other, the remainder having all been hit. It was now noon and no sign of our Train, and matters began to look serious. The men never murmured under the punishment they received in a blazing sun with but little water. When one considers that with the exception of myself it was the first time that any had ever seen a shot fired, it was a high trial, and they stood it well, steady as a rock and cool as cucumbers, as if they had been at it all their lives. The afternoon wore on, and the hail of shot, shell and rifle bullets never ceased.

'The ammunition gave out and water was gone, because not a man could be spared to get it, and then he would have to cross an extensive zone under a devastating fire. So we sat and suffered, but ammunition we had to have, and so it came, two of the men being hit getting it. At 4 p.m. we heard the welcome whistle of the Train in the distance, and on the instant the Chinese redoubled their fire, shell and bullet, and advanced more determinedly, but we drove them back. As the Train came in, it was our turn to advance and so up we got, fixed bayonets, and after them. The 600 men, Russians from the Train, poured out in hot pursuit on our right flank, and under cover of the two 6-Pounders on the Train and 9-Pounder on the Platform, we went for them. The enemy fired wildly for a short time and then up they all got like an enormous covey of partridges and bolted. If we had only had a Squadron of Cavalry! Then ensued the most extraordinary sight that ever was seen. Japs on the left, then ourselves, French and Russians, about 1,200 of us going into line as hard as ever we could, a regular steeplechase right up to the railway embankment, where we halted a second and poured three volleys into the village, a long straggling place. We were 200 yards ahead of any others and went clean through, driving all before us, and then fired the whole place, and returned to find the Russians, Japs, and French (who were very sluggish) fallen in waiting for us.

'The Russian Colonel came round and made a most complimentary speech to the men. Shortly after, we were enfiladed by a number of the enemy who had collected on our right flank. The Fort which had ceased firing, now opened again with shrapnel, but doing little harm. I asked the Colonel if we should not go on and take it, striking while the iron was hot, but he demurred, said his men were tired and it was late.

'If we had only captured the Fort then and there, which I firmly believe we could have done with little loss, how very different the next month or six weeks would have been. From it we could have dominated the native city and prevented the erection of Batteries. In fact it would have made it impossible to put Tientsin in a state of siege.

'The incessant demands from the Germans had become a byword in the Settlement and an infernal nuisance. Time after time they would send messages to say that they were being heavily attacked, and unless reinforcements came they would have to abandon their position. Out would go our men at the double, probably having just come in from a long day in the trenches or on Patrol, only to find that there was not a man (and never had been) in sight, so I had to give the German Officer, Lieut. Kuhne, a piece of my mind, and inform him that in future he would not get any reinforcements from us.

'*Tuesday, June* 19*th*. Next morning at 4.30 the bombardment of the Town and Station recommenced with fresh guns. At 6 a.m. they opened on the Settlement with 2 guns in a cutting of the Railway Embankment, only 1,000 yards from the Settlement. With these they were doing a great deal of execution shelling the Town Hall, where the women and children were, and the Club which was turned into the Hospital, so that had to be stopped at all costs. To do this, I proposed to take 3 Companies and advance under cover of the Houses of the Village opposite to within 600 yards and then through some orchards which lay between the village and the embankment, which I was told was full of ditches and banks, making good cover for skirmishing, while two Companies of the Russians should come down the Railway and attack from our left. So we sent to Col. Wogack, who replied that he had sent the two Companies, so I got our 3 together and crossed over the river and passed through the village and extended 2 Companies in skirmishing order across the orchards, keeping one in reserve and advancing about 100 yards. The enemy spotted us and opened a tremendous rifle fire from the embankment, which was lined with some 2,000 of them, so we lay flat and waited for the Russians, who were slow in coming along. After half an hour they appeared, during which time the fusillading was incessant and we had had several casualties. Poor Donaldson was shot through the lungs. When the Russians appeared, we advanced, and the Chinese opened a furious fire, and they bolted, taking their infernal guns, so although we did not capture the guns, we shot them out of their position and so saved the Settlement from a most disastrous Cross-fire. But we paid for it, having four officers hit and twelve men, none killed. Poor Donaldson was very bad, and I did not think we should ever get him back alive. Stirling was hit in the thigh, breaking the leg, and Powell in the right chest just touching the lung, and I was hit in the left arm just below the shoulder, a narrow squeak for the artery. Twenty minutes afterwards, I was hit again in the left wrist almost identically the same place as Colville, our late skipper, which was an extraordinary coincidence. We all went off to Hospital and dished up and went to bed.

'*Wednesday, June 20th.* Shell, shell all day from every gun they could get to bear. The rifle fire on our different positions was not nearly so heavy and they made no systematic attack at any one point. Nevertheless, the men were much worried by the different calls for assistance from the different points.

'This of course was very flattering, but entailed a deal of walking and humbugging the men about, very often unnecessarily, as "Wolf" was continually being cried when there was no Wolf. Russians, Germans, Americans, and even the French, used to come to us for assistance when it was required.

'*Friday, June 22nd.* I persuaded the Doctors to let me out of hospital, and so out I came, my arm in a sling, rather weak from loss of blood but otherwise all right. Again we suffered from the incessant shelling, which was becoming painfully monotonous, and every house had two or three shells through it, and many were the narrow escapes that took place. Mr. Cousens had five, one crashing through my room, smashing everything inside and setting fire to my bed, the shell bursting after getting inside, the fragments passing through all my clothes and destroying everything. Many also were the unfortunate victims that were killed or mutilated beyond recognition day by day, but luckily no women or children were struck, all being tucked away in the cellars, and the civilian men were able to place themselves in a place of safety. Our losses during the last 5 days had mounted up to over 100 per day or nearly 600, which was excessive. We were ourselves surrounded and cut off from everywhere, and with no communications from the S.E. or Taku, so were unable to move. Our ammunition was fading away, and the Russians said that, if the next four days would be the same as the last four days, all their ammunition would be exhausted. In fact, we knew nothing and had to act in the dark and simply hold on.

'We had a consultation of the Commanding Officers, and the Russian Colonel solemnly rose to his feet and calmly proposed that we should evacuate Tientsin during the night. All the women and children, of whom there were some hundreds, and the sick and wounded, of whom there were 400, should be escorted by the Germans, Austrians, Italians, French and Japanese, while the Russians and British should hold Tientsin until noon and then retire and form the rearguard. It was the maddest, wildest, damndest, rottenest scheme that could emanate from the brain of any man. With the C.-in-C. Seymour and the remnant of 2,000 men within 8 miles looking to us for help, with 28 miles between us and the coast filled with a supposed army of 20,000 men, and without even knowing if we could get through, or if there was a place to retire on, or if our men held the Forts or the enemy, it would mean consigning ourselves to a general massacre. When I heard it I nearly burst, and nudging Capt. Bayly I said: "Sit on his head." He did not want much nudging. He got up with a face like a peony, and swore lustily, which flattened the whole thing out. The Russian plan received no support and so fell flat.

'*Saturday, June 23rd.* At daylight they again commenced shelling the town and surrounding buildings, nearly succeeding in setting them on fire, which would have been a catastrophe. We heard about 8 a.m. the sound of rifle firing down the river, and the look-out reported what appeared to be troops advancing up the river-bank. Without doubt they were our Relief Column from the fleet, and at 11 a.m. the advance guard, consisting of a half Company from the *Alacrity*, marched in under Cradock, and the way was once more opened to Taku and the coast. A great weight was lifted off our minds. Soon they came straggling in without much law and order, deadbeat, 500 sailors and 300 Welsh Fusiliers, 100 Americans and *Terrible*'s Marines, and remainder of the Marines from the Fleet. Almost simultaneously with the arrival of the Relief Column the bombardment ceased and did not commence again all day, bringing with it a real sense of relief, making, by its very quietness, one feel as if we were at peace with all the world.

'*Sunday, June 24th.* A perfectly peaceful day, not a shot fired on either side, but we made preparations to go for the relief of the C.-in-C. at Hsi-ku. We started with a Force consisting of 500 Seamen under myself, 180 Marines under Luke, 150 Welsh Regiment, 100 Americans, 70 Italians, all under Captain Cradock, to go to the Russian Camp. After losing our way in that short distance, we eventually arrived, and started off again with 900 Russians and 100 Germans, making altogether 2,000 men under my old friend Colonel Schirinsky. We followed the Great Wall, which traversed the surrounding country and completely gave us cover from the Forts, and although owing to the want of guides mistook our way, eventually arrived at the river, where we became exposed for the first time to the shell-fire from the Forts.

'The horses had all to be swum across, and the men scrambled over the broken-down Bridge, but after we were once over, we had no further difficulties to overcome and only met with an ineffectual shell-fire. We sighted some 1,000 Chinese Cavalry, who made off on receiving several volleys and a dose of Maxims. We sighted the White Ensign flying amongst some trees on the river, and eventually arrived at 10.30 a.m. [25th June] at the position where the C.-in-C. and his party had established themselves, which was a walled Arsenal of great strength, and could have been held, with ammunition and food unlimited, for ever. Everybody of course was delighted to see us. The C.-in-C. was looking very well. Jellicoe had been badly wounded, but was doing well; in fact, notwithstanding their want of medical stores and food, the wounded were doing extraordinarily well. We had two casualties in getting there, one midshipman and a stoker, and the Welsh Regiment had two men hit. With the Russians supplying the necessary Sentries, Pickets, Patrols (the Colonel saying he would not have any other nationality to assist him but the British), we then destroyed the Arsenal as well as we were able, and got everything in readiness to return to Tientsin. All the wounded had to be crossed over the river and proper stretchers made for them, but by 2 a.m. [26th June] everything was in readiness, and we started back with our 226 wounded men. It made a tremendous long line and would have been an easy one to attack, but without the firing of a shot we all got back into Tientsin by 10 a.m. fairly cooked, having been out 36 hours, and having begun the journey at the end of a long day's work.

'*Wednesday, June* 27*th.* Commenced making emplacements and gun mountings for 4-inch and 4.7 guns. The Chinese appeared to wake up again, and recommenced bombarding us and also attacking the Station. It was suggested by several of us that we should attack them and destroy their work, but it was not received with enthusiasm. Brigadier-General Dorward, the Commissioner of Wei-hai-wei, arrived to take command of British troops. During the day the men from the Wei-hai-wei Regiment, Hong Kong Regiment, and Welsh arrived.

'*Thursday, June* 28*th.* The East Arsenal was attacked and taken by the Russians with a force of British Blues, Marines, and Welsh Regiment. We lost very few, 3 killed and 18 wounded. The 4-inch Guns arrived (from the fleet), and for the next few days our time was spent in fixing them up on solid platforms, the difficulty being in getting them there.

'The enemy continued to bombard us by the hour, and we replied as best we could. The C.-in-C.'s idea now was to get the men back to their ships, as they were being relieved by the soldiers. In fact, all were sent down except the Tientsin Defence Force, now including the *Terribles* and the *Centurions*.

'Fresh troops arrived daily. Americans, French, Russians, a few Germans, and the remainder of the Hong Kong and Wei-hai-wei Regiments and 2,000 Japanese, very workmanlike-looking lot. Admiral Alexieff also came up, being the Senior Officer in Tientsin.

'Poor Donaldson died during the night, after having made a great struggle for his life, and we buried him in the little cemetery by the Recreation, where others of our dead had been buried. R.I.P.

'On July 2nd we took over the Railway Station with the French and Japanese, the Russians retiring back to their Camp close to the East Arsenal, and a hot time we continually had. Day after day, hour after hour, the shelling would go on from Batteries that they used to shift every night, making it difficult to locate, as they used smokeless powder. At one time they had 9 guns firing intermittently all day, assisted by a heavy rifle fire. Our engineers made no sort of attempt to build

Lieutenant David Beatty, D.S.O., R.N., 1898
(*Mayall & Co., Piccadilly*)

bomb-proof shelters or even trenches. I suggested that we should advance 100 yards and dig big trenches there during the night and leave the Station, which only provided a target for them to fire at. No, they would do nothing. The Chinese advanced to within 300 yards and dug themselves trenches, from which, if a man showed himself, they would pour in a heavy rifle fire. Consequently the losses of the forces at the Station were daily becoming alarming in their numbers. I then offered to take the *Barfleur*'s men, and during the night clear every Chinaman out of the trenches in front of the Station, which could have easily been accomplished by us, as we knew the road and the lie of the land, and with a comparatively small loss. The C.-in-C. was delighted and said "Certainly"—when in walked Dorward, who said it was madness and could not be done, and so the C.-in-C. veered round and said it was not to be. Two nights after, the Japs went out and cleared them out of it, but did not make a very good job of it, probably because they did not know the country. In the meantime we had fixed up our guns, and on the 4th July we opened fire on the Forts with all our guns and bombarded them for two hours. This shook them up and stopped completely their guns from firing.

'*July 6th*. We repeated the dose of shelling with all our guns simultaneously with a most salutary effect. But there was a small gun, which appeared to be under our very noses, that was annoying us intensely and doing us a lot of harm, damaging the Hospital and Gas Works. Bruce of the Wei-hai-wei Regiment thought that he had spotted it in the suburbs just beyond the French Concession, so asked for a force to go and try and capture it or else destroy it, so a mixed force was made up of Wei-hai-wei Regiment and sailors to sally forth and seize it. But on arrival they found that it was on the other side of the river and was not to be got at. But Bruce thought that, if he had a gun, he could knock it out. He was referred to me, and took a 9-Pounder of the *Orlando*'s at 3.30, and off he went with 200 Wei-hai-wei Regiment and an escort. At 4 p.m. a steamer, that we expected to clear, not turning up, I took 2 Companies to see what had happened with the Gun. On arriving at the point where the Taku Road meets the river, I found the Gun and Limber stuck, with the gun's crew and escort taking shelter amongst the ruined houses from a perfect hail of bullets and shell-fire that swept the street. It was impossible to leave the gun in the position it was in. Another minute and the limber boxes would be blown up, and it was the work of a second to get the gun's crew out and retire the gun. My 2 Companies I left behind the corner under cover, while I had with me Esdaile, my A.D.C., and Whibley, messenger. We retired the gun right back, but the difficulty was to get the Chinese Regiment to retire quickly and orderly. They were much demoralised, having had several casualties from shell and rifle fire and were all of a heap. Poor Bruce, in his endeavours to get them out, was struck in the stomach, the shot passing clean through his liver, and poor little Esdaile was accidentally hit by one of the damned Chinese Regiment. The bullet passed clean through him from below the shoulder to the same spot the other side. I eventually had to get a Company of sailors to cover the retirement. As it was, there was nearly a stampede. We eventually got them all out of it and retired ourselves with one man wounded. It was a merciful Providence that caused us to go and see what was going on, otherwise there would have been a catastrophe and a lost gun. But at what a price! My best Midshipman knocked over. The doctors gave very little hope from the beginning, but he lived for $29\frac{1}{2}$ hours, suffering the tortures of the damned, which he bore without a murmur. Up to the last he proved himself to be the best plucked one of a thundering good lot, never gave up, and talked of going home and getting all right again. No one had the heart to tell him the truth, and indeed there was no need. It was the worst that I have had, and I can never forget it. Bruce held on through a shocking night and eventually got through.

'On *July* 8*th* we started at 1 a.m. in two Battalions, to co-operate with the other British Troops and the Japanese and Americans in clearing the West side of the Town. We went out through the Taku Road Gate, and making a big detour came upon the enemy not in very great force. The Japanese who were in front soon had them cleared out with a few casualties. We then turned to the right and wended our way to the West Arsenal, which we found was not held at all, but were soon fired on by the Chinese from the City Wall. After much consideration the Japanese and the General came to the conclusion that they would not hold it, so after removing everything that was of value, and ruining what was not, we retired back to the Settlement very tired and dirty at 12 a.m.

'*July 9th.* The *Centurions* then went down, leaving us alone with Tientsin Defence Force.

'*July 10th.* The C.-in-C. followed after them, leaving Dorward to work his wicked will, and Bayly as Senior Naval Officer and old Burke.

'*July 11th.* At 2 a.m. the Chinese made a most determined attack on the Station, and we had to send reinforcements and ammunition. They had advanced in the dark right up to our trenches, and on the extreme right up to the railway line, and had established themselves in some trucks that were lying there, and were able to enfilade our people in the Station. But they were turned out and a number of them killed by the Hong Kong Regiment, who were coming up to reinforce. Some of the Chinese troops were actually bayoneted in the trenches. All this was an indication that we were just as much besieged as ever, so it was all the more necessary to clear our front once and for all by taking the Forts and Native City. On many occasions it had been suggested, and even arrangements made for concerted action among the Powers, but each time there was a hitch. First one was not ready, then another, so sickening each other that relations were severely strained. We ourselves were as bad, if not worse, than any, and were most unreasonable.

'*July 12th.* After a great consultation among the officers commanding, it was decided that a combined attack should be made on the Native City and Forts at daylight next morning.

'*July 13th.* At 2.30 a.m. we fell in 4 Companies Bluejackets, and being much reduced in strength, made only 2,240 all told. We with Americans, Japanese, and French were to make the attack on the City, while the Russians and Germans on the other side of the river were to make the attack on the Forts.

'We advanced to the West Arsenal without opposition, but

while there, the bullets began dropping among us very thickly from the City Walls and directed at the Japanese and Fusiliers inside the Arsenal Wall and to whom we were acting supports. We were lying out in the open without any cover in a stupid place, as the bullets kept falling all round, and only 500 yards in advance we could have had the advantage of the cover of the Arsenal Wall. We were told to halt where we were, so could not go on, but I sent a message to General Dorward asking him if we could come up under cover of the wall, and received a very unnecessarily rude message that we were to remain where we were until we received orders to move. The consequence was that poor Lloyd was killed, 3 men and 18 wounded while doing nothing. This was too much of a good thing, so sent another message reporting the fact of losing men fast. Consequently we were brought up to cover of the wall, which we ought to have been under all the time, and but for downright crass stupidity would not have lost the valuable lives that we did. The men under these most trying circumstances behaved admirably, not a murmur, all as cheerful as possible, in fact, laughing and chaffing all the time.[1] From the Arsenal Wall (under which were now collected Japanese, French, Americans, and ourselves) the City Wall was a distance of from 1,800 to 2,200 yards, the South Gate being directly in our front. This was to be attacked by the Japanese with ourselves and Fusiliers on their left, the Americans on our left, and the French on the right, but owing to stupid blundering on the part of the Americans, they got away on our right and fell into such a hot spot that we had to send reinforcements to extricate them. Phillimore,[2] with one *Barfleur* Company, found that the Americans had lost a lot of men needlessly from not taking sufficient cover, and so upset that they would neither move forward nor retire. In the meantime he brought back their wounded, whom they had left out where they had fallen. This they managed with the loss of only one man killed and one

---

[1] It was at about this time that Beatty, Major Luke, and Midshipman Guy all distinguished themselves by going backwards and forwards to assist in bringing in the wounded under the shelter of the wall. Cp. accounts of Admiral Sir Roger Keyes and Commander Basil J. D. Guy, V.C., on page 72. It is typical of Beatty's modesty that he refrains from mentioning this incident in his diary.

[2] Later Admiral Sir R. F. Phillimore, G.C.B., K.C.M.G., M.V.O.

wounded, and for which he afterwards got thanked by the American C.O.

'At 10 a.m., in the centre it had been reported by the Japanese General to General Dorward that the Japanese had burst the Gate and had established a footing in the Town, so he immediately ordered the 4-inch and 12-pounders to cease firing. We also ordered up all our supports, 2 Companies Blues and Marines, so away. . . .'

The journal stops here, but to continue the narrative:

The Japanese rushed in through the breach in the South Gate, closely followed by Beatty's marines and seamen. Other troops occupied the city walls, and the Russians reached their allotted position to prevent the escape of the enemy. There was much street fighting, in which the Royal Navy and Welsh Fusiliers played a distinguished part, and the whole city, with enormous quantities of material, was in allied hands by nightfall.

Three weeks later an allied force of about twenty thousand men set off to relieve the Legations at Pekin. Beatty, ignoring his wounds, had volunteered to go with this expedition, but the work of the Navy was over, and only a small naval detachment with guns on the new field mountings was required. His wounds, however, were more serious than he allowed people to believe, and the medical authorities would never have allowed him to undertake the trip. One of Beatty's greatest qualities was his refusal to admit defeat in pain, illness, or any other respect. His fortitude was tested on many occasions in the course of his life; it did not diminish as he grew older, and was ultimately the chief cause of his death. On this occasion at Tientsin, wisdom prevailed, and to his bitter disappointment he was invalided home.

Shortly before he left for England, he received the following letter from Captain E. H. Bayly, R.N., under whose able direction he had worked throughout the siege:

Tientsin,
20th July, 1900

MY DEAR BEATTY,

In parting temporarily, and only so, I hope, let me express to you what I hope you will find my official letters have always stated, my belief that you are one of the best and most loyal supporters that any man could wish to have in trying times, or I believe, in any others. Many an hour's work you have saved me at a good deal of trouble and pain to yourself, both before and after your wounds.

Your personal gallantry and disregard of danger need no remarks. They are known to all, Russians, Americans, any who have seen you, as well as to all of us, but perhaps no one has more noticed than I have, your endurance of suffering patiently when you might have well rested, because you would not put any work on others, or wanted to lighten anyone else's burden. I can never forget it, and I can only hope that those with more power to reward than I possess or am ever likely to possess will see that your services do not go unrecognised, though I am aware that your actions have not been governed by any desire but that of doing your duty.

Good-bye, and may good fortune attend you. I am too seedy to write or express myself as I should wish.

Yours ever,

(signed) EDWARD H. BAYLY.

Affairs in China no longer concern us, but to complete the story we need only know that the Legations were duly relieved on 14th August, 1900, after some heavy fighting. Pekin came under allied military control, and peace in China was shortly afterwards restored.

From Beatty's point of view the fighting had been hard and continuous during the bare six weeks he had been ashore, yet his experience had been totally different from that of the Nile campaign, less than two years back. There was none of the deliberate planning and intensive preparation which contributed so largely to Kitchener's success. There was no centralised control, and very often there was doubt as to who was in supreme command. In China unexpected situations were constantly cropping up to be dealt with by the men on the spot, of whom Beatty was not the least.

The enemy were well armed with modern weapons, and their artillery was a powerful factor in terrorising the civilian population, thus increasing the difficulties of the Tientsin garrison. For the greater part of the siege, the British naval brigade had to make the best of what they had got, even if it were only an antiquated muzzle-loading gun.

A civilian eye-witness says: 'No one who saw the Navy at work at Tientsin can feel any doubt about their efficiency. Whether bluejackets or marines, they were all equally good. They fought splendidly and their discipline was remarkable.'

This tribute would apply in full measure to Beatty as commander of the *Barfleur*'s men, who played such a distinguished part in the siege. Here, as in Egypt, Beatty was always to be found where the fighting was most severe, and here again, by virtue of his conduct in action, he attracted the attention of the Commander-in-Chief, who in his despatch of 8th July, 1900, said of him: 'Commander David Beatty, D.S.O., of H.M.S. *Barfleur*, although suffering from two wounds only partially healed, one of which is likely to cause him considerable suffering and inconvenience for some time, begged to be allowed to accompany the expedition for the relief of the forces under my command. He is thoroughly deserving of any mark of appreciation of his services.'

Roger Keyes, in his *Adventures Ashore and Afloat*, recorded memories which substantiate much of Beatty's journal: 'Beatty who, Captain Bayly has told me, had been the life and soul of the defence before the so-called Relief, was very down on his luck. His A.D.C. Esdaile had been mortally wounded beside him the day before. . . . Beatty cheered up when we talked of the morrow. He had been suffering very much for some days from severe wounds in the wrist and arm, but had refused to go on the sick list. He asked me to come as his A.D.C. in place of Esdaile. . . . The next morning, while it was still dark, we were waiting for zero hour in a narrow street and the Chinese were shelling the Settlement. Beatty and I were standing dismounted by our ponies, when some Japanese cavalry pushed their way past us . . . and Beatty got the end of a kick which cut his shin to the bone, to add to his pains.

'As our people were only in support, Beatty and I closed up with the Japanese, who were a pleasure to watch. Everything went according to plan. . . . Beatty's leadership like Cradock's was an inspiration . . . midshipmen and young ordinary seamen bore themselves like veteran soldiers.'

Describing events on 13th July, 1900, Keyes goes on to say: 'During the operation the American 9th Infantry got into an exposed position when in close formation. Beatty promptly rushed out a company of the *Barfleur*'s bluejackets to cover them. Beatty was determined that the naval brigade should not be behindhand, and at once led it forward to take part in the assault. . . . Beatty, his orderly, Major Luke, and Midshipman Guy all greatly distinguished themselves, going backwards and forwards and bringing in the wounded. I was told they all four deserved the V.C. Guy eventually received it.' [On Beatty's recommendation.]

Commander Guy[1] gives his own account of the incident in a private letter dated 9th February, 1949:

'Beatty was my boyhood hero, and I would have done *anything* for him. I have no doubt that it was partly this feeling of adoration for him, coupled with my sense of duty towards one of my own half-company (McCarthy, the Able Seaman who was wounded and whom I had been forced to leave in the open because I could not carry him by myself), that inspired me without a second thought to go back to help when I saw Beatty and two others bringing McCarthy along on a stretcher. I knew that Beatty had already one arm in a sling—he had been wounded some days before and had also been kicked by a mule and was limping into the bargain.

'It was the day, 13th July, 1900, we attacked and took Tientsin Native City, and the affair took place on a patch of open ground which we had to run across to reach the shelter of some mud huts a bit nearer the city walls.

'McCarthy, who was originally shot in the stomach, was hit again on the stretcher, this time through his forehead, which gave him a merciful release from several hours of pain.

'The two men with Commander Beatty and the stretcher were Major Luke, R.M.L.I., and a civilian whose name I cannot remember.

'The capture of the walled Native City pretty well ended our (H.M.S. *Barfleur*'s) participation in the Boxer War. Beatty's conduct throughout was an inspiration to all—of course, he was the only one in the ship who had any experience of active service before, and we all took our cue from him—he was always so cool and collected and absolutely fearless.

'About the only thing I can remember more is the cursing he gave me when I dashed back and tried to relieve him of his hold on the stretcher— "Get to hell out of it" was all the thanks I got ! but he must have made up for this in his report, for I had no idea that I had done anything special,

[1]Now Commander Basil J. D. Guy, V.C., D.S.O., R.N.

[72]

or even been recommended or mentioned, till one night months later I was walking up and down the quarter-deck, when I heard my name read out by a signalman who was taking in a signal giving the names of promotions, decorations, etc., of those mentioned in the *Gazette* for the affair.

'Major Luke was lucky, two narrow shaves, a bullet traversing his cap and cutting his hair, whilst another took a nip out of his ear.

'I found out afterwards that I had two holes through the inside of my left sleeve about elbow height, but exactly when that happened I do not know.'

As the Navy had borne the heat and burden of the Boxer campaign, and had come out of it with so much honour, the officers who had distinguished themselves were well rewarded: Seymour was awarded the G.C.B. Four captains, Bayly, Burke, Callaghan, and Jellicoe, each got the C.B. Rear-Admiral Bruce, the second-in-command of the squadron, got the K.C.M.G., and five lieutenants got the D.S.O. Major L. S. T. Halliday, R.M., and Midshipman B. J. D. Guy were each awarded the V.C. Four commanders, including Beatty, were specially promoted to captain, with seniority, dated 9th November, 1900, and six lieutenants, including Roger Keyes, were promoted to commanders.

Beatty's position on the list of commanders was two hundred and eighteenth. He had served barely two years in that rank, and was only twenty-nine years of age. The average age of a captain at that time was forty-two, so his promotion caused considerable stir in naval circles, but did not surprise the British public, who had not forgotten his reputation as a fighting leader in the Nile campaign of two years ago. There was no surprise at Beatty's promotion in another important quarter, his own ship H.M.S. *Barfleur*. Her torpedo officer, Lieutenant Field, says: 'As Commander of the *Barfleur*, which included his taking command of the force landed (from *Barfleur*) to safeguard the European residents at Tientsin, his characteristics of leadership and readiness to take responsibility were always in evidence, and although he was wounded early in the operations, he continued to retain command of the force until we were relieved. As official record will show, he was promoted for his service during this period, and we his shipmates were the losers, as we were deprived of his company and leadership under which the *Barfleur* was such an efficient and happy ship.' A worthy tribute from a junior officer who in later years became Commander-in-Chief of the Mediterranean Fleet and also First Sea Lord.

CHAPTER FOUR

1900–1901
MARRIAGE

BEATTY had fallen deeply in love with Mrs. Tree before he sailed for China. They wrote impersonal letters to each other for about eight months, and after that the correspondence ceased. Then gossip reached Beatty that she was inclined to be flirtatious. Beatty remained faithful, but pride and possibly discretion prevented him writing to her again. She was surprised to find his letters had ceased, as she was not accustomed to losing admirers, and at heart she still loved him.

Having lost touch with him, she enquired as to his whereabouts and was startled to learn that he had been seriously wounded and was expected soon to arrive in England. To his surprise and delight he received, on his arrival at Portsmouth, a letter and telegram from her. He did not immediately answer them, as he had to consult a surgeon and go into a nursing-home. On 15th September, 1900, he replied:

I have just returned from the surgeon . . . a Mr. Marmaduke Shield . . . he said it would be necessary to operate, and the sooner the better. It was the only chance I had of recovering the use of my hand and that was very doubtful, so I am going to a nursing-home on Monday to be operated on, when I shall know the worst.

Now then a much more important matter—YOU. In your letter you said I did not seem to care for you so much as I have done, and I was to tell you if it were so, and not allow you to live in a fool's paradise. Great Heavens, if you could only imagine the fool's paradise that I was thrown into until a few months ago and taste of it only the smallest portion, I could find it in my heart to forgive you out of sheer pity. But as it is, I will tell you what occurred in my little world and how certain facts have been striking me and with what result. Some months ago all letters from you ceased absolutely and entirely. I was in a position unable to write,

not knowing whether you got the letters or not, and therefore not knowing whether I should be doing you infinite harm by writing. . . . Week
after week went by, month after month, and I had not a particle of a
word from you and I did not think you could have had much difficulty
in sending me a short note. And letters came from other people telling
me, merely in a conversational gossipy way, which is the curse of civilisation, that you and X. were never seen apart, and continually in each
other's pockets, and this by people who did not even know what you are
to me, so under the circumstances what was I to think? . . . I am not
easy going and have an awful temper, so can you blame me if I had a
credence in it, having nothing from you to help tide me over the pain
and keep up my faith? . . . I landed [from China] with my heart full of
rage, and swore I did not care if I ever saw you again or if I were
killed or not. And now I have arrived with the firm determination not
to see you at all in my own mind.

I got your letter which had no effect, and then your wire which
reduced me to wax, but with the resolve that you should tell me all about
it . . . so great is the joy at seeing you, to me, the sweetest creature on
God's earth, but you admit you are an awful flirt. I honestly think you
forgot me for a period, which was dissipated by the fact of my being
wounded, which gave me your sympathy and pity which now you think
is love, and you do not think I care for you so much as before.

Great heavens, do you think if after all that I have heard, after all the
resolves that I have made never to see you again, all the miseries I have
suffered, that I would come to you at all if I did not still love you?
Unfortunately, I shall go on loving you to the bitter end, and now
if this operation does not go right what use to you is a one-armed
individual?

If your father wishes to see so uninteresting a person shortly, he can
find me at the address I gave you. You have offered no explanation
of the things that you have said, and if you do not want to, you
need not. It could not prevent my loving you, if it were all true,
because that could never change. To me always a Queen if not quite
always mine.

Good-bye,

JACK. [The Sailor.]

Ethel Tree was well aware of the power her beauty gave her
to make men do her bidding. She would bow to the will of no
man, but she met her match in David Beatty.

She wrote a noncommittal reply, which he answered just
before the operation.

Nursing Home   (*20th Sept.*, 1900)

If your father is anxious to see me, he had better come here at once, and you sweetheart can come with him, but I must actually see him by myself I think. The morning is the best time, after the doctors have finished with me. I shall look forward to the interview.

The question that is bothering you is what can I do with a wife when I go to sea? Well, there are 40,000 answers: first, I have not got a wife; second, I haven't gone or got to go to sea; third, I may, between ourselves, be promoted, which would put off the question for two years; fourth, I may go to the Admiralty; fifth, if I go to sea, I only go as far as the Mediterranean, where it is possible for a wife to go too. Sixth, I should only be away in the next three years for a very short time and not far off. It is hardly worth going on, is it?

The operation proved to be a very tricky one, as the nerve had to be freed from the muscle in which it had become embedded, and Beatty was under chloroform for one and three-quarter hours. The result was highly satisfactory, and after a few days he returned to his father's house at Bilton Park, Rugby. He was out hunting three weeks later; needless to say, against the doctor's orders.

Walter Cowan records: 'A fragmentary memory of those days in the Dunchurch (North Warwickshire) country, hounds running well and three of us sailors, Beatty, Powlett,[1] and myself, fell in a row jumping into a road, Beatty handicapped by his wounded arm from China.'

Although Mrs. Tree had been living at Compton Verney, Warwick, apart from her husband, for close on two years, there was no official separation. Beatty, having declared his love for her, urged extreme discretion. They met occasionally in the hunting field. There were no clandestine meetings and they were never seen alone in public. His doubts about her conduct while he was in China soon disappeared; he wrote: 'Because I love you and trust you, and because I trust you you can do no wrong.' Their secret was well kept and was only known to Beatty's sister (Mrs. Courage) and Mrs. Tree's father. Mr. Marshall Field at first opposed any question of marriage, but on realising Beatty's sincerity and determination, he abandoned all opposition, and tried to influence his son-in-

---

[1] Later Vice-Admiral A. T. Powlett, C.B.E.

law to give his daughter her freedom. It was foreign to Beatty's nature to have to wait for anything, and there was no sign from Mr. Tree that he would divorce his wife on the grounds of desertion. Even so, Beatty's letters to her at this time, although betraying impatience, are written with delicacy and sometimes with beauty of expression.

Darling mine, if something doesn't happen soon to clear the air and bring us closer together, I feel like going off my head and becoming a raving lunatic and the burden of it all seems more than I can bear and I am in that state you quoted from Longfellow. Do you remember? it has been in my head ever since:

> 'My heart is hot and restless
> My life is full of care,
> And the burden that is laid upon me
> Seems greater than I can bear.'

It is so dreadfully applicable . . . one cannot live on hope alone. It is such small comfort after two long wearisome years, and without an active useful life to occupy the mind it lies like a lump of lead across my heart without the symptoms of a silver lining anywhere.

In his anguish he went to Mrs. Robinson, a fortune-teller well known in London Society. This woman gave such an accurate forecast of Beatty's future that in later years, when he was baffled by the unknown, he would seek her views. He never allowed himself to be influenced by them in professional matters, but he probably derived a certain amount of solace from them if they coincided with his wishes.

It happened that he visited Mrs. Robinson on the day he learnt that he was promoted to Captain. In a letter to Ethel Tree, written on the same day, he tells her of the significance of this early promotion and what it might mean to them both.

(10th Nov., 1900)

I want your sympathy and approbation and your dear arms round my neck to tell me you understand and approve of the honour which has been bestowed upon me and made me the youngest Post Captain by 6½ years in the Service, and I am so glad of it, because it brings me more near to you, and is a somewhat small token that you are not throwing your dear love away on a worthless object. . . .

He then records what Mrs. Robinson had told him:

She informed me I had the most interesting hand she had ever seen, but I presume that is a stock phrase. It was marked with a most extraordinary continued line of success, and I was to occupy in the future some high Government office of great power. It sounds like a fairy-tale. I was to see much more active service, all of which would lead to the right end and also to be again wounded but come up smiling and quite all right. She was very accurate as to the past, and told me many things of great interest which described events perfectly, and then told me of an influence that had entered my life two years ago and then partially disappeared, at one time entirely, to reappear again about the present time. . . . In the end, twelve months from now, all would be right and perfect, and I was to have an exceedingly happy married life. I should shortly take some short journey over the sea . . . my luck was to be and had been proverbial and quite extraordinary. I would go through many dangers but without effect on me. . . . I was to have some great stroke of fortune which would place me far ahead of my contemporaries. In fact, you never saw such a life as you and I are going to have . . . like a fairy-tale. She was in a great state about it, and said that whatever difficulties got in the way, they would all be overcome, and I should have a great success. Everything is nice and nothing bad, so I think she is a perfect fortune-teller as in the story-book! My life is to be the stormiest, most exciting, and successful that ever was seen, accompanied by perfect married bliss. . . . Do you want to see me again after all this and can you stand a stormy life? What she told me of the past I had almost forgotten and how my successes started four years ago, which was quite accurate. Thank heavens I have no superstition, or I should be expecting the world to turn upside down to satisfy the demands of this good lady and my longings. She tells me that I am to get the use of my arm completely, which is reassuring; in fact, she told me nothing which was not pleasant, which I suppose is her trade.

At about the same time Beatty heard that Midshipman Guy, who had fought at his side in China, had been awarded the V.C. He immediately tells Ethel:

. . . My Midshipman has got the Victoria Cross. Isn't it splendid? The Queen's sanction came up yesterday, but is not out yet. I am perfectly delighted, but hope it won't spoil him. Don't say anything about it until it is out: the first Mid. to get one since the Crimea. . . . The Governor tells me it was high time I got married, and he knows a lovely young creature of 20 summers with 11,000 a year who would take me. . . .

The heartening effect of Mrs. Robinson's rosy forecast did not last long. Beatty felt intensely lonely, and suffered from severe fits of depression.

15th Dec., 1900

Oh dear, oh dear, when is it going to be that I shall get more than a letter? It is so small and makes one feel dissatisfied with the work of fate or whatever it is that persists in keeping us apart, and I simply hunger for more and wish I could put the clock on 8 months, and that thought is so very unsatisfactory, as it insinuates such an absolute waste of life, in fact, every hour spent away from you is an absolutely wasted one, and the feeling, instead of getting better, is getting worse. . . . I simply can't make myself do anything except think, think until the brain feels like cracking and all other things fade away to a mere insignificance, which in itself is truly appalling and, if I were not so magnificently selfish, would become a madness, but my selfishness saves me from that and the worldly side of things in general appeals to me too much to even allow of such a state of blessedness, and so I have to wait and let the hours drag by one by one until I shall be permitted to see you again. . . .

23rd Dec., 1900

. . . I often feel as if they ought to have an earthquake or something just as startling to shake half the people out of their humdrum existences and then stand off and see what they would do. There always appears such a terrible sameness about the days, year in and year out, that I wonder often that more people don't go mad. They do the same things, eat the same things, think the same thoughts, and say the same idiotic things. . . . Am I a nasty, cantankerous, cross-grained beast always dissatisfied and grumbling? . . . I feel that I am very worldly and a slave to that most capricious mistress ambition, which is never at rest, but always pushing me along some rocky path. You, sweet one, will have to defend me from that.

His only solace was hunting, and while hacking homeward he would sometimes go out of his way to visit the spot where they first met.

I went to the same old gate at Cook's Gorse, and everything came back to me as of old. I could see you sitting there on your brown horse exactly where I saw you first, and it all seemed as if it had happened only yesterday instead of two years ago. . . . Do you think it will be very long before we can be together always—see the same things at the same time and breathe the same air?

Gunboats in action
on the Nile, 1896.
Drawing by Montbard
from a sketch by
H. C. Seppings Wright

On another day, while Beatty was indulging his romantic fancy at this place of happy memory, his horse shied and nearly unseated him. He was superstitious enough to believe that the horse also had seen the vision of the lovely lady on the brown horse, so indelibly fixed in his own mind. Superstition comes naturally to an Irishman, and Beatty was no exception to the rule. Fifteen years later, when he was Commander-in-Chief of the Grand Fleet, he would astonish the officers and men on the Flagship's bridge by solemnly bowing three times to the new moon. He had only one wish: that the enemy might be delivered into his hands at the earliest possible moment. This was shared by all on board, and in the watches of the night it was not uncommon to see a group of elderly officers going through the same ritual on the quarter-deck.

On New Year's Day, 1901, he wrote to her:

I have a confession to make: a great calamity occurred to me last night and has taken and destroyed one of my treasures, all through my own carelessness, and I can't get over it. The glass in the frame of your photograph got cracked, and so I removed the photograph from underneath, as it is bad luck to keep anyone under broken glass. Last night, going to bed, I propped your dear photograph up against the outside of the frame with a candle in front to shine on it as I always do, so that I can see you the last thing before I blow it out. Somehow, while I was turned round, the picture fell over the top of the candle and I never noticed it. When I turned round again, there it was utterly destroyed. Oh dear, oh dear, I nearly had a fit, as it was the one that looked straight at me as if it was looking straight into my heart. Wasn't I a fool? I could hardly sleep a wink from thinking of it, and now how can I ask you for another when you will see how little care I take of things? It was all my anxiety to be able to see it properly and an abominable carelessness on my part. But you will give me another one, won't you? I promise it shall never happen again, and I shan't be content until I hear from you that you will.

Although Mr. Marshall Field could not be expected to look with favour on the break-up of his daughter's marriage, he showed the greatest tolerance to Beatty, who was on friendly terms with the rest of the family. The chief difficulty lay in the fact that Mrs. Tree had a son. So for six weary months there was deadlock, but during that time the influence of some good friends began to make itself felt. Tree became convinced that his wife would never return to him, and in March 1901 he instructed his solicitors to take divorce proceedings in the U.S.A. against his wife on the grounds of desertion. The decree was granted on 12th May, 1901, and the following extract states the facts:

'Arthur M. Tree *v.* Ethel F. Tree (defendant)

'The defendant wilfully and without any reasonable cause therefor deserted the complainant and absented herself from him for a space of more than two years prior to the filing of the bill... Marriage is hereby dissolved. Further ordered, adjudged and decreed that the complainant have the exclusive care, custody and control and education of Arthur Ronald L. F. Tree, the infant son of the said parties. And that defendant shall have access to said child wherever he may be residing as often as she may reasonably request the same.'

In this affair all parties behaved with delicacy and restraint, and there was in consequence no serious disturbance in the relations between the families concerned. Beatty's father had been told nothing and apparently had no suspicion. He got a severe shock when young David told him that Ethel Tree had obtained her freedom, and that he intended to marry her almost immediately. According to Beatty, 'the old man fell on the flat of his back in a fit. When he came round he took it well'. The main thing that worried him was the effect it might have on his son's career. On being reassured on this point, and having learnt how the affair had been handled, he gave them both his blessing and said he would attend the wedding. After all, his son had not been a co-respondent; his name was never mentioned in the case, and in the eyes of the law Ethel was a free American woman, unknown to English law-courts. There had been no scandal, for during the time that the gossips might have been busy, he was in China, while she was flirting with someone else. The restraint and discretion which governed his handling of the affair after his homecoming afforded no scope for wagging tongues. Beatty wrote to Ethel:

NAVAL AND MILITARY

Hurray! I knew it was coming all right, and now it is all over. Thank the good God, and you can begin again. I'll be with you almost at once, say 10 o'clock, or you would never get dressed at all. God bless you, my own darling.

They were married by special licence at St. George's, Hanover Square, Register Office, on 22nd May, 1901. He was thirty years of age and she was twenty-seven.

The Beattys were well off. Ethel enjoyed a large income from the Marshall Field millions, and in the early days of their marriage she received an allowance from her father. This was generous, enabling them to live very comfortably, and to maintain their position in social and sporting circles. They were both popular, and had many invitations to stay in the houses of the oldest English families. She was naturally extravagant and had very little idea of the value of money. This led her into furnishing too many houses, and they found difficulty in settling down. They took a place in Leicestershire for hunting, a house in London, and a grouse moor in Scotland. She brought him great beauty, a passionate though jealous love, and wealth. She could ride a straight line to hounds and showed interest in the sea by buying a steam yacht. They were good companions, but both possessed implacable wills calling for unusual powers of harmony. His will was the stronger and was dedicated to a cause far greater than himself, whilst hers was mainly concerned with getting her own way. The Navy meant everything to him, and she knew from the beginning that she could have her way in most things, provided she left him full scope with his work and encouraged him in his career. Although she often used the weapons of the spoilt child, resorting at times to tears, they were blissfully happy, and it seemed that nothing could prevent their marriage continuing with the success which crowned their first years together.

It is the wish of the family that Beatty's private life should be included to some extent in his biography, for indeed his life-story would be incomplete without it. On the other hand, this book is an attempt to determine Beatty's place in history as one of Britain's greatest fighting admirals, and space will allow only a glimpse of his married life, chiefly as seen through the medium of his letters.

Beatty wrote to his wife almost daily when they were apart, and although she would often reply by telegram, she conscientiously preserved all his letters. These would fill volumes, and perhaps one day may be brought to light in their entirety, but for our present purpose it is sufficient to quote only those which are relevant to his naval career.

CHAPTER FIVE

1902–1910
YOUNGEST CAPTAIN TO
YOUNGEST ADMIRAL

ALTHOUGH Beatty had been able to hunt throughout two seasons and even took part in point-to-point races, his arm still bothered him. He underwent rigorous electrical treatment, but it was not until June 1902, two years after he had been wounded, that he was officially declared by a naval medical board to be fit for service afloat. He was most anxious to get to sea, and was highly delighted when appointed on 2nd June to command the *Juno*, a cruiser in the Mediterranean.

British naval policy at this time was based on the two-power standard, which laid down that the strength of the Fleet should be equal to that of any other two naval powers. The British Fleet was rapidly expanding to meet the open challenge implied in the German Navy Act of 1900 and Germany's avowed intention of building up a Colonial Empire. The expansion had begun when the British Navy had but recently emerged from the era of masts and yards. Obsolete designs and weapons were being replaced by the products of the scientist and engineer at a pace which outran full consideration of their use in war.

The Navy was fortunate, however, in having three such distinguished officers as Sir John Fisher, Sir Arthur Wilson, and Lord Charles Beresford in command of its principal fleets. These admirals were fully alive to the danger of war in the not too distant future, and appreciated the need for training officers and men to the highest standard of efficiency in handling their weapons and in working the ships that carried them. Sir Arthur Wilson ('Tug Wilson') was the Commander-in-Chief of the newly formed Home Fleet. He had been one of the first torpedo specialists, and had gained the V.C. in Egypt, but above all was a consummate seaman. No man was therefore better qualified to lead the Fleet out of its peace-time groove to a realisation of all that would be required of it in war. In matters of duty he was hard as granite, and under his command the Home Fleet became virtually a 'School for Battle'. At sea his ships were kept on a war footing by day, and were often darkened and manœuvred without lights at night. The men called him 'Old 'ard 'eart'.

Service in the Home Fleet was not popular, but it warned officers of the realities which lay ahead, and many admirals and captains who fought in the war had good reason to be grateful to 'Tug Wilson' for teaching them to take for granted risks and dangers that might have appalled men of lesser experience. He was a sailor first and last; but he was also a tactician who studied tactics by practical use of the Fleet he commanded. The lessons, however, he kept to himself, so, unfortunately, there was no record of them for the education of the younger officers.

Beatty well knew 'Tug's' reputation, and on taking the *Juno* to sea for the first time, was glad to find himself attached temporarily to the Home Fleet, and quickly put on his mettle in manœuvres under this hard-bitten sea-dog. He described the manœuvres as being most strenuous, and confessed that he 'was seasick and bad tempered most of the time'. On one occasion, when ordered to take up station on the cruiser screen, he crossed the bows of the flagship. This being entirely contrary to naval etiquette, the Commander-in-Chief at once asked for his reason. Beatty promptly replied: 'It was the quickest way to my station.' No impertinence was intended: the Fleet was engaged in war exercises, and Beatty, being as war-minded as his chief, felt that finicking formality of this kind should give way to tactical requirements. This view clearly appealed to the admiral, for he made no further comment. After the exercises Beatty sailed to the Mediterranean, carrying out gunnery practices on the way. The results were disappointing; in fact, the general standard of the ship's efficiency fell sadly below his expectations, and he told his officers in no uncertain terms that they must do better.

He wrote to Ethel:

GIBRALTAR, H.M.S. *Juno*   (27th *Aug.*, 1902)

I was terribly disappointed that you broke down at the last moment, and I was a silly fool ever to have made you come down to Weymouth at all. . . . When we went, we steamed past His Majesty in the yacht, and then turned back and steamed towards him again, and so it was pitch dark before we really got away. . . .

Saturday. Again we have been hustled about a good deal by Wilson at Steam Tactics. . . . I cannot think it would be of use to join your father, who always has the most depressing effect upon you. Whereas at Wemyss and Dunrobin they would tend to cheer you up. . . .

Monday. We have had a very busy day, and it appears to me that I have made myself excessively disagreeable to everyone. The old Commander is a dear old thing, but is very trying at times. . . . Tomorrow we do some Prize Firing, and I hope the beggars will shoot straight. It will not be for lack of practice, as we had them at it all day with poor results. The only one who never fails is the trusty Whalley, who made magnificent shooting. . . .

AT SEA BETWEEN GIBRALTAR AND MALTA   (1902)

I walked over the Gibraltar Dockyard, which is a truly remarkable achievement. They have now cut away hills, mostly of solid rock, by hundreds of square yards, and pushed the sea back half a mile to find room in which to cut and make the Dockyard, and what was originally a bare coast-line they have turned into a mighty harbour. It makes one stop and think when one realises that the greater part has been accomplished in six years, and there is no end to the might of science and brains today, but as Mr. Tommy Bowles says in the House, these millions and years of labour are practically at the mercy of a few good guns of the unenterprising Spaniard at Algeciras. Such is the frailty of common sense in big undertakings.

So Beatty was one of the first to appreciate the vulnerability of the mighty Gibraltar. He would have marvelled even more had he lived to see the successful efforts made forty years later to push back the sea still farther in order to establish a single airfield.

Malta brought him nostalgic memories, but soon he was indulging in his favourite sports of polo and racing. Many of his old shipmates were there, and they had a happy 'China' reunion at the Sliema Club. He learnt from them that other ships had also done badly in their firing and that the *Juno* was by no means the worst. On his return to the ship he sent for his gunnery officer and, mellowed by good wine, took back some of the rude remarks he had made to him.

Although Beatty was a hard taskmaster, he soon won by his personality the loyalty and affection of his ship's company, and it was not long before the *Juno* was top ship of the Fleet in certain exercises and drills. Coaling ship was regarded as a competitive evolution, so Beatty invented a method of his own to increase the rate of getting the coal aboard.

He tells Ethel about it:

H.M.S. *Juno* (*4th Oct.*, 1902)

That wretched collier did not get alongside till 11 p.m.; we started at 11.30 and finished at 1 a.m. The men worked like Trojans, and got the 166 tons in at the rate of 110 tons an hour when they had never done more than 64 tons an hour before in the three years they have been in the commission. Even the Commander was smiling, although at first he was much annoyed because I had torn up his arrangements and made him carry out mine, but the end justified the means, and the old dear doesn't bear any malice. We all sat down to a sardine and onion supper afterwards, a great success, like so many Christy Minstrels [black with coal dust], and consequently did not get to bed until 2.30 a.m., which was bad training for tonight, when we shall have to break the blockade.

The *Juno* was nearing the end of her commission when Beatty took her over, being due to pay off at the end of the year. He spent only three months in her with the Mediterranean Fleet, but during this short period took part in three large-scale manœuvres, and witnessed the introduction of wireless telegraphy as a means of signalling. After leaving the *Juno*, he stayed in the Mediterranean, first in command of the *Arrogant*, and then, in October 1904, in command of the *Suffolk*, a modern cruiser of the County Class. Lord Charles Beresford was Commander-in-Chief and Sir John Fisher had just started his remorseless term of office as First Sea Lord. The Fleet was continuously engaged in manœuvres, of which Beatty was critical, complaining in many private letters that the exercises were too artificial and bore little resemblance to conditions likely to be met with in war. 'Too much of a set piece', he wrote, 'where everyone is told where to go and what to do'; and again: 'Everything we do is of the most childish description and not in any single feature can it resemble the real thing. They had far better have spent the money in trying to improve the shooting. . . . We have sacrificed all our gun-practice and torpedo runs. There are only the two policies—we can think of. One is a bold one risking something, or a masterly inactivity risking nothing. Anything in between must be absurd. Still, there it is, and all I have to do is as I am told.'

Many complex problems remained to be solved. The speed of ships was increasing rapidly, the range of guns and torpedoes was lengthening, ships of all classes were growing in size. Wireless telegraphy had reached a stage where ships could communicate when out of sight of each other. Oil fuel was soon to begin replacing coal, and submarines were doing their trials at sea. All these new factors had their influence on strategy and tactics, and were of absorbing interest to Beatty. His vivid imagination and foresight enabled him always to examine the problems against the dark background of war. Naturally out-spoken, and with no false notions about seniority, he never hesitated to express his views officially to the Commander-in-Chief, where the seeds fell not on stony ground, and unofficially to his colleagues, who in most cases being much older than he was, regarded him with feelings of the greatest suspicion. 'All very well for him,' they thought; 'he's got lots of money and can say what he likes.' Nevertheless, the name of *Suffolk* became a household word for smartness and efficiency which outlived her time on the station. His youth made him a baby amongst the admirals and captains, but the same youth enabled him to mix freely with the younger officers and to pick up their ideas. Beresford, as a fighting admiral and brother Irishman, had the greatest affection for Beatty, and their friendship lasted unimpaired throughout the days of the Beresford-Fisher controversy which threatened some years later to split the Navy—but has no place in this biography, as Beatty most wisely kept clear.

It was not always plain sailing for Beatty: he had his set-backs. Once when the *Suffolk* was doing a full power trial on passage to Malta her boilers started priming. The Chief Engineer advised the Captain to reduce speed. Beatty, who wanted to get back to Malta as soon as possible, complied to a certain extent, but kept the ship going at a speed above the prescribed limit, causing serious damage to the machinery. Beatty accepted full responsibility and there was talk of a court-martial. On hearing this his wife is said to have remarked: 'What!—court-martial my David? I'll buy them a new ship!' Several different versions of this story were repeated in the Fleet.

On 22nd February, 1905, a son and heir was born. He was christened 'David Field' at Malta before a happy gathering of naval officers and their wives. An amusing letter survives from Mrs. Watkins, the English choir-mistress in Malta:

David Beatty was Captain of the *Suffolk*. The little church was full of the rank and fashion of Malta, and practically everyone was chattering and talking. Mrs. Beatty introduced me to Captain Beatty. I beckoned him to come out of the church and I said, 'I have spent three years trying to teach the choirboys to reverence the House of God and you bring your friends here and treat the church like the lounge of a theatre! Please stop it.' Captain Beatty was quite charming, and immediately stopped all the noise, and his son was admitted a member of the church in decency and order.

On 19th September, 1905, Beatty was succeeded in command of the *Suffolk* by Captain Rosslyn Wemyss, and about twelve months later was appointed to the unique post of Naval Adviser to the Army Council. His work for the next two years was mainly concerned with liaison duties between the Admiralty and War Office. Previous service with the Army in the field had equipped him with a knowledge of military affairs, which enabled him to see the soldiers' point of view and so promote co-operation between the two services. His presence at the War Office was of the utmost importance, as plans were being formulated for the transport of an expeditionary force to French ports in the event of war. This was the only shore appointment, excluding training courses, held by Beatty from the time he first went to sea as a Naval Cadet till he reached Flag rank, a fact which is conveniently forgotten by those who try to make out that he lacked sea experience.

On leaving the War Office in December 1908, Beatty took

over the command of the battleship *Queen* in the Atlantic Fleet, which consisted of six battleships and some smaller ships under Prince Louis of Battenberg. The Germans were now building with feverish haste. Public opinion in England was thoroughly aroused, and pressed for a more rapid expansion of battleship strength. Sir John Fisher, on the crest of the wave, was following up the new 'all big gun' experimental *Dreadnought*, with eight super-dreadnoughts, and at the same time was scrapping ruthlessly every ship he considered to be useless and redundant. He was also concentrating the flower of British naval strength in home waters. The Atlantic Fleet formed part of this concentration, but when based at Gibraltar also provided a link with the Mediterranean, frequently taking part in manœuvres with the Home Fleet on the one hand and with the Mediterranean Fleet on the other, sometimes combining exercises with both. Beatty quickly attracted the attention of his chief, for on 7th July, 1909, Prince Louis, in a letter to Mrs. Beatty, wrote: 'It will probably give you pleasure to know that your husband's handling of *Queen* is the best in the Squadron.'

In Beatty's own letters to his wife, he criticises some of his senior officers, and continues to complain that the fleet exercises and gunnery practices bore no relation to the realities of war. He takes particular exception to Admiralty interference in manœuvres, and asserts that some of them were designed for political motives rather than for honest investigation of current problems. His letters are devoted almost exclusively to naval matters, and he keeps on reminding her that war is inevitable, and that the Navy to him must come before everything. It is hardly surprising that she was not altogether pleased with this outlook.

BEREHAVEN, H.M.S. *Queen*   (*9th Feb.*, 1909)

I was glad to hear you went to see the *Englishman's Home* [a play written to awaken the British people to the danger of invasion by Germany] and enjoyed it. I've no doubt if they form provincial companies to perform it all over the country it may do good. . . . That it will ever serve any real purpose as regards the invasion of England is ridiculous. That could only take place if the Navy ceased to exist, and when that happens, well, we can prepare for the worst. . . . In the evening I dined with Prince Louis, who was very pleasant.

Speaking of his new command Beatty says:

H.M.S. *Queen* (13th Feb., 1909)

There is good material, and if I can't make a smart ship out of it I'll give up the sea and take to growing cabbages. Poor Prince Louis has taken to his bed with the influenza. . . . I was glad to hear Charlie Beresford was gay. I saw in the paper he had secured an influential birthday party. Little good I am afraid it will do him. Next month he will be relieved and be at a loose end. Well, he has done his time and, if he goes into Parliament, will be a sore thorn in Jacky Fisher's side, which won't be any harm.

BANTRY, H.M.S. *Queen* (14th Feb., 1909)

Another Admiral has unexpectedly retired, which only leaves ten in front of me on the list, which means four since 1st Jan. At that rate I shall not be very long here, but should like to remain sufficiently long to see my endeavours bear fruit if they ever will. I had the three other Captains to dine with me last night. I shall get all the Commanders to dine with me tomorrow night, and so get acquainted with them and the young ideas in the Fleet. They ought to be more interesting than the Captains.

BANTRY, H.M.S. *Queen* (16th Feb., 1909)

So I take it, the Main Fleet is to be composed of four Divisions: North Sea Div. under Admiral May who will be C.-in-C.; Channel Div. under Milne; Atlantic Div., Prince Louis; Home Div., Nevill. We are to have our refitting base at Gibraltar and two Home Bases in Home Waters, one at Dover and one here, and our cruising ground will be the Irish coast. . . . It is a better and more wholesome, though very strenuous existence, and I shall be in the end all the better for it, though exile it is from all I care for and have to live for. Do you remember once you complained that I wanted to be tied to your apron strings? The comic side of the remark struck me at the time that it could even be applied to a Naval Officer. However, you have your strings free now, so make the most of it, for I shall be back again tied up before so very long. I should like to have a peep every now and then of my two treasures just to help me on the way.

BANTRY, H.M.S. *Queen* (19th Feb., 1909)

I have just returned from a good long walk to Glengariff, but it was a good deal farther than I thought, a good twelve miles there and back, so I am keeping myself pretty fit against the time when the fittest will be likely to be most successful as per old General French. It seemed just as if it were yesterday that I was there, and certainly not seven long years, no not long years but full years. It was just the same. The hotel has improved. I went in and saw the rooms we had, and my heart ached with longing for my Tata [his pet name for Ethel].

BABY DAVID'S DAY (22nd Feb., 1909)

Our little loved one is the gigantic age of four. You said in one of your letters that 'Baby David was playing with your vanities that you have to use to make you look young'. I like that coming from you who look so youthful, and that you, a woman in the prime of life, should commence on such aids is simply ludicrous.

BANTRY, H.M.S. *Queen* (20th Feb., 1909)

We had our first competition with the Fleet yesterday in mooring the ship and we beat them all to blazes. The band is doing very well, although not brilliant, but we want sadly a good 'Cello player and First Violin. . . .

Tell Obby Beauclerk [Duke of St. Albans] I like *The Rise and Fall of the Netherlands*. I also found Putnam Weale's book *The Coming Struggle in Eastern Asia* most interesting. I am thrilled with Carlyle's *French Revolution*, which I read slowly and at intervals. A little goes a long way, as you must read every word and no skipping or else you lose the context. . . . My opinion is that Austria and Servia are as near blows as makes no matter, and I can't see how it can be avoided, unless Austria entirely alters her attitude. Furthermore, if it does come, Russia can't sit idle and watch Austria absorb Servia, so in she comes. Then arises the question of the Triple Alliance, and in how far Germany is involved to support Austria. It is a nice point, and I cannot see Germany doing nothing. Then where is our friend France and the Russo-Franco Alliance, backed up by the spirit which they like to make out pervades the whole of France, but in reality does not, namely, the one desire of a War of Revenge for 1870? *Alors*, where are we? The whole of Europe will blaze if it once starts, and the outlook at present is of the worst. [A perfect prophecy of events in 1914.]

He has his lighter moments, as in the dance at Queenstown described below, but his mind keeps coming back to the international situation.

QUEENSTOWN, H.M.S. *Queen* (2nd Mar., 1909)

Such a debauch. We bumped and banged away with glorious creatures we've never seen before and never shall see again, and Admirals and Midshipmen, with intermediate ranks thrown in, vied with each other as to who should last the longest. Needless to say the Midshipmen won in a canter, in fact, the girls nearly stampeded the lot in their endeavour to secure a Mid each time. . . . It is extraordinary how in great crises the Great Diplomatic Power of Russia always adds to its reputation where others fail, and there can be no question that in that field their superiority is beyond all question. . . . It is not realised in England how very near the whole world is to an appalling conflict which is treated in the usual light and airy way by the British public led by the British Press. Your wire just received.

Sir John Fisher, the First Sea Lord, was being heavily criticised at this time for encouraging his friends in the Fleet to write privately to him about the capabilities of other officers.

Beatty, who hated any suggestion of the Service being tainted with intrigue, admired Fisher's motive, but he disliked his methods and his friends.

Lord Charles Beresford openly attacked Fisher in the House of Commons and the Press, and the duel overhung the Navy like a pall. Except for opinions expressed to Ethel privately, Beatty remained neutral. He owed much to Lord Charles, but in time to come he was to owe more to Fisher.

DEAL, H.M.S. *Queen* (*8th Apr.*, 1909)

McKenna was asked in the House about the letter produced by Sir George Armstrong, and his reply was that it was written by Captain Bacon, a highly trusted officer, and he had read it and could see nothing wrong in it. That is a nice sort of admission; wasn't it practically countenancing the method of espionage that has been brought into force by our friend Fisher?

Beatty himself had strong views about his senior officers, but he reserved these confidences for his wife's private ear. He is thrilled with the prospects of manœuvres and action.

DEAL, H.M.S. *Queen* (*10th Apr.*, 1909)

We are off this afternoon, and then for the North Sea and manœuvres day and night. I hope and pray we shall have plenty of it. When I am on the job I like lots of it, and I can't stand Fleet work, which constitutes lying in harbour and doing nothing. . . .

CROMARTY, H.M.S. *Queen* (*14th Apr.*, 1909)

In the midst of a naval whirl, 21 battleships, cruisers galore and torpedo craft, a truly fine sight. Many admirals and not one that inspires a great deal of confidence except Prince Louis, and his birth qualifications are against him. [Sadly prophetic.]

I went on board to see May, the Admiralissimo, who was very nice and pleasant but not a man that impresses me as being possessed of the qualities of a Great Commander. I saw Prince Louis also and had some good news which I must impart to you. We are not going to Galway or to Ireland at all, but are going to do our gunlayers' practice at the mouth of the Medway, that is to say, off Margate. . . . This ship has been told off by the Admiralty to carry out a series of experiments with shrapnel shell for night defence. . . .

KIRKWALL, H.M.S. *Queen*   (19*th Apr.*, 1909)

Drilling all morning, not so successfully as I could wish. We were first ship only three times and third twice; considering we are a newly commissioned ship not bad, but we must be first every time in future. . . . Have you found any Soothsayers at Mentone? All my midshipmen except four have gone, and we have got twelve new ones from another ship, and they are the most dreadful lot of youths I have ever seen, dirty, untidy, unhealthy-looking young rascals. It appears they have never been taken care of in the other ships they have been in. Consequently, the moral standard is low. I dare say we shall get them right in time, but they are dreadful at present.

DINGWALL, H.M.S. *Queen*   (20*th Apr.*, 1909)

Your dear flowers arrived last night, poor sweet things, crushed and mostly dead. They could not stand the transition from the sunny balmy air of the South to the bleak Northern atmosphere, so they just died, but their fragrance remained, and they are symbolic of the South and they come from my sweetheart. . . . So you remember the little fern that my sweet boy bought for his daddy long ago. It is still going strong and growing into a magnificent bush and always sits on my table.

[Ethel Beatty at this time was in the South of France.]

AT SEA, H.M.S. *Queen*   (24*th Apr.*, 1909)

It is a beautiful morning. We are just passing Flamborough Head in Yorkshire, a great bluff that sticks out into the sea like the nose of a shark, and the land falls away from it each side, and it's fascinating to look at. It's so very solid and homely. There is always something very comforting to a sailor in sighting land, homeland in the early morning, and I am sure he is fonder of it then than at any other time. It tells him he hasn't slipped off the edge yet, and loves the smell of the brown earth that always comes with it. . . . You remember when reading Nelson's letters; I remembered what a whining peevish man he seemed by them, how they were mostly taken up by the bad health he truly enjoyed. I know better now, poor dear, there was little else for him to write of. Think of it, week in, week out, month in, month out, up to the space of three years and never put foot on shore and with a rotten constitution, but then, he had the hope strong in him that if he stuck it out he would reap his reward by meeting and annihilating the French. He did, poor Nelson, at Trafalgar, and it was worth it all to have a glorious end like that, worth three years of anybody's life. We have no reward on the horizon, so we grumble and growl at being three days at sea, hence a useful example of the ways and thoughts of men and of how circumstances alter cases, because we are no worse and hope we are nearly so earnest and just as keen.

H.M.S. *Queen* (28th Apr., 1909)
They have been again at McKenna in Parliament, and he has acknowledged our inferiority to Germany in the matter of docking accommodation for *Dreadnoughts*—to the effect that we have no docks capable of taking a *Dreadnought* on the eastern coast to Germany. Fine—and I hear that the House of Lords are going to ask questions out of Capt. Bacon's letter. The poor Admiralty will be worried into their graves if this continues much longer. . . . I have finished the book, *The City of Beautiful Nonsense*, and I think it is one of the most charming books I have read for quite a long time and I am sure you'll love it. Guns go off every minute, air is full of bombardment. The Gunnery Lieut. Lewin will finish up in a lunatic asylum if it continues much longer. He works like a brick.

Referring again to the Bacon letter, he says:

Matters have gone from bad to worse, an enquiry will do good *if* done properly but *not* a public one. That can do no good and an infinite amount of harm. . . . Asquith, Edw. Gray, Haldane, and Lord Crewe, two lawyers and two gentlemen, they ought to arrive at something, and if they will only make a scapegoat to stamp out this accursed spirit of espionage, jealousy, and time-serving initiated by Fisher, they will earn the gratitude of the country as a whole and the Navy in particular. . . . I just paddled round the streets of Dover, visited the few shops we had visited together, the Chemist, Flower, and Antique shop, not to buy anything, but for just the associations. Poked my nose into the Burlington and sorrowfully wandered on—and then came on board. I like being on board best when you are not near me, unless I have something definite to do, because I write to you and it brings you so much nearer to me. Now

Portrait of David Beatty by Philip de Laszlo, July 1911

I am beginning again. There is no doubt I love you, oh, my Tata, too much, with a big big *too*. Never mind, I wouldn't change it, and you'll have to bear with it right unto the end when you are a dear, soft-voiced, gentle, white-haired old lady with a charm all your very own that can have no imitation.

OBAN, H.M.S. *Queen* (22nd *June*, 1909)

. . . Unless the elements come to our aid and we enjoy thick weather to cloak our movements from the hosts of cruisers that the enemy have, we are bound to be caught. With luck they ought to be interesting, but on the other hand very little will turn them into a fiasco. And as far as we can judge, the Admiralty are interfering to such an extent that they can hardly fail to track us, nothing of practical value, in fact, only what the Admiralty wish, so that they can turn to the country and say, 'Look what fine fellows we are and what a strong position the manœuvres have proved that we have our Fleet in. . . .'

I dined tonight with Prince Louis, who as always is charming and simple and yet all there. Curzon-Howe, I sat next to, is always nice to me. He is a very good sound man, with streaks of brilliancy clouded by a somewhat distorted view of human nature. Young and active for his years, clear-sighted and with good sense, delightful manners and charming to talk to, and yet there is something that is there, which, when the time comes, would either produce a genius in the art of Naval war or a stubborn man that could not help but make the most terrific mistakes. Which is it to be? I am afraid the test will never arise in his time and perhaps it's as well. We are in the throes of coaling. . . .

OBAN, H.M.S. *Queen* (29th *June*, 1909)

We had a great day at drills yesterday, and were first or second in all and mostly first, so the *Queen* did well. But that is only a satisfaction to ourselves. . . . Old Curzon-Howe, our C.-in-C., has just been on board to see me, and was very perturbed, doubtful as to whether there would be manœuvres or not. The Admiralty as usual will tell them nothing. When a man arrives to the exalted position of C.-in-C., he should be treated with rather more consideration if not courtesy. . . . Have come to the conclusion that Charlie Beresford is getting an old man and ought to give up making speeches. It was mostly twaddle and full of innuendoes as to what he could say if he only would, which was worse than useless and not in very good taste.

(4th *July*, 1909)

We found our Allies at 9 o'clock last night and made our junction and, as it remained thick, it was a grand opportunity to exercise a little deceit, and by altering course judiciously and using the armoured cruisers to demonstrate in another direction, we could have led them a dance for several days. . . . Tomorrow we go to Foynes up the Shannon, and our C.-in-C. says he is going to stop there until the 14th, nine whole days. It is right up the river, so can do no firing or useful work of any sort. I think he must be going mad.

FOYNES, H.M.S. *Queen* (6th *July,* 1909)

Could stand it no more, so packed up my work, and proceeded ashore, blowing half a gale, and went for a jolly good tramp, finishing up running top speed 2½ miles without stopping, not bad for an old gentleman [He was thirty-eight!] who will be an Admiral before the year is out. But I drove the devils and cobwebs away, and came home and found your dear delightful letters from my beloved. I kept on reading until it was time to dress for dinner with Prince Louis, where I really was, for once, a success. . . . At Newmarket of course you were the best-dressed woman. You always are, only you won't realise it, and think I am an ass for telling you so. However, at times out of the mouths of simpletons and fools cometh much wisdom. I am glad the old King [Edward VII] and Prince of Wales [George V] had a yarn with you and were pleasant. . . .

H.M.S. *Queen* (11th *July,* 1909)

I went to lunch and met the Postman who had your letter which I tore from him, but had no time to read it, as I was already late and had two miles to walk. . . . It was the most delightfully amusing luncheon party, without meaning to be, you ever saw. I caught up with Rosie [Wemyss[1]] *en route*. It was typically Irish, old Victorian hideous mansion, the plaster falling off the walls, the inside mildewy, the door opened by a very old gentleman with a moustache in a very musty old suit of evening dress six sizes too big for him, gone at the knees, who ushered us into the Party of old Lord Monteagle waiting the arrival of Prince Louis with his daughter. It was exactly like a picture out of one of Lever's books. I took Rosie for a walk after, blowing a gale of wind, and we both never stopped talking.

BANTRY, H.M.S. *Queen* (14th *July,* 1909)

The sea fog rolled up and enveloped us as we left the Shannon, which increased the dangers of navigation and at the same time added an excitement to the hour, which prevented it from becoming humdrum and gave one something to overcome or compete against, which after all is half the joy of life. And there is something uncanny about booming along in a wet fog when you cannot see more than a 100 yards in front on either side. As we passed Kerry Head we could hear the shore birds piping their

[1] Afterwards Admiral of the Fleet Lord Wester Wemyss.

wild music; saddest and most delightful of all, two curlews calling to each other like the wail of two lost souls. I am sure, with the Greeks, that distressed souls take up their abode in wild sea birds, and then we steamed into the fog, which got thicker towards midnight, and really I think I enjoyed it, could see nothing, hear nothing except the wash of the water on the bow, and I sat on the rail of the bridge and opened my lungs and swallowed huge draughts of damp, soft, pure, warm air which had crossed the Atlantic from S.W. to N.E. and so was unpolluted for 10,000 miles, so felt it was doing me good, yes, I really did enjoy it, and Beaudon thought I was mad because I said what a nice night it was. And I pitied you in stuffy London surrounded by a polluted atmosphere and the crowds of hunters of excitement which is principally composed of doing something which others don't do and consequently the enjoyment lies in making one's friends envious, isn't it?

Scapa Flow, H.M.S. *Queen* (17th *July*, 1909)

The two days have been most productive, principally in demonstrating how unpractised our Admirals are in the manner and methods of handling large fleets. It is not their fault. We don't do enough of it, either sufficiently frequent or for sufficiently long periods to enable them to correct mistakes and put into full use the experience that is gained even by two days' continual manœuvring, but I think we lack a strong man sufficiently energetic, who would drive home the object-lesson of every mistake so that it should not be committed again. We have a very fine Fleet and the best materials. May the Lord help the Germans if they were to come along now. But we have eight Admirals, and there is not one among them, unless it be Prince Louis, who impresses me that he is capable of a great effort and 34 Captains among whom there is really fine material, which seems wasted for the want of a guide or leader. . . .

Ethel's letters were usually rather brief, and sometimes she would reply by telegram.

The London season was at its height, and having many admirers she was enjoying every moment of it. Although she knew that Beatty was fully occupied with his ship, she did not realise how much a letter describing all her doings and the silly little details of social life would mean to him in the solitude of his cabin when the day's work was done. A note of cynicism creeps into an occasional letter of this time.

Oban, H.M.S. *Queen* (21st *June*, 1909)

It's a terrible day, Sunday in Scotland, no mails, no golf, no nothing. . . . You said you have very little news to give me. Well, I fear that, if

there is no news to be obtained at Ascot during Ascot week, there is not
much chance from Oban. I should have liked to have had a peep at you
in your lace frock. There are tremendous descriptions in all the papers
of the clothes, even my stolid old *Times*. I suppose the usual party and
tuft-hunters anchored off the Royal Box gazing with longing eyes. Did
Lady Churchill have difficulty in beating off besiegers to her boxes, or
were there any amusing incidents attached to their efforts? Was there
nobody in that great throng of interest that you met or said anything of
interest? Surely it must have been the dullest of entertainments lasting
the inside of a week that produced absolutely nothing of interest beyond
clothes. If so, I am almost glad I was not there, but can hardly believe it,
especially as you were so busy. *Mon Dieu* what a life, which produces the
type depicted by Sargent in his portraits of the Restless *Great*? Ladies on
priceless sofas. No wonder he refuses to paint any more portraits, but has
begun to manifest a yearning for producing the Simple Life. Here we
have the Simple Life in truth, not even enlivened by hearing of the
doings of the gay world. I took old Packs[1] for a good 3½ hours'
walk over the hills and, being one of the few fine days, the views were
glorious.

At the end of July 1909, after the summer manœuvres, the
Fleet anchored off Southend in order to give taxpayers an
opportunity to see their money's worth. During the visit a
landing party of 1,200 officers and men marched through the
streets of London with Beatty in command. He and his men
created a deep impression as they marched past the Lord Mayor
at the Mansion House. They were entertained to lunch at
Guildhall, and in replying to the toast of the Navy, Beatty,
referring to a recent warning of Lord Rosebery, said: 'Never
in the history of the world had there been so overpowering a
preparation for war. The time must be drawing very close
when the efficiency of the Navy may be put to the test. In the
words of the hymn, and we are very fond of hymns in the Navy
on Sunday:

> *Principalities and Powers*
> *Mustering their unseen array*
> *Wait for thine unguarded hours.*
> *Watch and Pray.*

[1] Later Admiral Sir W. Pakenham, who became Beatty's Second-in-Command at
Jutland.

We are watching and praying, and we are praying that should the time ever come, we shall be found to conform to the words of the immortal Nelson that we have done our duty.'

For a short spell Beatty saw something of his wife, and was able to patch up the rift which threatened, and is liable to occur in, sailors' lives on account of enforced separations. The Atlantic Fleet remained only for a month or two in English waters, and then sailed away to its base, Gibraltar. Ethel did not follow him, so the correspondence was resumed:

GIBRALTAR   (23rd Nov., 1909)
Today I went out for my first hunt with the Calpe hounds. They were still cub-hunting, and then went to a larger cover on the side of the precipice. They soon found and we hurled ourselves down the precipice and along the side of another most precipitous hill covered with large boulders and scrub, and ran vigorously for about ten minutes into a similar place. It certainly has its excitements, and so can imagine could be great fun. The much-despised (by you) *Blue Moon* went like an Angel. How she kept her feet I don't know, but I left it all to her and she never failed. . . . The Field was most amusing, mostly mounted on little rats of ponies, a most melancholy sight climbing the mountain with legs almost trailing on the ground. The Female was wonderful in its hideosity, but poor things, they didn't know it. It was a perfectly heavenly afternoon, the air like wine and the scenery beautiful. . . . I see that Admiral Sturdee is to relieve another Admiral in Home Fleet. There remains one more to be appointed, and then possibly some of those that have been left out might be induced to retire as hopeless.

GIBRALTAR, H.M.S. *Queen*   (5th Dec., 1909)
I see Bacon has departed, so actually am the Senior Captain in the British Navy, a proud position, but just now would rather be the Junior Admiral, but I can't think that it will be long deferred. . . . Just come back from another day's hunting with the Calpe. It is a rest cure if you like. There was a good scent, and hounds flew over the most impossible country for about 20 minutes.

GIBRALTAR, H.M.S. *Queen*   (7th Dec., 1909)
I had a letter from Captain Madden this morning, (he is Private Secretary to the First Lord) to say that the latter had instructed him to say that the Treasury sanction and an Order in Council had been obtained empowering the Admiralty to promote me to Flag Rank the next vacancy that occurs. So that is all right isn't it? Let us hope the

vacancy will occur before very long. You might ask Jimmy when Admiral Henderson is going to retire?

GIBRALTAR, H.M.S. *Queen*   (*10th Dec.*, 1909)

You never mention politics in your letters, but do you never hear an expression of opinion worth quoting, or is the subject tabooed as being too ordinary and uninteresting among the intellectuals? We in the Navy are naturally much interested, as the result will have very important and far-reaching results upon the Service, also on our Foreign Relations with our great Rivals, which must cause anxiety to all those in the Navy who look ahead or think about the future at all. But the idle public are as blind in England as they were in Russia before the Russo-Japanese War. Please God we shall not have such a rude awakening or unhappy issue as they had. But in view of what we *Know*, one cannot but have serious misgivings, and I should describe the outlook as gloomy in the extreme, whichever Party wins. I fear we are not governed by any Office by that single purposeness, which alone can command success and which we know is being put to such effect by the Germans. I don't suppose you have seen, considered or heard mentioned the German Naval Estimates. Such purposeness is illustrated by the toast drunk every night in every German-Man-of-War 'To the Great Day'. While we waste our time listening to the quarrelling of Politicians and Admirals which provide the necessary copy for the newspapers and topics for discussion in the Fleet. What we truly need is a *man*, a big man who knows what is required and will get it, but I fear the national characteristic is against any such man making himself heard and felt until the moment arrives, and in the preceding phases everything is left to the claptrap of the small politician. It was ever thus, history repeats itself. When the blow falls we shall be unprepared, suffer many losses, and lose many lives and valuable assets, and the disasters will themselves breed the man and the strong points of the national character, and out of the debris we shall dig our way to a successful issue. [Another remarkable prophecy.]

Meanwhile Ethel paid a visit to Mrs. Robinson (the fortune-teller), but this time Beatty is sceptical:

H.M.S. *Queen*   (*13th Dec.*, 1909)

I was black and blue all over one side this morning after my adventure with the tree in the cork woods. They are wonderfully hard, these cork trees, and it is quite extraordinary that people are not killed galloping through them. . . . Silly Mrs. Robinson, she has a good memory to repeat herself. And if she goes on long enough she is bound to be right, as in my profession I am bound some time or other to go upon some sort of expedition which comes under the heading of mission, but she has been foretelling it now for *five* years. You think it's the Prince and Princess going to South Africa in September? I hope not, as I should like our autumn at Invercauld and have no desire to turn into a Court appendage.

The *Queen* remained at Gibraltar while most of the other ships went home for Christmas. In spite of his bright prospects in the Navy, he gives way to depression in his loneliness, and has doubts about his wife's happiness:

H.M.S. *Queen*   (*Christmas,* 1909)
    The men had a very quiet but enjoyable Christmas. The ship was beautifully decorated. . . . I do hope, dear one, you are *happy*. It struck me very forcibly on my return that you did not seem so, and the afternoon we went down to Brooksby [their house in Leicestershire] I felt as if I was an ogre dragging you to some fearful place that you dreaded. You see, dear, your happiness is the one thing I have to live for, and if only you are happy and contented, so am I, but I fear I am making a hash of it somehow, and at times it appears that the point of a rift in the lute is inclined to show and I can't think why, but have a sort of intuition that it is there. God knows I do not want to force myself at all times down your throat, but give me your confidence in *all things*. By plain speaking half the misery in the world could be done away with. . . . A new year is about to begin. I shall arrive at a higher status in Life at the same time with greater responsibilities and possibly greater opportunities, of which I shall want to make the most, and the first essential must be that I have you on my side, your advice, your assistance, and your confidence in all things. . . . I have my many faults. No one can see them more than you; won't you out of kindness point out where I fail, and in what I upset you, as it would appear that I do at times? You have the instinct and could put your finger on the sore spot if you could only speak frankly and tell me wherein I fail, for I truly feel that I do fail, and I do so want to succeed in making you happy and not rub you up the wrong way. Will you try to understand me and this rigmarole?

Owing to the expansion of the Fleet, officers were passing through the Captains' list more rapidly than usual, and at the end of 1909 Beatty found himself at the top of the list without having completed the six years' service required by peace-time regulations for promotion to Flag rank. While serving as a

Captain, he had commanded three cruisers and one battleship, all working with the principal fleets. His total time at sea in this rank was, however, only three years and five months. He had served two years at the War Office, and the rest of his time as a Captain (three years and seven months) had been spent on half-pay. Prince Louis, foreseeing the danger that the Navy might lose one of its most promising officers, informed the Admiralty that something would have to be done. Their Lordships[1] were well aware of the position and, supported by Prince Louis, obtained a special Order in Council stating that 'this officer was seriously wounded in action in China, and was consequently prevented from receiving an appointment for a considerable period. We beg leave humbly to recommend that Your Majesty may be graciously pleased by your Order in Council to sanction the promotion of Captain David Beatty, M.V.O., D.S.O., A.D.C., to Flag rank in his turn, notwithstanding the regulations above referred to.' Accordingly His Majesty graciously sanctioned the promotion of Captain David Beatty to Rear-Admiral on 1st January, 1910, when he was just under thirty-nine years of age, the youngest Flag officer in the Royal Navy in over a hundred years. Prince Louis at once wrote his congratulations:

> CUMBERLAND LODGE,
> WINDSOR
> (*2nd January*, 1910)

MY DEAR BEATTY,

Many thanks indeed for your kind wishes for the New Year which we reciprocate most warmly. I quite agree that the performance of *Queen*'s Engine-room personnel was quite excellent, and I shall take an early opportunity of expressing to the Engineer Commander my high appreciation.

To reach Flag rank at your age is indeed a matter for congratulation, and should I be honoured with any more sea Commands after my present one, I could not wish for any better assistant than you.

I am indeed sorry not to be able to take leave of you in the midst of the Fleet and to get your brother Officers to meet you at dinner in my cabin for the last time.

---

[1] The Board of Admiralty at this time included Mr. Reginald McKenna, Sir John Fisher, Sir Francis Bridgeman, and Sir John Jellicoe.

Of the *Queen* under your command, I can only say that my involuntary wish was that the other ships might be as good.

Hoping to see you both in London.

I am,

Yours sincerely,

LOUIS BATTENBERG.

The Times of 3rd January, 1910, commenting on Beatty's promotion to Rear-Admiral says:

'Rear-Admiral Beatty will not only be the youngest officer on the Flag list, but will be younger than over 90 per cent. of the officers now on the captains' list. . . . He attains Flag rank at the age of 38, a circumstance which is without precedent in modern times, except in the case of Royal Princes, and to find a similar rate of advancement it is necessary to go back to the Eighteenth Century, when Rodney was a Flag officer at 31 and Keppel at 37.'

His new promotion created even greater stir in conventional naval circles than his early promotion to captain. There was some justification for this, as he had spent so much time as a captain on half-pay. On the other hand, he had done a reasonable quota of sea time, and it is probable that he gained more in wisdom and breadth of view from the distinguished people he met in Society and as Naval Adviser to the Army Council than he would have done in orthodox shore appointments.

On 2nd April, 1910, to his delight, a second son, Peter, was born.

Although Beatty enjoyed to the full 'the blessings of the land', his enthusiasm for serving at sea never flagged. He was far more interested in the proper employment of the Fleet in war and how to use weapons than in the technical details of their construction. This was a time when naval thought was tending to become immersed in the intricacies of material, and the study of strategy and tactics suffered accordingly. There was no Staff College, and no time in an officer's career when he was obliged to study naval warfare. In the words of Mr. Churchill: 'At least fifteen years of consistent policy was required to give the Royal Navy that widely extended outlook upon war problems and of war situations, without which seamanship, gunnery, instrumentalisms of every kind, devotion of the highest order, could not achieve their due reward.'

In an attempt to remedy this state of affairs a war course for senior officers was instituted at Portsmouth for the purpose of studying strategical and tactical problems. Beatty attended one of the courses in the spring of 1911, working under Sir Henry Jackson in the same class as Stanley Colville, Cradock, and Chatfield. On taking leave of his family, he told his eldest son, now aged seven, that he was going back to school. Young David replied, 'Oh, Daddy, I hope you won't get whipped!'

In a letter to Ethel, he gives his impressions of Portsmouth:

Here I am in fresh pasture trying to find my way about, but have not been here for so long that it is difficult enough, and as usual everything seems very small and insignificant. Every item is redolent of the Navy and its belongings, which gives one the feeling as of going home, and I seem to recognise everybody in the streets, as it is one of those places that essentially never alters in a 100 years and the inhabitants go with it, and it only wakes up when the Channel Fleet come home or when there is a big Naval Review, and now it is its very sleepiest. . . .

CHAPTER SIX

1911–1914
THE GREAT OPPORTUNITY
Naval Secretary · Battle cruisers

EXCEPT for the three months when he was doing the war course, Beatty remained on half-pay for the two years following his promotion. He had only himself to blame, for he refused an appointment as Rear-Admiral Second-in-Command of the Atlantic Fleet offered by Mr. McKenna, the First Lord. This was a courageous decision on Beatty's part, as vacancies for junior Rear-Admirals were few and far between, and it naturally brought Beatty into disfavour with their Lordships. Beatty, however, had complete confidence in himself and an uncanny prevision of his own destiny. He was always ready to throw the dice with Fate. If Fate favoured him he felt he could not be thwarted. He knew he could serve his country best in some independent Command, the bigger the better, and it was against his nature to accept an appointment at sea where the ships were out of date and where he would be obliged 'always to follow in the wake of the Flagship'. For him it was all or nothing, and he was content to wait on half-pay until his destined opportunity turned up. It did.

On 25th October, 1911, Mr. Churchill took over the office of First Lord of the Admiralty, with 'my mind full of the dangers of war'. Churchill had followed Beatty's career with some interest. He had witnessed his exploits on the Nile and at Omdurman. He remembered a certain gunboat supporting the 21st Lancers when his own fortunes were attached to that famous regiment. He knew Beatty's war record and his reputation as a hard and fearless horseman. Admiralty opinion of Beatty at this time was adverse, and most of the Sea Lords were against offering him any further employment. They had not forgiven him for refusing what they themselves regarded as a suitable sea appointment. Churchill took a different view: 'My first meeting with the Admiral induced me immediately to disregard this unfortunate advice. He became at once my Naval Secretary.'

They got on very well together: 'We perpetually discussed the problems of a naval war with Germany. It became increasingly clear to me that he viewed questions of naval strategy and tactics in a different light from the average naval officer. His war experience on land had illumined the facts he had acquired in his naval training. He was no mere instrumentalist. He did not think of material as an end in itself, but only as a means. He thought of war problems in their unity by land, sea, and air. . . . I was increasingly struck with the shrewd and profound sagacity of his comments expressed in language singularly free from technical jargon.'[1]

Beatty, as we know, had no fear, moral or physical, and it is probable that his sincerity and outspoken presentation of his beliefs impressed Churchill more than anything else. They worked together as though they expected Germany to strike on the morrow, and both were aware that a wider outlook was needed towards war.

The First Lord's fertile brain had its complement in Beatty. Being well ahead of their time, both saw clearly the need for an organised body within the Navy to examine the problems lying ahead.

In the absence of any Staff invested with this duty, Beatty for a time virtually acted as Churchill's staff-officer. Examples of his work are preserved by his family. They are all in his own handwriting and afford a revelation, not only of his industry, but also of his knowledge of the 'art of the Admiral'. At Brooksby, on Easter Day, 1912, he wrote a long and deeply considered paper on dispositions to be taken up by the Fleet in event of war with Germany.

Beatty's proposals are similar in essence to the measures finally adopted in the British War Plan. While recommending Scapa, Cromarty, and Rosyth as bases for the Battle Fleet, he calls attention to their vulnerability to attack by submarines, destroyers, and minelayers, stating that: 'The safety of the Fleet

---

[1] *World Crisis* 1911-14, Winston Churchill.

from such attack can only be assured by keeping the sea with constant change of position rather than at rest in an anchorage.' He advocates a strong concentration of cruisers, destroyers, and submarines to be based at Harwich and Yarmouth for offensive operations in the Heligoland Bight and to cover the eastern approaches to the English Channel.

He surmises that the Germans will probably use their Navy:

'(1) To interrupt and destroy British overseas trade.

'(2) To endeavour to reduce the British main fleet by destroyers, submarines, and mines before giving battle with their entire available forces.

'(3) To hold the North Sea for a sufficient time to enable the British Isles to be invaded.'

There are many other papers dealing mostly with tactics and kindred subjects: the functions of the battle cruisers, lessons learnt at manœuvres, employment of the French Fleet, the offensive use of destroyers. All are sound in principle, but sometimes not too well expressed. Beatty must have burnt much midnight oil over them, and Churchill probably tore his hair reading them. Both must therefore have welcomed the day when the First Lord's efforts to introduce a War Staff at the Admiralty at last bore fruit. Somebody was required to do the thinking and planning, but in the words of Mr. Churchill: 'The dead weight of professional opinion was adverse. They had got on well enough without it before. They did not want a special class of officer professing to be more brainy than the rest.'[1] It may seem amazing that such a view could have prevailed at a time when no Sea Lord, with the exception of the First Sea Lord, was individually responsible for strategy and tactics. The Board as a whole were collectively responsible, but each member was fully occupied administering his own department, advised to a large extent by the Civil Service.

A start had been made, however, two years previously by Sir Arthur Wilson, who appointed Captain S. R. Fremantle[2] to assist him in working out the details of a naval War Plan. This was so secret that only a few senior officers were aware of

[1] *World Crisis* 1911–14, Winston Churchill.
[2] Later Admiral Sir Sidney Fremantle, G.C.B., M.V.O.

its existence. Nevertheless, it provided a good and valuable basis for the War Staff to work on.

One of Beatty's principal duties as Naval Secretary was to 'oil the wheels' of Admiralty procedure, and in this respect he did much to help his chief in getting the work of the War Staff recognised and appreciated. It was only after the War Staff had been allowed to get seriously down to work that their Lordships began to see the vastness and complexity of the problems of war, and were indeed grateful for professional naval assistance. Nevertheless, prejudice against the naval staff officers, 'ink slingers', was strong throughout the Navy, and it took a World War to remove it. The smoothness with which most operations ran in the Second World War as compared with the First is sufficient testimony to the wisdom of Mr. Churchill's inception of the Naval Staff, and Beatty was there when it happened.

In those spacious days the Admiralty had at their disposal a magnificent yacht, the *Enchantress*. She was a miniature liner of about 4,000 tons, with a Board Room, a good cellar, and extensive accommodation for official guests and their wives.

Mr. Churchill made full use of her, frequently visiting the Fleet and dockyards.

Apart from work, Beatty was seldom happy in the Admiralty yacht. The social environment bored him, so when he got the chance he would slip away for a game of golf with one of his friends in the Fleet.

Admiralty Yacht (*4th Feb.*, 1912)

Bitterly cold and a heavy blizzard blowing. Two inches of snow fell in under 4 hours. A ship in this weather is to be avoided, but I've been able to do a good deal of work. Three times I've pounded in the snow round the Yard with the First Lord, and have had some useful conversations with him and others towards settling many knotty points. And as I am the only Naval representative on board, under no circumstances except the most urgent could I have conscientiously got out of it. But I do hate these trips in the *Enchantress*, but I am such a selfish brute.

Admiralty Yacht (*28th March*, 1912)

What a day yesterday. . . . I hope it will improve before morning or our firing will be much upset. The First Lord, Winnie, waits for a telegram in the morning to decide whether we return tomorrow night or not. It all depends on the state of the Cabinet, and whether they feel strong enough to get on without him. I shall try to go and play golf with George Warrender this afternoon. I am very glad I came down, as I had two hours' solid conversation with Winston, and in consequence matters are better and my mind is not so perturbed as it was about questions of grave importance, and we see things from the same point of view, and consequently there will have to be some very considerable alterations made in the many schemes that have been evolved without the proper consideration. I think he had rather a shock at first, but in the end saw things with my eyes. But whatever happens it will be done without causing any breach in the relations between me and the First and Second Sea Lords. So if nothing else happens, my journey here will have been a fruitful one from many points of view.

At this time the Beatty home in London was Hanover Lodge, a large house standing in its own grounds on the edge of Regent's Park. Ethel was on the Continent, so he gives her the latest news of the children:

HANOVER LODGE   (*18th Apr.*, 1912)
Have not a moment to spare. It never seems to get less. Winston has to be back on Saturday, as he is going for a trip in *Enchantress* with Lloyd George, and it appears I have to be on a Committee Saturday morning. I am certainly not going in *Enchantress* with Lloyd George, and told him so. I hope all is well with you. The family are flourishing. Peter and David came into the room at 8 this morning as usual. Peter kept saying 'Mum Mum Com', and she wouldn't come, which distressed him greatly. He stuck it for 20 minutes, and then could bear it no longer and waddled off to his Nan Nan, but at lunch he was very well and happy and was quite nice to his poor Dadda. . . . I can't get over the *Titanic* disaster, but it has brought out the best in the Nation, played out as we are. No panic, not a man away from his post, and all went to the bottom doing their duty. Only men saved, those required to manage the boats. Could the French or any other nation have shown a finer picture?

PORTLAND HARBOUR, *Admiralty Yacht*   (*8th May*, 1912)
The King arrived this morning, but the weather was much too thick to permit of any practices at sea taking place. So he has spent the time in visiting ships, watching aeroplanes and hydroplanes, and going down in submarines. Tonight we go aboard the Royal Yacht for the usual banqueting, which is very tiresome and very stiff. However, we shall see all the Admirals and many friends, which will be pleasant.

In May 1912, Mr. Churchill took the *Enchantress* to the Mediterranean to investigate strategical problems, to visit the Fleet, and to inspect naval establishments. Mr. Asquith and members of his Cabinet, Sir John Fisher, Prince Louis, Lord Kitchener, and senior military officers were accommodated on board, and many important decisions on policy were made there. The company at times seems to have been a little over-powering, for Beatty confesses that he was frequently bored.

Oh dear, I am so tired and bored with the whole thing and the party on board bores me to tears. Winston talks about nothing but the sea and the Navy. Old Asquith spends his time immersed in a Baedeker Guide and reading extracts to an admiring audience. Prince Louis is of course charming, but *not* terribly exciting. Then there is Miss Hozier, who is the youngest and brightest of the lot. The two crushed Private Secretaries and myself, voilà! I can bear it no longer. . . . Don't say a word to anyone about my coming back. It would never do, but I really cannot stand any more of it, although of all the lot on board I like Winston the best. He is sincere, he does not enthuse, he is keen, and he is appreciative of the Navy, so should not like to hurt his feelings and it will have to be managed skilfully.

Nevertheless, Churchill kept him busy, calling for his views from time to time on matters of strategy. Amongst the papers written for his chief by Beatty in the *Enchantress* is one dealing with naval war dispositions and the part to be played by France in the Mediterranean. Being typical of his style of writing in those days and his prophetic insight, it is quoted here in full from the original manuscript:

'*Conclusions*

'1st. Absolutely essential that an agreement should be come to with France, that she is to take over the burden and responsibility of maintaining a Force in the Mediterranean of such a strength as to deter Italy and Austria from actively joining Germany in a war with G.B. Further, that France should state in this event what force she would consider it would be necessary for G.B. to maintain in Mediterranean waters to make certain of a successful issue to a conflict of G.B. and F. against I. and A. That is to say, G.B. should be ready at all

Portrait of Ethel Beatty by Philip de Laszlo, December 1911

times to supply the balance of strength to make victory certain if F. will provide the equality.

'2nd. Conclusion that with the withdrawal of the battleship strength from Malta a strong force of submarines and destroyers should be stationed there so as to make the attempted reduction of the island a hazardous and improbable eventuality even by the full strength (naval) of Austria *or* Italy. And that the island should be provisioned to a full four months' standard and the Garrison increased to withstand the possible landing of 20,000 men.

'That a strong Force of submarines and destroyers should be stationed at Alexandria, to deter any large expeditionary force being conveyed *by sea* to Egyptian soil. This force would at the same time be available to control the exits from the Suez Canal and the Dardanelles. To enable this force to lie undisturbed and free from molestation, it would be necessary to erect defences of such a strength as to deter any serious attack from an armoured Force.

'3rd. That if the battleships are removed from Malta to Gibraltar, to meet the important question of the prestige of G.B., the squadron should still retain the title of Mediterranean Battle Squadron, i.e. Fourth Battle Squadron Home Fleet followed by in brackets (Mediterranean Battle Squadron) and at intervals when convenient should cruise in the Mediterranean.

'Arising out of No. 1 Conclusion: It would strengthen the chances of arriving at a proper and equitable agreement with France if we are committed to withdraw the battleships from *Malta* (not Mediterranean), that we should *immediately* strengthen the cruiser force in the Mediterranean by an addition of two battle cruisers to be increased to three by 1st May, 1914, when the comparison of the Forces of I. and A. with F. will be unfavourable to F., and that the world should be informed by an authoritative statement that the withdrawal of the Mediterranean battleships is not the intention, that under present circumstances it is desirable to shift the strategic position of those B.S. from Malta to Gibraltar, where they will be immediately available under *all* circumstances.'

Beatty was more at home with the sword than with the pen,

but as we shall see later, his literary style in official and semi-
official papers improved considerably with practice. Irrespective of style, however, his strategic ideas were always sound.

His letters to Ethel tell us all we need know about this
cruise.

NAPLES, *Admiralty Yacht*   (*24th May*, 1912)

I hope you enjoyed your entertainment of last night and all went well
with you. I am sure you looked far nicer than anybody else, and I should
have loved to have seen you in your costume with your wig and hair
poudré. We arrived here from Elba this morning . . . nothing to remind
one that it was once the resting-place of the Great Emperor. That old
rascal Fisher arrived on board directly we got here looking very well and
young, never stopped talking, and has been closeted with Winston ever
since, wasn't that something to come to Naples for? Do not mention in
conversation to *anyone* that Fisher is in close confidence with Winston.
It would be most injurious to the Service, if it ever got out, and the Navy
would hate it. I took the opportunity to bolt to the shore and send you a
wire, but found them together still on my return and they are spending
the afternoon together. Prince Louis hates it and keeps out of the way
also as much as possible. . . . *If I break* away, I shall be home by the 6th,
and will come with you to the Ball, but won't dance in the Quadrille,
but you must be ready to get me a costume to wear or I shouldn't be able
to go.

NAPLES, *Admiralty Yacht* [on passage to Malta]   (*25th May*, 1912)

I shall certainly make a pilgrimage to Capua,[1] the shrine of Baby
David. That great event only seems the other day, and when I look at
the harbour here and the Stradas I used to wander in $2\frac{1}{2}$ years ago, it
seems literally as if it were only yesterday. I visited Pompeii today. The
buried City arrived at a height of civilisation that we have not reached
yet, and the decoration of some of the houses would make your mouth
fairly water. . . . There is not too much time for philandering. I like Miss
Violet Asquith better than I did, extremely intelligent and talks well.

MALTA, *Admiralty Yacht*   (*29th May*, 1912)

We arrived in due course and found Malta enjoying the luxury of the
usual Sirocco wind which reduces everybody to the condition of a rag.
. . . Borda,[2] very gloomy at the prospective absence of the Mediterranean
Fleet, says everybody will starve, the usual idea that the Navy was only
created to keep the Maltese from starving. Kitchener came on board

---

[1] Young David was born at Capua Palace, Malta.   [2] A Maltese contractor.

looking very well and sent many messages to you, quite delighted to come in a cruiser and have some fresh air. Had his usual joke about Egypt being the only place to get soldiers and sailors from. . . . Tomorrow we spend the day inspecting the Dockyard, and there is to be a Conference in the evening on the Mediterranean question, for which I have to collect most of the material, and is of extreme importance. Tonight we dine officially with the Governor . . . just leaving for this infernal banquet.

Admiralty Yacht   (*1st June*, 1912)

The Prime Minister is in an awful fuss, as his colleagues want him to come home, and he jibs and keeps sending wires for more details. I thought of going with him, but there is a chance he won't go, in which case I should be stranded and then should be beat. The old Silly won't make up his mind and I can't risk it. The C.-in-C. is going to let me have the *Hussar* to go to Sicily in, which, though not saving time, will be more comfortable than the dirty *Carola*. We've had a very busy day from 8 o'clock this morning and now are going to have a Conference Dinner Party of Prime Minister, Lord Kitchener, Winston, Prince Louis, and self, so it will be interesting, and am moving in the highest intellectual circles, so must keep my wits about me. I've rarely had a busier three days.

There were very good reasons for Beatty getting home as soon as possible. The annual manœuvres were in course of preparation and, as Naval Secretary, he had much work awaiting him at the Admiralty concerning the selection of captains to command the many ships preparing to take part.

* * * * *

In the summer of 1912 highly important large-scale manœuvres, employing every available ship, were carried out in the North Sea to investigate the problem of intercepting the German Fleet in time to prevent its covering a landing of troops on the East Coast of England. Mr. Churchill, probably with an eye to confounding the critics, but primarily to test Beatty's capacity as a Flag officer at sea, gave him command of an armoured cruiser squadron of six ships with his Flag in *Aboukir*.

They were all old ships, and had been in reserve with skeleton crews for some years. On 2nd July they were brought to full strength by reservists called up from civil employment. Beatty was given ten days to get his ships into fighting trim before 'zero day'. He assembled the squadron off the Isle of Wight, and kept them at sea doing tactical and gunnery exercises for the whole of the 'working-up' period. After being inspected by Mr. Churchill and the Board of Admiralty, his ships took up their war stations on 12th June, and played their part in the big manœuvres for about a fortnight.

Beatty's handling of this squadron and how he dealt with various situations evidently came up to the First Lord's expectations, for in the spring of the following year Mr. Churchill 'had no doubts whatever' in appointing him 'over the heads of all' to command the Battle Cruiser Squadron, 'that supreme combination of speed and power'.[1]

Beatty hoisted his flag in the *Lion* at Devonport on 1st March, 1913, having selected as his Flag Captain Ernle Chatfield,[2] whom he had previously 'tried out' in the *Aboukir*. Chatfield was a proved seaman, having successfully commanded two battleships and a cruiser, and having also been entrusted with the command of the P. & O. liner *Medina* when she took Their Majesties King George V and Queen Mary to India for the Delhi Durbar in 1911. Chatfield had also been a gunnery specialist, and had strong views on modernising gunnery methods and bringing them more into line with the reality of battle than the prevailing artificial conditions of target practice. There can be no better proof of the wisdom of Beatty's choice than the fact that the two were together on the same bridge at sea from the time Beatty hoisted his Rear-Admiral's flag in the *Aboukir* in 1912, to the day his Admiral of the Fleet's Union flag was hauled down in the *Queen Elizabeth* in 1919.

Here is Chatfield's first impression of Beatty:

'I quickly realised that I was with a man of exacting character. Each ship Beatty had served in from the rank of Commander he had brought to a high state of efficiency. He had a love of doing everything at high pressure and high speed. This was not a pose: it was entirely characteristic: whether at

---

[1] *World Crisis*, 1911–14.
[2] Afterwards Admiral of the Fleet the Rt. Hon. Lord Chatfield, G.C.B., O.M.

sea or in the hunting field . . . yet he had a great power of restraint when he judged it to be necessary.'[1]

Beatty spent only one day in the *Lion* while she was at Devonport. The ship was refitting, so he went to Monte Carlo. Many naval people would have expected him to create a good impression by taking an early interest in his new Flagship. Beatty held a different view; in his opinion it were better to leave the ship alone at such times and let the Flag Captain 'get on with it'. He was well aware that much thinking had to be done about the employment and administration of his squadron, but this could be done equally well at Monte Carlo undisturbed by the clatter of riveters and the hurly-burly of a dockyard port. Anyway, he would have his holiday when he, and only he, thought fit. Audacity was in his nature; it was impossible to think of his ever being fussed.

At the end of his holiday, while returning from Monte Carlo to take over the finest naval command in the world, his thoughts were with his wife and family.

(*25th March*, 1913)

A line as we pass through Paris. I hated more than anything leaving you and my babies and the sun. But it has got to be. We all have our duties to perform in the world, some one way and some another, and I think, after all, mine is not a bad way. It has appalling moments, but then it has splendid compensations which make up, and which, if we led the humdrum life and never parted, we should never have, and one does feel that after all one is doing something for the State.

On the next day he was at sea.

H.M.S. *Lion*   (*26th March*, 1913)

My first trip in the Battle Cruiser Squadron came to a successful ending at midday without any contretemps or misadventure. It's wonderful how these huge ships toss about, but it is a good sign, as it proves them good sea-boats, which is the saving clause. I have only three ships, a fourth turns up tomorrow, the *Invincible*, and the *Princess Royal* I don't know when. There is some delay about her refitting. . . . With the fall of Adrianople and the prescribed limitations by the Powers of the North, all cause of a possible war seems disappearing . . . postponed for at least a month. I took Chatfield ashore to play golf. . . .

[1] *The Navy and Defence*, Lord Chatfield.

Your wire of yesterday just received. Well, love, you might be a little more communicative. It's only twopence a word. Give me a shilling's-worth and say how the weather is. It brightens me up for instance to know the weather is fine.

According to the dates on these two letters he seems to have cut things rather fine; this, however, was not unusual.

Lieut. R. Schwerdt, a young officer in the *Lion*, describes a short conversation he had with Beatty in the early hours of the morning when the Fleet was anchored off Weymouth some weeks later:

'I had the Middle Watch, the barge was in at Weymouth to meet the Admiral who was returning from London by a train arriving about midnight. As the Admiral did not arrive, the Captain came up to me and told me he was going to bed. The Battle Cruiser Squadron was sailing at daylight, and I was to tell the Admiral that the squadron was in all respects ready for sea. About 3 a.m. the Admiral returned, and I gave him the Captain's message. After a few enquiries regarding the weather and the barometer, he bade me good night and then added as an afterthought, "Let the barge's crew have a lie-in: I'm sorry I'm late, but I hired a taxi in Piccadilly and told him to drive to Weymouth and the damned fellow lost his way twice.'

At the end of March Beatty was at sea with his squadron taking part in exercises with the Home Fleet under Admiral Sir George Callaghan. One of these was designed to demonstrate to the French Minister of Marine, who was the guest of the Board of Admiralty in the *Enchantress*, the tactical potentialities of battle cruisers. It was a typical 'set piece'. The two battle fleets approached one another until they were at a prearranged distance apart, when the Battle Cruiser Squadron had to deploy and cut across the enemy's van at high speed.

Unfortunately, a tramp steamer got in the way between the lines, preventing Beatty from deploying in time, and the whole show was a failure. All in the Battle Cruiser Squadron had hoped to share in the glory of Beatty's dashing manœuvre before such an important audience, but he was in no way perturbed. On meeting the Commander-in-Chief in the Fleet

Flagship later in the day, Beatty at once opened the subject: 'Well, sir, that was unfortunate; the two fleets were much too close to start with, and of course the battle cruisers had no room to manœuvre. . . . I hope the First Lord is not very disappointed.'[1] How many would have dared to beard the Commander-in-Chief in his own den and get away with it?

Beatty thought deeply about the function in war of his powerful and speedy squadron. The latest ships, *Lion*, *Princess Royal*, and *Queen Mary*, could steam at a maximum speed of over twenty-eight knots, and the older ships *Indomitable* and *Indefatigable* could do twenty-six. Until recently no other heavy ships in the world could attain such speeds, but the Germans had adopted a similar design, and some of their battle cruisers were already in commission. Beatty, having decided that his squadron must be trained to manœuvre in close order at the highest speed possible, announced that the next series of tactical exercises would be carried out at twenty-four knots. Never before had this been done with such large ships, and when Beatty was questioned on the wisdom of it he replied, 'Are we going to fight at twenty-four knots or not? It is more likely we shall steam at twenty-seven knots and leave the lame ducks behind'; which is exactly what happened a year later at the Battle of the Dogger Bank.

High-speed tactics became normal routine in the Battle Cruiser Squadron, disclosing conditions of vibration and heel which had their effect on gunnery. Chatfield therefore came forward with proposals for carrying out target practice at high speed. Beatty agreed, but gunnery in the Navy was in the grip of the 'Inspector of Target Practice', who insisted on standard conditions for competitive firings, limiting ships to a speed of 14 knots and a range of 9,000 yards; as a result, the competitive element tended to obscure the true purpose of destroying the enemy. Beatty eventually got his way, and with the connivance of the Commander-in-Chief carried out a practice designed by Chatfield to simulate battle conditions. Two large targets were towed as fast as the hawser would permit, five battle cruisers approached at a speed of twenty-three knots, deployed, and opened fire simultaneously at a range of 16,000 yards.

[1] *The Navy and Defence*, Lord Chatfield.

Chatfield says that the practice completely proved its value, bringing to light the inaccuracy of the British range-finders at long range and high speed. The Admiralty were critical, and told the Commander-in-Chief that such a practice should have had their approval beforehand. 'Their Lordships frowned and the Inspector of Target Practice was disturbed. But David Beatty was pleased; he saw clearly his task in the coming war.'[1]

The next step from Beatty's point of view was to correlate high-speed tactics with high-speed gunnery in co-operation with light cruisers and destroyers. To this end, with the blessing of Callaghan, his Commander-in-Chief, many exercises were planned, carried out, and the lessons recorded. Beatty was ably assisted on the tactical side by his talented flag commander, the Hon. Reginald Plunkett,[2] who not only designed many of the exercises to meet the requirements of his Chief, but also analysed them afterwards, taking care that the lessons learnt were circulated and understood. All this enabled Beatty to consolidate his views on the functions of the battle cruisers, which he set down in his own handwriting in September 1913, as follows:

'(a) To support a reconnaissance of fast light cruisers on the enemy coast at high speed.' [This was successfully carried out by Beatty a year later at the Battle of Heligoland.]

'(b) To support a blockading force.' [The idea of a close blockade was abandoned as a result of experience gained in recent large-scale manœuvres.]

'(c) To form support between the cruiser force and the battle fleet when cruising.' [This was a normal duty prevailing throughout the war.]

'(d) To support a cruiser force watching the Enemy's Battle Fleet.' [Again a normal duty.]

'(e) Finally, to form a fast division of the Battle Fleet in a general action.' [This became part of the Commander-in-Chief's battle plan, and was successfully carried out by Beatty at Jutland.]

These functions, after being examined and amplified by the Commander-in-Chief, were embodied in the battle orders.

---

[1] *The Navy and Defence*, Lord Chatfield.
[2] Later Admiral the Hon. Sir R. Plunkett-Ernle-Erle-Drax, K.C.B., D.S.O.

Beatty worked in close co-operation with Callaghan in matters of strategy and tactics, and it is a tribute to the knowledge and foresight of these great leaders that the principles accepted by them subsequently endured the test of war.

'This idea of Admiral Beatty as a thoughtful strategist and tactician, planning in advance how best to utilise his forces and how to train his Captains, may appear strange to readers who have been taught by post-war writers that Beatty was a mere Prince Rupert, dashing and happy-go-lucky in the spirit of the hunting field. . . . Beatty had complete command of himself; confident in his own judgment, he was able by careful mental preparation to decide rapidly on his next step without hesitation or visible anxiety.

'In the innumerable long walks we had together ashore, he would discuss all the war problems whose coming he foresaw. No one could live in continual touch with him without being affected by his force of character and fearlessness; nor fail to feel his own confidence and determination strengthened by contact with him.'[1]

All who have served close to Beatty, on reading these words of Chatfield, will involuntarily exclaim: how true! Others who may wish to seek conviction on this aspect of Beatty's character have only to read his letters here published, where they will find that, much as he enjoyed the fleshpots at appropriate times, the Navy in war was always his paramount interest.

Here is a good example of his mental preparation and foresight:

GLENGARIFF, H.M.S. *Lion*   (4th *Apr.*, 1913)

We spent the day doing practice at anchor, so I trotted my round little Flag Lieutenant for a good long walk ashore. I like him very much, more so than I did my first one. In fact, I like all my staff. They are all intelligent and charming. . . . The Germans are fairly setting about creating a formidable Aerial Force, and it behoves us to move rapidly and provide the means of defeating them, and I am busy preparing a scheme for the defence of our ships, which at present are absolutely at their mercy, a little matter that has been overlooked in the past with a possible case for disaster if we are not prepared.

[1] *The Navy and Defence*, Lord Chatfield.

He wasted no time in getting to know the officers and men of his squadron, for to lead them successfully in battle he must know them, and they must know him. He also took care to see that the lessons learnt in manœuvres were not forgotten.

BANTRY, H.M.S. *Lion* (6th *Apr.*, 1913)

I am commanding quite a respectable force here, two Battleships, eight First-Class Cruisers and Battle Cruisers, six Minelayers, and two fast new Light Cruisers, so we are somewhat congested. I spend most of the day, when not at sea, writing and inspecting. The former takes most of my time and my mornings are very full, seeing officers who arrive and trying to keep pace with the paper work. I go ashore and play golf in the afternoon and return about five, when I find time to read, and after dinner I spend time again writing and am kept at it until midnight, most nights. In fact it is midnight now and I haven't wasted many minutes during the day, which gives me a sense of satisfaction, whether one has accomplished anything or not, and so the days go by. Tomorrow, Sunday, I have a busy day inspecting one of the ships and seeing the men. I step on board to Church, and make everybody's acquaintance and get to know them and they get to know me, which is a good thing for us all. Monday we are out firing all day, in fact I am taking the Squadron out and go aboard each ship as she fires, which means a busy day, as we shall be at it all day. And so the world—our little world, goes round—no better and no worse.

H.M.S. *Lion*, at sea (9th *Apr.*, 1913)

We left Berehaven last night, and have been exercising at sea most of the day with varying results, but, I hope, much instruction certainly to myself. I learnt a great deal of the greatest value. The great difficulty is to drive the lessons home and see that none are forgotten. Therefore one has to look at everything from the schoolmaster's point of view, so that nothing is lost that comes from experience. . . . We arrive at daylight tomorrow and spend the next two days in coaling and conferring, both of which very necessary adjuncts of the Naval Service. . . . The famous system seems to have done you very well, and every letter reports a winning of from 150 to 200 francs, which ought to pay household expenses if you stopped: at that rate you would get quite rich, but I dare say by this you have lost it all again.

Beatty had certain little affectations, the 'three button' monkey jacket, the rakish cap, and the slightly 'horsy' cut of his clothes. He had also a strange habit of making faces. For no apparent reason he would screw his face up into a fearsome grimace and hold it quite unconsciously for a minute or two. Yet he hated publicity. While the family was at Monte Carlo they met Mr. Filson Young, who was a friend of Sir John Fisher and well known as a novelist and journalist. Beatty was furious when he heard that Filson Young had published, without permission, an article about him.

H.M.S. *Lion* to HANOVER LODGE (*11th Apr.*, 1913)

I hear there is a long article on the subject of my humble self in last *Saturday Review* signed by *Signifix* which is fulsome in its laudatory tone. This is Filson Young, I feel sure. I wish to Heavens he wouldn't. I personally hate it and it does me no good. Everybody naturally asks how much did I pay for it and classes me as an advertiser, which, whatever my faults are, I am not. I suppose he thinks that he is making me, as he said the Journalist Stevens made Kitchener. I don't like it, I don't want it, and I won't have it, but how am I to stop it? Thank the Lord he hasn't very much left to say from all accounts, and it will die a natural death. But it does me harm in the Navy, who can't abide the advertisement of a newspaper, and those that don't know me, of which there are thousands, will wrongly construe it.

(*12th Apr.*, 1913)

. . . I have read the *Saturday Review* article. It's dreadful, and makes me go hot and cold all over. Thank the Lord I've met only two who've read it, and though connected with, don't belong to the Navy, i.e. Eddy Marsh who thought it *divine* and Charles Cust who thought it disgusting and wanted to know how much I had paid for it. I wish they wouldn't write about me. It's an awful mistake. Nobody has achieved anything after being puffed up like that before he has ever done anything at all. So I am a goner, and of course they'll think I said it myself. That is the worst of journalistic friends and scribblers. They think only of good copy and that's all I am fit for.

About eighteen months later Filson Young, through the influence of Fisher, got himself appointed to Beatty's staff as intelligence officer. The staff was too short-handed and too overworked to carry an untrained passenger, so Filson Young did not stay long.

Throughout the year the Fleet was being continually exercised in preparation for the war that was to come.

Mr. Churchill as First Lord never missed an opportunity to see the ships at work.

H.M.S. *Lion.* To Paris   (*11th Apr.,* 1913)

No letter from you, dear heart, on arrival at Portland, simply because you will not direct your letters as I keep asking you to do—H.M.S. *Lion,* First Battle Cruiser Squadron. . . . Winston has written to ask if I can take him out with me for the manœuvres or rather the tactical exercises, which commence on Monday, so of course I shall, and I hope to be able to squeeze some sense into him, and something useful out of him for the good of the Squadron in particular, and the Service in general. It will add to the excitement, anyway, as he will want to know so much, but I hope it is not his intention to make a general practice of it, fond as I am of him.

During this strenuous year Beatty formed a high opinion of his Commander-in-Chief, Sir George Callaghan, and since we know how critical Beatty was of his senior officers, we can take it that the training of the principal Fleet for war was in good hands.

H.M.S. *Lion.* To Monte Carlo   (*13th Apr.,* 1913)

I am sorry you lost *all* you won. You could not have followed the system religiously to lose 1,500 francs in 11 *coups.* You must have been in a hurry to get rich quick and so were led to your undoing. Yes, I saw that Longmore[1] was going to be married, perhaps his wife will put a stop to his flying, which will be a pity, as we haven't too many first-class in the Navy. I dined with the C.-in-C. last night and met all the Admirals and most of the Captains, and had a tremendous talk of shop. He is a nice old thing, George Callaghan, and full of sound common sense, which is something to be certain of in these days. We are off tomorrow as soon as I can get Winston on board. . . . I will send you a letter by him.

Ethel Beatty, having been accustomed all her life to getting her own way, got a severe rebuff from her husband for suggesting to high authority that the movements of the Battle Cruiser Squadron might be arranged to suit her convenience.

Portree   (*9th May,* 1913)

You must not bother Prince Louis or Winston by asking them where we are going to and to send them [the First Battle Cruiser Squadron]

[1] Later Air Chief Marshal Sir Arthur Longmore.

here or there because you want to spend Whitsuntide with me. It won't do. It's good enough for the War Office but not for the Admiralty, and they have a good deal to do without having to consider which port will suit the wives best. I wrote to Prince Louis myself urging him to send us back to the East Coast, if all danger of complications were passed, so that we could get on with our practices which we cannot do here, and he will think that it is collusion between us, which is the last thing I should like him to think of, and I wish now I had never written to him. . . .

Ethel came to Invergordon while the squadron was there for a brief visit. Beatty felt homesick after she had gone, and consoled himself by granting some well-earned leave to the Scotsmen in his command. The concession was deeply appreciated, especially as the railway fares to Scotland from the ships' home ports in the south (where leave was normally given) were far beyond their scanty means.

INVERGORDON, H.M.S. *Lion*   (*30th May*, 1913)

I am giving leave for four days to all the Scotchmen, who will rejoin us at Queensferry, which has pleased them, and it's a good thing when we are in these waters to give leave to the men who live in these parts and it naturally saves their pockets. . . .

[To David Junior.] What do you think of my *Lion* [the ship's crest] on the paper? Isn't he a beauty and fierce-looking? Take care of your Mummy and Peter.

The summer manœuvres were again designed to try out means of preventing the 'Germans' (Red) under Jellicoe from landing a raiding force on the East Coast of England. At the same time the *real* Germans were busily engaged in war exercises of their own off the Norwegian coast.

H.M.S. *Lion*   (*24th June*, 1913)

Old Brock [Captain O. de B. Brock], in the *Princess Royal*, got lost, and I had a job to find him. Lucky we weren't required as fighting unit before nine o'clock this morning. He did not turn up until then, but now we are united. We hear wireless reports of all sorts of alarms going on in the southern area, and I expect Jellicoe is doing exactly what I said he would do. . . . I gather that four battleships and four cruisers escorted the transports to some landing-place between Yarmouth and Flamborough Head and are endeavouring to land. . . . Meantime our C.-in-C.

[125]

is dashing down there, but will arrive too late I fear. We are moving in support, unruffled and undisturbed except by the noise of German guns, who are not very far away on the Norwegian coast at exercises also. We have a great deal of interference from the wireless, which always chips in when we commence signalling with such regularity that it has all the appearance of being done on purpose.

H.M.S. *Lion*   (*25th June,* 1913)

I have just heard that the 'Red' have landed 36,000 men at Grimsby and have decamped with the loss of one battleship, some destroyers and submarines, and done exactly what I said they would do. Now we must wait for the next move. In the meantime we are ambling up and down doing nothing but burn coal.

KIRKWALL, H.M.S. *Lion*   (*20th July,* 1913)

Dined last night with the C.-in-C. who was very despondent about the manœuvres and the ridiculous conditions thereof, and told me Winston was to arrive here on Tuesday with Sir John French and Sir Reginald Custance in the *Enchantress,* so I said he would have a great opportunity of pointing out his opinion of the whole thing, which cheered him up. Winston would appear to be like the Great War Lord of Germany travelling about with a Naval and Military adviser. I hope he does come, and will give us the opportunity of telling him what we think of the absurdity of all the conditions.

KIRKWALL, H.M.S. *Lion* to the Yacht *Sheelah*   (*18th July,* 1913)

I sent you a wire yesterday to be careful David did not fall overboard, because I dreamt he tumbled down a cliff into the sea, and it gave me such a shock that I wired you to be careful. I thought forewarned was forearmed. Dreams always go by contraries, but it made me nervous.

In the spring of 1914 the Fleet was fully occupied with exercises and target practices, in which the battle cruisers acquitted themselves creditably. Pleasure and relief from the monotony was felt when the news came that certain squadrons were to pay courtesy visits to continental ports. And when it was known that Admiral Sir George Warrender was to take the Second Battle Squadron to Kiel, it seemed that the war clouds were dispelled, at least for a time.

Beatty was entrusted with two important diplomatic missions, first to visit Brest, and later Riga, Reval, and finally

Kronstadt. He sailed from home waters in February 1914, with the battle cruisers *Lion, Princess Royal, Queen Mary,* and *New Zealand.* At Brest they had a great reception, and were much impressed with the evident desire of the French to play their part with us at sea, in the event of war. This visit was primarily of professional interest, as it was known that close co-operation between the British and French Fleets would be necessary to give full effect to the war plan. Beatty writes to Ethel about the entertainments.

Lion, BREST   (*12th Feb.,* 1914)

We went to a banquet at the Préfecture and tackled a very long dinner with hundreds of wines of different colours, all of the same taste and all very nasty. You never heard such a polyglot of languages. Only two of them *would* or could speak English, so we had to wrestle with them as we could. He was a nice old boy the *Préfet Maritime,* and the other I had to contend with was an enormously fat old man. Mercifully they were both very fond of the sound of their own voices and both never stopped talking except when eating, and then they did not want to be interfered with, so I sat there and smiled, and they thought I talked French very well. Then we came to toasts, and I loosed off mine in *French*!!! which was very well received. I learnt it by heart and didn't forget a word. Anyway, the British officers understood it. We got away fairly early, which was the best thing about it. Today it is blowing like blue fury with heavy rain squalls, which they tell me is the prevailing type of weather here. However, I had to go and call upon the General, the *Sous-Préfet,* and the Mayor. . . .

Lion, BREST   (*16th Feb.,* 1914)

Only one more day and then we are off. . . . We had a great football match with the city, initiated by the Syndicalist Mayor, who was very anxious to make a ceremony of it, so Chatfield, I, and the Secretary trotted off and sat in a *Tribune d'honneur* for half an hour, and then had to return on board to receive the officials and their ladies who were coming to take tea. We defeated the Frenchmen, but they played extraordinarily well and they really were just beaten. The Tea Party was a great success. It mercifully stopped raining. We had the massed bands on board, which made a deuce of a noise, which they seemed to like. They wandered all round the ship, which they thought was magnificent, and then became very gay and danced round the upper deck. There were some funny old trouts and some spritely young ones, but no raving beauties. The Flag Lieutenant and Secretary enjoyed themselves. . . .

The visit to Russian ports, which took place in June, was quite another story. Apart from the interesting navigational experience of taking heavy ships through the Great Belt into the Baltic, the time in harbour was spent in one continuous round of gaiety punctuated by rigid ceremonial. On the first evening at Kronstadt, Beatty and a large number of his officers were entertained to dinner in the Russian Flagship, and learnt there for the first time the colossal capacity for food and liquor of their hosts. The British officers, having been received with due ceremony, soon found themselves standing at a high table crammed with cold dishes of all sorts: goose, salmon, and trout beautifully garnished, the predominant feature, of course, being fresh caviare in large bowls, with outsize tablespoons for helping. The drinks were mainly sherry and vodka. When everybody had eaten their fill, one British officer thanked his host for a delightful supper. The Russian, looking at him in amazement, replied, 'Supper? This is not supper. This is the Zakuska; in a moment we start dinner!' And sure enough the party moved to another large cabin, where they sat down to a seven-course dinner, with champagne and more vodka, not rising till well into the morning.

Here is an extract from the diary of Lieut. R. Schwerdt, R.N., of the *Lion*, describing a dinner-party in a Russian warship: 'The first thing is "Grace", which the funny old ship's pope says facing the Ikon, then Zakuska.... Then we sat down to dinner: soup, junket, cheese patées, salmon, crayfish, chicken, and ices. . . . Drinks were champagne, claret, hock, and sherry. Every five minutes everyone clinked their glasses and had to empty them. After dinner they produced an enormous cup and handed it round. As each fellow got it, the others shouted "*Pedada! Pedada!*" clapping their hands until it was empty, when it was immediately refilled and passed on to the next victim. . . . There was clog dancing going on, and some were doing the Russian dance on double knee, but one was never allowed to be without a drink. Odd speeches were made and drowned in shouts. People put each other's caps on, Jones looking comic in one of their green soldier and Sampson in one of their naval caps.'

The ceremony of *Pedada* later became a feature of gunroom

The Home Fleet moving off from Spithead, summer 1914
Photograph lent by Dr. Oscar Parkes, O.B.E.

| ST. VINCENT | THUNDERER | MONARCH | CONQUEROR | ORION | AUDACIOUS | K. GEORGE V | NEPTUNE | TEMERAIRE |
| MARLBOROUGH | COLLINGWOOD | SUPERB | BELLEROPHON | CENTURION | AJAX | HERCULES | COLOSSUS | IRON DUKE |

guest nights in the *Lion*. In this burlesque, Burghersh[1] the Sub-Lieutenant, acting as High-priest, would hand a bedroom utensil (kept for this purpose only) full of beer to the guest, and as he drank, the midshipmen, in their part of acolytes, would chant in chorus '*Pedada! Pedada!*' clapping their hands and stamping their feet.

The ten days at Kronstadt were a heavy strain. The men were treated with the same lavish hospitality, but most of them could not stomach the caviare, which they called 'fish jam'. Vodka, however, was more to their liking. There were banquets and theatres at St. Petersburg, and the usual time of returning on board was 5 a.m., making it difficult to fit in the Russian hours with ship routine. Various small craft, including a small imperial yacht, were placed at the disposal of the British squadron, and were continually employed ferrying the officers and men to and from St. Petersburg along the Neva.

Beatty and his captains lunched *en famille* with the Tsar at his country palace of Tsarskoye Selo, being driven there in gilded coaches with coachmen and footmen in golden livery and cocked hats. Chatfield said he felt like Cinderella going to the ball. But the illusion was spoilt at the end of the journey by the Russian liaison officer whispering in Spickernell's[2] ear, 'You give the driver five roubles!'

In spite of the discomfort of wearing full dress, the luncheon was delightfully informal. The party sat at small round tables with the Tsar at one, the Tsarina at another, and the four Grand Duchesses each presiding at the others. A few days later, the Royal Family honoured Beatty by lunching with him on board the *Lion*. Mrs. Beatty and Lady Gwendolen Churchill, who had followed the squadron in Beatty's yacht *Sheelah*, were also present. The Tsar inspected the ship's company, and afterwards, at his own request, visited the turrets, magazines, and shell rooms, showing great interest in all he saw. His dignity and charm reminded everyone of their own King. The four Grand Duchesses, looking most attractive in white frocks with black sashes, were well looked after by some of the junior officers. It was a novel experience for girls in their position;

[1] Later the Earl of Westmorland.
[2] Paymaster-Commander Frank Spickernell, the Admiral's Secretary.

they saw little of life outside the Royal circle, and did not disguise their enjoyment of it all.

Beatty and his officers, being naturally anxious to return, in full measure, the hospitality they had received, decided to give a ball on a scale hitherto unheard-of even in Russia. The number of guests to be asked was over two thousand, which was beyond the capacity of the Flagship. So the *New Zealand* was secured alongside the *Lion*, one ship providing the ballroom and the other the cloakrooms and supper room. The upper decks were encased by red and white striped awnings. Covered gangways connected the two ships. Flowers, flags, and even fountains completed the illusion that the dance was taking place in some fairy palace, and not in a battle cruiser.

Chatfield, who took over the responsibility for the catering, says: 'Our experience had shown us what Russian society and appetites expected. Mr. Woodley, the Admiral's steward, came to the rescue. We made about two hundred circular tables from rum casks and planking, to seat six at each. These were arranged on the *Lion's* quarter-deck. The champagne was a problem. After ten days of fleet entertainments, it was getting scarce even in St. Petersburg. Woodley ransacked the Embassies and procured a hundred dozen bottles. Twenty whole salmon, averaging about twenty pounds apiece, each on a block of ice, formed the centre-piece of the Zakuska, with innumerable dishes and mountains of caviare. . . . It was a perfect night and all went well.'[1]

On the 28th June, while the great entertainment was at its height, the Archduke Ferdinand of Austria was assassinated in the streets of Sarajevo, in distant Serbia. The significance of this act, which precipitated the war, being immediately appreciated in Russia, placed Beatty in an awkward position. His mission was largely diplomatic, and as so often happens in the Navy, the British Admiral found himself with no brief, faced with a political problem of the utmost delicacy. Beatty was fortunate in having the British Ambassador, Sir George Buchanan, so close at hand, but he was not always present when Beatty had to reply in Moscow and elsewhere to eulogistic speeches by the President of the Duma and other highly

---

[1] *The Navy and Defence*, Lord Chatfield.

placed Russian officials. The Admiral, even after having consumed a jorum of champagne and knowing himself to be proclaimed in the Press as the friend of Russia, never put a foot wrong.

He made most of his speeches in French, and took endless trouble in preparing them. Having decided what he was going to say, he would send for Spickernell late at night, and having provided him with a comfortable chair and a whisky-and-soda, would walk up and down the cabin rehearsing his speech until he felt that he had got it right or 'Spick' had fallen asleep.

Beatty and certain officers of his flagship, by invitation, spent several days in Moscow and were sumptuously entertained. High officials there took pains to point out that the City crest, St. George and the Dragon, was the same as that used on British coinage.

When the squadron left Kronstadt at the end of June, the Tsar also went to sea in his large yacht *Standardt*, and witnessed for the first and only time in his life heavy ships doing tactical exercises in close order at twenty-five knots. There could have been no better way of impressing on him the naval might of Great Britain than this silent demonstration of efficient ship handling.

In July Beatty, having been awarded the K.C.B. in the Birthday honours, received his Knighthood from the King on arrival in England. The London season and the usual round of social and sporting events, culminating at Goodwood, were in full swing. At the same time the Army was quietly calling up its reserves, and the Navy had assembled the whole of its fighting strength at Spithead for a test mobilisation. H.M. King George V reviewed the Fleet, and it was intended that the ships should disperse afterwards, the first-line ships giving leave and the Reserve Fleet ships paying off. At the last moment, however, Prince Louis of Battenberg, who was now First Sea Lord, directed, with the approval of the Board, that the Fleet was to remain fully mobilised, and by 1st August all ships were at their war stations.

Events moved with dazzling quickness. Beatty in the long-term view was certain war would come, but at the eleventh hour he could not believe it was imminent. He writes to Ethel:

Lion [at sea]   (*30th July*, 1914)

I was very distressed at leaving you all alone yesterday morning, but you had little David, who is a host in himself, to take care of you. I expect you found London in a turmoil when you got there. I hope you were able to glean some news. . . . We steamed slowly away and turned East in the Channel when out of sight but, of course, ran into a Cross-channel steamer, who would have reported us certainly. However, we were alarmed during the day by telegrams from the Admiralty, and last night we made certain that this morning would see us at war, but it has not come, and I feel in my bones that it won't. Everybody in every country, who thinks, seems to be of the opinion that it has got to come sooner or later, but I fear we are too well-prepared this time for it to happen; with the exception that we are short of cruisers, we could not be in better circumstances, and I feel that luck would be too great to permit of me going to war in this ship and in command of this fine squadron. No one could be better placed. I do not want to go to war, but if it has got to come I should like it to come now quickly while I am where I am. We have been busy all yesterday and to-day making preparations. Last night we bolted through the Straits of Dover with lights out. All the Fortresses round the coast are mobilised, and we watched with interest the big searchlights at Dover. You must not mention to a soul where we are or where we went. You can say we are at sea, and the newspapers will provide you with the rest. We shall in all probability remain at sea until it is necessary to coal, when ships will go in one by one to fill up. I shall not go in with *Lion*, but remain out and change on to another ship. But I will send you a wire and letters by the ships going in, which will be in 4 days or so. The situation is so acute that it cannot last in such a condition for any length of time. It is bound to get better or worse. Mercifully the weather is very fine and our visibility extraordinary. We passed the French ships which conveyed Poincaré to Russia. They were scattering off home as fast as they could go in a terrible fuss.

Jellicoe has been appointed 2nd in command of the Home Fleet, which I think is a good thing, as he is the C.-in-C. designate after Callaghan.

Lion [at Scapa Flow]   (*2nd Aug.*, 1914)

We are enveloped in fog, with our nets out ready for most things. We spent all yesterday getting rid of superfluities and still preparing. I am writing you at 4 a.m., when everything is at rest. It is quite daylight, and has been for over an hour. We received telegram at 2 a.m. that they had mobilised the Reserves, all of them, which means that as far as the Navy is concerned we can do no more in preparation. . . . Keep a strong heart, dear one, you have much trouble, trial, and tribulation before you. We've lived for 40 years in peace and comfort, and now we are to be put to the test. It is good for us, will strengthen us, and we shall be better men and women for it in the end now we have come down to bedrock. . . . It would not be safe for *Sheelah* to go up the North Sea when the trouble starts, as there will be mines all over the place which we know of but she couldn't. This quite private, of course. Later she might get as far as Rosyth. She could anchor well up the Firth. You might consider the desirability of offering the *Sheelah* to the Admiralty for purposes of sick, etc. I spent my time visiting my ships and watching over their preparations, which are complete now. My Captains are splendid, and are not easily rattled. Whatever comes the battle cruisers will give a good account of themselves. We are at 4 hours' notice and consequently ready to move.

On 3rd August Beatty was given the acting rank of Vice-Admiral, so as to clarify his position in command when operating with other units of the Grand Fleet. This was a timely measure, for on 28th August, exactly two months after the great ball at Kronstadt, Beatty was leading his squadron into the Battle of the Heligoland Bight, where other British commands were involved.

CHAPTER SEVEN

1914

THE BATTLE OF THE HELIGOLAND BIGHT

Outbreak of war · Lack of defended bases · A brilliant achievement

THE task of the Royal Navy in war is to deny the use of the sea to the enemy, and to keep it open for the free passage of the merchant ships and transports of Britain and her Allies.

The surest means of completing the task would be to destroy all enemy naval forces, which indeed was the hope of all the officers and men of the Royal Navy, but this could not be fulfilled unless the enemy were to put to sea with the intention of giving battle. If the enemy fleet chose to remain in its defended harbours, no means existed for digging it out. Even if it sailed on some specific operation, hoping to avoid battle, early location would be needed to foil its purpose.

During the latter part of the eighteenth and early part of the nineteenth centuries a distant watch could be kept on Brest from about thirty miles to seaward for long periods between gales. One of the major problems in 1914 was how to maintain a similar blockade of the German naval bases in the Baltic and Heligoland Bight. The old navigational dangers of inshore shoals and adverse winds had been replaced by the modern dangers of mines and submarines, but the problems remained much the same, and were closely studied by the Admiralty in the years immediately preceding the war.

The plan finally adopted, and faithfully adhered to throughout the whole war, was to maintain a distant blockade at the exits from the North Sea, so as to prevent German armed ships from reaching the main ocean trade routes and to protect the British Army's oversea communications. Small forces were also distributed at suitable ports to prevent raids on the east coast.

Submarines were given the dangerous task of patrolling the estuaries of the German rivers, and for a short time a force of semi-obsolete cruisers was allocated an equally dangerous patrol area in the western approaches to the Heligoland Bight. Over and above these standing arrangements, a powerful striking force of light cruisers and destroyers, under the command of Commodore R. Tyrwhitt,[1] was based on Harwich for the purpose of sporadic incursions into the German Bight. Behind all these dispositions lay the might of the Grand Fleet at Scapa Flow; a huge force of modern battleships, battle cruisers, cruisers, and destroyers, ready at any moment to sweep out across the North Sea.

In accordance with this plan, Beatty reached Scapa with the Grand Fleet on 31st July, 1914. Immediately after coaling he was ordered to take the First Battle Cruiser Squadron at high speed to the Fair Island Channel (between the Orkneys and Shetlands), for the Admiralty believed a raid on the Shetland Islands might be attempted. On 4th August, while he was at sea straining his eyes for the first sight of a German warship, two events of vital importance took place. That morning he was informed that Sir John Jellicoe had relieved Sir George Callaghan as Commander-in-Chief, and that the Grand Fleet was already at sea under Jellicoe's command. At midnight he learnt that Britain was at war with Germany. His reaction to the change of command at such a critical moment was primarily one of indignation at the rough manner in which his old chief and brother Irishman had been treated.

With characteristic moral courage Beatty sent a telegram of protest to the First Lord and First Sea Lord, who incidentally had also received telegrams from no less a person than Jellicoe himself, one of which read:

Am more than ever convinced of vital importance of making no change. Personal feelings are entirely ignored in reaching this conclusion.

And again:

Yours of Second. Can only reply am certain step contemplated is most dangerous, beg that it may not be carried out. Am perfectly willing to

[1] Afterwards Admiral of the Fleet Sir Reginald Tyrwhitt, Bart., G.C.B., D.S.O.

act on board Fleet Flagship as assistant if required to be in direct communication. Hard to believe it is realised what grave difficulties change Commander-in-Chief involves at this moment. Do not forget long experience of Commander-in-Chief.[1]

Callaghan enjoyed the full confidence of the Fleet, had been long in command, and it was largely owing to him that the Fleet was in a state of immediate readiness for war. On the other hand, Beatty had a high admiration for Jellicoe, with whom he had served in the Boxer Campaign in China, and whose ability, both as an administrator at the Admiralty and as a Flag Officer at sea, he was able to appreciate from personal experience.

Beatty's reaction to the declaration of war is well illustrated by his own words in a message he addressed to his ships' companies: 'We must not forget at this moment how much we owe to those who have gone before us and have created the Fleet as it now is: those who worked so arduously and so long, to be ready for such a moment as has now been forced upon us. How they would have wished to be here! We are indeed fortunate, as we are proud, to be where we are, and to prove ourselves worthy to use the great weapons they have forged.'[2]

He wrote to Ethel:

Lion (*5th Aug.*, 1914)

We are at war, as you well know, the long-talked-of and much-dreaded has happened, and we are to be put to the test. After all, I can hardly realise that it is so, and it seems as if it was only in a dream that I ever heard of such a thing. It is a cruel war, because there never has been any reason for it. We have been forced into it, entirely through the rapacity and thirst for power and a large portion of the world, by Germany. Never in the history of the world has there been so little reason or so little cause.

We left Scapa in a hurry Monday night to support cruisers who were investigating a report that Germans were landing in the Shetlands. Before doing so I went on board the ships and harangued them. The enthusiasm was immense. I have never seen such a magnificent and cheerful spirit. War was a certainty at the time and we all knew it. We

---

[1] *Life of Earl Jellicoe*, Admiral Sir R. Bacon, p. 199.
[2] *Navy and Defence*, Lord Chatfield, p. 123.

dashed out and spent the night, which mercifully was short, at the guns, as we shall for the next months. Yesterday we were told war would be declared at midnight. Had a scare last evening. *Queen Mary* of course started it, and reported two enemy cruisers in sight. Away I went with *Queen Mary* top speed to find it was only old Packs [Rear-Admiral Pakenham] pottering off to coal. Afterwards a quiet night, in which you will be surprised to hear I slept like a baby for the short spell off I took and am as fit as a fiddle this morning. We received a Royal Message from the King and also the news that the C.-in-C. has been relieved by Jellicoe. I fear he must have been taken ill. It is a terrible handicap to start a war by losing our C.-in-C. and it will break his heart. Jellicoe is undoubtedly the better man, and in the end it will be for the best, but he hasn't the Fleet at his finger-tips at present, and I do not think is very well either. I am not anxious and feel am able to deal with situations as they arise, if I could only have word with Jellicoe and learn his views. I knew poor old Callaghan's, but this is different, and one of the curses of changing horses in the middle of the stream. . . . The Secretary, Spickernell, rejoices that he has already gained a medal. All the Staff doing well. My cabin is being dismantled to remove woodwork, otherwise we are much the same as ordinary manœuvres. I got your wire of congratulations which was quick and very very welcome before I left. I send you the addresses of four young women who are engaged to be married to men on board whose banns have been published on board. Will you write to them and tell them to be of good cheer. They are all well. I think they would like it and show them that there is somebody in the world who takes an interest in them. We are making history now, and it shall be a page that will not be behind those of the glorious past, so courage, sweetheart.

Ever mindful of his men, Beatty wrote a few weeks later:

Lion   (*20th Aug.*, 1914)

I've used up the money for the horses to look after the wives and those dependent on sailors belonging to the squadron who are in a bad way. You see, there will be heaps of money coming in for spectacular Funds like Millie's [Millicent, Duchess of Sutherland] and the Prince of Wales's Fund. But nothing to help the wife and children of the poor badly paid sailor, stoker, etc. I am starting funds on board all the ships to go into the case of every man and see that his dependents are cared for, and am applying the money to that end, which is sorely needed. I get something out of it too, because the sailor who knows that his dear ones are being looked after will be happier in his mind and will work better and more cheerfully for that knowledge. Millie will get tons of money. The trouble is to spend the money to the best advantage and at once. All is well, well fed, well housed, plenty to think about and now well stored with sleep. The waiting is the part that tires one, never relaxing a second because never certain when the blow will fall. But be sure we shall be ready when it does, the sooner the better. The *Invincible* will join up before long, so we shall be well off then for ships.

Immediately after hoisting his flag in the *Iron Duke*, Jellicoe learnt from the Admiralty that German armed merchant ships were about to break out of the North Sea with orders to attack the trade routes. Losing no time, he at once put to sea with the whole fleet. At the same time he directed Beatty to sweep towards the Norwegian coast with his battle cruisers and cruisers. The only German armed merchant ship actually passing through the North Sea at the time was the *Kaiser Wilhelm Der Grosse*, a Norddeutscher Lloyd steamer of 14,000 tons, lately converted into an auxiliary cruiser. She managed to escape, however, by making skilful use of Norwegian territorial waters during the dark hours. The Grand Fleet returned to Scapa, and after the strenuous task of coaling, sailed for a strategic position in the central North Sea, in order to be at hand should the High Seas Fleet attempt to interfere with the passage of the British Expeditionary Force across the Channel.

Certain ominous events which occurred during this cruise were destined to have a serious influence on British naval strategy. Shortly after the Fleet left Scapa, and while some of the battleships were engaged in target practice, the *Monarch* reported having been attacked by a submarine. Later on, the *Iron Duke* and *Dreadnought* sighted periscopes. All three incidents occurred north of the 58th parallel, and it seemed incredible (at that time) that enemy submarines could be operating so far from home. Indisputable evidence came on the morning of 9th August, when the cruiser *Birmingham* rammed and sank the German submarine *U15* in the northern North Sea.[1] There was, however, no proof that *U15* had come from Germany, and the Commander-in-Chief concluded that the enemy submarines must be operating from an

[1] 58° 35′ N., 1° 10′ E.

advanced base, possibly on the Norwegian coast. Nevertheless, the fact remained that enemy submarines *were* operating in northern waters, and, in consequence, the German High Command must know that the British Fleet was concentrated at a northern base. The paramount concern at the moment was the safe passage of the Expeditionary Force to France, and it was expected that the enemy, being aware that the Grand Fleet was in the north, would strike a blow at the cross-Channel transports before Jellicoe could intervene. The enemy made no such attempt.

As long as he could keep his fleet at sea, the Commander-in-Chief felt he could cope with the submarine menace, for he had adequate destroyer screens to protect the battle fleet, and moreover, the capital ships themselves, moving on zigzag courses at high speed, offered no easy target for a submarine.

The Grand Fleet could not, however, remain at sea at high speed for long periods without refuelling, and the fuel endurance of the destroyers was much less than that of the big ships. The only convenient bases in the North Sea where the whole Fleet could be accommodated were Scapa and Rosyth, but neither was protected against submarine attack. Since the British margin of superiority over the German Fleet in battleships was narrow, the Commander-in-Chief had to guard against the enemy attempting to reduce this margin by underwater attack before the High Seas Fleet committed itself to battle.

Jellicoe decided, therefore, to establish another fuelling base at Loch Ewe, so as to avoid the danger of having the whole Fleet concentrated while at anchor. Although Loch Ewe was completely devoid of defences, a certain measure of security could be obtained by fuelling portions of the Fleet there as well as at Scapa, Cromarty, and Rosyth. This system prevailed until the defences of Scapa were completed at the end of the year.

On 15th August the Grand Fleet swept across the North Sea towards the German coast, south of Horns Reef. At the same time Tyrwhitt, with his Harwich Force, together with some older cruisers, swept the southern area towards Terschelling. The only enemy sighted was a solitary submarine. It was a typical operation, and the forerunner of many which were part of the general plan. Every sweep was a direct challenge to the Germans to come out and fight if they dared. As a rule no enemy vessels were seen, proving that the British controlled the North Sea.

The Grand Fleet at sea was an awe-inspiring sight; a solid phalanx of twenty or more mighty battleships in five or six columns, zigzagging from starboard to port with military precision, at a speed of eighteen knots, each column screened against submarine attack by destroyers. Thirty miles ahead a scouting screen of light cruisers covered a front of 120 miles. Between the cruiser screen and the battle fleet lay Beatty's battle cruisers, where they could conveniently support the scouting cruisers and assist them to locate the enemy fleet. Beatty's main task was to destroy the German battle cruisers, as these powerful ships formed the hard core of the enemy's advance forces. This object was ever present in his mind, and governed his tactics during the whole time he commanded the scouting forces of the Grand Fleet.

During the first three weeks of the war, the Grand Fleet was almost continually at sea, except for uneasy intervals for fuelling in defenceless harbours. At this pace the strain on ships and crews was very heavy. The High Seas Fleet, on the other hand, remained dormant behind the defences of the Heligoland Bight, refusing to be tempted by the British coat-trailing operations in the North Sea and the bait offered by the British troopships in the Channel.

Beatty writes to Ethel:

Lion   (*24th Aug.*, 1914)

We are still wandering about the face of the ocean and apparently get no nearer to the end, in fact we have not begun yet. This waiting is the deuce, and as far as we can see has no limit. We are entirely in the hands of our friends the Germans as to when they will come out and be whacked. We have established economic pressure of a very thorough character, and have trailed our coats for him to come and tread on them, but he refuses to come and we can do no more. . . . News is confined to telegrams from a German source called *Norddeutsch*, which continually reports magnificent victories won by the Germans all along the front, which are immediately contradicted by the telegrams we get from *Poldhu*, which were amusing but have now become boring, and we wonder what is the truth.

We have our own scares daily about every three or four hours, which always fizzle out to nothing. . . . For thirty years I have been waiting for this day, and have as fine a command as one could wish for and can do nothing. Three weeks of war and haven't seen the enemy.

The feeling of enthusiastic expectancy on the part of the officers and men of the Grand Fleet was beginning to give way to boredom and disappointment, when a brilliant offensive movement by Beatty produced results beyond expectation.

In the south the British light forces, working from Harwich under Commodore Reginald Tyrwhitt and the submarines under Commodore Roger Keyes,[1] had been far from idle. They had made deep incursions into the Heligoland Bight, and some of the submarines, with great gallantry and complete disregard of the ever-present danger of minefields, had actually penetrated right into the mouths of the German rivers. Thus Keyes had already acquired a mass of valuable information about the enemy's movements and system of defence. Accordingly, on 23rd August, Keyes proposed to the Admiralty that an operation should be carried out with the object of destroying enemy patrol craft in the Heligoland Bight and stirring the Germans into action. His plan was for Tyrwhitt's destroyers from Harwich to creep into the Bight from the northward, and cut off the enemy patrols from their bases during dark hours, then sweep from east to west in daylight, destroying all enemy ships encountered. At the same time, Keyes and his submarines would lie off the estuaries of the German rivers, and attack enemy heavy ships if they ventured out.

The Admiralty approved the plan, and ordered Rear-Admiral Sir Archibald Moore[2] with the battle cruisers *Invincible* and *New Zealand* from the Humber, to support Tyrwhitt's flotillas at a distance of about 50 miles, while Rear-Admiral A. H. Christian, with Cruiser Force C, consisting of five old cruisers of the *Cressy* class and the light cruiser *Amethyst* patrolled the southern end of the Bight off Terschelling.

All these forces were under direct Admiralty control, and

---

[1] Afterwards Admiral of the Fleet Lord Keyes, G.C.B., K.C.V.O., C.M.G., D.S.O.
[2] Rear-Admiral Sir A. G. H. W. Moore, K.C.B., C.V.O.

the date of the operation was fixed for 28th August, 1914.
Jellicoe, though Commander-in-Chief Grand Fleet, knew
nothing of the plan until the afternoon of 26th August, when
the following signal reached him from the Admiralty:

It was decided last night to occupy Ostend with 3,000 Marines to
relieve the German pressure on the left wing of Allied Army. Belgian
forces have broken out of Antwerp and are attacking German communications. The ships will arrive off Ostend this afternoon, landing
commencing today or tomorrow morning. This flank attack may cause
some movement of the High Seas Fleet.

A destroyer sweep of 1st and 3rd Flotillas from Harwich, with submarines suitably placed, is in orders for Friday from east to west, commencing between Horns Reef and Heligoland, with battle cruisers [from
the Humber] in support.

It will be noted that the greater part of this signal refers to a
totally different operation, the occupation of Ostend. The
Grand Fleet is not even mentioned, yet the Admiralty state
there is a possibility of the High Seas Fleet coming out.

The Commander-in-Chief immediately suggested the co-
operation of the Grand Fleet, and in later signals showed his
uneasiness and desire for information. However, he soon
received instructions that the Grand Fleet was 'not required',
but that the First Battle Cruiser Squadron could support 'if
convenient'. Jellicoe accordingly ordered Beatty to proceed
with his squadron, together with the First Light Cruiser
Squadron (Commodore W. E. Goodenough), to a position
some seventy miles north of Heligoland, where he would meet
Rear-Admiral Sir Archibald Moore and the two Humber
battle cruisers at 5 a.m. on 28th August. Thus, almost as an
afterthought, it came about that the three Grand Fleet battle
cruisers (*Lion, Queen Mary, Princess Royal*) and six light
cruisers (*Southampton, Birmingham, Nottingham, Lowestoft,
Falmouth, Liverpool*) were added to the forces detailed for this
operation.

When Beatty left Scapa in the early hours of 27th August,
he had only a vague idea of the plan. Neither he nor the
Commander-in-Chief had been informed of the type of enemy
forces likely to be encountered. The British forces from the

Humber and Harwich were known to be acting under Admiralty direction, but nobody had been told who was to command the operation.

At 8 a.m. Beatty signalled to the First Battle Cruiser Squadron and First Light Cruiser Squadron in company with him:

We are to rendezvous with *Invincible* and *New Zealand* in lat. 55° 10′ N., long. 6° E. at 5 a.m. [28th August] to support destroyers and submarines. . . . Operation consisting of a sweep of a line north–south true from Horns Reef to Heligoland to westward . . . know very little, shall hope to learn more as we go along.

He learned more at noon, when the Admiralty gave him the positions through which Tyrwhitt's destroyers would pass during their sweep of the Bight. Beatty was asked how he proposed to act in support. He replied that the light cruisers would follow the destroyers at a distance of ten miles, and that the battle cruisers would conform to their movements, keeping to the north-west of them.

The Admiralty passed this information on to the other forces taking part, but by a regrettable oversight the signal was not retransmitted from Harwich, and consequently the British flotillas and submarines were totally unaware that a Grand Fleet detachment was to support them.

At dawn on the morning of 28th August, Tyrwhitt's forces sighted columns of smoke to the north which were assumed to come from hostile ships. They were in fact from the First Light Cruiser Squadron, but fortunately, in spite of poor visibility, 'the challenge' saved the situation, and a disaster was averted. To Tyrwhitt's enquiry, 'Are you taking part in the operation?' Goodenough replied: 'Yes, I know your course and will support you. Beatty is behind us.'

At 5 a.m. Moore, with his two battle cruisers from the Humber, joined Beatty according to plan at the rendezvous, and informed him of the movements of British submarines in the area. The situation was at last clear to all except Keyes and his submarines, who still knew nothing of the presence of Beatty and Goodenough.

The British force advanced into the Bight on a southerly

course towards Heligoland. Tyrwhitt led the Third Flotilla of sixteen L-class destroyers. His flagship was the new light cruiser *Arethusa*, which had left the builders' hands only three days before. Captain W. F. Blunt, in the light cruiser *Fearless*, followed two miles astern, leading the First Flotilla of fifteen modern destroyers, while eight miles astern of them was Goodenough with six modern light cruisers.

Beatty with five battle cruisers was forty miles away to the north-west. It had been a part of the plan to hold this southerly course till 8 a.m. when the whole force would turn westward, covering a broad front in line abreast. The activities of Keyes' submarines working close inshore, however, stirred up a hornets' nest earlier than expected. At 6 a.m. the Germans sent out their Fifth Destroyer Flotilla to hunt a British submarine which had attacked one of their patrols. An hour later some of their destroyers were sighted at intervals by Tyrwhitt and his Third Flotilla, who immediately opened fire and gave chase. Blunt followed suit, and so it came about that, quite early in the day, the whole British destroyer force was deflected from the original plan, and was steaming at high speed towards Heligoland in pursuit of the fleeing enemy.

The visibility rapidly closed down to 10,000 yards, and the enemy were lost in the mist, but the British destroyers had been able to damage a few enemy ships at long range. Meanwhile, some German light cruisers had appeared on the scene to cover the retirement of their retreating flotilla. The first to appear out of the mist was the *Stettin*, which at 8 a.m. came into action for a few minutes with the *Arethusa* and *Fearless* on opposite courses, and retired behind Heligoland.

The British forces were now well within sight of Heligoland and within easy range of the shore batteries, which, however, did not open fire, as they could not distinguish friend from foe.

The next German ship to appear was the *Frauenlob*, and a fierce encounter took place between her and the *Arethusa* at a range of only 3,400 yards. It was now that the *Arethusa* felt the effects of having just left the builders' hands. The mechanism of all her six-inch guns jammed, with the exception of one. She was hit in the engine-room, but in return shattered the *Frauenlob's* bridge, forcing her to retire. At about this time an

'The Wounded Lion' by W. E. Wylie, R.A.

Picture shows the *Lion* in tow of the *Indomitable* approaching The Forth Bridge
after the Battle of the Dogger Bank

unfortunate Norwegian steamer unwittingly became involved in the fray. First of all she was fired at by the *Stettin* in mistake for a British minelayer, and later by the British Third Flotilla in mistake for a German minelayer. The crew not unnaturally took to their boats.

At 8.12 a.m. Tyrwhitt re-formed his flotillas and began a drive westward. This soon brought him into contact with enemy destroyers returning homeward from their outer patrol line. Some of these escaped round the flanks of the British forces, but the destroyer *V*187 was overwhelmed and quickly sunk. An incident now occurred which had far-reaching results. Keyes, in the destroyer *Lurcher*, sighted the ships of the British First Light Cruiser Squadron, and being totally un-aware of their presence in the area, reported them as hostile. This led Tyrwhitt to turn back with his flotillas to assist him and, at the same time, to request Goodenough to chase the new-comers. In other words, Tyrwhitt was inadvertently asking Goodenough to chase himself! Keyes, however, soon recognised the silhouette of Goodenough's flagship, the *Southampton*, but not in time to prevent one of his submarines from attacking her. Fortunately, the attack failed, and no damage was done, but the incident led Goodenough to with-draw from an area which he now knew to be occupied by British submarines. The sweep continued westward with the crippled *Arethusa* lagging behind.

It was now nearly 11 a.m. The British forces had already been in the Bight for some four hours, and as they had been in contact with the enemy, it was clear that strong enemy counter-attacks must be expected at any moment. These duly material-ised shortly after 11 a.m., in the form of independent attacks by three more German cruisers, the *Strassburg* and *Köln* from the south-east, and the *Mainz* from the west. Their attacks were badly timed, but had the effect of splitting up the British flotillas, causing ships to lose touch with one another in the thick weather. Tyrwhitt, in his crippled flagship the *Arethusa*, became involved in a hot action with the *Strassburg*. Com-menting on this action in his despatch, he says: 'We were receiving an almost accurate fire from the cruisers, salvo after salvo falling between ten and thirty yards short; but not one

shell hit. Two torpedoes were fired, well directed, but short.'
The *Strassburg* was driven off by the British destroyers. The
Mainz, on the other hand, had joined action with part of the
First Flotilla, which led her northward into the arms of Goodenough, hastening south on Beatty's orders to the scene of
action. After a stubborn fight she became enveloped in flames,
and was finally sunk.

It was comforting for Tyrwhitt to know that at least one of
his opponents was being effectively dealt with, but the respite
was short-lived, for very soon the *Strassburg* and *Köln* again
appeared. At 12.30 p.m., the situation was looking extremely
serious for the British. The *Arethusa* and three destroyers had
been seriously damaged, and would have to be extricated from
the Bight. Four more German cruisers, the *Stralsund*, *Stettin*,
Danzig, and *Ariadne*, were converging on the *Arethusa*. Blunt
in the *Fearless*, with a division of destroyers, gallantly engaged
them, thus drawing the fire from the *Arethusa*, but he could do
little against such overwhelming odds.

Suddenly, when all seemed to be lost, there appeared out of
the mist to the north-west the huge forms of Beatty's battle
cruisers steaming at full speed, with the *Lion* in the van. Their
timely arrival completely turned the issue of the day, and to the
hard-pressed British destroyers it seemed as if a miracle had
happened.

A young lieutenant (Oswald Frewen), then serving in one of
Tyrwhitt's destroyers which had been damaged, describes the
scene from their point of view:

The *Mainz* was immensely gallant. The last I saw of her absolutely
wrecked alow and aloft, her whole midships a fuming inferno. She had
one gun forward and one aft still spitting forth fury and defiance, like
a wild cat mad with wounds. Our own four-funnelled friend recommenced at this juncture with a couple of salvos, but rather half-heartedly;
and we really did not care a d——, for there straight ahead of us in lovely
procession, like elephants walking through a pack of 'pi-dogs', came the
Lion, Queen Mary, Invincible, and *New Zealand*, our battle-cruisers.
Great and grim and uncouth as some antediluvian monsters, how solid
they looked, how utterly earthquaking! We pointed out our latest
aggressor to them, whom they could not see from where they were,
and they passed down the field of battle with the little destroyers on their

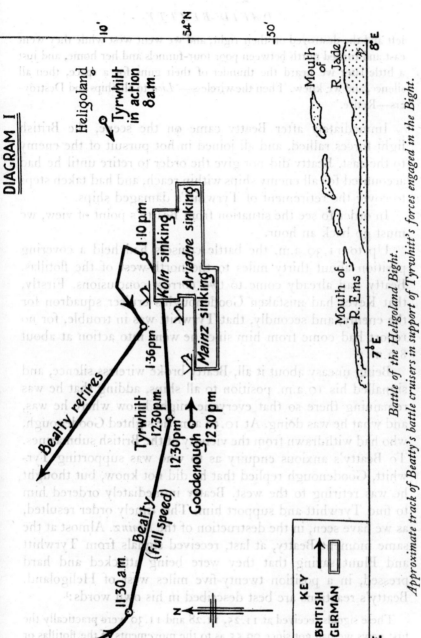

DIAGRAM I

Heligoland

Tyrwhitt
in action
8 a.m.

1·10 pm

Koln sinking

Ariadne sinking

Mainz sinking

1·36 pm

Beatty retires

Mouth of
R. Ems

Tyrwhitt
1230pm

Goodenough
1230 pm

12·30 pm

Beatty
(full speed)

11·30 a.m.

Mouth
of
R. Jade

KEY

——— BRITISH

▬▬▬ GERMAN

N

Battle of the Heligoland Bight.

Approximate track of Beatty's battle cruisers in support of Tyrwhitt's forces engaged in the Bight.

28th August, 1914.

8°E

7°E

6°E

54°N

-10'

50'

left and the destroyed on their right, and we went west while they went east and turned north between poor four-funnels and her home, and just a little later we heard the thunder of their guns for a space, then all silence, and we knew. Then the wireless—'*Lion* to all Ships and Destroyers—Retire.'

Immediately after Beatty came on the scene, the British light forces rallied, and all joined in hot pursuit of the enemy to the east. Beatty did not give the order to retire until he had accounted for all enemy ships within reach, and had taken steps to cover the retirement of Tyrwhitt's damaged ships.

In order to see the situation from Beatty's point of view, we must go back an hour.

Up to 11.30 a.m. the battle cruisers had held a covering position about thirty miles to the north-west of the flotillas. Beatty had already come to two correct conclusions. Firstly, that Keyes had mistaken Goodenough's cruiser squadron for the enemy, and secondly, that Tyrwhitt was in trouble, for no report had come from him since he went into action at about 8 a.m.

Being uneasy about it all, Beatty broke wireless silence, and signalled his 10 a.m. position to all ships, adding that he was remaining there so that everyone might know where he was, and what he was doing. At 10.50 a.m. he sighted Goodenough, who had withdrawn from the vicinity of the British submarines. To Beatty's anxious enquiry as to who was supporting Tyrwhitt, Goodenough replied that he did not know, but thought he was retiring to the west. Beatty immediately ordered him to find Tyrwhitt and support him. This timely order resulted, as we have seen, in the destruction of the *Mainz*. Almost at the same moment Beatty, at last, received signals from Tyrwhitt and Blunt saying that they were being attacked and hard pressed, in a position twenty-five miles west of Heligoland. Beatty's reactions are best described in his own words:[1]

These signals received at 11.25, 11.28 and 11.30 were practically the first news we had got since 09.55 as to the movements of the flotillas or the result of an action which had apparently been in progress for three and a half hours. The situation appeared to me to be extremely critical; the flotillas had advanced on their sweep only ten miles since 08·00, and

[1] Vice-Admiral's Despatch of 30th August, 1914.

thus were only twenty-six miles from an enemy base in their rear, with another base twenty-five miles on their flank . . . there was the possibility of a grave disaster.

At 11.30 I therefore decided that the only course possible was to take the Battle Cruiser Squadron at full speed to the eastward. To be of any value, the support must be overwhelming and carried out at the highest speed possible, and, as there were indications of three or four enemy ships, one of which was reported a large cruiser, I did not deem the Light Cruiser Squadron, two of whose ships were detached, to be strong enough to deal with the situation sufficiently rapidly.

I had not lost sight of the danger to my squadron from the following:

(1) Enemy submarines.
(2) Our own submarines.
(3) The possible sortie of a large enemy force.

(1) I discounted by the fact that our high speed made their attack difficult, and the smooth state of the sea made their detection easy.

(2) I discounted, partly for the same reason and partly because I had now been able to communicate with Commodore (Submarines) [Keyes], who informed me that our submarines were twenty miles to the eastward. This gave room to manœuvre and his presence was some measure of protection.

(3) I discounted, because our force was so powerful that we could only have been stopped by a Battle Squadron, which was unlikely to be out in time if we were sufficiently rapid in our support.

Accordingly, at 11.35, the battle cruisers turned east-south-east, and hastened at full speed towards the action now taking place on the threshold of the enemy's main base. Thus at 12.37 p.m. Beatty made his dramatic appearance. A minute later the *Lion* opened fire on the cruiser *Köln* who, turning south-eastward, managed to cling to the edge of the haze and presented a poor target. Nevertheless, she was repeatedly hit, and was eventually sunk by two heavy salvos. Only one man was saved. Another enemy cruiser, the *Ariadne*, who appeared ahead, crossing from port to starboard, was quickly despatched, but the *Strassburg* and *Stralsund*, taking advantage of the haze, managed to escape to the east.

At 1.10 p.m. all contacts with the enemy forces having been lost, Beatty made the general signal 'Retire'. Fifty minutes later, strong German reinforcements were crossing the bar of the outer Jade. Beatty's main concern now was to ensure the safe withdrawal of all British forces from the Bight, not an easy task, owing to the damaged state of the *Arethusa* and the destroyer *Laurel*. Both were taken in tow by the old cruisers *Hogue* and *Amethyst*, which had moved up from their patrol line off Terschelling. Beatty remained in the vicinity until all the British ships were out of danger.

There is no doubt that Beatty, by his prompt action, had turned into a victory what would otherwise almost certainly have been a disaster. His decision to lead his heavy ships into the dangerous waters of the Bight was a hard one to make. He had pondered all the risks and methodically discounted them one by one. Even so he was a little uneasy, and said to his Flag Captain (Chatfield), 'Am I justified in going into that hornets' nest with these great ships? If I lose one it will be a great blow to the country'. He knew only too well that the margin of superiority in battle cruisers over the enemy in home waters at this time was only one ship. Beatty could temper boldness with caution. Having weighed up the situation, he acted with vigour and determination, and as a result, three German cruisers and one destroyer were sunk. Truly Fortune had favoured the brave.

Captain Chatfield and other officers who stood on the bridge, as the *Lion* led her consorts at full speed into the unknown perils of the Bight, all vouch for the confidence inspired by Beatty's leadership. He was highly elated at the prospect of battle. The greater the danger and the graver the emergency, the clearer his brain and the quicker his decision. It was the first time he had led heavy ships into action, and the same qualities of courage and leadership which he had previously displayed on active service were immediately apparent to all.

Although the Battle of Heligoland was indeed a marked success for the Royal Navy, the action disclosed grave defects in staff work. Ships had not only failed to report the position of the enemy, but also their own positions, and until Beatty's presence had been disclosed to all, no one knew for certain who was in supreme command. This naturally created confusion, which in turn was increased by the thick weather.[1] At

---

[1] Captain Chatfield's report states that the *Lion* engaged the enemy at ranges of 5,000–7,000 yards, and even then was losing sight of her targets as ships disappeared in the mist.

such high speed in restricted waters the battle was indeed a severe test, and had it not been for Beatty's individual dash and gallantry, which enabled him to arrive at the right spot at the right time the whole operation might well have ended in disaster.

The almost total breakdown of the *Arethusa's* armament demonstrated the danger of sending a brand-new ship straight from the builders' hands into battle. That she was able, in these circumstances, to damage and drive off one of the enemy cruisers reflected great credit on Commodore Tyrwhitt and his ship's company.

The mistakes on both sides were the natural outcome of many years of peace. The Germans failed to concentrate their cruisers before falling upon our flotillas, and this undoubtedly saved the *Arethusa* and prevented other British losses. Hesitancy on the part of the German High Command to send out heavy ships in support of their patrols enabled Beatty to get his lame ducks out of the Bight without further damage.

The moral effect of the action was profound, and the results were far-reaching. Coming as it did just after the retreat from Mons, it served to put heart into the British Army and the whole country.

Deep depression ran through the German Fleet. The officers and men felt strongly the humiliation of having allowed the British heavy ships to penetrate with such amazing audacity close to the very coast of the Fatherland, where they had inflicted punishment on German ships, causing the loss of more than a thousand officers and men, including two Flag officers. This demonstration of the traditional spirit of the British Navy caused the Kaiser to decree that his ships were not to be risked, and that all Fleet sallies must be approved by himself.

On his return to Scapa, Beatty was somewhat upset by an embarrassing incident. As the battle cruisers passed through the lines of Grand Fleet battleships they were heartily cheered. Beatty felt that the circumstances did not warrant such a joyous reception, for to his mind the action had been no more than a normal operation of war. Unfortunately, the *Lion's* anchor was jammed in the hawse-pipe, and she had to turn round and come down the line again. This encore invited more cheers, most of the men thinking it had been done for their benefit. Beatty was annoyed, as he knew very well that ill-disposed contemporaries might misconstrue the motive. He was consoled, however, by a friendly signal from another Flag Officer saying, 'It seems that your anchor was rammed home as hard as your attack'.

On arrival in harbour he sent off this modest account of the battle to Ethel:

Lion   (29th Aug., 1914)

Just a line to say all is well. I sent *Liverpool* into Rosyth today with some prisoners and wounded. We got at them yesterday, and got three of their cruisers under the nose of Heligoland, which will give them a bit of a shock. The ones in the *Liverpool* were all that were saved out of one ship, and alas none were saved from the other that sank. A third disappeared in fog in a sinking condition, and I doubt if she ever got back. I could not pursue her further, as we were too close already, and the sea was full of mines and submarines and a large force might have popped out on us at any moment. Poor devils, they fought their ships like men and went down with colours flying like seamen against overwhelming odds. We take no credit for such, but it was good work to be able to do it within twenty miles of their main base, Heligoland, with the whole of the High Sea Fleet listening to the boom of our guns. We could not afford half measures, and had to go in and out as quickly as possible. Three of our Light Cruiser Flotilla Cruisers got badly knocked about and one or two destroyers. But the supporting force Light Cruiser Squadron, which did very well and sank one ship, and my battle cruisers had no material damage, only a few hits and only one casualty, very slight. The Flag Lieutenant (Seymour) trembles because he thinks he'll have to be bled. Don't say anything about this until you read of it in the Press, because I am not sure I am justified in telling you so much. Everybody on board is well, and the letting off of guns and doing execution did them all good. But it was sad seeing a gallant ship (*Köln*) disappear. That is a side of the picture that I cannot permit myself to think about, and only remember that if we had not been there in time, one of ours would have had the same fate.

On the following day he wrote:

(30th Aug., 1914)

The Admiralty has announced the result of the operation in the Heligoland Bight, so there is no need for secrecy on my behalf. We got back out of it quite safely, and I think gave the Germans a jolly good shock right at their door which will upset them. We got all our vessels out of it safely, which was an *intense* relief. At one time I thought we should never do it, but by hard steaming, thanks to old Green,[1] the *Lion* fairly flew 28 knots, and left the *Queen Mary*. Even Captain Hall admits it, and were just in time. It was an anxious 4 hours from 10 till 2, and then it got a little better, but it was not until 6 p.m. I felt they were all safe, so all is well, but 1 officer and 7 men were killed in *Arethusa* and 15 wounded. She apparently bore the brunt of the destroyer engagement. There were others in different ships and destroyers, but not many. I think it will have a very good moral effect on our fellows and proportionately demoralising effect upon the enemy. Three cruisers and a number of destroyers is a considerable loss. . . . I think an invasion on a small scale would do the country a lot of good. . . . I hope the poor German wounded were not very bad. Two poor fellows died in *Liverpool* on the way. Whatever their faults they are gallant and fight like men and indeed are worthy foemen. I have the *Inflexible* with me now and hope to exchange her with *New Zealand* and eventually to get them all in my clutches and then I think we can surely make them sit up. Our day,[2] Friday 28th, was also Plunkett's birthday, which brought us luck. He grinned all over.

From August to November, in Mr. Churchill's words, 'except for furtive movements by individual submarines and minelayers, not a dog stirred'. This period of enemy inactivity gave a much-needed respite, enabling the defence of British bases to be completed, and the position of the Grand Fleet to be consolidated. Jellicoe had no intention of 'letting sleeping dogs lie', so just to make sure, a well-planned repetition of the Heligoland Bight operation was carried out on 10th September, in the hope of drawing out the German heavy ships. Beatty, with six battle cruisers, supported the light forces as before, and this time was, himself, supported by the Commander-in-Chief with the whole Grand Fleet. Not a single enemy ship was sighted. The effect of this bold sweep was largely a moral one, and the enemy, becoming more apprehensive than ever, took immediate steps to lay extensive minefields in the waters of the Heligoland Bight.

In Beatty's own words:

[1] Later Engineer-Captain Sir Percy Green.　　　　[2] Lady Beatty's birthday

We wandered out into the North Sea and patrolled for Tuesday and Wednesday and Thursday, had another look into the Bight, but they knew we were coming and not a soul was in sight. I made certain they would be ready for us and give us a warm welcome, but no. I fear we gave them much more of a shaking than we thought. They haven't recovered from that yet. I fear the rascals will never come out, but will only send out minelayers and submarines. They seem to have a blight on them, and wanting in initiative and dash with their battle cruisers. They could have done so much by this time if they had set their minds to it. It really is very disappointing, and looks as if we should go through the war without ever coming to grips with them. Such a thought *is* more than I can bear. . . .

Beatty quite naturally expected some commendation from the Admiralty for his conduct in the battle of Heligoland, but no word of encouragement appeared to be forthcoming. He tells Ethel about it:

Lion (*2nd Sept.*, 1914)

I had thought I should have received an expression of their appreciation from Their Lordships, but have been disappointed, or rather not so much disappointed as disgusted, and my real opinion has been confirmed that they would have hung me if there had been a disaster, as there very nearly was, owing to the extraordinary neglect of the most ordinary precautions on their part. However, all's well that ends well, and they haven't had the opportunity of hanging me yet and they won't get it. Now this is entirely between you and I. Don't breathe a word of this to a soul, but it's on record. Anyhow, I received a most charming telegram from the Prime Minister of Canada to myself, officers and men. They did not leave us at rest long, just time to coal and get some more ammunition and we are now scouring the sea again. The ships' companies are full of beans, and that little shooting and getting into touch with the enemy did them no end of good and they feel warriors now. Of course, those entertainments are the easiest part of our job and not to be compared with the weary hours of looking out without much release to the strain, which is far and away the worst side of our picture. I had a long letter from Filson Young, who has gone off to sea as the official chronicler of naval events. He would hate it if he was here now. . . . I can only trust our friends the Russians are the victorious ones. Little Von Essen has done nothing up to now except some of his ships have blown themselves up apparently on their own mines. The German cruiser *Madgeburg* ran ashore, which with the three we sank, *Köln*, *Mainz*, and *Ariadne*, will make a big hole in their cruiser force. They seem to be terribly busy laying mines, which is all right as long as we can locate them, which fact has saved us from a disaster up to now. They borrowed the *New Zealand* from me the other day to operate down south and sent me the *Inflexible,* but I have managed to change it and get my *New Zealand* back again, which is a good thing, and I shall get the *Tiger* in about 3 or 4 weeks, so shall have my 4 pussy cats then. . . . We had a terrible scare last night, sighted a lot of vessels without lights, so turned round after them and followed for some time, trying to get the right side of the moon, so they should not see us and we could get a good view of them. This required great restraint on our part, as it is everything to get in the first blow. After an hour we got to a good position, when I thought they looked uncommonly familiar, and so challenged them, when they turned out to be our own destroyers. They were never so near being blown out of the water before. There is something wrong somewhere which would permit them being in a position in which we both run such unnecessary risks. War is bad enough without adding to it by making stupid mistakes of that nature.

The Admiralty's appreciation of Beatty's conduct in the battle of the Heligoland Bight eventually reached him at the end of October, two months after the battle.

The Commander-in-Chief,   Admiralty,
H.M. Ships and Vessels,
Home Fleets   *22nd October,* 1914
Sir,

Their Lordships have read this report with much satisfaction, and I am to request that you will convey to Sir David Beatty their appreciation of the resolution and promptitude shown by him in bringing his squadron into action with decisive effect, notwithstanding the risks which he had to face from submarines and floating mines.

I am, Sir,
Your obedient Servant,
(*signed*) O. Murray.

Vice-Admiral   *29th October,* 1914
First Battle Cruiser Squadron

I have much pleasure in forwarding this expression of Their Lordships' appreciation, with which I most fully concur.

(*signed*) J. R. Jellicoe,
Admiral.

CHAPTER EIGHT

1914
THE SCARBOROUGH RAID

The submarine danger · Withdrawal to the West coast ·
Frustration

MEANWHILE during September, in spite of repeated protests by the Commander-in-Chief, the work of defending the North Sea bases had proceeded all too slowly. Submarines had been reported inside Scapa Flow, though not actually there, and in the Firth of Forth. The policy of keeping the Fleet at sea for long periods was continued, thus rendering the distant blockade almost wholly effective. No important warship had been sunk by submarines, and there had grown up a certain feeling of over-confidence that the new weapon need not be taken too seriously. So light-heartedly was the menace regarded, that capital ships would actually stop at sea to examine merchant ships for contraband. The inevitable shock came on 22nd September, when the cruisers *Hogue*, *Cressy*, and *Aboukir* were torpedoed in quick succession, with a total loss of 62 officers and 1,397 men, while patrolling at slow speed off the Dutch coast under the direction of the Admiralty. By some miracle these old ships had been able, for six whole weeks, to keep watch on the very doorstep of the enemy without once being molested. The heavy loss of life and ships was due to the surviving cruisers hastening, one after the other, to the aid of their stricken consorts, and then stopping to pick up survivors.

On 23rd September, 1914, Beatty wrote to Ethel:

In the middle of the night we heard of the terrible disaster to the *Aboukir*, my old ship, that I first hoisted my flag on board and so had a considerable affection for, the *Cressy*, and the *Hogue*, all of my old squadron. We heard the *Aboukir* crying out yesterday morning, and we thought there was something wrong, although she was over 400 miles away, but never contemplated it was a disaster of the magnitude that it is.

Three fine ships and the greater part of 2,200 men that can be ill spared. It was bound to happen. Our cruisers had no conceivable right to be where they were. It is not being wise after the event, but I had frequently discussed with others that sooner or later they would surely be caught by submarines or battle cruisers if they continued to occupy that position. It was inevitable and faulty strategy on the part of the Admiralty.

On 2nd October, 1914, the Grand Fleet took up positions to prevent enemy warships from breaking out of the North Sea while the convoy carrying the Canadian Expeditionary Force was crossing the Atlantic, and it soon became apparent that attempts were being made by German submarines to attack the Fleet. Acute apprehension for its security while anchored in ill-defended bases was now shared by the Commander-in-Chief and the Admiralty, so on 16th October the whole Fleet left the North Sea for harbours on the west coast of the British Isles. The Commander-in-Chief took the major portion to Lough Swilly, in the north of Ireland, and Beatty, with the First Battle Cruiser Squadron, went to Loch-na-Keal, in the island of Mull. This movement was intended to enable the Fleet to carry out gunnery practices in waters reasonably immune from enemy submarines, but the exodus left the East Coast of Britain open to attack. The German Navy, however, being still numbed by the shock of Beatty's victory in the Bight, were in no mood for taking the offensive.

They confined their activities to submarine operations and indiscriminate mine-laying, and by a stroke of luck succeeded in laying a minefield in the very area off Lough Swilly selected by Jellicoe for his gunnery practices. The Germans had chosen this area in the hope of destroying British merchant ships using the North Irish Channel, but it was the battleship *Audacious* which fell a victim. The mines had been laid by the auxiliary cruiser *Berlin* after an adventurous outward passage through the British blockade. On her way home the *Berlin* entered the neutral port of Trondheim, rather than risk the return passage through the North Sea. Little did her crew, languishing interned in the Norwegian mountains, dream that they had inflicted such a heavy blow on the British Battle Fleet.

Although Beatty fully recognised the need for moving the

Fleet from the North Sea as a temporary measure, such an ignominious withdrawal from the main naval theatre of war was more than he could bear in silence, so he lost no time in expressing his views by private letter[1] to the First Lord. This was quite a proper course for Beatty to take, as he had served as Naval Secretary to Mr. Churchill.

SIR DAVID BEATTY TO FIRST LORD[1]

H.M.S. *Lion*,
17th October, 1914.

(Private)

I take the opportunity of an officer going to London in charge of signal books to write you of what goes on. I have written you before, or rather to Hood for you. I think it is right that you should know how things generally affect the Fleet. I trust that you will take this as it is written, in fact I know you will, as being written with only one idea of service to the country. I write as I do because I know that the plain truth at times such as these is the only thing worth hearing, and because you are the one and only man who can save the situation. Even at such times, official documents, requisitions, and demands are of little value; they are met at once, I admit, but without understanding the time value of all that lies behind them.

At present we feel that we are working up for a catastrophe of a very large character. The feeling is gradually possessing the Fleet that all is not right somewhere. The menace of mines and submarines is proving larger every day, and adequate means to meet or combat them are not forthcoming, and we are gradually being pushed out of the North Sea, and off our own particular perch. How does this arise? By the very apparent fact that we have no base where we can with *any* degree of safety lie for coaling, replenishing, and refitting and repairing, after two and a half months of war. This spells trouble. It is a perfectly simple and easy matter to equip Scapa Flow, Cromarty, and Rosyth, so that vessels can lie there undisturbed to do all they want, and for as long as they want, provided material and men are forthcoming. The one place that has put up any kind of defence against the submarine is Cromarty, and that is because at Cromarty there happens to be a *man* who grapples with things as they are, i.e. Commander Munro, and because they have trained artillerymen to man their guns. That was one of the best day's work you ever did when you insisted on taking the defences there in hand. At Rosyth it appeared to me in September when there, that to deny access

[1] *World Crisis*, 1911–15, Winston Churchill.

to submarines and destroyers was a fairly simple task; it was an awkward place to get into, but when once in, it ought to be, and could be, very easily made a safe asylum for vessels in need of rest, repair, fuel, etc. At Scapa, something has been done towards blocking the many entrances, but that is all. I am sure that all the brain and intellect at the Admiralty could devise a scheme or method of defence which would make the anchorage practically safe, and which could be done in a fortnight. No *seaman* can dispute that these three bases could have been made *absolutely* safe from submarine attack during the two and a half months that the war has been in progress. As it is, we have been lulled into a sense of false security, because we have not been attacked before; but I can assure you that it has literally been recognised by all that it was only a question of time when we should have this sense rudely shattered. . . .

The situation as it is, we have no place to lay our heads. We are at Loch na Keal, Isle of Mull. My picket boats are at the entrance, the nets are out, and the men are at the guns, waiting for coal which has run low, but ready to move at a moment's notice. Other squadrons are in the same plight. We have been running now hard since 28th July; small defects are creeping up which we haven't time to take in hand. Forty-eight hours is our spell in harbour, with steam ready to move at four hours' notice, coaling on an average 1,400 tons a time; night defence stations. The men can stand it, but the machine can't, and we must have a place where we can stop for from four to five days every now and then to give the engineers a chance. Such a place does not exist, so the question arises, how long can we go on, for I fear very much, not for long, as the need for small repairs is becoming insistent.

The remedy is to fix upon a base and make it impervious to submarine attack; as I have pointed out I am firmly convinced this can be done. . . .

You might be told that this idea of making the entrances secure is chimerical. This is not so; and I will guarantee that if the Fleet was instructed to defend the entrances to the ports named, and was provided with the material, they could and would devise not one but several methods which would satisfy most requirements, and which would keep out submarines. If the Fleet cannot spare the time and labour, turn it over to Commander Munro and give him a free hand and what labour he requires, and he will do it in a fortnight.

I think you know me well enough to know that I do not shout without cause. The Fleet's tail is still well over the back. We hate running away from our base and the effect is appreciable. We are not enjoying ourselves. But the morale is high and confidence higher. I would not write thus if I did not know that you with your quick grasp of detail and imagination would make something out of it.

Beatty's letter did not differ in substance from the many official ones on this subject addressed to the Admiralty by the Commander-in-Chief. Beatty considered Scapa too far north to ensure the interception by ships based there of enemy heavy forces attempting a raid on the east coast of England. It was no easy task, however, to make Rosyth secure for the whole Grand Fleet, and priority was given to the preparation of Scapa as a defended Fleet base. Steps were taken to prepare Rosyth for the Battle Cruiser Force as a preliminary measure, but even this did not fully satisfy Beatty, who later on pressed strongly for the Humber also to be got ready for his battle cruisers in order to place them as near as possible to the enemy.

An important change, which Beatty felt deeply, took place at the Admiralty towards the end of October, when his old friend, Prince Louis of Battenberg, in response to uninformed clamour about his German antecedents, voluntarily resigned from the post of First Sea Lord.

The war at sea was going none too well. There had been naval losses for which the Prince was made the scapegoat. His timely mobilisation of the Fleet before the outbreak of war, the successful transportation of the British Expeditionary Force to France without the loss of a single man, and the British naval victory of the Heligoland Bight had apparently all been forgotten. Truly the 'Hosannas' of today are the 'Crucify' of tomorrow. It was left to his two sons, the second Marquis of Milford Haven, a distinguished gunnery officer, and the first Earl Mountbatten, whom the world well knows, to show that Great Britain has seldom had sailors more loyal or useful to the State than those who came from this great family.

At the beginning of November Beatty wrote to Ethel:

Lion (*2nd Nov.*, 1914)

Well, Prince Louis has gone. . . . You were quite right. They have resurrected old Fisher. Well, I think he is the best they could have done, but I wish he was ten years younger. He still has fine zeal, energy, and determination, coupled with low cunning, which is eminently desirable just now. He also has courage and will take any responsibility. He will recognise that his position is absolutely secure and will rule the Admiralty and Winston with a heavy hand. He has patriotism, and is a firm believer in the good qualities of the Navy, that it can do anything and will go anywhere, and please God we shall change our present method for a strong offensive policy. . . . I trust old Charles Beresford will have the decency to sink his differences with him and not stump about the country endeavouring to calumniate him as he has done in the past. As it is, our principal and almost overwhelming handicap in the struggle of Nations is and has been our Administrators. Even now, as far as the Navy is concerned, we want a Kitchener at the head. We are only playing at war. We are all nervous as cats, afraid of losing lives, losing ships, and running risks. We are ruled by Panic Law, and until we risk something shall never gain anything.

All right, my dear, we *will* give each mess in each ship a Turkey for his Xmas dinner. It will mean something like 250 Turkeys. . . . I am inundated with letters from fellows to join the battle cruisers, and Filson Young writes once a day. Persistence will win if determined enough. Poor old Kit Cradock has gone, at Coronel, poor old chap. He had a glorious death. His death and the loss of the ships and the gallant lives in them can be laid to the door of the incompetency of the Admiralty. They have as much idea of strategy as the School Board boy, and have broken over and over again the first principles.

Meanwhile, the Admiralty had accepted Lady Beatty's offer of the yacht *Sheelah* as a hospital ship, and in this capacity she was stationed at Rosyth. A large part of the cost of fitting out was borne by Lady Beatty, who, acting on the advice of Sir Alfred Fripp, furnished an operating theatre which became a model for other hospital ships. She did not at first grasp that she could no longer control the *Sheelah's* movements, so the Admiral reminds her that the yacht is now under Admiralty orders:

(*28th Oct.*, 1914)

I am glad Arthur Balfour came and looked at the *Sheelah* and recognised the good work you are doing, but I think he is wrong when he says the German Navy won't come out, and I am sure they will sooner or later when they have weakened us something with their mines and submarines. . . .

No, my dear, you cannot move the yacht, because she is really not under your command, is an Admiralty vessel, and cannot move without instructions from the Senior Naval Officer present. As to yourself I would, of course, love to have you come wherever I am, but it would not do. I have set my face against other officers having their wives come, and I cannot go against my own decisions in this matter. It would not be right and it would not be fair. This I am sure you will see. When we go to Rosyth, which we are quite likely to do when they have it properly defended, it is another matter, because you are living there.

During the first week of November signs of activity in the German Fleet drew the Grand Fleet back to Scapa. The Battle Cruiser Squadron was immediately sent on a cruise in the southern North Sea to show the enemy that the British Navy intended to hold its grip on these waters.

On 6th November Beatty received a valuable reinforcement when the new battle cruiser *Tiger* joined his flag, but by the middle of the month this welcome increase was more than wiped out by Admiralty orders detaching the *Invincible*, *Inflexible*, and *Princess Royal* from his squadron. These ships were required for operations against Admiral von Spee who, with superior force, had destroyed Rear-Admiral Cradock's squadron at the Battle of Coronel in the South Pacific on 1st November. As the world knows, the move resulted in the victory of the Falkland Islands, when Vice-Admiral Sturdee, whose squadron included the *Invincible* and *Inflexible*, avenged Cradock's defeat. The Admiralty decision to send these power-ful ships so far afield was taken in face of grave risk, since their absence left Beatty with only four battle cruisers against Hipper's five. Indeed, the difference in strength between the British and German Fleets during the last months of 1914 was very small. Several new ships were nearing completion, but had not yet joined the Grand Fleet, the battleship *Audacious* had been lost, and four battleships were refitting as a result of the strain imposed by constant sea-keeping. Nevertheless, the policy of sweeping the North Sea, combined with 'pin-prick' operations by light craft and aircraft in the Heligoland Bight, was continued.

About the middle of November Beatty frankly confessed to Ethel that he was beginning to feel the strain.

Lion   (*17th Nov.*, 1914)

The anxiety of this sea life with the valuable machines and the valuable thousands of lives depending on you is very very great and makes a very heavy burden and responsibility to carry. I can but do my best and make ready to meet every eventuality that experience has taught me and, having done all I can, the result must be in the lap of the gods. We get back to coal with a feeling of thank God I've got in again, and yet when we go out again, that same day or the next, we are filled with hope that perhaps this time the opportunity will come, and think of nothing else and it never comes. Surely this is the hardest and most cruelly trying kind of warfare. And one has to be cheerful and encouraging to the others and binge them up to live in hope every time that this is *the* time. . . . The enemy are playing their game well in trying to *wear* us down, to upset one's nerves and make us do foolish things, but they won't succeed, and whenever I begin to think in the strain I have written, I pull up and say that is what they want, so I shut down on it, and only write it to you, but it is not true.

Beatty also expressed his anxiety to the First Sea Lord (Fisher), who replied sympathetically but forcibly:

I much appreciate your letter. Don't be downhearted. The German Admiral is now singing, 'It's a long way to Tipperary'. Sir E. Grey told me last night the Germans propose landing a hundred thousand men in Tipperary. Some Society is encouraging the Germans. Sein Fein, or some name like that, and we have discovered a nest of Irish-American traitors at Berehaven, but none of it matters. The great art of perspective has been missed by the Germans in their conduct of war, and alas, it has been missed in the conduct of the British Navy. Never such utter rot as perpetrated by Sturdee [as Chief of the War Staff] in his world-wide dispersal of weak units. Strong nowhere, weak everywhere. One battle cruiser in each ocean, with its attendance of tramps at £3 10*s.* a ton, fitted with wireless, would have cleared the world of German pirates and saved the Cradock disaster. One Armadillo can lick up millions of ants, and the bigger the ant the more placid the digestive smile. The *Black Prince* is bustling home to join you, so also *Duke of Edinburgh*, *Warrior*, *Minotaur*, *Defence*, and a flock of light cruisers. It's not numbers that tell, but gunneries. The *Scharnhörst* salvos did the trick on Cradock. Gunnery, gunnery, gunnery, all else is twaddle. Hit the target. I am too busy for more now. I'll finish in another letter. This is only the preamble.

Beatty felt keenly the absence of the *Princess Royal*, as she was of the same class as the *Lion* and *Queen Mary*. He did not hesitate to tell Fisher that the older *New Zealand* would have been a better choice.

To this Fisher replied:

(Private) *(28th Nov.,* 1914)

I admit the force of all your arguments. It's probable that at this very moment the *Princess Royal* is bagging the *Karlsruhe*, as the *Karlsruhe* has just sent her decoy the *Crefeld* to entice the *Lusitania* to come to her 'sinking' assistance. We have nought else that can catch the *Karlsruhe*, and the eventuality, not yet improbable, has still to be faced of the *Scharnhörst* and Co. [von Spee's squadron] coming through Panama Canal to New York to release the mass of armed German liners ready there to emerge into the Atlantic. Why the *Vaterland* has not 'nipped out' already is beyond me. Remember, the last new German battle cruiser, the *Derfflinger* or some such name, is even later commissioned than the *Tiger*, and we know has had very little gunnery practice, so I don't think you are in a bad way if you concentrate yourself, as I know you are doing effectively, on getting the *Tiger* into fighting efficiency. We can send up any number of anything animate or inanimate to help you, if you send me personal telegram. As I told Jellicoe, had I known of the *New Zealand* having more coal endurance, I would have taken her. I am in the position of a chess-player coming into the game after some damned bad moves have been made in the opening of the game. It's very difficult to retrieve a game badly begun.

Beatty's anxieties were more than justified, for never again during the whole course of the war was the situation so favourable for the Germans to challenge the Grand Fleet in battle. But the restrictions placed upon the High Seas Fleet by the German High Command after the British victory off Heligoland still prevailed, and the enemy fortunately was as yet totally unaware of the identity of the ships detached to deal with von Spee. Enemy minelayers, however, had been most enterprising, and had laid a large minefield extending from the Farne Islands to the mouth of the Humber. Until the limits of this field had been determined, Grand Fleet ships were not allowed to approach within sixty miles of the East Coast.

The great news of Admiral Sturdee's splendid victory off the Falkland Islands reached the Admiralty on 9th December. Beatty wired his congratulations to the First Sea Lord (Fisher), who was not slow in pointing out, in his reply, the part he had played in bringing it about.

(11th Dec., 1914)

Your kind telegram much appreciated. Sturdee's mob asked to put off sailing from Devonport till Friday, 13th Nov. (Imagine being such d——d fools as to sail on a Friday and on a 13th!) The answer went 'sail Wednesday', and we added a postscript they might embark the Dockyard if they liked. And they left! They only reached von Spee to the very minute! Hustle is a good word! Things done in a hurry are always done the best. Nelson said the whole secret of success in war was being there one-quarter of an hour before the other chaps. That was as nearly as possible Sturdee on von Spee, but perhaps it was ten minutes. The *Princess Royal* left direct for Scapa Flow day before yesterday 'with all convenient despatch' from Jamaica.

Although the victory had established British command at sea in the Atlantic, the likelihood of the Germans taking advantage of their favourable margin of battle-cruiser strength in home waters was increased. The enemy now knew for certain that the *Inflexible* and *Invincible*, which had taken part in the battle, were absent from the North Sea.

The Admiralty was fully alive to the danger, for on 11th December they warned Jellicoe to be prepared for a German sortie, and three days later sent him the following signal:

From Admiralty,   14*th Dec.*
To C.-in-C., H.F.   *Sent* 2130
                                              Not to be sent by W/T
523. Good information just received shows that German First Cruiser Squadron with destroyers leave Jade River on Tuesday morning early, and return on Wednesday night. It is apparent from information that the battleships are very unlikely to come out. The enemy force will have time to reach our coast. Send at once leaving tonight the Battle Cruiser Squadron and Light Cruiser Squadron supported by a Battle Squadron, preferably the Second. At daylight on Wednesday morning they should be at some point where they can make sure of intercepting the enemy on his return. Tyrwhitt, with his light cruisers and destroyers, will try to get into touch with the enemy off the British coast and shadow him, keeping Admiral informed. From our information the German First Cruiser Squadron consists of four battle cruisers, and there will probably be three flotillas of destroyers. Acknowledge.

It will be noted that the Admiralty decided the strength of the force to carry out this operation, but left its disposition to the Commander-in-Chief. Although it was considered in Whitehall unlikely that the German battleships would come out,

[165]

Jellicoe was not wholly satisfied, and added another cruiser squadron. He also represented to the Admiralty that Tyrwhitt's destroyer flotillas from Harwich should be near the British heavy ships in case an engagement became imminent.

The Commander-in-Chief's final directions were: the Second Battle Squadron (Sir George Warrender) from Scapa, with the First Battle Cruiser Squadron (Sir David Beatty) from Cromarty, Third Cruiser Squadron (Rear-Admiral W. C. Pakenham) from Rosyth, First Light Cruiser Squadron (Commodore W. E. Goodenough) from Scapa, were to be in position 54° 10′ N., 3° 0′ E. on a line joining Heligoland and Flamborough Head (about 100 miles from the English coast) at 7.30 a.m. on 16th December, 1914. As it was impossible to foretell the exact spot where the enemy would strike the coast, this position was selected as being the most favourable for intercepting him on his return. The enemy minefields, off the English East Coast, having been freshly laid, had only recently been located within broad limits; it was necessary, therefore, to give them a wide berth. On the other hand, the Germans, knowing their exact position, would be able to venture between the mines and the coast without risk.

Beatty was at Cromarty when he received the Commander-in-Chief's orders to join Sir George Warrender's force off the entrance to the Moray Firth at 11 a.m. on 15th December, 1914.

It was a terrible morning, blowing a full gale, the seas running confused and high against the strong tide of the Pentland Firth. Warrender was obliged to leave his destroyers behind at Scapa, and to send back two light cruisers, the *Boadicea* and *Blanche*, which had suffered severe structural damage from the heavy seas.

Beatty, with his four battle cruisers, being in more sheltered waters, was able to take with him two divisions of the 4th Destroyer Flotilla (seven destroyers) from Cromarty, and effected his junction with Warrender according to plan. Pakenham's cruiser squadron of four ships joined at 3 p.m., and the whole force was concentrated before dark, steaming south for the rendezvous. Beatty's battle cruisers were in the van, five miles ahead of the Second Battle Squadron. The First Light Cruiser Squadron was on the starboard beam of the battleships. The Third Cruiser Squadron was on the port beam, and the seven destroyers were ten miles east of the battleships.

Beatty had received no details of enemy movements before leaving Cromarty, but Warrender gave him all available information by visual signal, stating that a raid by enemy battle cruisers on Harwich or the Humber was probable. Warrender also announced his intention to steer east after reaching the 7.30 a.m. position in order to be certain of cutting the raiding force off from its base. If nothing happened by 10.30 a.m. he intended to turn westward and steer towards the Yorkshire coast. The battle cruisers, cruisers, and light cruisers were to spread to the west as a lookout screen in the direction whence the enemy force might be expected. Beatty asked for more information about enemy mines off the East Coast. Warrender replied that the battle cruisers were not to go inside a line drawn 149° from position lat. 56° N., long. 0°. This implied that all waters within fifty to sixty miles from the English coast were regarded as dangerous.

The night was overcast and moonless, and the destroyers soon lost touch with the main body. At 5.20 a.m. on 16th December they engaged an enemy force of cruisers and destroyers. There was a brief confused battle at close range in the pitch dark, in which the *Lynx*, *Hardy*, and *Ambuscade* were damaged. As day dawned, Commander Loftus-Jones in the *Shark* sighted five destroyers to the east, and although he had only four with him, closed at full speed and opened fire. The German destroyers retired eastward, and at about 7.10 a.m. a four-funnelled armoured cruiser resembling the *Roon* appeared behind the enemy smoke. The Germans continued to retire, and the *Shark*'s division kept touch at a distance of about four miles. At 7.50 a.m. three more German cruisers appeared, which compelled the gallant *Shark* to fall back to the south-west towards Warrender.

All this was going on north-eastward of Warrender's force, and the trend of operations opened the distance between the destroyers and the main body to thirty miles. The reports from the destroyers were of a very sketchy nature, merely conveying to Warrender that enemy light cruisers and destroyers were somewhere to the east. He therefore continued steering towards the rendezvous. At 7.30 a.m. the *Shark*'s report of the *Roon*, which had been delayed in transmission, came in. On hearing of the presence of this heavy cruiser, Beatty, with the battle cruisers and First Light Cruiser Squadron, turned eastward in pursuit. This move had Warrender's approval. The Third Cruiser Squadron, being too slow to keep up with Beatty, remained with Warrender's battle squadron.

The cruisers which the *Shark* had encountered in the bleakness of the dawn were in fact outposts of the High Seas Fleet, but Loftus-Jones did not know it.

Beatty continued pursuit till 8.54 a.m., by which time he had intercepted three wireless signals:

(1) From *Shark* that she was being chased to the west by cruisers.

(2) From the light cruiser *Patrol* that she was heavily engaged with two battle cruisers. No position was given, but it was known that the *Patrol* belonged to the 9th Destroyer Flotilla patrolling inshore off the Yorkshire coast.

(3) From Scarborough to Admiralty, that the town was being shelled at 8.30 a.m.

Beatty concluded that enemy forces were evidently north-eastward and westward of him. That those to the east were nearer to him, and that the *Shark* was leading them towards him. What was to be done?

He decided to turn north in order to meet the *Shark*, and at the same time cut the line of retreat of the enemy reported off the English coast. The *Patrol*'s signal had also reached Warrender, but not the one from Scarborough. Thinking that the *Patrol* was off Spurn Head, he ordered Beatty to join him on a course for the Humber.

At 8.56 a.m. both Admirals received an authentic report from the Admiralty that Scarborough was being shelled. Beatty, without hesitation, ignored Warrender's instructions and steered straight for Scarborough, informing Warrender that he was doing so. The First Light Cruiser Squadron, which was spread to the north of Beatty, had picked up the British destroyers, and all followed Beatty's movement to the west at full speed.

By 9.20 a.m. two further signals had been received from the Admiralty by Warrender and Beatty:

(1) 'Three dreadnoughts reported firing on Scarborough and enemy light cruiser off Hartlepool 0850'; and

(2) 'Three dreadnought battleships reported off Scarborough at 0900.'

Warrender was now also steering for Scarborough, and by 9.35 a.m. the British forces were in two main groups; the Second Battle Squadron and Third Cruiser Squadron being about ten miles astern of the battle cruisers and First Light Cruiser Squadron, all steering west.

A big question now faced the two British commanders. Should they take their heavy ships into the mined waters? There was no information as to whether the enemy bombarding forces had left the coast or were still near Scarborough and Hartlepool. In his anxiety to make contact at all costs, Warrender directed Beatty to send Goodenough with the First Light Cruiser Squadron through the minefield to locate the enemy. At the same time, he asked the Admiralty if the heavy ships could do the same. Another obstruction lay in Beatty's path. This was the south-west patch of the Dogger Bank shoal, which, although covered to at least a depth of seven fathoms, was strewn with many wrecks, and had barely sufficient water to allow heavy ships to pass over it at high speed. Beatty altered course north-west to pass north of the shoal, informing Warrender that he thought the enemy were working up the coast northward. This opinion was based on the information that the enemy were off Hartlepool. He did not know that two separate forces had in fact bombarded Scarborough and Hartlepool.

Warrender agreed with Beatty, and expressed a hope that the battle cruisers would cut off the enemy north-west of the Dogger Bank. Meanwhile, a most important piece of information came in from the Commander-in-Chief, Grand Fleet, to the effect that a gap about twenty miles wide was believed to exist in the German minefields leading towards Scarborough and Whitby, and that the enemy raiding force would probably come out that way.

Both Beatty and Warrender now steered for the gap—

Beatty to the north with his light cruisers spread ahead to cover the gap in the order south to north: *Southampton, Birmingham, Nottingham, Falmouth.* It was blowing hard from the north-west, with rain squalls reducing the visibility to barely a mile, so the two British heavy squadrons soon lost sight of each other.

At about 11 a.m. Warrender received a reply from the Admiralty about the minefield: 'Enemy is probably returning towards Heligoland; you should keep outside minefield and steer so as to cut him off (1030).' Nevertheless, the westerly movement of the British forces continued, but the weather conditions became so bad near the English coast that Beatty was obliged to reduce speed to eighteen knots. At 11.25 a.m. the *Southampton* (Goodenough's Flagship), the southern ship of the screen, suddenly in the driving rain came upon some enemy light cruisers and destroyers. She was then about six miles on the *Lion*'s port bow, but not in sight of her. These enemy light cruisers belonged to the German raiding force, and had been ordered home by Hipper owing to stress of weather. They were quickly identified as hostile, and Goodenough at once turned to engage them, reporting their presence to Beatty and Warrender. The enemy broke away to the south, returning the *Southampton*'s fire, and a running fight began, the *Southampton* being supported by the *Birmingham*, which had moved across at the sound of gunfire. On account of the bad visibility and the high sea, however, the firing was ineffective on both sides. Meanwhile, the *Nottingham* had lost sight of the *Birmingham*, her neighbour on the screen, and began to move across to regain touch. She was slightly on the *Lion*'s starboard bow, so the movement was seen by Beatty who, wishing to retain a screen ahead of him, gave orders for her to resume her station for look-out duties. On account of the thick weather, however, there was some doubt about the *Nottingham*'s identity, and in order to make sure that the signal should not be made to the wrong ship, it was addressed to her as 'Light Cruiser'. Unfortunately, the signal was interpreted as addressing 'All Light Cruisers', with the result that it was passed by the *Nottingham* to the whole screen, including, of course, the *Southampton* and *Birmingham*, both at that moment in action with enemy cruisers. On its receipt Goodenough turned the *Southampton* and *Birmingham* once more to the west, and in consequence the action was broken off and touch lost.

Beatty's object was to destroy the enemy battle cruisers, but up to that moment he had received no report of their whereabouts, except the *Patrol*'s signal stating that she was in action with two of them, but making no mention of any position. The reports received from Admiralty and Scarborough had stated that 'dreadnoughts' were bombarding Scarborough. Beatty, therefore, acted correctly in directing the *Nottingham* to keep her place on the look-out screen, so that he might have warning of the approach of heavy ships from the direction of Scarborough. The idea of calling off the *Southampton* and *Birmingham* never entered his head. In fact, such a thought would have been hateful to him. He was, therefore, astonished when he learnt that Goodenough had lost touch with the enemy. The following signals passed between them:

From Beatty to Goodenough:
  'What have you done with enemy light cruisers? (12.00).'
  Reply: 'They disappeared steering south when I received your signal to resume station.'

From Beatty to Goodenough:
  'When and where was enemy last seen? When you sight enemy engage him. Signal to resume station was made to *Nottingham* (12.20).'

This regrettable misunderstanding, as we have seen, was caused by a technical error in signalling and lack of means of identifying ships in thick weather. Goodenough, who throughout the war proved to be one of the greatest cruiser commanders, felt he was being reprimanded unjustly for obeying the direct order of his chief. Beatty, on the other hand, knew, in his own mind, that he had never given such an order. However, both Beatty and Goodenough had plenty to think about, and the incident was dismissed from their minds, to be cleared up in subsequent investigation.

At 11.45 a.m. Beatty learnt, from an intercepted signal, that enemy battle cruisers had been off Scarborough at 8.30

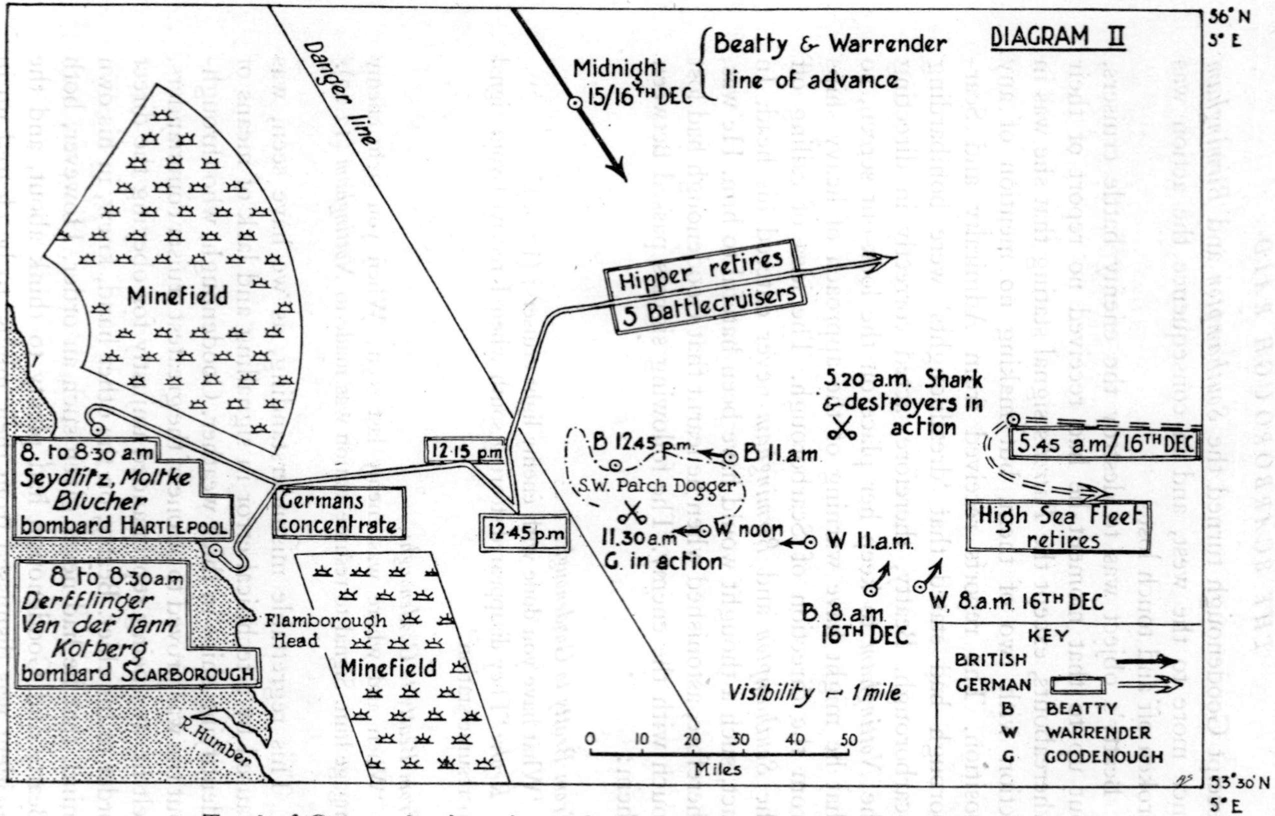

56° N
5° E

DIAGRAM II

5.45 a.m./16TH DEC

High Sea Fleet retires

W. 8.a.m. 16TH DEC

KEY

BRITISH B BEATTY
         W WARRENDER
         G GOODENOUGH

GERMAN

B. 8.a.m 16TH DEC

Beatty & Warrender line of advance

5.20 a.m. Shark & destroyers in action

B 11a.m.

W 11a.m.

Hipper retires 5 Battlecruisers

Midnight 15/16TH DEC

B 12.45 p.m.
S.W. Patch Dogger
W noon
11.30 a.m.
G. in action

Visibility ~ 1 mile

0   10   20   30   40   50
Miles

Danger line

12.15 p.m.

12.45 p.m.

Germans concentrate

Minefield

Minefield

Flamborough Head

Minefield

R. Humber

8. to 8.30 a.m. Seydlitz, Moltke Blucher bombard HARTLEPOOL

8. to 8.30 a.m. Derfflinger Van der Tann Kolberg bombard SCARBOROUGH

53° 50′ E
5° E

Track of German battle cruisers after bombarding Scarborough and Hartlepool.

a.m., and in the vicinity of Hartlepool at 8.50 a.m. There had clearly been two groups; whether these had now joined forces or not was not known, but it was evident that they must still be well to the west of the British ships. Beatty therefore continued to steer for the gap, with the light cruisers spread ahead.

At 12.10 p.m. Warrender, who was about fifteen miles south-south-east of Beatty, steering for the southern edge of the gap, suddenly encountered some enemy cruisers and destroyers. He immediately turned north-eastward to engage, but they escaped in the mist. He informed Beatty, who correctly inferred that they were the same force which Good-enough had engaged forty-five minutes earlier. Beatty also felt reasonably sure they were part of a look-out screen ahead of the German heavy ships. In order to cut them off it was impera-tive to keep east of the enemy now retiring homewards through the gap. Beatty, therefore, reversed his course to the east. This course would ultimately have brought about a contact with Hipper's battle cruisers had they continued to steer for their base. The German scouting forces, however, had already provided Hipper with comprehensive reports of the British battleships which they had sighted. From this information he concluded that two British battle squadrons lay between him and his base, so at 12.45 p.m. he made a drastic turn to the north and escaped.

This abortive action was a bitter disappointment to the British commanders groping for their prey in heavy seas and blinding rain, yet Providence was on their side.

The general situation on the early morning of the 16th December was very much in favour of the Germans. At mid-night Hipper, steering for Whitby with his five battle cruisers, passed fifteen miles ahead of Warrender. Here the German force divided, Hipper taking the *Seydlitz, Moltke,* and *Blücher* to Hartlepool and sending the *von der Tann* and *Derfflinger* to Scarborough. Meanwhile, Admiral von Ingenohl, with the whole of the German High Seas Fleet of some twenty battle-ships and attendant cruisers and destroyers, was steering west from a position about twenty miles north of Heligoland. This course would have taken him to a position about thirty miles north-west of Warrender at 7.30 a.m., where he could have cut off the British forces from their base. A bird's-eye view of the situation at 5 a.m. on 16th December would have revealed vast German forces and a comparatively small British force converging on the same area. But such a view was denied to the commanders taking part: so when von Ingenohl's scouting forces blundered into the British destroyers in pitch darkness at 5.30 a.m., he concluded that they were part of a screen covering the whole British Grand Fleet. Having regard to the Kaiser's instructions that the High Seas Fleet was not to risk an action with the British Fleet outside the Heligoland Bight, he reversed the course of his mighty fleet and steered for home, leaving his advanced force under Hipper without support. Nobody on the British side, not even the Admiralty, had any idea that the High Seas Fleet was at sea. In fact, the British commanders had been told by the Admiralty that the German battleships 'are very unlikely to come out'. Loftus-Jones in the *Shark* little knew that his gallant offensive action against the enemy cruisers and destroyers in the early hours of the morning would have the effect of causing the German armada to retire.

The British battle cruisers had had a lucky escape in more ways than one. During the critical period after the bombardment when Hipper was steering in Beatty's direction, Beatty's battle cruisers and Warrender's battleships were fifteen miles apart, separated by the south-west patch of the Dogger Bank. Visibility was less than a mile. Hipper, being unaware that the two British squadrons were so far apart, decided to turn northward to avoid them. If he had continued his easterly course, he would in all probability have run into Beatty. Hipper had with him the five battle cruisers, *Seydlitz, Derfflinger, Moltke, von der Tann,* and *Blücher,* while Beatty had only four. The action would have been fought at short range, and Beatty would have been caught at a disadvantage, as Warrender was too far away to support him.

It was not until 2.25 p.m. that the British commanders learnt, from the Admiralty, that the High Seas Fleet was at sea. By this time Hipper had got clear away to the north, and the German Battle Fleet was well on its way home, too far east to be of any consequence.

The British forces reluctantly turned homeward, unaware of how narrowly they had escaped disaster.

The operation is a good illustration of the realities of naval war, and it would be difficult to criticise any of the decisions made by Warrender or Beatty. Both Admirals did their utmost to come to grips with an enemy who was anxious to avoid them, and was moving at high speed in an area containing shoal waters and minefields in visibility which was often less than one mile. The British signal communications were not always helpful, the reports of the enemy from the Admiralty arrived too late, and those from the scouting forces were often in error. No scientific means had been devised at that time to synchronise the relative positions of ships out of sight of one another, and there was no radar. Consequently, the situation was obscure during its most critical phase. Hipper being near the coast was more certain of his position, and having been kept well informed of the movements of the British heavy ships, he was able to make full use of the low visibility to avoid them. The German High Command had the Kaiser to blame for the lack of offensive spirit shown by the Commander-in-Chief of the High Seas Fleet which, as we have seen, turned and fled ignominiously home after a brief contact with a few British destroyers.

Shortly afterwards Beatty expressed to Ethel his heartfelt disappointment at the result of the Scarborough operations. He did not at this time know all the facts.

Lion   (*20th Dec.*, 1914)

I am feeling better now, but the happenings of the past week have left a mark which nothing can eradicate except the total destruction of the enemy's battle and other cruisers. We were within an ace of accomplishing it the other day. We had overcome all sorts of minor difficulties, and we had made an excellent spot and arrived at the exact strategical situation. Our advanced ships had sighted them and then!!! I can't bear to write about it. And I can think of nothing else. . . . Your letters are a great help, and although you say you have no news, it is always news to me to know that you are all well and the little things you do each day. As to telling you things, I tell you all I can, and all I know that is proper for me to communicate. . . . If we had got them Wednesday, as we ought to have done, we should have finished the war from a naval point of view. . . .

LETTERS TO LADY BEATTY

21st September to 12th November, 1914

The following extracts are from some letters written by David Beatty to his wife during the period under review in the preceding chapter.

(21st Sept., 1914)

This roaming about the North Sea day after day with no prospect of meeting an enemy vessel I think is the heaviest trial that could be laid on any man, added to which the anxiety of the mine or submarine always present provides a situation which requires the highest forms of philosophy to compete with, to prevent it from clouding one's judgment. Here have I the finest striking force in the world, 6 Battle Cruisers and 6 Light Cruisers, and for all we can do, they might be Thames barges under any circumstances. We can never do anything because we are never in the right place. Who at the Admiralty is responsible for one's movements I do not know, but it is not the C.-in-C. He concurs with me. Not a word of this to a soul. I must not criticise. It is most improper, but my digestion, under continual disappointments, is giving way and my temper is becoming damnable.

I see in the *Poldhu* [radio news report] that the *Carmania*, the ship we went to U.S.A. in, had a 2-hour set to with a German armed merchant vessel and sank her. That was splendid, a regular old-fashioned mill, but one of our small cruisers was caught apparently at anchor at Zanzibar undergoing repair and disabled by a German, which was bad work on our side. Also Troubridge[1] is being brought home to have the question of the escape of the *Goeben* and *Breslau* enquired into. I suppose it will be hard swearing between him and old Arky Barky.[2] I am indeed sorry, but failures must be explained, and it is correct and sound on the part of the Admiralty to insist on adequate explanation.

Lion   *(29th Sept.,* 1914)

Blowing very hard with a bad sea. Sunday night and Monday morning it was a full gale and it was not pleasant. I haven't a dry spot in my cabin. The decks leak like a sieve, and it's like living under a perpetual shower-bath. It reminded me of the *Typhoon* by Conrad. We lost a top-gallant

---

[1] Rear-Admiral E. C. T. Troubridge, C.B., C.M.G., Commanding 1st Cruiser Squadron, Mediterranean.
[2] Admiral Sir Archibald Berkeley Milne, Commander-in-Chief Mediterranean.

mast with the wireless, and a gun went overboard, so it has been no joy, and this is the fourth day, one of which we practically spent hove to. It has been bad for some of the destroyers and two of our submarines. I don't know what has happened to them, but hope they will turn up all right. However, we continue our roaming about the sea. . . . Last time we had news it was so terrible, long lists every day of casualties in France, that one didn't want to go into harbour. So many we know have been taken, and the proportion of officers to men seems too high, as if they were foolish and exposed themselves too much, which is a foolish way of losing your life. Poor little David Bingham and Percy Wyndham, the two poor wives will break their hearts.

. . . Cramb is no doubt very correct as to the attitude adopted towards us by Germans. It will be a rude awakening to find that we are not the decadent race they expected to find simply because we haven't talked war and have talked about peace. They are evidently one of the lost tribes, and are going to remain lost for all time. Ever since the Roman Empire they have striven in the same way to achieve Empire, and it has always ended in the same way. Frederick the Great, the greatest warrior Germany ever produced, declined the job when the aspiring ones invited him to consider the time opportune to create a German Empire, by saying it would not be worth the trouble.

Lion　　　　　　　　　　　　　　　　　*(Sunday, 4th Oct., 1914)*

I had a great compliment paid me. A man who had served with me in the *Barfleur* and left the Navy twelve years ago went to British Columbia and has done well farming. On the outbreak of war left his farm and sailed for England to come and serve with *me*. He turned up on Friday smiling all over, ready to do anything he said! I loved the little book you sent me, wonderful language and so simple. I can well understand the German point of view and their hatred of us. Old Treitschke was, with his religion of valour, a splendid apostle.

I loved the bit about poor Scott and the Death of Heroes, didn't you? and the pursuit after the illusion of the Glory of Battle. Please God it will never be realised that it is an illusion. That is what the commercial critics of luxurious lives in England have been trying to prove for ages, but they haven't succeeded yet. Witness the heroic deeds of the Army in France, and our Navy, when its turn comes, will prove the same. The Pacifist has once again been proved in the wrong, or that the time is not yet when 'Man in his war against the vast sorrow of existence and pain declares there shall be no more war'. Without war nations cannot exist and with war they die and crumble to nothing. It's a paradox, but true.

Lion (*12th Oct.*, 1914)

Hall[1] has been appointed Director of Naval Intelligence at the War Staff. I am very sorry to lose him, but it will save his life. He could not last if he continued as he is. I think he has reached the limit of human endurance. I hear one of Winston's Naval Brigades has already been demolished and lost itself in Holland. I call it iniquitous calling it a Naval Brigade which in no respect it is.

. . . Surely the *Bon Dieu* will not permit this wholesale slaughter to continue indefinitely. I see French in his letter to Milly gives it a year. I fear it will take a long year and this winter there will be terrible suffering.

Lion (*19th Oct.*, 1914)

The Admiralty have a very difficult problem in front of them which will take them all their time to solve at this juncture, so much having been left undone in the past years and no steps having been taken to correct in the $2\frac{1}{2}$ months we have been at war. If we only had a Kitchener at the Admiralty!! How easy everything would be.

I hear that some of our destroyers have flattened out 4 German destroyers. This will counteract the raid of the enemy submarines on our Northern Patrols, not that they have been successful beyond sinking the poor old *Hawke*. The loss of life there was very great. The sad thing is that they go without striking a blow, without seeing the enemy, and without getting warmed up with excitement. Surely it is the most cold-blooded way of taking your departure from this world, and calls for a high quality of discipline to sustain the ships' companies through the uncertainties of the dangers of the sea. However, we can get used to anything in this world, I suppose, given time and experience. . . . I would like to command a cavalry regiment for ten minutes in a rough and tumble.

Lion (*23rd Oct.*, 1914)

Another gale, from the eastward this time. It did not blow nearly so hard, but we got very wet and shipped tons of water, principally because we had to steam through it. My cabins were again flooded out. It drips everywhere. It's just like living in a large wet case with water dripping from the roof. I've written to Lady Henry Grosvenor. I am sorry for her, parting with both her sons to go to the front, but as she says, she is proud to let them go. . . .

(*26th Oct.*, 1914)

I am glad to know that *at last* they are taking steps to deal with the Alien question, which is indeed a very serious one. I am sorry for poor

[1] Captain W. R. Hall, R.N., then commanding the *Queen Mary*.

Minna [a German maid], but it can't be helped, and I am sorry for you to be without her, but it shows thoroughness in some region which, unfortunately, does not extend everywhere, but will before long, or I am much mistaken. I sent Plunkett to London with some secret books and a confidential letter[1] to the First Lord which I felt bound to send him, and to make representations on certain matters which are of the most profound importance, and I am glad to say that he took them all and has acted upon them and consequently things are beginning to move and I feel better. It is satisfactory to know that he will listen to somebody, if it is only me. From Plunkett's account of things it appears at the Admiralty they are in that sublime state of mind that they think everything is going well, and is for the best in the best possible way. If they only knew what the Navy afloat thought!

Lion   *(27th Oct.,* 1914)

I am glad you like my Despatch [Heligoland]. I made it as straightforward and simple as possible, and there was certainly nothing meriting butter.

Lion   *(30th Oct.,* 1914)

They have had a tremendous lot of casualties in the Cavalry of late; oh dear, oh dear, I'd give anything to be there, and would give up my battle cruisers if I could command one regiment of Cavalry. Our lot is terribly irksome here. I have 5,500 men and four magnificent machines pining for something to do and we can do nothing. All our time is taken up avoiding submarines.... We hear in the Poldhu[2] that Prince Louis has resigned. . . . Now they have resurrected old Fisher. It does not matter who goes there as long as it is somebody that can get something done and I feel he'll be all right. . . . But where are the young men? We want young virile active men and we don't seem to possess one. It is lamentable. I cannot see Winston and Jacky Fisher working very long together in harmony. They will quarrel before long. The poor Navy, it's terribly sad, but nothing matters if we can get some proper policy initiated. . . . I heard from Page that all the horses were well, but if the country wants them they must go. This is not the time for half-measures, and we must not keep them back. Except little Merve, I would rather shoot him, as he is no longer very young.

Lion   *(3rd Nov.,* 1914)

I am sorry Filson Young thinks I am so inarticulate. I hope the Admiralty don't think so, or perhaps that is why I cannot always get done

---

[1] See page 158 (Letter to First Lord).
[2] News broadcast from Poldhu W/T station.

the things I am always asking for. He has been bothering me again. I told him I had no room, and he had better get at his friend Fisher. Dear heart, I did not tell you I was going to Cromarty because I did not know until just before we went there, and if I had known I should *not* have told you for reasons which I have already given and which you understood. Your idea of the Christmas Box is a beautiful one, *but* I think savours too much of self-advertisement, which I dislike intensely, whacking out photographs of myself *all* round, so we won't do that. I was thinking what I could do. I gave the *Lion* a Turkey for each Mess last year. But if I gave each Mess in each ship a Turkey, I don't think we could find enough. It would mean about 200 odd and cost about £100, which is a lot. I might give them all a goose, which would be cheaper, but I don't like thinking of the money side in times such as these.

Lion   (5th Nov., 1914)

. . . News just received of an action in the Pacific.[1] Poor old Kit Cradock has been badly knocked and lost the *Monmouth* and the *Good Hope*, but I expect he has damaged severely some of the enemy ships. I don't understand it. The Germans had a concentrated force of two big cruisers and three small ones against his force, so I fear he saw red and did not wait for his proper reinforcement the *Canopus*. He is a gallant fellow, and I am sure put up a gallant fight, but nowadays no amount of dash and gallantry will counterbalance great superiority unless they are commanded by fools. He has paid the penalty, but doubtless it was better to have fought and lost than not to have fought at all. Darling, my 1st Lieut. in *Queen* was in the *Good Hope*, and poor Peter Willoughby and the Musgraves' boy were in the *Monmouth*, which I hear went down with all hands.

[1] The Battle of Coronel.

CHAPTER NINE

1915

THE BATTLE OF THE DOGGER BANK

FROM the German point of view the bombardment of Scarborough, Whitby, and Hartlepool was a highly successful operation. Owing to low visibility on the coast, the presence of the enemy ships was entirely unsuspected until they opened fire, and during the bombardment the light cruiser *Kolberg* was able to lay a hundred mines off Filey without being detected. Although the bombardment lasted only twenty minutes, casualties suffered by the civil population were heavy: at Scarborough 17 killed and 99 wounded; at Hartlepool 103 killed and 344 wounded; at Whitby 2 killed. There was a great public outcry, and many questions were asked why the British Navy had failed to prevent the raid. This was exactly what the Germans wanted, for they hoped the Admiralty would succumb to public pressure and split up the Grand Fleet to take up defensive positions along the English coast. The Admiralty, however, were not to be drawn, especially as recent events had shown that a detachment of the Grand Fleet could be surprised in southern waters by the whole German Fleet.

Beatty had often advocated that the battle cruisers, being essentially a scouting force, should be based nearer the enemy, either in the Forth or in the Humber. Their high speed would enable them to avoid action with a superior force of German battleships, while at the same time they would be in a better strategic position to bring to action and destroy the raiding enemy battle cruisers.

The Admiralty and the Commander-in-Chief agreed with this view, and on 21st December, 1914, Beatty was directed to establish a permanent base for the battle cruisers and First

Light Cruiser Squadron at Rosyth. The Battle Cruiser Force, however, was to remain an integral part of the Grand Fleet. If the German Battle Fleet put to sea, it was Beatty's duty to do his utmost to bring it to action with the Grand Fleet, and then take up a position in the van, in accordance with the Commander-in-Chief's battle plan.

Almost immediately after Beatty's arrival at Rosyth, he was ordered to join the Grand Fleet in an extensive sweep of the North Sea, arranged to coincide with a raid on Cuxhaven by aircraft from the small seaplane carriers *Engadine, Riviera,* and *Empress.* Christmas was spent at sea, but ships' companies were able to enjoy their Christmas dinner, as the raid proved to be abortive, and the ships returned to harbour without incident. A gale sprang up that evening, which will long be remembered by those who took part in the operation as one of the worst of the war.

On the 15th January, 1915, an importantre organisation came into force. Beatty's battle cruisers were formed into two squadrons, the First Battle Cruiser Squadron, comprising *Lion, Queen Mary, Tiger,* and *Princess Royal,* and the Second Battle Cruiser Squadron, consisting of *New Zealand* and *Indomitable.* Rear-Admiral Sir Archibald Moore was appointed as second in command with his flag in the *New Zealand.* Three days later Beatty was off again to support Tyrwhitt's light forces in an uneventful sweep through the Heligoland Bight. These oft-recurring sweeps of the southern North Sea were necessary at this time to guard against raids on the English coast, and to prevent any attempt on the part of the enemy to block east coast ports, such as Harwich, where the entrances were narrow.

The Germans were equally nervous lest the same thing might be done to them, and two days after the British forces had left the Bight, the Admiralty learnt that the German Commander-in-Chief, Admiral von Ingenohl, intended to send Hipper's scouting forces on a reconnaissance sweep towards the Dogger Bank. Shortly after noon on 23rd January, the following signal reached Beatty from the Admiralty: 'Get ready to sail at once with all battle cruisers and light cruisers and sea-going destroyers. Further orders follow.' The scene at the Admiralty is authoritatively described by Mr. Winston Churchill:[1]

'Wilson[2] and Oliver[3] had already drawn on the Chart, with what afterwards proved to be almost exact accuracy, the probable line of the enemy's course. Our intention was that the British forces should meet and be united at daybreak at some point about ten miles behind the enemy after he had passed westward, and consequently be between him and his home. We discussed whether we would run the risk of a more adventurous scoop, such as a rendezvous for our ships still farther to the eastward. This would give more certainty of being between the enemy and his home, but also more chance of missing him if the weather became thick. Remembering what had happened on 16th December [Scarborough], this last possibility seemed a very serious one. Thus the rendezvous was fixed for seven o'clock the next morning (the 24th January), in 55° 13′ N., 3° 12′ E.'

Beatty's force was to be the spearhead of the whole operation. Other dispositions were: Tyrwhitt, with three light cruisers and two and a half destroyer flotillas from Harwich, was to join Beatty at the rendezvous at 7 a.m. on the 24th. Vice-Admiral Bradford, with the old Third Battle Squadron, popularly known as the 'Wobbly Eight', and the Third Cruiser Squadron from Rosyth, was to be some forty miles north-west of Beatty in a position to intercept Hipper if he should come north. Bradford, who was senior to Beatty, was instructed not to interfere with ships under Beatty's command. The Commander-in-Chief was to take the Grand Fleet to sea from Scapa and steer towards the Third Battle Squadron. Owing, however, to the great distance of Scapa Flow from the scene of operation, a junction between these forces was not possible till later in the day. The British submarines were to take up their usual intercepting position between Terschelling and Borkum Riff. The plan was well conceived; all responsible commanders knew what to do and what their colleagues were doing.

On the evening of the 23rd January, 1915, Beatty sailed

[1] *World Crisis*, 1915, Winston Churchill.
[2] Admiral of the Fleet Sir Arthur Wilson.
[3] Later Admiral of the Fleet Sir Henry Oliver.

with the First and Second Battle Cruiser Squadrons and First Light Cruiser Squadron (Goodenough). Intelligence gleaned through the interception and deciphering of enemy signals in the famous Admiralty Room 40 proved extremely accurate. So in the darkness of the night Beatty from the north-west with five battle cruisers[1] and four light cruisers, and Tyrwhitt from the south with three light cruisers and thirty-five destroyers, were converging on Hipper, who had with him four battle cruisers, four light cruisers, and twenty-two destroyers. The German Admiral was unsupported by the High Seas Fleet, but believed that all British heavy ships were in harbour.

Beatty was in the highest spirits at the prospect of action, and gave no sign of feeling the heavy responsibility that rested on his shoulders. According to his usual custom, he dined with his staff in his normal quarters, and was a gay and entertaining host. Like a true leader he trusted his officers, and being content to leave the navigation to his well-tried Flag Captain, Ernle Chatfield, retired to rest early, and enjoyed a good night's sleep.

The *Lion* reached the rendezvous punctually at 7 a.m. while it was still dark, and Beatty turned south to meet Tyrwhitt. Almost immediately gun flashes were sighted to the south-south-east, followed by a signal from the *Aurora*, one of Tyrwhitt's light cruisers, that she was in action. She had in fact engaged the *Kolberg*, the port wing ship of Hipper's cruiser screen, in a short indecisive duel.

The situation remained obscure, for it was not yet daylight. Beatty, knowing the rough direction of the enemy, ordered all ships to give chase, with the result that Goodenough, in the *Southampton* about five miles to the east of the *Lion*, sighted the German battle cruisers right ahead.

Hipper at once turned south-eastward in the direction of home, and Goodenough led his squadron to a position on the port quarter of the enemy ships, whence he could report their movements. Beatty ordered his five battle cruisers to work up to full speed, and the chase was on. Here was a situation after Beatty's own heart. Dawn was just breaking. At 8 a.m. the quarry was in sight, fine on the *Lion*'s port bow, only fourteen

---

[1] The *Queen Mary* was in dock.

miles distant, with at least 150 miles to go before reaching the protection of the German shore defences. Visibility was good, and the sea calm. A fresh breeze from the north-east gave Beatty the lee gauge, which ensured that the smoke from his own guns and funnels would not obscure his line of fire.

Hipper, under the impression that the British force was the same squadron of battleships he had located off Scarborough about a month previously, thought he had the heels of them, so did not immediately increase to full speed. On account of the smoke from his own squadron, he was not able to identify the British ships as fast battle cruisers till 8.40 a.m., when the range had closed to 25,000 yards, and it was too late for him to avoid battle.

Beatty, meanwhile, had ordered every ounce of steam, and, as a 'touch of the spur', had signalled a speed of twenty-nine knots which, as he well knew, was one knot more than the designed speed of his fastest ship! The three leading ships, the *Lion*, *Tiger*, and *Princess Royal*, had worked up to about twenty-seven knots, but the two older battle cruisers, the *New Zealand* and *Indomitable*, could do little more than twenty-five, and slowly dropped astern.

The German squadron, now retiring in the order *Seydlitz*, *Moltke*, *Derfflinger*, *Blücher*, was equally handicapped by the speed of the *Blücher*, which was only twenty-three knots. Some of Tyrwhitt's destroyers and light cruisers were striving to get ahead of the enemy to deliver a torpedo attack, but the pace was too hot, and their smoke was obscuring the range. Beatty, having decided that he could destroy the enemy by gunfire, ordered these light craft to get out of the way, and at the same time formed his battle cruisers on a line of bearing to port (echelon) in order to give each ship a clear line of fire.

At 8.52 a.m. the *Lion* fired a ranging shot at the *Blücher*, the rear ship of the enemy line, which fell short. By 9 a.m. she was within range, so Beatty gave the general order to open fire, and all ships concentrated on her at an opening range of 20,000 yards.

Conditions, however, were none too easy for either side on account of the German funnel smoke, but by 9.20 a.m. all heavy ships, except the *Indomitable*, were in action. The

Germans concentrated their firing on the *Lion*, and the British continued to concentrate on the *Blücher*.

As the range closed, the *Lion* correctly shifted her fire to the *Derfflinger*, next ahead of the *Blücher*, and shortly afterwards, when all the German ships were within effective range, Beatty ordered a ship for ship distribution of fire. His intention was that the *Lion* should engage the leading enemy ship (the *Seydlitz*); the *Tiger* the *Moltke*; the *Princess Royal* the *Derfflinger*, and the *New Zealand* the *Blücher*. The *Indomitable*, lagging in the rear, was still out of range, and this led to an unfortunate misunderstanding: for the *Tiger* included the *Indomitable* in her calculation, and followed the procedure for five ships *v.* four, which laid down that the two leading British ships should concentrate on the German flagship. The *Princess Royal* and *New Zealand*, on the other hand, had correctly interpreted Beatty's signal, and were engaging the *Derfflinger* and *Blücher* respectively. Thus the *Moltke*, the second enemy ship, was not engaged. To make matters worse, the *Tiger's* shells were falling a long way over her target, and she mistook the splashes of the *Lion's* shells for her own. The enemy gun flashes were also mistaken by some observers for shell bursts. This was understandable, as the enemy's smoke made spotting very difficult, and it was the first time in history that heavy ships had been in action at such a long range. On the other hand, Goodenough had a clear view from the disengaged side and sent valuable reports to Beatty of the fall of shot.

By 9.30 a.m. the range was down to 17,500 yards, and shortly afterwards the British scored their first success. A shell from the *Lion* penetrated the after-turret of the *Seydlitz*, exploding all cordite in the handing-room and working-chamber. The door leading to the adjacent turret was opened by men endeavouring to escape, with the result that the flames spread to that turret, producing further havoc. Thus one shell killed the crews of both turrets, and had it not been for the prompt action of the executive officer in flooding both magazines, the ship would probably have been lost. As it was, she took in many tons of water aft and settled by the stern.

The immediate result of this hit was a call for help by Hipper to the High Seas Fleet, which was still in harbour.

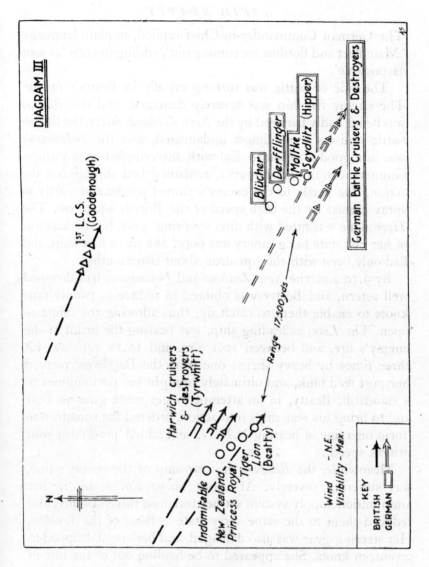

Battle of the Dogger Bank.
Situation at 9.25 a.m., 24th January, 1915.

The German Commander-in-Chief replied, in plain language, 'Main fleet and flotillas are coming out', adding in code 'as soon as possible'.

The tide of battle was turning rapidly in Beatty's favour. The enemy flagship was severely damaged, and the *Blücher* was being badly battered by the *New Zealand*. So far, the British battle cruisers were almost undamaged, and the *Indomitable* was in a good position to deal with any crippled enemy ships. Gunnery conditions, however, remained bad throughout the action, due partly to the enemy's funnel smoke and partly to spray caused by the high speed of the British squadron. The *Tiger* alone was fitted with director-firing[1] gear, but on account of her raw state her gunnery was poor. She was a new ship, and had only been with the squadron about two months.

By 9.50 a.m. the *New Zealand* and *Indomitable* had dropped well astern, and Beatty was obliged to reduce to twenty-four knots to enable them to catch up, thus allowing the range to open. The *Lion*, as leading ship, was bearing the brunt of the enemy's fire, and between 10.1 a.m. and 10.18 a.m. was hit three times by heavy shells; one from the *Derfflinger* pierced her port feed tank, and ultimately brought her port engines to a standstill. Beatty, in an attempt to get more guns to bear and to bring his rear ships into action, ordered the squadron to 'form on a line of bearing N.N.W.' and added 'proceed at your utmost speed'.

Meanwhile, the *Blücher*, the rear ship of the enemy's line, was suffering severely. At about 10.30 a.m. a hit in her ammunition supply system set her foremost turrets on fire, and reduced them to the same sorry state as those of the *Seydlitz*. Her steering-gear was also damaged, and her speed dropped to seventeen knots. She appeared to be hauling out of the line in an attempt to escape, so Beatty ordered the *Indomitable* to intercept her.

The *Lion* was also feeling the effects of the blows she had received and was gradually dropping astern. As the other battle cruisers began to overtake her, Beatty realised that it was a question of now or never. At 10.35 he ordered a turn of one point towards the enemy, and at 10.45 another, followed

---

[1] A device for firing the guns from a central controlling position aloft.

by the signal, 'Close the enemy as rapidly as possible consistent with all guns bearing'. At 10.50 the *Lion* received a hit which put her last remaining dynamo out of action, and robbed her of all electric power, light, and radio. At this moment the *Tiger*, *Princess Royal*, and *New Zealand* swept past her, and there occurred an event which had most disastrous consequences.

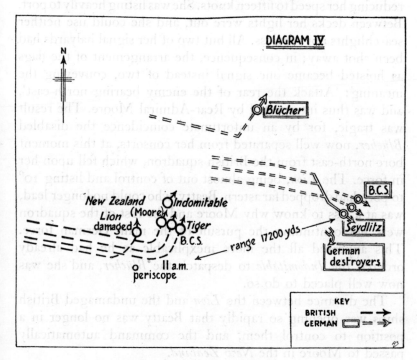

Battle of the Dogger Bank.
Situation at 11.4 a.m., 24th January, 1915.

A submarine was reported on the *Lion*'s starboard bow. Beatty himself said he saw a periscope,[1] and believing he was running into a submarine trap, ordered the squadron at 11 a.m. to turn together 90° to port. This manœuvre inevitably opened the range and, anxious not to lose touch with the retreating enemy, he decided a few minutes later to turn north-east and then when clear of the wake of some enemy destroyers suspected of mine-

[1] Subsequent investigation by N.I.D. suggests that this was probably a torpedo surfacing at the end of its run fired by the German Destroyer *V5*.

laying, he would resume the chase. Accordingly he ordered his flag lieutenant, Ralph Seymour, to hoist two flag signals 'Compass B' (Course North-east) and 'A.F.' (Attack the rear of the enemy). No difficulty had been experienced hitherto in getting signals through, but the *Lion* was now in a critical state. She had received fifteen hits. Her port engines were stopped, reducing her speed to fifteen knots. She was listing heavily to port. Between decks her lights were out, and she could use neither searchlights nor wireless. All but two of her signal halyards had been shot away; in consequence, the arrangement of the flags as hoisted became one signal instead of two, conveying the meaning: 'Attack the rear of the enemy bearing north-east', and was thus interpreted by Rear-Admiral Moore. The result was tragic, for by an unfortunate coincidence the disabled *Blücher*, now well separated from her consorts, at this moment bore north-east from the British squadron, which fell upon her in force. The *Lion*, being almost out of control and listing 10° to port, had dropped far astern. Beatty, who could no longer lead, was at a loss to know why Moore and the rest of the squadron were not continuing the pursuit of the main German force. This appeared all the more inexplicable as he had already ordered the *Indomitable* to despatch the *Blücher*, and she was now well placed to do so.

The distance between the *Lion* and the undamaged British ships was opening so rapidly that Beatty was no longer in a position to control them, and the command automatically passed to Moore in the *New Zealand*.

In desperation Beatty made one last effort to get the hounds on to the proper scent. He ordered Seymour to hoist the traditional signal, 'Engage the enemy more closely', but found to his dismay that the flag group had been removed from the signal book since Nelson last used it at Trafalgar. The only alternative which could be found was 'Keep nearer the enemy'. This signal was hoisted, but it was too late, for the *Lion* had dropped far astern, and smoke prevented it from being read. The squadron therefore continued to close the unhappy *Blücher*, while the remaining German ships made good their escape.

In a final desperate attempt to retrieve the situation, Beatty

ordered the destroyer *Attack* alongside the *Lion*, and jumping
on board directed her young commander to take him at full
speed to the *Princess Royal*. He reached the scene of action at
noon, just as the flaming *Blücher* was on the point of capsizing,
and the British battle cruisers were retiring north-westward.
He ordered the squadron to reverse their course and continue
the chase to the south-east, while he himself rehoisted his flag
in the *Princess Royal*. Further pursuit was hopeless. As described by Seymour: 'It was like trying to win the Derby after
a bad fall at Tattenham Corner.' At 12.45 p.m., therefore, he
reluctantly turned westward, and the battle was over.

His chief anxiety was now the wounded *Lion*. He ordered
the *Indomitable* to take her in tow, and directed all available
destroyers to protect her against submarine attack. The delicate
operation of towing this great ship, listing heavily with many
tons of water inside her, was successfully accomplished by
Captain F. W. Kennedy, who got her into Rosyth Dockyard
in the early morning of 26th January. It had been hoped to
take the *Lion* to the Tyne, which was nearer at hand, but in
her present condition her draught was too great for that river.
She was towed at slow speed by two hawsers, one of which
endured the passage, but the other had to be replaced several
times. Inside the ship there was a sinister silence: no hum of
fans, no throb of engines, and no rush of water along the hull.
Down below it was pitch dark, and the stagnant air was charged
with the fumes of high explosives tainted with the sickly smell
of chloroform. A few weeks afterwards the *Indomitable* was
presented with a silver trophy in the form of a guardian angel
bearing the inscription: 'From the Captain and Officers of
H.M.S. *Lion* to the Captain and Officers of H.M.S. *Indomitable*
to commemorate a very excellent 6½-inch hawser.'

Hipper was obliged to leave the doomed *Blücher* to her fate,
for all his ships, with the exception of the *Moltke*, had been
severely damaged and were on fire. The *Seydlitz* had six
hundred tons of water on board and her two after turrets were
completely knocked out. The *Blücher* fought gallantly to the
end, and it was only after having been hit by seven torpedoes
fired by the *Arethusa* and Tyrwhitt's destroyers that she rolled
over and sank. While the British light craft were picking up

survivors, a Zeppelin, accompanied by a seaplane, hovered overhead dropping bombs indiscriminately on her own countrymen struggling in the water, and on the British ships trying to rescue them. During the battle the total British casualties were fifteen killed and thirty-two wounded, and German 954 killed and 80 wounded. One hundred and eighty-nine Germans were captured.

In Great Britain elation was felt that a naval battle had been won without loss, but the victory might have been complete had Beatty been able to retain his leadership. At the Admiralty satisfaction was felt that once more the organisation for deciphering enemy wireless signals had proved trustworthy and effective. The failure to follow up the initial success was attributed to the misreading of Beatty's vital signal, and Moore was exonerated on the ground that he had obeyed what he had believed to be its purport. On the other hand, with Beatty out of the fight, Moore, on assuming command, had a unique opportunity to use his own initiative and continue the pursuit in spite of his interpretation of Beatty's signal. Had he done so he would have acted in accordance with the real intentions of his chief, and would in all probability have annihilated the whole German squadron. Unfortunately, Moore had taken up his appointment as second-in-command to Beatty only a few days before the battle, so there had not been time for him to get to know the principles which guided his chief in the conduct of the battle cruisers. Had he served with Beatty a little longer, he would have learnt, as Nelson's captains had learnt, that he could do no wrong if 'he laid his ship alongside the enemy'. All signals made by Beatty, prior to the tragic moment when he could no longer lead his squadron, had made it clear beyond doubt that Hipper's main force was the objective. To anyone who knew Beatty there could have been no other.

Mr. Winston Churchill remarks: 'The victory of the Dogger Bank brought for the time being abruptly to an end the adverse movement against my administration of the Admiralty, which had begun to gather. Congratulations flowed in from every side, and we enjoyed once again an adequate measure of prestige. The sinking of the *Blücher* and the flight, after heavy injuries, of the other German ships was accepted as a solid and indisputable result.'[1]

In Germany there was a corresponding feeling of despondency and dissatisfaction, relieved only by the knowledge that their ships had fought gallantly, and that German gunnery and shells had proved efficient. It was felt that the operation had been badly planned and deserved its fate. The blame for withholding the support of the High Seas Fleet fell naturally upon von Ingenohl, its Commander-in-Chief, who was ordered to haul down his flag, and was relieved by the Chief of the Naval Staff, Admiral von Pohl.

The experience gained on the German side at the battle was of inestimable value to the enemy in testing the ability of his ships to stand up to heavy shell-fire. The turret explosions in the *Seydlitz*, and the exposed nature of the ammunition supply in the *Blücher*, called attention to the need for adequate anti-flash arrangements and magazine protection, which were promptly put in hand.

Up to the end of 1913, British gunnery training had always been based on the assumption of close action at moderate speed. Beatty foresaw that the Fleet would have to pass through long range at high speed before reaching short range. In the spring of 1914, he persuaded the Commander-in-Chief (Callaghan) to allow him to carry out a firing practice in strikingly similar conditions to those experienced in grim reality at the Battle of the Dogger Bank.

It was not generally appreciated, however, that at long range ships would be vulnerable to enemy salvos plunging through the decks, and thus the need for adequate horizontal armour to protect magazines was not yet realised. None of the British battle cruisers experienced turret explosions during the battle similar to those in the *Seydlitz*, so it was not till many months later, after the *Queen Mary*, *Invincible*, and *Indefatigable* had been lost at Jutland from this very cause, that the bitter lesson was brought home and the necessary modifications applied to the British ships.

Although Beatty was a brave leader ready to do and dare all, his actions were always carefully thought out beforehand. He

[1] *World Crisis*, 1914–15, Winston Churchill.

foresaw with uncanny accuracy the situations that might develop and how to deal with them. Thus in battle he had complete command of himself, and trusting in his own judgment would make decisions without hesitation or visible anxiety. 'He used his staff when he wanted to, but he never leant upon them.'[1]

[1] *The Navy and Defence*, Lord Chatfield.

CHAPTER TEN

1915–1916

DAYS OF TENSION

*Rosyth · Letters from Lord Fisher · Formation of Battle
Cruiser Fleet · Lessons of experience · The men round
Beatty · Gunnery efficiency · Enemy activity*

ON his return to Rosyth, Beatty was much heartened by
many congratulatory messages, notably one from his
Commander-in-Chief, Sir John Jellicoe:

I have waited to congratulate you on your fine achievement until I
could do so by telegram [land line]. Please accept for yourself and all
under your command my warmest thanks for all you have done and my
sincere appreciation of the result of your efforts. The successful return
of the *Lion* is a fine feat, reflecting the greatest possible credit on all
concerned.

Beatty himself felt bitterly disappointed, and his own view
was shared by no less a person than that hard-bitten old seaman,
Lord Fisher, the First Sea Lord, whose first comment on hearing the result of the battle was: 'Why didn't he get the lot?' He
criticised Beatty's ninety-degree turn to port to avoid the
submarine, on the grounds that no enemy submarines were in
the vicinity. This knowledge may have been available to the
Admiralty, but Beatty did not possess it at the time, and had
every reason to beware of submarines in view of the loss of the
three British cruisers off Terschelling only four months
previously. He was also influenced by the threatening position
of the German destroyer flotillas which, as he states in his
despatch, were getting into a favourable position to attack
him with torpedoes. As it happened, his sudden turn completely
frustrated Hipper's intention to deliver the attack, and obliged
him to recall his flotillas.[1] On the other hand, Beatty was

_____
[1] *Admiral von Hipper*, Waldeyer Hartz, p. 153.

[195]

perhaps over-cautious in making such a large turn, thereby appreciably increasing the range, but it must be remembered that this was the first naval battle to be fought at such high speed in home waters. The loss of a few minutes of time by signal delay and other causes materially altered the whole situation. Beatty's decisions at this critical moment had to be made under heavy fire in a split second from the sloping bridge of a listing ship, which had borne the brunt of the battle and had suffered severe damage. Instead of making the signal 'Attack the rear of the enemy' he would perhaps have been better advised to hoist the one flag signal 'Chase', which he had already used in the early stages of the action and which could hardly have been misinterpreted.

When the official reports of the action had been examined, the reasons for the German escape became clear. Beatty retained the full confidence of the Admiralty and also of the Commander-in-Chief. Moore was appointed to a foreign command, but there is no record that Beatty asked for his relief. It was not in Beatty's nature to shirk responsibility, in fact he sought it, and when he got it, took it for better or worse. He knew that in the circumstances an unfortunate choice had been made by Seymour in the arrangement of the signals ordering a return to the pursuit, and also that Moore had correctly interpreted the literal meaning conveyed by the flags as hoisted, although he had completely misunderstood their real intention. In his published despatch Beatty makes no reference to Moore and accepts full responsibility for the escape of the enemy, though he hints that they got away because he was no longer in a position to lead his squadron. He knew that the disappointing sequence of events had to some extent been due to the unfortunate shooting away of most of the *Lion*'s halyards, and he retained complete faith in his signal officer.

Lord Fisher, as First Sea Lord, was writing regularly to Beatty. The following letters are of historic interest, and typical of Fisher's quaint literary style.

(*25th Jan.*, 1915)

A few lines of sincere gratitude for your good fight. I feel the death of Engineer-Captain G. C. Taylor most acutely. You don't know what a faithful and loyal friend he was to me. It will be interesting to hear how your firing affected the German ships. The *Seydlitz* and *Derfflinger* (but don't mention this fact to a soul . . .) had to hustle into dock, and yet not one single casualty in *Derfflinger*. I suppose the *Lion* hit a German mine. I do hope you will be able to repair her rapidly—as these incidents will be repeated as the *Lutzow* is coming along for early commission. Sad that *Queen Mary* was away. I won't burden you with more. Don't trouble to reply: you will be too busy. Jellicoe will never be in it—he is too far off at Scapa—he might as well be at Timbuctoo. He ought to be at Rosyth, as you ought to be at the Humber now the submarine defence is finished and eight berths ready.

Strictly Private and Confidential   (27th *Jan.*, 1915)
    I've already written to tell you that you're splendid, but I cannot understand when you were left behind in *Lion*, why *Tiger* and *Princess Royal* absolutely unharmed did not go on and finish off *Derfflinger* and *Seydlitz* very heavily on fire (both of them) (I hear this from an eye-witness) and both seriously damaged, and this cessation of fighting takes place at noon, when still 3 hours off the enemy's minefields (or possibly 4 hours). You are mistaken about the enemy's submarines—we know from themselves exactly where they were—hours off you. I've only time for this very hurried line, but it is simply incomprehensible to me why Moore discontinued the action at noon when the *Seydlitz* and *Derfflinger* both heavily on fire and very badly damaged and they had to scuttle into dock with great urgency and a very great number of killed. It's quite terrible to me that they should have been allowed to go free at noon. What possible explanation is there? What excuse have we to offer?

Private and Personal   (31st *Jan.*, 1915)
    I've quite made up my mind. Your conduct was glorious. 'Beatty beatus.' He [Moore] was a long way ahead, he ought to have gone on, had he the slightest Nelsonic temperament in him, regardless of signals, like Nelson at Copenhagen and St. Vincent. In war the first principle is to disobey orders. Any fool can obey orders. Half an hour would have finished the *Derfflinger* and *Seydlitz*.

Private   (3rd *Feb.*, 1915)
    Winston gave me a delightful account of his stay with you. I sympa-thise with you preferring Cromarty to Rosyth, but if you had been at Cromarty, we couldn't have had *Blücher*. It's 150 miles too far off. Nevertheless, I admit there are big compensations, but to go out in daylight with a lot of large ships and the German submarines is a very

serious risk—on the other hand, less risks of mines at Cromarty than Rosyth. I agree with you about Cowan, he ought to have gone to *Tiger*. Myself, I have a very great opinion of Pakenham.[1] 'He's a brave man.' (Togo said this of him to the Mikado.) We want brave men, any bloody fool can obey orders. What we want is a man who can disobey orders and win victories like Nelson at Copenhagen and St. Vincent.

(6th Feb., 1915)

Herculean efforts are without doubt in progress to repair *Derfflinger* and *Seydlitz*. So we may indeed have them ready before we have repaired *Lion* and *Indomitable*. So don't relax your vigilance and readiness and gunnery training. The *Lutzow* (a little faster than *Derfflinger*, I believe) will be ready soon now. At last the world is seeing that the battle cruiser is the 'breath of life'. (Lucky I got two more laid down of 33 knots the first week I arrived at the Admiralty, against great opposition.) All the d——d rabble that yelped at my heels are dumb dogs now. D——n 'em, and they will be damned. I always love Joseph's answer to his brethren, 'Fear not—am I in the place of God?' He knew they would get their reward all right, where the worm dieth not and the fire is not quenched. This is war time, and we can't have any d——d folly about suscepti-bilities. Don't you worry about any odium—I will take that and love it.

P.S.—I am too pressed to write more, I began at 3 a.m. today.

(8th Feb., 1915)

With the activities of threatened 20 German submarines in Channel and Irish Sea, it's not possible to have heavy ships coming south for repair, which is why *Lion* and *Indomitable* have been arranged to be repaired up north. I hope you'll make the dockyard workmen in *Indomitable* com-fortable, and then they will work harder. I forget if I told you, we have started two new 'Light Cruisers', which will join your flag next Decem-ber. They carry 15-inch guns, only 21 feet draught of water, and go 33 knots. Radius of action 11,000 miles. A surprise packet for Tirpitz. We are keeping it so secret that the whole correspondence about them is only on one half-sheet of notepaper, with Lloyd George's initials for $2\frac{1}{2}$ millions sterling to pay the bill. I will get you the model to look at. They are gems. I don't believe the Battle Squadrons will be in this war— the 'Battle Cruisers' will finish the job, if only their gunnery is perfec-tion. Imagine the *Invincible*, which was leading ship and did the whole fight and sunk the prize gunnery ships *Scharnhörst* and *Gneisenau*, had not one single person killed or wounded. The *Invincible* hit first, hit hard and kept on hitting. And yet, my dear friend, I was vilified by

[1] Admiral Pakenham was with Togo in his flagship at the battle of Tsu-shima.

Custance, Beresford, and a whole mass of others for introducing those 'hybrid monsters', the Battle Cruisers.

(9th Feb., 1915)

Now that I am so busy dragging masses of weights and luxuries out of the *Warspite* to make her go faster, 27 knots, I hope, and be a fit companion to *Indefatigable, New Zealand* and *Australia*, it occurs to me whether all your ships have any excess weights that could be got rid of so as to make all of them faster. You might let your clever young men look into this. For myself I cannot understand on what earthly grounds you keep your ships full of coal and oil in the restricted area of the North Sea fighting—at the very most you would not in any fight you can imagine want to go more than 500 miles at top speed, so why carry enough to go about 3,000 miles, and make yourself go slower and carry all that damnable dead weight of unnecessary fuel? Had you gone two knots faster on Jan. 24, you might have finished them off before the big fiasco. The Engineer-in-Chief asked me yesterday why the *Tiger*, with her big excess of speed, did not pursue the flying enemy—instead of answering him I talked about the weather.

Secret *(12th Feb., 1915)*

A few lines to tell you that all our intelligence points to all future fighting being in your hands, and that the German High Sea Fleet won't come out for a big job. They'll emerge and retire, but the new *Lutzow*, the *Derfflinger*, the *Seydlitz*, and the *von der Tann* will try an escapade *à la* Scarborough just for half an hour's bombardment of our coast in the break of dawn, and nip back with mines dropping freely behind them and submarines in front of them to waylay you. They are in holy terror of the 13½-inch guns and the Big Speed of the *Lion* and *Tiger*. Those two ships can outstrip them. (Apparently *Queen Mary* and *Princess Royal* much slower—why?) So you've got to get the gunnery of the *Lion* and the *Tiger* to the very best pitch of perfection.

> '*There's a beauty in the bellow of the blast,*
> *There's a glory in the growling of the gale,*
> *There's an eloquent out-pouring*
> *When the* Lion *is a-roaring*
> *And the* Tiger *is a-lashing of her tail.*'

Private *(5th March, 1915)*

I've had a big fight to get you Pakenham [to command the Second Battle Cruiser Squadron]—fierce endeavours in other directions— *Pakenham is a brave man*. Also Pakenham believes in you. *We must have officers who believe in their Admirals instead of back-biting them.* But what can you expect when Sir Gerard Noel writes to the First Lord protesting against my being at the Admiralty and saying, 'God help the Navy'? We have laid down 187 new ships since 15th Nov. (*four of them battle cruisers of 33 knots and 15-inch guns*) and *all of them will be fighting within a year.* God *is* helping the Navy.

Secret

I think about 8th March to 20th March the German Fleet may come out.

Postscript—Gospel Truth

Press cutting—'Lord Fisher, notwithstanding his 74 years, is full of health and vigour and enthusiasm. No one is prouder of the exploits of Sir John Jellicoe and Sir David Beatty.'

Private (5th March, 1916)

A mutual friend spoke to me this evening of an excellent letter you are supposed to have written to the Prime Minister, and it moves me to write you a line of hearty praise, as no one now seems to have any courage to do anything, and the Naval situation is perilous owing to lethargy, apathy, inexperience, and ineptitude. As a Yankee wrote me yesterday of the Admiralty, 'Even the decisions are indecisive'. Which I think is rather sweet.

Your friend Filson Young has played me the dirtiest trick conceivable in setting *The Times* against me. He appears to be bosom friends with the Editor of *The Times*. However, I won't trouble you with the story, it's ignoble, and after all, what does it matter? The Right will conquer in the end.

Beatty's answer is here quoted as being typical of his forthright manner in dealing with high authority.

Lion (8th March, 1916)

Thank you for your letter, which I found on my return.

Yes, I wrote to the Prime Minister, and hope that it was of some assistance to him.

I am sorry Filson Young has been playing dirty tricks. It is in the air and very catching.

Here we hear nothing and know less, and only wait for the day to come before it is too late.

In the mildest terms this weather is damnable.

Early in February 1915, the Battle Cruiser Force was reorganised at Rosyth with the new title of Battle Cruiser Fleet, and Beatty was reappointed in command, with his existing rank of Acting Vice-Admiral. The status of the *Lion* was raised to that of Fleet Flagship, and the remaining battle cruisers were organised, as they became available, in three squadrons of three ships each, making a total of ten battle cruisers in all. In addition to the main body, the First, Second, and Third Light Cruiser Squadrons and the 13th Destroyer Flotilla, a total of thirteen light light cruisers and sixteen modern destroyers, were also included in the new organisation.[1]

In fact, all the scouting forces of the Grand Fleet, with the sole exception of the Fourth Light Cruiser Squadron and some armoured cruisers, were placed under Beatty's command. Each squadron was homogeneous, the ships being organised according to their age and class; the whole force having a speed of at least twenty-five knots. Although his responsibilities had been greatly increased, Beatty remained as before under the supreme command of the Commander-in-Chief, who allowed him complete freedom of action within the framework of the strategical plan and the Grand Fleet Battle Orders.

The German battle cruisers, having been severely crippled, were not expected to give trouble for some time, so Beatty was able to take stock of his experience in encounters with the enemy. Not the least of his problems was how to obtain an accurate picture of the relative positions of opposing forces during operations at sea. The method in use was simple enough: ships would report by radio the bearing and distance of the enemy, giving their own positions at the time of sighting him. There was no radar, and wireless direction-finding between ships was in the stage of early experiment. The accuracy of these positions depended upon the calculations of individual navigators who, as every sailor knows, could not be certain of their whereabouts within a mile or so when out of sight of land. This liability to error would be greatly increased in thick or cloudy weather, when no celestial observations are possible, and the navigator has to rely on his

---

See Appendix IV. In the new organisation, the First Light Cruiser Squadron (Goodenough) became the Second Light Cruiser Squadron.

own estimation of speed and course; a method known as 'D.R.', or dead reckoning. Furthermore, ships operating in widely separated areas would be affected by different conditions of wind and tide. Thus, on the occasions when the Grand Fleet sailed from Scapa, while Beatty sailed with his scouting forces from Rosyth, there was no means of determining accurately the positions of the two fleets relative to one another, unless they came into visual contact. To obviate this difficulty, Jellicoe planned, whenever possible, that a junction should be effected before entering an area where the enemy might be met. Strategical considerations, however, usually prevented this being accomplished, notably before the battle of Jutland.

The task of plotting the reported positions of the enemy in correct relation to the British forces was a formidable one, so Beatty applied for a navigating specialist to be appointed to his staff for this work. When the young officer[1] duly arrived on board the Flagship he was told to report to the Admiral at once. Beatty, who was in his bath, summoned him to enter the bathroom, and gave him his brief in the following words: 'I have sent for you because my navigator has quite enough to do taking the squadron from one place to another and keeping us off the rocks. Your job is to tell me, at any time, where the enemy is, not only his big ships, but his little ships, his mines, his submarines, and everything that is his. Thank you—run away.'

These instructions issued from the depths of a bath virtually gave birth to a system which, after many vicissitudes, became universal, but did not reach perfection till the introduction of high-frequency direction finding and radar in the war of 1939–45. It is now known as the 'Action Information Organisation', employing in large ships not less than forty officers and men.

The idea of a staff of specialists to assist the Admiral was beginning to take shape in 1915. Beatty had around him the same staff which had served him well in peace-time, but it was too small to cope with the many problems of modern war and the administration of the newly-formed Battle Cruiser Fleet. The heat and burden of most of the staff work fell on the Flag

[1] The biographer.

Captain, Ernle Chatfield, who not only acted as Chief of Staff, but also carried the heavy responsibility of commanding the *Lion* with her company of over a thousand officers and men. He was also responsible for co-ordinating the gunnery of the squadron, and his expert advice on matters of fighting efficiency had to be available to the Admiral and to all ships in the Fleet. at all times. The strain on this great sea officer must have been severe; but he never showed any sign of it. Chatfield was the embodiment of all that was admirable in the naval officer of his day. He came from a naval family steeped in the best traditions of the Service, and being well aware from his early youth that the great test would come, had always imposed upon himself a rigid self-discipline. Although a first-class shot and devoted to sport, he would not allow these things to intrude upon his naval duty, and so when he reached captain's rank at the early age of thirty-five, he had achieved a perfect balance of physical and mental fitness. On the *Lion*'s bridge he was imperturbable. Beatty and Chatfield were complementary one to the other. Beatty's chief concern was to bring about the destruction of the enemy, and it was Chatfield's business to see that the Battle Cruiser Fleet was kept in the highest state of efficiency for this task. Soon after the Battle of the Dogger Bank, Chatfield was ordered to take the *Lion* to the Tyne for repairs. At this time Beatty was flying his flag temporarily in the *Princess Royal* (Captain O. de B. Brock),[1] and there was much to be done in reorganising the Battle Cruiser Fleet, particularly in regard to training and administration. The appointment of an experienced officer as Chief of Staff became, therefore, an urgent need. Beatty naturally turned to Chatfield, but reminded him that if he accepted the appointment he would have to relinquish command of his beloved *Lion*. Chatfield felt that in command-ing the *Lion* he was filling an historic rôle, and it was to him the finest job in the Navy. To have become Chief of Staff would have been an advancement, but he decided to remain as Beatty's Flag Captain and retain command of the officers and men who had served him so well. Beatty approved, and selected Captain R. Bentinck[2] as his Chief of Staff. Here again Beatty

[1] Later Admiral of the Fleet Sir O. de B. Brock, G.C.B.
[2] Later Admiral Sir Rudolf Bentinck, K.C.B.

showed his good judgment. Bentinck's personality inspired confidence. He was a man of fine physique with the features of a Roman patrician; a born aristocrat of the old school, yet always approachable; tactful but strong. In Beatty's own words, 'He was a tower of strength', and so acted as a bastion between the Admiral and the countless officers who sought interviews during the day.

Beatty himself was always approachable when important problems arose. On many occasions he would send for young officers who had ideas or 'brain-waves', which he would not hesitate to adopt if in his opinion they had practical value. The most fruitful of these was a scheme for destroying enemy submarines put forward by his own secretary (Spickernell) in co-operation with Lieutenant J. B. Glencross.

The German submarines at the time were attacking British fishing trawlers on the surface by gunfire. Spickernell suggested that a British submarine should be towed submerged in place of the trawl. As soon as the trawler was attacked, she was to slip her tow, leaving the British submarine with a sitting target.

Beatty immediately directed that the plan was to be executed. Two trawlers, the *Taranaki* and *Ratapico*, with two C-class submarines, were detailed for the task, and within forty-eight hours the *Taranaki* destroyed a submarine. Four more fell victims to this ruse before the enemy got wise to the idea. Although Beatty was always accessible, he would never allow himself to become immersed in technical detail. He regarded himself rightly as the supreme user of the instrument—it was the business of the staff to see that all the cogs worked smoothly, and from Beatty's point of view this could best be judged by results.

In order to serve his country with maximum efficiency, Beatty took great care to keep himself physically fit, so when Bentinck and the augmented staff had got into their stride, Beatty designed for himself a routine which he stuck to throughout the war whenever the Fleet was at Rosyth. At seven every morning he landed for an hour's fast walk round the dockyard, sometimes rowing himself ashore in the skiff. The forenoon was occupied attending to correspondence and giving important interviews. He was an exceptionally quick thinker, and had the invaluable faculty of being able to pick out at a glance essential points in a paper and give the required decision. In consequence his 'IN' basket was usually empty, but he had another basket labelled with an abbreviation for 'Balderdash', to which he committed all ill-conceived schemes or excuses. Many an officer was chastened by the thought that his 'explanation' had been sitting in the B-basket for some weeks.

Beatty, like Nelson, was a prolific writer, and most of his views on policy, strategy, and tactics are to be found in his private letters to statesmen, senior officers of all three Services, naval friends, and to his wife. He did all his writing standing up at a special desk with long legs, 'because,' he said, 'too much sitting gives you a "tummy".'

When Lady Beatty was in London he wrote:

Princess Royal   (*12th March*, 1915)
My usual controversy going on with the Admiralty. If it is not one subject it is another. It is quite extraordinary how constant it is and how arguments or argumentative matter accumulate. It makes it quite a relief to get to sea to escape from it all. We were disturbed in the middle of the day by reports of heavy firing out to sea which has not been definitely cleared up yet. But it startled old Lowry,[1] and kept me more or less tied to the ship. I fancy it must have been patrol vessels firing at either a real or an imaginary submarine. . . . . I feel I shall be a very old and dull human being by the time the war is over, and fear I am far from being a bright, cheerful, or interesting companion. My head is generally full of schemes of an uninteresting character, and I must be to you a very dull person just now. So I am glad you have gone south to London. It will brighten you up, and you will see and be with people who are more interesting. . . . . All my *real* thoughts are with you. I am a queer creature, but my heart is yours.

While Captain Ryan was improving the anti-submarine defences in the Forth, Beatty wrote:

Princess Royal   (*15th March*, 1915)
Great excitement, everybody very busy. Even old Lowry is getting a move on. Submarine has been knocking at the door all day, and they have located him near Oxcars with microphone. I popped down to see what I

[1] Admiral Sir R. Lowry, K.C.B., Commander-in-Chief Coast of Scotland.

could do, but of course nothing, and cannot afford to be away from the ships, but I feel sure they'll make a mess of it, and they ought to get him this time. Old Lowry plaintively bleats what a pity Ryan[1] isn't here to work the microphone, which amuses me, as he never fussed about it before. And says I am afraid he'll have gone before Ryan gets back. . . . If they hunt him with sufficient determination night and day, they are bound to get him in the end. Oh dear, I wish I was not stuck to these big ships. I am sure I could catch him, but I suppose one cannot do everything, but these spells of inactivity and wrestling with the Admiralty and the C.-in-C. now are making a crabbed old man of me. They have taken my beautiful repair ship away from me now, just as we were getting everything fixed up and making it into a self-contained concern, but she has to go out to the Mediterranean, so I suppose it is a case of necessity. I am sending the Secretary away for a few days to have a night in a bed and a rest. Eight months in the same spot, same faces, the same atmosphere, is trying to anybody, and we are beginning to dislike each other.

Princess Royal   (*14th March,* 1915)

No sooner is one difficulty overcome than another crops up. The *Lion* will be ready and completed Saturday next, which will be a great thing to get her out of the repair stage. It is nice to have a change and see other people and hear other points of view, although I do not suppose London is a very cheerful spot just now. . . . I should like a change also, if only for forty-eight hours, and sleep in a comfortable bed. It is just on eight months since I have been more than four hours out of my ship.

When young David went to school for the first time, Beatty wrote to Ethel:

Lion   (*21st Sept.,* 1915)

Keep your courage up. It will be a dreadful day for you leaving little David at school, and I wish I could be with you to support you. It is one of the penalties of bearing sons, but one that will bear fruit in the end, and the sacrifice will be repaid tenfold when you see him grow up into an intelligent, self-reliant, and capable man, which he could never attain unless he was pushed out of the nest and made to look for himself. He is indeed fortunate, and I have no fear for him. It is you, dear one, which causes me to grieve for. And you must bear it best you can. We have a Boxing entertainment in the Light Cruisers, which I shall have to attend today and tomorrow.

[1] Captain C. P. Ryan, R.N., in charge of anti-submarine experiments.

While the enemy were inactive, opportunity was taken to refit the *Lion* and give leave to her ship's company. He wrote:

Lion   (*22nd Nov.*, 1915)

The horrid Forth, like a great ditch full of thick fog which makes everything so cold. My great Barns of Cabins are like Vaults. I never get them warm. . . . There is no joy in life under such conditions. But on board the *Lion* there is the exception. She goes off to dock tomorrow, and they all go on five days' leave, and they are simply bubbling over with the joy of it. I turn over to *Queen Mary* with the Sec. and Flags, and they can get their leave afterwards. It will do them all no end of good, a change of scene and company. They will come back like giants refreshed. Even Chatfield is smiling. Peter is very well. I haven't seen him today, as I have been stuck on board hoping to go to sea. It's a wonderful thing Hope. We live on it, month in and month out. It's all that's left, and I don't give up. My time *must* come. If it wasn't for it I should chuck and try something else. To live in times like these and be condemned to this existence without something to come would be unbearable, without hope, and it makes me go cold all over to think that there isn't a chance in front of us.

After lunch he would spend about an hour at work before going ashore. His wife and family lived at Aberdour House, a comfortable old-fashioned country house overlooking the Firth of Forth, about six miles from Rosyth. Its greatest asset for Beatty was a good hard tennis court, where he played strenuously most afternoons. If the weather was unsuitable for tennis, he would play golf, or go for long walks, generally with Brock, Pakenham, Cowan or Chatfield, who were his closest friends, but all his officers were welcome at Aberdour. He returned on board at 7 p.m. and always dressed for dinner. He attended regularly the weekly ward-room cinema shows, and even if the Fleet were proceeding to sea, would see the programme through, relying on his Flag Officers and Captains to take their squadrons and ships past the well-known but tricky navigational hazards of the Firth of Forth anchorage. During the whole war he rarely if ever slept ashore.

Beatty kept close touch with his men. In the Fleet regattas he rowed in the veterans' skiff, and always won his race. He seldom missed the ships' concert parties and boxing matches, where, in a friendly atmosphere, he would take the

[207]

opportunity to address the crews and fire them with his own ardent desire to come to grips with the enemy. Later on, when he was Commander-in-Chief, speaking to 18,000 officers and men of the Grand Fleet after the boxing finals, he urged them to be patient, which he knew was dull, and reminded them that history repeated itself, and that the fleets of Hawke, Cornwallis, St. Vincent, and Nelson had all endured the same weary waiting. Nevertheless, they had had their Day. If our day came, it could only have one end—the complete annihilation of the enemy. Then he paraphrased Shakespeare's famous lines spoken by Henry V before Agincourt:

> *'And gentlemen of England now a-bed*
> *Shall think themselves accursed they were not here,*
> *And hold their manhood cheap while any speaks*
> *That fought with us on our Great Day.'*

This roused the men to such a pitch that they threw their caps in the air and cheered him again and again. As he walked away, dockyard workmen and sailors crowded round him, leaning forward to get a closer glimpse of him. Roger Keyes, commenting on this scene, says: 'He is a great man, there is no mistake about that, and the Fleet know it.'[1]

On another occasion it happened that Harry Lauder, the famous Scottish comedian, was present. Beatty, after he had finished his address to the men, turned to his guest and asked him to say a few words. Lauder, being a true artist, did not wish to steal Beatty's thunder or to create an anti-climax. Springing to his feet he gazed fixedly in silence at the two huge turret guns overhanging the platform, and then, after a few moments, he faced his audience and said: 'My, I wish I could see them vomit!' Thus effectively adding to the strength of Beatty's remarks.

Beatty was amply rewarded by the magnificent fighting spirit shown by his men, both in victory and adversity. At the Dogger Bank, when he was boarding the destroyer *Attack* to continue the chase of the fleeing enemy, the men on the upper deck of the crippled *Lion* spontaneously cheered him, a group of stokers shouting: 'Well done, David, finish 'em off!'

[1] *Naval Memoirs*, 1916–18, Sir Roger Keyes, p. 106.

His magnetic personality had that uncanny quality of getting through to all those he commanded, and drawing from each one of them confidence and admiration.

He encouraged his officers and men to take as much exercise and recreation as possible. Normally the Fleet kept steam for full speed at four hours' notice, but this was shortened to two and a half hours, and then one hour, if the situation required it. At long notice the officers were allowed to visit Edinburgh, but were subject to immediate recall. The dress prescribed was monkey jacket, with flannel trousers, and this led to many sartorial variations. The senior officers, including Beatty, in their brief spells of leisure naturally wished to get away from their plentiful gold lace, so wore monkey jackets with no distinguishing marks. Some of them, on more than one occasion, were mistaken for their own stewards.

Beatty's intimate assistants were his Flag Captain, Chief of Staff, Flag Commander, Flag Lieutenant-Commander, and Secretary, all of whom had their meals with him. The Flag Commander was the Hon. Reginald Plunkett,[1] a tall, good-looking sports-loving Irishman, who, like his Chief, had unlimited courage and imagination. It would be no exaggeration to say that he proved to be the ideal staff officer. Scholarly and intellectual, he had studied war and the employment of modern fleets in battle all his naval life, and yet had found time to become a torpedo specialist. As there were plenty of good 'torpedo men' in the Fleet, Plunkett devoted much time and energy to working out tactical problems and advising Beatty on the best methods of bringing about the swift destruction of the enemy. He was an ardent believer in the offensive, which fitted in well with the pattern of warfare as seen by the mind's eye of his Chief. In battle he was never absent from the Admiral's side. At the Dogger Bank, it was Plunkett who remembered Nelson's 'Engage the Enemy more closely', but found to his dismay that it did not appear in the modern signal book. Many years of study, backed by war experience, had put Plunkett well ahead of his time in matters of naval thought. Later, when he was Director of the then newly formed Naval Staff College at Greenwich, and also while holding

[1] Later Admiral the Hon. Sir Reginald Plunkett-Ernle-Erle-Drax, K.C.B., D.S.O.

important Flag appointments, he took every opportunity to impress upon the younger generation the paramount importance of the offensive in war—a doctrine which was readily accepted, and bore much fruit in the War of 1939–45. He was always a keen believer in night fighting, and did much to increase the efficiency of the Fleet in this respect. He is the only flag officer who in the course of his career has been Commander-in-Chief at Plymouth and also at the Nore.

Ralph Seymour, the Flag Lieutenant-Commander, carried out the duties of Fleet Signal Officer. He had a cheerful disposition well suited to Beatty's temperament. He was not a fully qualified signal specialist, but was an able and far-seeing officer of courage, zeal, and energy, who from his own battle experience did much to improve the signal organisation of the Fleet. Beatty had a great affection for him, and referred to him as 'my little round Flag Lieutenant'.

The officer most closely in touch with Beatty was Frank Spickernell,[1] his secretary. In pre-war days, when an Admiral's staff consisted of only two or three officers, the Secretary was the Admiral's principal personal assistant and confidential adviser. He controlled the Admiral's office, which handled all correspondence, secret ciphers, and documents, so his power was enormous. War experience had quickly brought home to flag officers the need for fully trained executive officers and specialists to assist them in the many ramifications of staff work. In big commands such as the Battle Cruiser Fleet, where the staff had to be greatly increased, care had to be taken that the new staff officers should be fitted into the existing organisation without upsetting it unduly. Much depended upon the Secretary if this was to be done without friction.

Spickernell, who was then only twenty-nine, was blessed with a keen sense of humour, quick brain, personal charm, and great tact. He welcomed the change, and in consequence Beatty's staff, as it grew in size, continued to work in harmony as a team irrespective of rank or branch. Spickernell knew his Chief inside out, his loyalty and affection for him were unbounded, and many officers have reason to be grateful for the wise counsel of this very young secretary.

[1] Later Paymaster-Captain Sir Frank Spickernell, K.B.E., C.B., D.S.O.

The rest of the year 1915 was uneventful for the Battle
Cruiser Fleet. In Flanders there was stalemate, and a serious
shortage of ammunition was being felt by the Army. In order
to assist the Government in their munition drive, Beatty
introduced in the Fleet a system of voluntary production of
small parts. All officers and men responded heartily, and every
evening in the dog watches while the ships were in harbour,
Beatty and his officers could be seen breaking their finger-
nails on the hand production of grummets for army shells.

On 9th August, Beatty was confirmed in the rank of Vice-
Admiral at the early age of forty-four, by which time the *Lion*,
having completed her repairs, had resumed the duties of Fleet
Flagship, the *Australia*, *Invincible*, and *Inflexible* had returned
from overseas, and for the first time the Battle Cruiser Fleet was
at full strength. The German High Seas Fleet lay quiescent in
its bases, but there was much enemy submarine and minelaying activity, which kept the British destroyers and light
craft fully occupied. Beatty did all he could to keep the gunnery
efficiency of the Fleet at a high standard, but was handicapped
by the lack of a firing range in the Firth of Forth, which was
too narrow to permit full-calibre shoots from heavy guns. The
Commander-in-Chief, however, had established a full-calibre
range west of the Orkneys, where ships could exercise in
comparative safety from submarines, and arrangements were
made for Beatty's force to visit Scapa at frequent intervals for
gunnery practices and tactical exercises with the Grand Fleet.

By this means the battle cruisers enjoyed the same practice
facilities as the rest of the Grand Fleet, and Beatty was able to
keep in personal touch with Jellicoe. Later, when the outer
defences of the Forth had been completed, a gunnery range
for sub-calibre practice was established in the Firth, thus
enabling ships at Rosyth to be constantly exercised. About
this time Commander Sidney Bailey[1] joined Beatty's staff as
Fleet Gunnery Officer, easing the burden of co-ordinating and
directing the gunnery of the Fleet borne hitherto by the re-
doubtable Chatfield, who had recommended Bailey as 'one of
the best gunnery officers in the Navy'. The gunnery of the
Battle Cruiser Fleet could not have been in better hands.

---

[1] Later Admiral Sir Sidney Bailey, K.B.E., C.B., D.S.O.

In January 1916, there was an important change of command in the German Navy. Admiral von Scheer became Commander-in-Chief of the High Seas Fleet, and boldly announced his intention of coming to 'close grips with England'. He implemented this threat by carrying out some abortive 'tip and run raids' at scattered points on the East Coast of England. In response to each of these alarms Beatty went to sea, but the raiding force, after firing only a few ineffective rounds into British territory, made off at high speed before he could intercept them. This change of heart on the part of the Germans was significant, so Jellicoe retaliated by increasing his offensive sweeps into the Heligoland Bight, together with minelaying operations, and even air attacks by seaplanes on shore objectives. These air attacks were ticklish operations. The seaplane carriers (converted channel steamers) had to stop off the enemy coast to hoist out their aircraft, while destroyers and cruisers, supported by battle cruisers, patrolled near at hand ready to ward off enemy counter-attacks and pick up returning air crews. Although the damage done by the aircraft would probably be negligible, the air operations were attractive as a means of drawing enemy naval forces towards the carrier, and this indeed happened on the early morning of 25th March, 1916.

The selected air objective was the Zeppelin base at Hoyer, on the Schleswig coast, near the Island of Sylt. The seaplane carrier *Vindex*, escorted by five light cruisers and thirteen destroyers from Harwich, under Tyrwhitt, was entrusted with the task. Beatty, with the whole Battle Cruiser Fleet, cruised in general support over the horizon to the north. The *Vindex* successfully launched her aircraft in a position near the Vyl lightship. Meanwhile, some of Tyrwhitt's destroyers, waiting close inshore to pick up returning seaplanes, attacked an enemy patrol six miles north of Sylt and sank two armed trawlers. During this engagement one of Tyrwhitt's destroyers, the *Medusa*, came into collision with another destroyer, and lay helpless. Tyrwhitt at once rushed to the rescue, and as soon as the *Medusa* was safely in tow of the flotilla leader *Lightfoot*, he ordered the whole force to retire westward, but speed was greatly reduced on account of the tow. This unfortunate incident took place in sight of the enemy coast, so it was not very long before hostile aircraft were over the British force reporting their movements and dropping bombs, fortunately with little effect.

For Tyrwhitt the situation was perilous in the extreme. He was only too well aware that the German High Command had enjoyed full knowledge of his presence ever since early morning, and that strong enemy forces would already be on their way to intercept him. At noon Beatty was only twenty miles from Horns Reef light vessel, and no more than fifty miles westward of Tyrwhitt's force. Half an hour later Tyrwhitt was ordered, by the Admiralty, to withdraw. So slow was his retirement, however, that it was not till 4 p.m. that he sighted Beatty's battle cruisers steering southwards across his course ahead. Beatty held on towards Heligoland till 5.30 p.m. before turning back, and it was dusk before the two forces were close together again.

Meanwhile, the sea had been rising rapidly, a gale sprang up, and hour by hour the wind increased in violence. At 7.40 p.m. the *Medusa* was still barely fifty miles west of Horns Reef when her tow parted. Tyrwhitt could do no more; under stress of weather the damaged destroyer was abandoned, and eventually became a total loss.

The troubles of the night were far from over. It was exceptionally dark, and at 10.15 p.m. Tyrwhitt steamed straight into a flotilla of enemy destroyers. Both sides were taken by surprise, but by skilful manœuvring Captain Loder-Symonds in the *Cleopatra* rammed and sank one of the enemy. Unfortunately, at this moment the *Undaunted*, the cruiser next astern, collided with the *Cleopatra*. Although the *Cleopatra* was able to maintain full speed, the *Undaunted*'s bow was badly damaged, and she rapidly lost touch with the Commodore. She was, however, able to struggle into the Tyne, where she was soon rendered fit for service. Reports of the mishaps which had occurred created a state of acute anxiety at the Admiralty, where it was known that German cruisers, battle cruisers, and destroyers were searching for Tyrwhitt. Orders were accordingly sent out to Tyrwhitt at 4.35 a.m. on the 26th to sink his disabled ships and retire. Beatty, however, had seen here an opportunity of bringing the enemy to action. He reasoned correctly that the enemy, knowing Tyrwhitt's approximate position, would be searching for him to the westward. Addressing his Chief of Staff, he exclaimed:[1] 'If I continue on a westerly course, I shall probably run into their destroyers in the dark, and lay myself open to night attack, but if I go back into the Heligoland Bight I will be in a good position to intercept them on their return in the morning. If I meet Hipper and his battle cruisers I can deal with them. If their Battle Fleet is also out, I can retire on the Grand Fleet.' Being uncertain whether the Grand Fleet had yet put to sea, he informed the Admiralty of his intentions.[2] The Admiralty did not immediately approve, but finally relented,[3] and Beatty accordingly turned once again south-eastward towards the enemy coast. He spent the forenoon of the 26th off Horns Reef, covering the northern approaches to the German bases, but to his great disappointment sighted nothing. Tyrwhitt joined him at noon with his three remaining light cruisers, while Jellicoe, with the Grand Fleet, was steaming south at full speed. Beatty, however, soon received information from the Admiralty that the German forces at sea had turned for home on account of the bad weather. His own force was running short of fuel, and so, at 2.15 p.m. on the 26th, he set course for Rosyth, after spending twenty-seven hours in German waters, vainly hoping to bring the enemy to action.

In vivid contrast the German forces had been timid in their movements. Hipper and his battle cruisers, supported by two squadrons of battleships, were at sea during the night of 25th–26th March, but did not advance beyond Sylt, because, according to their own account, the weather was too bad for destroyers. They never, in fact, got within sixty miles of Beatty. It is worthy of comment here that Beatty, on no occasion throughout the whole war, ever allowed either gales or fog to prevent him from carrying out his avowed intention. If the seas were heavy he sent his destroyers home, and carried on without them, relying on the high speed of his cruisers and battle cruisers as a protection against enemy submarines. No fog ever stopped him from leaving harbour.

---

[1] Eye-witness.   [2] Signal 279 of 25th March, 1916, S.O.B.C.F. to Admiralty.
[3] Signal 663 of 26th March, 1916, Admiralty to S.O.B.C.F.

The spring of 1916 was full of alarms and excursions, and the Battle Cruiser Fleet was constantly at sea to counter enemy movements reported by the Admiralty. During the afternoon of 22nd April, in a sweep towards the Skagerrak, the battle cruisers, while zigzagging at twenty knots, ran suddenly into a thick belt of white fog before anyone was aware of its existence. The phenomenon is by no means new to those who know the North Sea: the fog, being the same colour as the sky, creates a false horizon, and without warning, ships are enveloped and visibility reduced to a few yards. Beatty immediately ordered the Fleet to reduce speed and cease zigzagging, but there was no time to prevent a collision between the *Australia* and *New Zealand*. The two ships came in contact nearly broadside-on, the *Australia* being severely damaged in two places, and though quickly placed in dockyard hands, had to be written off as a fighting unit for many months to come— a serious loss at this critical time.

In the brief spells at Rosyth, the Battle Cruiser Fleet was kept at immediate readiness and no shore leave given. In the *Lion*'s gunroom this situation inspired a 'hymn of hate' sung by the midshipmen, who, naturally resenting long periods of confinement in their ship, were getting somewhat bored with the many wild-goose chases to sea, and no sight of the enemy. So they sang:

> '*We hate this bloody war,*
> *It gives us all the blight,*
> *We cannot go ashore,*
> *And yet we cannot fight,*' etc.

Although at Rosyth there was very little social life ashore, many officers had established their families in the neighbourhood. The strain on the wives must have been great, for they would often wake in the morning to find the anchorage empty and the whole fleet gone, and never knew whether they would see their husbands again.

Beatty's house at Aberdour was only nine miles from Rosyth but he could not visit it when the Fleet was at short notice for going to sea, which was the usual state of affairs at this time. Ethel, who was not accustomed to staying for long in one place, grew restive and sometimes fretful, giving him the impression that he was not always welcome on the few occasions he could get to Aberdour. In his distress he wrote to her:

Just after I had telephoned you that we were at too short a notice for me to come to Aberdour, I got orders putting us back. I did not want to upset your arrangements by telephoning again, and as I was very gloomy I thought I would go for a good tramp. It's the best thing for me when I get the Blues, which I fear I do rather too often now. At times our inactivity frets me to such an extent that I can hardly bear it. The greatest war of all time is proceeding, the finest deeds of heroism are being performed daily, the dreams of the past of glory and achievement are being uprooted and proved impossible of accomplishment. The country is in such need, the spirit is so willing, and yet we are doomed to do nothing, achieve nothing, and sit day after day working out schemes that will never be carried out, and endeavouring by pen and paper to impress the Admiralty with the possibility of our doing something, even small things, and are met with a stone wall. You are quite right. It is infernally foolish to fuss. You can imagine that it is painful, humiliating almost, to see all the ideals and hopes of one's life being rent in twain and reduced to nothing; at times I feel I can't bear it, and I have to preserve a hopeful aspect, to keep on smiling and saying our time will come when I feel in my heart that it never will. Tata dear, do not be too matter of fact, try to understand me. I would gladly give my life to strike a real blow, to achieve a success, to destroy this cursed and poison-ous enemy. I think of nothing else, and the futility of it all gives me the Blues. And then you accuse me of being cross, bad-tempered, saying cutting things which indeed were far from my thoughts or intention. I fear this has become an obsession which won't come out, and caused you to acquire an antipathy to me. I had got rid of the devil or thought I had. Perhaps he left a mark behind and made me look bad-tempered, cross, what you will. Truly I am not fit for the society of anybody but those who have *got* to *be* with me. I express myself badly perhaps, but to hurt your feelings is the last thing in the world I wish to do. Try and believe me.

She did not respond as he would have wished, so a month later he wrote again with no regard to self:

You must give me a little more time to get accustomed to the new conditions and your changed feelings. You see in the past you have spoilt me horribly and have given me so much love and sympathy that it is difficult to realise that I must do without it or without so much of it. It is unfortunate (for me) that it should come at a time when one can do with so much more. No doubt when the war is over, if we are still alive, I shall be able to secure as much as anybody could want, but then the pressing need for it will have passed. However, let me impress upon you that I am really tumbling to the altered conditions, that I in no way wish to monopolise your entire life, that I have no wish to be the orbit, against your will, round which everything will revolve, to be the centre of your efforts to live, as you put it, and makes me a horribly selfish egotistical person. I truly am not that really. I know you did not mean to imply that I was, but that is what it came to. That is altered for ever. I realise you like to be more independent and indeed am thankful for it, and all I ask and wish is that you should do exactly as you wish at all times, all I truly care for is that you should be happy and contented. . . . I have read the Archbishop's Letter to the Fleet, and I do not agree with you. . . . He simply states the plain facts, and they are simple enough, but when represented in simple language it comes rather as a surprise to the inarticulate ones. It is true that for 12 months the Fleet has been enduring the strain of *immediate readiness* for battle. For the first five months we were constantly at sea. We had no harbours secure from danger. We were constantly in foul weather moving at high speed without a light to show where our next-door neighbour was. Anyone who had any idea of what fleet work was would readily recognise that the strain and the risk of moving these monsters about was considerable. As the A.B. put it, we had all the strain and responsibilities of war without the thrill of battle, and one might well add with the quite horrible prospect of being sent into the next world by agency of the mine or torpedo from the submarine. All that was welcomed, and I think I can truly say was far preferable to the subsequent six months, during which the inactivity has added a burden far harder to bear than the over-activity of the first period. You judge everybody in the Fleet by me. I am having a perfectly easy and comfortable time. Not so the men. They haven't their wives and families here. They can't go ashore. They are as a fact allowed ashore for a march for $2\frac{1}{2}$ hours in one day out of eight. They are almost in reach, in sight of their homes, but they can't go. And yet their spirit of cheerfulness is wonderful. They have played the game, and they might so easily have not done so, and if I ask them to do a big thing I know that I can depend upon them. They have not performed heroic deeds as their brothers have in Flanders or Gallipoli, but they can and they will when the time comes. If you think of what the fact of being immediately ready for battle means in mind and spirit as well as in organisation and detail, you will realise that it is not a frame of mind or condition

of life that one wants to dwell in longer than can be helped and one would
be glad to relax. No, my dear, I don't think the Archbishop over-stated
the case for the sailor. If applied to me or the Captains perhaps yes, but
not to the men, of whom he was talking.

Although Beatty had this great worry on his mind and
accuses himself of being bad-tempered, he showed no sign of
it to the officers and men of his flagship. In fact, they marvelled
at his serene calmness and cheerful outlook during the weary
months of waiting.

During the month of May there was a feeling of great
tension in the Battle Cruiser Fleet. The ships' companies
knew that in recent sweeps they had once or twice narrowly
missed an encounter with the High Seas Fleet, notably after
the German raid on Lowestoft on 25th April, 1916. On this
occasion, Beatty sighted the smoke of the retreating enemy
battle cruisers too close to their own coast for him to continue
the pursuit. The German Commander-in-Chief (von Scheer),
however, had seldom ventured far beyond the confines of the
Heligoland Bight with his heavy ships, and information from
German sources indicated that it was part of Scheer's plan to
avoid action with the Grand Fleet until it could be reduced by
attrition. The Lowestoft raid had been designed with the
object of forcing dispersion on the British Fleet in response to
popular clamour from the East Coast towns.

Another significant factor was the apparent cessation of
enemy submarine activity against merchant shipping, and
an ever-increasing number of reports of their presence in
the North Sea. Although this was actually a political move
resulting from U.S. protest, it fitted in well with Scheer's
attrition plan. By the middle of May all available German
submarines were stationed off the British bases and across
routes which the Grand Fleet might be expected to follow
in an advance to the south. Scheer hoped, not only to reduce
British strength by these dispositions, but also to gain valuable
information of British movements. This concentration of
enemy submarines had no effect whatever on the freedom of
movement of the British heavy ships, but it indicated that
Scheer might be contemplating some bigger and bolder move,

Great and continuous vigilance was therefore more than ever necessary.

At the end of the month the Admiralty received information confirming their suspicions that Scheer was about to put to sea. Whereupon the squadrons and flotillas of the Grand Fleet slipped the leash and headed for the coast of Jutland.

CHAPTER ELEVEN

1916

THE BATTLE OF
JUTLAND—I

*Opening phase · The run to the south · Beatty and
Hipper: the gun duel and destroyer attack · Beatty sights
the High Seas Fleet*

THE following account of Beatty's part in the Battle of
Jutland is based, not only on personal experience, but also
on the results of subsequent professional investigation. The
biographer was on the bridge of the *Lion* throughout the action,
having the duty of plotting the positions and movements of
British and German units, and keeping Beatty informed of the
general situation. After the war the biographer served on the
directing staff of the Royal Naval Staff College (1921–3), on
the instructional staff of the Royal Naval War College (1932–4),
and held the post of Director of the Royal Naval Staff College
(1936–8). In these establishments, lectures and demonstrations were given to each course of officers with a view to
stressing the lessons of the battle and studying the application
of tactical principles. The demonstrations were based on
authoritative information from both British and German
sources, and it was customary at the Staff College to invite
senior officers who had held important commands in the battle
to give their views. Free criticism and discussion were encouraged. Thus, after many years of careful and unbiased
examination under the fierce light of professional criticism, the
picture may now be said to have become clear in its essentials.

The writer is mainly concerned with Beatty's part in the
battle, and relies for his facts, not so much on his own experience, for memory is fickle, but on the cold analysis of his
brother officers. The reasons for certain decisions taken by his
chief are known to him, and can be confirmed by Admiral of

the Fleet Lord Chatfield, Admiral the Hon. Sir R. Plunkett Ernle-Erle-Drax, and Captain (S.) Sir Frank Spickernell, all of whom were on the bridge of the *Lion* with Beatty from the start of the battle-cruiser action, to the time the enemy battle cruisers disappeared for the last time into the mist, a beaten foe. It is too easy to criticise leaders when sitting in comfort with all the facts available and explanatory diagrams at hand for reference. One is apt to forget the real conditions which existed at the time, when all that could be seen were often the dim outlines of a few ships, vanishing before it was possible to distinguish friend from foe. A very effective method of bringing officers back to reality during demonstrations at the Staff College and Tactical School was for the instructor to super-impose a circle of visibility on the diagram under discussion and say: 'That was all the Admiral could see at the time—now what would you have done?' So, in considering the difficulties which confronted Jellicoe and Beatty on that memorable day, one must try to visualise the battle as seen from the bridges of their flagships.

The sequence of events which brought about this mighty clash of arms is too well known to require repetition. In brief, von Scheer, in pursuance of his policy to entice away a portion of the British Fleet and then fall upon it before the Grand Fleet could come to its support, planned an operation in which his light forces and battle cruisers were to attack shipping off the Norwegian coast and in the Skagerrak. Meanwhile the High Seas Fleet was to remain about fifty miles away to the south, ready to pounce on any British detachment which might be sent to deal with the raiders. Before putting this plan into action, he placed strong submarine patrols in positions where British warships might be expected to pass. It was the presence of these submarines, as we have seen, which gave the British Admiralty the first indication that the enemy was contemplat-ing some operation, probably on a major scale. So from Scheer's point of view they were not entirely beneficial.

The date finally selected by Scheer, after several postpone-ments, was 31st May, 1916. By a strange coincidence, Jellicoe had also prepared an operation for 2nd June, which was in essence the same as Scheer's, for it was designed to draw

enemy forces into the Skagerrak and destroy them with a
superior fleet.

The Third Battle Cruiser Squadron, under Rear-Admiral
the Hon. Horace Hood, was detached from the Battle Cruiser
Fleet at the end of May for routine gunnery practices at Scapa
Flow. Jellicoe, therefore, at Beatty's request,[1] despatched in
exchange Rear-Admiral Hugh Evan-Thomas with four battleships of the fast Fifth Battle Squadron to join Beatty at Rosyth
and to act as a supporting force. These battleships had much
greater offensive power and ability to stand punishment than
the battle cruisers, but their speed of twenty-five knots was
some two and a half knots less. It was not fully realised at the
time what a valuable replacement they were, because the
previous experiences of the British battle cruisers in action had
given no indication of the weakness of their magazine protection against plunging fire. Beatty had every reason to be satisfied
with the force entrusted to his command, for although the
Australia had not yet returned from dockyard hands, he had
six battle cruisers to oppose Hipper's five, and in addition he
could rely upon the close support of four of the latest and most
powerful battleships in existence. His three Light Cruiser
Squadrons of four ships each were at full strength, and the
13th Destroyer Flotilla, led by the light cruiser *Champion*, had
been reinforced by eighteen destroyers from Harwich and
Scapa, making a total of twenty-nine destroyers.

On 30th May, the whole of this force was concentrated at
Rosyth ready to carry out the impending operation in the
Skagerrak. During the forenoon the Admiralty intercepted a
warning signal from Scheer to his patrolling submarines,
which confirmed suspicions that something was afoot on the
other side of the North Sea, so they told Jellicoe that there
were indications that the German Fleet might be putting to sea
early on the following morning. Jellicoe immediately cancelled
his own projected operation, and ordered all units of the Grand
Fleet to have steam at short notice.

At 6 p.m., the Admiralty informed both Jellicoe and Beatty

---

[1] Private letter from Beatty to Jellicoe, dated 7th May, 1916: 'I should like 3rd
B.C.S. to go to Scapa for exercises. Will you send 5th B.S. to take their place, as
Australia will not be back until 10th June.'

that the Germans intended to carry out some operation on 31st May, leaving by the eastern route and Horns Reef. Jellicoe was ordered to concentrate the Grand Fleet eastward of the 'Long Forties' (about ninety miles west of the entrance to the Skagerrak) and await eventualities. He accordingly directed Beatty, with the Rosyth Force, to be in a position lat. 56° 40′ N., long. 5° E. at 2 p.m. on 31st May, and informed him that the Grand Fleet would be in lat. 57° 45′ N., long. 4° 15′ E. at that time. He further instructed Beatty that if no news had come in by 2 p.m. he was to stand towards him and get into visual touch. It was Jellicoe's intention that the whole Grand Fleet, with Beatty's scouting forces spread well ahead, would then sweep south-eastward towards Horns Reef.[1] This plan was simple and sound. Beatty's rendezvous had been fixed seventy miles to the southward of the Battle Fleet, so as to ensure that the waters between the British coast and Jellicoe's line of advance should be well swept by Beatty's widely spread cruiser screen, before the final concentration.

All units of the British Fleet were clear of their bases by 11.30 p.m. on 30th May. Only two enemy submarines were sighted, one by Beatty's force and the other by the Second Battle Squadron from Cromarty on its way to join Jellicoe. The advanced forces of the German Fleet did not clear the River Jade till some two and a half hours later.

It is creditable to Admiralty Intelligence that their information should have been in time to enable the Grand Fleet to get well into the North Sea before the High Seas Fleet had left harbour, and it also speaks well for the vigilance of British coast patrols that only two of a large number of enemy submarines were able to sight units of the British Fleet.

Admiralty Intelligence, however, was silent during the morning of the 31st. Scheer, on the other hand, had received reports from the two submarines already mentioned, misleading him to believe that only detached units of the British Fleet were at sea, which would have suited his plans admirably.

By noon the two hostile Fleets were converging on one another, as shown on Diagram V. The diagram represents the viewpoint of a bird of limitless vision, and it is most important

---

[1] Commander-in-Chief's telegram addressed to Beatty.

to realise that at this moment neither Jellicoe nor Beatty had any definite information that the German Fleet was at sea, while Scheer believed that only detachments of the British Fleet were likely to interfere with his operation. In fact, these two great armadas, 150 British and 101 German warships, com-

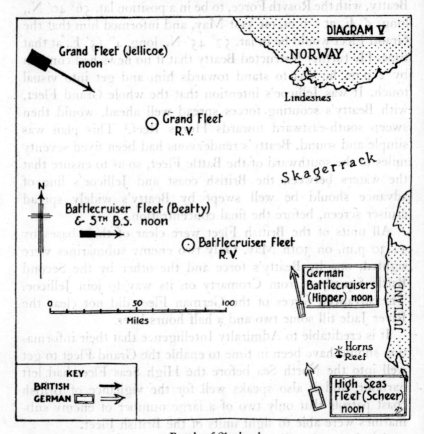

Battle of Jutland.

Situation at noon, 31st May, 1916, showing hostile fleets converging.

prising the naval might of the two nations, were drawing closer to each other, but neither side knew that the other was at sea in strength. It may seem strange that such a situation could arise, but in those days naval air reconnaissance was almost non-existent. Scheer had hoped to have Zeppelin cover, but this did not materialise. Beatty had the seaplane carrier *Engadine* with

The Battle of Jutland by W. E. Wylie, R.A.

Picture shows the *Lion* in foreground in action with German battle cruisers at about 6.5 p.m. The *Defence* and *Warrior* have just passed across the *Lion's* bows

him, but the range of her few seaplanes was very limited, and once they had flown off the water it was problematical if they would ever return. It was not possible to maintain an air reconnaissance patrol for any length of time, so it was the usual practice to conserve the seaplanes until there was some indication that the enemy was in the immediate vicinity. Thus, information of enemy movements depended wholly on the limited vision of Beatty's scouting cruisers, spread on a line extending about 100 miles across his front.

The fog of war was further intensified for the British by an Admiralty signal informing Jellicoe and Beatty, at about 12.41 p.m., that although the enemy had made all preparations to sail, there was no definite news, but directional wireless had placed the German Flagship in the Jade at 11.10 a.m. on 31st May. Both admirals naturally concluded that this operation, like so many previous excursions, was likely to end in disappointment. Nevertheless, Jellicoe's original plan remained unchanged, and Beatty, at 1.30 p.m., redisposed his forces in preparation for turning to the north to meet Jellicoe. The cruiser screen was swung to a line E.N.E.–W.S.W. so as to cover the front of the Grand Fleet during its advance to Horns Reef, and the Fifth Battle Squadron was stationed five miles, 325°, from the *Lion*. This disposition was designed to assist Evan-Thomas in taking up his appointed station in the van of the battle fleet after the junction between the two fleets had been effected (see Diagram VI). According to the Grand Fleet's battle orders, the prescribed distance between the battle cruisers and Fifth Battle Squadron, while cruising as part of the Grand Fleet, was ten miles. In the circumstances, Beatty wisely reduced this to five miles, to ensure closer support if required.

At 2.15 p.m., Beatty reached his rendezvous and turned to N. by E. to meet the Grand Fleet as ordered. At the same time he made a signal to Evan-Thomas, now ahead of him, to look out for Jellicoe's advanced cruisers. This was normal procedure, probably resulting in all eyes on the bridge of the *Barham* (Evan-Thomas's flagship) being turned northward and thoughts centred on the business of effecting the junction. There was no reason why Beatty should have arranged other-

wise, for the Admiralty had so recently informed him that the
German Fleet Flagship was still in harbour. About a quarter of
an hour later there came a sudden awakening for all. Commodore E. S. Alexander-Sinclair, in his cruiser flagship

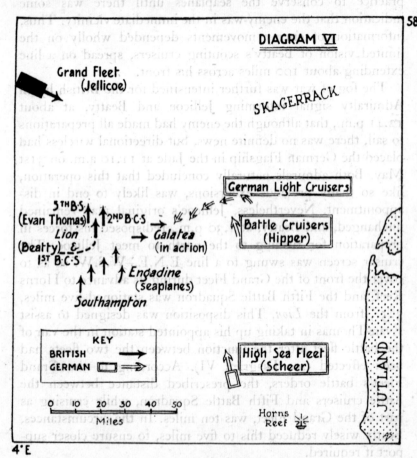

DIAGRAM VI

Battle of Jutland.

Situation at 2.30 p.m., 31st May, 1916. First Contact.

Galatea, occupying the most easterly position on Beatty's
cruiser screen (about thirty miles east of the *Lion*), sighted a
Danish steamer blowing off steam. On closing to investigate,
Alexander-Sinclair found that she had been stopped by enemy
warships, and at 2.20 p.m. he signalled on full-power wireless:

'Urgent. Two cruisers, probably hostile, in sight bearing E.S.E., course unknown. My position lat. 56° 48′ N., long. 5° 21′ E.' On receiving this report, Beatty decided to set a course to get between the enemy and his base, and accordingly, at 2.32 p.m., he turned the Battle Cruiser Fleet to S.S.E. The turning signal, made by flags, was not seen by the *Barham* owing to the heavy smoke belched forth by the battle cruisers in pressing on steam. In any case the *Tiger*, as repeating ship, should have passed it on by searchlight. Beatty was unaware that Evan-Thomas had neither received the *Galatea*'s enemy report nor the turning signal. Some critics have said that the *Barham*, on seeing Beatty turn, should have followed suit. Unfortunately Evan-Thomas did not receive the *Galatea*'s signal until some five minutes later than Beatty, and since his last orders were to look out for the Grand Fleet, he might reasonably have assumed, at first, that Beatty was probably adjusting his position prior to meeting Jellicoe.

At 2.38 p.m., Evan-Thomas, realising the true situation, also turned to S.S.E. This was six minutes after Beatty, and since the two squadrons had meanwhile been steaming in opposite directions, the gap between them had widened to nearly ten miles.

For Beatty to have waited for the battleships would have been unthinkable. It was his first duty to locate the enemy at the earliest possible moment, and support the cruisers already in touch. He had visualised the situation in a flash and acted immediately.

There was nothing rash in this split-second decision, which incidentally was fully approved by the Commander-in-Chief in his despatch,[1] and endorsed by the enemy.[2] As far as Beatty knew, the High Seas Fleet was not at sea, and even if he were to meet their battle cruisers, his experience at the Dogger Bank would justify him in thinking that his six battle cruisers would be more than a match for Hipper's five. He had yet to learn of the superiority of German material and ship construction. His duty, as Commander of the British scouting forces, was clear. He must find the enemy. And with this

[1] Commander-in-Chief's despatch of 18th June, 1916.
[2] German Official Account, p. 47.

object in view, guided by reports from Alexander-Sinclair, who was drawing the enemy westward, Beatty gradually hauled round to the eastward so as to close him. The nature of the *Galatea's* reports left no doubt in his mind that the German battle cruisers were supporting their cruisers, although Alexander-Sinclair had not yet been able to identify them on account of smoke.

At 3.8 p.m., at Beatty's order, a seaplane from the *Engadine* took off from the water. Owing to low thin cloud the aircraft did not fly above 1,000 feet, and owing to poor visibility was not able to keep the British and German ships in sight at the same time. She made three reports of enemy cruisers, but sighted nothing bigger before she was compelled to come down owing to a broken petrol pipe. The pilot, Flight-Lieutenant F. S. Rutland, R.N., and the observer, Paymaster G. S. Trewin, R.N., who were fortunately picked up, had the distinction of being the first airmen to take part in a naval battle.

At 3.15 p.m., Beatty was steering north-east at 23 knots. He had not exceeded this speed, which gave the Fifth Battle Squadron a chance to catch up. Evan-Thomas did his best to reduce the gap by cutting corners, while the battle cruisers were working round to the north-eastward. Meanwhile, Alexander-Sinclair, who had correctly appreciated Beatty's intention to get between the enemy and his base, deliberately drew their cruisers north-westward. Napier, with the Third Light Cruiser Squadron, turned to support Alexander-Sinclair, and the Germans also conformed to the westerly movement.

The effect was that Beatty and Hipper were each denuded of a scouting screen in the direction it was most needed, and in consequence, at 3.25 p.m., the two hostile groups of battle cruisers suddenly found themselves in sight of one another. So the ring was cleared for the opening round of this titanic struggle. Both antagonists had met before, and both intended that this time it would be a fight to a finish. The enemy bore E.N.E. and were steering north-west. Beatty immediately turned east, and increased speed to 25 knots to try to keep between the German ships and their base. Hipper, observing this movement, reversed his course by turning in succession to starboard.

Both admirals now informed their respective Commanders-in-Chief by wireless of the situation. Beatty's report of the enemy, sent at 3.40 p.m., was further amplified four minutes later by the cruiser *Falmouth*, giving the latest details of Hipper's movements. Jellicoe, at this time, was about sixty miles to the north and Scheer fifty miles to the south, but neither yet knew that the other's battle fleet was at sea.

At 3.45 p.m. Beatty, who was rapidly closing Hipper, formed line of battle on a line bearing north-west from the *Lion*, on a course E.S.E., in the order *Lion, Princess Royal, Queen Mary, Tiger, New Zealand*, and *Indefatigable*. Meanwhile, the Fifth Battle Squadron had shortened its distance to about seven miles to the north-west and were pressing on at full speed.

Beatty says in his report: 'The visibility at this time was good, the sun behind us, and the wind south-east. Being between the enemy and his base, our situation was both tactically and strategically sound.' The visibility, as it happened, was extremely patchy. It was one of those typical North Sea summer days with a thin white mist varying in intensity and having too much humidity for the sun to break up. We have already seen how the seaplane found the cloud base no higher than 1,000 feet. Unfortunately, the western horizon was clear, so to the enemy the British ships were sharply silhouetted against a blue sky, and so also would be the splashes of German shells falling around them. Due to these conditions, the British range-finders gave readings far in excess of the actual range, which caused Beatty to hold his fire a little longer than necessary.

From the *Lion*'s bridge the dim outline of the German ships could be seen, but no details could be picked out. They were steering south-east in the order *Lutzow, Derfflinger, Seydlitz, Moltke, von der Tann*. At 3.48 p.m. the gun flashes of their first salvos rippled down their line, stabbing the haze, and a few seconds later the reassuring roar of the *Lion*'s first salvo rent the air. The shells from both sides fell well over the target.

Beatty, as advised by his gunnery officers, believed he had

opened fire at 18,000 yards, when in point of fact the range was only 15,500 yards, and both squadrons were closing rapidly. When the battle opened Hipper was steering S.S.E., with a flotilla of destroyers ahead of him. His cruisers, having been drawn westward by the *Galatea*'s action, were now well astern of him. Beatty was steering E.S.E., but on realising that the range had dropped to 15,000 yards, he turned parallel to the course of the Germans, thus holding his overlap to the south, at a good fighting range. Ahead of him were the *Champion* and destroyers of the 9th and 13th Flotillas, and also Goodenough, with the Second Light Cruiser Squadron, forming a screen to cover Beatty's van. This distinguished officer, with his great experience of cruiser work in war, had been carefully watching the situation. He had wisely refused to be drawn by the north-westerly movement of the First and Third Light Cruiser Squadrons, but had placed himself instead where the 'eyes' of his cruisers were most urgently needed—to watch the southern horizon.

The Germans found the range very quickly. Four minutes after opening fire, the *Lion* was hit twice. A minute afterwards the *Tiger* was also hit. Both sides made slight alterations of course to confuse the fire of their opponents. The Germans were undoubtedly enjoying more favourable visibility, which, with their world-famed optical instruments, they were quick to exploit. Von Hase, the gunnery officer of the *Derfflinger*, has remarked: 'At the longest distance I could make out all details of the enemy ships, as for instance all movements of the turrets and individual guns. . . . The north-west wind was blowing the smoke of the English guns between them and us.'[1] No such accuracy of detail was vouchsafed to any British observer. In support of this the German official account[2] justly remarks: 'At first the firing from the British ships was slow and uncertain owing to low visibility and unreliable range finding.' An impression of this stage of the battle from the British point of view can be obtained from the narrative of an eye-witness[3] on the *Lion*'s bridge, written a few days after the battle:

'The first German salvos fell well over us, but within four

---

[1] *Kiel and Jutland*, by von Hase, p. 152.   [2] German Official Account, p. 58.
[3] The biographer.

minutes we were hit twice. On the bridge we were blissfully ignorant of the fact that two large shells had exploded in the ship: the rush of wind and other noises caused by the high speed at which we were travelling, together with the roar of our own guns as they fired, four at a time, completely drowned the noise of bursting shell.

'There was no doubt, however, that we were under heavy fire, because all round us huge columns of water, higher than the funnels, were being thrown up as the enemy shells plunged into the sea. Some of these gigantic splashes curled over and deluged us with water. Occasionally, above the noise of battle, we heard the ominous hum of a shell fragment and caught a glimpse of polished steel as it flashed past the bridge. One of these went clean through the plotting room and dislodged the clock. It was a Service clock, however, and seeming to realise the importance of its duty, continued to tick merrily as if nothing unusual had happened!!

'By four o'clock the range had come down to 14,000 yards, and we were at close grips with the enemy. His fire was phenomenally accurate, and we were being hit frequently. I glanced aft over the upper deck and saw one of our boats on the booms going up in a cloud of splinters. We hoped the enemy was being similarly punished, but the five shadowy forms, with sporadic tongues of fire leaping from their guns, were apparently none the worse, and we could not tell what damage we were doing to them, as it was difficult to see the splashes of our shell in the white mist.

'At about this time a bloodstained sergeant of Marines appeared on the admiral's bridge. He was hatless, his clothes were burnt, and he seemed to be somewhat dazed: on seeing me he approached and asked if I were the captain. While directing him to the compass platform above my head, curiosity got the better of me, and I asked him what was the matter: in a tired voice he replied, "Q turret has gone, sir. All the crew are killed, and we have flooded the magazines".

'I looked over the bridge. No further confirmation was necessary: the armoured roof of Q turret had been folded back like an open sardine tin, thick yellow smoke was rolling up in clouds from the gaping hole, and the guns were cocked up in the air awkwardly. It was evident that Q turret would take no further part in the battle. Strange that all this should have happened within a few yards of where Beatty was standing, and that none of us on the bridge should have heard the detonation.

'But a naval battle is a strange experience—almost uncanny. Apart from the noise of gunfire, and the shrieking of the wind, events move so rapidly that the mind seems to lag behind. Fortunately for the *Lion* the mind of Major F. J. W. Harvey, R.M.L.I., the officer in charge of Q turret, did not lag behind when disaster came upon him. With his dying breath he gave the order to close the magazine doors and flood the magazines: the action taken by the turret's crew in response to this order immediately before they themselves were killed not only saved the ship, but enabled the defects in the system of protection of the ammunition supply to be brought to light afterwards. [For this great deed Major Harvey was awarded a posthumous V.C.]

'By a bit of bad luck the shell happened to strike the turret at the joint between the front armour plate and the roof plate. If it had struck either of these plates a direct blow, the thickness of the armour would have prevented any serious damage being done, but striking at the only weak point, the shell detonated inside the turret, killed the entire gun's crew, and caused a fire in the gun-house. This fire set alight some cordite charges which were in the cages for reloading the guns; the resultant flash passed down the trunk into the magazine handing room and thence escaped through the "escape trunk" on to the mess deck, where it finally dissipated itself.

'By the time the flash reached the handing room, the crew of the magazines had just closed the doors; some of them were found dead afterwards with their hands on the door clips. Their work was done, and the ship was saved.

'Everyone in the path of the flash was killed, including a Surgeon-Lieutenant and his stretcher party who were stationed just above the "escape hatch". The clothes and bodies of the dead men were not burned, and in cases where the hands had been raised involuntarily to protect the eyes, the parts of the face actually screened by the hands were not even discoloured, indicating that protection against cordite flash should be a matter of no great difficulty. [Measures were taken subsequently to provide this very necessary protection against flash.]

'While out on the bridge I took the opportunity to have a look down our own line. How magnificent our ships looked with their huge bow waves and flashing broadsides. Astern of the rear ship was a colossal pall of grey smoke. I gazed at this in amazement, and at the same time tumbled to the fact that there were only five battle cruisers in our line. Where was the sixth? What ship was absent? Could it be that cloud of smoke? The unpleasant truth dawned upon me that the cloud of smoke was all that remained of the *Indefatigable*. I glanced quickly towards the enemy. How many of them were afloat? Still five.'

The destruction of the *Indefatigable* was the first serious loss to the British. At 4.2 p.m. a salvo from the *von der Tann* struck her stern. An explosion followed, and she hauled out of the line. She was hit again near her fore turret, then there was another explosion, and she turned over and sank. Meanwhile Evan-Thomas had succeeded in closing the rear of the enemy, and at 4.8 p.m., in swift vengeance, the leading ships of the Fifth Battle Squadron opened fire, first on the *von der Tann* at a range of 19,000 yards, and four minutes later on the *Moltke* as well. The German Official Account says: 'The end ships of the German line were thus exposed to a regular hail of fifteen-inch projectiles, *von der Tann* being hit almost immediately'.

At 4.10 p.m. the *Lion*'s main wireless was shot away, but the *Princess Royal*, her next astern, was instructed to retransmit Beatty's signals passed to her visually, which inevitably caused some delay. The pressure on the British battle cruisers at this time was heavy, and to bring relief, Beatty ordered the 13th Flotilla and other destroyers favourably placed to attack the enemy with torpedoes. By 4.15 p.m. the destroyers were a mile ahead of the *Lion*, and moving over to attack. At about the same time Beatty, with traditional tenacity, boldly turned 45° towards the enemy to close the range, which had opened to 18,500 yards.

In spite of the loss of the *Indefatigable*, the situation at 4.20 p.m. began to look more favourable for the British. The whole Fifth Battle Squadron was rapidly coming into action. The enemy battle cruisers *Moltke*, *Seydlitz*, *von der Tann*, and *Lutzow* had all been heavily hit, and Beatty's destroyers were in a good position to deliver their attack. Beatty says in his despatch: 'From 4.15 p.m. to 4.43 p.m. the conflict between the opposing battle cruisers was of a fierce and resolute character. . . . Our fire began to tell, the accuracy and rapidity of that of the enemy depreciating considerably.' Speaking of the same phase of the action, Hipper says: 'It was nothing but the poor quality of the British bursting charges that saved us [the Germans] from disaster.'

Beatty's optimistic outlook, however, soon received another shock. At 4.26 p.m. a second catastrophe overtook his fleet. The *Queen Mary*, which, according to German accounts, had been shooting most effectively, suddenly blew up. She disappeared almost instantaneously in a huge column of grey smoke rising to a great height. While the *Tiger*, the next astern, was passing through this dense smoke cloud, observers were amazed to see vast quantities of official forms and sheets of paper whirling about. It was thought afterwards that these must have been suddenly released from an airlock which had formed in the offices situated in the stern of the stricken ship. Midshipman J. H. Lhoyd-Owen,[1] one of the survivors, described what he saw as he emerged from the after turret: 'An appalling scene greeted my eyes. I could see neither funnels nor masts. A huge column of black and yellow smoke shot with flame hung like a funeral pall over the forepart of the ship, casting a lurid glow over the scene. The masts and funnels had fallen inwards. . . .' While the survivors were in the water, salvos of heavy shell from the German battle cruisers fell around them, and after being rescued by the destroyer *Laurel*, the gallant little band took part in an action against the enemy battle fleet on that very night.

Chatfield, who was standing beside Beatty on the bridge of the *Lion* at the time of the disaster, says: 'We both turned round in time to see the unpleasant spectacle. . . . Beatty turned to me and said, "There seems to be something wrong with our bloody ships today", a remark which needed neither comment nor answer. There *was* something wrong. . . . Beatty was

---

[1] Now Commander J. H. Lhoyd-Owen, R.N.

ostensibly unaffected.' His main concern was still the destruction of the enemy, and this feeling of 'will to win' permeated every man under his command.

An incident which might have had serious consequences for those on the bridge occurred in the *Lion* about this time. A signal boy happened to see a large unexploded German shell lying close to a fire raging near the fore funnel. He reported to the signal officer (Seymour), who immediately ordered its removal, and a party of signalmen and boys rolled the dangerous object over the side—an action reminiscent of Beatty's gallant deed on the Nile.

According to individual records the officers and men in the remaining battle cruisers refused to believe that they had suffered more severely than the Germans. To those who were in a position to see both sides, the fact that five German battle cruisers remained afloat after two of the British battle cruisers had gone was a little disquieting, but the thought of retirement never entered anyone's head. Few of us had even fleeting glimpses of the action, and the general attitude of mind is well expressed in the following extract[1] from the diary of an officer in the Fifth Battle Squadron: 'We never dreamt that it was one of our own battle cruisers—but it was the *Indefatigable*, and over a thousand dead men lay in her wreck. The same thing occurred when we passed the wreckage and the survivors of the *Queen Mary*. Even when a man on some wreckage waved to us, we thought it must be a German wanting to be picked up. I have often thought since, how well it showed the confidence that we had in our own fleet that no one for a moment imagined that one of our own ships would be sunk so soon.'

Beatty grimly held his course S.S.E., keeping within effective range, and there was no slackening of the British gunfire, which was clearly beginning to tell. Although his squadron had been badly mauled, he knew that his ships had their teeth into the enemy and he did not intend to let go. At 4.28 p.m., shortly after the destruction of the *Queen Mary*, Hipper turned his squadron 56° away from Beatty, and from that moment no further damage was sustained by any British battle cruiser during the run to the south.

[1] *The Fighting at Jutland*, Lieuts. H. W. Fawcett and G. W. W. Hooper, R.N.

It is perhaps surprising that Hipper, knowing that he would very soon have the support of Scheer's battle fleet, should not have pressed in to exploit the success he had gained by sinking the *Queen Mary*. Apart from the fact that he was being heavily punished by the surviving British battle cruisers and the Fifth Battle Squadron, the explanation is that the British destroyer attack ordered by Beatty was now developing, and Hipper, following rigidly the orthodox counter accepted in both navies, made a broad turn away to avoid their torpedoes.

The British destroyers, led by Commander the Hon. E. B. S. Bingham in the *Nestor*, attacked with the greatest determination and courage. They were met by the German cruiser *Regensburg* and fifteen destroyers, and a fierce 'dog fight' took place between the lines, the ships engaging each other at point-blank ranges as low as 600 yards. In spite of having only twelve destroyers against the stronger German force, Bingham sank two of the enemy. He forced his way under heavy fire with the *Nestor*, *Nomad*, and *Nicator* to within 3,000 yards of the German battle cruisers, and fired ten torpedoes into their line. He was followed by the *Petard*, *Nerissa*, *Turbulent*, *Termagant*, and *Moorsom*, which made a second attack, and subsequently got in some shots at the van of the German battle fleet before retiring. The *Nestor* and *Nomad* were brought to a stop, and later sunk by the German battleships after the *Nestor* had fired her last torpedo at them. As a result of these attacks the *Seydlitz* was hit by one torpedo, but although she took in a good deal of water, she was able to hold her place in the line. The British destroyers attacked with such ferocity at so close a range that they were able to bring their small 4-inch guns into action against the big enemy ships. According to von Hase, in the *Derfflinger*, this was by no means a futile effort. 'They had damaged our wireless aerials and gunnery control wires. After the action, an officer found an unexploded 4-inch shell in his bunk.' The damage done by the guns of the British destroyers, however, had no effect on Hipper's tactics. It was the threat of their torpedoes that caused him to turn farther and farther away, and at 4.36 p.m. he was steering east, almost directly away from Beatty, thus breaking off the action. The Germans themselves admit: 'This attack [by the British destroyers], executed with great resolution, just at the sinking of the *Queen Mary* and immediately before the arrival of the German Battle Fleet, did much to relieve the pressure on the British line, as it forced the German battle cruisers to turn away *at the decisive moment.'* [Biographer's italics.][1]

Meanwhile, at 4.33 p.m., came the first news that the High Seas Fleet was at sea. Goodenough, in the *Southampton*, who was scouting some five miles ahead of the *Lion*, reported by searchlight that he had sighted the enemy battle fleet steering north.

This was the supreme moment of Beatty's career, and another split-second decision was required of him. The High Seas Fleet was not in the River Jade, as the Admiralty had believed. It was just over the horizon and steering straight for him. Thanks to Goodenough's cruiser screen ahead, Beatty was not taken by surprise. Jellicoe was hastening to his support from the north, and provided that Scheer could be tempted to hold his present course, a clash between the two battle fleets was inevitable. The responsibility of bringing about a fleet action in conditions favourable to the British Commander-in-Chief lay wholly in Beatty's hands. It was most unlikely that Scheer would know that the Grand Fleet was approaching, and it was Beatty's duty to keep him in ignorance, by preventing the German battle cruisers from sighting the Grand Fleet. Hipper, however, had temporarily broken off the battle-cruiser action, thus giving Beatty sufficient respite to locate the High Seas Fleet, and if possible lead it towards Jellicoe, sixty miles to the north. Beatty made good use of this opportunity, and steered for the *Southampton* to see for himself. Almost immediately a forest of masts and funnels appeared on the southern horizon, where the visibility happened to be clear. Without hesitation, Beatty, at 4.40 p.m., swung his battle cruisers round in succession 180° to starboard, to a northerly course, and settled down at full speed to close the Commander-in-Chief by the quickest route. As soon as he was steadied on his course to the north, Beatty reopened fire on the German battle cruisers, which had again come within range. At 4.45 p.m. the Fifth Battle Squadron was well in sight, coming down

---

[1] German Official Account, p. 78.

on the opposite course on Beatty's disengaged side (Diagram VII). Beatty's squadron at this time is described by a navigating officer in the Fifth Battle Squadron: 'The battle cruisers were

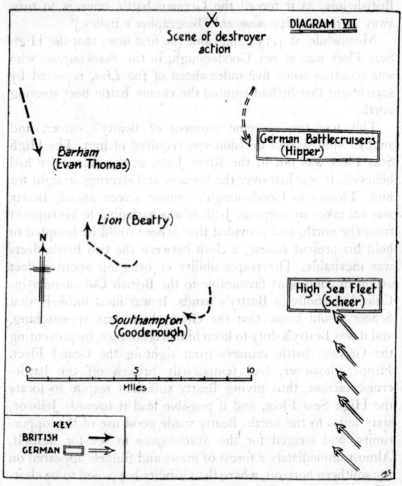

Battle of Jutland. Situation at 4.48 p.m.
Beatty sights High Seas Fleet, and retires to North, Goodenough in touch.
31st May, 1916.

a splendid sight as we passed them; they were firing fast and furiously in perfect station, with blank spaces of *Queen Mary* and *Indefatigable* filled up. They seemed as full of fight as ever.'[1]

[1] *The Fighting at Jutland,* Fawcett and Hooper.

Beatty warned Evan-Thomas by flags of the bearing of the enemy battle fleet, and at 4.48 p.m., just before the two squadrons came abreast of one another, he hoisted the signal ordering him to turn 180°. Evan-Thomas did not turn till 4.57 p.m., and this delay brought his squadron under the fire of the battleships in the van of the High Seas Fleet. On the other hand, he was able to give as good as he got.

With dramatic suddenness the scene had changed. Up to the moment when Goodenough sighted the High Seas Fleet, Beatty had no idea this mighty force was at sea, and now the Germans, in hot pursuit, were totally unaware that they were being led into Jellicoe's clutches. Hipper had thought earlier in the day that he was leading the British battle cruisers to certain destruction, but defeated his own object when he broke off the action to avoid the torpedo attack. Within a quarter of an hour the tide of battle had turned in favour of Beatty.

CHAPTER TWELVE

1916
THE BATTLE OF
JUTLAND—II

*The run to the north · Beatty achieves his object · Contact
with Jellicoe · Battle cruisers in the van · Final
encounter · Disappointment*

BEATTY had now accomplished faithfully and well the
first part of his task. He had located the German High
Seas Fleet, and his cruisers were keeping in touch with it.
Reports of the enemy's movements and composition of their
battle fleet were being passed to Jellicoe, now some fifty miles
away to the north. The *Lion's* wireless being out of action,
Beatty's report of the enemy at 4.45 p.m. had to be passed
through the *Princess Royal*, and was received by the Commander-in-Chief in a garbled form. It is important to remember
that the British battle fleet from Scapa and the Battle Cruiser
Fleet from Rosyth had been at sea for about seventeen hours
without establishing visual contact with one another. On
account of poor visibility, few ships of either force had succeeded
in fixing their position by celestial observation. The reports of
the enemy's position reaching the Commander-in-Chief from
various units of Beatty's force were therefore based on individual dead reckoning and inevitably lacked accuracy.

Beatty's next task was twofold. He had to get into visual
touch with Jellicoe as soon as possible, and he had at all costs
to prevent Hipper from sighting the Grand Fleet and giving
early warning to Scheer of its approach and disposition. Beatty,
knowing full well that Hipper would not venture far beyond
the close support of the German battle fleet, decided to make
as much distance as possible in advance of him, so as to be in a
favourable position to head him off before the British battle
fleet came on the scene.

The Battle of the Dogger Bank: '*Seydlitz* on Fire'
Photograph lent by Dr. Oscar Parkes, O.B.E.

The Battle of Jutland: '*Seydlitz* badly damaged'
From 'The Fighting at Jutland', by Fawcett and Hooper

The Fifth Battle Squadron, which was more than a match for the already damaged German battle cruisers, was well placed to cover Beatty's temporary retirement, and had sufficient speed to extricate itself from too close contact with the van of the High Seas Fleet. Moreover, the longer range of its 15-inch guns should have enabled Evan-Thomas to keep the leading battleships under fire, without dangerously exposing his own rear ships. Unfortunately, owing to the conditions of visibility, Scheer had the Fifth Battle Squadron in view before Evan-Thomas had sighted the High Seas Fleet, and the *Malaya* came under heavy fire at the turning-point. Nevertheless, the prospects for the British at that moment were bright, though success depended largely upon the visibility, which was very tricky. The remaining four British battle cruisers, *Lion*, *Princess Royal*, *Tiger*, and *New Zealand*, were in good shape, all their guns were in action, with the exception of two turrets. All four ships were under control and could maintain full speed. Morale was high; the knowledge of the loss of the *Indefatigable* and the *Queen Mary* was shared only by a few observers who kept it to themselves. This was fortunate, for if the vulnerability of the British ships had been generally known, the effect on the men might have been disquieting. Beatty knew, of course, but it made no difference to his conduct of the battle and the execution of the plan he had in mind. A lesser man than he might have acted differently.

The action continued on a northerly course with renewed violence, the *Lion* being hit twice without serious damage.

One of these hits, however, caused a temporary interruption to the navigation of the flagship, creating an embarrassing situation for the biographer, who says in his personal narrative: 'I was working on the chart in the Admiral's Plotting Room (immediately below the compass platform, where Beatty was standing) when I felt the deck under my feet give a sudden heave. At the same moment the chart table, over which I was leaning, split in the centre and the windows fell in, exposing the chart and myself to the full blast of a head wind.

'I placed both hands on the chart, but the wind was too quick for me, and before I could realise what had happened, the chart was torn in two, and the business half of it flew through the window. I last saw it fluttering over the sea like a frightened seagull.'

It transpired that a shell explosion had started a fire which had ignited some cordite charges lying near to the 4-inch guns underneath the bridge. Since this gun-deck was an open space, the cordite did not explode, but the gases were sufficiently compressed to cause the bridge to buckle slightly, and this in turn caused the chart table to split and the windows to fall in.

The narrative goes on:

'I climbed on to the compass platform and reported the incident to the navigating officer (Arthur Strutt), who was keeping the reckoning in his notebook, but could not leave the compass. He handed me the book and told me to get another chart and plot it all over again. D. B., who was standing beside him, having heard the order, turned to me and said, "Mind you get a check from the *Princess Royal* [our next astern]."' This was typical of Beatty's coolness and clarity of mind in the height of action.

The range was opening rapidly as the British battle cruisers raced northward to close the Grand Fleet, and at 5.12 p.m. the German fire ceased altogether. The Fifth Battle Squadron now bore the brunt of the action until 5.30 p.m., when it too drew out of range. Evan-Thomas had succeeded in the difficult tasks of keeping the German battle cruisers fully occupied, and also inflicting punishment on the van of their battle fleet.

The German Official Account states that the battleships *Grosser Kurfurst* and *Markgraf* and the battle cruisers *Lutzow*, *Derfflinger*, *Seydlitz*, and *von der Tann* were all hit. By this time all heavy guns of the *von der Tann* were out of action, but 'the captain decided to remain with the squadron so that the enemy, having to take this ship into account, would not be able to strengthen his fire against the other battle cruisers'. She was, in fact, nothing more than a helpless decoy.

While all this was going on, Goodenough, with the Second Light Cruiser Squadron covering the rear of the Fifth Battle Squadron, had remained in close touch with the enemy battle fleet: too close, in fact, for the visibility was poor, and he was determined to get full information about them. Thus, his four light cruisers came under the fire of ten German battleships for at least half an hour, at ranges varying from 14,000 to 20,800 yards. Goodenough, when asked later how he managed to avoid being hit, replied: 'Simply by steering straight for the splashes of the last enemy salvo!' the idea being that the next salvo was unlikely to fall in the same place. Anyway, the system worked successfully, much to the annoyance of Scheer, who wrote: 'Their vague and purposeless hurrying to and fro led one to think that our fire had reached them and that the action of our warships had so surprised them that they did not know which way to turn next.' He would have been even more irritated had he known that Goodenough was able, from this time onwards, to get through a continuous series of comprehensive wireless reports, giving to his Commander-in-Chief the strength, course, and position of the enemy battle fleet and battle cruisers.

At 5.26 p.m. Beatty, having decided that he had drawn far enough ahead of Hipper and that the time was ripe to head him off, signalled: 'Prepare to renew the action.' He then turned 45° to starboard, and at 5.40 p.m. opened fire on the enemy battle cruisers at a range of 15,000 yards. The Fifth Battle Squadron, still on its northerly course, also came into action on the enemy's quarter, the *Warspite* and *Malaya* continuing to engage the van of the enemy battle fleet.

The visibility had at last turned in Beatty's favour, enabling him to inflict heavy punishment. The *Lutzow* (Hipper's flagship) was hit twice with heavy shell; the *Derfflinger* was heavily hit in the bow at 5.55 p.m. and 'began to sink by the head owing to the inrush of water';[1] and the *Seydlitz* received several hits and was on fire. Seizing his advantage and determined that his adversary should not catch even a glimpse of the Grand Fleet, now about to come on the scene, Beatty relentlessly held his easterly course across the German van, bending back the head of their line, and forcing them, at 6.5 p.m., to retire under the cover of the guns of their own battle fleet (Diagram VIII). The Germans frankly acknowledge Beatty's success at this critical moment: 'Hard pressed in this way and unable to return the fire, the position of the German battle cruisers soon became unbearable.'[2] Hipper tried to relieve the situation by

[1] German Official Account, p. 89.   [2] Ibid., p. 89.

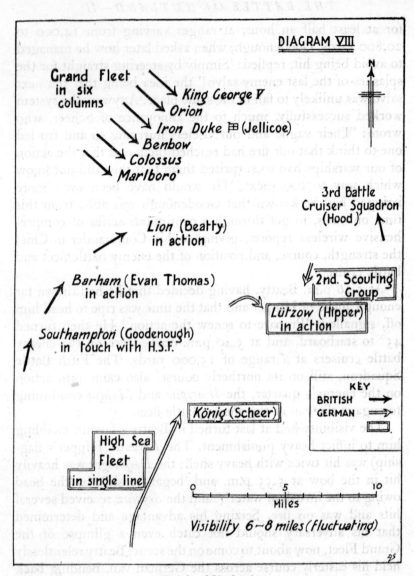

DIAGRAM VIII

N

Grand Fleet
in six
columns

→ King George V
→ Orion
→ Iron Duke ⊞ (Jellicoe)
→ Benbow
→ Colossus
Marlboro'

3rd Battle
Cruiser Squadron
(Hood)

Lion (Beatty)
in action

Barham (Evan Thomas)
in action

2nd. Scouting
Group

Lützow (Hipper)
in action

Southampton (Goodenough)
in touch with H.S.F.

KEY
BRITISH →
GERMAN ⇉

König (Scheer)

High Sea
Fleet
in single line

0   5   10
Miles

Visibility 6–8 miles (fluctuating)

Battle of Jutland.

*Situation at 6 p.m., showing Beatty forcing Hipper to retire and German
light cruisers retiring after action with Third Battle Cruiser Squadron.*

31st May, 1916.

ordering his destroyers to attack, but this move was frustrated by the sudden arrival, at 5.55 p.m., of Rear-Admiral Horace Hood with the Third Battle Cruiser Squadron, barely discernible in the banks of haze to the eastward.

This squadron, as will be remembered, had been at Scapa for gunnery practice, and when the Grand Fleet sailed, Jellicoe ordered it to take station well ahead on the Fleet's eastern flank. As soon as he learnt that Beatty was in action, he directed Hood to go immediately to his support. On account of differences in dead reckoning, Hood's course took him far to the eastward of the scene of action. In fact, he might easily have missed the battle altogether had not the light cruiser *Chester*, some six miles to the westward of him, stumbled into the Second Scouting Group of Hipper's light cruisers. Hood immediately came to her rescue, and within five minutes had damaged severely the *Wiesbaden*, *Pillau*, and *Frankfort*, before they escaped into the mist. The surprise appearance of the Third Battle Cruiser Squadron to the north-eastward drew away the German flotillas ordered to attack Beatty, and also prevented them from interfering with the deployment of the Grand Fleet. The Second Scouting Group, being taken by surprise, reported to Scheer that they had encountered 'several battleships' which caused him to miscalculate the position of the British battle fleet relative to himself.

Thanks to Beatty's offensive tactics and Hood's action, no German scouting forces were now sufficiently far advanced to give Scheer warning of the close proximity of the Grand Fleet. At 5.56 p.m., when Beatty was tenaciously forcing Hipper away from the direction of Jellicoe's approach, battleships of the Grand Fleet appeared suddenly on the *Lion*'s port beam about five miles distant. This contact was earlier than expected, and Beatty had achieved his purpose only in the nick of time.

In order to get a broader picture, we must go back two hours to see how the situation presented itself to the British Commander-in-Chief. At about 3.45 p.m., when he learnt that Beatty and Hipper had first joined action, Jellicoe ordered the battle fleet to proceed at twenty knots on a course south-east by south, towards the combat. His ships were in six columns, each in line ahead, with their leaders abeam of the Flagship.

There were four ships in each column, making a total of twenty-four battleships. The First Division, led by Vice-Admiral Sir Thomas Jerram in the *King George V*, was on the eastern flank (port wing). The Sixth Division, led by Vice-Admiral Sir Cecil Burney in the *Marlborough*, was on the western flank, while the Commander-in-Chief, in the Fleet Flagship *Iron Duke*, was at the head of the Third Division, just east of the centre. This arrangement was known as 'cruising formation', and was designed so that the divisions could quickly turn into single line of battle, by following their leaders in the direction ordered for deployment. Battleships, however, take some time to turn, and at least ten minutes must elapse while they move from cruising formation into line of battle. In misty weather, when gun range is greater than visibility, the Commander-in-Chief must exercise the finest judgment in deciding the direction in which to deploy, so that all his guns will bear on the enemy ships as soon as they appear. Time is the vital factor, because if caught in cruising formation, the Commander-in-Chief would be at a serious disadvantage. Early warning of the approach of the enemy battle fleet is therefore essential.

In the absence of Beatty's scouting forces, the Grand Fleet was screened ahead by a line of armoured cruisers of the *Defence* class. These ships, being out of date, lacked the speed for this duty. In consequence, they never succeeded in reaching their allotted stations, and were only six miles ahead of the battle fleet when the enemy was ultimately sighted.

The first intimation Jellicoe received that the High Seas Fleet was at sea came in the *Southampton*'s enemy report, despatched at 4.38 p.m., whereupon he informed the Admiralty and all concerned that a fleet action was imminent.

From this time onwards the *Southampton* continued to send a series of reports, from which the Commander-in-Chief learned the composition of the enemy fleet, that the German battle cruisers had closed their battle fleet, and that all were coming north towards him. These reports, however, when considered in conjunction with those from the *Lion* and *Champion*, were at variance in regard to the position of the enemy. Two more reports, based on direction-finding wireless, received from the Admiralty at 5.5 p.m. and 5.33 p.m., as it happened were fairly accurate. These also differed from the others, and Jellicoe was suspicious of them, partly on account of the erroneous information received from the Admiralty that morning, and partly because he considered that directional wireless was not always reliable. Apart from individual discrepancies, a constant and more serious error was the basic difference between the calculated position of the Grand Fleet and that of the Battle Cruiser Fleet. As already mentioned, the two forces, having set out from different bases some seventeen hours previously, had been subject to different conditions of weather and tide, and furthermore the Rosyth force had been in action for several hours, whereas the Scapa force had maintained a steady course for most of the time. It so happened that the *Iron Duke*, by her own reckoning, was four miles northwest of her true geographical position, and the *Lion*, by her reckoning, was seven miles east of her actual position. The accumulated error of the two Flagships was therefore about eleven miles in an E.S.E. direction, and since the *Lion* had not been sighted by any ships of the battle fleet, no one was yet aware of this large discrepancy. The general trend of all the reports, as plotted in the *Iron Duke*, led Jellicoe to expect that the enemy battle fleet would be sighted right ahead at about 6.30 p.m., if they held their present course. In other words, he believed them to be six miles farther eastward and about nine miles farther off than they actually were.

It came as a shock, therefore, when the cruiser *Black Prince*, occupying the extreme westerly position on the cruiser screen, reported at 5.42 p.m. that she had sighted the enemy battle cruisers five miles ahead of her. This screen, as previously mentioned, was only six miles ahead of the battle fleet, so the *Black Prince's* report, if correct, implied that the enemy battle cruisers were only eleven miles away, and well to the westward of Jellicoe. In fact, it placed them twenty miles farther northwest than the *Southampton's* reports had done. This appeared so improbable that the Commander-in-Chief correctly assumed that they must be our own battle cruisers. Confirmation came a few minutes later when the *Marlborough*, leading the starboard wing division of the battle fleet, reported that she could see the British battle cruisers on her starboard bow. Jellicoe quickly realised that the enemy fleet was much farther to the westward than he had been led to expect from the wireless reports. At 6 p.m. he sighted Beatty's battle cruisers about five miles distant, heading across his bows on an easterly course, hotly engaged with an unseen enemy. He asked the *Lion*: 'Where is enemy battle fleet?' but Beatty, being fully occupied at the moment trying to prevent Hipper from sighting the Grand Fleet, and being unable to see the High Seas Fleet, could only reply that the enemy battle cruisers whom he was fighting bore south-east.

Jellicoe, meanwhile, turned the leaders of his battle fleet columns together to starboard in order to make some ground to the west, which brought his divisions into echelon. Realising from Beatty's signal that the enemy might come into sight at any moment, instead of in twenty minutes' time as he had calculated, he resumed his original south-easterly course, which brought his column leaders abeam again and more handy for deploying into line of battle.

The visibility was about seven miles, and was appreciably less than gun range. It was, therefore, a matter of vital importance that the Grand Fleet should be formed in line of battle with all its guns bearing on the enemy fleet as soon as it appeared through the mist.

On a clear day, this would have presented no great difficulty, but the Commander-in-Chief could see only a curtain of mist and smoke ahead of him. Beatty's battle cruisers, shrouded in smoke, were still on his starboard bow, crossing from west to east, their gun flashes piercing the murk. Which way should Jellicoe turn? His first inclination was to turn to starboard (westward), as all the signs of battle were in that direction, but this manœuvre might place him at a serious tactical disadvantage, with his weakest ships in the van, impinging almost directly on the High Seas Fleet. He decided, therefore, to deploy to port, and keep between the enemy and their coast. Before committing himself, he still hoped for a report of the enemy's relative position from some British ship which had both fleets in view, for only then could he gauge the exact position of the enemy relative to himself.

The Fifth Battle Squadron at this moment was suitably placed to give the required information, but no report of any sort had come from them. A signal from Hood on the extreme eastern flank would also have helped, but he too was in action and had remained silent. In the words of the official historian:[1] 'No time was to be lost if the deployment was to be made in time. . . . Beyond a few miles, everything was shrouded in mist; the little that could be seen was no more than a blurred picture. Above all was the roar of battle, both ahead and to starboard. In this blind distraction Admiral Jellicoe had to make the decision upon which the fortunes of his country hung.'

Beatty, meanwhile, had forced Hipper back on Scheer's van, and while so doing sighted the enemy battle fleet. He immediately signalled: 'Have sighted enemy battle fleet bearing S.S.W.' This vital information reached Jellicoe at 6.14 p.m., and was confirmed a few minutes later by a report from Evan-Thomas. All doubts were now set at rest. Jellicoe ordered the battle fleet to deploy into single line ahead, with the port wing column leading, on a course south-east by east. This manoeuvre brought the ships of the starboard wing column into the rear of the line, and a few minutes later they came into action. Jellicoe in his despatch states: 'Firing was general in the battle fleet . . . only three or four ships being in sight at a time from the van and centre, although more were visible from the rear. Ships fired at what they could see when they could see it.'

It has been said that Beatty could have given Jellicoe some idea of the position of the enemy battle fleet when he first sighted the *Iron Duke*, but he was at that moment engaged in fierce combat with Hipper's battle cruisers, and at least an hour had passed since he had last seen the enemy battle fleet. An inaccurate or estimated report of their position at that critical moment might have done more harm than good. Some critics have gone so far as to suggest that Beatty should not have run out of sight of the High Seas Fleet. If he had adopted this course, he would have reached visual touch with Jellicoe much later than he did, and would not have been able to get far enough ahead of Hipper to ride him off. He knew that the Fifth Battle Squadron, covering his retirement, was in touch

[1] *History of Naval Operations*, Corbett, vol. III.

with the enemy battle fleet, and that it had the speed and gun power to look after itself. He also knew that Goodenough and his cruisers were providing the Commander-in-Chief with a constant flow of comprehensive and accurate reports. He did not and could not know that a combination of ill-luck and human error had caused the positions of the enemy to be calculated on a basis some eleven miles to the east of that of the Commander-in-Chief. In spite of this, however, it was Beatty's brilliant handling of the battle cruisers which gave Jellicoe those few vital extra minutes required for his deployment.

Nothing like enough credit has been given to Beatty for his masterly tactics in the critical half-hour before the two main fleets clashed. By foresight and strong offensive action he forced Hipper to retire, thus denying to the German Commander-in-Chief the vital information that the British battle fleet was not only uncomfortably close, but was actually deploying into line of battle across his bows, and placing him in a tactical position of great difficulty.

Full appreciation of Beatty's conduct, however, comes from the enemy, who frankly admits that Scheer had been placed in a 'tactically untenable position by an outflanking movement of Beatty's'. Scheer himself says that he was taken completely by surprise: 'Suddenly the German van was faced by the belching guns of an interminable line of heavy ships extending from north-west to north-east.'[1]

The situation was a desperate one for Scheer, who through Beatty's action and Hood's routing of the Second Scouting Group had blundered into the very situation he was so anxious to avoid, an embarrassment from which he never recovered.

At 6.36 p.m., on realising that his position was desperate, Scheer turned all his ships together 180° back to the westward and broke off the action. His simultaneous turn, which extricated the German battleships from a seemingly hopeless position, had not previously been considered practicable in the Royal Navy, and no counter-measure had been devised to meet it. By a brilliant and unforeseen manœuvre, Scheer had saved his fleet from almost certain destruction.

Meanwhile, at about 6.30 p.m., Beatty took up his allotted

German Official History, pp. 96 and 109.

[250]

position in the van ahead of the First Battle Squadron, as prescribed in the Commander-in-Chief's battle orders. In doing so, he had passed between the two battle fleets, and had some difficulty in avoiding collision with the armoured cruiser *Defence*, flying the flag of Rear-Admiral Arbuthnot, which was advancing to locate the enemy. A few minutes later this gallant ship met her doom through pressing in too close to the German battle line.

Evan-Thomas, when the Grand Fleet turned to deploy, was about five miles astern of Beatty. It was not possible for him, therefore, to follow Beatty to the van without masking the fire of the British Fleet, so he took up his alternative position in the rear of the line, as prescribed in the Battle Orders.

The Third Battle Cruiser Squadron, led by Admiral Hood in the *Invincible*, came into view on the *Lion*'s starboard bow and, having put to flight the Second Scouting Group, took up station about two miles ahead of Beatty. At the same time (6.25 p.m.) the German battle cruisers suddenly appeared out of the mist to starboard of Hood's Flagship, at a range of 9,000 yards. Hood immediately opened fire, and the shooting of his squadron is described by both sides as being magnificent, the *Lutzow* and *Derfflinger* being hit several times.

Hood pressed home his attack, and it was an inspiring sight to see this squadron of battle cruisers dashing towards the enemy with every gun in action. On the *Lion*'s bridge we felt like cheering them on, for it seemed that the decisive moment of the battle had come. Our feelings, however, suffered a sudden change, for just when success was in our grasp, the *Invincible* was hit by a salvo amidships. Several big explosions followed, great tongues of flame shot out from her riven side, the masts collapsed, the ship broke in two, and an enormous pall of black smoke rose to the sky. One moment she was the proud flagship full of life, intent on her prey; the next, she was just two sections of twisted metal, the bow and the stern standing up out of the water like two large tombstones suddenly raised in honour of a thousand and twenty-six British dead; an astonishing sight, probably unique in naval warfare.

Von Hase, who as gunnery officer of the *Derfflinger* was

responsible for dealing this terrible blow, says: '. . . At 6.29 p.m. the veil of mist in front of us split across like the curtain of a theatre. Clear and sharply defined we saw a powerful battleship . . . at 6.31 the *Derfflinger* fired her last salvo at that ship. Then for the third time we witnessed the dreadful spectacle that we had already seen in the case of the *Queen Mary* and *Defence*.'

Immediately afterwards, the German battle cruisers turned sharply away, disappearing into the mist. Beatty followed in support of the remaining ships of Hood's squadron, and while passing the wreck of the *Invincible*, observed some survivors on a raft who cheered the *Lion* as she passed. Their spirit remained unshaken by this dreadful experience, although their hope of rescue was slight. Fortunately for them the destroyer *Badger* happened to be near at hand, so Beatty ordered her to pick up survivors. Only six were saved, including the gunnery officer, Commander H. E. Dannreuther, and the torpedo officer, Lieut. C. S. Sandford. In the words of an officer of the *Badger*: 'The Commander (Dannreuther) was marvellously self-possessed. I can hardly understand to this day how a man, after going through what he had, could come on board from the raft as cheerily as if he was simply joining a new ship. . . . He had merely—as he put it—stepped into the water when the fore-top came down.'[1] Dannreuther attributed the disaster to one shell which penetrated the roof of the *Invincible*'s midship turret, bursting inside and causing two magazines to blow up. Had it not been for Major Harvey, the *Lion*, on an earlier occasion, would have shared the same fate (see p. 232).

In their encounter with Hood, the enemy battle cruisers had once again been heavily punished, and had conformed to Scheer's general retirement. The *Lutzow* had a heavy list, and her bows being deep in the water, she could take no further part in the battle. As his flagship was a wreck, Hipper left her at about 7 p.m. in the destroyer *G*39. He intended to transfer his flag to the *Seydlitz*, but found this impossible, as she was flooded up to the middle deck forward. It was not until 9 p.m. that he managed to board the *Moltke*, and resume command of

---

[1] Commander Dannreuther was in the fore-top directing the fire of the *Invincible* when the ship blew up.

his squadron. The *Derfflinger* was also in a sorry state, with all her signalling gear destroyed and water streaming in through a huge gap in her bows. Her captain, although he was not able to communicate with other ships, led the battle cruisers until Hipper could find a flagship. The *von der Tann*, as will be remembered, was ineffective, as all her turrets were out of action. Of the German battle cruisers which had started the day so hopefully, only the *Moltke* remained serviceable. But in spite of the damage they had sustained from British gunfire, they were all still afloat. How different was the story of the *Queen Mary*, *Indefatigable*, and *Invincible*; all three had disappeared beneath the waves after sustaining not more than five hits. Beatty's comment to Chatfield earlier in the day had proved to be regrettably true: there *was* something wrong with our ships.

By 6.40 p.m. Scheer had completed successfully the difficult manoeuvre of turning his long line of ships together 180° away from the solid phalanx of battleships with which Jellicoe had confronted him. Only the low visibility had made this possible, otherwise his whole line would have been raked by the overwhelming fire of the Grand Fleet. The turn had been very difficult to detect, as only a few German ships at a time had been visible to the British. Several British battleships, and the cruiser *Falmouth*, of the Third Light Cruiser Squadron, observed it, but not one of them told the Commander-in-Chief. Goodenough very soon saw the need to push in with the Second Light Cruiser Squadron towards the enemy, in order, as he says in his despatch, 'to observe the enemy's rear more closely, their course being in doubt'. Napier, with the Third Light Cruiser Squadron, was in a good position to observe the enemy's van, and was ordered later by Beatty to do so. This was essentially the light cruisers' task, but a delicate one, because in the existing conditions of poor visibility they would be subjected to the concentrated fire of the German battle fleet at the instant they came into view, as happened in the case of the *Defence*.

At 6.55 p.m. Scheer decided to make another thrust against the British line, and at the same time ordered his flotillas to attack. Just before he reversed his course, the British Second

Light Cruiser Squadron broke through the mist, and immediately came under a very heavy fire at close range from the German battleships. Goodenough, however, got off unscathed, and at 7.4 p.m. was able to give the vital information to the Commander-in-Chief that the enemy battle fleet was advancing on a course E.S.E. Jellicoe, meanwhile, had turned to the south and formed his divisions so that they would be across the enemy's line of approach. Scheer, therefore, for the second time found himself under a dense hail of shells to which he could only make a very feeble reply, and at 7.18 p.m. he was once again, after suffering heavy punishment, compelled to reverse his course and retire. This turn was observed by Goodenough, but his wireless report was not received by Jellicoe till 7.45 p.m. Owing to the fluctuating visibility, the British found it difficult to detect whether the sudden disappearance of the enemy ships was due to a thickening of the mist or to a turn away. At the same moment Beatty reported from the van that enemy destroyers were approaching. A massed torpedo attack on the battle fleet seemed imminent, so Jellicoe adopted the long-foreseen counter-measure of turning his fleet away from the approaching torpedoes, as previously proposed by him and approved by the Admiralty.[1] A turn of 45° to port in two parts was completed at 7.25 p.m., and at the same time the Fourth Light Cruiser Squadron, and half of the 11th Flotilla, advanced to break up the attack. A few torpedoes crossed the British line of battle, but these were avoided by individual ships.

At 7.35 p.m. the Commander-in-Chief turned back to south by west and formed single line, but the turn away had increased the distance from the enemy by at least 4,000 yards. Beatty at this time was steering south-west, about six miles on the starboard bow of the leading British battleship, *King George V* (Vice-Admiral Jerram). Beatty had not conformed to the easterly turn away of the battle fleet, and could still see what he believed to be the enemy's van (actually it was their battle cruisers). To quote his despatch: 'At 19.32 my course was 212° (S.W.), speed 18 knots, the leading enemy battleships bearing 291° (N.W. by W.). . . . The destroyers at the head of

---

[1] Letter from Commander-in-Chief to Admiralty, dated 30th October, 1914.

the enemy's line emitted volumes of grey smoke, covering their capital ships with a pall, and at 19.45 we lost sight of them.'

Beatty reported the position of the enemy at 7.40 p.m. and again at 7.45, giving their course as south-west. He wished to close the enemy van, but in the low visibility he felt, quite rightly, that it would be unwise to press into close range of the enemy battle fleet without battleship support. At this moment he was steering 23° nearer to the enemy than the leading British battleships, and from the *Lion*'s bridge, the van of the British battle fleet appeared to be steering too far to the east. He therefore made the following wireless signal to the Commander-in-Chief: 'Urgent. Submit van of battleships follow battle cruisers. We can then cut off whole of enemy's battle fleet.' This signal was transmitted at 7.47 p.m., but was not received in the *Iron Duke* till 7.54 p.m. The Commander-in-Chief, when he saw it about 8 p.m., immediately approved, but his signal ordering the Second Battle Squadron in the van to conform did not reach Jerram[1] till 8.10 p.m. In the twenty-three minutes which had elapsed since Beatty had made his request, the situation had changed completely, because in the meanwhile Jellicoe, at 8 p.m., had turned the whole battle fleet to the west, taking it nearer the enemy than the course Beatty was steering. In fact, when Jerram ultimately received the signal, the British battle cruisers were out of sight.

Beatty was fully justified in making the signal; the Commander-in-Chief's prompt approval and his order to the battle fleet to steer west goes to show that the two leaders in the height of battle were in complete accord.

Beatty now ordered his light cruisers to get into touch with the enemy before dark, and at 8.17 p.m. turned to the west in support. Almost immediately the German battle cruisers came into sight, and Beatty opened fire at a range of 10,000 yards. The enemy, being in no state to renew the action, retired to the westward under a heavy smoke screen, but not before they had suffered further damage. The *Derfflinger*'s last turret was put out of action, and the *Seydlitz* lost all her forebridge personnel. Hipper had just decided to board the *Moltke*, but

[1] Vice-Admiral Sir Thomas Jerram, K.C.B.

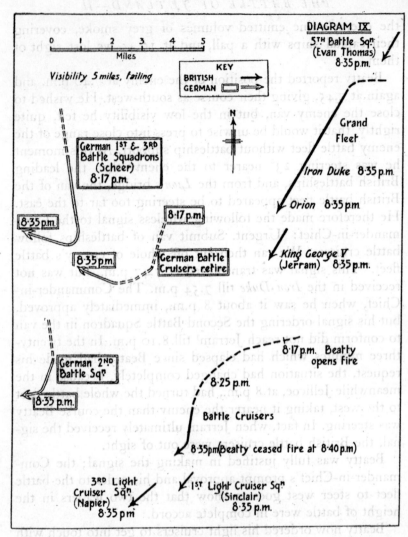

Battle of Jutland.

Situation between 8.17 and 8.35 p.m., showing Beatty's pressure on German van in last big-ship engagement.

31st May, 1916.

had to postpone doing so for another hour. She had 1,000 tons of water in her when he eventually got on board.[1]

Beatty next sighted the six pre-Dreadnought battleships of the German Second Squadron, which comprised the German van. These ships also turned away to the west after being fiercely engaged at 8,000 yards. This was the final encounter between capital ships, so Beatty had the honour of firing both the first and the last salvos in combat with capital ships in the Battle of Jutland—an achievement which speaks for itself.

Scheer, who was steering south with the main German battle fleet, on seeing the results of Beatty's action, turned once again to the west away from the direction of the German base. The Grand Fleet, steering west, was now about eight miles to the eastward of the High Seas Fleet, and Jellicoe, seeing the flashes of Beatty's guns, turned south-west to close the battle cruisers. This brought the Fleet again into line ahead, but the Commander-in-Chief could not see the enemy, and as firing died away at about 8.40 p.m., he asked Beatty for their bearing. There was unfortunately a hitch in transmission, and Beatty's reply did not get through till 9 p.m. Describing the situation at 9 p.m., Jellicoe says in his despatch: 'Darkness was now setting in; the mist was increasing, and it became necessary to decide on the future course of action. The British Fleet was between the enemy and its base. . . . I rejected at once the idea of a night action between heavy ships (as leading to possible disaster), first owing to the presence of torpedo craft in such large numbers, and secondly, to the impossibility of distinguishing between our own and enemy vessels. Further, the result of a night action under modern conditions must always be very largely a matter of chance. I was loath to forgo the advantage of position which would have resulted from an easterly or westerly course, and I therefore decided to steer to the southward, where I should be in a position to renew the engagement at daylight; I should also be favourably placed to intercept the enemy should he make for his base by steering for Heligoland or towards the Ems and thence closing the north German coast.

'Further, such a course enabled me to drop my flotillas

[1] *Life of Hipper*, von Waldeyer Hartz, p. 210.

astern, this at one and the same time providing the battle fleet with a screen against attack by torpedo craft at night, and also giving our flotillas an opportunity for attacking the enemy's heavy ships should they also be proceeding to the southward with the object of regaining their bases.

'Accordingly, at 9 p.m. the fleet was turned by Divisions to the south and formed in Divisions in line ahead disposed abeam to port, columns one mile apart, the object of the close formation being that the Divisions should remain clearly in sight of each other during the night in order to prevent ships mistaking each other for enemy vessels.'

Beatty, at 9 p.m., was midway between the two fleets, about six miles in advance of the leading battleships. In his despatch he says: 'I continued on a south-westerly course with my light cruisers spread until 21.24 [9.24 p.m.]. Nothing further being sighted, I assumed that the enemy were to the north-westward, and that we had established ourselves well between him and his base. . . . My position, course, and speed had been made to Commander-in-Chief at 19.40, 20.40, and 21.00, the latter signal giving the bearing of the enemy as N. by W., steering W.S.W., which, as near as could be judged, was correct.

'At 21.16 I received a signal from Commander-in-Chief that the course of the fleet was south.

'In view of the gathering darkness and for other reasons, viz.:

(*a*) our distance from the Battle Fleet,

(*b*) the damaged condition of the battle cruisers,

(*c*) the enemy being concentrated,

(*d*) our strategical position being such as to make it appear that we should locate the enemy at daylight under most favourable circumstances,

I did not consider it desirable or proper to close the enemy during dark hours.

'I therefore concluded that I should be carrying out the Commander-in-Chief's wishes by turning to the course of the Fleet, reporting to the Commander-in-Chief that I had done so. . . .

'My duty in this situation was to ensure that the enemy could not regain his base by passing round the southern flank of our forces.'

Sir Julian Corbett, in his *History of Naval Operations*, says: 'Nothing could have more nicely interpreted what was in Admiral Jellicoe's mind.'

Both Jellicoe and Beatty had gauged the position of the German fleet more or less correctly, *but not its course.*

Beatty, having continued on a south-westerly course for twenty-four minutes after the battle fleet had turned to the south, had passed in the darkness eight miles ahead of the van of the High Seas Fleet, which by now was also steering south, but he did not know it. At 10 p.m. the general situation was briefly as follows: the British battle fleet, steering south in cruising formation, lay eight miles E.S.E. from the High Seas Fleet, which was in line ahead, feeling its way on a south-easterly course towards the British rear. Scheer had sent all his destroyers to attack the British battle fleet, but they failed to locate it. The events of the night have been fully dealt with elsewhere, and since Beatty took no part in them they have no place in this narrative.

As is well known, Scheer made a third thrust to break through the British fleet, and this time he succeeded in passing astern of it and escaping home by way of Horns Reef. While doing so he was attacked by the British flotillas, and both sides suffered losses and damage. There were other encounters between light craft, notably a fierce night action at point-blank range between the Second Light Cruiser Squadron and Fourth Scouting Group, which took place five miles west of the *Iron Duke*, at about 10.30 p.m. Goodenough was well prepared, and answered their 'challenge' by opening fire. His flagship *Southampton* torpedoed and sank the *Frauenlob*, but there were many casualties on both sides.

This encounter was observed by the Commander-in-Chief and confirmed his belief that the enemy were still to the west of him, which indeed they were at that time. The *Lion*, throughout the night, was some ten miles south-west of the *Iron Duke*, and Beatty had no inkling of what was going on. He, like his Commander-in-Chief, still believed the enemy fleet to be to the north-westward, and was hoping to intercept it at dawn if Scheer attempted to approach his base by the southern channel. At 10.41 p.m. the Admiralty informed the Commander-in-

Chief that the German battle fleet had been ordered home on a course S.S.E. by E., which indicated that the enemy would make for Horns Reef. This information was discounted by

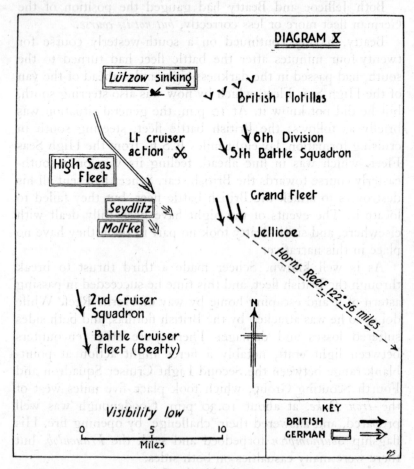

Battle of *Jutland*.

Situation at 11 p.m., *showing Scheer hauling across to pass round rear of Grand Fleet.*

31st *May,* 1916.

Jellicoe for reasons given in his biography,[1] and owing to the state of the *Lion*'s wireless, it was not received by Beatty.

The night was uneventful for the British battle cruisers.

[1] *The Life of Earl Jellicoe*, Admiral Sir R. Bacon, p. 289.

Nothing was sighted and nothing happened. They were too far distant to see the gun-flashes of the action taking place to the north-east while Scheer was forcing his way through the British flotillas. So, as all seemed to be quiet in the direction of the Grand Fleet, Beatty had no reason to alter his view that the enemy were to the north-west, and that the Grand Fleet lay between them and their base.

When he had last seen the enemy battle fleet just before dark, it was steering south-west, so at 4 a.m., having seen a Zeppelin heading west, he asked Jellicoe if he could make a sweep in that direction. Shortly afterwards, however, the Commander-in-Chief gave him the disheartening news that the enemy had returned to their base.

Beatty closed the battle fleet at 5.20 a.m. on 1st June, and then went off to look for enemy stragglers, notably the *Lutzow*, which was thought to be still afloat; actually she had been sunk by her destroyer escort. The captain of the *Lutzow* (von Harder) reporting the loss of his ship, says:

'After it became clear that it was not possible to save the ship, because she had 8,300 tons of water in her and was on the point of heeling over, I decided to send off the crew so as to save them from disaster. By 3.45 I had got them all, the wounded included, into the destroyers which had come along-side. I myself was the last to leave the ship after many enthusiastic cheers had been given for His Majesty the Kaiser, our leaders Scheer and Hipper, and the good ship herself. She was so down by the bows that the water came up to the control tower and the stern was right out. On my orders the ship was sunk by a torpedo fired by *G*38. She heeled over, and after two minutes swiftly sank with her flag flying.'

The *Seydlitz*, drawing forty-two feet of water, grounded first off Horns Reef and later in the Amrum channel. She had 5,300 tons of water on board, her bulkheads had given way, and she was only saved by the timely arrival of pumping ships from the dockyard.[1]

The power of the German battle cruisers to withstand punishment was the result of careful investigation initiated by Tirpitz before the war, and German thoroughness ensured

---

[1] *The Life of Hipper*, p. 220.

that the crews were trained to reduce the effects of damage to a minimum.

As the North Sea had been cleared of enemy ships, there was nothing more to be done, and the British Fleet set course for its bases.

In the forenoon of 1st June, all ships held a funeral service for those who had given their lives in the battle. The chaplain of the *Lion*, the Rev. C. W. Lydall, having been killed, the Flag Captain took the service. Beatty, deeply moved, stood on the poop behind Chatfield, while ninety-nine bodies of the flagship's company were committed to the deep, in the traditional manner of seamen.

In the afternoon Beatty came into the *Lion*'s chart-house. Tired and depressed, he sat down on the settee, and settling himself in a corner he closed his eyes. Unable to hide his disappointment at the result of the battle, he repeated in a weary voice, 'There is something wrong with our ships', then opening his eyes and looking at the writer, he added, 'And something wrong with our system'. Having thus unburdened himself he fell asleep.

The damage to the *Lion* brought to light for the first time how local the blast effect of high explosive could be, when restricted by compartments. This became common knowledge after experience of air bombardment in the Second World War, but at Jutland those of us who had seen great ships blow up as a result of a single hit were surprised to find after the battle the wardroom of the *Lion* in exactly the same state of tidiness as it was when we last saw it. In the early afternoon of the 31st, when the bugle called the ship's company to action stations, the wardroom servants had just completed laying the long table for 'seven-bell tea'. Some fourteen hours later the furniture was found to be still intact. The cups, saucers, and plates of cake were all in proper array, and even the flowers stood proudly in their vases, as if in defiance of the death and devastation that lay on the other side of the bulkhead.

The navigating officer was less agreeably surprised, on reaching his cabin, to find that a large shell had passed right through it, causing a fire of such intense heat that everything was pulverised except the steel heads of his golf clubs, huddled together in the corner where the bag had rested.

The Battle Cruiser Fleet reached Rosyth at 9 a.m. on 2nd June, sadly conscious of the gaps in their line. Nevertheless, the morale of the Fleet was high. The ships' companies had supreme confidence in their leader, and all who had been at close grips with the enemy had seen the German ships retreat as soon as they began to get the worst of it. They knew that the German battle cruisers were a spent force, whereas Beatty had still got six battle cruisers ready for action, while the battle fleet had suffered no loss. It is indeed a remarkable fact that, with the exception of the ships of the Fifth Battle Squadron, only one British battleship had been hit by an enemy shell. Above all, everyone knew that the High Seas Fleet had quitted the battlefield and steered for home, rather than fight to a finish on the following day.

They were fully justified in their optimism because, as the world knows, the High Seas Fleet made no further attempt to challenge the Grand Fleet in battle. In the words of a German naval critic, Captain Persius, written on 18th November, 1918: 'Our Fleet's losses were very severe. On 1st June, 1916, it was clear to any thinking person that this battle must, and would be, the last one.'

After arrival in harbour, Beatty's Flag-Lieutenant, Ralph Seymour, sent the Admiral's flag to Lady Beatty with a short note reminding her of the significance of this historic emblem:

6th June, 1916

MY DEAR LADY BEATTY,

I send you the flag flown by Sir David at the foremast head of the *Lion* during the action of 31st May. I send it you just as it was hauled down on our return to harbour, torn by the wind and dirtied by the smoke. I thought you would like to have it, as it is a thing which should be preserved as an emblem from which the enemy have invariably fled.

Rear-Admiral O. de B. Brock, who commanded the First Battle Cruiser Squadron, wrote on 7th June, 1916:

MY DEAR LADY BEATTY,

I meant to have written before this to tell you how thankful I am that David has come out safely; his life is worth the whole Battle Cruiser Fleet.

The way in which he led us into action was magnificent, and to fight under such a leader is a privilege given to few. My heart is full, and you may well be proud of such a husband.

Lord Charles Beresford wrote to Beatty on 9th July, 1916:

I have read the C.-in-C.'s despatch. Again let me express to you my unbounded admiration for your brilliant performance in the greatest naval battle of all time. How splendidly you were supported by those under your command.

If it had not been for your consummate skill (as the C.-in-C. states), there would have been no battle.

May you have another chance of adding to the glory of the British Navy.

CHAPTER THIRTEEN

1916–1917
THOUGHTS ON JUTLAND

Some controversial points · Lessons of the battle · Scheer
puts to sea again · Beatty becomes Commander-in-Chief.
Revision of the Battle Orders

THERE has been much controversy about the Battle of
Jutland. This was inevitable, as never before had two
such powerful fleets, armed with the products of modern
science, been ranged against one another in mortal combat.
Owing to conditions of visibility and the lateness of the hour,
no decision was reached before the German Fleet, by skilful
manœuvring, finally escaped from the scene of battle, leaving
the British Fleet, with an ample margin of strength, in full
control of the North Sea. The test of battle brought to light
defects in the system of command, tactical doctrine, ship construction, and armament hitherto undetected on account of
insufficient war experience and the absence of an adequate
system for studying the problems of war.

When things do not go quite right, people look for a scapegoat, and so, not for the first time in British history, the man
selected was the Commander-in-Chief. Beatty also came in for
a share of malicious criticism and calumny, although he had
defeated his antagonist in sustained action, and could not be
called to account for the design of the British battle cruisers.

After the war, with the inevitable post-mortem, the controversy reached its height because the bird's-eye view depicted
on diagrams could not always be identified with the situation
as seen by those in command when they made their decisions.
Owing to low visibility, no two commanders got the same view
of the action, and although 250 ships took part, there were
never more than three or four enemy capital ships in sight at
the same time from any point in the British line. Generally

speaking, the chief criticisms of Jellicoe's conduct of the battle were that he was over-cautious, that his control of the Fleet was too rigid, and that the battle orders which he had carefully prepared were likely to lead to an indecisive result. In the conditions prevailing, with the information available to him, he had reason to be cautious. He did not know what was going on behind the curtain of mist. It seemed to him at the time that he would be throwing away his superiority in numbers if he became involved in close action, when only a portion of his fleet could see the enemy. The rigid control of the Fleet was more a result of a system evolved from pre-war exercises, where artificial conditions tended to obscure situations which might occur in battle. Some critics have inferred that if Beatty had been in command the result would have been different, but Beatty too had an adequate amount of caution in his nature and, as we have seen from his despatch, he agreed with his chief that it would have been unwise to engage in night action with heavy ships. On the other hand, we know that Beatty's tactics in the gruelling test of the battle-cruiser action were governed throughout by the old principle, 'Keep nearer to the enemy'.

There grew, unfortunately, a tendency for the names of Jellicoe and Beatty to become associated in the public mind with two different camps of naval opinion. Self-appointed champions poured forth a stream of calumny and uninformed criticism upon one or other of the two admirals. This was deplorable, and gave a totally false impression of the relationship which actually existed between the two men. Like all great men, they had their differences, but no one could question Beatty's loyalty to his chief while he served under his command, and afterwards.

Having played the preliminary moves which led to contact between the main fleets, Beatty was naturally disappointed at the inconclusive result of the battle, but this did not lead him into paths of acrimony or public controversy. The Commander-in-Chief, having sensed Beatty's feelings, expressed his sympathy in his despatch:

'Sir David Beatty once again showed his fine qualities of gallant leadership, firm determination, and correct strategic insight. He appreciated the situation at once on sighting first the enemy's lighter forces, then his battle cruisers, and finally his battle fleet. I can fully sympathise with his feelings when the evening mist and fading light robbed the Fleet of that complete victory for which he had manœuvred and for which the vessels in company with him had striven so hard. The services rendered by him, not only on this, but on two previous occasions, have been of the greatest value.'

It is a measure of Beatty's greatness that he forbore to reply to his critics, being content to abide by the judgment of his countrymen and history.

Amid the general chorus of emphatic approval there were a few adverse comments on his leadership of the Battle Cruiser Fleet which, in justice to him, cannot be overlooked. Some of these have already been dealt with in the narrative, but there are others having wider implication, which must be treated separately.

It has been suggested that because the British lost two battle cruisers and the Germans lost none, Beatty was defeated by Hipper in the first phase of the battle. The question of victory or defeat is not a matter of material gain or loss; it is a question of which of the two antagonists achieved his purpose. This can best be answered in Beatty's case by summarising very briefly the results of his tactics.

His first task was to locate the enemy battle fleet. In this he succeeded, in spite of Hipper's efforts to prevent him.

His second task was to keep touch with the enemy battle fleet. His light cruisers did so.

His next task was to prevent Hipper from locating the British battle fleet. Beatty succeeded in this by fierce and determined action, in spite of having previously lost two of his ships.

A tribute to Beatty's tactics at this stage comes from the enemy. von Hase, the gunnery officer of the *Derfflinger*, writes: 'Actually Admiral Beatty, by completely outflanking us, in spite of our high speed, accomplished an excellent tactical manœuvre, and his ships carried out an admirable feat of technique. He accomplished the famous "crossing the T", compelled us to alter course, and brought us into such a position that we were completely enveloped by the English battle fleet and battle cruisers.'[1]

His final task was to take up his position in the van of the British line of battle, in accordance with the Commander-in-Chief's plan. In this he also succeeded, and before night fell, when the opportunity came, he led the battle cruisers into effective range, and again forced the enemy van to turn away, although in the meantime he had seen yet another of his vulnerable ships blow up.

In general, he achieved his purpose at every turn, and his victory over Hipper was complete. It is difficult to see how he could have done more.

The question has been asked, why did Beatty, in his preliminary disposition, station the Fifth Battle Squadron at so great a distance as five miles from him?[2]

In the prevailing conditions of visibility, five miles, as it happened, was the correct distance to enable Beatty to get Hipper to commit himself to action before Evan-Thomas appeared on the scene. If Beatty had placed the Fifth Battle Squadron any closer, they would have become part of his own fleet. Hipper, on finding himself confronted with such a superior force, would certainly have refused action, and there might not have been a battle at all. The Fifth Battle Squadron was a supporting force, and neither the Commander-in-Chief nor Beatty had ever intended it to be used as an integral part of the Battle Cruiser Fleet until battle was joined. In his despatch Beatty gives Evan-Thomas full credit for his 'brilliant and effective support'.

Arising out of the loss of the *Indefatigable*, *Queen Mary*, and *Invincible*, and the apparent inability of the British to produce similar instantaneous results against the enemy, critics have said that the gunnery of the British battle cruisers was of a low standard. Apart from the fact that this statement has been repudiated by the enemy, the data is too scanty and the conditions too variable to compare with any accuracy the shooting in battle of one squadron of the British Fleet with any other squadron. The gunnery officers of the Battle Cruiser Fleet had the highest qualifications and ability, and the gun crews were

---

[1] *Kiel and Jutland*, von Hase.   [2] See p. 225.

trained up to the same high standard as the rest of the Grand Fleet. Beatty himself took the keenest interest in gunnery progress, and was advised by Chatfield, who, in the course of his career, held most of the important gunnery posts in the Navy.

It is true that the ships based at Rosyth, on account of lack of defended water space, did not enjoy the same facilities for full-calibre practice as the ships at Scapa Flow, but this was partly remedied by periodical visits to Scapa by the battle cruisers.

In one of Beatty's private letters to Jellicoe, written three weeks before Jutland, he gives the Commander-in-Chief his views on the recent firings, and he comments adversely on the shooting of one of his battle cruisers, stating the measures he intends to take to improve it. Beatty did not take lightly his responsibility for the gunnery efficiency of his squadron.

According to the German Official History, Appendix 8, the hits received by the British and German battle cruisers were:

Lion	12	*Lutzow*	24
Tiger	17	*Derfflinger*	17
Princess Royal	9	*Seydlitz*	21
Queen Mary	5	*Moltke*	4
Indefatigable	5	*von der Tann*	4
Invincible	5		

We can assume that the hits on the German ships are assessed on the low side, especially as it would be difficult to count up the hits by 'shell of poor quality', which, according to the Germans, exploded on impact and did not penetrate the armour. The German assessment does not include the *New Zealand*. Although this ship fought gallantly in all Beatty's battles, she was only hit once and suffered very little damage.[1]

This is not the place to analyse the percentage of hits on the

---

[1] Shortly before the war, when the ship was visiting New Zealand, a Maori chief presented her captain with the traditional grass kilt of his race. During the ceremony he prophesied that the *New Zealand* would take part in a great battle, but no harm would come to the ship if the captain wore the kilt. Captain J. F. E. Green, who commanded the ship in the war, respected the superstition, and always wore the kilt over his uniform when the ship was in action.

enemy obtained by the British battle cruisers in the course of the day. There exists, however, a booklet written by a clergyman and scientist who made the attempt in genuine search of the truth:[1] This publication, and the German *Der Krieg zur See*, 1914–1918, *Nord See*, vol. V, para. 108, give a high estimate of the shooting of Beatty's battle cruisers.

Pastfield himself wrote, on 11th April, 1936, after Beatty's death: 'I think *New Light on Jutland* was as a *Nunc Dimittis* to Beatty. After what he went through at Jutland and the campaign of vilification to which he was subjected by some who preferred personalities to getting at the facts, I think *New Light* came as the shadow of a great rock in a weary land.

'I was in South Norway when Jutland was fought, within sound of the guns, and from the information which I made it my business to get, I was certain that when the German reports and histories were published they had concealed a great deal. Having a keen insight into German mentality through an exhaustive study of *Modernism*, I was able to see clues which others missed, and finally, after years of patient research, was able to publish *New Light* . . . the vindication of one of the world's greatest heroes. To carry on as Beatty did after ship after ship was blown up stamps him, as, to my mind, greater even than Nelson (this may be heresy, but I stick to my heresy). He was not merely a dour fighter, his courage was of the same order as his strategic insight.'

The Germans, in their official history, say that both the *Queen Mary* and *Invincible* were shooting magnificently before they blew up. The *Queen Mary*, in the competitive firings just before the war, held first place in the Navy, and so had the reputation of being one of the best shooting ships in the Fleet. The *Invincible* had only just completed her firing practice with the Grand Fleet at Scapa. The best gunnery in the world would not have prevented these ships and the *Indefatigable* from blowing up after receiving only five hits. The cause lay, not in the quality of British gunnery, but in defective design, which was a matter quite outside Beatty's control.

On the German side, Tirpitz had directed that their capital ships should be 'unsinkable gun platforms', and no design was

[1] *New Light on Jutland*, the Rev. J. L. Pastfield, M.A.

approved for final construction until after exhaustive experiment and test. He held the view that a ship, no matter how heavily damaged in battle, could always be repaired, provided that she could reach port, and how right he was. Jellicoe, in his despatch, says: 'The facts which contributed to the British losses were first, the indifferent armour protection of our battle cruisers, particularly as regards turret armour and deck plating, and second, the disadvantage under which our vessels laboured in regard to the light. Of this there can be no question.'

It is now generally recognised that the Germans were superior to the British in the quality of their optical instruments, their magazine protection, the watertight subdivision of their ships, and their shells.

In spite of these disadvantages and his own surmise of their existence early in battle, Beatty never wavered in his offensive action against Hipper at the decisive moment. The 'will to win' of the British ships' companies was strong enough to enable their leader to achieve his purpose at all times, in spite of the weakness in material. In general, it is fair to assume that if the British battle cruisers had been as well and stoutly built as the German, the relative losses would have shown a great superiority in the fighting ability of the British Fleet.

The allegation that the British light cruisers failed to keep touch with the enemy battle fleet after the main fleets had become engaged, thus depriving their Commander-in-Chief of a clear picture of the situation, is a fair criticism. On the other hand, the German Commander-in-Chief was no better served by his scouting forces. His so-called 'blows' at the Grand Fleet were delivered blindly, and on each occasion during daylight he was compelled to make a hasty retreat, thankful for the mist that covered him. If British cruiser work had been perfect, this 'safety curtain' would have afforded him no sanctuary. Perfection, however, can only be achieved by constant practice, and although the British cruisers had been frequently exercised in their duties with the battle fleet in tactical exercises, the actual conditions of a fleet action in low visibility had never before been experienced, and, wireless organisation being in an early stage of development, signals took time to get through. The British cruisers did their work well in locating the enemy in the first place, but with the notable exception of Goodenough's squadron, they did not maintain touch with the High Seas Fleet after battle was joined—a most difficult task in low visibility, as light cruisers cannot remain long within sight and gun range of a hostile battle fleet. The gallant Arbuthnot, in a single-minded effort to accomplish this dangerous feat with the heavy cruisers *Defence* and *Warrior*, was frustrated because the *Defence* blew up under his feet and the *Warrior* was put out of action in the space of a few minutes. These ships, however, being slow and cumbersome, were quite unsuited for such work, whereas the light cruisers, with their easy manœuvrability, were specially designed for it. Goodenough's handling of them from the time the enemy was first sighted, throughout the period of the battle to the moment when he conducted a successful night action against an enemy cruiser squadron, is universally regarded as being exemplary. It is significant that Goodenough was the only cruiser leader who had fought with Beatty in all his previous engagements, and had learnt, through war experience in North Sea conditions, exactly how to interpret his intentions.

At Heligoland and Scarborough, in the early days of the war, there had been misunderstandings arising from mistakes in signals. It soon became evident to Goodenough, however, that he had the full confidence of his chief, and was expected to use his own initiative in applying correctly the principles of cruiser work, which had been agreed and understood.

Beatty's views on the employment of cruisers in battle are contained in the following extract from his Battle Cruiser Orders: 'It is of paramount importance that an enemy force, once brought into action, should not escape in fog, under a smoke screen, or in gathering darkness. . . . It therefore becomes the duty of subordinate leaders to anticipate executive orders and act in the spirit of the Commander-in-Chief's requirements. There are only two, and they are simple: so long as the enemy heavy ships remain afloat, we must "locate and report", "attack and destroy". But to perform either duty without the other is to fall short of that co-ordination which ensures success; nor should it be thought that to perform one efficiently it is necessary to abstain from the other.'

Commanding officers who had served under Beatty in action soon came to learn that they could do no wrong in his eyes if they did their utmost to bring about, directly or indirectly, the destruction of the enemy.

It was a matter of extreme urgency after the battle to analyse the lessons learnt. The staffs of Jellicoe and Beatty worked day and night in close co-operation and harmony to achieve this end. Apart from tactical matters, the chief problems to be solved were how to improve the quality of the projectiles and also how to protect the ships against cordite explosion. Chatfield, working closely with Dreyer[1] and strongly supported by the Commander-in-Chief and Beatty, succeeded in getting the Admiralty to carry out experiments without delay. 'These trials (of the shell) exposed a situation so disturbing as seriously to affect the fighting power of the Fleet.'[2] The story of how the Navy eventually got its new shell is told in Lord Chatfield's book and need not be repeated. The vulnerability of magazines caused grave anxiety, but the evidence obtained from the *Lion* and other ships enabled certain preventive measures to be taken against cordite flash penetrating the magazines. It was too late, unfortunately, to make any change in armour protection, although ships under repair and in construction were slightly improved in this respect.

* * * * *

There was no sign of activity on the part of the German High Seas Fleet until August 1916, when the presence of enemy submarines taking up strategic dispositions in the North Sea became known to the Admiralty. On the night of 18th August, Scheer once again put to sea in support of a raiding operation against the Yorkshire coast. The Grand Fleet, having been warned by Admiralty Intelligence, left their bases about the same time, concentrating at daylight with Beatty's battle cruisers thirty miles ahead of the Battle Fleet on a southerly course. It is clear from Scheer's orders that he had no intention of committing himself to a fleet action, but hoped, as before,

---

[1] Captain F. C. Dreyer, C.B., Flag Captain to the Commander-in-Chief, and afterwards Director of Naval Ordnance.
[2] *The Navy and Defence*, Lord Chatfield, p. 154.

to draw the British forces across a submarine network. Perfect weather enabled the High Seas Fleet to advance with caution behind a screen of Zeppelins, which in due course warned him of the British approach. At 2 p.m., when Beatty, with his ships prepared for battle, was only about forty miles away, the German Fleet turned and fled for home. Scheer's plan, however, succeeded in one respect: his submarine traps were well laid, causing the Grand Fleet an anxious return passage. The signal 'submarine in sight' was flying almost continuously at the yard-arm of one or other of the British ships, and two of Beatty's light cruisers, the *Nottingham* and *Falmouth*, were torpedoed and sunk. On the other hand, the German battleship *Westfalen* was hit by a torpedo from a British submarine, but, in keeping with the German tradition of unsinkability, she was able to return to harbour without assistance.

One may wonder why the Germans who, by this time, must have known that they excelled in ship construction and material, did not venture upon another trial of strength with the British Fleet. The explanation is simple enough: the high quality of the British personnel, especially under stress, was known to the enemy and had been proved in battle. The spirit of the Grand Fleet, in spite of two years of monotonous waiting, compared well with that of Nelson's men in their weary months at sea before Trafalgar, and Jellicoe and Beatty will ever be associated with the maintenance of this heritage. After the battles of Heligoland and the Dogger Bank, the name of Beatty was just as great a bogy to the German sailor as Drake had been to the Spaniards. Even at Jutland, although the German ships remained afloat throughout the battle, the punishment they received from the Battle Cruiser Fleet was sufficient to damp their enthusiasm for another encounter. Subsequent events leading to mutiny in the High Seas Fleet demonstrated to the world how much the British seaman was feared. This truth is inescapable.

* * * * *

In the latter part of 1916, British merchant-ship losses from enemy submarine attack increased to an alarming extent, and Jellicoe was appointed First Sea Lord to cope with the danger. He was succeeded as Commander-in-Chief, Grand Fleet, on

27th November, by Beatty, with the acting rank of Admiral. The transfer took place at Rosyth, the First Lord of the Admiralty, Mr. A. J. Balfour, travelling north to confer with the two admirals and to explain the reasons for the change. Thus, at the age of forty-five, when most of his contemporaries were still on the captains' list, Beatty took over the command of the most powerful fleet the world has ever seen or is likely to see again. He chose as his flagship the modern *Queen Elizabeth*, because she had the speed to enable him at short notice to get to the most favourable position for exercising supreme command in battle. During the three months while his new flagship was being refitted and equipped for her duty, Beatty flew his flag in the *Iron Duke*, thus providing an opportunity for the officers and men who had worked close to Jellicoe to get to know his successor. It did not take long for Beatty's magnetic personality and power of leadership to be felt by the whole Fleet. Alexander-Sinclair[1] writes: 'At the first meeting of Flag Officers on board *Iron Duke* at Scapa on his taking command, Beatty was the youngest man in the cabin, and some, I think, were senior in the service to him. Before the meeting there was evidently a good deal of tension, but his tact and manner generally at the meeting killed any jealousy or doubt that may have existed, and everyone left in high spirits. He was a natural leader.'

As Beatty's promotion to acting-admiral took him over the heads of eight vice-admirals, one or two changes in Flag appointments within the Fleet became necessary. Sir Cecil Burney was relieved in the command of the First Battle Squadron and also as second-in-command of the Grand Fleet by Vice-Admiral Sir Charles Madden, who had been Jellicoe's Chief of Staff. This was an excellent appointment, indicating continuity of policy and loyalty to the new leader. Vice-Admiral Sir Thomas Jerram, commanding the Second Battle Squadron, was relieved by Sir John de Robeck, of Dardanelles fame. Vice-Admiral Sir Doveton Sturdee, the victor of the Battle of the Falkland Isles, preferring to waive his seniority rather than miss the chance of another battle, requested that he might remain in command of the Fourth Battle Squadron.

[1] Rear-Admiral E. Alexander-Sinclair, C.B., M.V.O.

Beatty gladly agreed, the sentiment being so much after his own heart. Rear-Admiral W. C. Pakenham succeeded Beatty in command of the battle cruisers, which, being reduced in numbers, were reorganised under the title Battle Cruiser Force.

Rear-Admiral O. de B. Brock, from the First Battle Cruiser Squadron, became Beatty's Chief of Staff. Chatfield continued to be Flag Captain, commanding the *Iron Duke* and later the *Queen Elizabeth*. Captain the Hon. Hubert Brand took over the duties of Captain of the Fleet, being responsible for administration and supply. Beatty's old staff accompanied him to the Grand Fleet with the exception of Bentinck, who was later given command of the Fourth Light Cruiser Squadron, and Plunkett, who, on promotion to Captain, took command of the minelaying cruiser *Blanche*.

Captain the Hon. Arthur Strutt, Beatty's navigator at Jutland, became Master of the Fleet. Jellicoe offered to leave behind any members of his own staff whom Beatty might require. This offer was gladly accepted, and several 'key' positions, such as Fleet Wireless Officer and Staff Officer Operations, were filled by officers with experience of the Grand Fleet.

Very shortly after Beatty had taken over the command, Chatfield came to him with the disturbing news that no annihilating victory over the German Fleet was likely until all the existing shell had been replaced by a more effective type.[1] Beatty, as Commander-in-Chief, thought only in terms of annihilation, but it would be necessary literally to pound enemy ships all day with 'dud' shell, as had been done at Jutland, before they could be put out of action. Even with superior numbers, it was doubtful if there would be time to destroy the enemy during daylight in North Sea conditions. Beatty summoned his Flag Officers on board the *Iron Duke*, and after explaining the position to them, directed that on no account must the Fleet be told this unpalatable truth. Dreyer had stated that the Admiralty hoped to re-equip the Fleet with effective shells before the summer of 1918. This meant that Beatty had to endure the thought that the next battle, like its predecessor, might be inconclusive. The crushing victory at which he aimed was now more difficult to achieve. He showed

[1] *The Navy and Defence*, Lord Chatfield, p. 156.

no sign of being depressed by this terrific handicap. It was not a matter to be brooded over. The battleships were to be trained to bring a heavy concentration of fire to crush the van or some selected portion of the enemy's line, even in the fleeting opportunities of low visibility. Short-range wireless telegraphy in the gunnery control of ships was required, and special equipment had to be provided. Thanks to the efforts of Chatfield, who was assisted on the wireless side by Major B. C. Gardner, R.M., and Commander Somerville,[1] a system of concentration of fire designed to fit in with Beatty's intended tactics was quickly introduced, and the Fleet exhaustively trained in it.

Beatty made it clear, however, that he had no intention of relying on the gunnery duel alone for victory. There were other ways of destroying the enemy. The destroyer flotillas must be trained and organised to attack the enemy rather than to defend the battle fleet. A place must be found for submarines in his plan of battle. Full use must be made of aircraft, and the battle fleet must, if possible, press in to close range, where it was hoped the shell might be more effective.

Although still undaunted, Beatty felt that someone should eventually be called to account for a state of affairs which had so reduced the offensive power of the Grand Fleet. He sent for Chatfield and, handing him a letter in his own handwriting, he asked him to read it, and then said: 'If I am killed so also will you be probably. This letter, if the Fleet ever fail to do all that is expected of it in action, will place the blame where it should lie, and not on the shoulders of the officers and men of the Fleet when I am unable to defend them.'

The letter was intended to convey to posterity the truth about the shell; Beatty said he was sending it to his bank, only to be opened if he were killed in action.[2]

One of the most important tasks which faced Beatty as Commander-in-Chief was the revision of the Battle Orders, so as to embody the lessons of Jutland and his own tactical convictions. There was no question of overthrowing, with one stroke of the pen, the ideas of his predecessor.

[1] Later Admiral of the Fleet Sir James Somerville, G.C.B., D.S.O.
[2] *The Navy and Defence*, Lord Chatfield, p. 158.

Jellicoe had trained the Grand Fleet from the first day of the war. Since then the strength of the Fleet had been steadily increased, but at the beginning there was little margin of superior strength over the German High Seas Fleet, whilst the defences of the Grand Fleet bases were utterly inadequate. In these conditions, to Jellicoe it was essential that 'he should not risk the Grand Fleet', and in this view he was undoubtedly supported by most of the officers in his fleet, and also at the Admiralty. His tactics were framed accordingly, and properly represented the official view.

By January 1916, Jellicoe had issued to the Fleet the 'Grand Fleet Battle Orders', consisting of seventy pages and diagrams, revised and reprinted as new ideas formed and new units joined. They were in force at the Battle of Jutland, and dealt very fully with cruising dispositions during the approach and the duties of battle cruisers and cruisers in a fleet action.

The ruling principle in the Battle Orders was that the battle fleet as a whole should keep together and form one line of battle. Attack by a division or squadron on a portion of the enemy's line was not encouraged. In the words of the Commander-in-Chief: 'Action on approximately similar courses will be one of the underlying objects of my tactics.' Reliance for a decision was placed mainly on the gun duel.

A section dealing with the deployment of the battle fleet was accompanied by a diagram showing the positions which the Commander-in-Chief desired should be occupied by the various units. It was intended primarily as a guide, but when put to the test of battle, some commanders are alleged to have thought more of getting into their correct positions on the diagram than of destroying the enemy. Although the exercise of initiative and decentralisation was provided for, this did not come naturally to senior officers, who throughout their careers had been subject to a highly centralised system of command. In practice they expected the Commander-in-Chief to control the whole battle fleet, and having unbounded confidence in Jellicoe, preferred to leave as much as possible in his hands. Over-centralised control was also largely due to training under peace conditions, where the fleets were much smaller when split in two for tactical exercises, and of course there was no noise and smoke of battle. The Commander-in-Chief's intentions regarding the tactics he would adopt in battle were fully described in the Grand Fleet Battle Orders, including his decision to turn the Fleet away from the enemy flotillas if they were observed to be favourably placed for a massed torpedo attack. Jellicoe did not come lightly to this decision. It was only after careful investigation and conference with his Flag Officers that he informed the Admiralty by official letter, in October 1914, of his intention, stating that he felt 'such tactics, if not understood, may bring odium upon me'. Their Lordships approved his tactics, informing him of their full confidence in his contemplated conduct of the Fleet in action.

This method of countering a massed destroyer attack was practised in both the British and German Fleets. Hipper used it to avoid the torpedoes of Beatty's destroyers at the climax of the first phase of the battle, and in doing so broke off the action.

The primary duty of destroyers, as defined in the Grand Fleet Battle Orders, was to prevent the enemy destroyers from delivering an attack on the British battle fleet. This also conformed to Admiralty ideas, and was based on the knowledge that the British destroyers carried a heavier gun armament than the Germans. Beatty held the opposite view.[1] He believed in using destroyers offensively in a fleet action, and when he launched his attack against Hipper, Commander Bingham, as we have seen, made good use of his guns in forcing his way through the defending enemy flotilla.

The tactical doctrine which governed the conduct of the Fleet at Jutland had, however, been evolved from pre-war study; and Jellicoe himself, as a result of experience in action, had made some amendments in the direction of greater flexibility.

The essential changes that Beatty had to make were to reduce centralisation and, above all, to stress the importance of the offensive spirit and devise tactics conforming thereto.

Beatty had always been keenly interested in tactical problems. His vivid imagination enabled him to foresee situations which might arise in battle, and he spent much time in thought

[1] Official letter No. 0122 of 4th June, 1913, Beatty to Callaghan.

and discussion on the tactics he intended to adopt. This is evident from the many papers he put forward to his Commander-in-Chief, from the time he took over command of the battle cruisers in 1913. He had always visualised that his battle cruisers would have to fight at high speed, and he had insisted upon carrying out exercises in peace-time at speeds and ranges he would expect to use in battle. These conditions also affected the cruisers and destroyers, which had to work with him at high speed, bringing to light certain deficiencies, such as lack of fuel capacity to keep at sea for any length of time.

The question of handling a massed fleet of thirty battleships in a manner best suited to bring about the annihilation of the enemy was, however, a different matter. A few days after Beatty arrived in the *Iron Duke* at Scapa Flow, he took the whole Fleet to sea for a period of intensive exercises, practising various deployments as prescribed in the existing orders. His conduct of the Fleet, described by one flag officer as being masterly, quickly established the confidence of everyone in their new leader.

After this valuable experience, he set his mind to revising the Battle Orders, and directed Commander R. M. Bellairs, who had served on Jellicoe's staff, to examine the various problems and generally edit the work. Beatty felt that the title 'Battle Orders' implied a too-rigid control, so, on 12th March, 1917, he issued a printed covering memorandum of two sheets, entitled the 'Grand Fleet Battle Instructions'. These brought clearly and briefly to the notice of all flag officers and captains the strategical and tactical principles which would govern the Commander-in-Chief's conduct of the Fleet in battle. Dealing with the torpedo menace, a paragraph stated that in normal conditions the divisions threatened would turn *towards* the attack, because to turn away would run them out of gun range too quickly.

Beatty was anxious to have his intentions in regard to the offensive use of destroyers promulgated as soon as possible, so that the flotillas might be exercised, and the commanding officers acquainted with the tactics they were to employ in battle. Accordingly, on 20th January, 1917, he issued a special memorandum emphasising the importance of developing the attack at the earliest possible moment, of firing the maximum number of torpedoes, and not retaining torpedoes on the off chance of a more favourable opportunity occurring later.

In February 1918, the title 'Battle Orders' was abolished, and the series was reissued in two parts:

(i) The Grand Fleet Battle Instructions.

(ii) The Grand Fleet Manœuvring Orders.

The first part dealt with guiding principles and general instructions for the conduct of the Fleet in action. It was intended to be digested at leisure, and need not be taken on the bridge at sea. The second part contained detailed orders for the Fleet leaving and entering harbour, cruising formations, and all information likely to be required at sea. This arrangement was designed to prevent the Commander-in-Chief's intentions becoming lost in a mass of detail, and proved to be most satisfactory.

In these modifications to Jellicoe's Grand Fleet Battle Orders, there was a definite change in the emphasis placed on attacking the enemy even at some risk, and allowing more scope to individual initiative.

The two leaders, throughout their careers, had proved that they were each endowed with moral and physical courage of the highest order. While they were together in the Grand Fleet, Jellicoe, like Cornwallis, had held firmly the sure shield of England, while Beatty, like Nelson, had wielded the flaming sword of the offensive.

Beatty assumed the command of a fleet considerably superior to the enemy and blessed with adequately protected bases, a fleet brought by Jellicoe to a high standard of efficiency, but handicapped by defective shell. Beatty had the abiding faith of Nelson, amounting to a complete certainty that he was fighting for a righteous cause, and that when he met the enemy he would, with God's help, utterly defeat it. He had the same instinct as Nelson for battle, and proved it in August 1914, when in misty weather he led his battle cruisers up the Bight, almost to within range of the guns of Heligoland. He proved it again during the battle of Jutland by his tenacity and offensive spirit in closing the enemy, even after suffering heavy losses.

To THE EDITOR OF

H.M.S. "LION'S" SEARCHLIGHT.

On this the 2nd Anniversary of the action of the 24th Jan. (Dogger Bank) my thoughts turn to the Lion. For a message, I can only repeat to you my Christmas message to The Fleet. "May the desire of our hearts be accomplished in 1917" There can be no relaxation until the decisive blow for this wicked Peace has been struck and won

David Beatty

Facsimile of personal message from Admiral Beatty to his old flagship, "The Lion."

The following example is typical of his audacity. During the run to the north, with the High Seas Fleet close behind him, the Fifth Battle Squadron, steering south, came in sight nearly ahead, while Beatty was still engaged with Hipper's battle cruisers. A staff officer asked him, would he wish the Fifth Battle Squadron to pass him on the engaged or the disengaged side? The former would have brought fresh guns to bear, and have given a respite to our battle cruiser squadron, which had already lost two of its number. Wise tactics perhaps, cautious tactics certainly, would have dictated a move whereby the Fifth Battle Squadron was brought down between our battle cruisers and the enemy. But Beatty, rapidly weighing up the pros and cons, replied: 'The Fifth Battle Squadron must pass on our disengaged side.' The critic may say: 'Bad tactics; Beatty should have given place to the heavier and more powerful ships.' This, however, might have caused Hipper to turn away and place himself safely out of range. Anyway, the final results fully justified Beatty's confidence and audacity, for from that moment his ascendancy over Hipper was complete.

This sound instinct for the offensive is to be found in all great leaders. Many of our admirals had it, and many of our generals. It was probably the same instinct, supported by faith in a righteous cause, which gave our sailors and soldiers, even in the blackest hours of the war, an unconquerable faith that wherever they could meet the Germans on equal terms they would infallibly defeat them. When our leaders and their men are imbued with that spirit, the history of Britain proves them to be invincible.

On 16th February, 1917, Beatty hoisted his flag in the *Queen Elizabeth*. The whole staff turned over, together with some of the ship's officers from the *Iron Duke*. Chatfield says of them: 'Never was a better team collected together, never a happier atmosphere, seldom such a keen and enthusiastic ship's company as that of the *Queen Elizabeth*, devoted to their Commander-in-Chief, and determined that his Flagship should be worthy of him.'

While the Grand Fleet was at Scapa Flow, Beatty wrote regularly to his wife at Aberdour House, near Rosyth. The letters were taken there by the officer carrying official despatches to the port admiral, so Beatty was able to talk a little more frankly than he would have done if he had sent them through the post. His revelations, though at times indiscreet, are of historical interest, and the series provides an accurate narrative of events from his own point of view.

H.M.S. *Iron Duke*   (*7th Dec.*, 1916)

. . . For the first time since I took over my new duties, I begin to see light and have got ahead of my work. I have started several campaigns which has kept me busy, but they are well under way, and I have been able to get the Cabinet to take an interest in them. When I see Carson,[1] I hope to be able to enforce some further attention. One hour's conversation is worth pages of writing.

The Grand Fleet   (*21st Dec.*, 1916)

We arrived today after a cruise with the whole Fleet, which was, as far as an exercise is concerned, a very instructive and interesting one. All the admirals have just left me, and said it was the best that they had ever had, which was something. Even Madden [his second-in-command] enthused over it. At any rate it was very valuable in many ways, and being the first time the battle fleet had been to sea with me, it was satisfactory. Packs[2] will agree that it was good. He did very well in the battle cruisers. It was strange seeing the dear things booming along from the outside, and they looked fine, and I envied him being in command. The weather was fickle. On the whole we were lucky, but it was the cause of a terrible disaster. Two of the battle cruisers' destroyers had been detached by Packs because one had its steering gear gone wrong and he sent the other with it to look after it. They collided in the middle of the night, blowing a gale with a very bad sea, and both sank. I am afraid the loss of life is considerable, but might have been worse. I heard of it and luckily was not very far away, so sent them 1 cruiser and 4 destroyers. . . . It seems

[1] Sir Edward Carson, First Lord of the Admiralty.
[2] Rear-Admiral W. C. Pakenham.

[284]

that about 6 officers and about 45 men were lost in the *Negro* and 8 men
in the *Hoste*. I hope to get Sir Edward Carson up to Edinburgh about the
4th. Could you put him up about then? The difficulty would be his
secretaries. Those sort of fellows never travel about without one or two,
and they are a nuisance. . . . You must not mention anything of my
movements. . . .

The Grand Fleet   (*23rd Dec.*, 1916)

In times like these, it seems out of place to talk of happiness and Peace
upon earth, Christmas festivities, etc., but it is right to let this cursed war
interfere as little as possible with the pleasures of the little ones. At
Aberdour they will be happy. I shall go to sea tomorrow. Things might
happen on Christmas Day. The Huns like Festivals, and we are on the
qui vive. Is President Wilson insane? I never heard or read such rubbish.
The *Scotsman's* leader of yesterday sums it up beautifully in the most
dignified and restrained fashion. . . .

I have many irons in the fire just now, and am steeped in work, which
is good for me, but my day is twenty-four hours too short. And I have
great difficulty in getting any exercise. O. de Brock [his chief of staff] has
developed a tremendous capacity for work, and is perfectly excellent,
clear as a bell, and is of the very greatest assistance in the most unexpected
way. Chatfield and Tommy Brand are both also doing nobly, and I could
not have better assistants. I hope to have everything cut and dried to
bring as many of the battle fleet, which means *all* the battleships, down to
Rosyth as soon as the defences are complete. This will entail giving the
battle cruisers a spell at Scapa, but that will be good for them. But don't
say anything about it. I've got my way over the *Queen Elizabeth*, and
shall turn over to her when she has been refitted and repaired about the
end of January. I am sure the change is a sound and desirable one in
every way.

The Grand Fleet   (*Xmas Day*, 1916)

I hope the boys spent with you a Happy Day. Indeed, I know they
did. You always make everybody happy—that is your own particular
charm. We did not go to sea last night after all, as the enemy evinced a
certain activity which made it desirable we should be kept full up with
fuel, and we have been at short notice instead and nobody allowed ashore.
The men enjoyed their Turkeys, and I received all sorts of nice messages
to convey to you their appreciation of your thought for them all in little
laboured speeches learnt by heart. . . . I made the Sec [secretary] play the
part of Santa Claus and go round and put your gifts in the respective
stockings. They [the staff] were all so pleased you had forgotten nobody.

.... I haven't heard further from Carson, but I shall in any case come down and bring a battle squadron with me, probably the 5th. It's good to move them about.

The Grand Fleet   (1*st Jan.*, 1917)

Many good wishes to my dear ones for the New Year. How time slips by, too fast by far, but while this war is on, Time is nothing. This is the 3rd New Year. How many more are to come and go, and where shall we all be at the end of it ? . . . Mercifully I am terribly busy. John de Robeck already looks ten years younger since he came up. These cursed submarines of the enemy are doing untold damage, and will continue to do so until they take the question in the right way, and if they don't we shall very shortly be brought to our knees. It is truly terrible the prospect if somebody cannot be moved, but we will see. But this is absolutely for your eye only.

I should like to get away and not hear of ships, mines, submarines, sweeps, sinkings, and the many small tragedies that are always happening, but thank God these times are rare and at long intervals. I must go on until the end.

Grand Fleet   (22*nd Jan.*, 1917)

I am afraid you will be feeling very sad and depressed at the departure of little David. These partings are terrible, and one never seems to get used to them, but they are inevitable, and if the boy has got to be brought up properly, it must be impressed on his youthful mind the necessity of keeping engagements, no matter how disagreeable. You will say this is not very consistent with my telegram to keep David if you are not better. That is just the exception which proves the Rule, and all Rules are made to be broken. . . . I should like to know what Carson thought of his visit to the Fleet, and whether all that I told him really sank in. Time is the one thing that I cannot get the authorities to understand.

Grand Fleet   (25*th Jan.*, 1917)

We have had a French Admiral Chocheprat here presenting Légion d'Honneurs in great profusion, a very charming fellow, who was intensely interested at seeing the Grand Fleet. Was most enthusiastic and flattering in his allusions to the British Navy. We had a most impressive ceremony on board here, and he showed us how decorations really should be presented. . . . He, poor man, has suffered terribly during the war. He said three fine sons all gone and he has nothing left, the last and youngest only a week before he came up. He was very pathetic, and we sobbed on each other's shoulder, when he pulled himself up and said, *Eh bien, c'est pour La Patrie.* The tragedies of this cursed war—they will never cease and fairly shake one to one's foundation.

France is now one great family and their sorrows are my sorrows and their triumphs my triumphs. I explained this to him, and he said, 'You will be my son. In France Papa Joffre is known by everybody and David Beatty also is known by everybody, nobody else.' It is pardonable to be proud when one is told that, though it is only delightfully expressive of the pleasantness of a French gentleman. . . . I was glad to hear the hydrophones had located the sub. west of May Island, but why didn't they act on the information and hunt him? . . .

Grand Fleet   (28th Jan., 1917)

I have got most of my lambs back in safely, so a weight is off my mind or rather lessened. I cannot think a raider got out this time, as we had two good lines to catch him and he never appeared. . . . The encounter they had in the south was under very difficult conditions, very dark and freezingly cold, so much that the ships were a sheet of ice-frozen spray when they returned. Our boats sank one and another got into Ymuiden and will take no more part in the war. She was hammered out of all recognition by the *Simoon* before she blew up, torpedoed by a submarine they think. I think the enemy were thoroughly well frightened and will not be in a hurry to repeat the adventure. But it is a great pity they didn't get more. On a dark night, travelling at twenty-five knots in different directions, it seems difficult to get or expect any success.

Grand Fleet   (1st Feb., 1917)

The battle cruisers have arrived safely and I have had a long talk with Packs. He has the right ideas in his head, and I feel would do the right thing in the presence of the enemy, which after all is something. It is the administrative work which is badly done. . . . He will learn, especially as I am pointing out his mistakes and never lose an opportunity. Still, he is such a gentleman that he (like many others would) never takes offence or tries to shirk the question, so I have hopes. . . . I have got in a lot of my ships this morning and feel better about them, but I must send out a lot more to keep fairly on the move. The Huns have pronounced a War to the Knife policy with the sub., and trying to sink everything they see. I thought they had been doing that all the time. I was glad when Lord Milner and his party got safely across.[1] They were sent up in my care and so were an additional anxiety. The *Queen Elizabeth* is now on my mind, as she is at Newcastle, and I have got to get her to Rosyth, and they are laying mines to catch her. I have sweepers in all directions.

[1] Mission to Russia via Kola Inlet.

Grand Fleet (*3rd Feb.*, 1917)

... Her [German] Fleet is still intact. She is suffering from the effects of our blockade, and her rulers might well say that the time has arrived when the Fleet must do something and endeavour to raise the blockade by an attempt to defeat us on the sea. In exactly the same way that Napoleon did when he sent Villeneuve out to be defeated at Trafalgar against the advice of all the Naval Authorities. . . . We are not quite prepared yet. There are portions of our Service I find which are not instilled with the right spirit. It's not their fault, poor dears; they have had bad times and have been treated abominably, nobody to look after them, and their morale has sunk below our standard. I've only just found it out; give me another month and they will be all right. The heart is there, but has been crushed in the most extraordinary way and wants reviving. I must not say any more.

Grand Fleet (*9th Feb.*, 1917)

I am sending the battle cruisers back this evening. I hope they won't get into trouble on the way down, and I hope to follow on the Monday. . . . I fear I shall not be able to stop down at Rosyth for more than a week, on account of the astounding activity of the enemy submarines prevalent at this time, and it may forebode further activity on the part of the Main Fleet; in any case, I cannot be separated from my Fleet, and the Firth of Forth is not ready yet to take us all and I do not like dividing the Fleet. I am sure that is unsound, and I have always said so, and I shall stick to it. When there is room for everybody there, then I will bring them all down, but not before.

Grand Fleet (*21st Feb.*, 1917)

I have been up to the neck in work ever since I got back, and O. de Brock says he will go on strike if it continues. I like my *Queen Elizabeth*. She is very much more comfortable at sea than the *Iron Duke*, and it is no trouble to her to travel at a high speed. I was a little nervous at getting out of Firth this time, as the fog had interfered with the sweeping arrangements, but we struggled out all right. . . . I hope you will be able to hear something of the Fisher intrigue. I heard that I am the subject of wrath now, and I must be got rid of at all costs, that I am quite the wrong man for the job. It does not disturb me in the least.

Grand Fleet (*1st March*, 1917)

We have been at sea all day and part of the night, which gives me a bit of a rest, as I get away from the telegraph line.[1] Four years today since

---

[1] While in harbour the Fleet Flagship was connected to the shore telegraph system.

I joined the *Lion*. It seems to me as if it were not more than two, and three months I have been in command of the Grand Fleet and we have not struck the enemy a severe blow yet. We have got some submarines, but that is not what is required to satisfy the longing to do something. I keep on saying to myself patience, just have patience, but it is hard to act up to that. We have had our disappointments and our disasters too. This morning a destroyer went out on patrol at 5.30 and at 6.10 she ceased to exist, simply disappeared. There was an awful explosion, and not a vestige of her was left except a little wreckage and a few dead bodies. It must have been a mine floated in to the coast from a minefield that was laid eighteen months ago, 85 fine fellows in one pouf. It is terrible and nothing to show for it. Such is life, and death is but a bend in the road of Life. And after all, nothing really matters. In a few short months it is forgotten or remembered as an incident. But it is hateful to be blown up in such a manner without striking a blow. . . . I am glad you told Masterson Smith that I liked having Carson come up and see me. It is good for him to get the views of the Fleet, and he can balance them against those of the Admiralty which, as we do not always see eye to eye, is a good thing for him and for the prosecution of the war.

Grand Fleet (6th *March*, 1917)

I was very glad indeed to see that the King had awarded the posthumous honour of the Victoria Cross to the gallant Commander Loftus Jones who was killed in the *Shark* on 31st May (Jutland), somewhat belated, but better late than never. And all the survivors got the Distinguished Service Medal. When does David come home for his holidays? I hope they are getting enough to eat at his school. I hear potatoes are very hard to get, impossible in some places. It won't do to have him underfed, better to be uneducated.

Grand Fleet (14th *March*, 1917)

We have had some losses and some fine fellows have just disappeared, no more, nothing to show where or how, but they just don't come back. The silence of it is uncanny and has a baneful effect, but I keep it to myself, and others take their place. I am wondering how long it can go on. We have been successful again, and are to the good on the balance, and I think shall in the end be able to stand it longer than they can. This gambling with men's lives is making an old man of me and worse than any general action. But it must go on, and we must not run back, but prosecute our purpose up to the hilt. . . . We have had three undoubted successes lately. This for you only. It is something to hearten one up. But it is a wearing-out game and leaves an indelible mark behind.

Grand Fleet   (*16th March*, 1917)

But really we are doing well. We sunk a raider this afternoon. Dear old Martin Leake had a battle.[1] Just had a wireless. Most people thought my dispositions were wrong, but they were proved right, unless I wake up and find it a dream only. I've had so many disappointments lately. This is for you only. *Do not say a word*, but I must tell you. We've paid for what successes we have achieved. The war is, from the sea point of view, in a very much more active and moving condition than it was.

Grand Fleet   (*March*, 1917)

We returned this morning after a cruise with the battle fleet in the North Sea for three days. This will account for no letter. . . . Carson's speech read very well. He told them what his public will think—a great deal, and I do not think anything he said will have any bad effect anywhere. I certainly think the British public will be able to realise more readily the difficulties of the situation. . . . Really and truly, I do not think Fisher has any chance of getting back as 1st Lord or 1st Sea Lord. He is *too old*, and that you cannot get over. As for John Jellicoe, I do not think he has any desire to return to the Grand Fleet. Do you think they would agree to my being turned out?

Grand Fleet   (*March*, 1917)

So old Fisher says I will let the Grand Fleet down in gunnery, does he? I know where he gets that from. It might interest him to know that the general opinion of the *Fleet* is that we have advanced more in our gunnery methods in the last three months than we have the previous two *years*. This is a fact. It was said by one distinguished officer after the 31st May [Jutland] that the reason we lost three battle cruisers that day was because the battle cruisers shot so badly. It has since transpired that on that occasion the enemy was hit by the *battle cruisers* a great deal more than we were hit, and the reason they did not suffer immense damage was because our projectiles were not capable of penetrating the enemy's armour. Similarly, if we had had decent projectiles on the 24th Jan. [Dogger Bank], we should certainly have destroyed three of the enemy's ships instead of only *one*. Lord Fisher was the First Lord of the Admiralty at the time. . . . However, I think at present we can afford not to take too much notice of the vapourings of these old gentlemen. But what is a matter of consideration, is where does he get his information from and his views? They certainly are not his own. I am glad you have got the

[1] On 16th March, 1917, H.M.S. *Achilles* (Captain Martin Leake, R.N.), with Armed Boarding Steamer *Dundee* (Commander S. M. Day, R.N.R.), while on Northern Patrol, sank a German Armed Raider attempting to break out for operations on the trade routes.

Chatfield baby his mug. His name is *Ernle* David Lewis Chatfield. I have now completed three months in command, and am grateful indeed that we have been vouchsafed such a spell of on the whole fine weather.

The Grand Fleet   (*18th March,* 1917)

I've just seen old Martin Leake very elated in his dry way. He did very well and made a good job of it, no survivors. Somebody whispered into his ear submarine, so he remembered the old *Pathfinder* and took no risks, though he was somewhere near the North Pole. It is not clear whether she [the enemy raider] was a new one going out or the old going home. When he saw her first she was going toward home, but it might well have been the other way. In any case, it was a splendid thing getting her and justifies a good deal that I have been trying to do. . . . We had a very good week last week, one Raider and four Subs., but very dear we have paid for it, but is more than balanced. Still, it is very wearing, and I am rapidly ageing. If we could only get to grips properly I should be rejuvenated. I return you Marie Corelli's flowery effusion, but it is very nice and very true about you and your gallant heart. Really, dear one, you are a good and beautiful fairy Princess, and have brought sunshine and happiness into many a sad household. The poor Czar, I am truly sorry for him, but there was nothing else to be done. He was so entirely under the thumb of the Czarina who was extremely stupid and wrong-headed to say the least. They appear to have managed it very quietly without too much violence. Grand Duke Cyril did not take long to range himself on the side of Duma and Grand Duke Nicolas has apparently been a moving spirit. Once they settle down they will be persecuted by them with greater vigour. [A true forecast of tragic events.]

Grand Fleet   (*28th March,* 1917)

Just a line to catch *Princess Royal,* which is now returning to Rosyth. Something has gone wrong inside, and she is *hors de combat,* which is indeed a very serious matter at this juncture of the war, because I feel that something might happen at any time now and her loss is a considerable reduction in our strength in battle cruisers and will take a month at least to put right if not more. Poor little Cowan [Captain of the *Princess Royal*] is in a terrible state of anxiety, but it cannot be helped, and we have to face it. I am sending you some curious things made out of some of the wood that was washed ashore from the wreck of the *Hampshire. . . .* The outlook on the sea does not improve. Raiders get out apparently when they like, because the sea is large and we have an insufficient number of ships to patrol the vast waste spaces and the Admiralty will not introduce the system of Convoy. The enemy subs. are sinking ships by the score, and they will not take advice, or if they do they will not adopt it in its entirety. . . . I hope to be down on the 4th or 5th if things are sufficiently quiet, and I hope to get Sir Edward Carson and the Prime Minister up at that time and make an effort to startle them into doing something different to what we are doing now.

Grand Fleet (*30th March*, 1917)

I do not see how we can continue losing ships at the rate we are doing. I feel that we are living on a volcano, and that we shall suddenly wake up and find that we cannot go on. I shall be glad to see Sir Edward Carson again. I have just had a wire from him saying that the Prime Minister cannot get up at Easter, but he will come on the 13th. (This is a secret, so don't mention to *anyone*.) So I shall probably be delayed in arriving at Rosyth, as I cannot afford to be away from the Fleet for more than a week. I must see the Prime Minister and put my views before him, so I sincerely trust that nothing will interfere with that plan. I shall get down on the 6th. It will be nice to see you and the boys again, and nothing but the advent of the enemy shall interfere with that. They seem to have had some terrific rumours down South this week. All caused by that silly old man French, supported by our old friend Fisher, who have made up their minds that we are about to be invaded and consequently caused shocks all round. You must not begin to wonder who is going to win the war, because it is a certainty that we are, in spite of all the handicaps we make for ourselves by our muddling methods and crass stupidity. We have the very finest human material in the world, who simply cannot be defeated, but the many mistakes drag it out so long and increase the suffering so much that it makes one angry. In the end we shall win because we are right, our cause is just, and our hearts are in the right place, but the end is not in sight yet.

Grand Fleet (*1st April*, 1917)

Everything as far as the Fleet is concerned is going like hot cakes and all my admirals are in good humour. I am feeling elated. I hope not unduly so. But everybody is pulling together in the Fleet. There is no friction and no *jealousies*, and they all tell me they think we are more efficient. I must not buck about it or shall have a heavy fall, but cannot help being puffed. We are now getting ready for a new fine-weather campaign against the submarine in these latitudes, but fear it is little we can do when we consider the whole areas we have to operate in, but live in hopes of some successes. Really, we are too far away from the root of the evil and cannot expect overmuch. They must be tackled nearer home.

CHAPTER FOURTEEN

1917–1918
COMMANDER-IN-CHIEF, GRAND FLEET

*The anti-submarine campaign · Beatty starts a convoy
system · The 'Theatre Ship' · Battle of 17th November,
1917 · Admiral Rodman and the Sixth Battle Squadron
Scheer's last sortie · Defeat of the enemy submarine*

ON 3rd December, 1916, Sir Henry Jackson, who was
about to be relieved by Jellicoe as First Sea Lord, wrote
to Beatty:

I wish, however, we could see a solution to the submarine trouble,
especially against neutral shipping. The neutrals won't help us to help
them to protect their ships, as all, without exception, are frightened of
Germany and none is frightened of us. The strong and ruthless hand in
war goes far towards obtaining victory.

Beatty received this letter only a few days after he had
assumed command of the Grand Fleet, when he was fully
occupied with problems affecting its employment. Nevertheless,
he had given deep consideration to the submarine question,
and had directed a section of his staff to examine it and make
proposals for the early introduction of convoys in the North
Sea.

The situation became acute in February 1917, when
Germany abandoned the idea of seeking a decision at sea with
her battle fleet, and concentrated her naval effort on unrestricted submarine warfare. Beatty was not aware of this
decision. From his point of view, the High Seas Fleet
remained 'in being' as a bulwark behind which the Imperial
Navy could build up its submarine strength. It stood for the
control of the Baltic and inner waters of the Heligoland Bight.
He could not send a detached force into the Baltic, for it would

have to be based there, and would soon fall a prey to superior German forces using the Kiel Canal. For similar reasons it would be impossible to maintain a detached British force permanently watching the German harbours in the Heligoland Bight. As long as the High Seas Fleet remained concentrated, Beatty had to keep the Grand Fleet ready for battle. It was impossible for him to destroy the enemy unless they emerged from the protection of their shore defences, willing to fight. The choice of time and place lay with Scheer. Beatty, therefore, could not relax his vigilance, so destroyers and light craft, included in the Grand Fleet plan of battle, could only be spared for anti-submarine operations in the vicinity of the Fleet base. These operations naturally aroused his hunting instinct, and being fully alive to the deadly threat to the national existence, he used every means in his power to destroy enemy submarines passing to and from the Atlantic through the Northern Approaches.

The existing British counter-measures, such as patrols and hunting forces in focal areas, Q ships, and scattered and sparsely laid minefields, had proved quite powerless to check the drain on the nation's life-blood. Merchant-shipping losses jumped to over 875,000 tons in April, 1917,[1] and the situation was grave indeed. In Beatty's words, 'It looked as if the Germans might strangle us with their submarines before either our army or our blockade strangled them'.

Beatty by now had formulated his own ideas about the submarine war, believing that he for one could see a solution. To his mind big problems required big measures, and he did not hesitate to point out in strong terms to the Admiralty that 'the existing policy of dropping driblets of mines in wide areas was quite ineffective'. If the German fox was to be 'stopped in his earth', a thousand British mines must be laid for every hundred scattered off the German rivers hitherto.

He asked for the co-operation of the Ministry of Munitions, and was amazed to learn that it had no responsibility for mine production, a defect which was remedied later. He also advocated the complete blocking of the Dover Strait, and was in favour of using submarines to hunt submarines in narrow waters.

[1] British, 545,282 tons; foreign, 329,825 tons.

As the number of auxiliary patrol craft had risen from 745 in December 1914 to 2,556 in December 1916, he urged that officers dug out from retirement should be replaced by experienced young officers on the active list for directing anti-submarine operations.

Above all, he was a firm believer in the convoy system, which had not yet been introduced on a large scale. He argued that from an offensive point of view, submarines would be attracted to the convoys, where it would be easier to find and destroy them. These views he set out in a strong letter, on 30th April, 1917, to Sir Edward Carson, the First Lord of the Admiralty (see Appendix VI). Beatty had cut away the undergrowth, laying bare the essentials of the problem, and his recommendations were the measures which eventually defeated the enemy submarine. There was nothing new about them. In fact, the introduction of the convoy system was being considered by the Admiralty, but Beatty could not tolerate half-measures or delay, and whenever he felt convinced of the right course of action, would ignore official procedure and hammer away at the responsible authority until it was adopted.

The Admiralty had pinned their hopes on certain new weapons,[1] but Beatty approached the problem on tactical and strategical grounds. His continuous pressure on Ministers[2] was undoubtedly one of the main factors in overcoming the strong opposition to the introduction of convoy which existed in some highly influential quarters at the time.

Growing impatient with the delay, he sought permission to run convoys of allied and neutral ships to and from Norway under his own direction. The Admiralty approved with some misgiving,[3] and Beatty, having already organised the system in co-operation with Admiral Sir Frederick Brock, the Admiral Commanding the Orkneys and Shetlands, got it started before the end of April. It was a complete success, for convoys of up to a dozen ships passed daily to and fro across the North Sea with negligible loss from submarine attack. A month later the first Atlantic convoy sailed from Hampton Roads.[4]

During the summer of 1917, H.M. King George V

---

[1] *Official History of Naval Operations*, vol. IV, p. 380.   [2] Ibid., vol. V, p. 17.
[3] Ibid., vol. IV, p. 383.   [4] Ibid., vol. V, p. 392.

honoured the Fleet with a week's visit to the Fleet Flagship. He and Beatty had been shipmates in the old *Alexandra* and shared many memories. The King, always a keen sailor, visited every class of ship, from the latest battleship to the humblest trawler. After his visit he wrote to Beatty on 1st July, 1917, in his own handwriting:

I wish to thank you for all your kind hospitality while I was on board the *Queen Elizabeth*. I was quite delighted with everything you showed me, and I must say I was deeply touched with the splendid welcome I received from the officers and men of the Grand Fleet, which I greatly appreciate. Their spirit is magnificent and all the ships most efficient. I have had a long talk with Jellicoe and he told me that they are building 13 knot trawlers for escorting convoys, etc., which will be able to keep the sea better and longer than destroyers. He quite agrees that he should be in touch more often with you, and that Oliver[1] or Brock[2] should go up and down between you and him whenever possible.[3] He told me he tells you everything that is being done and any new ideas he has.

The Chief of the Imperial General Staff, Field-Marshal Sir William Robertson, also visited Beatty at about this time, with the news that the Government was planning a major offensive in Flanders, north-east of Ypres, which was to be supported by a landing of troops to attack the enemy's flank near Zeebrugge. The Prime Minister (Mr. Lloyd George) had suggested that the battle cruisers, or possibly a squadron of battleships, might support the landing. Beatty, who considered the whole plan ill-conceived and lacking time for the necessary preparations, suggested that officers with experience of combined operations in the Dardanelles, such as de Robeck and Keyes, should be consulted. In any case, he would not allow any detachment of force which might impair the Grand Fleet's readiness for battle. During the discussion Beatty, becoming slightly impatient, asked: 'Who thought of this?' 'Lloyd George,' said Robertson. 'What does he know about it, anyway?' Robertson, who was a friend of Beatty's, replied in his Scotch accent with a pawky

[1] Vice-Admiral Sir Henry Oliver, Deputy Chief of Naval Staff, Admiralty.
[2] Rear-Admiral O. de B. Brock, Chief of Staff to Beatty.
[3] Beatty had written many letters to the Admiralty urging closer co-operation between the Naval Staff and himself.

smile: 'Well, David, you see, Lloyd George is like a *vurrgin*. He thinks he knows, and he does know. But he hasn't had the *expeerience*!' Beatty was adamant in his opposition, and went so far as to say that too many troops were being held in England as a defence against invasion, and that most of these should be sent to France. He pointed out that defence of the English coast was the Navy's responsibility, and gave assurance that, so long as the Grand Fleet remained concentrated, he could prevent invasion, thus freeing the Army for a major offensive. No further attempt was made to divide the Fleet, and nothing more was heard about landing the Army on the heavily defended Flanders coast.

In October, a great combined anti-submarine operation by Grand Fleet destroyers and submarines, working with mine-layers and mine-net drifters, resulted in the destruction of three submarines. The operation, although seriously curtailed by bad weather, was successful, but could not be repeated, owing to the ever-increasing demands for convoy escorts. It was not possible to supply enough destroyers for anti-submarine work in addition to convoy, and at the same time keep the Grand Fleet ready for battle. The latent power of the High Seas Fleet was exerting its influence in no small measure. The need for its destruction was paramount, and Beatty was taking no chances by weakening the Grand Fleet. Only light escort forces could, therefore, be provided for the protection of the Scandinavian convoys, and it was clearly a question of time before one of them would be attacked by fast enemy surface warships. This happened twice during the autumn of the year.

On 17th October, 1917, two of the latest German cruisers, the *Brummer* and *Bremse*, intercepted a convoy of twelve merchant ships bound for Lerwick from Bergen. The two escorting British destroyers, *Mary Rose* and *Strongbow*, advanced gallantly to the attack, but having no chance against such overwhelming odds were quickly sunk. The enemy then destroyed all but two ships of the convoy, and made their escape. Beatty, having been warned by the Admiralty of possible enemy activity, had spread some eighty of his available cruisers and destroyers on patrol across the North Sea. The German cruisers, making full use of their high speed, had managed to get through undetected, proving, as Beatty had feared, that intercepting measures could not be relied upon to stop a 'tip-and-run' raid of this nature.[1] Had it been possible to use some of the patrolling cruisers and destroyers as additional convoy escorts, the story might well have been different.

About a month later the same thing happened again. A small convoy of six merchant ships bound for Norway, escorted by only two destroyers, the *Partridge* and *Pellew*, was attacked by four enemy destroyers of the largest and fastest type. Once again the escort was overpowered, and on this occasion the whole convoy was sunk. The *Pellew*, however, although heavily damaged, managed to escape under cover of a rain squall. The German destroyers, by following the Norwegian coast and returning home by the Skagerrak, unfortunately succeeded in evading the Third Light Cruiser Squadron which was endeavouring to intercept them.

These two German successes came as a very unpleasant shock to the British public, for by this time the convoy system had been adopted in the Atlantic and other oceans, and was proving itself a successful counter against enemy submarines. People had begun to breathe again. The loss of a whole convoy at one fell swoop was so disturbing that many questions were asked in the House of Commons. As a result the Admiralty ordered a court of enquiry into the losses. Beatty, who had accepted full responsibility for the strength of the escort, but not for the time of sailing the convoy which was a matter for the Admiralty, was therefore the principal witness. He naturally took great exception to an order directing him to submit the names of the court for Admiralty approval. This procedure, while depriving him of his constitutional authority, implied that he might 'pack the court'. He was highly indignant, but knowing that Sir Eric Geddes, the new First Lord, was about to visit the Fleet, complied with the order. At the end of the visit, Geddes asked if there were anything else he wished to discuss. Beatty told him very plainly that he and his flag officers had felt deeply insulted by the Admiralty order. Geddes promised to look into the matter, and asked what action he would wish him to take. Beatty replied that a letter of apology

[1] *Official History of Naval Operations,* vol. V, p. 159.

would suffice. A few weeks later Beatty pointed out that no letter had yet been received. In response to this reminder the apology eventually arrived, and was read out to the flag officers in Beatty's cabin on board the *Queen Elizabeth*.[1]

The court found that in the circumstances the dispositions for the protection of the convoy could not have been improved. A complete flotilla was required to provide continuously two destroyers for each convoy, and no more could be spared from the Fleet. Unfortunately, the only additional support readily available in 1917 consisted of old armoured cruisers too slow to cope with fast enemy craft. It did not require a court of enquiry of his own flag officers to tell him how to deal with a situation which was developing as he had expected. The enemy was growing bolder, and Beatty saw in the Scandinavian convoys a bait by which strong enemy forces might be lured into northern waters and brought to action.

In November 1917, there occurred an unprecedented event. The United States, which had entered the war in April, sent a battle squadron to join the Grand Fleet, the American admiral placing himself without reservation under Beatty's command. It had been known for some weeks that the Americans were coming, and there was much speculation as to how a foreign squadron, hitherto accustomed to peace-time routine, could suddenly graft itself on to a Fleet which had been at war for over three years. All doubts were quickly dispelled by the personality of the American admiral himself.

Hugh Rodman, the 'Kentucky Admiral', on learning from the United States Navy Department that he was to take his squadron to Scapa Flow, asked specifically that he should be given no instructions beyond the routine orders for sailing. In his own words:[2] 'I realised that the British Fleet had had three years of actual warfare and knew the game from the ground-floor up; that while we might know it theoretically, there would be a great deal to learn practically. There could not be two independent commanders in one force if our work was to be harmonious, and the only logical course was to amalgamate

---

[1] Eye-witness, Rear-Admiral E. S. Alexander-Sinclair.
[2] *Yarns of a Kentucky Admiral*, by Admiral Rodman, p. 268.

our ships and serve under the command of the British Commander-in-Chief. This I explained to Admiral Beatty on our
first meeting, and said I was ready to give him my loyal support
in every way. I told him if he would confide in me in the same
way and trust me, I would, during our stay in the Grand Fleet,
adopt the same code of signals, visual and otherwise, even their
secret code, which I promised never to divulge.'

Beatty took to him at once, and the two leaders became firm
friends. Later, when at Rosyth, Rodman and his officers were
constant visitors to Beatty's home at Aberdour, where they
found much in common with their American-born hostess.

Beatty, reciprocating Rodman's wishes, included the United
States squadron in the fighting organisation of the Grand Fleet,
as a wing division with the title of Sixth Battle Squadron. There
were six[1] battleships: the *New York* (Flagship), Captain C. F.
Hughes, U.S.N.; the *Texas*, Captain V. Blue, U.S.N.; the
Wyoming, Captain H. Wiley, U.S.N.; the *Arkansas*, Captain
W. Bullard, U.S.N.; the *Florida*, Captain T. Washington,
U.S.N.; and the *Delaware*, Captain A. Scales, U.S.N. Within
three days of their arrival they were taking part in a full-scale
Fleet operation, apparently having no difficulty in conforming
to British tactical manœuvres. It is a tribute to American naval
training that the British signal codes and methods were so
quickly assimilated. There were certain aspects, however,
where skill could only be acquired by long experience of war
conditions, such as keeping accurate station at night with no
lights showing. One pitch-black night, when the Grand Fleet
was at sea in columns five miles apart, with the Sixth Battle
Squadron five miles astern, Beatty received a signal from
Rodman: 'Have lost *Delaware*'. Beatty, knowing full well what
had happened, signalled: 'I hope she is not sunk', which drew
the reply: 'No, just mislaid!' Next morning at dawn the smoke
of a warship was observed on the horizon ahead of the Fleet.
As smoke is always an object of suspicion at sea in war-time, all
ships went to action stations, but the stranger was soon
identified as the *Delaware*, which, in attempting to regain
touch with her 'next ahead', had passed unseen between the
lines of British battleships.

[1] The number of ships varied according to requirements.

The strong tides in the Pentland Firth were at first a little disconcerting to the newly joined squadron, as it was a unique experience for them to pass suddenly from the placid waters of Scapa Flow into a tideway of eight knots, in company with other squadrons of battleships. Rodman, with the Sixth Battle Squadron, being the last to leave the Flow in numerical order, was somewhat alarmed to see the battleships of the divisions ahead being thrown as much as forty-five degrees off their course as the tide struck them. He described the scene thus: 'They seemed to be heading in all directions like a lot of scared sheep.'

The Sixth Battle Squadron, however, soon got accustomed to the strange ways of the North Sea, and took its turn with the rest of the Fleet in escorting convoys, and supporting cruiser operations. Sometimes Rodman would be the senior officer with British Flag Officers under his command. It made no difference, since he and his squadron were accepted as an integral part of the Grand Fleet. Rodman says: 'When the Grand Fleet is mentioned, our thoughts naturally turn to the Commander-in-Chief, Admiral Sir David Beatty. A man of rare accomplishments, a natural-born, tried, trusted, and gallant leader who would fight at the drop of the hat. He has my greatest admiration. It was an honour and a pleasure to serve under him, and I shall always treasure the friendship and comradeship engendered during our service with the Grand Fleet.'[1]

Admiral Sims, the Commander-in-Chief of United States naval forces in European waters, tells us that 'Beatty's intention to run all justifiable risks if a chance presented of defeating the German Fleet was as well known to the Germans as to ourselves'. Beatty was so highly thought of in America that the U.S. Navy planning section always took his character into account when considering problems of North Sea strategy. '. . . After we had sent five of our battleships to reinforce Beatty's fleet, this topic became even more interesting to American naval men.'[2]

Towards the end of 1917, the situation was further relieved by the arrival of American destroyers. These reinforcements

[1] *Yarns of a Kentucky Admiral*, p. 266.
[2] *The Victory at Sea*, by Admiral W. S. Sims, U.S.N., p. 152.

enabled the convoy system to be extended in all oceans and the anti-submarine forces round the British Isles to be strengthened. From then onwards shipping losses steadily diminished.

The easy co-operation between the British and United States Navies prevailing on all stations was a marked feature of the war at sea. It was simply a question of give and take, and came quite naturally to the seafaring men of the English-speaking peoples. Almost as quickly as the Americans adapted themselves to the ways of the Royal Navy, the British began to understand American colloquialisms and their subtly concealed humour. At Queenstown, the United States anti-submarine forces were controlled by a British admiral whom they called 'Uncle Lewis'.[1] One day he received a signal from a U.S. destroyer on patrol. 'Have sunk German submarine in position lat. 51° 30′ N., long. 8° 10′ W. Where am I ?' 'Uncle Lewis', being somewhat puzzled, sent for his U.S. interpreter, who without hesitation gave the answer: 'Top of the class !' This laconic reply was immediately flashed back to the delight of the ship's crew.

One of the most important anti-submarine measures in the North Sea during 1917 was intensive minelaying. As the year advanced, the supply of mines had increased satisfactorily, and a large number of minefields were laid across the Heligoland Bight. Unfortunately, it was not possible to prevent the enemy from sweeping channels through fields near his own coast. On the other hand, the area could be extended by the continuous laying of additional mines on the outer perimeter farther and farther to seaward, thus compelling the German sweepers and their escorts to operate at increasing distances from their bases and bringing them within reach of Beatty's light forces. This plan worked well. At frequent intervals British light cruiser squadrons attacked the sweepers, so the enemy, after suffering some losses, began using battleships to support them. Hoping to surprise these heavy ships, Beatty decided to send a strong force to the edge of the minefields, where sweeping was known to be going on. It consisted of the new cruisers *Courageous* and *Glorious*, the First and Sixth Light Cruiser Squadrons, accom-

[1] Admiral Sir Lewis Bayly.

panied by destroyers, and supported by battle cruisers and the First Battle Squadron.

At dawn, on 17th November, 1917, the British cruisers and destroyers fell upon a group of German sweepers operating on the Horns Reef–Terschelling line. The visibility was low, and while the attack was developing, four enemy light cruisers appeared. On seeing the British force they turned and fled down the swept channel under cover of a smoke screen, closely pursued by Rear-Admiral Trevylyan Napier in the *Courageous*, Commodore Walter Cowan with the First Light Cruiser Squadron, and Rear-Admiral Alexander-Sinclair with the Sixth Light Cruiser Squadron. The battle cruiser *Repulse* (Rear-Admiral R. Phillimore) joined the chase in support of the light cruisers. There was a hot running fight, with hits sustained on both sides, but gunnery conditions were very difficult, as the retreating enemy kept up a continuous smoke screen, consequently neither force could see their targets, and owing to the danger of mines, neither could deviate from the channel. At 9.30 a.m. Napier, having only scanty information concerning the positions of the various minefields, directed his own squadron and the *Repulse* not to advance any farther. The two light cruiser squadrons continued the pursuit. The *Repulse*, ignoring her recall, remained in close support, but when they had advanced thirty miles between the minefields, two German battleships appeared and attacked them with heavy salvos. Alexander-Sinclair and Cowan had no choice but to retire, hoping the enemy would follow them back to open waters, where Madden, with the First Battle Squadron, and Pakenham, with the Battle Cruiser Force, were eagerly waiting. Beatty's hope was not fulfilled. The German battleships, no doubt remembering his tactics at Jutland, refused to be tempted, and the British reluctantly withdrew from the Bight.

Except for a few enemy minesweepers, there were no losses on either side, but the intrepid character of the British attack in such dangerous waters and so near the German naval bases not only had a demoralising effect on the enemy, but also materially assisted the British anti-submarine campaign. The enemy realised that systematic minesweeping so far afield could no longer be carried out with impunity, and in consequence, the British rate of laying mines began, at last, to exceed the enemy rate of sweeping them up. The channels to and from the German North Sea bases were frequently closed, and an ever-increasing number of enemy submarines had to be diverted through the Kattegat into the Baltic, which weakened their striking power.

By the end of the year, the measures Beatty had advocated for countering the submarine onslaught were beginning to bear fruit under the able direction of the Anti-Submarine Division, which had been established by Jellicoe at the Admiralty. The calls on the Fleet for every type of warship to assist in the campaign were ever-increasing, and Beatty, with true strategic insight, felt that the time had come to define clearly the function of the Grand Fleet. Hitherto his object had been to seek out and destroy the High Seas Fleet, but this, for reasons already explained, was proving impossible to achieve. The matter being of such grave importance, and victory over the submarine being within grasp, Beatty attended a conference at the Admiralty on 2nd January, 1918, to discuss future policy. At the request of the Admiralty the Commander-in-Chief expressed his views in a forceful letter, which was later laid before the War Cabinet:[1]

So long as he [the C.-in-C. High Seas Fleet] remains in his harbours, [wrote Beatty] he is in a position to operate on interior lines and with such forces as he may choose against our vitally important mercantile traffic with the Scandinavian countries. His interior position, and the presence of his agents in neutral ports from which convoys sail, facilitate the execution of surprise attacks with forces stronger than our covering forces. To take an extreme case, it is obviously impossible to have the whole Grand Fleet covering the convoy, whereas it is possible for the whole High Seas Fleet to effect a surprise attack with reasonable prospect of escape to their bases. . . .

He reminded the Admiralty that the new type of shell had not yet been supplied to the Fleet, and that he would have to go into action with ineffective projectiles. Was it wise, in these circumstances, to try to force a Fleet action? Beatty considered that it was not.

[1] *Official History of Naval Operations*, vol. V, p. 206.

The foregoing review [he concluded] represents the situation as I see it. If correct, as I believe it to be, and accepting the principle that trade must be protected, the deduction to be drawn is that the correct strategy of the Grand Fleet is no longer to endeavour to bring the enemy to action at any cost, but rather to contain him in his bases until the general situation becomes more favourable.

The Admiralty agreed, and measures were taken to intensify minelaying in the Heligoland Bight, in order to restrict the movements of the High Seas Fleet, while the British counter-offensive against submarines was working up to its climax.

Beatty's ultimate object still remained the destruction of the High Seas Fleet, but the defeat of the submarine was of over-riding importance. There was nothing illogical in the change. The new policy was simply the correct application of the principle of concentration at the decisive time and place. The place was the trade routes and the time was the present. Beatty emphasised, however, that he was taking a grave strategical risk in providing continuously so many destroyer escorts for convoys, unless the Admiralty could be sure of obtaining early information of an impending move of the High Seas Fleet.

The advent of the American battle squadron enabled a division of battleships to be spared for the protection of the Scandinavian convoys. At first this could not be done very frequently, but with such strong escorts the same flow of trade could be maintained by running larger convoys at longer intervals, and from January 1918 to the end of the war, 3,862 merchant ships sailed across the North Sea in convoys of sixty ships at a time, with a total loss of only 0·4 per cent.

By the spring of 1918, the battle fleet was spending more time in harbour than had previously been the custom, thus easing the strain on machinery and liberating the flotillas for anti-submarine work. About once a month the Commander-in-Chief would take the whole Fleet to sea for tactical exercises, paying particular attention to enemy reporting, cruiser work, and massed destroyer attacks. Offensive operations were going on all the time in the form of submarine hunting, harassing enemy patrols, and minelaying. The war for the little ships was strenuous indeed, and being often in touch with the enemy, their morale was high. The battleships, on the other hand, absorbed a far greater proportion of the personnel, so other means had to be found to relieve monotony and prevent boredom while the Fleet was in harbour.

One of the store ships had been converted by Jellicoe into a veritable 'Army & Navy Stores', with various departments where the officers and men of the Fleet could purchase from white-coated shop-assistants practically everything from sports gear to caviare. Another store ship, the *Gourko*, was used as a theatre in her spare time, thus providing stage and seating accommodation, which otherwise would have to be rigged on a warship's quarter-deck. The usual practice was for the *Gourko* to spend three days alongside any warship wishing to stage an entertainment. The first day would be for rigging and rehearsal. On the second day the show would be given to the warship's crew, and on the third day officers and men from other ships in the Fleet would be invited to attend. If the warship happened to be ordered to sea in the middle of a show, the *Gourko* would slip her wires and part company, taking everything with her except the cast and audience. The services of the *Gourko* were much in demand, ships vying with one another to put on the best show. There was plenty of talent in the Fleet, and as time went on a very high standard was achieved. Costumes and wigs were hired from London. Lighting effects, equal to the best London theatres, were devised by the ship's torpedo party, giving intense pleasure to the men who planned and operated them. An augmented orchestra from the Royal Marine band was ensconced in the orchestral pit below the stage, the ship's bandmaster in tails and white tie getting the thrill of his life conducting a chorus of highly talented Welsh miners, in concert with his orchestra.

As no women were available, the female parts were usually taken by young midshipmen, beautifully bewigged and frocked, among whom was Lord Louis Mountbatten, then serving in Beatty's flagship.

There was plenty of variety in the type of entertainment. The *Warspite* won a high reputation by presenting a complete light opera based on Edward German's 'Merrie England'. The *Queen Elizabeth*, being Fleet Flagship, feeling she must outclass them all, astonished the Fleet by putting on a Russian Ballet to the music of Liszt. Those of us who took part in this had reason to appreciate the strenuous nature of the training that ballet dancers must undergo. The company rehearsed for months before the event. The only space available in the ship for this purpose was the submerged torpedo flat, where the deck, being oily, caused some bad falls, and in one case a broken leg.

On the big night when the show was given to the Fleet, the most popular item was the Second Hungarian Rhapsody, which worked the ballet up to a frenzy; any lack of terpsichorean skill being obscured by the wild enthusiasm of the dancers, who were enjoying themselves even more than the audience. At the end the whole audience, including Beatty, rose to their feet demanding an encore. The dancers, on the other hand, having danced at high speed for ten minutes, were none too eager to comply. As one of them said afterwards: 'It was like hearing the distant voice of the referee at a boxing match announcing that there would be an extra round of one minute!' Unfortunately for them, it was not a matter of one minute, it had to be ten minutes 'all out' or nothing.

Thanks to the tact of Surgeon-Commander Digby-Bell who, in addition to his skill as a doctor, possessed considerable histrionic ability, the audience was kept quiet long enough to enable the dancers to recover their breath. After a spell of five minutes, when they had been suitably refreshed, the curtain went up, and to the joy of the sailors the gallant troupe did it all again. It was touch and go. As the curtain descended on their final bow, three members of the ballet fell flat on the stage, and had to be carried off in a state of complete exhaustion.

Beatty was an ardent theatre-goer, and seldom missed a show. These entertainments, usually attended by over two thousand officers and men, made it possible for his personality to become known outside his own Flagship. At the end of the performance he would address the men, always on the same theme: 'Soon they [the High Seas Fleet] will have to come out, and there is only one thing for us to do. Annihilate them.' His optimism was infectious and could be felt throughout the Fleet. Chatfield says: 'It is to David Beatty's everlasting credit that during these monotonous and testing two years he maintained the spirit of the Grand Fleet, its efficiency, harmony, and cheerfulness at the highest possible level.' In their preparation and presentation, the theatrical entertainments refreshed the minds of many men, recalling nostalgic memories of the last leave, and bringing to them the latest song hits, such as, 'If you were the only girl in the world', 'Roses of Picardy', 'Pack up your troubles', and 'Keep the home fires burning'. The theatre ship played no small part in upholding the morale of the Fleet during these weary months of waiting.

Beatty, ever mindful of the welfare of his men, was kept in touch with individual ships through 'Tommy Brand',[1] the Captain of the Fleet, a cheerful, twinkling little man who always seemed to have time to discuss anything with anybody. He was an expert at pouring oil on troubled bald heads, and helping commanding officers with their problems. In consequence he knew everything that was going on. Although the men were happy enough, there was a strong feeling that their friends in the Army and in the little ships were getting all the fighting. No one could have been more sympathetic with this point of view than Beatty, and towards the end of 1917 he had seen an opportunity to grant to a selected few their hearts' desire. The Admiralty had decided to block the harbours of Zeebrugge and Ostend, which had long been used as bases for enemy submarines. Outstanding officers and men were needed, and Beatty had immediately offered the services of six hundred from the Grand Fleet. His offer was gladly accepted. The question of calling for volunteers, however, presented some difficulty, for there was no doubt that every man in the Fleet would offer his services. Secrecy was essential, so Brand was deputed to arrange privately with individual captains for the provision of suitable volunteers from their ships. By this means a magnificent body of men were spirited quietly away on various pretexts to undergo four months' intensive training for 'hazardous service'. Their ultimate achievement now has its place in British naval history.

On 12th April, 1918, the whole Grand Fleet moved to Rosyth, which henceforth became its permanent base. The

---

[1] Later Admiral the Hon. Sir Hubert Brand, G.C.B., K.C.M.G.

anchorage had the advantage of being nearer the enemy, but it was very congested, and the strong tides made manœuvring difficult. At no time, however, did these conditions prevent Beatty from taking his 150 ships to sea by day or by night, or in dense fog. There were some hairbreadth escapes and a few unfortunate mishaps, but as a rule the superb seamanship of the captains and navigators overcame all hazards.

Meanwhile, unknown to the Admiralty, Scheer was preparing to execute the very plan that Beatty had foreseen: 'To take the High Seas Fleet to the coast of Norway, to sink another convoy and its escorting cruisers under the eyes of the neutral skippers; to overwhelm a battle squadron almost within sight of the Norwegian coastguard stations and lighthouse keepers; and to do all this whilst the British armies in Flanders were reeling under the German onslaught would be a success of the first order.'[1] Scheer had learnt from past experiences that he must at all costs get his Fleet to sea without the movement becoming known to the British, otherwise he would have to fight Beatty and the whole Grand Fleet, which was the last thing he wanted. Secrecy depended upon the suppression of wireless signals of a non-routine nature. Accordingly, on the evening of 22nd April, 1918, he concentrated all available ships in the Heligoland Bight, clear of the German rivers, but within the mined area, under the pretext of carrying out routine exercises and drills. While all this was going on Admiral Keyes was delivering his attack on Zeebrugge, and Tyrwhitt, with the Harwich Force, was patrolling between Brown Ridge and the Texel, to prevent enemy interference with that operation. There being no sign of any threat to Keyes, the Admiralty informed the Commander-in-Chief that all seemed quiet in the Bight.

Scheer's quarry, a large Scandinavian convoy with its escort, covered by the Seventh Light Cruiser Squadron and the Second Battle Cruiser Squadron, left Selbjorns Fiord on the afternoon of the same day for the Firth of Forth. Scheer, observing strict wireless silence, reached the end of the German-swept channel by the evening of the following day without being detected, and Beatty was again informed that all was quiet.

[1] *Official History of Naval Operations*, vol. V, p. 282.

Shortly after leaving the mined area, however, some of the enemy ships were sighted by a patrolling British submarine. The weather was thick, and the submarine commander mistook them for British warships working in support of mine-laying operations which had been going on incessantly. He therefore made no report, and the British Commander-in-Chief remained unaware that the High Seas Fleet was at sea.

On the morning of the 24th the convoy reached the Firth of Forth safely, while Scheer, with his vast armada, was warily groping for it along the Norwegian coast. Off Stavanger the *Moltke* developed serious engine trouble, which brought her to a standstill. Scheer ordered the battleship *Oldenburg* to take her in tow, and turned back with the battle fleet for the Heligoland Bight. Not wishing to abandon the operation completely, he directed Hipper to take the battle cruisers as far as Slotterö, where, having found nothing, they also turned for home at high speed. The wireless signals which had been exchanged between Scheer and Hipper on account of this incident were picked up by British directional stations, and at last Beatty was informed that some large operation was actually in progress. He immediately raised steam for full speed, and cleared the Firth of Forth in the early afternoon of the 24th, with thirty-one battleships, four battle cruisers, two cruisers, twenty-four light cruisers, and eighty-five destroyers. He was short of battle cruisers, for the Second Battle Cruiser Squadron was already covering the outgoing convoy which Beatty had allowed to sail from the Forth, being confident that he could deal with Scheer without dislocating the normal flow of trade.

The High Seas Fleet, however, had been retiring south all day, and by nightfall had passed ahead of the Grand Fleet's line of advance. The British submarines patrolling the edge of the minefields in the Bight were now well on the alert; one of them, *E*42 (Lieutenant Charles Allen), got a torpedo into the crippled *Moltke*, but unfortunately she did not sink.

During the afternoon of the 25th, after learning from the Admiralty that the High Seas Fleet had reached its base, Beatty carried out a sweep to the north of the minefields before returning to Rosyth.

So ended the last sortie of the High Seas Fleet. It failed

because Scheer, through faulty intelligence, had miscalculated the date of sailing of the convoy by twenty-four hours. Likewise Beatty, through lack of information and an error on the part of a submarine commander, was too late to intercept the enemy.

Meanwhile, the counter-measures against submarines were being intensified. They included a colossal mine barrage, sponsored by the United States, stretching across the North Sea, between the parallels of 59° and 60° N., from the Shetlands to the Norwegian coast. In areas where the mines were laid deep, a constant patrol of yachts and trawlers was maintained to force down the submarines, or attack them when they came to the surface. Beatty never like the idea of the barrage. Apart from the possibility of restricting the movements of the Grand Fleet, he considered it a dissipation of effort, and believed that better results could be obtained by increasing the number of mines in the Bight and Kattegat. Moreover, except by coercing Norway, there was no way to prevent the enemy from using Norwegian territorial waters to circumvent the barrage at its eastern end.

At a conference held in the *Queen Elizabeth* at the end of August 1918, Beatty stated that it would be most repugnant to himself and to the officers and men of the Grand Fleet to force our way into the territorial waters of a small but high-spirited nation. This, said the Commander-in-Chief, 'would constitute a crime as bad as any the Germans had committed elsewhere'.[1] However, there was no need even to discuss such measures, because by this time the rate of production of merchant ships was far outstripping their losses, while these were steadily diminishing. The submarine war had been won, the German Navy was losing heart, and the British armies were advancing in Flanders.

[1] *Official History of Naval Operations*, vol. V, p. 349.

LETTERS TO LADY BEATTY

April 1917 to September 1918

Beatty's personal narrative in this series of letters covers events described in the foregoing chapter, and a good deal more. Lady Beatty being at Aberdour, he only wrote when the Grand Fleet was based at Scapa, so after April 1918, when he moved the Fleet to Rosyth, his letters cease, except for short periods when he came north again for gunnery and tactical exercises.

Grand Fleet   (*23rd April*, 1917)

We arrived safely this morning. We had a good passage, but the first part was full of shocks, as just before we got to May Island we heard that mines had been discovered to the north of the channel we were to go out by. And seven miles to the eastward of May Island they reported an explosion on the starboard bow and a ship on fire. We had just time to see an unfortunate steamer standing on its tail and disappear about two miles off. It all happened in two minutes. The question was—was it a mine or a torpedo? If the former, it was dangerous to turn round, as we were on the top of the mine-field, and if the latter (a submarine), it was dangerous to go on. I considered the latter was the least dangerous, and rammed the spurs into the good *Queen Bess* and we got through. The *Valiant* was ten miles astern, and so I stopped her and sent her back. I sent one of my destroyers to pick up what they could find of the crew of the unfortunate steamer, and they picked up 13 floating in the water, which I fancy was the whole crew, as she was a very small steamer, and I think now it must have been a submarine that torpedoed her. It seems cruel that these poor little steamers should be sunk in this way. There never was a more cruel and heartless war than this one. . . . We got two Zeppelins yesterday in the North Sea, and up at this end we got two enemy submarines—*this last part is secret*. Our distant patrols got them during the week, so we haven't done badly lately. Perhaps the luck is going to turn. God knows we want a bit of luck just now.

Grand Fleet   (*25th April*, 1917)

Everything at present is given up to the defensive attitude, and even that is not being well done. I am terribly exercised over the question of getting the neutral traffic across the North Sea and down the coasts, and hope to establish a system. [Scandinavian convoys.]

Grand Fleet (*27th April*, 1917)

I pray, not for tranquillity nor that my tribulations may cease, but for opportunity and strength to overcome adversity and make use of opportunity when it comes. They always say opportunity makes the man, but what is more to the point is that man makes the opportunity, and that is where I am beat. I cannot see my way to make the opportunity. Can you help, dear one, with your clear-sighted view of things? . . .

Grand Fleet (*1st May*, 1917)

May day is anything but May like, and my small ships are getting sadly knocked about, but the weary work has to go on—hunting, hunting all day and night and endeavouring to protect the merchant craft. We have been successful up to now, and have not lost one that was under convoy. 'So be it said' touch wood, and we have brought over and down the coast a great number, but this cursed weather plays the devil with my escorting vessels, but I try not to grumble. The Press and the House are making a dead set at poor Carson [Sir Edward Carson, First Lord] and the stupid Admiralty.

Grand Fleet (*3rd May*, 1917)

I fear the agitation will result in removing Carson, who gave me the impression that he was only too ready to go the last time I spoke to him about it. I think with you, his heart is in the Irish question, and he feels that he has not much scope at the Admiralty, it being a very technical service, and that he must support his Naval advisers and does not like acting on his own initiative. Is it possible, do you think, under such circumstances, to do anything to pull the fat out of the fire? With an old vulture like Jacky Fisher sitting on the rail waiting for the corpse to give its last kick—the man who, if he gets there, has pledged himself to turn me out, as I am a danger to the nation, because I do fight the enemy when I meet him. Ye gods, was there ever such an astoundingly humorous situation? How they must laugh, and in the meantime our magnificent Mercantile Fleet is rapidly being destroyed. And the task is gradually assuming proportions that the Archangel Gabriel couldn't put right under six months. What is to be done? I've had my say, I will wait and see what happens to that, and if no attention is paid I must reconsider. There is not a man that I know of who could go to the Admiralty and put it right, *not one*, unless it's Winston! It's very late. I am going to bed and will send by *Renown*.

Grand Fleet (*6th May*, 1917)

I was glad to hear Ryan was getting on with aeroplane control. He certainly does work hard, and I wish everybody was as keen as he is.

[313]

I am pressing Carson to have his very valuable services recognised in the next Birthday Honours List, and I hope he will get the Bath, but don't tell him so or he may be disappointed. . . . There seems to be the makings of an upheaval at the Admiralty, so my representations have borne fruit. Lloyd George and Curzon visited it together, and turned them upside down and made themselves very unpopular. I doubt very much whether any very great real good will come out of it, unless they have a general clear out and put it on a sounder and more practical basis. I have not heard anything more as to my coming down, so I do not anticipate that it will be likely now. Perhaps it's as well. I am better here, but I should like to shake them out of their complacency. I am sorry to hear about the Red Flags in the pockets of the Dockyard men. As long as they keep them in their pockets it's all right. Weren't they harmless pocket-hankies? Red is the colour they favour most. I heard from Mr. James yesterday. They are going to plough up all the beautiful grass fields in Leicestershire. It is right, but it is hard to see them go.

Grand Fleet   (*8th May*, 1917)

   I see there is a large amount of criticism being levelled in the Press at inactivity of the Grand Fleet. They will be wanting my head on a charger soon. . . . I find, on looking up my old papers, that I made suggestions on 8th Dec., 1914, which, if they had been accepted, would never have permitted the submarine menace to reach the proportions it has now. . . . The Admiralty again once more seem to be the target at which all and sundry are letting fly. There are rumours of change, but I pity any poor devils that have to go there and work under the present regime. It is simply impossible to make it a success. Nothing but a clean sweep would be of any value. They will tinker with the question and call the same people by different names, and all will go on as before, until another disturbance greater than the last will have an uprooting effect. I am not consulted and do not know what is going on. I have given Carson my opinion, and I doubt if he is strong enough to take it. But we shall see. Of one thing I am certain. I have no idea or liking of leaving the Grand Fleet and clearing up the mess for them. I can do my duty best by keeping the Fleet ready and prepared against the day, which cannot be far off, when we shall have to fight like the devil, after which I am prepared to do anything.

Grand Fleet   (*11th May*, 1917)

   I have come to the conclusion that I must move very warily. If I attack the Admiralty too vigorously and *successfully*, it will end in my having to go there, and that means leaving the Grand Fleet, which I should not like, and moreover I do not think would be a good thing. I also am of the opinion (perhaps I am biased) that of the two appointments, i.e. C.-in-C. or 1st Sea Lord, the most important one from the national point of view is the Grand Fleet. If that went wrong or if it did not succeed in destroying the enemy for a second time on meeting them, then we may as well put the shutters up. We should be done. I can still harass the Admiralty and goad them into doing something before it is too late. . . . We are out of luck at this end. We have had many hunts after the Subs, but have always, when it has come to the final blow, just missed the shot, five in the last week, too sickening. They have always been saved by a hair's-breadth. But our turn will come. We have harassed them, and have had only two ships torpedoed out of 150 in the last fortnight, and these old merchant craft are terribly slow and the days are getting very long.

Grand Fleet (18*th May*, 1917)

[After hearing that his eldest brother, Charlie Beatty, had died of wounds.]

I am quite stunned by the blow, and words fail to express what I think and what I feel. They are so useless and are of no avail. I don't understand what happened. I have lost my oldest, my truest, and best friend, and the world has lost the straightest and truest gentleman in it. Poor little man, his troubles are over, and I can almost feel that in some measure it is a release, as he felt bitterly his mutilated condition and that he was not doing anything further. His gallant soul fretted terribly. Thank God I saw him the other day, and Lu must take comfort in the fact that she has had him to herself for so long just before it happened. I have a telegram just come from Fripp that he died under an operation. I can hardly bear it when I think of all he suffered and how plucky he was. When I think of the happy days of long ago, when we grew up together, played together, fought together and hunted together, I can't write any more. Thank God I have much to do. We go out for exercises tomorrow. I shall be better when we come back.

Grand Fleet (22*nd May*, 1917)

The King very kindly sent me a nice telegram which I enclose. It is hard not to be thinking of poor little Charlie all the time when my mind is not occupied with my work. And it is so useless that it makes me angry. We had some busy days at sea and some very interesting exercises and deployments. I am working out some new tactics which I think promise well, but our opportunities are so few and far between, and the submarines are so numerous that it makes a great burden and responsibility taking the Fleet to sea purely for exercises, and yet, if we don't practise them, we shall do no good. . . . I haven't heard from Carson except a telegram asking for my views on a certain question. I have written him two letters of considerable length and importance lately, and have received no answer to either.[1] I will give him another 48 hours, and if I do not get an answer, I will send him a snorter. I expect the unfortunate man is thinking mostly about his pledges on the Ulster question, and doesn't know which way to turn to get out of an awkward situation.

Grand Fleet   *(24th May,* 1917)

Roger Keyes returned to the fold of the Grand Fleet yesterday very pleased with himself at having been presented with a son.[2] You must get me a mug for him, as he is another godson. . . . Sturdee is a great supporter of mine now. I have humoured the old beggar, and he is loyal and helpful and we get on very well. In fact, all my admirals are splendid, and help me enormously to keep things going, and all our relations are harmonious. Dear old John de Robeck is like a two-year-old, and you wouldn't believe he is the same man as joined up six months ago. Six months I have commanded the Grand Fleet now, and we haven't met the enemy yet. How many months are we to wait? I would not mind how many if I knew at the end we would get them, but it is the haunting fear that we never shall, and the Grand Fleet will never be able to justify itself, that is the fly in the ointment. I have been asked by several officers of high degree if it is my intention to recognise or celebrate the 31st May [Jutland]. My answer is that that was one of the saddest days of my life, on which I lost many old and valued friends and trusted comrades, and the Navy missed one of the greatest opportunities of achieving the greatest and most glorious victory and, therefore, it could not be in any sense considered a day for celebration. I like your idea of a Memorial Service. It must be that and nothing more.

Grand Fleet   *(27th May,* 1917)

Yes, there has been a moderation in the number of ships sunk, and we have been getting submarines, 3 up here last week, I think all fairly good and substantial cases. Yes, you are right, Carson is a politician first and a patriot second. He wrote me that he was unable to write before because he had been so busy over the Irish question! . . . All the Captains tell me that we have made immense strides in the gunnery of the Fleet. I know that, but it is a good sign when they come and tell me so, and I don't think I have made them unhappy or discontented.

[1] Appendix VI.
[2] Later Lieut.-Col. Geoffrey C. T. Keyes, V.C., killed in the 1939–45 war.

My dear little Talbot[1] has joined the *Birkenhead*—be kind to him when he comes to Rosyth. . . . I got such a dear letter from Charlie to be sent to me if anything happened to him. It is terribly sad getting a letter like that. It was written just before he went to France 2½ years ago.

Grand Fleet   (*29th May*, 1917)

I return you the battle cruisers, I trust safely, and hope you will have, as I am sure it will be, a nice Service on the afternoon of the 31st. I think their sojourn up here has done them good, and I pray that the lessons that have been learnt have been rammed home. I have done my best to do so, and it is all important that they should stick. I shall get the Second B.C.S. up here shortly and give them a go. It will do them good, also old Lambert and his lot, Second Light Cruiser Squadron. I think and hope got another Sub, making 4 for the week, but this is for your information *only*. I have laid traps in many places, and am always changing them, but chances are not very good. . . .

Grand Fleet   (*31st May*, 1917)

It hardly seems a year since that terrible day when we might have accomplished so much and our failure to do so has cost us dear, when those great ships and gallant lives were lost [Jutland]. As time goes by, one realises more clearly the opportunity that was missed, an opportunity that will never recur, and what would have been easy then will be infinitely more difficult in the future. Fate is not over-generous in the matter of giving opportunities, and if you miss one you never get another. However, I console myself with the thought that the Battle Cruiser Fleet did all that it could have done, and that next time, if Fate is kind and gives us a next time, the battle fleet will have their chance. The weary waiting is hard indeed, but the sailors are so extraordinarily happy and cheerful through it all, bless them, that they help me in the execution of my duties. We are never still all day and manœuvring about, and all acknowledge that we are advancing in efficiency day by day . . . until our great day comes to prove that it has not been all wasted effort. The fly in the ointment is the dread that that day may never come and all our efforts will have been in vain. I never allow myself to think or speak of such a possibility, but at the back of my mind it is always there like a nightmare. I hope that your [Memorial] Service this afternoon was a success, which I am sure it was, as everything that you do is well done. I am sorry that the other battle cruisers did not get down in time, but they did not get their firing finished until this afternoon. . . . I am not surprised to hear that Sir Edward Carson can realise what the defects at

[1] Captain H. F. G. Talbot, D.S.O., R.N., had served with Beatty on the Nile.

the Admiralty are. They are as plain as the nose on your face, but if he is fussed over Ireland, he won't give much time to so little a thing as that!! These politicians are all alike.

Grand Fleet   (*4th June*, 1917)

I have been out all day exercising with the destroyers, a great gathering, and only returned very late, and am as usual, when I go away from the telegraph, deluged with questions. I got a wire that they have given Ryan a C.B. I am delighted. Nobody deserves it more. I suppose there is a great list, no doubt most of them well deserved, but sure to be full of those that are not. I hear Jellicoe is very seedy and has had to go away for a rest. The submarine menace is no more in hand to-day than it was 3 months ago. They might flood the Admiralty with civilians and soldiers, but it will serve no purpose unless the heads change their views and adopt the strongest measures.

Grand Fleet   (*19th June*, 1917)

I feel all the better for my short visit, and it was a rest and a delightful change to see you and little Peter, but we have got to pay for it now. I am in the middle of a big operation against enemy submarines which I pray may be successful. I have denuded myself of all Destroyers, Subs., Patrol-vessels, Sea-planes, Air-ships, etc., in the effort, so the Fleet is immobilised for the time being. It's no use pecking at it.

Grand Fleet   (*20th June*, 1917)

Every day we get reports of opportunities missed fire, sheer bad luck, not the fault of our fellows. It really is rather crushing, and they are working like blacks and feel the disappointment more than I do, poor dears. Their hearts are in the right place and in time it must tell. The King arrives tomorrow. . . . I shall have to work double tides while he is here. . . . He brings with him seventeen journalists, two cinemato-graphers, two photographers. What are we to do with them?

Grand Fleet   (*22nd June*, 1917)

The King arrived last night in a howling gale of wind. Mercifully I have got the Electric Light Bath, so popped him into it. He had just come from an intense heat-wave, so the change was very severe. We then had the most terrific thunderstorm lasting for hours, which of course elected to break upon us as the unfortunate admirals were coming on board to dinner. So they arrived like drenched rats. The King was followed by a regiment of Press men, and included cinema operators of every description. They were brought across the Pentland Firth in the ordinary mail-steamer. At the best of times it is not pleasant, but last night it tried these unfortunate gentlemen very highly, and I believe the scene on board beggars description. Three nearly died, and had to be hoisted on board a limp mass of inert humanity. One was senseless and a complete collapse. They will have some startling things to say about Scapa. This morning it was still blowing very hard, so had to abandon our program and spent the morning going round the ship, which pleased the King and interested the men enormously. We then had him photographed. We were then bagged by the cinema man in every conceivable position. What happened to the Journalists I do not know. I sent him [the King] off to lunch with Madden and go round some of the ships, so I think he is quite happy. The teetotal business is a severe trial.[1] The old boys don't get communicative without drink of some form or other. No luck with the Subs, have seen many, harassed them, and no doubt have counteracted what was a very determined attack upon our trade, but we have not been successful in getting more than one up to this.

Grand Fleet   (*24th June*, 1917)
    What with Monarchs and Submarines, we are having a hectic time. No program has been of any use, as it simply could not be kept, but we have struggled along supported by Barley Water!! . . . And he is sympathetic with our troubles and difficulties. . . . In the evening I took him out in the *Queen Elizabeth*, and we did a shoot with her and the Fifth Battle Squadron, after steaming round and round like a dog after its tail until the weather cleared. I was rather afraid of stopping out too long, as the enemy Subs are always about, and it would have been a tragedy if we had been torpedoed with him on board. . . . I hear of more rumblings of discontent at the Admiralty's conduct of the war. . . . I have been very careful to explain that my relations with Jellicoe are very friendly. I think he has enjoyed his visit. He dined with me each night and lunched with the different Admirals each day, and was very funny as to the food they gave him to eat. When he returned today from lunching with old John de Robeck, he said he had had nothing to eat that he could eat. I said we had had some excellent dressed crab, whereupon he said he would have some!! The things you sent me were of great value. . . . I hope the garden is coming along nicely and the roses behaving themselves.

Grand Fleet   (*29th June*, 1917)
    We are very busy still hunting Subs, and got another day before yesterday, but these odd ones here and there are not sufficient. We must

---

[1] His Majesty, as an example to the nation, had banished from his table all wines and spirits for the duration of the war.

do much better than that or we shall be defeated. The situation is very serious and I feel very powerless at present. I shall be glad when O. de Brock [Chief of Staff] returns tomorrow night, and perhaps he will bring me some encouraging news, or I shall be compelled to present an ultimatum to them [Admiralty]. You will rejoice with me to hear that they have promoted Flags [Seymour] and Strutt[1] the one to be a Commander and the other to be a Captain. They are at present imbibing strong drink to a chorus of congratulations. I have packed old Sturdee off on a fortnight's leave and intend to do the same with all my Admirals in turn. They pretend they do not want it, but all are really delighted to go, and I am sure it will do them no end of good.

Grand Fleet (*3rd July*, 1917)

I had a charming letter from the King thanking me for his visit and the care we took of him. It was nice of him to write, as he very seldom does do that, and it points to the fact that he really did enjoy himself and appreciated our efforts under difficult circumstances.

Grand Fleet (*6th July*, 1917)

I was very glad to hear your Concert was a success. How delicious to be able to sit in the garden and listen to really divine voices and good music. It fairly makes my mouth water. I wonder when I shall ever hear good music again or enjoy any of the pleasing amenities of life. After all, really good music is one of the most inspiring things in the world and helps to put one's thoughts on a higher plane. Instead I have to turn to wrestling with the Admiralty on paper, which I loathe. The situation is extraordinarily complex, and I simply cannot get on without discussions and must see the Admiralty officials. . . . I am not taking things too seriously, so don't fuss, dear heart, but they are getting seriouser and seriouser as Alice in Wonderland said, and I must ginger somebody up.

Grand Fleet (*11th July*, 1917)

A terrible calamity has befallen us, and one of my fine battleships blew up at anchor at 11.30 on Monday night. The poor old *Vanguard*, with 1,000 men on board.[2] In two seconds it was all over. The explosion was terrific. Two men and one officer only were picked up, and the latter died soon after. Luckily 15 officers were out of the ship on board another

---

[1] Master of the Fleet.

[2] The cause of the internal explosion which wrecked the *Vanguard* was never actually proved, but there is little doubt that the disaster was due to defective cordite, which became unstable at high temperatures. During the course of the war the battleship *Bulwark*, the cruiser *Natal*, the minelayer *Princess Irene*, and the monitor *Glatton* all suffered the same fate.

'The Surrender of the German Fleet, Admiral Beatty reading out the terms. Fore Cabin H.M.S. *Queen Elizabeth*, Rosyth, November 16, 1918. *Painted by Sir John Lavery, A.R.A. (Raphael Tuck)*

ship at the time. A boat's crew was away, and 3 officers and 50 odd men had been sent away on leave to make room for Admiral Sturdee and his Staff, who *were* going to turn over to her while his ship the *Hercules* was undergoing a refit. But fortunately for him and his Staff, I sent them on leave instead, or else he and all his Staff would have been among the victims. It is an overwhelming blow and fairly stuns me to think about. We expect these things to happen in the heat of battle, but when lying peacefully at anchor it is very much more terrible.

Grand Fleet (13*th July*, 1917)

We have had another success with the Subs. You can have no idea what a fillip it is to score even a small success in times like the present. The poor old *Vanguard* incident is fading away. It is wonderful how the sailors put these things out of their mind almost immediately. We were under the shadow of a great calamity one minute and it is almost forgotten the next. Such is life, and God knows I would not have it otherwise. The sailors are full of heart, but like children, forget at once. For instance today we had a great Boxing Carnival on the Island. I thought I wouldn't put it off, as it would help to make them forget, and bless them they enjoyed themselves largely for 9 hours, looking at men hammering themselves, 18,000 of them, an immense concourse. I went up for the Finals and presented the Prizes, and took the opportunity of talking to them and telling them what fine fellows they were. They were a very sympathetic audience. As for the poor old *Vanguard* lying at the bottom of the Harbour with 1,000 gallant souls on board, they had forgotten all about it, and I am glad it was so.

[Later in the year Beatty visited the Admiralty and afterwards wrote this letter to a friend.]

Grand Fleet (30*th Nov.*, 1917)

It is terribly unsatisfactory to go down there for so short a visit and to be boxed up all the time arguing and talking in the Admiralty. By the way, I see or rather read that the *Daily Mail* is conducting a most outrageous campaign vilifying the Admiralty in general and the unfortunate Jellicoe in particular. This is against all fair play. He cannot reply, and as long as he occupies the important and responsible position he does, he is entitled to some measure of protection against the Press. It is doing an immense amount of harm and no good. It is destroying confidence in the Directing Powers of the Great Service, and causing a feeling of disquiet and uneasiness in the higher direction which must have a baneful effect. It looks to me as if somebody in the Government was at the bottom of it. L. G. probably, or it would not be permitted. Fair criticism is one thing, but this is another. And if it continues, nobody is safe and nobody will be trusted. However, I hope it will all come out in the wash. What we want is a bit of luck just now. Not that I think the war or the Naval part of it is going to be won by good luck. Good direction and appreciation is generally rewarded by good luck and vice versa. . . .

Grand Fleet (*29th Dec.*, 1917)

Just a line in great haste. I always seem to be doing things against time nowadays. I was glad to hear from you that you all had a pleasant and quiet Xmas. Dear little Dadie's beautiful present of the little aquatints was delightful. Did he choose them himself? They are much admired, and my lovely kettle which I am now making tea with as soon as this mail goes. Really, it seems at times as if I will never get things finished. Have you seen old Lambert?[1] We gave him a good bucketing, and I fear it upset him inside. I've had to keep Jack Sinclair up here, as I wanted more light cruisers. . . . Did you hear about Lady X? She was driving her small car in Piccadilly and, wanting to turn up a side-street, put her hand out to stop the traffic, whereupon a man on the pavement kissed it. She had him arrested for assault, but the magistrate dismissed the case as frivolous, and said he could not recognise any assault.

Grand Fleet (*16th Jan.*, 1918)

I feel as if we were at the North Pole and expect to see Polar Bears wandering about. There does not seem any prospect of a change. I only hope and pray that the Huns are having it as cold as we are. The unfortunate train with drafts from the Fleet was snowed up for two days on the mainland, and all communication has been cut off north of Invergordon. It is still stuck in the snow and they are trying to dig it out, as they have no heat and no food.

It was a good thing for many reasons I came up. It is desirable that the C.-in-C. should share their troubles and there is much to be done.

Grand Fleet (*17th Jan.*, 1918)

My poor two destroyers [*Narborough* and *Opal*] had a terrible ending. They tried to make the anchorage in a blinding snowstorm which, of course, was wrong, and they paid the penalty, both running full tilt on to the rocks, where they were battered to pieces in a very short time. Only one survivor out of 180, and he had the most remarkable escape.

[1] Rear-Admiral C. F. Lambert, who had relieved Rear-Admiral Goodenough in command of the Second Light Cruiser Squadron.

He was thrown by the waves on to the rocks and, being a very strong man, clung on and dragged himself up the cliff and on to a ledge, where he remained through two nights very bitter, and was found the second day after. How he survived the exposure and the cold is remarkable, but he appears none the worse.

The snow was so thick and heavy that search-parties along the shore could not get near the cliffs, which were ten feet deep in snow, and it is feared that other men got ashore only to perish in the snow. It is very hard on them to have such a terrible end, especially during war, when they might have died fighting. But so it is, and it is no use crying over spilt milk.

Grand Fleet (*8th Feb.*, 1918)

No, I don't think it would be a good thing to whack out a lot of money.[1] Money is the one thing they do not want, and a bluejacket is a very funny fellow, and does not appreciate it when money is provided for him. He likes to feel that his own money is producing the good things that he likes, and then he takes more pride and notice in them. . . . That was a great misfortune, the torpedoing of the *Tuscania* full of American soldiers, and they saved *all* the officers and 2,011 men out of 2,156, which was a great performance, but 83 of the crew were lost out of 200, which shows that they stuck to their ship and did all they could to save those in their charge, another good mark for the British Mercantile Marine.

Grand Fleet (*14th Feb.*, 1918)

I pray they don't succeed in turning out Robertson, as he is a sound and able old man [Field-Marshal Sir William Robertson, C.I.G.S.]. If the Press and the politicians would leave the Army and Navy alone every now and then, it would help things along. And give them time to concentrate on the enemy instead of spending their time in trying to defeat the intrigues.

Grand Fleet (*29th March*, 1918)

The more one hears the more one is impressed with the great fighting qualities of the British soldier. The strange part is that for some reason or other he always has to face overwhelming odds. What would he do if the odds were overwhelmingly in his favour? It would seem that there was nothing that he could not do. . . . I think the last eight days have been the most appallingly anxious we have ever had. It is difficult to

[1] Lady Beatty's Jutland Fund, finally incorporated in the Royal Naval Benevolent Trust.

write, think, or do anything else but pore over the maps and wait for news. But we shall have to go on with our own job, and I am glad to say we have had some successes of a small but valuable character, and we are making the Hun dance to our tune now instead of the reverse, and we are surely getting him rattled. . . . I very nearly brought the Fleet south, but am marking time, and am quite ready to move at a moment's notice. This for you only.

Grand Fleet (*2nd April,* 1918)

There is no doubt Germany will not reap much benefit from her victory over Russia for some very considerable time to come, probably not before the autumn of next year. But it is a foolish man who attempts to forecast what will happen six months ahead and a wicked and unpatriotic man who talks of peace at all.

Grand Fleet (*5th April,* 1918)

I am sorry Richmond[1] has to go to the Admiralty, but I feel that he will do good work there. He has brains, has studied, and will, I hope, be a great help to me. He is of an independent character, and will always say what he thinks, which is one of the reasons I could not get them to take him there before.

Grand Fleet (*7th April,* 1918)

If he [the enemy] succeeds in breaking through and forces the British to wheel back for the defence of our Channel ports, it may be well worth his while to have a combined Naval and Military offensive, using his ships to destroy our communications across the Channel, even at the risk of being intercepted. If he fails, and fails badly, in sheer desperation he may be tempted to try a last coup at the British coast. We must always remember that he is ruled by a great Military Party who count risks and losses as nothing, who may make the same mistake as Napoleon did, and gamble upon obtaining a Naval victory. With such in my mind one cannot afford to run the shadow of a risk, as an indecisive action on the sea with the Main Fleets would amount to a German victory. Therefore, at all costs we must aim at annihilation. To obtain that is indeed a difficult problem, the North Sea is so small and the spread of ships so great that in a few hours the beggars can retire behind minefields and submarine screens in their own waters. I often wonder what Nelson would have thought of it. His high spirit would have chafed him to death by this time.

[1] Captain H. W. Richmond, commanding H.M.S. *Conqueror.*

[324]

Grand Fleet   (*No date*)

. . . If your young friends, when they condemn everything wholesale, would only provide me or you with some valuable suggestions as to how to improve matters, I should be eternally grateful. You must remember that destructive criticism carries with it no responsibility, whereas constructive criticism does. My one great difficulty is to get the younger officers to voice their views and ideas, and I think I can truthfully say that I have done my best to encourage it and to make use of it. I have started them writing essays on every sort of subject. I have given prizes for the best, and everybody in the Fleet knows quite well that if they send in anything it will receive sympathetic treatment. I have received much, but not enough and amazingly little of any real value. I don't tell them that, but ask them to try again. The result is I have a very poor opinion of the brains of any, old or young. I am always being told young so and so is so clever and can do this and that, and I catch hold of them and try and get something out, but the bubble always bursts, and I generally find they have earned their reputation by having a caustic tongue and a gift of criticising all that is done and being tried destructively. They can knock down, but they can't build up again. The old gentlemen can't either, but they have learnt a little wisdom and do not indulge so freely in damning everything and everybody.

Grand Fleet   (*24th June*, 1918)

We have been at sea all day, and have been very busy, and the results very satisfactory. At last am beginning to see the fruits of our labours, and feel that we really have made gigantic strides towards improving our efficiency and it was not only a chance success. Please God our time will soon come when we can put it to the test and reap our reward.

Grand Fleet   (*25th June*, 1918)

I hear there are all sorts of intrigues going on still to remove Haig from the command. Why or who or what is at the bottom of it I cannot understand, but intrigue is as the breath of life to some people, and it will no doubt go on until the end of the war whoever is in command. Doubtless they say the same about me, and no doubt I should be the last to hear of it. But what does it matter so long as one does one's best? Another gale is approaching just reported from the weather office. What a life!

Grand Fleet   (*26th June*, 1918)

Weather just awful, tinges everything with depression. Truly this is the most damnable place on earth. For four days it has been the same without respite. Even the Midshipmen are becoming depressed, and even the good news from Italy fails to cheer us up. . . . I had four Provincial Premiers and a Canadian Senator, a Mr. McLennan, a great friend of Ellen Hood's, up here yesterday. They came and dined with me last night, a very typical party worthy and full of Imperialism. They were thrilled with what they saw. We took them out to witness a firing of a Subdivision of Ships. So they had a good object-lesson in the might, majesty, and power of the Grand Fleet.

Grand Fleet (*4th July*, 1918)

Old Rodman and the Americans are busy celebrating the 4th July. I sent them over to the other side of the anchorage [Scapa Flow] to do what he liked. What they can do is hard to say. I shall be glad to get out of this place, and hope to be with you Sunday evening or Monday morning. Not a soul knows at this end of my intention, so it will be interesting to see if anybody knows at your end before they sail to meet me.

Grand Fleet (1918)

I had Mr. Gompers[1] to luncheon, a very quaint person, said to be the most powerful man in the United States. I cannot believe it. Think he was very nervous with us, fine old head, but very slow in his delivery, and talked as if he was making a speech, was very proud of the fact that he was a Cockney, and was much impressed by the sight of the Grand Fleet.

Grand Fleet (*Sept.*, 1918)

I cannot imagine that the morale of the German submarine crews can be maintained against the heavy losses they sustain when they hear on their return that the war is being lost on land. We hear that there has been considerable discontent showing itself in the Navy at Kiel, necessitating the presence of the Emperor. Well, there are two ways of looking at that. If there is real discontent, the best way to kill it is to send them to sea. On the other hand if there is no discontent, the advent of the Kaiser may be the preliminary to an undertaking by the Naval Forces; whichever way you have it, it might be said to portend the advent of the High Seas Fleet. . . . We know that of all things he is desirous of regaining his Colonies, and the latter without a Navy are of no value. Therefore, if he thinks there is any chance of securing his Colonies in the Peace Terms, he is not likely to risk the destruction of his Navy. On the other hand, if he recognises that he has no chance of recovering his Colonies after the war, then he may consider the possibility of attempting some great

[1] Mr. Samuel Gompers, an influential American labour leader.

blow with the High Seas Fleet. But generally speaking the prospects are poor. It is terrible to think that after all these weary months of waiting we shall not have an opportunity of striking a blow. But events are moving so rapidly just now that anything might happen. The advance of combined French, Belgian, and British troops under *Le Roi des Belges* is a moving and far-reaching effort, and may produce great happenings, eventuating in the clearing of Ostend, Zeebrugge, and Bruges, and this might cause Naval movement, hence I may return south at any moment.

CHAPTER FIFTEEN

1918
VICTORY

Anxious days · Beatty and the Armistice terms · Surrender

THE last two months of the war were anxious ones for Beatty. While watching the High Seas Fleet, he had to see that political considerations did not override the requirements of British naval strategy.

In a letter to a friend, Beatty says:

Grand Fleet   *Undated. Probably about 5th Oct.,* 1918

The nearer we get to the end of the Drama the closer shall I sit to my Seat in the Dress Circle and wish it was the first row of the Stalls. I have burst a bomb over the Admiralty today, and we must wait and see how they take it. It may require my presence south earlier than I intended. . . . The news continues superlatively good, and the Hun is making tracks out of Belgium or rather the Flanders coast part of it. Unfortunately, owing to the supineness of the Naval Direction of Affairs, he is getting away scatheless, and not being made to pay as he ought and that is heavily. That is another story and not a very pleasant one. But the dark clouds do appear to be rolling back and the prospects are good. . . . After much interruption I am able to snatch a moment to continue my scrawl. . . . Ever since the month of August it has done nothing but blow, and this cramps one's style terribly and knocks my poor small ships about. Telegram just come. Germany is squealing for a cessation of hostilities. It is not to be thought of for a moment just when we are getting some of our own back. And it behoves us to be more on the alert than ever. It is just at such times that they may be expected to do something desperate. It will have the effect of shaking the Turk in any case, and whatever happens with the Hun, I doubt the Turk remaining in the war after the end of this month. But it is simply inconceivable that we should dream of ceasing hostilities until we have everything that we want. No matter what comes of it. It is the 'Writing on the Wall'. And the utter defeat of the damnable Hun is not likely to be long delayed. But we *must never* return them their Colonies.

Scheer had become Chief of the German Naval Staff, and there were indications that he would order Hipper, who had succeeded him as Commander-in-Chief, to take the High Seas Fleet on a 'death-ride'. The German armies were in full retreat on the Continent, the Flanders naval bases had been evacuated, and the German submarine war on merchant shipping had practically ceased. Now or never was the moment for Germany to play her last card. Scheer and Hipper knew that Germany had nothing to lose by defeat at sea, but if their Fleet could achieve even partial victory, it would restore the prestige of the fighting forces, and have a favourable influence on peace negotiations. Beatty was well prepared for such an eventuality, and was confident he could annihilate the enemy. The Grand Fleet was fully concentrated at Rosyth, and was trained to the highest peak of fighting efficiency, its ships had received the new type of shell, and all were looking forward with the greatest enthusiasm to the moment, so often predicted by their Commander-in-Chief, when the High Seas Fleet would come out for the last round.

The prospect was pleasing, but the last round was never to be fought. On 5th October, 1918, the German Chancellor asked the President of the United States to bring about the immediate conclusion of an armistice on land, water, and in the air; consequently the allied Premiers directed their naval and military representatives at Versailles to prepare armistice conditions upon the basis of eight directing rules, which need not be repeated here. These outlined purely military conditions; there was only one naval clause, demanding the cessation of submarine warfare, and stating that the allied blockade would continue. Nothing was said about the surrender of the High Seas Fleet or the disposal of enemy surface warships.

Here was a striking example of the continental military mind in the flush of victory, completely forgetting that every British and American soldier, all their equipment, and every round they fired had been brought to France under the cover of the British Grand Fleet. The allied Premiers had also forgotten that the enemy submarine offensive could be built up and later renewed with greater vigour, so long as the High Seas Fleet remained in being.

In response to the Premiers' request, Foch and his staff produced draft armistice terms, which made no mention of naval conditions; while the allied naval and military representatives submitted another which laid down that the entire German Surface Fleet was to be interned, during the armistice period, in ports approved by the Allies.

It soon became evident that there was a body of opinion among the Allies, led by Marshal Foch, that was afraid to press the naval requirements too strongly, for fear the enemy should refuse to accept the terms as a whole, and so prejudice the rigorous nature of the military clauses. Foch went so far as to say that German submarines were the only section of the Fleet that need be surrendered, as they alone had done any harm. In the interests of British sea power, Beatty became very apprehensive, and flatly asked the Admiralty, 'Who wanted the Armistice?' If the enemy really wanted it they would accept any conditions, but if they only wished to gain time to escape utter defeat, the conditions must be so severe that they would either have to continue fighting or lay down their arms.

At this time Beatty and the First Sea Lord, Sir Rosslyn Wemyss, were in constant communication. On 10th October, Wemyss wrote:

MY DEAR DAVID,

I have just sent you a telegram suggesting that you should put off the refit of the *Queen Elizabeth*, and I now give you the reasons:

(1) The German reply to Wilson's Note will be made today (Saturday) and we know for certain that the reply will be conciliatory.

(2) The President will then have to formulate the terms on which an armistice will be granted. The naval and military terms which were agreed to at Versailles are hard, and it is not probable that the terms which will be put forward by Wilson will be anything else.

(3) We know that Berlin has declared that Germany is entitled to 'honourable terms'.

(4) If the new Government in Germany accepts the terms of the armistice, one of two things will probably happen:

(a) The military party will make a final effort to control the country by declaring a military dictatorship and by removing the new Government. This would certainly cause a prolongation of the war and *probably* involve a movement of the Fleet; or (*b*) If the terms are accepted and the military party are in no position to attempt action, the armistice comes into force.

Thus, in either case, the next fortnight will surely be one of the most critical of the war, and must be fraught with great possibilities, and every effort should be made to have the Grand Fleet ready for instant action with yourself present.

Events are moving rapidly, and one feels that even an hour may make the greatest difference in the situation, and it appears to me that we have arrived at a moment when either the war collapses or when the most likely psychological moment, if ever, has arrived for the High Seas Fleet to make some demonstration.

Yours in great haste,

R. WEMYSS.

The correspondence continued, Beatty writing in his usual forceful manner urging that the High Seas Fleet and Heligoland must be surrendered to him, as Commander-in-Chief in the North Sea. He also raised the question of opening up the Baltic and the immediate disclosure by the enemy of all minefields.

Wemyss was in agreement with most of Beatty's points, but reminded him with great tact, that some of our allies were more difficult to deal with than the enemy. Both admirals realised that letter writing was an unsatisfactory medium for discussing matters of such grave importance, and it was arranged that Beatty should attend a meeting of the War Cabinet on 21st October (Trafalgar Day) to consider the Naval terms of an Armistice proposed by the Admiralty. Beatty was loath to leave the Fleet, even for a day, at such a critical time, but the Admiralty assured him that the moment was propitious, and a special train having been placed at his disposal, he attended the meeting at 10 Downing Street. The views he expressed to the War Cabinet on this occasion are recorded in his own handwriting thus:[1]

'The Views of the Commander-in-Chief, Grand Fleet, as expressed at the War Cabinet meeting on Monday, 21st October, to the Cabinet as a whole, and to individual members of the Cabinet on the subject of:

---

[1] MSS. in possession of Earl Beatty.

"THE NAVAL TERMS OF AN ARMISTICE"

'1. I assumed that the object of the war was: "The destruction of German Militarism."

'From the Naval point of view: "The destruction of German Sea Power."

'2. I asked whether the general circumstances of the war from the military point of view made it necessary or desirable that we should have an Armistice? If the answer was in the affirmative, I recognised that the Naval terms proposed would most certainly prevent it at this juncture. If, however, the enemy condition was such as would cause them to accept the Military terms as outlined by the Field-Marshal, then it was possible that they would accept also the Naval terms.

'3. The Military successes have been great, and the Military terms are commensurate with their achievements. The Navy made them possible and therefore shares in them.

'The Navy also has won a great Passive Victory, has swept the enemy from the seas, rendered secure the vast lines of communications with our Allies, and permitted the trade of this country, necessary for existence, to continue. Because ours is a Passive Victory, it is no reason why the Empire should not reap the fruits of that Victory.

'4. We have built up a great Military organisation, but the British nation still exists on Sea Power. Although a platitude, it is one which will bear constant repetition, that even though we gain many victories on land, one defeat at sea and the Allied cause is lost. Inversely we may be defeated and crushed on land, but if we maintain our supremacy at sea, the Empire will weather the storm.

[How true this proved to be in 1940!]

'Therefore, in framing our Naval terms, since the existence of the Empire depends on our Sea Power, we must ensure that no fleet in being is left which can threaten our supremacy. No compromise on this vital point is possible.

'If there is to be elasticity in the terms of the Armistice, it must be on the Military side and not on the Naval side.

'It must be our particular care to safeguard the Naval side

of any Armistice with the enemy. Our Allies as land powers may be expected to safeguard the Military side.

'5. The question as to what approximation the Terms of Armistice should have to the Terms of Peace.

'It was apparently the opinion of the Cabinet that the time between arriving at an Armistice and signing the terms of Peace would be long, even possibly as much as twelve months. It was also accepted that after living under conditions of an Armistice for so long, the possibility of returning to war conditions was highly improbable.

'During the Armistice, and in arranging the Terms of Peace, assuming the best will in the world, friction was bound to arise between the Allies, which would be intensified by the action of Germany, who would devote every effort to sowing dissension.

'These factors make it very desirable that the terms of the Armistice should be as nearly as possible the Terms of Peace. Therefore the Naval Terms of the Armistice must be stiff, and such that will achieve one of the objects for which we are fighting: "The destruction of German Sea Power."

'6. To achieve the destruction of German Sea Power and reduce Germany to the status of a second-rate Naval Power, it is necessary to lay down in the Naval Terms of the Armistice conditions which would be commensurate with the result of a Naval action, i.e. the result of the Armistice should be what we expect would be the result of a Naval action as regards the relative strength of the two forces. The question had been asked whether it would not be sufficient for the Enemy to surrender the whole of their Submarines without humiliating them to the extent that would be entailed by surrendering the ships laid down in the Naval terms.

'The Power behind the Submarine warfare of the enemy is the High Seas Fleet. Remove that Power and the Submarine menace would completely collapse. The removal of the High Seas Fleet would allow of the whole of the Forces of the Grand Fleet being set free to tackle the Submarine menace at its source, i.e. the Enemy bases.

'The Bases could be ringed in by Mine Barriers, obstructions and nets, which could be guarded by comparatively light Patrols, which could be continuous and of sufficient strength as circumstances required.

'The removal therefore of the High Seas Fleet means the removal of the one Naval menace—the Submarine.

'On the other hand, if we insist on the handing over of Enemy Submarines and leave the High Seas Fleet intact, then the position of affairs, so far as the relative Naval strength is concerned, is precisely the same as that which obtained at the commencement of hostilities.

'During four years of war the enemy has built up a huge Submarine Fleet. In four years of peace he can do all and more than this, and with the High Seas Fleet in being, and assuredly stronger than ever, Germany will again menace the Sea Power of Great Britain. As a consequence, Sea Power being vital to our existence, excessive expenditure on armament will be entailed at a time when the economic effect of such expenditure is likely to be serious.

'Remove the power of the High Seas Fleet now, and definitely reduce the continental nation of Germany to that of a second-rate Naval Power, corresponding to her geographical position and requirements, and *our* position at sea is at once secured. The threat of the Submarine disappears, and Great Britain in the future will be spared a race with Germany for sea supremacy.

'In stating that Germany should be reduced to the status of a Second-class Naval Power corresponding to her requirements, it is assumed that there was no intention of returning her lost colonies.

'7. It is noted that in the exchange of Notes between President Wilson and the enemy, the Naval side of the matter had not been referred to. Doubtless President Wilson, in using the term "Military", intended it to include Naval, Army, and Air questions. This, however, was not clear, and Germany will certainly, and in fact has, kept the discussion to the land side only.

'It is very essential that the Naval side should be kept clearly before the Allies and dealt with separately and apart from the Military side.'

Meanwhile, great vigilance was necessary at Rosyth. Enemy submarines were massing in the North Sea: a clear indication that the High Seas Fleet might put to sea at any moment. As the war against merchant shipping had ceased, the Admiralty countered this move by placing all available anti-submarine craft at Beatty's disposal. In addition, they sent Captain W. W. Fisher, R.N.,[1] the able Director of the Anti-Submarine Division, to assist him in the control of anti-submarine operations. Fisher wasted no time, and was soon at sea in the destroyer *Swift*, supervising dispositions with the object of keeping the submarines 'down'. His measures were so effective that the Rear-Admiral Commanding the Second Battle Cruiser Squadron, on return from a sweep across the North Sea in late October was able to report that only one torpedo had been fired at his squadron. This was most reassuring, indicating that the Grand Fleet, with its full complement of destroyers, could move in any direction without undue risk of loss from submarine attack. On 26th October, Wemyss wrote:

MY DEAR DAVID,

Thank you very much for your letter and the memo which have been of the greatest assistance to me. We have had two or three Cabinet Meetings and also one Board Meeting since you left London, always on the same subject. As you can easily imagine, it has been most difficult to get any satisfactory conclusion out of the War Cabinet. They are always inclined not to come to any strong decision and leave matters in a nebulous state; however, under the circumstances, I think we are as favourably placed as can be. The whole Board are unanimous on our pressing the business. I have had many says at the War Cabinet, and they are really very impressed with the fact that so far as the Naval terms are concerned it is impossible not to embody terms of peace in the armistice.

I am going off to Paris tomorrow. We have an Allied Naval Council on Monday, the results of which I have not the slightest doubt of, and feel perfectly certain that I can carry them all with me, and I therefore look forward to a unanimous resolution to put before the Supreme War Council at Versailles on Tuesday. The crux will, of course, come then, but the Board of Admiralty have very satisfactorily strengthened my position. The First Lord accompanies me, and he will be at Versailles

[1] Later Admiral Sir William Fisher, G.C.B., C.V.O.

and will back me up at the final business. More than this I can hardly tell you at the present moment, because although I might dilate for hours upon the various forms which different arguments have taken, I have given you the general results. . . .

The situation is most extraordinarily interesting, and we are quite prepared to further strengthen you with destroyers. . . .

I am very glad you have taken Fisher. I think that, under the circumstances, he will be of tremendous use to you. There is nobody who has quite the same knowledge of all the various appliances and how to use them as he has, and I trust that you will find his presence of assistance.

I am very pressed with work, and hardly have time to get my meals, so forgive my rather cutting short this letter. All good luck to you, and I do hope to God that your long and anxious time of waiting may shortly be brought to a close with a glorious and splendid victory which you and the whole of the Grand Fleet so richly deserve.

Yours ever,

(*signed*) R. WEMYSS.

It was clear that the Admiralty still believed the High Seas Fleet would come out. The situation for Beatty was unique: while keeping his finger on the trigger to deal the 'coup de grace' to Scheer if he should emerge from his base, he had at the same time to be ever watchful that there should be no weakening of the Armistice terms, which might deprive Great Britain of the fruits of victory at sea.

He expressed his views in a private letter to a friend:

Queen Elizabeth   (*31st Oct.*, 1918)

. . . At present the talking party are hard at work at Versailles, and I trust they won't let us down. The fear is that the politicians will overcome the Naval and Military opinion. Rosy [Wemyss] is none too strong and hasn't very strong convictions, and so might easily be talked round. But I doubt if he would commit himself before communicating with me. But one never knows. I think the public would support me if it came to a tussle, but the word *Peace* has a very alluring sound, especially when they are cold and hungry. Another question which weighs on my mind—are we in the Grand Fleet to be cheated out of our reward of breaking the Sea Power of the Hun for ever? I do not think so if the talking gentlemen at Versailles don't let us down. If they are firm, the High Seas Fleet must have a run for his money, and it may happen at

[336]

"The Day of Surrender" Beatty 21.11.18

Admiral Beatty acknowledging the cheers of the men of the Grand Fleet

any moment, but it won't be until the very last thing, a forlorn hope to give him a better position from which to talk of Peace. It would be a very bad thing for the country if our great Fleet never has an opportunity of showing its power in a more demonstrative manner than it has. The public are very short-sighted, and would murmur at the necessity of expending large sums on the maintenance of the Sea Power if they had no *ocular* demonstration of its power to command the Seas. Just received Telegram: Hostilities with Turkey cease today 31st.

Although Wemyss had got his way with the Allied Naval Council, the continental school of thought in the Supreme War Council considered the Naval terms too severe.

On 2nd November, the First Lord (Geddes) wrote:

The German terms are approved in so far as the surrender of the 100 submarines goes, but as regards the battle fleet, the fear is that if we pitch the terms too high Germany will refuse them and there will be another year of bloodshed without any real compensatory advantage. It is thought that surrender of the whole of the ships recommended [by Beatty] is too severe.

On 3rd November, Wemyss wrote in the same strain, adding:

We have had discussions with the Prime Minister, and if we are absolutely obliged by order of the Supreme War Council to ease up our Naval terms my idea is . . . that we should intern the whole lot in some neutral port without their ammunition. . . . I could wish that it were as easy to compete with our friends as it is with our foes.

On receipt of this disturbing information, Beatty protested violently to Wemyss by telegram, followed, on 5th November, by a letter which is so typical of Beatty's moral courage, prevision, and intense patriotism, that it must be quoted in full:

5th November, 1918

As stated in my telegram of yesterday, I was very perturbed at the underlying tone of your letter, which indicated that the Supreme Council might override the Naval Council. You speak about, 'If we are obliged to ease up our Naval terms', also 'If our terms are put down by the Supreme War Council, we can do nothing but enter a protest'.

There must be no question of the Naval terms being overridden. It is vital to the country that they should be recognised as the very minimum: our great efforts during the war will otherwise have been largely nullified.

I note that Heligoland has been omitted from the terms, which means that Germany, with any fleet of battleships at all, can menace the Sea Power of this country with her submarines.

I am surprised that such an important alteration in the Naval terms had not been communicated to me. If it had been communicated, I should certainly have increased my demands as to the number of battleships to be surrendered.

I would remind you that I represent a very large proportion of the best Naval opinion in the service, and that the Prime Minister recognised this, *vide* the decision at the War Cabinet on 21st October, that the Admiralty and Commander-in-Chief Grand Fleet should examine the question of what would be the minimum for us to accept.

Nothing has been done to give effect to this. I have previously stated that I was prepared to come down or send a representative as the situation demanded.

With regard to the question whether the enemy ships should be surrendered or interned, or some one and some another, the First Lord, in his letter to Murray on 2nd November, put the matter quite clearly, i.e. that it must either be surrender of all the ships recommended, or internment of all the ships recommended, with a clear understanding that all the ships recommended must come out of Germany's hands.

I read that to mean—never returned to Germany.

It is very satisfactory to note that the Allied Naval Council stand firm on their decisions.

Unfortunately, however, you state they may be overridden; and that if this is done you can do nothing but enter a protest. I assume the protest would take the form of the resignation of the Board of Admiralty as a whole.

I do not believe that the country would stand that on a question so vital to our future.

I attach a summary of the contents of this letter for convenience of reference.

I do not wish to be egotistical or to put my finger into pies which are not my concern, but for four years and three months I have been closely connected with the war in the decisive area, for the last two years in command and directly responsible. Perhaps, therefore, it may be admitted that I am in a position better than any to realise what it means to have a powerful German Fleet, supplemented by a large number of submarines, ready on his selected day, to come out and fight.

I am confident of the ability of the Grand Fleet to deal with the enemy Fleet both now and in the future.

Success, however, could only be expected at the cost of vast casualties, and my experience has shown me that, should the enemy be favoured with the best of the luck, fogs, fluctuating visibility, he will be compensated in a large measure for the inferiority of his forces.

Survival of the German Fleet in any strength will throw upon us the necessity for continuous increase of armaments.

We must not, therefore, in a short-sighted endeavour to accelerate the advent of peace, waive any of the conditions which we know to be essential for the safety of the Empire.

History will never acquit us if we miss the present opportunity of reducing effectively the menace to our sea power.

(*signed*) DAVID BEATTY.

SUMMARY

The Allied Naval Council has agreed to terms which, to the surprise of the Commander-in-Chief, Grand Fleet, do not include Heligoland.

They have been asked to reconsider and reduce their terms, with the result that they were unable to revise their recommendations.

So far so good.

The First Sea Lord's letter, however, implies that the Supreme War Council may reduce the terms recommended by the Allied Naval Council and that the Allied Naval Council can do no more than enter a protest.

The omission of the surrender of Heligoland makes it all the more imperative that the list of ships named for surrender should be strictly adhered to, and no compromise can possibly be accepted, unless we are to stop a long way short of the objects for which we have been fighting for $4\frac{1}{2}$ years.

As the Naval terms affect this country to an infinitely greater degree than any other, it is assumed that the form of protest to be entered by the British Naval representatives, in the event of the terms being reduced, would be the resignation of the Board of Admiralty as a whole.

The correspondence went on, but when it tended to become heated, Wemyss, who had much in common with Beatty, wrote: 'Whatever happens, do not ever let the shadow of a misunderstanding come between you and me.'

Meanwhile, at Wilhelmshaven, Scheer and Hipper were striving with great energy to get the High Seas Fleet to sea and provoke a Fleet action while the negotiations were going on. Their intention was to move south, and 'they had planned a stroke similar in its objects to the Dutch attack upon the Medway' at the end of the second Dutch war.[1] Hipper gave the order to sail late in the evening of 29th October. This, however, was disobeyed by the crews, and in many ships the stokers drew fires. During the preparation for sea, the German seamen had guessed their Admiral's intention, and were determined to prevent it. Hipper immediately dispersed the Fleet to various anchorages, and hundreds of men were arrested.

Reliable intelligence from Germany was difficult to get, and it was not till some days later that the Admiralty were able to tell Beatty that the expected German sortie would not take place. On 5th November, Wemyss wrote to Beatty:

The state of affairs in the High Seas Fleet is not very clear. . . . The crews of some of the ships or of some of the shore establishments have mutinied, and are under the control of the 'Soldiers Council', whatever that may be. . . . We may look forward to one of two possibilities:

(1) Such events as have happened forcing the High Seas Fleet out as a desperate action;

(2) The disintegration being so great that they cannot possibly come out.

By the time this letter reached Beatty, the German armies were in headlong flight, and it had become clear that the naval mutiny was part of a general revolutionary movement in Germany. The Allied Naval Council at once redrafted their armistice conditions, and the Supreme War Council, over-ruling Marshal Foch, decided that the German Fleet must be interned in an allied port.

A 'red herring' was introduced by President Wilson, who wished a clause to be inserted relating to a doctrine known in the United States as 'Freedom of the Seas', but as none of the Allies could understand what this meant, it was wisely shelved until the Peace Conference. In the end, the British and French delegations met Herr Erzberger and his German colleagues at 7 a.m. on 8th November, in a railway carriage on a siding in

[1] *Official History of Naval Operations*, vol. V, p. 369.

the Forest of Compiègne. The British delegation, under Wemyss, was wholly naval, and the French, under Marshal Foch, were all soldiers.

Erzberger had no definite instructions, but had been given full powers. Wemyss and Foch, in presenting the terms, had powers to treat on technical points. Three days later, at 2.15 a.m. on 11th November, 1918, Erzberger accepted the terms, and Wemyss lost no time in obtaining allied agreement that the German Fleet should be interned in Scapa Flow. Furthermore, it was decided that Beatty should enforce the naval clause relating to its surrender and internment. Time was short, and since there did not appear to be any stable Government in Germany, Beatty was instructed to get into direct wireless touch with the German High Command. Eventually it was arranged that Rear-Admiral Hugo Meurer would act as plenipotentiary for the German Navy, and would arrive at Rosyth in the light cruiser *Königsberg* on 15th November.

Beatty's innermost thoughts are contained in a letter to a friend dated 12th November, 1918. The last few lines are an uncanny forecast of things to come a quarter of a century later.

The Fleet, my Fleet, is broken-hearted, but are still wonderful, the most wonderful thing in Creation, and although it would appear that they never can achieve their hearts' desire, they preserve a cheerfulness that is extraordinary. But we are not at the end of the Book yet, only nearing the end of a Chapter, a sinister and poisonous Chapter badly ended, but we have more to follow in which the Fleet will have a great part to play. I had most of my Captains and Admirals on board this morning, and with them to support me, I feel we could go anywhere and do anything. All suffering from a feeling of something far greater than disappointment, depressed beyond measure. But they respond gallantly and sink their feelings in their attention to duty. I enclose you a note I got from one of my Admirals which I am terribly conceited to be terribly proud of. So you will treat it carefully and *return it to me*, as I treasure it greatly. That heartens me more than anything else could, and your dear letter inspires me to sink all feelings except those of attention to *duty*. Am I writing like a copy-book for the young? God knows I don't feel like that. That is a truly British sentence, isn't it? but then I am of the Irish persuasion, with a dash of French in me. On the top of it all is the feeling that we are not going to win in the Council all that our great silent victory entitles us to. That is Hell. We have unfortunately those in a position to give advice who are not imbued with correct appreciation of the situation and who are incapable of interpreting correctly the needs of the Nation, who are inclined to be jealous, and for that reason are not ready to receive suggestions from those who have thought of nothing else for 4½ years. So the situation is that I am jamming down their throats what I consider the correct solution and they don't like it and don't ask for it and I cannot force them to swallow it. In the meantime the country is being let down by a crew who cannot realise the vastness of our efforts and who are being overruled by another crew who are strong in the Council Chamber but who have accomplished but a 100th part of our share, i.e. Americans, French, Italians, Portuguese, and *others*. I do not believe we near the end yet. Nearer, yes. But what are we going to do when we have defeated the cursed Huns under one constituted authority and on being defeated they down it and produce another which disagree? The only thing is to sail into their poisonous country and wreck it and take what we want and put the fear of God, Truth, and Justice into them, represented by the British Tommy.

When the *Königsberg* duly arrived on the evening of the 15th November, Admiral Meurer signalled that the 'Sailors' and Workmen's Delegates' on board insisted on accompanying him to the *Queen Elizabeth* for the negotiations. Beatty promptly replied that he would only meet an officer of flag rank, and that no one but the Admiral and his staff were to leave the ship. Meurer later thanked Beatty for this courtesy, stating that it was the first time for some weeks that his rank had been recognised!

The German Admiral and his staff arrived on board the *Queen Elizabeth* at 7.30 p.m. on 15th November, and were formally received in silence by Rear-Admiral Brand and Captain Chatfield, wearing swords. It was dark, and a strong electric light was focused on the gangway, behind which Sir John Lavery, the official artist, did a rapid sketch of the scene. This method of securing a pictorial record of such an historic event was chosen in preference to the more modern and brazen one of subjecting the victim to the fire of flashlight photography. Among the British officers present, there was a feeling of some sympathy for Meurer, who, apart from suffering in his flagship the gross indignity of being under the supervision of a Communist mob, was about to negotiate the surrender of the Fleet he loved so well.

After exchanging salutes, Brand led the German officers down the companion ladder to the Admiral's dining cabin, where Beatty was seated at the table, with Madden, his Second-in-Command, on his right, and Brock, his Chief of Staff, on his left.[1] Immediately behind Beatty hung an old naval print of Nelson, and in the centre of the table, before him, was a bronze lion, a sharp reminder to the Germans that British naval traditions are hard to break. As Meurer stood facing Beatty, the proceedings were opened thus:

Beatty: Who are you?

Meurer: Rear-Admiral Hugo Meurer.

Beatty: Have you been sent by Admiral von Hipper as his plenipotentiary to arrange the details for carrying out the terms of the armistice which refer to the surrender of the German Fleet?

Meurer: Yes.

Beatty: Where are your credentials? Pray be seated.

After the credentials had been examined, Beatty handed to Meurer a paper printed in two parallel columns. On the left were the armistice conditions, and on the right the arrangements with which Meurer was expected to comply. Meurer replied that he could not immediately answer all the questions put to him, and requested permission to communicate at once with his High Command. This was granted, and Meurer left the Flagship.

Beatty's own account of these dramatic events is given in two letters to a friend:

(*19th Nov.*, 1918)

I have been so terribly busy with all-night sittings with Enemy delegates and I have to carry out all the Terms of the Naval Armistice which has kept me fully employed. I am now in the position of commanding the High Sea Fleet as well as the Grand Fleet, which is a big business, and am now arranging for some Autumn manœuvres with the two

[1] There were also present: Rear-Admiral the Hon. Hubert Brand, Captain Ernle Chatfield, Paymaster-Commander F. T. Spickernell, Commander R. M. Bellairs, and Commander W. T. Bagot (interpreter). At certain stages Vice-Admiral Sir M. Browning and Rear-Admiral Sir Reginald Tyrwhitt also attended.

Fleets.[1] As we are enveloped in fog, it may lead to all sorts of difficulties and regrettable incidents if things go wrong that one has to be especially careful. . . . I will write you more fully an account of my meeting, which was most dramatic with a strong tragic element, but I haven't time now.

(26th Nov., 1918)

I simply haven't a moment. I hardly leave the ship. Two hours is the most I've done for a long time, and even that has been rare. . . . I am beginning to wish we were still at war. This Peace business makes me tired, all hopes destroyed, all ideas of glorious achievement gone by the board, nothing but an immense drudgery and masses of problems which there seems to be great difficulty in solving. It all began with the advent of Admiral Meurer. You would have loved that. It was dramatic and tragic to a high degree. He arrived on board at 7 p.m. pitch dark, aided by a thick fog, in which he could see nothing and had no idea he was surrounded by the greatest Fleet in the world. I arranged a most beautiful setting. My dramatic sense was highly developed at the moment. When he marched up the gangway he was met by a blaze of light from groups of the strongest electric sunlights which lighted the gangway and the path to be trod from there to my hatchway. Outside the path everything was inky black and perfect stillness. Actually on the edge of the Path of Light, half in, half out, was a line of the fattest Marine sentries about two paces apart with fixed bayonets upon which the light gleamed. Wherever he looked he met a bayonet. He was met by Tommy Brand and Chatfield, who were frigidity itself. The wretch nearly collapsed on the Quarter-deck, and his party were led to my cabin, where I met him supported by my Second-in-Command (I wish he hadn't got a beard. I nearly asked him to take it off. It spoilt the scene), Osmond de Brock, Tyrwhitt, and several members of my staff. I wouldn't accept him as being what he said he was, until he produced documentary evidence in support of his statement and identified his Staff. Having 'Pray be seated', I read him my prepared instructions and refused to discuss them, but said they must be thought over and answered on the morrow. They were greatly depressed, overwhelmingly so, and I kept on feeling sorry for them, but kept going by repeating to myself: *Lusitania*, Belgian atrocities, British prisoners, and I won in a trot. So much so that Meurer, in a voice like lead, with an ashen grey face, said: I must think the Commander-in-Chief is aware of the condition in Germany, and then in dull, low, weary tones began to retail the effect of the Blockade. It had brought Revolution in the North which had spread to the South then to East and finally to the West, that Anarchy was rampant, the seed was sown.

[1] Operation ZZ. See Appendix V.

It remained for the harvest of human lives to be reaped in the interior of Germany as well as on the frontiers. Men, women, and children were dying of starvation and dropping down in the streets and died where they lay. Children under six were non-existent, that Germany was destroyed utterly, the latter with a wail in his voice. It had no effect. I only said to myself: Thank God for the British Navy. This is your work. Without it no victory on land would have availed or ever been possible. I told them to return with their answers in the morning. He then informed me he had three delegates of the Sailors' and Workmen's Council outside who were anxious to take part in the conversations. I naturally said I knew them not, and did not intend to know them better, which was the one source of relief to the Stricken Party. And they stepped out into the darkness and fog to do the twelve miles back to their ship. I retired and was nearly sick. They returned the next day, still in the thickest fog I've seen in the Firth of Forth. It was a fine achievement on the part of the *Oak*[1] in getting them through but very late, and they brought their replies. Generally speaking they would agree to anything. They raised points here and there which were firmly squashed. They queried about the honour of their submarine crews being possibly assailed, which nearly lifted me out of my chair. However, I scathingly replied that their personal safety would be assured, which would doubtless satisfy their honour. In any case it's different to ours, and we wouldn't waste time over it. When it came to signing the documents I thought he would collapse. He took two shots at it, putting his pen down twice, but we got him over it, and they returned into the fog in grim silence. If I could draw I would make a glorious picture, but it would require a Leonardo da Vinci to do it well. It was very poignant all the time and rather wearing. It was curious, all the time he was in the Firth of Forth it was the thickest fog imaginable. He never knew that he passed through lines of the finest ships in the world. They were just out of sight. I think the *Bon Dieu* was kind to him in that. The next act in the Drama I must keep for another letter. You will have read most of it in the papers. They were rotten bad accounts that I saw and it was a wonderful day. Enough of that. The next Tragedy was a telegram last night that my beloved David had got pneumonia. That was a blow I was not prepared for. Poor Tata got the telegram at the same time, 10.15 p.m., and we had a brief and tragic conversation over the telephone. Luckily she was alive and got packed, and I met her at Inverkeithing at 11.30 and got her a place in the Naval Train and she went off full of courage but in dreadful distress. I sent Dr. Hill with her, and she got down to Osborne (cursed spot) this afternoon. He is much better, thank God, but my dear it makes my heart

[1] H.M.S. *Oak*, destroyer attached for duty with the Fleet Flagship.

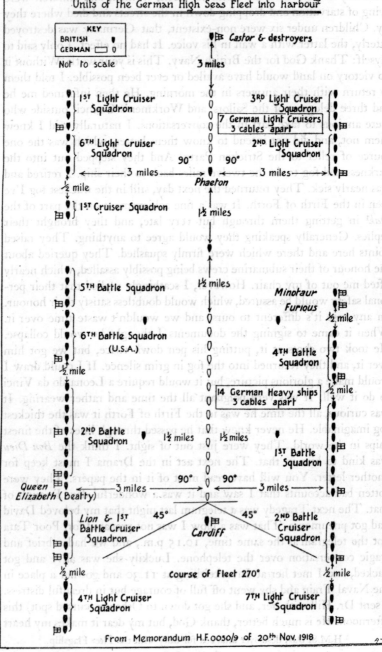

DIAGRAM XI

Order of the British Grand Fleet escorting
Units of the German High Seas Fleet into harbour

KEY
BRITISH ⊞
GERMAN ☐ 0

Not to scale

Castor & destroyers
3 miles

1ST Light Cruiser
Squadron

3RD Light Cruiser
Squadron

7 German Light Cruisers
3 cables apart

6TH Light Cruiser
Squadron

2ND Light Cruiser
Squadron

90°   90°
— 3 miles —   — 3 miles —

Phaeton

½ mile

1ST Cruiser Squadron

1½ miles

1½ miles

5TH Battle Squadron

Minotaur
Furious

½ mile

6TH Battle Squadron
(U.S.A.)

4TH Battle
Squadron

½ mile

14 German Heavy ships
3 cables apart

½ mile

2ND Battle
Squadron   1½ miles   1½ miles

1ST Battle
Squadron

90°   90°
Queen   — 3 miles —   — 3 miles —
Elizabeth (Beatty)

Lion & 1ST   45°   45°   2ND Battle
Battle Cruiser   Cruiser
Squadron   Cardiff   Squadron

½ mile   ½ mile

Course of Fleet 270°

4TH Light Cruiser
Squadron

7TH Light Cruiser
Squadron

From Memorandum H.F.0050/9 of 20th Nov. 1918

stop still thinking about it. Poor Tata did not get to London until 11.30 and drove straight across to Waterloo and caught the 12.30 down. She must be half dead with emotion, distress, and fatigue. I am only waiting up here for news. I pray my God, I pray hard that the little chap will be all right. It is terribly hard that he should be in distress now.

Three further meetings were held, and final arrangements made for all German submarines to surrender to Rear-Admiral Tyrwhitt at Harwich, and the surface ships to Beatty in the Forth, prior to internment at Scapa Flow.

In the early morning of 21st November, 1918, the light cruiser *Cardiff*, flying the flag of Rear-Admiral Alexander-Sinclair, stole quietly out of the Firth of Forth, on perhaps the most stirring mission a British warship has ever had to perform. She was to meet the German battle fleet, and lead it to a pre-arranged rendezvous with the British Commander-in-Chief. Shortly afterwards Beatty left harbour with the whole Grand Fleet, consisting of no less than thirteen squadrons, in two huge columns. The German ships were sighted about 8 a.m. Their fleet consisted of nine modern battleships, five battle cruisers, seven modern light cruisers, and forty-nine destroyers, all in single line ahead, with the *Cardiff* in the van. Forty miles west of May Island, the *Cardiff* led the German Fleet between the two British columns, approaching on an opposite course. As soon as they were in position, Beatty turned the Grand Fleet 180°, which placed him abeam of the German Flagship. This manœuvre, which was beautifully executed, brought the two Fleets into three columns, with the Germans in the centre, all steering for the Forth (Diagram XI). Describing the scene, Admiral Rodman, U.S.N., said the *Cardiff* reminded him of 'the old farm in Kentucky, where many times he had seen a little child leading by the nose a herd of fearsome bullocks'. In the early afternoon the German Fleet anchored off Aberlady Bay, while the Grand Fleet proceeded to its anchorage above the Forth Bridge. In the British Fleet the feeling was more of sober triumph than of jubilation. Everyone had good cause to remember the tough fighting qualities of the German warships, now mere impotent hulks with demoralised crews. As of old, the great traditions of the British fighting seamen had prevailed, not only in battle, but in the dull routine of keeping open the sea communications through-out a long, weary war. Adversity never dismayed them. Victory they took as a matter of course.

The officers and men of the Grand Fleet all knew how much they owed to Beatty's inspiration and leadership. While the ships, big and little, passed the Fleet Flagship, one by one, they gave vent to their pent-up feelings by cheering their Commander-in-Chief as few men have ever been cheered before. But Beatty felt that it was not to himself that thanks should be given, so in words reminiscent of Nelson's signal after the battle of the Nile, he made a general signal to the British Fleet: 'It is my intention to hold a service of thanks-giving at 6 p.m. today, for the victory which Almighty God has vouchsafed to His Majesty's arms, and every ship is recommended to do the same.'

When the last ships had gone by, and the *Queen Elizabeth* had secured to her buoy, Chatfield asked Beatty to address the ship's company assembled on the quarter-deck. Beatty, know-ing that the men's thoughts were his own, expressed them in a very few words. Then, as if wishing to escape from it all, he made for the ladderway leading to his cabin. To the delight of the ship's company he suddenly stopped, and with the familiar flash of the eye and a smile on his lips, said: 'Didn't I tell you they would have to come out?'

Among the many congratulations received by Beatty, the one that pleased him most came from Field-Marshal Sir Henry Wilson, expressing laconically the result of the war in terms of traditional British strategy: 'You have given us their army and we have given you their fleet.'

Lord Charles Beresford wrote:

(24th Nov., 1918)

Your letter of the 21st Nov. is the most interesting and historical of the many in my possession, written at 6 a.m. on a day when the prestige and glory of the Grand Fleet under your command have really won the greatest sea victory of history. All our hearts go out to you and your splendid officers and men in their disappointment at there being no naval action, but a bloodless surrender is really a more brilliant achievement, illustrating the superb discipline, strength, and organisation of the forces under your command. You have added to your own renown, and the traditional glories of the British Navy, and all your old comrades of days gone by regard you with feelings of unbounded respect and affection.

A remarkable testimony came from Rear-Admiral W. R. Hall ('Blinker Hall', the famous Director of Naval Intelligence):

Standing outside the Fleet as I have done for the last four years, I know, as few others can, what great work you have done and how little it is known and realised. I know no one who could, in the midst of a great war, have successfully changed the mental attitude of the Fleet towards the conduct of war from a defensive to an offensive attitude, and this, if I may venture to say so, is your great triumph, for it is one of character.

The dramatic finale to this historic day had yet to be enacted. At eleven o'clock Beatty had signalled to Admiral von Reuter: 'The German Flag will be hauled down at sunset today, Thursday, and will not be hoisted again without permission. 1104.'

Whether Beatty had the right to make such a signal has been questioned, but he was not concerned with legal niceties or the continental school of thought at such a moment. He would organise the surrender in his own way, and being still at war, he felt that it would be intolerable to have enemy ships flying their national flag in a British harbour. So, at dusk, as the sky reddened over the Scottish hills, and the buglers of the British Fleet sounded the call of 'Sunset', the ensigns of the Imperial German Navy fluttered slowly down for the last time. And darkness closed like a curtain on the final act of this mighty drama of the sea.

1919–1927
THE FIGHT FOR SEA POWER

Naval pay · Public speeches · Admiralty tribute
Promotion to Admiral of the Fleet · Thanks of Parliament
Earldom · First Sea Lord · Washington Conference
Cruiser crisis · Offer to resign · Beatty gets his way
Collective security · The first Chiefs of Staff Committee
Government appreciation

AFTER the German Fleet had been safely tucked away at Scapa Flow under guard of a British squadron, Beatty had many post-war problems to consider. The most urgent and the one nearest to his heart was the welfare of the men who had served him so well. He wasted no time in getting the views of the officers and men who had joined for the period of 'hostilities only'. These represented about 40 per cent. of the war-time ships' companies, and had fitted in well with the fighting organisation which was based on the solid rock of the professional officers and 'long-service' ratings. All wished to return to civil life as soon as possible, not because of dislike of service afloat, but because they knew only too well how inadequate were the existing scales of pay in the Navy to meet the high cost of living.

Beatty, who had already made representations to the Admiralty about the need for an increase of pay for regular officers and ratings, saw at once that something must be done, so he directed Rear-Admiral Goodenough to form a committee, within the Fleet, to investigate and report. Goodenough, having examined ratings of all branches, stated that the men had given their evidence clearly and with sincerity, and that some of the facts brought to light were most disturbing. Goodenough's report recommended large increases in pay, and also suggested that any announcement by the Admiralty of changes in pay and conditions in the Navy should be accompanied by logical reasons expressed in language which would be easily understood by all on the lower deck.

The Admiralty had, in fact, issued, on 27th December, 1918, a memo desiring it to be known that 'the whole question . . . has been engaging their attention, etc.' Shortly afterwards they were suddenly confronted with a letter from Beatty endorsing forcefully Goodenough's recommendations, and acquainting the Board with the views of the officers and men now serving afloat, and the true conditions of their domestic life. This proved to be the much-needed 'spur', but it was not until May 1919, after prolonged discussions with the Treasury, that justice was done, although marriage allowance was denied to the officers. This delay of six months created a certain distrust of Whitehall, but the men knew, thanks to Beatty's prompt action, that their officers had done everything in their power for them, and confidence in their leaders never wavered. The measure, when it eventually materialised, did much to alleviate distress, and successfully checked any discontent which might have raised its head during the dangerous transition period from war to peace.

Besides concern for his men, Beatty had also to think about his duty to the public. With his usual prevision he foresaw that the Navy would shortly be cut to the bone unless somebody with knowledge and authority could tell the people all that the Navy had done for them in the war, and how much their future prosperity depended upon it. The old lines of Nelson's day were often in his mind:

> '*God and the sailor we alike adore*
> *When danger looms, but not before.*
> *The danger past, both are alike requited,*
> *God is forgotten and the sailor slighted.*'

His opportunity came very soon when he was invited to become a Freeman of all the great cities and principal towns in Great Britain and the time-honoured guilds of the city of London. He was made an honorary member of Lloyd's, and later was elected Lord Rector of Edinburgh University. At the ceremonies held in his honour, he took care to impress upon everyone how much sea power meant to England. He was gifted with an unusual power of oratory. The short, clipped, forceful delivery was always lightened by touches of humour. His distinguished bearing, immaculate appearance, and flashing eye all contributed to a magnetic personality which held his audience in rapt attention from first to last. At Edinburgh, in January 1919, having referred to the close connections between the city and the Fleet throughout the war and the tireless work of the hundreds of small craft manned by Scottish fishermen, he said: 'The officers and men of the Fleet have shown that the trust which the country reposes in the Navy is not misplaced, and that today the sure shield is as sure as ever it was. They have earned the gratitude of the country, and [referring to naval pay] the country must not forget that the labourer is worthy of his hire. . . . I can say that the whole of the Fleet, from the Commander-in-Chief to the last joined boy, is a band of brothers.' To the delight of his Scottish audience he concluded this speech by quoting from Robert Burns:

> *'Be Britain still to Britain true*
> *Amang oursels united.'*

At Liverpool, in Grand National Week, 1919, addressing a vast audience, he said: '. . . In the necessary struggle for retrenchment, economies must be applied with wisdom and a proper understanding of the problems before us. . . . Only so shall we avoid impairing the essential efficiency of the Great Navy. The Navy is a shield and not a rattling sabre. We are a sea race, we came into being by the sea, and we exist by the sea.'

Beatty's term of service as Commander-in-Chief of the Grand Fleet was drawing to a close. Sir Charles Madden was to relieve him in the spring of 1919 as Commander-in-Chief of the peace-time Atlantic Fleet, and it was generally expected that Beatty would become First Sea Lord. He was ready and willing to accept this appointment, because he wished to bring fresh to the Admiralty his war experience and knowledge. He was anxious to reorganise the Fleet and the Staff on modern lines before other influences got to work, and to take his place

King George V and the Prince of Wales with Admiral Beatty, Rear-Admiral Hugh Rodman, U.S.N. and Vice-Admiral W. S. Sims, U.S.N., on the quarter-deck of the American flagship *New York*, 1918

in the front rank against any attempt to tamper with British sea-power. On the other hand, Wemyss, who was heavily committed with the politicians and allied admirals in the drafting of peace terms, naturally did not want to go until he felt he had completed his task. The Government decided that Wemyss should continue in office for another six months, and in Beatty's personal interests it were better perhaps that he should have a rest. During the whole course of the war he had taken no leave, and although his family lived close to Rosyth, he slept in his flagship every night.

Their Lordships had no doubts about Beatty's outstanding ability as a leader and administrator, and he could expect no greater tribute than this deeply considered appreciation of his services:

ADMIRALTY, S.W.1
5th April, 1919

SIR,

1. On the termination of your appointment as Commander-in-Chief Grand Fleet, I am commanded by my Lords Commissioners of the Admiralty to place on record their high appreciation of the eminent services which you have rendered to the British Empire during the war.

2. My Lords desire to pay their tribute to those qualities of resolute leadership, unerring insight, and quick decision which were early revealed by your achievements in battle, and which throughout the war have been a source of admiration and confidence to your countrymen.

3. They also desire to record their satisfaction with your administration and organisation of the Grand Fleet. Few beside the Board of Admiralty and your own Staff can fully realise what prevision, judgment, enthusiasm, and unremitting industry have been required in the officer upon whom it has ultimately rested to keep a force of this size, with so many complex parts, continuously and under all conditions at the necessary pitch of efficiency and preparation for immediate action. In the successful performance of this duty you have, as Their Lordships are aware, been greatly assisted by your Staff and by the various Flag Officers and their Staffs, whose services you have brought to the notice of the Board.

4. In the midst of all these heavy responsibilities you have shown a constant solicitude for the welfare of the Officers and Men serving under you, which is in accordance with the finest traditions of the Service, and has made you a beloved as well as a trusted leader.

5. The hauling down of your Flag marks the close of one of the greatest chapters in the history of the Royal Navy, and it is a chapter that Posterity will always associate with your name.

I am,

Sir,

Your obedient servant,

(signed) O. MURRAY.

On 3rd April, 1919, Beatty and Jellicoe were both promoted to the Navy's highest rank, Admiral of the Fleet. Beatty immediately sent a telegram to his old chief: 'Grand Fleet tender heartiest congratulations on your high promotion.' Jellicoe replied: 'Please convey my warmest thanks to the Grand Fleet for congratulations. It is especially pleasant to me, as it will be to the Grand Fleet, that you are similarly honoured.' A special Order in Council was required for these promotions, as the authorised number of Admirals of the Fleet was only three, and there were no vacancies. Beatty was only forty-eight, an age when most of his contemporaries were still on the captains' list. It was the second occasion in his career when an Order in Council had to be invoked to secure his promotion. In fact, every step in rank since he had been a lieutenant was in the nature of special preferment, and each was at the hands of different Boards of Admiralty. He became a commander by special promotion at the age of twenty-seven. After only two years' service in that rank he was specially promoted to captain, not only for war service, but also for his marked ability as an executive officer. He reached Flag rank when he was just under thirty-nine, the youngest Flag Officer in over a hundred years.

Nelson became a rear-admiral a few months over thirty-eight, and in many respects the early careers of the two admirals were similar. Both were country bred. Both lived dangerously, and first attracted public attention by their conduct in action, and curiously enough were wounded when fighting ashore. Neither had any fear of authority—nor did they hesitate to quarrel with it if they felt that the views they held were in the best interests of their country. Although loved by the people, they had no undue regard for public opinion so far as it affected themselves, and each fell in love with a married woman. Beatty was denied his Trafalgar, but his bloodless victory was even more complete.

Beatty flew the union flag[1] at the mainmast of the *Queen Elizabeth* from 3rd April to 7th April, 1919—the only occasion when an Admiral of the Fleet, apart from royalty, has commanded the battle fleet of Britain. After he had said farewell to the officers and men of his flagship on the quarter-deck,[2] his flag was hauled down, and the Grand Fleet ceased to exist, the units being re-formed on a peace-time basis as the Atlantic, Home, and Mediterranean Fleets. Four months later he was created an Earl, and thanked by Parliament, who voted him £100,000 for his great services in the war. As the North Sea had been his war, and Brooksby his favourite residence, he chose the title of Baron Beatty of the North Sea and Brooksby.

In appreciation of his leadership and his efforts on their behalf, the men of the Fleet invited him to be their guest of honour at a dinner in Portsmouth Guildhall. His car was dragged through the streets by a gun team of seamen, and the people of Portsmouth turned out in their thousands to bid him welcome.

An extract from the City of Portsmouth Corporation Records describing this occasion says:

'Portsmouth witnessed a scene on 22nd September, 1919, unparalleled in the naval annals of this country. The Lower Deck of the Fleet entertained at a banquet Earl Beatty, the late Commander-in-Chief of the Grand Fleet, and a distinguished company of naval officers. The spectacle of a Commander-in-Chief sitting between a chief writer and a petty officer, and of other Admirals of the Fleet being the guests of the Lower Deck was absolutely unique and unprecedented in naval records. The stirring scene at the end of the gathering, when sixteen bells were struck to show that a new era had been commenced, was eloquently prophetic of the future relations between the higher and the lower branches of the Service and the Navy in general.'

Beatty remained officially unemployed for six months. During this time he and his wife took a holiday on the Continent, visiting Mediterranean ports in their yacht *Sheelah*. Much

---

[1] The distinguishing flag of Admiral of the Fleet.　　　　[2] See Appendix VII.

as he needed respite, the tour developed into a triumphant progress, and he found himself unable to avoid visits to some of the principal capitals.

Meanwhile, there grew in England a feeling that Beatty's experience and advice should be at the disposal of the Government, and there was general satisfaction when his appointment as First Sea Lord and Chief of the Naval Staff was announced. He took office on 1st November, 1919. Mr. Walter Long was the First Lord, and all the naval members of the Board had served in the Grand Fleet under Beatty's command. They came as a fresh breeze from the sea, and with a determination that the dust which had accumulated in a century of civil administration should neither be thrown in their eyes nor allowed to clog the wheels of progress. The Naval War Staff, having proved itself to be indispensable, had been organised by Jellicoe to meet the current requirements of war, with extra divisions to deal with operations, plans, training, anti-submarine warfare, and convoys. The First Sea Lord, being responsible for policy, had automatically become Chief of the Naval Staff, and he was assisted on the staff side by two Flag officers, also members of the Board. But the basic organisation of the Admiralty as a civil establishment remained untouched, and it was not long before an agitation started in Government circles and the Press to cut down the Naval Staff. Beatty, while being fully alive to the need for economy, realised that the lessons of the war could not be co-ordinated and the Navy of the future could never be developed on modern lines unless the Naval Staff was firmly established with power and prestige as an integral part of the Admiralty.

Professional thought and experience were needed just as much in ship construction and material as in the realms of strategy and operations. Economy could be effected by reducing the number of *ad hoc* divisions and sections which had grown during the war. Efficiency could be increased by employing a smaller number of highly qualified officers in essential departments dealing with plans, operations, training, and the development and use of material.

Chatfield, who had been serving as Fourth Sea Lord for some months before Beatty took office, had given much thought to this important question, so Beatty had him transferred to the staff side of the Board, as Assistant Chief of the Staff to work out the new organisation.

The First Lord, Mr. Walter Long, describing this in his speech on policy accompanying the Naval Estimates on 12th March, 1920, said: 'Under this organisation war experience will be fully laid to heart and the lessons applied to naval training and progress. . . . By neglect of that experience there would be a real danger of embarking on expenditure on wrong lines, the building of wrong types of vessels, incorrect tactics, and faulty training of personnel.'

Shortly after he came to the Admiralty, the controversy over the Battle of Jutland reached its height. Naval writers all over the world were publishing their views about the battle, but no official report, based on post-war analysis, had come from either British or German sources. In January 1919, the First Sea Lord (Wemyss) directed Captain J. E. Harper, R.N., to prepare a report of the battle. This was completed on 12th February, 1920, and Beatty was in favour of publishing it as soon as possible. He asked, however, that some of the diagrams should be re-examined, as they did not seem entirely correct. Nor were they. Indeed, it was an impossible task, with the data available, to construct an accurate diagram showing for the whole period of the battle the correct positions of all ships relative, not only to one another, but also to the enemy. This latter point was particularly relevant, for meanwhile important information from Germany had become available[1] which materially affected the report.

Another obstacle presented itself. In August 1920, the publishers of the *Official History*, being written at the time by Sir Julian Corbett, hearing of the Harper Report, sent a letter of protest against its publication, on the plea that it would be detrimental to the sale of the *History*, for which they had exclusive rights.

Beatty's views on the question at this time are recorded in a draft minute in his own handwriting:[2] 'We are of opinion that in view of the fact that Sir Julian Corbett's account will

---

[1] Admiral Scheer's *High Seas Fleet*, and correct lists of German losses.
[2] MSS. in possession of Sir Frank Spickernell, K.B.E., C.B., D.S.O.

shortly be produced, it would be better to place all the information in the possession of the Admiralty at his disposal, including Harper's final proof and plans.' This was the course adopted.

Meanwhile, requests were coming from the Staff College and from senior officers at sea for a staff appreciation of the battle. This, being confidential, would not affect the sale of the *Official History*. The Harper Report was not suitable for the purpose, being nothing more than a bald chronological account of the movements of squadrons and flotillas.[1] Beatty accordingly instructed the Director of Training and Staff Duties Division (Captain Walter Ellerton) to prepare a full appreciation of the battle. The task was entrusted to Captain Kenneth Dewar, R.N. (now Vice-Admiral retired) and Captain A. C. Dewar, R.N. (retired), of the Historical Section of the Division. Both these officers were Gold Medallists of the Royal United Service Institution. Lieutenant J. F. Pollen, R.N., who had helped to prepare the Harper Report and had constructed the diagrams, also assisted in compiling the staff appreciation. None of these officers had served with Beatty, and none of them had any bias or prejudice in the matter.

In reply to critics who inferred that Beatty had influenced the authors, Vice-Admiral Dewar states: 'I can only say that neither Lord Beatty nor anyone else attempted, either directly or indirectly, to influence their work, and that he did not even see the appreciation until its completion. I had only one interview with Lord Beatty, when I asked him whether the appreciation was to be confined to a plain narrative or to include comments on tactics and command. He replied that an intelligible and accurate account was the main thing, but that we should endeavour to bring out its lessons.'[2]

The authors had at their disposal all available information, including the German material coming in, and the view that this gave of the action completely vindicated Beatty's tactics throughout the battle. Their appreciation was used, together with the Harper report, by Sir Julian Corbett in compiling his account of the battle which appeared in 1923, in vol. III of

---

[1] 'Record of Battle of Jutland,' by Captain J. E. F. Harper, M.V.O., R.N., 1919–20, published in 1927 (H.M.S.O.), Cmd. 2870.

[2] *The Navy from Within*, by Vice-Admiral K. G. B. Dewar, C.B.E., p. 267.

the *Official Naval History*. The publishers' objection to the issue of a report no longer held good, and though the Staff Appreciation remained confidential, an abridged edition (*Narrative of the Battle of Jutland*) was issued in 1924, with the omission of various comments on tactics and methods of command.

This led to enquiries in the Press and elsewhere as to the reasons for withholding the publication of the Harper Report, and certain critics ill-disposed to Beatty encouraged the idea that it contained information which he wished to suppress.

Beatty preferred to ignore all criticism, but in order to allay this unfounded suspicion and assuage controversy, the Admiralty eventually published the Harper Report on 10th May, 1927, with an explanatory note stating that the object of publication was to give a clear idea of the limitation of its form and scope and 'to dispel the idea that there is any mystery, sensational evidence, or criticism contained in it'. After its publication not a word was heard of the dark secrets it was supposed to contain.

Beatty would not consent to the Staff Appreciation being made public in its entirety, and thereby suppressed the view it presented of his leadership and tactics, which redounded so greatly to his name and fame.

* * * * *

The problems facing Beatty as First Sea Lord were unprecedented in magnitude and conflicting in nature. He knew well the urgent need for economy, but at the same time he was determined not to accept any measure proposed by the Government, or anyone else, which might impair the efficiency of the Navy or weaken Britain's position as the leading sea power. In a speech to the Highland Society on 29th March, 1920, he said: 'The economical side requires a note of warning. You cannot have a valuable thing without paying for it.'

Beatty's attitude to retrenchment was that the strength of the post-war Fleet must be based on quality rather than quantity, and all reductions were to be carried out in the light of this principle. He had to move quickly, however, to make sure that money would be forthcoming for the constructive measures he had in mind, before the economy wave, then gaining impetus, swept away the just with the unjust.

Being well aware of the importance of science in modern war, and appreciating that the development of the ships and weapons of the future must keep pace with scientific progress, Beatty strongly supported the creation of the Department of Scientific Research and Experiment. This proposal was initiated by the Controller of the Navy, Rear-Admiral W. C. Nicholson, in charge of material development, and was finally approved by the Board.

Dr. Frank Smith was appointed Director, and he established himself with a strong team of scientists next door to the National Physical Laboratory at Teddington—a timely step which later produced far-reaching results.

Beatty approached with caution the controversial question of the use of aircraft for naval purposes. The Admiralty, under his leadership, were prepared to give full support to the new Air Ministry. They were ready and willing to co-operate, provided that the Navy retained operational control of its own aircraft in the Fleet Air Arm, and such others as might be employed on work directly concerned with naval operations.

In a speech at the Lord Mayor's banquet on 9th November, 1923, Beatty made this remarkable prophecy: 'The fleets of the future will be commanded by naval officers with as intimate a knowledge of the air as of the gun and submarine . . . and it may well be that in the future the Commander-in-Chief of a fleet with his staff will be quartered on board an aircraft carrier.'[1]

Practical experience soon made it clear that an air wing of the Navy was more consistent with maritime requirements than a naval wing of the Air Force.

The Air Ministry, on the other hand, thinking more of the strategical independence of the Royal Air Force than the needs of sea power, insisted on keeping the Fleet Air Arm within their own organisation, retaining responsibility, not only for the design and supply of material, but also for training naval personnel in their air duties.

---

[1] The Commander in-Chief of the Home Fleet now flies his Flag in an aircraft carrier.

In this the Air Ministry were supported by certain sections of public opinion, who took the extreme view that the devastating effect of air power would render navies impotent and armies useless. In consequence, the Fleet Air Arm remained nobody's child, in spite of Beatty's claim to full custody.

The need for a satisfactory solution was on Beatty's mind almost to the day of his death. In fact, one of the last letters he ever wrote warned the public that the existing system had failed, and asked for a judicial enquiry into the question. It was not until a year later, in 1937, that the Government finally decided that the administration, operation, and training of seaborne aircraft were to come wholly under naval control. The influence of aircraft carriers on strategy in the World War of 1939–45 proved the wisdom of this decision.

Beatty's task as First Sea Lord was made no lighter when Admiral Sir Percy Scott opened a campaign in the Press against the capital ship. 'What is the use of a battleship?' he asked. 'Do away with these useless expensive Leviathans and we shall save millions.' The air enthusiasts took up the cry. Why spend six million pounds on a battleship when a single aircraft costing only a few thousand pounds could sink her with bomb or torpedo? The present-day reader, viewing the problem thirty years later in the light of scientific development after the Second World War, might well think that Scott was right, for there are only two battleships in full commission in the world today, and none is under construction. The reason for this happy state of affairs is not far to seek. No potential enemy possesses modern battleships powerful enough to threaten the communications of the Western Powers on the high seas.

If Beatty had submitted to the popular clamour to abolish the battleship, neither aircraft nor submarine would have prevented the *Bismarck*, *Tirpitz*, and other German surface warships from destroying whole convoys far out to sea in the war that was to come. The *Bismarck* and *Scharnhörst* met their fate on the high seas at the hands of battleships, and it was fear of the British Battle Fleet that kept the *Tirpitz* shut up in a Norwegian fiord, a sitting target for air attack.

Cunningham's epic struggle to keep open British sea

communications in the Mediterranean is a classic example of the skilful use of battleships. The four old battleships which had fought in the Fifth Battle Squadron with Beatty at Jutland dominated the naval situation in the Mediterranean a quarter of a century later.

In 1920 Beatty said: 'In our opinion the capital ship remains the unit on which sea power is built up. Nevertheless, it must be emphasised that, although the battleship remains, its type may require to be altered. . . . It is even possible that the present battleship will change to one of a semi-submersible type, or even a flying type, but such types are visions of the far future, not practical propositions of the moment. By gradual evolution and development the types forecasted may arrive, but the immediate abandonment of the capital ship in favour of a visionary scheme of aircraft and submarines would leave the British nation destitute of sea power and without the means of progressive training.'[1]

Beatty was anxious that the views of the Naval Staff on this and other matters of policy should be made known to the public, so Mr. Walter Long agreed to include them in his statement to the House of Commons on the Navy Estimates of 1920. They were accepted without serious dissent, and Beatty felt that his hand was strengthened. Lord Selbourne, who had held the office of First Lord some years previously, wrote to him:

Yes, I read the paper on Naval policy which accompanied the First Lord's statement, and I cannot tell you what pleasure it gave me. I felt sure it was yours, and, so far as my opinion is worth anything, I think you are absolutely right, and I was glad that the answer to Fisher and Scott came so quickly.

The Cabinet, however, had no wish to be rushed into expenditure on new construction, so a subcommittee of ministers was appointed to examine the whole naval position with special regard to the capital ship. It included Mr. Bonar Law (Chairman), Mr. Winston Churchill, Mr. Walter Long (First Lord), Sir Robert Horne, Sir Eric Geddes, and Admiral of the Fleet Earl Beatty. After a preliminary meeting Long wrote

[1] Beatty's notes for First Lord's statement on Navy Estimates, 1920.

to Beatty: 'I think you were masterly. I have never heard such powerful statements from a First Sea Lord.' Mr. Long fell ill, and was unable to attend any further meetings, so the whole burden of the Navy's case fell upon Beatty, who, quite unabashed by such a formidable gathering of ministers, proved himself to be as effective at the council table as he had been in command of fleets at sea. In a letter to Long reporting progress, he said:

I pointed out that time was of the utmost importance . . . that unless we were authorised to commence building ships in the summer of 1921 we should drop from the position that we have held for the past three hundred years to that of taking third place as a sea power in the world, and that we should never be able to regain our present position without incurring great cost. . . . I pressed most earnestly that a definite decision should be come to at the earliest possible moment. I informed the meeting that as regards the vital question of the capital ship, the Admiralty's mind was made up, and that we did not consider it necessary to make any further investigation into the lessons of the war than those that we had already made.

The subcommittee continued its sittings into March 1921, and finally confirmed the necessity for building four more capital ships, and this was approved by the Cabinet. In his first year at the Admiralty Beatty had done well.

* * * * *

Beatty had the gift of being able to 'live' any part that he was called upon to play. His power of concentration was phenomenal. Those who knew him at the Admiralty remember him in three distinct rôles: 'the elder statesman', 'the admiral', and 'the sportsman'. On days when he had to attend a Cabinet meeting or mix with ministers, he would appear at the Admiralty elegantly dressed in morning coat, dark striped trousers, a fairly high collar adorned with a black satin cravat held by a tiepin with a single pearl. He attached importance to the psychological effect of dress, and was determined to be at no disadvantage in any company. On such days he would be even more dignified than usual, and more aloof than was natural to him, giving the impression of a statesman whose mind was occupied with problems on a far higher plane than the every-day work of the Admiralty. But this was no mere acting, for indeed he *was* a statesman, and ministers soon came to learn that they were dealing with a man on their own level, if not above it.

Before presenting his case to the Cabinet, he would get Spickernell to cross-examine him from the opposite point of view, and the two would argue far into the night. Beatty had an infinite capacity for taking pains, and in consequence was never at a loss in the councils of the great.

When presiding over staff conferences on purely naval matters as Chief of the Naval Staff, he was very much the admiral. Sometimes the conference would be over before those present had time to collect their thoughts, which was not surprising, as Beatty would take each item on the agenda and answer it himself. He did not discourage discussion. He was so sure of himself, and such a master of his subject, that the officers present felt complete confidence in his judgment. They were not afraid to speak. They just knew that there was nothing more to say. On one occasion a young staff officer, finding himself swept on to the next item before he had time to say his piece, whispered a protest to his next-door neigh-bour (Sir Roger Keyes), who appeared to show no interest. Just as the meeting was about to break up, and there was silence all round, Keyes turned to the young man, and said, 'Go on, tell *him* all about it!' Beatty listened attentively and then replied, 'I quite agree. Why didn't you say so before?'

We get another glimpse of Beatty at the Admiralty from his personal messenger, a pensioner who had served there under many Sea Lords. Recalling their habits, somewhat in the manner of a keeper at the Zoo, he said: 'Most of 'em 'as a bit of bird-seed for lunch, and don't leave the office. The Earl was different; 'e would saunter across to the Carlton Hotel, and 'ave a gentleman's lunch with a nice glass of brandy, and come back here all smiles, smoking a fine cigar.'

On summer evenings, when he could look forward to a game of polo or tennis after office hours, Beatty would be in the highest spirits, treating everyone, from Sea Lords to messengers, as if they were his best friends. While playing games, or hunting, or taking part in the sports he loved, he would seem to have not a care in the world. Yet he was not a happy man, for behind it all there was an ever-increasing anxiety about his wife's health and the stability of his home life.

Ethel Beatty was suffering from a severe nervous breakdown which was aggravated by her restless disposition. She could not stay in one place for any length of time, and sought distraction and cure abroad. She wanted Beatty's undivided attention, and in her state of mind could not understand why his duties should prevent him being with her. While she was in the South of France he wrote to her:

(23rd Jan., 1921)

The whole of the future of the Empire depends upon this question [Cabinet investigation into new construction] and incidentally our own future also, because if it goes against the Admiralty, I do not remain First Sea Lord. You may today think that would be a very good thing, but you would not think so in six months' time, and also would not wish me to be false to the trust that is imposed upon me all for the sake of 48 hours. . . . In any case, I know in your heart of hearts you would not have me go down to history as the First Sea Lord of the day who made so bad a struggle that our rulers gave up the heritage of the command of the sea which we have held for over 300 years. You won't say, 'You are always putting your wife second, and that I ought not to bother about it'.

And again:

(25th Jan., 1921)

Once the Committee have made their decision, my business is done, and the Government act as they think best. If it is as it should be, well and good, if not, then I remove myself, and they can get somebody else. I shall then be entirely at your disposal, and you can do what you will. But once gone, I never return, and my connection with the Navy is severed for ever. That alone gives food for thought, and is not to be undertaken lightly. To join the masses who have nothing to do is not altogether a pleasant prospect.

*   *   *   *   *

In July 1921, the President of the United States invited Great Britain, France, and Italy to send representatives to Washington for a conference on the limitation of naval armaments. Great Britain was prepared to restrict her Navy to meet the barest needs of imperial defence, and the question of analysing these requirements was the responsibility of the Admiralty.

Taking everything into consideration, the British Government decided that the size of the Navy should be equal to that of the strongest Naval Power, and on this basis the Admiralty was instructed to work out their proposals for Washington. It was by no means an easy problem, since British naval requirements are unique. The country itself is utterly dependent for its existence on overseas trade, and the security of the Empire as a whole depends upon sea communications with Great Britain. All this was clear enough to Beatty and those who held the burden of responsibility for the defence of the Empire, but it was not clear to the man in the street in England, although better understood by his compatriot overseas. So, in the face of an hysterical public outcry at home for peace at any price, and the claims of the air enthusiasts that they could revolutionise warfare, Beatty and his colleagues, with full knowledge of the dangers which lay ahead, had to frame proposals which would ensure that British naval strength would not fall below that of any other Power. It was impossible to measure comparative strength with a 'yard-stick', as British sea communications, being spread all over the world, required for their defence a proportionately larger number of cruisers than other nations. Moreover, the battle fleet, being the cornerstone of the whole system of naval defence, could not be reduced beyond parity with another power. Even if parity were accepted in principle, the question of quality in ships was even more important than quantity. All British battleships were of pre-Jutland design, and could not be compared with those recently laid down by foreign Powers, embodying all the lessons which the Royal Navy had learnt in the hard school of war.

Beatty went to the United States, accompanied by his wife and his secretary, Frank Spickernell, as guests of the American Legion, a month ahead of the official British delegation. This was a wise move on his part, because being *persona grata* with the United States Navy, he was able to sound American opinion beforehand on the whole question of limitation of armaments, and at the same time to put the British case to influential American citizens.

He was given a magnificent reception. At Washington a squadron of United States cavalry met him in the station yard and escorted his car to the house of Mrs. Field. The speed of the motor-car did not seem to worry either the driver or the escort; the horsemen went off at full gallop, maintaining their ranks with ceremonial precision. The road was slippery, and there were tramlines. Then came a right-angle turn, where several horses slipped, unseating their riders. The ranks were quickly closed, and the gallant band continued on its way at full gallop. Beatty, being a horseman himself, was glad when the drive was over. Next morning, when the car arrived to take him to the White House, he saw that he was again to be honoured with a cavalry escort. Not wishing to hurt anyone's feelings, but having a natural concern for the horses, he told Spickernell to ask the Commanding Officer if they might go a little slower this time. As a result the party proceeded with less élan, but with greater dignity.

After being received by the President, he went to New York, where he was given the Freedom of the City, and entertained by important public bodies, including the Pilgrims. Describing a dinner in New York, he writes to Lady Beatty in Washington:

New York (to Washington)   (*28th Oct.,* 1921)

. . . After shaking hands with a thousand citizens sat down at 8.15 to dinner. However, Mr. Chauncey Depew made a charming speech and said a lot of nice things about me. My effort was very well received. They were very enthusiastic, and as it was a very representative crowd from the heart of the U.S.A., it was a good opportunity. Today I lunched with the financial Magnates of Wall Street, who were all very agreeable. . . . Then went into the crowd in the streets and assisted in welcoming old Foch. They gave him a very good reception and he looked very pleased, but he has aged a good deal, I thought. He will have some difficulty in standing the Kansas City business. I am not looking forward to it. Four nights in the train does not appeal to me as much as it does to you. I have just received a telegram that the Cabinet wish me to place the Victoria Cross on the grave of the Unknown Warrior on Armistice Day.

All the officers in the United States Navy who had served under his command in the Grand Fleet, 'Comrades of the Mist', entertained him at dinner. He visited Chicago, Kansas City, Philadelphia, Washington, and Annapolis. At Chicago Beatty and Foch attended the unveiling of the war memorial. Grouped artistically round the steps at the base were some beautiful young women draped in diaphanous garments and each carrying a basket. Spickernell, who was standing close to one of them, asked her in a whisper who she was supposed to represent. 'Can't you see?' she replied coldly; 'we are the Vestal Virgins'. Spickernell dared not ask what she had got in the basket, but his curiosity was soon satisfied, for at the moment of unveiling, all the baskets were opened, and flocks of doves took to the air.

On the train from Chicago to Kansas City Beatty was accompanied by Mr. Calvin Coolidge, the Vice-President of the United States, known to his friends as 'Silent Cal'. He wore a very high top-hat, and throughout the journey sat bolt upright, hardly uttering a word. Beatty said that he reminded him of the sailor's parrot, "'E don't say much, but 'e thinks a lot!'

Beatty was accompanied everywhere by Mr. Houghton, a high-ranking police officer, who wore plain clothes, and was always immaculately dressed. He became a great friend of the party, and never failed to get them to the right place at the right time, in spite of dense crowds. He confessed that all he had to do was to tell the police that Beatty was an Irishman! At Chicago a man jumped on the running-board, and felt immediately Houghton's gun pressing his stomach. "'Ave a 'eart', said the man in unmistakable Cockney; 'I want to shake 'ands with the Admiral. I was one of 'is stokers in the *Lion*!'

As the United States in those days was suffering from prohibition, the British naval team brought their own wine and spirits suitably camouflaged in despatch-cases and other innocuous-looking packages. They also took the precaution to post sentries to guard the cellar where the precious liquor lay, but their defence measures proved to be inadequate against the highly specialised American 'rum runners', who broke through a wall at the back and took all. Thus were the British

Admiral of the Fleet, Sir David Beatty on the quarter deck of the *Queen Elizabeth*

deprived of a lubricant for oiling the wheels if controversy became acute.

The Washington Conference opened on 12th November, 1921, and the United States startled the world with the announcement that they were prepared to sacrifice thirteen out of the sixteen capital ships then under construction, subject to maintaining parity in this class of vessel with Great Britain. This was accepted by Great Britain, provided that the 'quality' of her capital ships in the post-war fleet should be of the same standard as other nations'.

The question of capital ships having been settled more or less satisfactorily, Beatty's main concern was to see that British cruiser strength would not fall below the limit prescribed for the protection of the Empire's many lines of sea communication. He found, rather to his surprise, that there was considerable support for the British point of view in official circles in the United States, and in consequence no limit was fixed at the Conference for the maximum number of cruisers to be allowed to each Power. A maximum size of 10,000 tons, with 8-inch guns, however, was laid down for cruisers, which was in excess of British requirements. A large number of ships of 7,000 tons, armed with 6-inch guns, would be more useful for trade protection than a smaller number of heavily armed ships of 10,000 tons. Yet, as in the case of the capital ship, if other nations built heavy cruisers, Great Britain must have them too, otherwise our smaller ships would be outclassed and outgunned.

The Washington Conference has been fully described elsewhere and its results are well known, the most notable being the termination of the Anglo-Japanese Alliance, and a ten-year holiday in the laying down of new capital ships. Great Britain was permitted to lay down two new battleships (*Nelson* and *Rodney*) to bring her up to the 'quality' standard of the post-war ships now under construction in the U.S.A. and Japan. These new ships, however, were to be limited to 35,000 tons, the maximum displacement for capital ships agreed at the Conference. The tenders for the four battleships already called for by the Admiralty had to be cancelled, as their tonnage would have exceeded this maximum. The fact that agreement had been reached on most points gave encouragement to the

'wishful thinkers' in Great Britain in their belief that all dis-
putes between nations could be settled by international conference within the framework of the League of Nations.

Beatty, scenting the danger on the home front, returned to
London after about a month, leaving Chatfield at Washington
to wrestle with the important technical problems of tonnage,
gun-power, and oil-fuel capacity. He found the feeling at home,
from the point of view of British naval security, even worse
than he expected. Highly placed politicians were openly
declaring that it was Britain's duty, in the cause of peace, to
give a lead to the rest of the world by disarming still further.

The responsible Ministers, being well aware that their term
of office was ephemeral, were not prepared to legislate for any
unpleasant situation which might arise in the distant future.
No conditions could, therefore, have been more difficult than
those in which Beatty and his colleagues worked to obtain a
measure of security for the British Empire. No better example
could be given of a 'prophet crying in the wilderness'. The
halcyon days Beatty had spent in company with Ministers in
the *Enchantress* before the war had taught him that the Achilles'
heel of the British politician was fear for his votes. So, working
on this knowledge, he never allowed an opportunity to pass,
when addressing public gatherings and official dinners,[1] of
impressing upon the people how much the Navy meant to
them. In consequence, his name was held in high esteem by
the public, which strengthened his position when dealing with
the Cabinet. Beatty could force the hand of the Treasury by
offering his resignation, but he had no intention of playing this
card except as a last resort.

One of the most ruthless assaults on Admiralty expenditure
came in the Report of the Geddes Committee, issued on 10th
February, 1922.

In accordance with custom, the draft of the Geddes Report
was shown to the Admiralty before publication, thus enabling
the Board to prepare a memorandum controverting its stric-
tures. The First Lord (Lord Lee of Fareham) was away from
office, so Beatty, as the acting head of the Admiralty, with Mr.
Amery, the Financial Secretary, as senior political member of

[1] See Appendix VII.

the Board, took full responsibility for the Admiralty reply, but the Government would not agree that it should be published with the report.

He wrote to Ethel at Biarritz:

(7th Feb., 1922)

The situation is developing in an unpleasant way. They are going to publish Geddes Report, but are not going to publish any reply. Of course, that means we will come in for a great deal of abuse, and I am afraid that my leaving England at this juncture will look like running away. But I am quite prepared to leave for Biarritz at a moment's notice and leave the yapping dogs to abuse to their hearts' content.

The Geddes Report itself was made public on the morning of Friday, 10th February, 1922, and the same evening Beatty, on his own initiative, issued the Admiralty statement. This caused a mild sensation, some of the evening papers showing placards with the words: 'Admiralty reply. Geddes Report torpedoed.'

As the Admiralty counter-proposal was based on principle rather than expediency, Beatty felt confident of public support, and went to Biarritz to join his wife, who was ill. Mr. Amery, having been left in political charge, had to bear the brunt of Cabinet displeasure. After returning to the Admiralty, Beatty wrote to Ethel:

(23rd Feb., 1922)

The battle rages on, and still we keep our heads above water, and on the whole I think holding our own. Winston and Birkenhead have supported us nobly and are continuing to do so. I think therefore we shall win in the end and defeat the Geddes Committee side. If not, a break in the Cabinet is certain, and after that anything might happen.

(25th Feb., 1922)

I did not write yesterday, as I went down to Brooksby by the late train and had a hunt with the Cottesmore, the first time this season. . . . The Geddes Committee having published their last report, we also fired off another round. . . . We have held our own, and as far as I can see have the sympathy of practically the whole community and of the Man in the Street.

In the end, a Cabinet Committee appointed to examine the Geddes Report largely upheld the Admiralty point of view, and when the Lloyd George Government fell, Amery became First Lord.

Beatty succeeded in getting the Government to implement the Washington decision for Great Britain to lay down the two post-war battleships *Nelson* and *Rodney* in 1922, but there was difficulty about the cruiser programme. In facing the Cabinet, Beatty stated that the abandonment of the Anglo-Japanese Alliance had greatly increased our naval commitments in the Far East, both in peace and in war. Not only would it be necessary for us to keep a fleet there, but we would also require to modernise the base at Singapore and maintain Hong Kong to enable the Fleet to operate. He fixed the total number of cruisers of all types which would be required by the British Empire in war at a minimum of seventy, including modern light cruisers already in service. These, however, had been designed mainly for North Sea warfare, and new ships able to operate in any part of the seven seas would be wanted in course of time to replace them. He therefore submitted to the Government a modest programme of construction, to be spread over several years, for a number of small cruisers, armed with 6-inch guns. He pointed out that the laying down of two or three ships each year would have the advantage of keeping the ship-yards going and ensuring continuity of design.

Foreign competition, however, forced Beatty's hand, compelling him to shelve for the time being his moderate proposals. The United States, Japan, and the European Powers were devoting their full building capacity to large cruisers of 10,000 tons, and Great Britain could not afford to be left behind in the construction of these powerful ships. This made the Admiralty case more difficult, as the British equivalent (County Class), being a new design, would be far more costly to build than developing existing types with their standardised 6-inch guns.[1] Nevertheless, Beatty insisted that his fixed total of seventy cruisers must include a quota of large cruisers at least equal to that of any single Power, therefore the construction of the five ships approved in principle after the Washington

[1] Cost of County Class cruiser was £2,097,663.

Conference was a matter of great urgency, and must be provided for in the Navy Estimates of 1924.

The Labour Government came into power on 22nd January, 1924. Mr. Ramsay MacDonald's Cabinet accepted Beatty's view, and the House of Commons passed the Navy Estimates by a large majority. As the feeling in the country was strongly against armaments, this was a great personal triumph for Beatty, and he expresses his satisfaction in a letter to Ethel:

The Admiralty (*23rd Feb.*, 1924)

It is extraordinary to note the result of the Division in the House of Commons on the question of cruisers. Only 73 Liberal Members supported the Motion, that is, voted against the Admiralty. Over 20 Liberal Members and the whole of the Labour Party and the whole of the Conservative Party supported the Admiralty, including extremists of every description, Pacifist, Communists, Socialists. It really is a very remarkable result and one which gives ample food for thought. The Prime Minister must see, and I think does, what an immensely strong position it puts him in. Who would have thought, a few years or even months ago, that we should see an overwhelming majority of the House support the proposition of a strong Navy? ...

In the following year the Conservative Government, having been returned to power, did not take kindly to the Admiralty proposals for still more County Class cruisers, and made no provision for them in the Navy Estimates of March 1925. The First Lord (Mr. W. C. Bridgeman) stated, however, that proposals for new construction would be laid before Parliament at a later date after a Cabinet enquiry.

During a discussion with Ministers on the cruiser question, Churchill passed a note privately to Beatty:

I don't see how even if you had your 70 cruisers against (say) 50 hostile you could bring in the food and trade otherwise than by convoy; and if convoy were adopted, would these lolloping gazelle cruisers [advocated by Beatty] be the best vessels to guard them? Would no small rhinos or wart-hogs, even if slower, be a better type? W. S. C.

The crisis came in July 1925, when Mr. Bridgeman and Beatty went together to the Prime Minister and told him that they would be compelled to resign if the Government refused to act on the advice of the Board of Admiralty. Beatty's action was known in the country, and came as a shock to the complacency prevailing. A section of the Press renewed the cry that navies were out of date, and that an air force could provide all the defence that was necessary.

The Admiralty's case, however, had been well prepared on the unanswerable basis of the country's dependence on overseas trade and the need for protection of the ships that carried it. The day was still far distant when heavy cargoes could be carried by air, and no aircraft as yet had the range to give protection to merchant ships against any form of attack in the wide spaces of the ocean.

The Government had no case beyond the parrot cry of economy, but those who had the interests of the country at heart realised that to forgo insurance is poor economy. The Cabinet, fearing the publicity of Beatty's resignation, came to a compromise, and the Prime Minister (Mr. Baldwin) announced on 23rd July that agreement with the Admiralty had been reached.

If agreement had not been reached, Beatty, freed from office, intended to put the Admiralty case to the nation from the floor of the House of Lords, and had his speech prepared ready to deliver immediately following his resignation. Although the need for this did not arise, the concluding sentences are here quoted, as they show how deeply he felt about it:

'My Lords, for the past five years and nine months I have been serving my country as First Sea Lord under four successive Governments, and in my endeavour to meet the urgent needs of economy and financial stress I have had to reconcile my duty to preserve the Naval Power of the British Empire with the unenviable task of reducing that great Service which made victory in the Great War possible.

'I have had to acquiesce in and recognise the necessity for the destruction of many magnificent vessels, and for the axing of many gallant and efficient Officers and Men, all sacrificed to the need for economy, many of whom were personal friends and gallant comrades who had proved their worth by their loyalty and devotion to duty, and to whom I owe far more than I can ever repay for their support in those days of trial and tribulation.

'During the past ten years I have had to take upon myself many responsible decisions, but I can assure Your Lordships that I have never before taken a more responsible decision than I do now, and that I would be not faithful to what trust the country has in me, nor could I look in the face any one of my comrades of that Great Fleet it was my proud privilege to command, if I could not now take upon myself the responsibility of saying that the Government of this country are asking the Board of Admiralty to assume a responsibility which they are not capable of fulfilling.'

In the end Beatty succeeded in getting his full quota of fifteen large cruisers, thus enabling Great Britain to hold her own with other Powers in this new class of warship. The Australian Government proved, not for the first time, to be a friend in need by laying down at their own expense two of these costly ships.

Throughout his term of office Beatty made it quite clear to the world in general that he would oppose any reduction in the number of cruisers. Seventy was the bare minimum to meet the needs of the Empire, and he would never agree to base our sea security on figures which another nation considered sufficient for itself. He had not forgotten his history. In 1798 Nelson said, 'Was I to die this moment, "Want of frigates" would be found stamped on my heart'. And in 1805 he wrote to the Admiralty:

With great deference I venture by Your Lordships' desire to state my opinion of the necessity of a constant succession of frigates[1] and fast sailing sloops being employed for the protection of our Commerce and the destruction of the Enemy's numerous privateers. . . .

It was not until three years after Beatty had left the Admiralty that weaker counsels prevailed, and British sea power was threatened by the London Treaty of 1930. Parity in cruisers and destroyers was surrendered to the United States, and the replacement of our remaining pre-war battleships was postponed for five years. This was strongly criticised and hotly opposed by Beatty in the House of Lords. On Trafalgar Day, 1933, in an after-dinner speech, Beatty recalled:

'At Geneva in 1927 there was an attempt to alter this

---

[1] The frigate was the forerunner of the modern cruiser.

[cruiser minimum], but I am glad to say it failed. It was left until the London Conference, in 1930, that we departed from our hitherto accepted principle and allowed ourselves to be tied down to accept a quantum of 50 cruisers and parity with the United States, instead of the 70 cruisers which had always been accepted as our minimum number required for the work to be done. It is not—and I want to make this quite clear—it is not the parity with the United States that I cavil at or quarrel with. If she wants as many as we do, why not? But I do say this, that the acceptance of 50 cruisers to do the work of 70 was a grave and deplorable blunder.'

The 'cold war' which Beatty had to wage throughout his term of office for British maritime security was on two fronts. He had to fight on the international front with the uneasy feeling that any concession he might make to a foreign Power would be well received in some circles at home as a welcome economy. He was not deceived by this, and he made no concessions abroad. On the home front he knew, as well as any Cabinet Minister, the pressing need for economy, but he would fight to the last ditch any measure which might weaken basically the strength and efficiency of the Royal Navy.

The main battle at home was between the Admiralty and the Treasury, and the Chancellor of the Exchequer was aware that his toughest opponent in the fighting services was the First Sea Lord of the Admiralty. The Chancellor's task was not so difficult, as he had merely to provide the cash to meet the popular needs of the moment. Beatty, on the other hand, had to get the cash to prepare for sinister possibilities that no one wished to be reminded about, the majority of the people being under the hypnotic influence of collective security, and having high hopes of the millennium it would provide.

Another difficulty Beatty had to contend with was the 'Ten Year Rule', created by the Government to assist the Treasury in resisting expenditure on the fighting services. In the belief that war had been outlawed and renounced by most nations as an instrument of policy, the Government had the temerity to declare, in a secret instruction to the heads of the Navy, Army, and Air Force, in 1919, that there would be no great war for ten years.

Beatty at once saw a loophole, and working on the assumption that the Navy was to be ready for war in ten years' time, he pointed out that certain cuts could not be recovered by 1930, and that the new construction he was proposing would have to be ready by that date. The Cabinet would not accept this argument, and countered it by deciding that the Ten Year Rule should start afresh each year. In other words, the fighting services were to be at ten years' notice for war. Further protest was unavailing, and the immediate effect was to increase the power of the Treasury in curtailing naval expenditure. Beatty followed the policy of agreeing to considerable cuts in the branches of the tree, but he resisted strongly any attempt to tamper with the roots. In this he was well justified, for in spite of the prevailing atmosphere of blind optimism, there were many calls upon the Navy during Beatty's term of office.

In 1920 a strong fleet, including a battle squadron, had to be sent to the Bosphorus, as the Turks had become aggressive, and were in process of driving the Greeks out of Anatolia. The British Fleet remained there, acting also in support of the army at Chanak, for nearly three years, and was a powerful influence as a background to the delicate negotiations, which terminated in the Peace of Lausanne. On 20th September, 1922, Beatty and the Foreign Secretary (Lord Curzon) attended a meeting at the Quai d'Orsay to dissuade our French and Italian allies from evacuating the Chanak area, and so leaving the British to meet alone a possible Turkish attack. There was much plain speaking, Curzon and Beatty urging strongly that allied control of the Dardanelles should continue. Curzon said that he did not think that Mustapha Kemal would be so foolish as to hurt a Frenchman, but even if the risk had to be faced, 'Surely it would be more seemly than running away, so as to leave only English to be shot at!' Beatty said, 'The Navy could of course only control the sea. An attack by an army on the lines apprehended by Count Sforza [the Italian representative] would be a military situation. If instructions were given to the Navy in sufficient time to remove or destroy all craft on the southern shore, it would be possible to prevent the Turks passing from the southern to the northern shore even in the Bosphorus. The Kemalists would have to build new boats or swim!'[1] Since those days British prestige in Turkey has always been high, and there could be no better example of the use of the Fleet as an instrument of peaceful policy.

Mr. Amery, the First Lord, in his statement on the Navy Estimates (1923–4) said in the House of Commons: 'The political value of the Naval Forces employed in the Mediterranean during the past year and during the recent protracted negotiations with Turkey needs little emphasis. At a critical period of these negotiations they played a considerable part in the maintenance of peace.'

A powerful squadron was also required in China, not only to show Japan that we had no intention of abandoning our Far Eastern commitments, but also to protect British interests in a much-disturbed land.

There were many other calls on ships and squadrons in the interest of peace and humanity: notably in Ireland during the Sinn Fein trouble, and in the United Kingdom during the periods of acute industrial unrest. On such occasions, sailors were often used to carry out the military duty of assisting the police to preserve the peace. During the dock and railway strikes, warships were employed distributing yeast round the coast, and submarines provided electric power in the docks. Yet while the Navy was working hard in the interests of peace and security, public faith in the League of Nations was undiminished, and the cry for disarmament was intensified.

The United States had already abandoned the League, and Japan and Germany walked out later when it suited their interests. In 1935, eight years after Beatty had left the Admiralty, the inevitable crisis came when the Emperor of Abyssinia applied for the protection of the League against the aggression of Italy. As the world knows, sanctions were invoked largely at the instigation of Great Britain, but when the League looked round for collective security to enforce them, the only instrument ready to hand was the British Fleet. France was unwilling to play, but Great Britain did not fail. The same people in England who had proclaimed that armaments were the cause of war, and who had either advocated or

[1] Notes taken at the Conference by Sir Frank Spickernell.

condoned the reduction of the Fleet to a shadow of its former self, were now loud in their demands for its use in implementing a collective security which did not exist. History can show no greater paradox. Thanks to Beatty's prevision ten years previously, the seagoing Fleet, although emaciated by the Ten Year Rule and the drive for economy, was ready for war. Ships were called in from all over the world to join the main concentration at Alexandria, and peace was preserved at the expense of Abyssinia. Little did the world know that the reserves of ammunition and dockyard repair facilities were just enough to see the Fleet through one major battle.

Although Beatty naturally could not have foreseen that the first threat of war would arise in the Mediterranean, he fully realised that if the Fleet were to operate in any part of the world, defended bases with docks capable of taking our largest ships must be provided. Far Eastern waters were completely lacking in this respect, so Beatty got the Government to agree to the gradual development of such a base at Singapore. There was strong opposition to the project, and progress was so slow that Beatty deemed it necessary to address Members of Parliament on the question. He impressed upon them that Britain had to fulfil her obligations for the defence of her Far Eastern colonies and the Dominions of Australia and New Zealand, all of whom were prepared to contribute in one way or another to the defence of the Empire as a whole. He remarked that the people of the Dominions seemed to understand the importance of sea power better than our folk at home.

In 1925 the whole question of the defence of British bases overseas was being considered as a long-term policy. The Royal Air Force was desperately short of fighter squadrons, and the Air Ministry was anxious to avoid too many commitments abroad. They proposed to the Committee of Imperial Defence that Gibraltar should be omitted from the list of bases requiring fighter defence, because, so they said, weather conditions in a 'Levanter' (east wind) would prevent flying on many days of the year. When Beatty heard of this he sent for a staff officer of the Admiralty Air Division, who records the interview thus: 'Beatty was most indignant, and asked if I agreed with the statement. I said "No", adding that during the war we had a few flying boats at Gib. under the command of Major Barnby, R.M., and that I believed they did a lot of flying. Beatty asked if Barnby was still serving. I said I thought so, but did not know where. "Look him up in the Navy List." I did so, and found he was at Chatham. "Get him on the telephone, and find out if he can produce definite evidence, a photograph or something." Barnby was playing tennis, but was brought to the telephone, and eventually remembered a photo in his family album showing a flying boat in the air, and in the background the characteristic "Levanter" cloud covering the top of the "Rock". I told Barnby to hold the line, and reported to Beatty. "Tell him to come to the Admiralty at once, and bring his book with him." "He was playing tennis, sir, and is in flannels." "I don't care if he's in his bath. Tell him to come as he is." Beatty took the photo with him to the Committee of Imperial Defence, and fighter defence for Gibraltar was included in the plan.'

The regrettable differences which arose between the Admiralty and the Air Ministry in those days can be traced to the system whereby the Chancellor of the Exchequer decided for himself what proportion of the national expenditure could be spared for defence as a whole. This led to a tendency on the part of the fighting services to scramble for the leavings —a most undesirable state of affairs which, although relieving to some extent the Chancellor of his burden, placed heavy responsibility on the chiefs of the services, stimulated rivalry between them, and was detrimental to the security of the Empire.

In 1926, when Mr. Churchill was Chancellor, and the 'Ten Year Rule' was still in force, Mr. Baldwin, the Prime Minister, took a step of the highest constitutional importance. He created the Chiefs of Staff Subcommittee, charged with the duty of 'co-ordinating the functions and requirements of the Navy, Army, and Air Force'. Beatty was appointed its first chairman, and the memorandum inaugurating this important instrument of high command is with the Beatty family.[1]

The Chiefs of Staff Committee fulfilled a long-felt need, and soon became the corner-stone of the British system of high

[1] See Appendix VIII.

command, hitherto somewhat loosely knit. Although its functions were advisory, it derived executive power through the Prime Minister, as he, being chairman of the Committee of Imperial Defence, could preside, when necessary, over the Chiefs of Staff Subcommittee.

In October 1926, the Prime Minister deputed Beatty, as Chairman of the Chiefs of Staff Committee, to address all the delegates then attending the Imperial Conference, giving them the views of the British Government on the strategical aspects of Imperial Defence. Speaking on behalf of all three services, he emphasised that the responsibility for the defence of the sea communications of the Empire was not a matter for the Navy alone, but a joint one affecting the Navy, Army, and Air Force of the Mother country and the Dominions.

In modern war quick decisions are essential, and these may require to be translated into action by one or all of the fighting services or even the whole nation. The Chiefs of Staff Committee provided a means of co-ordinating policy and action at short notice without having to call a meeting of the Committee of Imperial Defence or the Cabinet. The system worked perfectly in the Second World War, giving Mr. Churchill day-to-day contact with the Services he controlled.

The success of the Chiefs of Staff Committee is in a measure due to Beatty's personality and tact as their first Chairman. With true statesmanship he maintained harmony at a time when the Services were at variance, and on their joint behalf held his own when dealing with Ministers. In the following year, when his time at the Admiralty was drawing to a close, he received this letter from Sir Maurice Hankey, Secretary to the Cabinet and Committee of Imperial Defence:

OFFICES OF THE CABINET,
2 WHITEHALL GARDENS,
S.E.1
30th April, 1927

DEAR LORD BEATTY,

I am very sorry to see that you have decided to go. I can guess that your motives are generous and that you feel you must give others a chance. I dare say also that you will be glad to get out of the ties of office life.

Still, you will be very much missed. You are the only First Sea Lord

I have known in my twenty-six years' experience who could really talk on even terms to the highest Cabinet Ministers and stand up to them in argument. Fisher is an exception, but Fisher was a crank, and even he didn't really state a case clearly.

This has meant everything in starting the Chiefs of Staff Committee. Without a really first-class Chairman we might have failed, and that would have been disastrous. It might have brought a Ministry of Defence even.

You have tremendous achievements to your name, but your successful pilotage of the C.O.S. Committee through its early days will, I believe, be one of your great contributions to the Empire's Welfare.

I am glad to think how well I have always worked with you.

Yours very sincerely,

(*signed*) M. P. A. HANKEY.

Beatty held the position of First Sea Lord for seven and a half years—a longer time than any of his predecessors. In spite of many differences with the Cabinet, and one offer to resign, his term of office was twice extended. He served under four Prime Ministers—Mr. Lloyd George, Mr. Bonar Law, Mr. Ramsay MacDonald, and Mr. Baldwin—and held the confidence and respect of three different Governments—Coalition, Labour, and Conservative. He trimmed his sails to none of these, pinning his faith on the greatness of British sea power, and convincing them of their duty to maintain it at a standard not less than any single nation, however friendly. Beatty had no illusions about the need for economy in those days of financial stress, but he weighed financial problems always in the light of what he considered to be the country's interest. Although a realist, his imagination and his knowledge of human nature enabled him to form a true picture in his mind of things to come in the sphere of international relations, so he took care to prepare for the worst. During his term of office the average expenditure on the Navy was about ten per cent. of the total supply vote, which compared well with the pre-war figure of thirty per cent., and was not a large insurance premium to pay for safeguarding the prestige and interests of the British Empire.

On 30th July, 1927, Beatty was relieved by Admiral Sir Charles Madden, who had been his second-in-command in the Grand Fleet. Beatty's departure was regretted everywhere. In his dealings with Ministers he had been sincere, forthright, and, when necessary, implacable. His personality and his achievements had made a deep impression, not only on those who had contact with him, but on the whole country. Even his detractors were silenced, as there was nothing they could criticise in his administration. The pacifists respected him, because they could not, in honesty, contest his point of view and still profess to be patriots. The economists found difficulty in quarrelling with the validity of his figures. Foreign envoys could get no change out of him, either in conference or through the Government. All this is summed up admirably in a letter from the Prime Minister expressing the thanks of the Government for his services:

Prime Minister's Office,
10 Downing Street,
Whitehall, S.W.1
28th July, 1927

Dear Lord Beatty,

On your relinquishment of your appointment as First Sea Lord and Chief of the Naval Staff, I wish to place on record the thanks of the Government for the invaluable assistance you have rendered during the last eight years, following your great service in the war.

We all recognise that the period of retrenchment and economy which necessarily followed on the war has been one of exceptional difficulty for the Admiralty, and we greatly appreciate the continuous efforts you have made to achieve these objects consistently with the essential needs of naval defence.

As President of the Committee of Imperial Defence, I wish also to thank you for the prominent part you have played in the successful inauguration of the Committee of Chiefs of Staff, and for the promotion of that close co-operation between the three fighting services, to which the Government attach the greatest importance.

May I express the hope that, notwithstanding the completion of your term of office at the Admiralty, your services will remain at the disposal of the Committee of Imperial Defence?

Yours sincerely,
(*signed*) Stanley Baldwin.

The First Lord, Mr. W. C. Bridgeman, wrote:

29th July, 1927

I am sorry to be away on the last day of your time at the Admiralty in one sense, but glad in another, because it would have been a really painful thing to me to bid you an official good-bye after the three years of companionship in the work at the Admiralty.

By word of mouth it would have been difficult to express my gratitude to you for all your help, support, and instruction, and even by letter I can hardly say what I feel. I have had now a good many years' experience in various Government offices—but never have I come across a colleague with whom I could work as easily as with you, in calm as well as in troubled times.

You have never bothered me with unimportant affairs, and you have never let me run up against serious difficulties without pointing them out to me—and never have I had an adviser who was able to put a case more plainly or more concisely before me.

More than that, you have always been able to see the political trials of my position, though it is often held that the Royal Navy can see nothing outside their own Service. That is not my experience of those principal members of the naval side of the Admiralty Staff.

You have never spared yourself in time or trouble when we were pressed, and never lost your equanimity, even under the very trying circumstances which you and I had to go through together occasionally.

Beatty finally left the Admiralty, not only with the goodwill and admiration of the Navy, but also with the thanks of the Government for his invaluable assistance 'during a period of exceptional difficulty'.

The prophet who had cried in the wilderness had honour in his own country.

H.M.S. *Alexandra*, flagship of Admiral H.R.H. Duke of Edinburgh,
Admiral Beatty's first ship, 1886
Photograph lent by Dr. Oscar Parkes, O.B.E.

H.M.S. *Queen Elizabeth*, wearing the Union Flag, Admiral Beatty's
last ship, 1919

CHAPTER SEVENTEEN

1919–1927
LETTERS TO LADY
BEATTY

ONLY the bare narrative of Beatty's memorable term of office as First Sea Lord has been given in the preceding chapter. The measures introduced by him and the success of his policy are well known, but the anguish he endured at the zenith of his fame was his own secret hidden from all except his family and a very small circle of intimate friends.

For ten years Beatty's character was put to the test in the most trying battle of his career, the emotional conflict between his duty to the Navy in its hour of need, and his love for his wife, who was suffering from a nervous affliction for which neither he nor she could find a cure. Her illness took the form of severe depression, bordering on acute melancholia, but there were short spells of reasonable health, when the sun would shine, reflecting happiness in husband, sons, and household.

So great was his power of concentration that he was able, on entering his room at the Admiralty, to dismiss from his mind the cares and anxiety which overshadowed his home life. None of the Ministers or Admiralty officials whom he met daily would have guessed that while he was fighting with his customary zeal and courage to maintain British sea supremacy, his strength was being sapped by sleepless nights and precious time spent in trying to help his stricken wife back to health. When they were together he would read to her for hours, and at all times he had to attend to her business affairs, which were complicated only too often by her unpredictable changes of mind.

Her roving nature and restless spirit would not allow her to stay long in one place, so the family went from one home to another. The Mall House, in Admiralty Arch, was their official residence, where they lived for a year, but as Lady Beatty could not stand the noise of the traffic, they moved back to their own house, Hanover Lodge, Regent's Park. They also owned Reigate Priory, Surrey, Brooksby Hall in Leicestershire for hunting, and rented Grantully Castle in Perthshire for the shooting. They sold Hanover Lodge in February 1925, and six months later moved to 17 Grosvenor Square, which became their permanent London residence till the Admiral died in 1936. In addition, they had the steam yacht *Sheelah* where they sometimes found peace. Curiously enough, Lady Beatty was a good sailor, and, like her husband, was always happy at sea.

She spent the greater part of the year abroad, going from spa to spa, where, in their turn, famous continental doctors, such as Coué, Dengler, and Marten, brought temporary relief. While she was abroad, Beatty, hoping and praying for her recovery, wrote almost every day, and she, knowing the place he would take in history, carefully preserved all his letters. She liked to know all that was going on in political and high naval circles, so from these letters we get an idea of the complexity of the problems which confronted him at the Admiralty and elsewhere. The Admiral himself is speaking, and by his frankness reveals quite unconsciously his love of family, devotion to duty, moral courage, and disregard of self.

Palais de Bruxelles (*19th Feb.*, 1919)
[On a visit to the King of the Belgians.]

We arrived here after 11½ hours in the motor over the worst roads you ever saw. We are in the Regal apartments waited upon in Regal fashion, so assiduous and courtly that even Frank[1] in our presence never moves except backwards, bowing till he tumbles over the mat.

The Admiralty (*6th Aug.*, 1920)

We have brought it on ourselves by bad handling and lack of foresight [intervention in Russia], and now we are up against a problem which the British public haven't begun to realise is staring them in the face. It is rather like trying to fight a feather pillow which might at any moment turn into a granite rock. We can't hurt them and our blows may hurt ourselves.[2] However, the usual panacea, a conference between Millerand

---

[1] Sir Frank Spickernell.
[2] Another penetrating forecast of things to come. See also p. 57 & 94 for Beatty's assessment of Russian characteristics.

and Lloyd George, is to take place on Sunday at Philip Sassoon's mansion —Hythe, and I have to go down there. . . . That turbulent priest, Archbishop Mannix, is fairly upsetting authority, and foolishly they have taken him seriously and forbidden him to land in Ireland, as if it were possible to make the situation there worse than it is. Again the Navy has to come to the rescue, and we have to arrest him on the High Sea, which, in view of a gale of wind blowing off the Irish coast and the possibility that he will resist arrest, is not going to be easy or pleasant. More especially as all the Stokers on his ship, the *Baltic*, have threatened to do all sorts of things if he is interfered with. However, we are relying on the support of the Stewards and Cooks of the said ship and hope with their co-operation we shall triumph. It is *opéra bouffe*.

Lympne, Kent [At a conference of the Powers]   (*9th Aug.*, 1920)
    Replies from the Bolshy were not as expected, they never are, and required further and more violent discussion. The only force capable of doing anything at all is the British Navy, and we are to be sorely tried, and I fear it will be a very unpopular service. [Beatty was opposed to the use of British naval forces at this time in the Baltic and Black Sea.]

Hanover Lodge   (*10th Aug.*, 1920)
    I understand the House was thoroughly bewildered, but because L. G. was in good form from a histrionic point of view they cheered him and seemed satisfied which is more than I am. He says in any case we are not going to war and he is not going to risk the lives of any soldiers, but I suppose sailors don't count, as they certainly will have to undergo war risks without the honour and glory of being at war. I made a strong case for the Navy, and he fully understands and was good enough to say that I had made his position plain.

The Admiralty   (*10th Jan.*, 1921)
    We have been having tremendous arguments over China and what we should do. As usual, everything comes down to me, and I have had to prepare an appreciation of the situation and make recommendations. The Cabinet have accepted them *in toto* and telegraphed them verbatim to Lampson in China. It is annoying that this disturbance sadly interferes with my brief holiday.

Brooksby   (*18th Feb.*, 1921)
    I loved getting on a horse again and seeing hounds. . . . Slept like a log, walked in the garden . . . the birds were screaming their little souls out and everything is sprouting. We met near Lowesby. Prince of Wales

was out, enquired after you, and hoped you were better. I nearly killed him, he would follow me, and I landed him in the middle of a big stake and brush fence. Poor little boy is not a good horseman, and pulled at his horse at the critical moment, which landed him in it instead of over it. He had a bit of a shake, but was all right. . . . I have disagreed with Bonar Law and his version [new construction]. Luckily I have Winston on my side. . . . If it comes to the worst, they can kick me out, and you will have your wish, but it will not be a pleasant way to end my period of office, and I should feel I had been a Failure, but I do not think honestly that they will go to that length. I don't care if they do, as I shall feel that I have done my duty and am consoled by the thought that in any case you will be pleased.

Hanover Lodge (*21st Feb.*, 1921)

I had a long talk with the King this morning, who asked after you, was very sympathetic, and was really pleased to hear you were better. He was very strong in his support of the Admiralty policy, and said that he had tackled the P.M. . . . I dined tonight at the Grillions Club with a lot of funny old gentlemen, and had a great *entente* with a funny old Law Lord who drank a devil of a lot of port and got redder and redder until I thought he would burst.

Beatty took a short holiday in France at the end of May, combining business with pleasure.

Aix-les-Bains (*29th May*, 1921)

I have had long conversations with Grasset [a French admiral] and the Minister of Marine, and a lunch banquet with the latter, so I think I cemented the *Entente*, which is really the essence of what I am here for and to assure him that the Navy of England is always ready to assist France in her hour of need. . . . All we can do will counteract a good deal the feeling of soreness caused by the statements issued and speeches made by the Prime Minister. Among them at luncheon was old Zaharoff the Greek. I don't know how to spell his name or why he was there.

Aix-les-Bains (*30th May*, 1921)

I drank the beastly waters today and take the Bath tomorrow. . . . The French authorities will have the answers to my questions by Monday, when I pass through, so my visit will not have been wasted. At the lunch yesterday we were photographed in every sort of shape and form. Dennis[1] is a kind of King of Aix, and runs the whole place.

[1] Captain Dennis Larking, R.N. (retd.), a friend of the Beattys.

Aix-les-Bains (*1st June*, 1921)

A great deal more has come out of my visit than was ever anticipated, and I hear the Prime Minister is very pleased with the result, so that he is finding out that sailors can be diplomatic. . . . This place is extraordinarily empty and is all the nicer for that. . . . The Sec. [Spickernell] and I celebrated the 31st May [Jutland] in silence. . . . No one else noticed it. Memories are short.

Aix-les-Bains (*5th June*, 1921)

Dennis dragged me to the Casino last night for the second time, and of course I paid the penalty and lost my money. I am no good as a gambler, and have no card sense, and the atmosphere makes me feel sick, so it is no use my trying. However, I did not lose my head as well as my money, and only lost £30. . . . The Derby seems to have been a great race. I wish I had been there, as I certainly should have backed Humorist, and I always love the meeting where one meets so many old friends that one never sees anywhere else.

The Admiralty (to Biarritz) (*22nd Jan.*, 1922)

You have a great deal to live for. I am a public man, and I have a right to ask you to do all you can to make yourself well, so that you can be of assistance to me in my life. . . . Today I am fighting a terrible battle to preserve what can be saved of the Navy for the Empire, and it is the most difficult task I have ever had to do and more depends upon the result than anything we can imagine. I can throw up the sponge and retire from the contest. I have no doubt somebody will be found who could do it equally well.

Hanover Lodge (*23rd Jan.*, 1922)

We are now enveloped in the thickest fog you ever saw, just like Pea Soup. You can thank the *Bon Dieu* you are out of this. . . . It's hard work being Daddy and Mummy to two boys and do my work too. Poor lambs, they'll be back at school in a day or two, so I must do my best for them.

Hanover Lodge (*21st Feb.*, 1922)

Lee [First Lord] is so overwhelmed by the attack on him by *The Times* he can think of nothing else, which is a mercy, as he leaves the things that matter to me and is quite happy apparently in doing so. I went to the Pilgrims' Dinner tonight to Mr. Balfour. I thought it was a good thing to appear in public to show I was here, and paid the penalty in having to listen to a lot of boring speeches. They really seemed to me perfectly futile and said a great deal about nothing. A. J. B. has got old—very old. . . . Practically the whole of the Cabinet was in support, equally bored to death. The Ambassador lasted for 45 minutes, and nobody could understand a word he said. . . .

Hanover Lodge (*28th Feb.*, 1922)

You must not think there is a seething world of gaiety going on which you are not invited to . . . a succession of very heavy solemn collections of functions at Buck House [Buckingham Palace]. Curzon's parties have been very heavy political parties. . . . I went to the Abbey, which was full of every sort and kind, the King being a Great Democrat. The little Princess looked very nice. The Press are booming the wedding [the Princess Royal and Lord Lascelles] to keep the attention off the very many and dangerous situations all over the world. Tomorrow the Chancellor will make his statement, and I am afraid it will be a pretty poor one, but I've gingered Winston up to come to our rescue if he is not fair to the British Navy.

The Admiralty (*29th Feb.*, 1922)

I really do not know what to say as to your visiting Coué at Nancy. I cannot think you are a type of person who would yield readily to suggestion. Biarritz you find very dull, well, Nancy you would find infinitely worse and that would upset you. . . . I went to the Party at Buck House last night. . . . The King and Queen asked after you *very warmly* and hoped you would not hurry home in this weather. The King was very pleased with the Admiralty stand, and said we trust you not to let the Navy down. We had another Battle Royal this morning in full Cabinet and we are winning on points. . . .

Hanover Lodge (*March*, 1922)

Your telegram and letters fill me with joy. I can't tell you or even explain what a great weight has been lifted from my mind and how different everything seems in consequence. I first cried and then laughed and sent for Mam[1] to tell the great good news, and Mam beamed all over and danced round the room, and said I must write at once to David. It all seems so very wonderful, and yet, when you read the little book which I have just done again, so simple and straightforward, I think of it all day and say to myself, '*She is better. She is better*'. What a wonder man little Coué[2] is. . . . Indeed, the world seems a different place, and I did my work today with a light heart and everything seemed to come easy

---

[1] Mlle Kambly—Lady Beatty's secretary.
[2] Dr. Émile Coué, a famous mental healer.

to me. I was so bucked I took the Secretary down to the Priory to show
him what was wanted to be looked after. It was a bright afternoon and
everything looked so pretty and pleasant and the atmosphere was delightfully calm and soothing. . . . Mam went off to see Peter and will tell him
the good news.

Palais de Bruxelles [on a visit to the King of the Belgians]
(10th *May*, 1922)

. . . Finishing off with a terrific Banquet of over 250. Poor King Albert
suffers a good deal with his arm. I got at the Queen and told her of the
wonders of Coué, and it did not lose anything in the telling. She said she
would tell the King, but I must do so also. I will, if I get a chance, but
he is very difficult to get hold of quietly, and he hates talking about himself. We have just returned from visiting first the Panorama of the Battle
of Yser magnificently painted, and secondly the Tir National, the monument erected to those executed by the Germans, including Miss Cavell,
where our King laid a wreath. . . . I get so mixed with Kings and Queens
it is difficult not to mix them up.

The Admiralty (6th *Oct.*, 1922)

I was so glad to get your wire that you had seen Coué. I am sure the
little man will stabilise your whole state of mind. I comfort myself by
reading again the letters you wrote me the last time you were there.
They breathe such confidence that I have no fear as to the result. Here
we are again in the throes of a hectic time, and I spent last night up to 1.15
this morning at 10 Downing Street. Curzon has gone over to Paris this
afternoon to wheel Poincaré into line if he can [*re* Turkey]. The French
are deserting us at the critical moment, and I am sure the French Nation
would be horrified if they knew how the entente is being jeopardised by
his action.

[At about 6 p.m. Beatty himself was asked to join Curzon in
Paris. He caught the night train and had a filthy crossing in the old
Engadine.]

A month later Beatty went to Biarritz for a fleeting visit,
and on his return wrote:

The Admiralty (to Biarritz) (19th *Nov.*, 1922)

I hope you got over your terrible storm. You certainly sent me off in
a hurricane frame of mind. I can perfectly see your point of view, as I
have told you, but you never can see mine. As long as I have got a job
to do I have to do it. If I chuck my appointment tomorrow it would not
have changed the fact that I had to go back to stand by comrades and

support the Admiralty policy when they telegraph for me as they did.
. . . Bless you, sweetheart. Cheer up and get out of the habit of storming
at the things that cannot be altered. I pray for you all day and every day.

The Admiralty (12th Dec., 1922)

I hope and pray you recovered your equanimity. . . . Really, if you
think seriously of the situation, you will see how impossible it is becoming
for me. You are fast wearing me out.

Hanover Lodge (to Hyères) (26th Feb., 1923)

After you left I went to the Admiralty and then to St. Paul's to hear
that delightful organ and choir and to get calmed down. Trot brought
Chris to lunch, and I then went to the Queen's Hall to hear Tchaikovsky
music, which all helped to soothe my troubled spirit.

Hanover Lodge (2nd March, 1923)

As to David, you will have had my letter saying I would write to the
Captain of the *Thunderer* to let him go up to Hyères to see you. . . .
I went to see the King today, who asked after you, and sent you many
messages. He was very cheerful and was very pleased at his son's engagement. I asked what the Duke of York wanted for a wedding present and he
said a Dessert Service. . . . The King spoke to me about going to Rome
with him, but said if there was difficulty in my getting away he would
take Madden, as he is his principal Naval A.D.C. and he would take
Cavan instead of Haig this time. As he leaves on a Sunday and gets back
the following Sunday and spends 4 days in the train, I don't think I
should be missing much by not going, especially as part of the time he is
to be visiting graveyards.

Reigate Priory (4th March, 1923)

As regards the Priory, I quite understand you don't like it and are
anxious to get rid of it. But you cannot get rid of it in a hurry unless you
are prepared to lose a very large sum of money. Your fault is that you
always want to do things in a hurry. You no sooner have an idea than
you want to put it into effect at once. Well, that is a very expensive
luxury. When you bought it you were in a hurry, and consequently it
cost you a good deal more than if you had taken time over it.

The Admiralty (6th March, 1923)

. . . It lies within yourself to re-establish yourself, and the first thing
to do is to put away this unhealthy craving for always being in the swim.
People that are, are not, as you imagine, the happiest people in the world.

Living for excitement is the most exacting form of life. The more you get the more you want, and to miss anything is looked upon as a cruel blow. You have so much, old girl, and should be quite capable of making your own life a perfectly happy one. . . . I get so weary in thinking of it all, that at times I feel quite sick, and am incapable of doing my work properly, and I have a good deal on my hands just now. We are preparing for another great battle in Cabinet Committee over the Air question. It is a momentous question, and we cannot afford to be beaten over it. It takes a vast amount of preparation, and that alone occupies most of my time, and we stand or fall by the result. There is another question which also is a source of annoyance and anxiety, and that is the Jutland question, which is ever present and must be brought to a head. The solution is not easy. There are so many interests involved. The outstanding and only one which should be considered is what is best for the Navy. That is my guiding consideration. Now cheer up for Heaven's sake, and help me by being more reasonable and taking a more reasonable view of life.

The Admiralty (*9th March,* 1923)

The Naval Estimates were completed and laid on the table of the House of Commons. They were very well received, and at last our efforts in the direction of Economy are being really appreciated. It is as well, because we have reached rock bottom and can go no lower, and in fact they must increase from now on. It has always been represented to us by a succession of Chancellors of the Exchequer that the Financial Year 1923–24 was the critical one, that is the one in which we should have greater difficulty than in any other to make the Budget meet. . . . We have two principles accepted, which is the great thing, and 2 Battleships laid down and commenced, and next year we must begin on a Light Cruiser programme. The next thing which I hope we shall see is more than likely an attack upon us for not doing more. The great thing is for the public to think that they are guiding our policies and either checking our extravagances or urging us on to greater endeavour, and then they are quite happy.

(*22nd March,* 1923)

I dined last night at the Grillions Club. I sat between old Asquith and George Curzon. Balfour, Haldane, Austen Chamberlain, Baldwin, Birkenhead, Hugh Cecil, and Archbishop of York. They were very nice to me, and said I was to stick to the Admiralty.

The Labour Government came into power on 22nd January, 1924, with Mr. Ramsay MacDonald as Prime Minister,

Mr. Philip Snowden as Chancellor of the Exchequer, and Lord Chelmsford as First Lord of the Admiralty.

Hanover Lodge (to Hyères)   *(23rd Jan., 1924)*

Such a day—the old 1st Lord out and the new 1st Lord in, two Board meetings, and taken old Peter off to Eton and planted him securely there. . . . Today Amery has departed and the new 1st Lord is Lord Chelmsford, who was the Viceroy of India, and has now thought fit to join Labour and the Socialists. I should have preferred to have had a real Labour man. The Parliamentary Secretary is Mr. Ammon, who was in the P.O. as a clerk some years ago. The Civil Lord is Mr. Frank Hodges, an out and out Labour man. . . . I have just returned from the Londonderry Party at 11.30. You never saw such a Bear Garden in your life. There simply wasn't room to move and so I bolted. They have re-elected Baldwin as the Leader of the Unionist Party, and so I suppose things will go on much in the same old way. I wired you this morning that David had arrived at Singapore and all was well. That infernal place's name will be engraved on my heart. The struggles I have had over it are to be repeated more bitterly than ever and with doubtful results. . . . The crowd tonight was so great I never got up the front staircase at all, and I believe lots never got into the front door. It really was too ridiculous having so many at one sitting. You never saw such oddities.

Mentmore   *(Not dated)*

Harry Dalmeny[1] very kindly asked me to come here after hunting. It is pleasanter than spending the evening by oneself. . . . I have to prepare for the first assaults on the Navy by the new Cabinet, and we cannot afford to be defeated in the 1st round. There is a decided Press Campaign, one half of which (the stable half) represented by *Times*, the *Daily Telegraph* and some of the Picture Papers are on the side of the Admiralty and the other half against us. They try to represent that I am a Dictator and have bullied two Cabinets into swallowing schemes for the aggrandisement of the British Navy, but now I am up against the Labour Cabinet I am to face defeat. . . . I am not having a glorious time as you seem to think. I am having a rotten time, fraught with difficulties and anxieties, and my responsibility is great, and it does not help me by making me unhappy all the time. I am leading a very simple orderly life. My one relaxation is an occasional hunt and that you could hardly grudge me.

[1] Earl of Rosebery.

The Admiralty   (*25th Jan.*, 1924)

I have made the acquaintance of Mr. Hodges, the new Civil Lord, a regular Labour man, an intelligent face and good head on him. We made friends, and he seemed grateful that I didn't bite him or was disagreeable. He evidently has brains and a will of his own. Also I received the new Financial Secretary, Mr. Ammon, whom I told you of. He also is a typical Labour M.P., and I think we shall get on all right when we once get to work. I had a long conversation with Chelmsford and I like him. He seems reasonable and open-minded, but is in a very difficult position. I think he will see things from our point of view, and it remains to be seen what strength he has in the new Cabinet and if he carries enough guns.

The Admiralty   (*3rd Feb.*, 1924)

Just returned after hours of unpleasant and very controversial argument with the new Chancellor of the Exchequer in particular and the whole Cabinet in general. You will see how perfectly impossible it is for me to come rattling out to join you at Hyères and I am between the devil and the deep sea. The First Lord supported me nobly, but he is very pessimistic, and has just informed me that he did not see how he could possibly stop on in a Cabinet with the views expressed by Mr. Snowden. Of course, if that is the case, there will be a debacle, and I do not see how anybody can continue to attempt to administer the Navy under such conditions. In that case you may well see me coming out to you, having wiped the dust of the Admiralty off my feet. So for Heaven's sake do not be in a hurry to post home. . . . I am having a very difficult time and I simply cannot and will not run away from my difficulties. . . . If you could see the letters I get and the appeals I receive to stick it out and try and save the situation, you would realise the magnitude of my task and the heavy responsibility that lies on my shoulders just now, and I think you would be pleased that so many people have faith in me and would be proud of the part I am asked to play in the affairs of our distraught and wretched country.

The Admiralty   (*6th Feb.*, 1924)

We have to teach them Imperialism. With some it is easy, but with others it is difficult. For instance, J. H. Thomas, Stephen Walsh, and Clynes are already very sound on these questions, and Lords Haldane and Chelmsford ought not to require any teaching, merely being brought up to date. With those Five thinking together, we shall start with a fairly good nucleus to deal with the remainder. It is quite extraordinary the amount of real ignorance that exists in their minds on questions of the greatest importance.

The Admiralty   (*7th Feb.*, 1924)

However, we are getting on, and I think they are beginning to see that there is something in some of the arguments we use. My principal and most formidable weapon is that they cannot fail to comply with our demands without explaining to the Country that we are too poor to preserve our integrity on the Sea and they are not brave enough to do that. They would not last one hour in power if they were to say that, and they jolly well know it. I had a letter from David from Dar-es-Salaam. . . . If I could get one cheerful letter from you, that would help me more than anything else, but of course you are on my mind all the time and I can't get away from it. So struggle, dear heart, for the blessed boys and your devoted husband.

Hanover Lodge   (*9th Feb.*, 1924)

Have had a wearisome and tiring day of endless discussion and did not get away until 8.30, and as I have to go back to see the Sea Lords I came here to get some dinner. We shall have to come to some under-standing as to whether we can go on or not. The new Chancellor of the Exchequer, Mr. Snowden, is a bitter pacifist, and would do away with the Navy altogether if he had half a chance. I told them if they wanted to be defeated in the House they were going the right way about it. That is the last thing they want. . . . If they give in, well and good. If not, we can but go, and they will find some difficulty in finding others to take our places.

The Admiralty   (*15th Feb.*, 1924)

I do like our new First Lord [Chelmsford]. He is a gentleman and as straight as a line. He might not be of a very strong character, but we can help him and one can believe what he says. He is also a very hard worker and gets through a lot. The thorn in our side is Mr. Philip Snowden, the Chancellor, who is an out and out pacifist. Old Haldane has been a great help to us and supports us on every occasion, but I am afraid they are going to be difficult, as there are many pacifists among the junior officials. However my two, Mr. Ammon and Mr. Hodges, both men that count in Councils of the party, are seeing reason and are a help. I like Mr. Frank Hodges especially. He was the leader of the miners and led the big Strike two summers ago, a fine fellow with a good head on him, and I think he is a friend of mine now. You would like him. I asked old Asquith how long he gave the Govt. to remain, but he would not commit himself, but said L. G. had prophesied 6 months. As I said before, this is too much or too little.

Hanover Lodge (18*th Feb.*, 1924)

I went to see old Peter at Eton yesterday, and the first thing he said was, 'What a good thing Mummy isn't coming home. This weather would make her ill again'. We lunched together with Ava [Lord Dufferin, killed in Burma] and went for a walk in Windsor Park, but couldn't walk much because of the snow. It's a long sort of day, as I had to wait and give him tea with two other friends of his, and they filled themselves up with things they liked. The Dockers' Strike has started, and we have to take charge of things to try and prevent the country from being starved. How did you like old Dumesnil, the French Admiral? He is a nice old boy. I am glad you went and lunched with him. It all helps in maintaining the *Entente*.

The Admiralty (19*th Feb.*, 1924)

I do hope and pray you are sleeping better now. I suppose you worked yourself into a state of fury because you decided to stay on and then regretted it afterwards. When one does that, it always takes toll and has to be paid for. It had the effect upon me of keeping me awake all night for the last two nights. You see, there must be some telepathy between us, because I couldn't sleep either, just lying awake and thinking of you and the gigantic problem which is involved. My dear, please sleep or I shan't sleep. I have just heard from the 1st Lord that we are going to get our way over the Naval Estimates. Well, that is the first big fence. The next will be Singapore.

The Admiralty (21*st Feb.*, 1924)

We have won our first Victory over the Govt., but they have had some trouble over it in the House, and I had to go down to bolster them up and give them material. They are beginning to lean upon me, so that is to the good.

The Admiralty (22*nd Feb.*, 1924)

The storm burst last night in the House, and on the whole we came out of it very well. The P.M. thought it was sufficiently serious to tackle it himself, and so I had to provide him with the material. . . . I am now preparing my dossier for the Singapore question. It has been accepted reluctantly by 3 Cabinets representing Liberals and Conservatives in the Coalition and by *two* Conservative Govts. and has been endorsed by two Imperial Conferences, so to reverse the whole decision will be not easy. It is hard that I should have to spend my time educating Government after Government and have the same struggle almost every year. Still, it is my job, and if we succeed so much the more credit for the Admiralty.

Hanover Lodge (to Nice)   (*3rd March*, 1924)

I had a hectic day yesterday, and had not a moment to turn round, what with seeing the King, attending a Cabinet meeting, and looking after Peter, that I had no time to write. The King was very nice and asked after you in the most sympathetic manner, and said he hoped that the trip to the Fleet and Malta would do you good. . . . Old Peter is very well, has had a bit of a cold. I took him yesterday to see the Football Match between the Navy and Army, which filled him with delight, and was better for him than a Matinée. . . . We went to The Little Minister, which he liked very much. Today we are going down to the Priory, take our lunch and picnic there. Rosemary[1] took me to a Charity Dance at Philip Sassoon's for the Northern Hospital, a most awful squash.

Brooksby Hall   (1924)

I am hoping to hear by telegraph today that you have found the Villa satisfactory and comfortable. David and I came down last night. . . . We had a regular Quorn day and galloped about all day, never a respite. So had little or no conversation with anybody. It was very good from a hound's point of view, but not so good from the riding, but as I enjoy seeing hounds work it suited me very well. You won't be cross about all this when you know how good it is for the Boy, and better than hanging about London with no exercise. . . . If you make up your mind that it will do you good, it will, and then you will come home a different woman and be able to enjoy the Boys' holiday with them and me. Bless you, dear heart, do not harbour hard thoughts in your head about me, but be your generous self.

Hanover Lodge   (*5th March*, 1924)

I dined with the Londonderrys. I sat between the Duchess of York [Queen Elizabeth] and Lady Curzon. The former is a perfect little duck, one of the nicest little ladies I have met for years. . . . I see you are haunted once more by the inevitable and everlasting problem of clothes, and are now turning your attention to my clothes, as if your own were not a sufficient problem. . . . You were always the best and simplest-dressed woman without any fuss or trouble.

Hanover Lodge   (*24th July*, 1924)

It really is refreshing to get such a happy letter and it makes me a hundred per cent. happier to read it and to know that all is well and you are enjoying life. What a comfort to be in a climate that you know is

------
[1] Viscountess Ednam.

going to remain the same. . . . I dined with the Pilgrims to meet Hughes, Secty. of State [U.S.A.]. He was in great form and pleased with himself. . . . I am so glad and light-hearted to think you are so happy. It is the best news I've had for years, and I am ten years younger in consequence. What a wonderful effect a happy letter can have.

The Admiralty Yacht (at the Naval Review)   (26th July, 1924)

Here I am back once again in the old *Enchantress*. It is 12 years since I last slept on board her and spent half the night talking war with Winston. It is amazing looking back how much has happened, and happened in accordance with the views that were expressed then, years ago. . . . Last night we all dined with the King. He was in great form and pleased to get back on the sea amongst the sailors. The old Duke of Connaught and the Prince of Wales and Prince George were there, and I think they all enjoyed being together as sailors. It is the first Review since 1914, and will do an immense amount of good and be a great advertisement for the Navy. It was nice meeting all the sailors again and we talked until midnight. . . . We had our Prime Minister and M. Herriot from France and Thennis from Belgium on board, with many members of our Cabinet, and Freddy Dufferin as the Speaker of the Senate of Ulster and Vice-Admiral of Ulster.

The Admiralty   (28th July, 1924)

The Review has been hailed all round as a great success, and was made up in numbers of small craft, Minesweepers and Destroyers for lack of Battleships and Battle Cruisers. But one (I for instance) could not help reflecting on the Great Fleet that used to fill the Firth of Forth, and draw comparisons and think if the British public enthuse over the Force assembled at Spithead on Saturday, what would they have said, thought and written of the great Collection of Ships which surrounded me from 1916 to 1919? I think Herriot, the French Prime Minister, was much impressed, but he said little, and the members of the Cabinet, although Labour, from the Prime Minister down enthused tremendously and pledged themselves never to let the Navy down, so I think we have gained many adherents to maintaining an adequate Navy and the Naval Review of 1924 has served its purpose. . . . I had a telegram from Marie, Queen of Roumania, as follows: 'The King and I would be delighted to have you and your Party here at Sinaia first days of September, have a National Festivity in Transylvania it may amuse you all to see. If so, our Government will make arrangements for you all to be transported there— Marie.' I replied: 'I thank your Majesty for gracious telegram and invitation. We should be delighted to see National Festivity in Transylvania and to visit Sinaia. We have to reach Constantinople about 4 Sept.—Beatty.' That sounds as if it would be great fun.

The Admiralty (*29th July*, 1924)

Am having some trouble in the House of Commons over many questions which have become acute, but this Naval Review has changed their ideas and they are more amenable to naval suggestions. The Jutland publication [*Narrative of the Battle of Jutland*] has not yet raised a storm. That has got to come. At present the critics are collecting themselves before letting loose. . . . I have had a long letter from Sir Herbert Dering at Bucharest, who says they are all out to make our visit to Roumania an enjoyable one, and from his account it certainly ought to be very interesting. Don't forget about the Mosquito netting, as they are bad on the Danube.

Hanover Lodge (*October* 1924)

. . . And a nice mess the delegates at Geneva are getting into, so my advent has been very opportune and I have fairly shaken up the Foreign Office and the First Lord. The Delegates have been agreeing to things at Geneva that would render the Navy impotent or put it in such a position that could not be tolerated. I have now told them we at the Admiralty agree to nothing, and I am sending a Staff Officer, your Captain Pound,[1] off to Geneva first thing in the morning to point out the mistakes they are making. It was lucky I came back when I did, as the whole Protocol is to be accepted and signed on Monday and our foolish representatives were prepared to accept it. Of course, all this has kept me very busy. I did not get away from the Admiralty until 8 last night and at $\frac{1}{4}$ to 8 tonight. The King of the Belgians came and had a long yarn about his son Charles, who he says is recovering wonderfully well and wants him to complete his courses and become a Sub-Lieutenant. This I can manage for him.

The Admiralty (*4th Oct.*, 1924)

Since I have been back I have had masses of work. It seems that nobody would make decisions until I returned, and I have had piles of them. . . . The Navy was to be pledged as the weapon of the League of Nations. Did you ever hear such a notion? However representations to the P.M. made it clear, and we were able to stop them signing anything. We are now being accused of wrecking the League of Nations. The answer is: Is it possible that it can be such a fragile instrument?

[1] Later Admiral of the Fleet Sir Dudley Pound, G.C.B., G.C.V.O.

Admiral Beatty's famous
horse 'Gold Bridge'.
Portrait by Nina Colmore.

The Conservative Government came into power on 7th November, 1924, with Mr. Stanley Baldwin as Prime Minister, Mr. Winston Churchill as Chancellor of the Exchequer, and Mr. W. C. Bridgeman as First Lord.

Mr. Churchill wrote this personal letter to Beatty:

TREASURY CHAMBERS,
WHITEHALL, S.W.
11th November, 1924

MY DEAR BEATTY,

I am so grateful to you for your kind letter of congratulations.

I am one of your greatest admirers, and I never cease to proclaim you as an inheritor of the grand tradition of Nelson.

How I wish I could have guided events a little better and a little longer. Jutland would have had a different ring if the plans already formed in my mind after the Dogger Bank for securing you the chief command had grown to their natural fruition.

I live a good deal in those tremendous past days.

Once more my sincere thanks,

Yours ever,
WINSTON S. C.

Although Beatty had friends in the Cabinet, he was soon to find that the new Government, contrary to expectations, were less amenable than their predecessors in following his advice. Fortunately, Mr. Bridgeman saw eye to eye with him, and together they weathered many a storm. For the moment, however, all was peace, and his thoughts turned to Christmas and a happy family reunion. He writes to Ethel:

The Admiralty (*7th Dec.,* 1924)

When you are happy we are all happy, but when you are miserable we are all miserable. I felt that you will be with us shortly restored to your dear self and able to enjoy things with us all at the Priory for Christmas. That is a blessed thought to look forward to (please excuse smudge— my glasses fell off my nose) and it would be splendid to begin the New Year with you in good health and happy once more. . . . Everything is very peaceful here with the new Government and I like Bridgeman very much, a gentleman and easy to get on with.

The Admiralty (*9th Dec.,* 1924)

I went down to Hall Barn last night, old Burnham's place, where he entertained the King, and a curious party, consisting of old Lincolnshire, Desborough, T. P. O'Connor, Rudyard Kipling, Marshall Hall, Sir Charles Russell, Simon Lovat, Harry Stoner. A very good shoot, and I really enjoyed it, the first I have had and the last this year of any good. T. P. O'Connor is an engaging old man full of anecdotes, never stops talking.

This brief spell of tranquillity was but a lull. The storm broke again at the coming of the New Year.

The Admiralty (to St. Jean Cap Ferrat) (*6th Jan.,* 1925)

Yesterday I was vigorously engaged with Winston [Chancellor of the Exchequer], and I think on the whole got the better of him. I must say, although I had to say some pretty strong things, he never bears any malice and was good-humoured throughout the engagement.

The Admiralty (*8th Jan.,* 1925)

The 1st Lord[1] is a dear little man and I like him better than any we have had, honest and straightforward and a gentleman in the best sense. I feel full of confidence with him, which is more than I have ever done before.

The Admiralty (*10th Jan.,* 1925)

In the U.S.A. they are voting enormous sums to build a lot of Cruisers, are to lay down 8 at once. This makes it very awkward for us, and I am hoping it will assist us in the demand for 6 Cruisers this coming year. I do not think we shall have difficulty in making a really sound case, but the Economists have got their mind on a reduction of the Income Tax, for which they anticipate receiving much applause. If they persist it will show once again how penny wise and pound foolish our legislators are, and in the end they will incur a considerable amount of odium but there are none so blind as those who won't see.

The Admiralty (*13th Jan.,* 1925)

Winston Churchill appears to have accomplished something by his trip to Paris and will return tomorrow flushed with victory. We have a very important meeting on Friday on Singapore and the Far East Policy, which I have no doubt will give him a full opportunity of letting himself go and it will be difficult to restrain him. He will, I know, be all for cutting everything down, which we shall have to resist.

[1] Mr. W. C. Bridgeman.

The Admiralty (to Cap Ferrat)   (*22nd Jan.*, 1925)

There is no doubt that we have all got our Crosses to bear, but mine seems so varied and different that it is bewildering at times, the problems are so different and each so difficult. If they were all of the same kind it would be comparatively easy, but what with my public difficulties and private problems they seem incapable of solution. . . . For 4 hours we wrangled with Winston and the Treasury myrmidons and I think successful, but it was a hard struggle and takes a lot out of me to concentrate on gigantic figures for a prolonged period and have to battle with those whose life is spent in a maze of figures. . . . I got your letter about the sale of Carpets, Curtains, etc.

The Admiralty (to a Friend)   (*23rd Jan.*, 1925)

I have had such a hectic time the last month over this Cruiser building programme which reached crescendo state Tuesday or Wednesday and I had not a moment those days to do anything, even get to the telephone. . . . After a very bitter struggle we won our case for our poor Cruisers, but it had been very wearing and the continual bickering over the needs of the Navy is very trying and produces a hopeless feeling trying to convince people who have not the intelligence to see that without adequate Naval protection the Empire runs a very grave risk of ceasing to exist as an Empire. The Prime Minister, against the views of the intelligent gentlemen in his Cabinet, came down on our side, and so there it is, we get what we want but at a considerable cost of temper and bad feeling.

The Admiralty   (*24th Jan.*, 1925)

I think it might be possible to sell the *Sheelah*. Yachting generally is about to improve. But I think the best policy would be to charter her if we can get a good Charter for some time, and then if you want her in the Autumn you could use her and get your yachting free, as old Duke of Sutherland used to do. Today is a great anniversary for us. The Dogger Bank action 10 years ago. It doesn't seem so far away as that, and yet a tremendous amount has happened since that (what we thought) was a glorious day and it has been completely forgotten by everybody except the *Daily Telegraph* which had a long article by our old friend Filson Young.

The Admiralty   (*26th Jan.*, 1925)

That extraordinary fellow Winston has gone mad. Economically mad, and no sacrifice is too great to achieve what in his shortsightedness is the panacea for all evils—to take 1s. off the Income Tax. Nobody outside a lunatic asylum expects a shilling off the Income Tax this Budget. But he has made up his mind that it is the only thing he can do to justify his appointment as Chancellor of the Exchequer. The result will be a split in the Conservative Party and nothing else. As we the Admiralty are the principal Spending Department, he attacks us with virulence. . . . Poor old Bridgeman our 1st Lord takes a very gloomy view and sees his job fading away from him. But I have heartened him up a lot and I think he will stand firm. It's then a case of Winston coming off his perch or a split in the Govt., followed by the resignation of the Board of Admiralty. Every year it is the same struggle. We have won through up to now, but we are up against tougher stuff just now and it requires very careful watching.

The Admiralty   (28th Jan., 1925)

In the course of this work I have many ups and downs and many disappointments and some successes, and I am always battling with entirely changed conditions and points of view. Of course being a public man I am prepared to meet or ignore a great deal of criticism, some fair and honest but a great deal of which is neither. I try not to take notice of the latter, and have succeeded to a certain extent, but little drops of water wear away a stone.

Marlborough Club   (29th Jan., 1925)

I've had a rest from Winston the last two days, but it is the calm before the storm which will burst out next week. I think I have collected much evidence which will defeat him, and gradually am overcoming the views of some of the waverers who are undecided. By putting the whole thing on a higher plane and appealing to their patriotism, I find a successful method provided one is emphatic enough. I shall lose Roger Keyes shortly, as he is going to relieve O. de Brock [as Commander-in-Chief Mediterranean].

The Admiralty   (31st Jan., 1925)

I am very busy tackling the Chancellor of the Exchequer [Mr. Churchill], who has burst a bomb over us which he thinks will pulverise us, setting forth the extravagance of our claims. I am answering that to-morrow. In the meantime I've persuaded the First Lord to go and spend the weekend with the Prime Minister at Chequers and take him out for a long walk and talk sense to him. . . . Winston and I are very good friends, and there is no malice or bad feeling attached to it. . . .

The Admiralty (to Dr. Dengler's Sanatorium, Baden-Baden)
                                                    (*1st Feb.*, 1925)

We have suffered a severe blow from this Government . . . actually behaving far worse to us at the Admiralty than the Labour Party. Of course it is all Winston as Chancellor. He has gone Economy-mad, and the result is that the Govt. are not proposing to build any Cruisers at all. Well, this obviously has to be fought, and if I have never done anything else of any value for my country I must withstand this at all cost. I must stand and fight.

The Admiralty   (*3rd Feb.*, 1925)

I had a bad day yesterday and it continued till the small hours of the morning, that is, until 2 a.m. Bridgeman went down to Chequers to see the P.M. and table our Naval Estimates. In the meantime Winston had cancelled a memorandum to the Cabinet against Naval Expenditure which brought Bridgeman galloping back, and of course being a Sunday it was difficult to put hands on anybody and to prepare our case. . . . Today I had a long and wearisome day going over all the old ground, finishing up with $2\frac{1}{2}$ hours with Winston very amicable and friendly, but he says it is a very difficult position and it is not easy to bring our difficulties into line. Wires and letters pass in profusion, but I am bewildered by the change of plans and by the many proposals. . . . I am so infernally harassed at present by the Government over Estimates and Singapore which they are now at the 11th hour jibbing at that I have no time to turn round, and I have little or no time even to write letters except in the middle of the night, when I can be sure of not being interrupted.

The Admiralty (to Baden-Baden)   (*4th Feb.*, 1925)

I have to tackle Winston and had $2\frac{1}{2}$ hours with him this evening. It takes a good deal out of me when dealing with a man of his calibre with a very quick brain. A false step, remark, or even gesture is immediately fastened upon, so I have to keep my wits about me. We of course arrived at nothing, but I think I impressed upon him the difficulties of the situation from the Admiralty point of view, and how it comes to the fact that the Government must either reaffirm their policy or alter it.

We are working up a case for the Prime Minister to adjudicate on the differences which exist between us at the Admiralty and the Air Ministry. It is a question of vital importance to us, and therefore we have to be very careful in the preparation of the arguments.

The Admiralty   (*5th Feb.*, 1925)

I am having the devil's own time over Singapore. For $2\frac{1}{2}$ solid hours we argued and talked over a question which was settled, and has been again raised principally with the object of gaining time and indeed wasting time. It simply is monstrous. . . . I had to stop writing you and go and see the P.M. about the Estimates, and so brought this home with me and am writing after dinner. Little Bridgeman is leaving all the conversations about the Estimates with me. I do not think Winston will go into the last ditch, and although we are a long way apart just at the present we shall come together and find agreement somehow. Curzon told me he went to see you, but was unfortunate not finding you in. He has been very useful to me, and supported me nobly, principally because he dislikes Winston, so that he finds pleasure in our continued opposition.

The Admiralty (*7th Feb.*, 1925)

You say I am having an awful time with the Government which is true, but you add: they won't give in to you any more than the other Govts. have, and there you are quite wrong. The other Govts. have always given in in the end, and this Govt. is going to give in exactly as the others have done.

The Admiralty (*11th Feb.*, 1925)

Poor old Hanover Lodge, I shall be sorry to leave it, but you will be pleased and that's all that matters. The Obolenskys have bought it and got it very cheap. Well, it's gone now, and there is no more to be said. I am having such a bother over Naval Estimates that it is quite possible we shall not have the Mall House to go to soon, and then we shall *have* to go to the Priory, so better not sell that until we see where we are.

The Admiralty (*14th Feb.*, 1925)

I think I have now overcome them all and saved the situation. My meeting yesterday with the P.M. and the Chancellor was very fruitful, and the way is clear to an understanding which will preserve the issues for which I have been struggling. The struggle has been long and difficult, but I think all is well, and I shall certainly come to you in a fortnight's time for three weeks of peace and visit the Fleet.

You must have realised from my letters that I have been passing through a pretty hard time, and from day to day have not known what the outcome would be. I have a great responsibility on my shoulders, not only affecting the Service but the future of the Empire, and moreover affecting the lives and careers of many distinguished officers serving under me at the Admiralty.

The Admiralty (*16th Feb.*, 1925)

. . . You now say you will not sell Hanover Lodge. That is out of the question. *It is sold* and we have to be out by the 25th March. God knows

[406]

I did not want to sell it, but it was done at your express wish and what's done cannot be undone. I have heard of several houses, but I am not going to take the responsibility of selecting a house for you. We can manage quite well in the Mall House and at the Priory once the weather improves.

The Admiralty (to Nice)   *(23rd Feb., 1925)*
Every day this week is very full of meetings and Conferences. . . . Then again I have to arrange for everything to be moved from Hanover Lodge, because when we return Hanover Lodge will no longer be ours. It will be a great wrench. There are so many old and happy associations and one will miss many things, but no doubt one will find compensations elsewhere. It is quite unique and the only one of its kind left.

The King is going for a trip in the *Victoria and Albert*, and I am getting her ready for him, and she will go out to the Mediterranean. We shall get away in the *Bryony*[1] well in advance, and be at Pollenza with the Fleet there. I sent David a telegram yesterday. Of course I remember when he came into the world and what a wonderful day it was.

The Admiralty (to a Friend)   *(7th March, 1925)*
I am by way of sailing to go and join the combined Atlantic and Mediterranean Fleets at Pollenza in Majorca. *But* there is always a but. It may be that what I get tomorrow will prevent it and make me turn my head the other way. . . . I don't go near Monte Carlo, because it does not appeal to me, it is so tawdry and the humanity one meets is so disgusting.

H.M.S. Bryony (to a Friend)   *(15th March, 1925)*
I am resting in the bosom of my Fleets and am feeling consequently happier and more at home than I have been for some time. Here I am at Palma, Majorca, surrounded by 100 ships all flying the White Ensign, manned by the salt of the Earth, and the result is a healthier outlook on the problems by which I am surrounded.

H.M.S. Bryony (to a Friend)   *(19th March, 1925)*
It was nice to be on the High Sea again and amongst all the sailors. They are the nicest people in the world and were very kind and hospitable, and we all thoroughly enjoyed ourselves carrying out exercises, solving problems connected with the sea. In 24 hours I was an entirely different human being, no cold, and 20 years younger. It was such a relief to be away from the everlasting wrangling with the politicians and forget all

---

[1] A sloop attached to the Mediterranean Fleet.

about them and their weary intrigues. . . . I am busy inspecting and getting to the bottom of things before I send out any more ships, my intention being to re-distribute the Fleets and have the Main Fleet out here instead of in the Atlantic. Consequently, there is a lot to be done beforehand and arrangements to be made. I gather that the Italians in general and Mussolini in particular is disturbed at such a possibility, and thinks that the Mediterranean should be an Italian lake and we have no right to be here at all. Well, he is mistaken, here we are, and here we remain. I think I shall go and see him on my way home and talk to him like a *sailor*!

[From London] (to a Friend) (17th June, 1925)

Here we are very busy and involved in the arrangements for safeguarding our Nationals in China. Every ship in the Far East is stationed with that object in view, and owing to the policy of the Government in reducing our naval strength all over the world, the amount of protection is not as effective as we should have liked. However, it is an ill wind that does nobody any good, and you can imagine that I am making full use of the situation to strengthen my arguments as to the futility of doing anything to reduce our Naval strength and the urgent necessity of meeting my demands which are modest and the very least with which we can carry out our commitments. I went yesterday to Ascot. I had hoped to go again tomorrow but, alas, they want the Cabinet Committee to sit on the Naval Construction question, which is of such importance I must be here.

The Admiralty (1st July, 1925)

I dined with the Admirals and Captains of the Grand Fleet last night [in London], a very representative gathering of over 140 officers, many old friends who made enquiries after you, and many I had not seen since the old war days. Of course the greater number of them were retired, but still there were at least 75 Admirals present, and on the whole it was a great success. Jellicoe and I were the guests of the evening and we were like brothers. . . . I am just off to a meeting on the Security Pact with France, Germany, and Belgium, and there is further trouble over Morocco and the Tangier Zone.

The Admiralty (4th July, 1925)

I am glad you are reading Winston's book, which is very well written, but I do not think you are fair to him when you abuse him because he appointed Jellicoe to be C.-in-C. Everybody thought in those days that Jellicoe was the best admiral we had. He certainly was the cleverest, and because he failed on one particular occasion, which would have proved the greatness or otherwise of the man, I do not think can be put down to Winston. He has been a very good friend to me and has backed me many times under circumstances of great difficulty.

The Admiralty   (*7th July*, 1925)

We have reached an *impasse* with the Government on the cruiser question, and I do not see the way out. We have made our proposals as being the very lowest we can agree to, and they won't have them, with the result that somebody has got to give way completely and Willie Bridgeman [the First Lord] is as firm as a rock. Therefore the whole of the Admiralty is with him *en bloc* and I suppose we shall have to go. There can be no other way out. . . . On the top of it all comes the China situation, which seems slowly going from bad to worse under Bolshevist influence and in every place becoming more threatening to the unfortunate foreigner, and the loss of trade amounting to 250 millions a year, and there are people who talk of peace all over the world. . . . 'Shaky' Marshall[1] had a terrific party last night, 48 to dinner. Princess Mary was very charming. The dinner was followed by a Cotillion. I haven't seen one for years. I was lucky getting hold of Violet Mar[2] as my partner, and so we sat through it all. It was over by 12. I have just been telephoned for from the Cabinet Offices, and shall probably be there until a late hour.

The Admiralty   (*10th July*, 1925)

The situation is a little easier today and slightly more hopeful. The Prime Minister is more open to entertain the Admiralty views, and I hope will be induced to settle the question in our favour by himself stating in Cabinet that for many reasons apart from those considered by the Committee it would be to the advantage of the country to accede to the Admiralty demands. . . .

The Admiralty   (*11th July*, 1925)

Things look brighter again today. I have got Arthur Balfour to come down on our side, so far as it is possible to get him to come down on any side, and that will have a great effect on the remainder of the Cabinet. . . . Of course the Press are not helpful and make references of an unpleasant kind that of course the Admiral will get his way and cost the country more money on Naval Extravagances. . . . However, if A. J. B. will act up to his words, we shall be all right. Unfortunately, he has

---

[1] Mrs. Marshall Field, second wife of the first Marshall Field.
[2] Countess of Mar and Kelly.

[409]

retired to bed in an exhausted state, and may not be able to get out to voice his views. . . . No word from David, but in a letter I had from the C.-in-C. Atlantic, old Oliver,[1] he said David was very well and a splendid officer. The old man supports me and urges me to be firm, and says 'the Navy would never get on without me'. Simple and pleasant flattery that I swallow like jam. But it is nice to know that one's efforts are appreciated by the best men in the Service.

[Beatty got his way. In addition to six large cruisers (10,000 tons) laid down in 1924, four more followed early in 1926. These included the *Australia* and *Canberra* built to the order of the Australian Government, see page 374.]

The Admiralty (to Dr. Martin's at Freiburg) (16th Feb., 1926)

I am sitting on the office stool endeavouring to reconcile the maintenance of a Navy with the ideas of Economy which fills the minds of all men to the exclusion of everything else. It seems like a madness which assails them. All precautions are to be thrown to the winds to completely trust the goodwill of every Nation and give up everything which will take years to reproduce for the sake of saving a few millions to spend on making roads and pay out in doles to people who don't want to work. The one real danger, Russia, they ignore. . . . If Japan adopted the doctrines of Bolshevism, then we should have some trouble, and the Prophecies of the Pyramids would come true, that the Races of the North and East would join hands and sweep across Europe.

17 Grosvenor Square (26th Feb., 1926)

No letter from you today. You can have no idea how much I dwell on getting your letters in the hope that there will be some light, some ray of sunshine in them that will provide some hope. . . . I saw Birkenhead at the Committee of Imperial Defence. . . . He was moved to make a most eloquent speech pointing out the real peril with which we were faced and which I called their attention to six months ago. I feel in my bones that it is a very real peril, and unless we are careful will find us unprepared and we shall suffer as we have never done before. In fact, we have very stormy times ahead of us, not at home, but in the great world, and before very long Europe will become once again an armed camp.

17 Grosvenor Square (28th Feb., 1926)

You cannot realise how we clutch at straws and build up on them, all three of us. Consequently, when you wrote Peter you were really better and underlined it, we felt very exhilarated and happy. . . .

[1] Admiral Sir Henry Oliver.

The Admiralty (*11th March,* 1926)

I personally am all for a Minister of Defence in certain conditions, only I am afraid they would never accept my conditions, which are to do away with the First Lord, Sec. for War, and Sec. for Air, and let the one Minister do the lot, with the Naval, Military, and Air Officers chiefs in their own Departments without another Civilian over them. Then one might get a real working machine and certainly economy. As soon as I start that idea, it will no doubt put a stop to the whole thing.

The Admiralty (to Dr. Dengler's) (*26th Sept.,* 1926)

As we get older our ideas of life, our desires, and our wants alter, which necessitates a reshuffling of one's ideas and a recutting out and planning of one's life. They say that all ages have their compensations, but we have to adapt ourselves and our outlook to them. You keep harping on the fact that I want to enjoy life. Of course I do. Of course everybody does, but I do not want to do so at the sacrifice of somebody else, least of all you. . . .

The Admiralty (*11th Oct.,* 1926)

I quite understand the extraordinary recuperative power of the Germans, and by their industry they are gradually resuming their position in the world's trade. . . . Of course they all say they never wanted to fight England and it is perfectly true. It was the surprise of their life that we were quixotic enough to fight for the moral preservation of Treaties. And now they know better and have a far greater respect for us in consequence.

The Admiralty (*14th Oct.,* 1926)

The politician says there are no external dangers. That may be true, but if so, it is due to the fact that we are strong; directly we become weak, external dangers will grow up like mushrooms. . . . The Colonial representatives for this Conference are pouring in: Bruce and Mackenzie King we know, but Coates of N.Z. and Hertzog of South Africa are new. The former is very sound and sensible. The latter is a visionary and a dreamer, but I hope to give them something to dream about.

The Admiralty (*17th Oct.,* 1926)

Yesterday I attended a great Ceremony on the Horse Guards Parade of the unveiling of the War Memorial to the Guards. I had to go to represent the Navy. It was most impressive and rather sad. 17,000 serving and past Guardsmen marched past, the vast majority being civilians in a variety of garments, some very smart, some very much the reverse, but all very proud to be there. The long lines, which took over an hour to pass the Memorial, were full of pathos when one remembered that they represented the finest fighting material produced in the whole war by any country. I was glad to represent the Navy. I see that New York are just about to spread themselves in their reception of Marie of Roumania, and how she will enjoy it!

The Admiralty   (*17th Jan.*, 1927)

I had to come up over this China trouble, which is getting worse instead of better. I have a Squadron of Cruisers all ready to leave Malta, and am collecting 1,000 Marines which I can send off by Friday. . . . I have just returned from a stormy Cabinet meeting, at which I have succeeded in getting my way, and they have agreed to send a Brigade from India and get another one ready to follow as soon as possible, but it will take them five weeks to get there and that may be too late. . . . Old Balfour sent you his love! Very gay of him.

17 Grosvenor Square (to a Friend)   (*15th Feb.*, 1927)

The weather has fairly defeated me in my efforts to get exercise, because hunting is out of the question, and my shoulder is so infernally stiff and painful I cannot play golf, tennis or other games, so am reduced to walking, which is unsatisfactory and unsatisfying. I have given much time to the work entailed by the China situation, which is better now we have a complete Brigade at Shanghai, as we are so much the safer and there is no likelihood of a catastrophe there.

Weston Shifnal (to a Friend)   (*No date*)

I have been at some trouble to impress my views on the Cabinet, who are just now overcome with the effects of the Locarno Pact and visions of a world in perpetual peace and feel that the hour has come to go further than anybody else and make proposals for doing away with all forces which have been necessary hitherto for defence purposes. It is quite amazing the lengths that some of the members of the Cabinet will go in their enthusiasm and desire to make a *beau geste* to the world. . . . However, we have got our way, and the 'Dove of Peace' Robert Cecil has gone to Geneva with the strict instructions to refrain from suggesting any proposals and . . . only on the understanding that the United States and Russia will both come in.

17 Grosvenor Square (to a Friend)   (*21st April*, 1927)

China goes on, and wanders from one set of circumstances to another entirely different, which render all the provision we had made for the first set to be perfectly useless for the second set. The changes are so rapid and kaleidoscopic that there is no keeping pace with them. . . . It's no use screaming, and saying that if they do not do what we demand of them, we shall smack them, when there is nobody to smack, and no place on which to smack them, which is exactly the state of affairs out there at present.

The Admiralty (*26th May,* 1927)
. . . The Soothsayer, the finding the four-leaved clover, Dengler's confidence, all have reassured me and made me feel so much happier and confident that you will return your dear self.

17 *Grosvenor Square (to a Friend)* (*No date*)
We are now embroiled in a serious situation in Egypt. The Nationalists have taken the bit in their teeth and are being stupid, and think that because we are so involved in China we are not free to consider troubles anywhere else. It is the old old game of twisting the Lion's tail which they are so fond of playing at. However, we still possess a Navy, and two fat battleships at Alexandria and another at Port Said has put a different complexion on the situation and has brought them to reason, even if it is only temporary. What a world of unrest it is. We never seem to be without difficulties of an international character and I suppose never shall. They are very tiresome and wearing, because they all come down to be dealt with by the Service Chiefs, and the political gentlemen take refuge behind the advice we give them. If successful they never say thank you and if not they are quite ready to make us the scapegoats. Is it surprising that I shall not be displeased to be relieved from such an unenviable position and retire to the peaceful paths of a private life?

17 *Grosvenor Square* (*14th June,* 1927)
The P.M. said that he could not spare me to go to Geneva with all these very real troubles on hand, and he keeps bombarding me with questions all day long. . . . I am just off with old Peter to the Confirmation at Southwark Cathedral, and we shall both be thinking of you and praying for you to have courage and determination to stick it and recover. I am sure that *le Bon Dieu* will answer our prayers and give you the necessary strength.

The Admiralty (*15th June,* 1927)
Old Peter, Canon Davies, and I fell in at Southwark Cathedral last night for the Confirmation and all went well. It was a very simple service, followed by a simple and suitable address by the Bishop. We then

returned and had a late supper. . . . Tomorrow the Cabinet sit on the China question, which I have to attend, and I hope to be able to ginger them up. . . . They have just telephoned me to go to another meeting at the H. of C. Peter and I prayed for you last night, and we believe that our prayers will be answered very shortly.

The Admiralty (17th *June*, 1927)

First Lord and our Naval Delegates leave today and tomorrow for Geneva, and I do not envy them their task, and I have fairly tied them up so they cannot decide any important question off their own bat but have got to refer it to me first. My principal difficulty will be the Cabinet at home. However we shall see. I shall go to the Priory and spend a quiet Saturday and Sunday with David and Peter.

Reigate Priory (19th *June*, 1927)

Here we are the three of us quietly spending the week-end at the Priory. Everything very late, not one rose out yet. I think they are like us, waiting for you to return.

The Admiralty (21st *June*, 1927)

The King has announced his intention of coming to dine with me and the Senior Officers of the Navy at the Mall House on 7th July. I am glad he is able to come, as it will be the last year I can entertain him at a Dinner of that kind, and it has done an immense amount of good to the Service to get the Senior Officers to meet the King.

The Admiralty (22nd *June*, 1927)

The P.M. sends for me nearly every day. I cannot move from my office, as telegrams are coming in morning and afternoon which have got to be answered. Still, if you urgently want me, I will come. You must come first, whatever the cost.

Shortly afterwards Lady Beatty came home and the correspondence ceased. Beatty continued his fight for British sea power until the 30th July, 1927, his last day in office.

CHAPTER EIGHTEEN

1927–1936
'HOME IS THE SAILOR'

TWO days after he had left the Admiralty, Beatty wrote this letter to a friend:

THE PRIORY, REIGATE
(*1st Aug.*, 1927)

It is all over and I've left my office. My work with His Majesty's Navy has come to an end, and now I am at a loose end. I have had a hectic ten days to finish up with. This Geneva Conference has kept me busy up to the last thing, and I do not know what the outcome will be. But I am afraid that the compromising spirit will prevail among our representatives, and they will be manœuvred into accepting something which they shouldn't. Friday evening we had telegrams which indicated that, and they had a hurried Cabinet meeting, at which I was able to prevail upon the Cabinet to stand firm and orders were sent Geneva accordingly. But even now I feel they will be going back on it and eventually come to a compromise, which I for one would never accept.

However, I have done my best and am out of the hunt. It was a wrench in a way severing finally my connection with the Service in which I have spent my life. That, however, was inevitable, and all things both good and bad have got to come to an end. . . . I do not think that once I have settled down to the altered circumstances I shall have many regrets. But one never knows. We are strange creatures, and everything goes contrariwise and not as we expect it. . . . It is very peaceful, but Ethel is still very unhappy.

Beatty dismissed from his mind any thought of a high public appointment. To him the Navy meant everything, and feeling that he had done all that he could for the Empire, both in the Fleet and in the council chamber, he retired to the country with the satisfaction of duty well done.

Having handed over the torch, he devoted himself to helping his wife back to health, and his hopes were raised when, for a short time, she took to the saddle again, and rode with him in the hunting field. He writes to Peter about a hunter he has bought for her:

Mummy is better and quite cheerful. . . . Went over to Melton yesterday and bought a bay mare, very nice and good quality, which Beeby said was exactly Mummy's sort—very easy to ride and a perfect hunter. She liked it very much. I had a ride on it over there, and it certainly was a nice ride, easy action, smooth, with a very good mouth. Has been ridden by a Lady, and I think will do Mother well.

Ethel, however, preferred the yacht, and to please her Beatty would gladly give up his favourite sport to accompany her on a Mediterranean cruise.

In the spring of 1928, when young David was serving as a sub-lieutenant in the *Queen Elizabeth*, the flagship of Sir Roger Keyes, Commander-in-Chief Mediterranean, the attraction of seeing his son in the familiar environment of his old flagship proved too strong for Beatty, so he took the *Sheelah* on a private visit to Keyes at Malta. Shortly afterwards the Mediterranean Fleet went to sea for combined manœuvres with the Home Fleet, and Keyes persuaded Beatty to meet him at Gibraltar, where at Keyes' request he addressed the officers of the two Fleets in a memorable speech. Imagine Beatty's feelings as he looked upon the rows of faces and recognised friends and shipmates whom he had not seen since Grand Fleet days. He had once described them as 'the salt of the earth', for they were the men who had helped him forge the weapon that had forced upon the German Fleet the fatal choice of annihilation or surrender.

After saying farewell to the Fleet, he went with his wife to Seville for the Easter celebration, and then on to Madrid as the guests of King Alfonso.

Although Lady Beatty could brave any storm at sea, both he and she were powerless against the waves of depression that continued to assail her. In order to soothe her and take her mind off petty worries, he would read to her by the hour. The sympathy he gave her was all that a husband could possibly give. His deep unselfishness was remarkable, but he had moments of despair, and in a letter to a friend he comes near to admitting it.

S.Y. *Sheelah* (11*th March,* 1928)

I am not sure I am able to continue to compete with what is obviously an impossible task. . . . I try not to think of Brooksby, but it is very difficult, more especially as I hear that the hunting has been good and they have had very good sport. Well, I am out of it all, and there is no use grieving over it and filling oneself up with regrets.

In the summer of 1928, young David was appointed to the Royal Yacht, and after Cowes week he joined his parents and his brother, Peter, at Grantully. Here the whole family were together, and the two boys did much to ease the burden of their mother's ill-health. The invigorating Scottish air, the beauty of the Perthshire landscape, and the kind attention of many old friends took Ethel out of herself, and, according to young David, she was better there than anywhere else. They spent the shooting season of each year at Grantully, and they were happy months for Beatty. He described a day on the moors in a letter to Peter:

The last day on Grantully Beat was spoilt by the wind getting up very strong and all the birds went wrong, so we only got 68½ brace and should have got 120 brace, which would have been very good for 4 guns. We have killed just over 1,300 brace up to the 16th, and the weather has been so bad. . . .

Beatty and his wife were united in their affection for their two sons, whose future careers provided an absorbing common interest. Young David had proved himself to be a good naval officer and showed promise, but war seemed so remote and active service so improbable that he left the Navy in 1930 and took up a political career, being elected a Member of Parliament in 1931.

Peter followed the family tradition of breeding race-horses, which proved to be his true vocation, for he won the Derby with Bois Roussel in 1938. Neither his father nor his mother lived to see this sporting triumph for the family.

If the Admiral had been spared, he would have been sixty-eight at the outbreak of the Second World War, and had his health permitted, there is no doubt he would have sought active service. Anyway, he would have had the satisfaction of knowing that both his sons were serving in the Navy.

David commanded destroyers before joining the active branch of Combined Operations. He took part in the Dieppe raid in 1942, and commanded landing-craft in the Sicily and Calabria landings. He was awarded the D.S.C. and promoted to Commander for his war services.

Peter served as a lieutenant in the R.N.V.R., and volunteered for service with the Commandos, but was compelled to withdraw on account of trouble with his eyes. Unfortunately, their father did not live to see his grandchild, David's son, who by a strange turn of fate was born on 21st November, 1946, which was the anniversary of the surrender of the German Fleet.

The summer of 1931 was the last they spent together as a family at Grantully. Late in the year Ethel began to fail, and a difficult winter followed for them all. In the spring of 1932 she fell into a state of acute melancholia, and died on the 17th July at Dingley Hall, Market Harborough, where she was laid to rest. Among the sailors who were present at the funeral was Admiral Sir Walter Cowan. To him Beatty wrote:

My dear Old Friend.—Thank you so much for being at my side on the worst day of my life. As I said, we have been so much together in great days and sad days that one likes the support of old and tried friends. Thank you for your dear letter, it helped a lot.

Beatty loved her to the end. She had helped and inspired him, but in later years came to resent the claim that the Navy made upon him. Like many women born to wealth, she expected always to have her own way and could not bear to be thwarted. She was, in fact, jealous of his love for the Navy, and this was aggravated by her illness. Small things loomed large in her mind, and Beatty would give way to her in everything that did not intrude upon his work.

In the years of war Lady Beatty worked hard for the men of the Fleet and their families, and spared no expense in caring for the wounded. In addition to fitting out the *Sheelah* as a hospital ship, she maintained Brooksby Hall during the whole war as a convalescent hospital, and secured the services of Sir Alfred Fripp and Dr. M. Shields as consultants. She ran two Y.M.C.A. huts for sailors at the Fleet base on the Forth, and raised a considerable sum of money, registered as Lady Beatty's Jutland Fund, for the widows and orphans of men killed in the battle.

A month after her death Beatty wrote to the Duchess of Rutland:

Grantully Castle (*18th Aug.*, 1932)

I cannot get used to the altered circumstances. We are strange creatures and truly Conservative, and I miss poor little Ethel far more than I can say, forget all the difficulties and remember only the sweetness of her, and try and console myself with the thought that she is happy and at peace, and her turbulent soul is at rest. Time alone can help, or at least I hope so, and I have to keep a stiff lip to help the Boys along. They miss her terribly. She did so much for them. It all seems terribly strange at present. Every corner reminds one. It is hard to sever a link of 30 years of a very stormy life. We shall go on living at Dingley, and I want to sell Brooksby, and for the present to lease the Priory.

His life had indeed been stormy. In the Soudan, when there was no fighting on the river, he sought it on shore. In China he went where the fighting was heaviest and, although wounded, he volunteered for every expedition which held prospect of action. Twice in his life he came near to winning the V.C., once on the Nile and again at Tientsin.[1] He had led his squadron and fleet successfully in three naval battles, but for reasons beyond his control, absolute victory eluded him, except perhaps at Heligoland.

As Commander-in-Chief he was often engaged in wordy combat with the Admiralty. Yet he was not disloyal. In these quarrels there was no question of personal animosity. They were more in the nature of family differences, and he would not hesitate to close the ranks against irresponsible criticism.[2]

His implacable will usually prevailed, and so great was the confidence of the Government in his prevision and judgment, there was neither hesitation nor doubt in appointing him First Sea Lord and retaining his services in that office for the longest term in history. Here again, with a single-minded belief in the need for a strong Navy, he withstood the assaults of the Treasury and the supporters of the League of Nations. At the

[1] See pages 23 and 72.   [2] See page 321.

same time he managed to achieve considerable economies without disturbing the basic principles of national defence.

Through it all he had the ever-present worry of his wife's illness.

Enough has been said in this biography to enable the reader to judge for himself the true character of David Beatty, although some may think that his faults and mistakes have been overlooked. From a professional point of view, the biographer, with all the facts before him, can find few faults either in Beatty's conduct as a leader or in his outlook on policy, strategy, and tactics. This view seems to have been shared first of all by Kitchener in the Sudan and later by Mr. Churchill, and also by the four separate Boards of Admiralty responsible for his special promotion respectively to Commander, Captain, Rear-Admiral, and finally Admiral of the Fleet. In each stage of his career he was tested by different men in different conditions of service, and was never found wanting in any of the qualities required for high naval command.

In matters of policy Beatty could be hard and relentless even to friends in high places, if he thought they were not acting in the best interests of the Navy. Ministers failed to awe him, and he was sometimes bitterly critical of them. This attitude naturally led to differences of opinion with authority, and brought him some enemies. He hated intrigue, and always got what he wanted by the force of his personality and the clarity of his arguments.

Following one of Beatty's outbursts against the lenient terms which the Supreme War Council was about to offer for the disposal of the German Fleet, one Flag officer at the Admiralty remarked, 'The fellow thinks he is running the whole Navy'. Beatty had no illusions about his position as Commander-in-Chief Grand Fleet, but he could not tolerate any weakness on the part of the Cabinet or the Admiralty which would deprive his country of the fruits of victory at sea.

He instinctively got down to the essentials of a problem, and quickly recognised the principles which governed its solution. His great antagonist in the war, Admiral von Hipper, also had this gift, for he too held the view that 'a man who loses himself in trifles runs the risk of blurring his senses of the relative importance of things and wasting his energies in a false direction. A leader must view things from a height like an eagle, not grub in the depths like a mole'.[1]

Beatty and Hipper had many characteristics in common, and there was similarity in their upbringing and outlook. Hipper was born in the heart of the country, more than a day's journey from the nearest seaport, yet the call of the sea was irresistible, and all his life he had only two main interests, the Navy and sport. German naval officers have said of him, 'To know Hipper thoroughly it was necessary to have seen him in the woods and fields following St. Hubert rather than on the bridge of a ship'. After the war Hipper retired to the country, and as a result of over-strenuous indulgence in chamois hunting, developed serious heart trouble. When he died in 1932, at the age of sixty-nine, Beatty said: 'I am very sorry. One would like to express regret for the passing of a gallant officer and a great sailor.'

The two admirals had a mutual respect for the fighting qualities of each other, and the clearest vindication of Beatty's leadership is to be found in Hipper's biography and the German Official Account of the battle of Jutland. The situations when Beatty and Hipper met in battle have already been reviewed in these pages, and the facts presented should enable readers to draw their own conclusions. It is well to remember, however, that an admiral in battle must always be dealing with rapidly changing events, and the platform from which he directs operations is in the front line, subject to intensive bombardment from above and demolition from below. His decisions must be made instantly; the loss of two or three minutes of time may deprive him of the victory he so ardently seeks. Yet every order he gives is written down by his signal staff before being transmitted to his ships, some of which may be out of sight. So, provided that his Flagship survives, the signal log bears witness of his actions, to be examined at leisure by the historian. There may be no record, however, of the state of the signal equipment, which may have been wholly or partly shot away when most urgently required. The simplest way to obviate the difficulties of signal communication in battle

[1] *Admiral von Hipper*, by Waldeyer-Hartz.

would be for the admiral to make as few signals as possible, relying on his Flag Officers and captains to understand his intentions through personal knowledge of their chief.

It came naturally to Beatty, like Nelson, to trust his subordinates, and he took care to impress upon them individually in walks ashore his views on tactics and his intentions in battle. Senior officers who had served under his command long enough to learn his ways soon came to know what they were expected to do. Hence at Jutland Beatty made comparatively few signals. His tactics were based always on the principle of the offensive, and no captain could go wrong if he sought out and engaged the enemy. Some critics may say why then did he tell the Admiralty, in January 1918, that he did not intend to seek action with the High Seas Fleet until the submarine menace had been mastered? Beatty made this decision after characteristic deliberation. As we have seen, he had correctly regarded the High Seas Fleet as the bulwark behind which the enemy could build up their submarine strength, and while their fleet remained in being, Beatty had to keep the Grand Fleet concentrated and ready for battle. Towards the end of 1917, it became clear, through Admiralty intelligence, that the pick of the German officers and men had been transferred from the High Seas Fleet to their submarine service for unrestricted attack on British trade. Beatty then came to the conclusion that Germany had no intention of seeking another fleet action except as a last resort, so he released many of his light forces from the Grand Fleet for offensive operations against the greater menace. In fact, he took the offensive in the right direction at the right moment.

Beatty had studied closely the life of Nelson and drew inspiration from him. Mahan was his favourite authority, but the book that he prized most was an account of Nelson's death written by the surgeon of the *Victory* whose name was Beatty. The walls of the Admiral's cabins in the *Lion* and *Queen Elizabeth* carried a fine selection of old prints of Nelson and his battles. A neatly framed copy of Nelson's prayer for victory before Trafalgar lay on Beatty's desk, and another copy hung above the pillow in his sleeping cabin.

Those who served at sea with him were fired by the thought

that their chief was endowed with the immortal spirit of the world's greatest naval commander, and Winston Churchill has recorded how that gallant old warrior Pakenham once whispered in his ear: 'First Lord—Nelson has come again.'

It would be invidious to stretch the parallel too far. Circumstances have changed with the century and their achievements were different, but it can be truly said that Nelson and Beatty each in his day symbolised to the people of all nations the fighting spirit of the British Navy.

In religion, Beatty held the 'honest to God' belief of the sailor. He always attended Divine Service on board. Like Drake, Duncan, Nelson, and many another of our greatest leaders, he had a simple faith in the guiding hand of Providence, which explains, not only his phenomenal courage, but his splendid habit of being always ready to take a risk if the occasion required it. He was often heard to say, 'Oh, well, *le bon Dieu* will see to that'.

In reply to a letter from a religious society, he wrote:

H.M.S. *Lion*   (31*st Dec.*, 1915)
... England still remains to be dug out of the stupor of self-satisfaction and complacency which her great and flourishing condition has steeped her in. And until she can be stirred out of this condition, until a Religious Revival takes place at Home, just so long will the war continue. When she can look on the Future with humbler eyes and a Prayer on her lips, then we can begin to count the days towards the end. Your Society is helping to this end, and so helping to bring the war to an end, a successful end, and without success it cannot end.

His first act after the surrender of the German Fleet was to order a massed service of thanksgiving to be held simultaneously in all ships of the Grand Fleet.

After the war his religion took the practical form of supporting the needy, and taking an active interest in such schemes as the Dockland Settlements and Seamen's Institutions.

Yet he was no saint. He loved the joys of life and was intensely human. He was attractive to women and enjoyed their company. He was a good husband and devoted father, and never happier than when at home with his family.

Any faults that Beatty may have had are disclosed in his own letters. He confesses to being ill-tempered, yet no one who served with him ever saw a sign of it. On occasions he may have been ruthless, but he was a statesman as well as a warrior, and his forthright methods had but one aim——the good of the country. He had faults: 'But where was he to be matched in devotedness and gallantry? And what man of blood fiery as his ever fought so to subject it.'[1]

By breeding and inclination Beatty was a man of action. Like Nelson he had learnt the art of war in early command by sheer experience, and being a deep thinker, he had come to know subconsciously how to apply successfully its simple principles. He had the rare faculty of combining decision with vision in a flash, yet he was neither impetuous nor rash. He was serene in adversity, and in moments of crisis his brain worked with absolute clarity, his judgment was sound, and his decisions were the result of previous reflection and forethought. Above all was his dauntless courage, both moral and physical.

When he left the Admiralty at the age of fifty-six, Beatty was young in mind and body, and showed no outward sign of the strain and anxiety which he had borne. Physical fitness was almost an obsession with him, and during his long term as First Sea Lord he never missed an opportunity to get in a day's hunting. His favourite pack was the Quorn, and sometimes he would slip away late in the evening, follow hounds all next day, then go back to the Admiralty and work late into the night on papers which had accumulated in his absence. He played polo at Hurlingham, and on one occasion, comparatively late in life, he rode in a point to point, falling at the last fence with victory in sight. He liked to live dangerously, and the sports he loved best were those where risks could be taken, but Providence cannot be tempted too far, and he had more than his share of accidents.

In 1922, while driving near Reigate Priory, he wrecked his car by deliberately mounting a high grass verge to avoid a cyclist at a cross-roads. Beatty's breast-bone was broken, but his strength at that time helped a speedy recovery, though the injury led to recurring chest trouble.

In the hunting field, ignoring all risks, he had a series of accidents. In 1930 he broke an arm. Three years later, while

---

[1] *Beauchamp's Career*, a novel by George Meredith.

schooling a German horse imported from Ireland, he was badly kicked after a fall. His jaw was shattered, and he had to support it with his hand. Finding he could not remount without assistance, he led his horse across some fields to the main road, where he met a roadmender, who helped him into the saddle, and he rode home. Although suffering acute agony, he never lost consciousness, and later remarked jokingly to a friend:[1] 'Some prize fighters when hit on the jaw go down for the count —I was hit on the jaw by a *horse* which wasn't wearing gloves and I did not pass out.' Beatty's injury was far more serious than he thought. Several operations were necessary, and while recovering from these his jaw was tightly closed. For three months he had to be fed through a tube, and could only speak with difficulty. The following year he broke three ribs. All these accidents took their toll, but he would never admit that he could not be as active as any young man.

Like his father before him, he was always a good judge of a horse, and after Ethel died he was able to give more time to the race-course. His fame as an admiral and his keen interest in horses endeared him to the public, who instinctively recognised him as a worthy upholder of Britain's oldest traditions.

The most successful horse that he ever owned was 'Gold Bridge', a magnificent-looking chestnut of great character, and at one time the fastest sprinter in England. When 'Gold Bridge' went to the stud at Newmarket, Beatty would spend many an hour in his box appraising his good looks and looking forward to the day when his progeny would run in races.

Unfortunately, he did not live to see them run, but his good judgment has been confirmed, as the offspring of 'Gold Bridge' have won over a quarter of a million pounds in stakes.

In retirement Beatty kept himself fully occupied. He worked hard for the Dockland settlements, and was an active Chairman of the National Playing Fields Association and also King's College Hospital.

He continued to take an interest in naval affairs, and when well, would hasten to the House of Lords to oppose any measure which he felt would endanger British sea power. Two days before his final illness, being dissatisfied with the way things

Sir Frank Spickernell.

were going for the Fleet Air Arm, and being unable, because of his health, to use his personality in support of the case for the Navy, he wrote to the *Daily Telegraph*:

13th February, 1936

Sir—

I note that the unsatisfactory situation as regards the Navy's air weapon is again arousing correspondence in the Press.

Such correspondence is no doubt inevitable so long as the present situation is allowed to exist. At the same time it is undesirable that it should continue at a time when the Government itself is no doubt giving serious consideration to the uncertainty in the public mind on the whole vital question.

The important thing to remember is that the decisions given many years ago were considered by the Government of the day to be the best compromise that could be made pending experience. It is in my recollection that Lord Salisbury, who arbitrated on the question of the relations between the Navy and the Air Force, made it clear that in his view ultimately the Fleet Air Arm may become a special branch of the Fleet in all respects like any other. The situation today is that we have had more than ten years' experience and the present system has failed.

I am sure that neither through the Press, nor Parliament, nor by Political Committees will this question ever be satisfactorily settled. A proper judicial enquiry seems to be the only solution, in order that facts and not personalities shall be the deciding factor in making such a vital decision.

Yours truly,

(*signed*) BEATTY.

This was the last time that Beatty recorded his views on defence matters.

Although he would never admit it, the series of accidents which came his way in later life had undermined his health. His indomitable will enabled him to overcome the effects of the strain and anxiety he had suffered, but his power of resistance to physical ailments was beyond his control and his heart was tiring.

> '*It is not in the storm nor in the strife*
> *We feel benumbed and wish to be no more,*
> *But in the after silence on the shore,*
> *When all is lost, except a little life.*'[1]

[1] Lord Byron.

In November 1935, while he was lying ill with influenza and a high temperature, he heard of Jellicoe's death. On the day of the funeral, being determined to pay his last respects as a pall bearer, he rose from his bed against the advice of his doctor. In full-dress uniform, wrapped in a boat-cloak, he took his place beside the gun-carriage, and struggled along through three miles of London streets to the slow cadence of the funeral march. During a halt, a member of the staff of the *Star* newspaper, noticing how ill he looked, refreshed him with a glass of brandy, and Beatty marched on with the procession to St. Paul's Cathedral.

In January 1936, H.M. King George V died, and again the doctors forbade Beatty to face the cold winter's day. Dismissing their warning with the words, 'He was not only my King, he was my friend', he once again accompanied the slow-moving gun-carriage drawn by a hundred and fifty sailors from the Fleet.

Afterwards his heart trouble increased, and the doctors tried to keep him in bed. He refused to admit defeat, and one day, when Captain Grint[1] called to enquire how he was, Beatty said to him, 'You are going to walk with me to the Turf Club'. It was his last stroll, for on the next day he suffered a further attack and the doctors insisted that he should take to his bed again, and furthermore, if he hoped to recover, he must lie still as a log and not lift a finger to help himself.

This naturally was extremely irksome to a man of his character, and in spite of repeated warnings from the doctors and the entreaties of his sons, he found it impossible to carry out their instructions. The odds were too heavy against him, and he fell into his last sleep on the night of 11th March, 1936, in his London house, 17 Grosvenor Square.

Roger Keyes, who had visited him on the day previous to his first bad heart attack, wrote:

Only a few hours before the heart attack which laid him low, he expressed to me his deep anxiety about the state of the Navy, and his determination to fight again for those things which he considered to be essential for its efficiency. Throughout his illness, which he fought

[1] Captain W. Grint, late master of S.Y. *Sheelah*.

bravely and fearlessly, he continually expressed his concern for the Navy, and his hope for a happy issue out of the trials which beset it. His death is a national calamity. His wise counsel would have been the greatest value to the Government, and it is a tragedy that his gallant spirit should have passed at this critical hour.

Speaking of the end, his eldest son, David,[1] says: 'At 11 p.m. I went to say good night to him just after he had taken a small whisky and soda which he was allowed occasionally under the doctor's orders. He seemed much brighter, and when I asked him how he felt, said to me: "I feel much better, old man; I could ride from the Prince of Wales to the Coplow, now.[2] Good night, Sonny." These were his last words, after which he slept peacefully until about 1 a.m., when he had his final attack. The nurse called me, but by the time I reached him he had died.'

He would have chosen to be buried beside his wife at Dingley Hall, and had caused a space to be left for his own name on her memorial stone, but the nation claimed him as one of her most distinguished sons, so on 16th March, 1936, amidst the solemn pageantry that England reserves for her great, Beatty was borne through the streets of London to St. Paul's Cathedral. The union flag that covered the coffin was the same flag that had flown so proudly at the main-mast head of his Flagship when he reached the zenith of his career.

In the hallowed atmosphere of the great Cathedral, as the congregation sang 'Crossing the bar', the coffin was lowered gently into the crypt. In a moving address the Archbishop of Canterbury said:

'It may not be unfitting that one voice should try to express the admiration and gratitude of the great body of his fellow-countrymen. To them as to his comrades he was, as one of these comrades has said, "the very embodiment of the fighting spirit of the Navy". In him something of the spirit of Nelson seemed to have come back. As with Nelson—to use the words of the old Psalm—his was the ministry of a flaming fire.

[1] The second Earl Beatty.
[2] The 'Prince of Wales' and 'Billesden Coplow' are two famous fox coverts in the Quorn Friday country, where Beatty and his sons had had many a good hunt together.

The bust of Admiral Beatty by Feridah Forbes

'In him, as in Nelson, the fire burned as a passion for victory. In the days of the war his one consuming desire was to engage the enemy. When any tidings came that the enemy was coming out, he was like one of his own hounds set free from the leash. His signal at the Dogger Bank, "Keep closer to the enemy", though it miscarried at the time, expressed the very spirit of the man. In pursuit of victory he was ready to take all risks. As a horseman on shore he feared no fence. As a commander at sea he feared no responsibility.

'And now, from the body which we have laid to rest, that fiery spirit has gone. No more for him the fierce rush of his battleships through the hissing foam; no more the thrill of the hunt on shore. Yet why should we mourn? He is at rest.'

He lies close to the tomb of Nelson in the deep silence of the vaults, broken only by the voices of the choir and the sonorous peal of the organ.

> '*Here he lies where he long'd to be;*
> *Home is the sailor, home from sea,*
> *And the hunter home from the hill.*'

APPENDIX I

TRIBUTE FROM THE BRITISH PEOPLE TO ADMIRAL OF THE FLEET EARL BEATTY

(Hansard, 5th May, 1936)

The PRIME MINISTER (Mr. Baldwin): I beg to move,

'That this House will, tomorrow, resolve itself into a Committee to consider an humble Address to His Majesty, praying that His Majesty will give direction that a Monument be erected at the public charge to the memory of the late Admiral of the Fleet Earl Beatty, as an expression of the admiration of this House for his illustrious naval career and its gratitude for his devoted services to the State.'

For the second time within a few months the House is being asked by me to pass a Motion of this description. I know it will gratefully pass this Motion for a permanent memorial to the late Admiral of the Fleet Earl Beatty, as an expression of its sense of gratitude to the second of the two great sailors who bore on their shoulders the immense responsibility of command in the Great War. For nearly half the Great War Lord Beatty served under Lord Jellicoe. From November, 1916, until the end of the war he bore upon his shoulders that almost intolerable responsibility, the chief responsibility for the safety of our country. They were both great sailors, different of course, but those differences may well be explored by the historians. For me and for the House today, we seek, not to compare the measure, but merely to express our thankfulness that at the time of our country's need two such men as Jellicoe and Beatty were there to respond to the call.

As a sailor he was undoubtedly a figure which appealed to the imagination of the British people. There is no doubt that to our people, whether they live on the sea-coast, in the great towns, or inland, the Royal Navy is in some subtle way the repository of the spirit and tradition of our nation; and there is no doubt that instinctively our people seemed to recognise in Lord Beatty the sure successor to those men whose names were so familiar to them and whose sayings have almost passed into the conversation of our land. We think of Duncan, off the Texel, who, when he had taken soundings said: 'I have taken the depth of the water and when the *Venerable* goes down, my flag will still fly.' We think of Grenville who, dying, gave orders to scuttle his ship with all on board her lest she should fall into the hands of the Spaniards. We think of Raleigh driving his little ships into Cadiz harbour and answering the guns of the Spanish forts with an insolent flourish of trumpets. We think of Nelson at the Nile, when he

saw the ship of his great friend Troubridge run aground and he com-
miserated with him, 'while his more fortunate companions were in the
full tide of happiness'; and at Copenhagen when he said, as the battle
began, 'It is warm work and this may be the last moment, but, mark you,
I would not be elsewhere for thousands.'

When one thinks of these things one feels instinctively how Beatty
might have taken his stand by any one of these admirals, and how, had he
been in their place, what they said would have sprung naturally to his lips.
In Beatty, fighting his battles as he did from an exposed position which he
selected for himself on the compass platform high above the bridge, calm,
unruffled, and alert, our people rightly saw the embodiment of that
persisting spirit of the Royal Navy that has lasted through the centuries,
and has been the glory of the Navy and the pride of our country, an
inspiration, not only to the men who served with him, but to the people of
this country through the darkest days.

When I think of Beatty as the people thought of him, I like to think
of another aspect of him familiar to me but much less familiar to his
countrymen. Although a public figure, although gifted with all those
qualities that attract the admiration of mankind, spectacular qualities we
might call them in some ways, yet the man himself was fundamentally a
shy man, a man who disliked publicity, who never courted it, and who,
I rejoice to think, took no part in any of the controversies that have raged
since the war. He kept himself aloof from all those things. Men who
worked with him have often told me of the deep impression made on them
by his foresight, by his method, and by the gift of sheer hard work that he
brought to his profession, all of which things were precedent to the prompt
decision and the vigorous action for which the world knew him so
well.

Those qualities and a mind attuned to statesmanship were given in full
after the war, when he spent more than seven years at the Admiralty at
a time of intense difficulty for any First Sea Lord, at a time when, in the
hands of any lesser man, it might have been impossible to have accomplished what was done; for this great sailor, who had been in command
of the greatest naval force the world has ever seen, had in those years
immediately succeeding the war to turn the whole of his knowledge and
the whole of his skill to reducing that force to the very skeleton of what
it had been, to see that after those reductions what was left was as efficient
as it could be, on that comparatively slender scale, to see that all the changes
of personnel that had to be made, the dismissals, were done—hardship
there must have been in many cases—with as little hardship as possible.
These things he did, and he served four or five separate Governments,
all with the same devotion to duty and with the same loyalty. Those last

years of his service to his country showed a man no less great in any way than he had been at the height of his power with the Grand Fleet.

When that work was done, for a short time he enjoyed such rest as was more than due to him, but in those last months, in failing health, there were two calls of personal duty to which he with his nature would not fail to respond. He followed his brother admiral, Lord Jellicoe, to his grave, and later, on the occasion when most of us saw him for the last time and were struck only too sadly by his appearance, he followed his beloved King on the last march through London. His gallant spirit is now at rest, and it only remains for this House, as they will, to pay him with no dissentient voice that tribute that they reserve for men who have rendered superlative service to their country. There can be no greater honour to any man than that this House, as I have said on one previous occasion, should stand aside for a few brief moments from its constant strife, and unite to pay its tribute to those who have deserved well of the State. This, I am convinced today, we shall all do as one man in this House.

Mr. ATTLEE: I rise on behalf of the Opposition to support the Motion which has been so eloquently moved by the Prime Minister. My mind, like his, has gone back to that occasion only a few months ago when we were paying our tribute to Lord Jellicoe. Now we are considering the erection of a memorial to another great naval commander, Lord Beatty. One by one the great fighting leaders of the nation during the Great War are passing away. To many people the name of Beatty suggests a brilliant, impetuous leader, rushing into battle regardless of consequences. But he was far more than an impetuous and gallant leader. He was indeed brilliant, fearless, and vigorous, but his valour was controlled by a cool brain. In the heat of an action he could think swiftly and calmly. He would take risks, but only if the objects to be gained were commensurate. He was a born leader of men and had that gift of inspiring those who served under him with his own dauntless spirit. He was ever mindful of the welfare of those he commanded, both when at sea in the war and afterwards in time of peace. It was during his tenure as First Sea Lord that the Welfare Committees were set up for the men in the Navy. His name will be linked for ever with the achievements of the British Fleet in the Great War. He has taken his place with the great sea captains of the nation. For all those years after the war he served as First Sea Lord in most trying times, when inevitable Fleet reductions meant the infliction of hardship on his comrades in the Service. His monument, like that of Lord Jellicoe, will be a tribute, not only to him, but to the valour and devotion of all the men who served our country at sea during the Great War.

Sir ARCHIBALD SINCLAIR: I rise to support on behalf of my hon. and

right hon. Friends the Motion before the House, and to echo the senti-
ments which have been so eloquently expressed by the Prime Minister
and the Leader of the Opposition, of admiration of the character and
gratitude for the services of the great sailor to whose illustrious memory
it is rightly proposed to erect a monument. None I think can doubt that
history will assign to Lord Beatty a place in the company of Blake and
Nelson and of the greatest of our naval commanders, some of whose
names the Prime Minister was recalling to us this afternoon. Exactly
what that place will be I agree with the Prime Minister it is not for us
to attempt to estimate; but this I know, that I have never yet met an
officer or naval rating who served under Lord Beatty who did not say so
with a ring of pride in his voice. Of course we must erect a memorial of
stone so that he who walks the streets of the capital of the Empire shall be
reminded of its debt to a great leader of men. But his true memorial will
be less tangible; it will be part of the traditions of the Service to which he
devoted his life in peace and war. His strength, valour, and ardour, controlled by a keen, cool, and disciplined mind, were among the gifts which
he brought to the Navy which it will not relinquish at his death, for so
long as the British Navy sails the seas and so long as its fame endures, the
man we called Lord Beatty, the deeds he did and the inspiration he gave
will be freshly remembered; and so long will he hold a place of honour
in the hearts of the British people.

Question put, and agreed to.

Resolved,

'That this House will, tomorrow, resolve itself into a Committee to
consider an humble Address to His Majesty, praying that His Majesty
will give directions that a monument[1] be erected at the public charge to
the memory of the late Admiral of the Fleet Earl Beatty, as an expression
of the admiration of this House for his illustrious naval career and its
gratitude for his devoted services to the State.'

---

[1] A bronze bust and memorial tablet is now installed on the north side of Trafalgar
Square.

APPENDIX II
CHRONOLOGICAL RECORD OF SERVICES OF ADMIRAL OF THE FLEET EARL BEATTY

Born 17th January, 1871

Ship	Rank	Period of Service		Remarks
		From	To	
Britannia	Naval Cadet	15 Jan., 1884	14 Jan., 1886	
Alexandra	Naval Cadet	15 Jan., 1886	14 May, 1886	
Alexandra	Midshipman	15 May, 1886	20 July, 1888	
Cruiser	Midshipman	21 July, 1888	20 Oct., 1888	
Alexandra	Midshipman	21 Oct., 1888	19 Mar., 1889	
Duke of Wellington	Midshipman	20 Mar., 1889	14 Sept., 1889	
Ruby	Midshipman	15 Sept., 1889	13 May, 1890	
Ruby	Sub-Lieutenant	14 May, 1890	15 May, 1890	
Duke of Wellington	Sub-Lieutenant	16 May, 1890	10 June, 1890	
Ruby	Sub-Lieutenant	11 June, 1890	31 Aug., 1890	
Duke of Wellington	Sub-Lieutenant	1 Sept., 1890	1 Sept., 1890	
Excellent	Sub-Lieutenant	2 Sept., 1890	13 Jan., 1892	
Victory II	Sub-Lieutenant	14 Jan., 1892	4 Feb., 1892	
Nile	Sub-Lieutenant	5 Feb., 1892	6 July, 1892	
Victoria and Albert	Sub-Lieutenant	7 July, 1892	30 Aug., 1892	
Ruby	Lieutenant (seny. 25 Aug., 1892)	31 Aug., 1892	30 Sept., 1893	
Camperdown	Lieutenant	1 Oct., 1893	2 Oct., 1895	
Trafalgar	Lieutenant	3 Oct., 1895	18 May, 1896	
Victory I	Lieutenant	19 May, 1896	2 June, 1896	
Egyptian Government		3 June, 1896	19 Nov., 1896	Half Pay
Victory III for Ranger in command	Lieutenant	9 Jan., 1897	30 June, 1897	
Egyptian Government	Lieutenant	1 July, 1897	24 Oct., 1898	
—	Commander	15 Nov., 1898		Half Pay
Barfleur	Commander	20 Apr., 1899	12 Sept., 1900	Wounded
Duke of Wellington	Commander	13 Sept., 1900	30 Sept., 1900	
—	Captain	9 Nov., 1900		Half Pay
Juno	Captain	2 June, 1902	17 Dec., 1902	Half Pay
Arrogant	Captain	3 Nov., 1903	29 Sept. 1904	
Diana	Captain	30 Sept., 1904	11 Oct., 1904	
Mars	Captain	12 Oct., 1904	24 Oct., 1904	
Suffolk	Captain	25 Oct., 1904	19 Sept., 1905	
Victory I	Captain	20 Sept., 1905	14 Oct., 1905	
				Half Pay
Naval Adviser to Army Council	Captain	21 Dec., 1906	14 Dec., 1908	
Queen	Captain	15 Dec., 1908	3 Jan., 1910	Half Pay

Ship	Rank	Period of Service		Remarks
		From	To	
Naval Secretary to First Lord	Rear-Admiral (seny. 1 Jan., 1910)	8 Jan., 1912	1 July, 1912	
Aboukir	Rear-Admiral	2 July, 1912	27 July, 1912	
Naval Secretary to First Lord	Rear-Admiral	28 July, 1912	8 Jan., 1913	
				Half Pay
Lion	Rear-Admiral	1 Mar., 1913	2 Aug., 1914	
Lion	Act. Vice-Admiral	3 Aug., 1914	28 Jan., 1915	
Princess Royal	Act. Vice-Admiral	29 Jan., 1915	8 Apr., 1915	
Lion	Act. Vice-Admiral	9 Apr., 1915	8 Aug., 1915	
Lion	Vice-Admiral	9 Aug., 1915	27 Nov., 1916	
Iron Duke	Act. Admiral	28 Nov., 1916	15 Feb., 1917	
C.-in-C. Grand Fleet	(seny. 27 Nov., 1916)			
Queen Elizabeth	Act. Admiral	16 Feb., 1917	31 Dec., 1918	
Queen Elizabeth	Admiral	1 Jan., 1919	2 Apr., 1919	
Queen Elizabeth	Admiral of the Fleet	3 Apr., 1919	7 Apr., 1919	
President	Admiral of the Fleet	8 Apr., 1919	31 Oct., 1919	
First Sea Lord	Admiral of the Fleet	1 Nov., 1919	29 July, 1927	Half Pay

Died 11th March, 1936

APPENDIX III

REWARDS AND DISTINCTIONS OF
ADMIRAL OF THE FLEET EARL BEATTY
P.C., G.C.B., O.M., G.C.V.O., D.S.O., D.C.L. (Oxon), LL.D.

London Gazette	17th Nov., 1896	D.S.O. for services during Sudan operations.
London Gazette	1896	Awarded Medal with Hafir Clasp for Dongola Expedition.
London Gazette	30th Sept., 1898	Mentioned in Sirdar's despatch on Nile Expedition as having done good service.
London Gazette	7th Oct., 1898	Order of Medjidieh 4th Class.
London Gazette	15th Oct., 1898	Promoted for services on the Nile during Sudan operations.
London Gazette	9th Nov., 1900	Specially promoted to Captain for services China.
London Gazette	12th May, 1905	M.V.O. 4th class.
London Gazette	5th Nov., 1908	Unpaid A.D.C.
London Gazette	19th June, 1911	C.B.
London Gazette	22nd June, 1914	K.C.B.
London Gazette	20th June, 1916	K.C.V.O.
London Gazette	29th Aug., 1916	Military Order of St. George (4th Class).
London Gazette	15th Sept., 1916	G.C.B. Grand Officer of Legion of Honour, mentioned in despatches Battle of Jutland.
London Gazette	29th June, 1917	G.C.V.O.
London Gazette	11th Aug., 1917	Grand Officer of the Military Order of Savoy.
London Gazette	29th Aug., 1917	Japanese Order of the Rising Sun (Grand Cordon).
London Gazette	29th Nov., 1918	Grand Cordon of the Order of Leopold.
London Gazette	15th Feb., 1919	French Croix de Guerre (Bronze Palm).
London Gazette	17th Mar., 1919	Grand Cross of Star of Rumania.
London Gazette	3rd Apr., 1919	Specially promoted to Admiral of the Fleet for valuable services rendered during the war.
London Gazette	27th May, 1919	Grand Cross of Legion of Honour.
London Gazette	3rd June, 1919	Order of Merit.
London Gazette	21st June, 1919	Greek Order of the Redeemer Grand Cross.
London Gazette	25th June, 1919	D.C.L. (Oxon).
London Gazette		LL.D. (Aberdeen).
The Times	6th Aug., 1919	Created an Earl, and granted the sum of £100,000 by Parliament for valuable services rendered during Great War.
London Gazette	16th Sept., 1919	American D.S.M.
London Gazette	21st Oct., 1919	Titles conferred by the King— Baron Beatty of the North Sea and of Brooksby in the County of Leicester, Viscount Borodale of Wexford, and Earl Beatty.
London Gazette	22nd Jan., 1920	Chinese Order of the Excellent Crop 1st Class.
London Gazette	23rd Mar., 1920	Presented at the Admiralty with the Gold Medal of 'La Solidarad' by the Panamanian Delegate.
London Gazette	1st Nov., 1921	Grand Cordon of the Order of the Rising Sun with Paulowina.
London Gazette	29th July, 1927	Sworn as Privy Councillor.

APPENDIX IV

THE ROSYTH FORCE

The following ships and commanding officers sailed from Rosyth under Admiral Beatty's command, on the 30th May, 1916, and took part in the Battle of Jutland.

Lion Captain Alfred E. M. Chatfield, C.V.O. (Battle Cruiser Fleet Flagship).

Flying the flag of Vice-Admiral Sir David Beatty, K.C.B., D.S.O., M.V.O.

Captain Rudolph W. Bentinck, Chief of Staff.

1ST BATTLE CRUISER SQUADRON

Princess Royal Captain Walter H. Cowan, D.S.O., M.V.O.

Flying the flag of Rear-Admiral Osmond de B. Brock, C.B.

Queen Mary Captain Cecil I. Prowse.

Tiger Captain Henry B. Pelly, M.V.O.

2ND BATTLE CRUISER SQUADRON

New Zealand Captain John F. E. Green.

Flying the flag of Rear-Admiral William C. Pakenham, C.B., M.V.O.

Indefatigable Captain Charles F. Sowerby.

(*Australia,* flagship of this squadron, was absent refitting at Devonport ; the flag was flown temporarily in *New Zealand.*)

5TH BATTLE SQUADRON

Barham Captain Arthur W. Craig.

Flying the flag of Rear-Admiral Hugh Evan-Thomas, M.V.O.

Valiant Captain Maurice Woollcombe.

Warspite Captain Edward M. Phillpotts.

Malaya Captain the Hon. Algernon D. E. H. Boyle, C.B., M.V.O.

(*Queen Elizabeth* of this squadron was under refit.)

[437]

1st Light Cruiser Squadron

Galatea	Commodore Edwyn S. Alexander-Sinclair, M.V.O.
Phæton	Captain John E. Cameron, M.V.O.
Inconstant	Captain Bertram S. Thesiger, C.M.G.
Cordelia	Captain Tufton P. H. Beamish.

2nd Light Cruiser Squadron

Southampton	Commodore William E. Goodenough, M.V.O., A.D.C.
Birmingham	Captain Arthur A. M. Duff.
Nottingham	Captain Charles B. Miller.
Dublin	Captain Albert C. Scott.

3rd Light Cruiser Squadron

Falmouth	Captain John D. Edwards.
	Flying the flag of Rear-Admiral Trevylyan D. W. Napier, M.V.O.
Yarmouth	Captain Thomas D. Pratt.
Birkenhead	Captain Edward Reeves.
Gloucester	Captain William F. Blunt, D.S.O.

13th Destroyer Flotilla

Light Cruiser

Champion	Captain James U. Farie (Captain D. XIII)

Destroyers

Nestor	Commander the Hon. Edward B. S. Bingham.
Nomad	Lieutenant-Commander Paul Whitfield.
Narborough	Lieutentant-Commander Geoffrey Corlett.
Obdurate	Lieutenant-Commander Cecil H. H. Sams.
Petard	Lieutenant-Commander Evelyn C. O. Thomson.
Pelican	Lieutenant-Commander Kenneth A. Beattie.
Nerissa	Lieutenant-Commander Montague G. B. Legge.
Onslow	Lieutenant-Commander John C. Tovey.
Moresby	Lieutenant-Commander Roger V. Alison.
Nicator	Lieutenant Jack E. A. Mocatta.

(*Negro*, *Nereus*, *Paladin*, *Penn*, and *Pigeon* of this flotilla were away refitting, and *Nepean* remained in harbour.)

APPENDIX IV

PART OF 1ST FLOTILLA

Light Cruiser

Fearless	Captain Charles D. Roper (Captain D.1)

Destroyers

Acheron	Commander Charles G. Ramsey.
Ariel	Lieutenant-Commander Arthur G. Tippet.
Attack	Lieutenant-Commander Charles H. N. James.
Hydra	Lieutenant Francis G. Glossop.
Badger	Commander Charles A. Freemantle.
Goshawk	Commander Dashwood F. Moir.
Defender	Lieutenant-Commander Lawrence R. Palmer.
Lizard	Lieutenant-Commander Edward Brooke.
Lapwing	Lieutenant-Commander Alexander H. Gye.

(*Botha, Archer, Jackal,* and *Tigress* of this flotilla were away refitting, and *Phœnix* remained in harbour.)

PART OF 9TH FLOTILLA

Lydiard	Commander Malcolm L. Goldsmith.
Liberty	Lieutenant-Commander Philip W. S. King.
Landrail	Lieutenant-Commander Francis E. H. G. Hobart.
Laurel	Lieutenant Henry D. C. Stanistreet.

PART OF 10TH FLOTILLA

Moorsom	Commander John C. Hodgson.
Morris	Lieutenant-Commander Edward S. Graham.
Turbulent	Lieutenant-Commander Dudley Stuart.
Termagant	Lieutenant-Commander Cuthbert P. Blake.

Seaplane Carrier

Engadine	Lieutenant-Commander Charles G. Robinson.

APPENDIX V

THE LAST OPERATION

Copy of original order issued by Admiral Beatty

OPERATION ZZ

H.F. 0050/9
MEMORANDUM

Queen Elizabeth
20th November, 1918

1. OBJECT

To meet and escort to an anchorage in the Firth of Forth the ships of the German High Seas Fleet which are to be handed over for internment to the Grand Fleet.

2. FORCES EMPLOYED

Queen Elizabeth
Oak

1st B.S.	*Lion*	1st L.C.S.	*Castor*
2nd B.S.	1st B.C.S.	2nd L.C.S.	*Champion*
4th B.S.	2nd B.C.S.	3rd L.C.S.	3rd Flotilla
5th B.S.	1st C.S.	4th L.C.S.	11th Flotilla
6th B.S.	*Furious*	6th L.C.S.	12th Flotilla
	Minotaur	7th L.C.S.	13th Flotilla
		Fearless	14th Flotilla
			15th Flotilla
			20th Flotilla
			21st Flotilla

3. INTELLIGENCE

(*a*) The German Force to be handed over for internment on Thursday, 21st November, consists of the following vessels of the German High Seas Fleet:

Battleships:

Friedrich der Grosse, flying the flag of Rear-Admiral von Reuter, who is in command of the whole force (call sign IMA)

König Albert	*Kaiserin*	*Prinzregent Luitpold*
Kaiser	*Bayern*	*Grosser Kurfürst*
Kronprinz Wilhelm	*Markgraf*	

[440]

Battle Cruisers:

Seydlitz, flying the Broad Pendant of Commodore Tagert (call sign NCO)

Derfflinger   *Hindenburg*
von der Tann   *Moltke*

Light Cruisers:

Karlsruhe, flying the Broad Pendant of Commodore Harder (call sign WBD)

Frankfurt   *Nürnberg*   *Köln*
Emden   *Brummer*   *Bremse*

Destroyers:

50 of the latest destroyers from the German 1st, 2nd, 3rd, 6th, and 7th Flotillas.

(b) The force will approach rendezvous 'X', position latitude 56° 11′ N., longitude 1° 20′ W., on a course 270°, speed 10 knots, the leading ship passing the rendezvous about 0800 Thursday, 21st November.

(c) The order of the German force will be as follows:

    (i) Heavy ships in single line ahead, 3 cables apart, with the Battle Cruisers leading.

    (ii) Light Cruisers in single line ahead, 3 cables apart, the leading Light Cruiser 3 miles astern of the rear battleship.

    (iii) Destroyers in five groups, 3 miles astern of the rear Light Cruiser.

(d) The German vessels will have their guns in the securing position, trained fore and aft.

4. MOVEMENTS.

Leaving Harbour and meeting the High Seas Fleet

(a) Squadrons are to pass Black Rock Gate at the times shown in the table given in Enclosure 1, and are then to proceed in two lines as follows:

Squadrons in the *Northern Line* in the order:

            1st L.C.S. less *Phæton*
            6th L.C.S. less *Cardiff*
            1st C.S.
            Lion and 1st B.C.S.
            5th B.S.
            6th B.S.
            2nd B.S.
            Queen Elizabeth
            4th L.C.S.

are to pass North of May Island, and are then to proceed along the parallel of 56° 14′ N.

Squadrons in the *Southern Line* in the order:

> 3rd L.C.S.
> 2nd L.C.S.
> *Furious*
> *Minotaur*
> 2nd B.C.S.
> 1st B.S.
> 4th B.S.
> 7th L.C.S.

are to pass South of May Island, and are then to proceed along the parallel of 56° 8′ N.

Queen Elizabeth will adjust speed so as to pass May Island at 0800 Thursday, 21st November, and after passing May Island will maintain a speed of 12 knots.

At 0815, 21st November, squadrons are to be in station as shown in Diagram 1, Enclosure 2, *Lion* with 1st B.C.S. proceeding to the rear of the Northern Line, the 2nd B.C.S. to the rear of the Southern Line, the 4th and 7th L.C.S. dropping astern to give room for the 1st and 2nd B.C.S.

(*b*) *Cardiff* (towing a kite balloon, weather permitting), *Phæton*, *Castor*, *Champion*, and flotillas are to proceed in company well ahead of the 1st L.C.S. in time to arrive in position lat. 56° 11′ N., long. 1° 20′ W. at 0800, Thursday, 21st November, *Cardiff* and *Phæton* following the 13th Flotilla out of harbour.

After passing May Island, *Cardiff* and *Phæton* are to form 3 miles astern of the 13th Flotilla, which is to spread at daylight 21st November as a lookout screen.

(*c*) On sighting the German force, *Cardiff* and *Phæton* are to take station 3 cables ahead of the leading German heavy ship and light cruiser respectively. *Castor* is to form ahead of the centre line of German destroyers.

Flotilla leaders and flotillas are to form on the German flotillas in accordance with orders issued by the Commodore (F), copies of which are to be supplied to *Cardiff* and *Phæton*.

(*d*) In the event of the reckoning of the German Fleet being in error, *Cardiff* is to lead the German Fleet for a position 1 mile 180° from May Island. *Cardiff* is to report her position, course and speed by W/T as soon as formed up ahead of the German Fleet.

(*e*) On sighting the German Fleet, the Senior Officers of 1st and 3rd

L.C.S. are to alter course as necessary to allow the German Fleet to pass midway between the Northern and Southern Lines, at the same time making the signal by W/T: 'My course is . . .' Senior Officers of Squadrons are then to alter to this course and preserve their compass bearing from the Senior Officers 1st and 3rd L.C.S. respectively. On the Senior Officers 1st and 3rd L.C.S. resuming the original course, the same procedure is to be carried out, the object being to take up position preparatory to the signal 'W.L' being made.

(*f*) On the signal 'WL' being made by the Commander-in-Chief, leaders of divisions of the battle fleet and leaders of battle cruiser, cruiser and light cruiser squadrons will turn together 180° outwards, remainder following in succession, the British Fleet then assuming the order shown in Diagram 2, Enclosure 2.

ENTERING HARBOUR

(*g*) The Northern Line, with the exception of the 1st C.S., 1st and 6th L.C.S., is to proceed into harbour, passing north of May Island.

The 1st C.S., 1st and 6th L.C.S. are to proceed into harbour astern of the Southern Line.

(*h*) *Lion* and 1st B.C.S. are to wait in Largo Bay until the 5th B.S. has passed, allowing sufficient room for the divisions of the Northern Line to invert the line.

(*i*) Squadrons of the Southern Line, with the exception of the 7th L.C.S., are to turn 180° to port, battleships by divisions, the remainder by squadrons, by signal from the Admiral 2nd in Command when the leading ship of the 2nd B.C.S. reaches the meridian of 2° 30' W. They will be turned to the westward again and proceed into harbour astern of the German Flotillas by order of the Admiral 2nd in Command, 1st B.S., 2nd B.C.S., 2nd and 3rd L.C.S. anchoring in the berths shown in the anchorage plan (supplied to Flag Officers and Commodores).

(*j*) The 7th L.C.S. is to proceed into harbour direct, ahead of the German Fleet, taking station astern of 4th L.C.S. after passing Fidra Gap.

(*k*) On passing Fidra Gap, each division proceeding to the Fleet Anchorage is to invert the line by signal from its Divisional Commander, ships passing on the starboard hand of the ships ahead, leading ship maintaining the speed of the fleet, the rear ship increasing to 17 knots.

(*l*) As regards the German Force, from position 1 mile 180° from May Island *Cardiff* is to lead the German Fleet to pass 5 cables 360° from South Buoy (Light Fl. Red) of Fidra Gap, thence for Still Point, Inchkeith, bearing 242°.

After passing Fidra Gap *Phæton* is to alter to the southward till on line 'D' (*vide* anchorage plan) steering 242°, and lead the German Light Cruisers to the anchorage as shown on the plan.

After passing Fidra Gap, German ships should be ordered to form up according to the anchorage plan.

Castor is to lead the German Flotillas to their anchorage.

5. SPECIAL ORDERS

(*a*) One destroyer, detailed by the Commodore (F), is required with *Lion* and each flagship of the 1st and 2nd B.C.S., 1st C.S., 1st, 2nd, 4th, 5th, and 6th B.S. These destroyers are to take station 5 cables on the outer beam of their respective Flagships when the Fleet is in the cruising order shown on the diagram. Commodore (F) is to report the names of these destroyers to the Senior Officers concerned.

Oak is to work with the Fleet Flagship.

(*b*) *Fearless, Blonde, Blanche, Boadicea,* and *King Orry* are to act as repeating ships in the positions shown on Diagram 2, Enclosure 2.

(*c*) *Minotaur* is to follow *Furious* throughout the operation.

(*d*) Navigation lights are to be burnt whilst leaving harbour and until sunrise, 21st November.

(*e*) Balloons are not to be towed except by *Cardiff*.

(*f*) *Cardiff, Phæton,* and *Castor* are each to fly a Blue Ensign at the masthead.

Cardiff is to direct the movements of the German Main Force and order them to proceed, if possible, at a speed of 12 knots.

(*g*) Aircraft from local stations are to fly over the Fleet in accordance with the orders issued by the C.-in-C., Coast of Scotland, and A.C.A.

(*h*) One destroyer is to be detailed by the Commodore (F) for photographic duties, and is to embark photographers in the Penns p.m. Wednesday, 20th November.

(*i*) Before meeting the German Fleet, and until the signal is made to negative it, ships' companies are to be at 'CB' stations.

Turrets and guns are to be kept in the securing positions, but free. Guns are to be empty, with cages up and loaded ready for ramming home.

Directors and armoured towers are to be trained on.

Correct range and deflection are to be kept set continuously on the sights.

(*j*) Ships are to fly masthead flags from 0800 until sunset, 21st November.

(*k*) The Red and Blue Burgees will be the distinguishing signals for the Northern and Southern Lines respectively. For the purposes of W/T the Northern Line will be considered as Red Fleet, the Southern Line as Blue Fleet.

APPENDIX V

(*l*) German ships will be listening out on 800 metres. Should it be necessary to signal to them, plain language is to be used; the name of the officer addressed and ship of origin is to be included in the text.

THE FLAG OFFICERS, COMMODORES AND OFFICERS
IN COMMAND OF H.M. SHIPS OF THE
GRAND FLEET.

Admiral,
Commander-in-Chief.

Copies to:
Admiralty
Commander-in-Chief, Coast of Scotland
Admiral Commanding, Orkneys and Shetlands
Rear-Admiral Commanding, Harwich Force
Rear-Admiral (M)
Senior Naval Officer, Granton.
250–20/11/18.

APPENDIX VI

TYPICAL LETTERS TO THE FIRST LORD OF THE ADMIRALTY

1917–1918

A fortnight after Beatty had hoisted his flag as Commander-in-Chief of the Grand Fleet, Sir Edward Carson became First Lord of the Admiralty, and was relieved six months later by Sir Eric Geddes. Beatty lost no time and did not mince his words in presenting his point of view to these ministers. Space will only permit the publication of a few selected letters which illustrate the tone of correspondence and Beatty's anxiety to get things done. On 13th January, 1917, he wrote to Carson:

'The situation from the naval point of view as to success or failure may be summed up as to which Power, Germany or Great Britain, exercises the most effective Blockade. Great Britain is trying to strangle Germany by means of the Blockade maintained by the 10th Cruiser Squadron [a permanent patrol of armed merchant cruisers between Iceland and the North of Scotland] which is made possible by our command of the sea by surface vessels. But this Blockade is being eased up by the detachment of certain ships of the 10th C.S., which also makes it easier for the enemy to pass out raiders to assist the enemy's Blockade. The enemy are trying to strangle the Entente by means of the Blockade maintained by their submarines as rapidly as they can be built.

'Which side will be strangled first?

I enclose you a copy of a portion of a letter I wrote Mr. Balfour on 3rd July, 1915. The First Sea Lord (Jellicoe) when C.-in-C. wrote practically to the same effect at the same time. I give you this, not to say "I told you so", but to point out that the coming menace was foreseen.'

On 28th January, 1917, Beatty wrote again:

'I am perturbed about the mining policy and the intention to declare an enormous area dangerous owing to our mines. This is futile. 1st, in any case the area is much too big. 2nd, we have no mines. 3rd, our future supply is totally inadequate. To take a huge slice out of the North Sea and say that we are going to fill it with mines is to make us the laughing-stock of the world.

I leave to you which is sound. The war is not going to be won by proclamations. . . .

The Ministry of Munitions must produce more than 3,000 a month;

[446]

it is a very vital matter affecting the whole question of curtailing enemy submarine activity.

2,000 a week should be forthcoming in this country.

America could produce cases to any quantity. . . .

What is the reason that more mines cannot be turned out?

I understand from the First Sea Lord that the enemy is about to declare a blockade of our coast. I assume that our declaration of a huge dangerous area is to be the counterblast. As I said before, we cannot do it.

Therefore don't do it.

I have written a long letter to Jellicoe in the same strain, so please discuss fully the points raised.'

Carson felt that the naval problems under discussion required the attention of the Prime Minister, so he arranged for Beatty to meet him at Rosyth. Shortly afterwards, on 25th April, 1917, Carson wrote:

'Why there should be any disposition to refuse assistance from the Ministry of Munitions I have never been able to understand. I am very much perturbed as to the qualifications of S.N.O.s at various ports. . . .

However, I gather that the difficulty is that all the best men are afloat. I am glad the P.M. had an opportunity of meeting you and seeing something of the work.'

Beatty was far from satisfied, and replied immediately in a strongly worded letter dated 30th April, 1917, summarising his views:

'Your letter depressed me beyond measure.

It is inconceivable that we should not have been doing all within our power to meet this cursed menace.

It is incredible that the Ministry of Munitions should not have been called upon to assist before.

Five precious months have now gone, winter months, during which all arrangements could have been made for a vigorous mining campaign during the spring and summer, and we are very nearly where we were at the beginning of the winter.

It is heartbreaking to think of all the sacrifices that have been made, the gallant efforts of our glorious Army; and the Navy is losing the war as fast as the Army is winning it.

We are living on top of a volcano which will blow the Admiralty and the Navy to hell if we don't pull ourselves together.

The impression left on my mind after two days at the Admiralty was that there seemed to be a lack of concrete ideas and principles, that they were meeting troubles as they came, they were not foreseen, and cut and dried plans based upon sound principles were lacking. . . .

I know the Admiralty dislike intensely receiving suggestions, which makes them receive them in an antagonistic spirit; and, if they do adopt them, do so in a modified form which accepts the principle, but spoils the working by a lack of thoroughness which ruins the whole thing.

I propose mining the Bight. The principle is accepted, but they neglect to order sufficient mines upon which the whole thing is based.

I proposed using submarines to hunt submarines—the principle, after weeks of delay, is accepted, but it is done in a half-hearted way, which spoils the result.

I have suggested blocking the Straits of Dover effectively—the principle has been accepted ever since the beginning of the war, but has been non-effective owing to a faulty system. I produce a system and ask for its consideration. After ten days' delay I ask if any consideration has been given to it. After 48 hours I receive a reply that every consideration will be given to it—but the officer responsible for it, who could make it clear, after kicking his heels at the Admiralty for a week, is told that he is no longer required, and he returns north, not having seen a soul as to the value of his plan. It may be a good, bad, or an indifferent plan—I think it is good and worthy of consideration, and no consideration can be of value unless you have the man who conceived it there to explain it.

I suggested the use of ground mines. Ryan produced one three months ago, but the First Sea Lord knew nothing of it and nothing was done until I produced Ryan, and Jellicoe saw him.

I propose convoy of merchant traffic—after months of delay it is being tried in the North Sea. It may succeed, it may fail, but it is worth trying, and in any case it is better than a system which permits of 9 vessels being sunk in a very small area in the course of 6 days. While on this point I would say that I am sure we could conceive a plan which would relieve the enormous losses we have recently sustained in the Western Approaches to the British Isles.

We are not using the brains and energy of the youth of the service. You say that you are perturbed as to the qualifications of the S.N.O.s[1] at the various ports.

I do not wonder. We dig out old retired officers who are not capable of producing the energy and driving force required and the employment of whom is responsible for the loss of thousands of tons of valuable shipping.

We must destroy the fetish that exists that an officer with four stripes on his arm must be a better man than he with three. You have already moved in the right direction by making Dreyer the D.N.O.[2] and it is already bearing fruit of a most remarkable character and might well have saved us from disaster.

[1] S.N.O. means Senior Naval Officer.   [2] D.N.O. means Director of Naval Ordnance.

I have written to you at some length because I feel, as C.-in-C. of the Grand Fleet, that it is my duty to let you know my views, and I have marked it private and personal, because it is my private and personal opinion to which in our respective capacities you are entitled.

I wish to make it quite clear that I am not attacking the individual, but the system which has grown up and made such a state of affairs possible.

You will gather from my letter that I feel very strongly on the subject, that I write to you as the Head of the Navy who stands to me as my Father Confessor, and I am aware that what I have said will cause you considerable concern. . . .

I consider that the C.-in-C. Grand Fleet should be in much closer touch with the Admiralty War staff. At present we are at cross purposes. My only means of communicating my views or understanding the intentions and policy is by letter, an entirely unsatisfactory method. The personal touch disappears, letters can always be read in different ways, and this creates opportunities for innumerable misunderstandings which breed friction and doubt.'

Meanwhile, the First Sea Lord (Jellicoe) had reorganised the Naval Staff at the Admiralty, creating departments to deal specifically with the direction of anti-submarine operations and the organisation of convoys.

Some of the most capable officers in the Grand Fleet had been appointed to the Admiralty for these duties, and by the middle of the year most of Beatty's suggestions were being implemented, and there was a marked improvement in co-operation between the Admiralty and the Fleet.

On the 23rd May, 1917, Carson wrote:

'Ireland plus Admiralty is too much for anyone, but I suppose it cannot be helped. I will do my best to have your wishes met with a view to closer co-operation between the War Staff and the C.-in-C. . . . I dare say the new mine will be all right, but it is a long time coming.'

On 17th July, 1917, Sir Edward Carson was relieved in the post of First Sea Lord by Sir Eric Geddes. There was no immediate need for Beatty to open a correspondence with the new First Lord, as staff officers from the Admiralty were now paying frequent visits to the Fleet.

It was not until 25th September, 1917, that Beatty felt that the time had come for him to give Geddes a summary of his views on the grand strategy of the war, the co-ordinated employment of the fighting services, and the attitude to be adopted towards neutrals. He called for closer co-operation between ministries: 'Is it to be accepted that co-operation is at present of the closest description? I certainly am of opinion that it is not so.' This paper of Beatty's is too long to come within the compass of his biography, but the concluding paragraphs are quoted as being characteristic of him.

'As a final shot I would again urge the absolute necessity of not wasting time and giving weeks to consideration of the various schemes; if we are not very careful in this matter it will again be too late. When do you think you will be coming north to visit the Fleet? If possible, I should recommend that it should be as soon as possible, before the weather gets too bad.'

Geddes replied on 9th October in a guarded tone:

'I was very much interested in getting your letter and will give consideration to the points you mention.

I am afraid I see little hope of getting away from London for some time, although I would like very much to come up to Scapa and see you again. I hope, however, that when Wemyss is up with you, you will have a talk with him upon all these naval matters. As you know, I hold the view very strongly that it is for you naval officers to deal with questions of naval policy and tactics.

We appointed Wemyss for the very purpose of relieving the First Lord, and in order that he might take up these questions, and also at your urgent request we arranged that you should appoint a liaison officer with the Staff here to enable you to keep in touch with all channels through which you could make your views known, and I certainly hope that you will use these means which have been provided to the full.

You may rely on me doing whatever is possible for a civilian to do, but naval warfare must be run by the Navy, and cannot be run by a civilian.

As regards Pound, I am very glad indeed to hear that you found his visit of use. I think that the new organisation and the new officers appointed are beginning to work well. You may be perfectly sure that I will not urge Pound's removal to another position so hurriedly that there will be any break in continuity.'

Beatty took a poor view of the First Lord's reply, and promptly told him so. On the 12th October he wrote:

'Thank you for your letter. I quite agree with your view that the First Lord should not meddle with purely naval policy and tactics, and I had no wish to occupy your time with matters which were not your concern. The questions which I put before you involved the relations of Ministry with Ministry—Admiralty with War Office and Foreign

Office. National policy as opposed to Naval policy. That was why I wrote to you, as I have done in the past with previous First Lords.'

The correspondence continued in cold tones mostly on questions of the appointments of senior officers to important commands. The two men were taking each other's measure, and it was not until Sir Eric Geddes had met Beatty in November that ideas and points of view were freely interchanged between them.

After a year had passed, and the war was over, Beatty wrote on 14th November, 1918:

'Let me say at once that I realise fully all the difficulties that both you and the First Sea Lord have had to contend with, and that indeed I have no desire to embarrass or handicap you in any way whatsoever.

I feel that I can with perfect confidence leave the representation of what the Navy in general and the Grand Fleet in particular have done in your hands.

Let me say also at once that I have only one desire, to understand the Admiralty point of view, and where necessary to give them my view from the sea side of the question, and when a decision has been arrived at to loyally support and carry out the Admiralty wishes to the best of my ability. . . .

I am also quite sure that there are no real differences between us, and it only needs an hour's conversation to finally clear the air. I have never hesitated to state my views quite plainly on all questions relating to my command, even though I am aware that the Admiralty view is different.

I am sure that you will agree that this is my obvious duty.'

APPENDIX VII

SELECTED SPEECHES

1. *TRIBUTE TO THE UNITED STATES BATTLE SQUADRON*

At the end of November 1918, the United States Battle Squadron sailed for home. Just before their departure Beatty went on board the *New York*, and paid this high tribute to the officers and men of the American battleships:

'There is not much that I have to say, but what I do say I hope you will understand comes from the heart, not only my heart, but the hearts of your comrades of the Grand Fleet.

'I want, first of all, to thank you, Admiral Rodman, the captains, officers, and the ships' companies of the magnificent squadron, for the wonderful co-operation and the loyalty you have given to me and to my admirals; and the assistance that you have given us in every duty you had to undertake. The support which you have shown is that of true comradeship; and in time of stress, that is worth a very great deal. As somebody said the other day, "The fighting is now over, the talking is now going to begin"; therefore, I do not want to keep you here any longer, but I want to congratulate you for having been present upon a day which is unsurpassed in the naval annals of the world.

'I know quite well that you, as well as all of your British comrades, were bitterly disappointed at not being able to give effect to that efficiency that you have so well maintained. It was a most disappointing day. It was a pitiful day to see those great ships coming in like sheep being herded by dogs to their fold, without an effort on anybody's part; but it was a day that everybody could be proud of. I have received messages from several people, offering sympathy to the Grand Fleet, and my answer was that we do not want sympathy; we want recognition of the fact that the prestige of the Grand Fleet stood so high it was sufficient to cause the enemy to surrender without striking a blow.

'I had always certain misgivings, and when the Sixth Battle Squadron became a part of the Grand Fleet, those misgivings were doubly strengthened, and I knew then that they [the enemy] would throw up their hands. Apparently the Sixth Battle Squadron was the straw that broke the camel's back. However, the disappointment that the Grand Fleet was not able to strike their blow for the freedom of the world is counteracted by the fact that it was their prestige alone that brought about this achievement.

[452]

'I thank you again and again for the great part the Sixth Battle Squadron played in bringing about the greatest naval victory in history. I hope you will give this message to your comrades: "Come back soon. Good-bye and good luck!"'

2. *FAREWELL SPEECH TO THE SHIP'S COMPANY OF H.M.S.* QUEEN ELIZABETH, *5TH APRIL,* 1919

'I am taking this opportunity of saying good-bye to my shipmates, and in doing so I will read to you the last general order which I shall issue to the Grand Fleet:

"In bidding good-bye to the Grand Fleet, I desire to express to officers and men the deep regret which I feel at leaving those who have shared so loyally and devotedly the stress of the past years of war.

"In success, in disappointment, and in monotony, the spirit of the Fleet has been beyond praise, and the highest traditions of our great Service have been upheld.

"I leave in full confidence that the spirit of the Grand Fleet will remain, that the lessons learnt in the war will be laid to heart, and that the mutual respect and understanding which exist between officers and men will be maintained and fostered for the safety and honour of King and Empire."

'I need hardly say that my wishes as regards the *Queen Elizabeth* will be fulfilled. For over two years she has carried my flag under conditions unprecedented, and during that time the *Queen Elizabeth* has made a name for herself worthy of her position as the Fleet Flagship. In efficiency, in smartness, in cleanliness, and in good spirit, the *Queen Elizabeth* has shown an example to the rest of the Fleet which a Fleet Flagship ought to do.

'When my flag comes down, you will carry the flag of my Second in Command, and under him I am quite sure the reputation which the *Queen Elizabeth* has established will be maintained. You have to remember that the period in front of us is going to be different; reaction sets in, new features appear, and new difficulties arise, all of which have got to be overcome, but I am confident that in the future, as in the past, the *Queen Elizabeth* will live up to the reputation which she has made. It is a great one, and it will be difficult, but those who are going to be left on board can do it. The spirit of the *Queen Elizabeth*, and the spirit of the Grand Fleet, will remain. I thank you, Captain Chatfield, officers, chief petty officers, petty officers, and men, for your loyal and whole-hearted support during the two years past. Without that support my task would have been much more difficult.

'Recently, at Liverpool, you were able to realise something of the feeling in the country with which the Navy is considered. You were fortunate in being there, and I hope you will pass on to your friends in other ships the knowledge that you have gained that the people of this country are fully aware of what they owe to the Navy, and are full of gratitude to the Navy for the part that they have played. I was proud to have representatives of my Flagship to support me on that occasion. I received the Freedom, not as David Beatty, but as the representative of the Grand Fleet; the honour is to you as much as it is to me, and in all subsequent functions of that sort the honour that is being done to me embraces every man in the Fleet. I am the figure-head, I have to make the speeches, but you are really the recipients of the honour just as much as I am, but I think that at Liverpool they made that quite plain.

'It is good for you to know that the feeling in the country is what it is. Sometimes in the Navy we have a sort of feeling in our minds that because we are out of sight we are out of mind. That is not so. Therefore I would remind you that that feeling entails certain obligations upon us, that we have to continue to hold ourselves worthy of the trust, that unfailing trust, which England has in the great Service to which we all have the honour to belong.

'I now say good-bye to you. This to me is a sad day, because it brings to an end my service in the Fleet, and I may say my service afloat. I am still a servant of the State, and so long as I may be employed, or am employed in the service of the State or in the service of that great Service to which you all know I belong body and soul, you may depend upon my sympathising and assisting every man and officer of the Fleet in his just aspirations. What the future holds for us I cannot say; I will not prophesy. I thank you, and remember that, although I have gone, I still remain a comrade and a friend. Good-bye.'

3. *LORD RECTOR'S ADDRESS*

at Edinburgh University, 28th October, 1920

By Admiral of the Fleet Earl Beatty

Gentlemen—First I must express to you my gratitude for the very great honour you have conferred upon me in electing me to the Lord Rectorship of this University. I am, I believe, the first sailor to hold this honourable position, and have little qualification to follow the long list of great names which have adorned its history. I have no pretension to be placed in the same category as the famous men who have preceded me in office, and it would be presumption not to realise that my election by your free suffrages was a mark of your appreciation of the services of the Royal Navy during the Great War.

The subject upon which I should speak to you has caused me considerable thought. I cannot deliver an address which will rank with those of my predecessors. I have been brought up in a Service in which silence is a tradition, and I have read that Thomas Carlyle, the great Lord Rector of a former day, said: 'Silence withal is the eternal duty of man: he won't get to any real understanding of what is complex, and what is more than aught else, pertinent to his interests, without keeping silence, too.'

Today, however, in fulfilment of the duties of my office, I will endeavour with my limited capabilities to address you shortly on the subject of 'Sea Power'.

The lessons of sea power cannot be learnt too early, and even amongst the hard work of your undergraduate days you can find time to understand how sea power has created and made prosperous the greatest empires in the history of the world.

Although the value of sea power has been recognised in an undefined way all through the passage of history, it was not until recent times that a great student of the subject set himself to analyse and codify the lessons which might be learnt.

The work of the American, Admiral Mahan, was of great importance, and aroused many who were inclined to sleep. Nowhere was its effect greater than in Germany, where an overwhelming army had hitherto been regarded as the one requisite for the attainment of greatness.

Our own great Empire is the outstanding example of one that has been created by this power; and yet how little has been written—what a small share of time and effort is devoted to a study of this aspect of the past!

We live in a material age—material and practical; and it is necessary, therefore, that we should study the material and practical side of history. There is much in the history of the world which we can apply to ourselves; much that we can glean to assist in understanding the part that sea power has played in the destinies of empires; much to indicate that empires which have neglected it have crumbled and fallen by the way.

We are accustomed to associate sea power wholly with war and, indeed, since we stand or fall in war according to whether we are strong or weak, skilful or unskilful at sea, this is but natural.

Sir Walter Raleigh, in a discourse on the invention of ships, said: 'Whosoever commands the sea commands the trade; whosoever commands the trade of the world commands the riches of the world and, consequently, the world itself.'

Therefore it would seem that sea power means something more than the possession of fighting fleets, though it cannot exist without them.

The fleets, which are the expression of sea power to which we are accustomed to refer, are, and always have been, closely related to the commercial prosperity of the country.

The prosperity, and indeed the existence, of the country depends upon the mercantile marine; and protection against the attacks of the enemy on our mercantile marine is a primary business of our fleets.

Quoting again from Sir Walter Raleigh, he said: 'Peace is a blessing from God, and blessed are the peacemakers; therefore, doubtless, blessed are those means by which peace is gained and maintained: the which means of our defence and safety being shipping and sea forces, are to be esteemed as his gifts.'

Our powers of resistance to attack are measured in a high degree by the capacity and strength of our mercantile marine. This must depend, not only upon the number of ships composing our merchant fleets, but also on the hearts of those who man them.

Permit me to dwell for a moment on the great asset we possess in having a population endowed with the sea sense and sea courage essential to an empire in the development of its maritime policy. This priceless heritage, born out of our insular state, has been handed down and cultivated through the ages, and has proved of incalculable worth from the days of Spain's greatness, when British seamen resolutely refused to admit that she was stronger than England on the sea, until the present day, when in the late war our merchant ships refused to remain in harbour, notwithstanding the dangers introduced by an enemy who ignored or despised the custom of the seas in war.

The manner in which sea power plays its part in war is largely the outcome of the nature of war itself. Let us see how the British Empire is affected thereby. War is a struggle resulting from contending ideals. When a community holds a certain faith—a faith which may be expressed in terms of religion, of liberty of thought, of expansion of territory, of trade, or of mode of government—war results from a challenge of those convictions.

A community may attempt to force its religion, its trading policy, its theories of government upon other nations, in which case it acts aggressively; or, to defend its own religion, its trading policy, or its territory from encroachments, when it acts defensively.

The degree to which a people will persist either in supporting or in resisting a policy will be measured by the depth of its convictions, and the unanimity with which they are held. But whether the views are deep or shallow, whether they are those of a single ruling autocrat or of a whole democracy, personal inconvenience is, as a rule, the factor that decides whether a struggle shall continue.

That inconvenience may range from the loss of a crown with its revenues and privileges, to the loss of essential material needs of food and warmth, and restriction of the liberty of every person within the borders of the State.

The aim throughout war is to bring such pressure upon the enemy people that they will prefer to abandon their pretensions rather than continue to suffer the inconveniences to which the want of success of their armed forces has brought them.

These inconveniences are imposed in two ways: armies may invade the country and impose internal pressure by controlling the whole system of production, distribution, and administration; navies may impose external pressure by cutting off those supplies from overseas upon which the nation is dependent for its food, its clothing, its manufacture, its commerce, and its munitions of war.

Sea power is the principal means by which this external pressure can be exercised, and per contra by which such pressure can be resisted and the channel of supply be kept open.

The degree in which sea power can be operative varies, according to the geographical situation and resources of the country, and the state and condition of national development.

It is affected also by the political relations with, and the strength of, the countries whose frontiers march with its own.

Thus, some nations are but little susceptible economically to the pressure which sea power is capable of exercising, and would be affected to only a small degree by a temporary, or even a prolonged, seclusion from the outer world.

Such nations are not great world-wide Empires, and to them sea power may not be an essential asset, although desirable. But, to a great world-wide Empire like our own, which must get food from overseas, and can get it by sea routes only, sea power is not a desirable luxury: it is the essential condition of existence.

Without such power the British Empire would not possess liberty. Its every act, its very existence would depend upon the goodwill of other nations.

The realisation of Britain's dependence upon the sea is no modern discovery. Even when that dependence was far less than it is today, and when the keeping open of its doors was less difficult than now, the need was patent to our merchants and statesmen.

'The true interest of England is in its trade,' wrote the author of *England's Guide to Industry* in 1683. 'If this receives a baffle, England is neither able to support itself nor the plantations (as colonies were then called) that depend upon it, and then, consequently, they must crumble into so many distinct independent governments, thereby, becoming weak, will be a prey to any stronger power which shall attack them.'

Eleven years after this was written the Marquis of Halifax admirably stated the matter: 'The importance of our being strong at sea was ever very great, so in our present circumstances it is known to be much greater; because as formerly our force of shipping contributed greatly to our trade and safety, so now it is become indispensably necessary to our very being. To the question: "What shall we do to be saved in this world?" there is no other answer than this—"Look to your Moate". The first article of a Britisher's creed must be that he believeth in the sea. Without that there needeth no General Council to pronounce him incapable of salvation here.' The sea, said Halifax, had enabled his countrymen to become rich, quiet, and free. What it did for Englishmen then it does for the *whole British people* now.

By the sea we are enabled to keep open to us, even in war, the markets of the world. To all those markets which supply the shops you pass each day we can continue to have access so long as we have sea power. A short harvest in our part of the world, even in our own islands, need not disturb us, for we can make up the deficiences by buying where the harvests are good.

These same goods might be brought to us by others, in foreign bottoms, with the result that their cost would be greatly increased. But, during war, neutral shipping would require security, without which they would not sail; security might not be possible—then we starve. Therefore, for the maintenance of our sea power, a mercantile marine of our own is essential.

In the past it was the principal source of seamen for the Fleet: the reservoir from which we drew when the Navy expanded from peace to war strength. The ships furnished transports, which carried our expeditions to all parts of the world, and gave us the means of placing our troops where we wished on the Continent of Europe.

Wellington, speaking of the Peninsular War, said: 'If anyone wishes to know the history of this war, I will tell them it is our Maritime superiority gives me the power of maintaining my army while the enemy are unable to do so.' We could carry and maintain our troops; they could not.

Those transports and store ships, which have carried our soldiers to every corner of the world in the last three centuries, have been drawn from the mercantile marine; and unless that marine had been numerous, it could not, at the same time, have supplied both the needs of armies and the needs of the nation. More than that: in its very magnitude lies its power of resisting attack. Losses did not cripple it as they crippled less numerous merchant fleets.

This was a feature of all the old wars, but never has it been so pronounced as in the struggle from which we have lately emerged.

If, then, we should lose our ocean trade, if our sons should abandon the calling of the sea, then, notwithstanding we should pour our money upon our fighting fleet, we shall not remain what our ancestors made us—a Great Sea Power.

Admiral Vernon, who captured the Spanish town after which Portobello is named, said: 'I think our trade and navigation of more consequence to us than even that which is called the balance of power in Europe, because upon our trade and navigation depends our naval power; and while in this we are superior to France, we might preserve our independence, even though she were mistress of the whole continent of Europe.' This statement of Admiral Vernon suggests the answer to be given to the question, 'What need is there that we should remain a great sea power? Are there not nations fully as happy as we, unburdened by yearly demands for money for ships, men, and guns, for coal to drive battleships, instead of for lathes and looms, who enjoy that most treasured possession—Liberty?'

Yes, there are, but by what right do they possess liberty and independence? They enjoy Liberty by the virtue of the might of others. Switzerland is free, but although her independence had been granted by the treaty of Luneville in 1801, 30,000 French soldiers under General Ney occupied her territory to interfere in her domestic affairs in 1802. She is but one example.

When an individual like Alexander, Cæsar, Louis XIV, or Napoleon dominates and leads a people towards conquest, or when an overwhelming national idea takes possession of a nation, the rights of lesser people are swept aside. Provinces, states, duchies, republics, and kingdoms that cannot defend themselves are overrun and incorporated in the empire of their conquerors. Their independence is lost. Their nationals must submit to the laws of an alien. They may be annexed like the Low Countries in 1793, Schleswig and Holstein in 1866; or, like the Luxemburgers in the late war, conscripted and forced to fight in a cause they detest; or, like the Belgians, lose all civil liberty; or live as the Dutch lived, with the certain prospect of being engulfed at the next moment if Germany won the war.

Countries thus dependent upon the strength of others for the maintenance of their liberty cannot be called free.

Sea power has played its part in preserving their independence. Without sea power we should be even more helpless than they; nor could we have exercised that power for good which we believe we have exercised. Sea power is the defence of every portion in the Empire against such a fate.

It has defended our liberties, and prevented us from submitting to the successive aspirants to the hegemony of Europe.

When the England under the Commonwealth was the pariah state of Europe, the freedom of Britain was preserved by her sea power in the hands of Blake, Monck, and Deane. When Louis XIV and when Napoleon attempted to rule the world, sea power preserved us, and was a primary element in bringing about the failure of their plans. When Louis XV conquered Flanders, sea power forced him to restore it by counter conquest overseas.

However far back into history we may carry our researches, we find sea power in one or other of its modes of action—military, economic, or both—influencing the destiny of the world.

Historians of the early days have preached the gospel of sea power, and, as pointed out by Admiral Sir Cyprian Bridge in his essay, no historian before Mahan had evinced a more correct appreciation of the general principles of naval warfare than Thucydides. He laid stress on the words of Pericles, the first man of his time at Athens, ablest alike in counsel and action, and one of the greatest orators of all time who in urging the continuance of the war with the Peloponnesians said: 'The rule of the sea is indeed a great matter.' Decisive naval campaigns have had more influence upon the history of the world than land wars, notwithstanding the greater frequency of the latter.

From the earliest times, though known but dimly to history, we learn that through the trading fleets, which required as much protection in those days as in later days, the eastern trade was controlled and grew very rich, being developed by Solomon in partnership with the Phœnician King of Tyre. We have an early indication of the struggle for the eastern trade in the story of the War of Troy.

Troy controlled the land portage from the Ægean to the Black Sea. The trading vessels of those days not being able to negotiate the current and the strong north wind in the Dardanelles, the continuous voyage was interrupted, trade goods having to be carried overland from sea to sea. If continuous voyage had been possible, a great and devastating war might have been avoided.

Time does not permit me to dwell on the many struggles that continued through centuries for the command of the trade on the seas, which included the descent of the Indo-European races from the Grasslands of the Danube into Greece and the Islands, whence, as they learned to navigate the sea, they pushed out colonies along the north side of the Mediterranean. The southern side of the Mediterranean was controlled by the Phœnicians, who had been seafaring from the earliest days of their history, and had established a great trading centre at Carthage, with outposts in Sicily and Sardinia.

The greatest of the contests waged by the nations of the East against European states were the Persian Wars, the governing factor of which was sea power. Fortunate, indeed, was Greece that they possessed a citizen of transcendent genius in the person of Themistocles, who gauged correctly that the only means of defeating Xerxes and his Persian hordes lay in the possession of a strong navy. He it was who, correctly estimating the value of sea power, persuaded the Greeks to increase their fleet. The Athenians gave heed to his words, and gained the decisive victory of Salamis, thus saving Greece from Xerxes and from Oriental oppression.

From that time onwards sea power enabled the Athenians to monopolise the trade of the eastern Mediterranean and flourish exceedingly until, by the annihilation of her fleet at the great Battle of Syracuse, the Athenian Empire was crippled and began to decline.

We now turn to the part played by sea power in the maintenance of the great Roman Empire. The Romans did not at first recognise the value of this power, and the error came near to bringing about their early destruction. It was the presence of the Carthaginians in Sicily which taught them the lesson.

Carthage at this time controlled the trade of the western Mediterranean; such was the situation when the Romans realised the value of sea power. They learned to build ships, created fleets, and challenged the sea power of Carthage, and once more there commenced the battle for the trade routes.

After varying fortune the Romans triumphed, and finally held all the Mediterranean trade in their hands. Thus ended the first Punic War, practically decided by the victory of Catullus over the Carthaginian fleet off the Ægatean Islands.

The issue was again in the balance after the assassination of Cæsar, when Mark Antony, after the marriage with Cleopatra, endeavoured to establish a vast Oriental monarchy, and the Roman Republic was not safe until her dominance over the sea was secured by the Battle of Actium. The Roman Empire then commanded both east and western trade routes in the Mediterranean.

After the conquests of the followers of Mohammed, the trade routes to the East were closed to Western Europe, and new lines had to be developed with the Far East, which assisted in the development of the Hanseatic towns on the Baltic and the North Sea.

The Mohammedans conquered northern Africa from Egypt to the shores of the Atlantic with the aid of sea power. With such a long seaboard the maintenance of a large and efficient Navy became a matter of vital importance. The neglect of this essential factor is connected with the decline of the power of the Saracen and the success of the Crusades, which could not have been conducted without the Merchant Navies of the republics of Venice, Genoa, and Pisa.

It is true to say that the final effect in all these cases was produced by military operations, but it was the command of the sea which made these operations possible and, what was of still more consequence, enabled trade to be developed during their progress while depriving the enemy of the means of existence.

No better example can be found of the economic value of sea power than the rise of the Venetian Republic to the position of one of the most influential European states.

To obtain security for her eastern trade she persuaded the leaders of the fourth Crusade to divert their forces to Constantinople, which fell before the united efforts of the Venetians and the Franks in 1204.

The Frankish Empire did not last much more than fifty years, but Venice remained mistress of the eastern basin of the Mediterranean until the Turkish conquest of Constantinople.

The Turkish naval historian, Haji Kaliphah, tells us that after the taking of Constantinople it became necessary to build ships and armaments, and in 1470, for the first time, they equipped a fleet with which they drove the Venetians out of the Grecian seas.

For a hundred years the Ottomans dominated the Mediterranean, practically cutting off Europe from the East, until their defeat at the Battle of Lepanto, in 1571, put an end to their maritime dominion.

It was, however, during their command of the Mediterranean that a stimulus was given to the quest for other lines of communication, and the Cape route, discovered by Diaz in 1486, was opened up as a new channel for the eastern trade by Vasco da Gama in 1497.

Thus the Portuguese, who were springing into prominence at sea, circumnavigated the Cape, and, having penetrated into the Indian Ocean, challenged the Ottoman supremacy and reduced its resources.

By its action in Indian waters, Portugal exercised a great influence in bringing about the downfall of the Turkish dominance at sea.

With the consolidation of the Spanish monarchy and the incorporation of the navies of Aragon and Catalonia with Castille, a new sea power arose which extended east in the Mediterranean and west into the vast domain of the New World, founding colonies and acquiring great wealth.

The accession of the naval forces of Portugal made Spain supreme throughout the world, and her strength, her existence, depended upon the riches she drew from her colonies in the New World.

The story of how England challenged the sea power of Spain is known to you all.

The exploits of the great sea captains of the Elizabethan era form some of the greatest and brightest pages in the history of our islands: exploits which brought about the decline of Spain, and laid the foundations of what has been, and still remains, the greatest sea power of all time; the means whereby the British Empire came into being.

Religious persecutions, and so on, were contributory causes of the war; but the real bed-rock cause was rivalry for control of the sea and the trade routes.

Cromwell pursued the policy of the Elizabethans, and sent a fleet to the Spanish coast in 1656. Blake fought the Battle of Santa Cruz in 1657, and destroyed the Plate Fleet. The power of Spain declined, and Britain stepped into her place of supremacy in overseas trade from that day.

It was not an undisputed supremacy, the Dutch having secured the carrying trade of a great part of the world.

With the increase of her maritime commerce and her determination to compete in the trade which was being monopolised by the Dutch, Britain had to provide naval protection for her merchant fleets.

The efforts of the Dutch to exclude the British from their trade routes brought on the Dutch wars.

These were purely maritime wars to settle a maritime question, and are among the most interesting in the history of the world.

The third Dutch War, ending by the peace of Westminster, helped to place Great Britain in the position of maritime superiority, which she has continued to hold until the present day.

The economic influence of sea power, though less marked in the seventeenth- and eighteenth-century wars with France, was not absent from them. France was more productive, less ocean dependent, than Spain. Nevertheless, commerce was as necessary to her as to other Powers.

Although the losses suffered by French trade during these wars were, perhaps, not the decisive factor in the failures of Louis XIV and Louis XV, they had far-reaching effect, and if France had possessed and used successfully adequate sea power, her condition and situation would have been greatly improved.

On the other hand, Great Britain without her sea power could not have supported those struggles, kept together alliances, and furnished subsidies to pay the continental armies which resisted that series of great French marshals from Turenne to Saxe.

Later, Napoleon saw the possibility of undermining the power of Great Britain by reopening the eastern trade route through the Red Sea, and so establishing an alternative to the Cape route.

His machinations and schemes were brought to nought by the genius of Nelson, when he destroyed the French Fleet at the Battle of the Nile.

Finally, when Germany became the dominant Power on the Continent, she also felt the need for expansion in the furtherance of her schemes. She secured a strong position of advantage in railway communications with the East, and if her ambitions had not led her to force the pace and bring on the recent war, she would have controlled a large share of the eastern trade by the Berlin-Bagdad railway.

Once again, however, sea power exercised it preponderating influence on the situation.

This, gentlemen, is a brief survey of the principal wars from the earliest times to the present day, in which power of Empires has been decided through the command of the sea. What are the lessons to be deduced? What is the correct judgment which can be applied to present-day conditions?

Sea power is capable of exercising great pressure upon an enemy. The law of nations stands in the way of abuse of its power.

If a maritime state in an endeavour to increase its pressure upon an enemy uses measures which encroach upon the interests of neutrals, it risks raising against itself new enemies. Armed neutralities and coalitions may be brought into being against it.

The enhanced value of the command of the sea, when allied with land power, was plainly shown in the late war. Our statesmen of the past fully realised this, and though there was a school of thought which recommended isolation, our policy was to associate ourselves with military states who could provide what we could not.

This country is, and has ever been, one whose interests are bound up in trade. Trade calls for peace, so sea power, which cannot fully develop without trade, is, taken alone, of a non-aggressive character.

For sea power to become aggressive and a threat to the liberties of the world, it needs two conditions: the nation wielding it must dispose of great armies, or possess powerful and well-situated military allies; a common cause must bring the allies together. The policy of these allies must be a common policy.

We must assume that an alliance of several Powers will not be directed by the selfishness of one of them, and those of the sea power must be accepted and approved by the others.

This would provide a case very different from that in which the dual power is exercised by a single populous and military nation. Joint land and sea power united under a single head may be a real danger to the liberty of the world.

Neither democracy nor autocracy is free from the passions which produce wars; there are many examples in history which are familiar to all.

In these wars sea power had played its part, being diverted from the activities which, wisely used, help mankind to unite in common effort to develop the resources of the globe.

It is by trade and by science that we best serve the common interest. For the profitable pursuit of trade, peace and security are essential. By sea power is security gained. Without peace there is no security. Without security there is no trade. Without trade there is no sea power. Sea power is, then, essentially a power for peace; unaggressive itself, it is a shield against aggression. If wisely employed, it will not excite the odium of others, nor the suspicious jealousy that is the lot of those who pin their faith in armies.

Hence there is no greater fallacy than to speak of 'navalism' as the sea counterpart of 'militarism', or to refer to the British Navy as a baneful influence.

In conclusion, I ask you to bear in mind that history shows no instance of sea supremacy once yielded being regained.

Today we have to apply the lessons of the past centuries.

I have tried to indicate the part sea power has played in the history of the world.

We have established a great world-wide Empire based upon the sea—an Empire which is linked up by the sea.

It is a trust, a heritage, which has been handed down to us for safe keeping from the days of the great Elizabethan adventurers—Gilbert, Raleigh, Drake, Hawkins, Frobisher, Davis, Grenville, and Cavendish. We have to prove ourselves worthy by maintaining it inviolate.

Only by studying the lessons of the past and applying them to present-day conditions can we fulfil the destiny of the Empire.

You who are on the threshold of life, who have lived and, perhaps, fought through the greatest world struggle of all ages—a struggle in which sea power has enabled us to weather the storm—can serve your country well by spreading a proper understanding of that power.

It is during your academic career that you store up knowledge and learning which will avail you in the years to come, both for your own advancement and for the good of your country.

The influences of education are great. In all great crises of history it is those influences which have guided public opinion.

You, gentlemen, members of a great and illustrious University, in common with all other Universities of the Empire, have a great and grave responsibility to live up to its noble tradition, and in so doing impress upon those less fortunate the value of the lessons of history.

In your hands, in your knowledge, therefore, lies the power to lead. Let it be applied in all earnestness, in all sincerity, so that if we should, in the years to come, be faced with another crisis such as that through which we have just passed, we can feel that:

'Came the whisper, came the vision,
Came the power with the need,
Till the soul that was not man's soul
Was lent us to lead.'

4. *SPEECH BY ADMIRAL OF THE FLEET, EARL BEATTY, AT THE LORD MAYOR'S BANQUET,* 9TH NOVEMBER, 1923

It is my proud privilege to reply to the toast of the Royal Navy, and in occupying your time to listen to me, which I will endeavour to make as short as possible, I assume that the interest of the peoples of this Empire, is as great today in the well-being and efficiency of the British Navy as it ever has been in the past; and therefore if you will permit me, I will touch on some of the questions which have struck me will be of interest.

After the war, quite rightly and properly we commenced on the Navy, as did other Departments, with the reduction of ships, personnel, and material.

This policy, fateful as it was, has been carried out thoroughly and effectively, having due regard to the commitments of the Empire, which it is the duty of the Navy to safeguard.

In 1921, at the Imperial Conference which was then held, the naval policy of the Empire was laid down, that the needs of the Empire require the maintenance of a Navy at least as strong as that of the greatest Naval Power.

This was followed by the Washington Conference, where, as is well known, the strength of the Navies of the Great Powers was definitely laid down and accepted in so far as capital ships and aircraft carriers were concerned, in the ratio of 5 Great Britain, 5 United States, 3 Japan, 1·7 France and Italy. To all other vessels, such as Light Cruisers, Destroyers, Submarines, etc., there is no limit beyond that of limiting the size of the Light Cruiser to 10,000 tons.

It was recognised that our peculiar situation as an Empire called for very different treatment in the matter of Light Cruisers to other nations. This can easily be recognised as essential when it is understood and realised that this Empire of ours is a Commonwealth of Nations spread all over the world, whose lines of communication are the sea; and it is for the protection of those lines of communications that Light Cruisers are all-important.

Owing to the need for economy, our Light Cruiser building programme has not kept pace with the needs of the Empire. The Light Cruisers are wearing out; their lives are short, and the time has arrived when it is necessary to replace these worn-out vessels by new and up-to-date ships. The Prime Minister has already announced the forthcoming replacement of the [old] County Class which were specially laid down in 1901 for trade protection.

As I have said, the situation as regards capital ships was agreed to and decided for us at the Washington Conference, and the necessary steps have already been taken to provide the British Empire with her allowance of this type of vessel.

I think it would be as well to say something of this type of vessel. It is a type which has caused considerable controversy and comment, and therefore it would seem desirable that something should be said.

The question arises, What is a capital ship?—and it seems to me that it can be no better expressed than by defining it as an inexpugnable ship combining the greatest offensive powers with the greatest powers of defence, with the addition of speed and good sea-keeping qualities.

The capital ship of today has to meet very different forms of attack than ten years ago. Not only have guns and torpedoes developed immensely, but submarines and aircraft are additional weapons with which to threaten the life of the capital ship.

The gun of today has greater velocity and bursting charge. The protecting armour has had to be increased accordingly; this armour helps to deal incidentally with other forms of attack.

The increase in the efficiency of the torpedo has led to the adoption of new methods of protection. The submarine, which has increased the attack from that particular weapon, has necessitated the development of these new methods of protection. Anti-submarine methods have had to be devised to minimise this form of attack. These methods have made great progress, and the race between the submarine and the anti-submarine devices is somewhat the same as that between the gun and the armour. Today, the development of the anti-submarine is more than keeping pace with the submarine, and to the Power in command of the surface of the sea the submarine is not a great menace. To a Power weak on the surface of the sea it must remain a serious menace.

Then we come to the air.

In a certain limited radius of action aircraft are a menace to ships, but are not a menace sufficiently great that means cannot be devised whereby the capital ship cannot counter and defeat this form of attack.

In any case, the great oceans upon which our trade and communications are maintained are as free from air influence as ever.

In arriving at the decision that a capital ship can be produced which can withstand all the attacks to which it may be subjected, the opinions of naval officers who have had the greatest experience and are best qualified to judge both at the Admiralty and in the Fleets, have been taken into account. These opinions have been confirmed by the decisions of the United States of America and Japan.

Turning again to the question of the air as a new weapon of the Fleet, I would like to say that nowhere is the importance of this arm more fully recognised than in H.M. Navy, the development of which must be all-important to naval forces. It is not too much to say that in the future no ship and no fleet will be fully equipped for war without aircraft. Aircraft have become an additional naval weapon required by ships working on the surface of the water. A unit of the Fleet, such as a Light Cruiser Squadron, would not be complete without these aircraft, any more than it would be without guns or torpedoes, and the fleets of the future will be commanded by officers with as intimate knowledge of the air as of the gun and the submarine. The intelligent use of the air for reconnaissance purposes will improve the quality of the information which the admiral now possesses derived from Light Cruisers; and it may well be that in the future the Commander-in-Chief of a fleet with his staff may be quartered on board an aircraft carrier; during operations his Staff Officers being in the air, far in advance of the fleet, giving information which will enable him to so dispose his forces to obtain strategic and tactical advantages which would culminate in great victory. But let me add this—as in the case of the submarine, the full use, the freedom of action, and the value of aircraft working with the Navy can only be secured by the Power which commands the surface of the sea; without command of the surface the aircraft could not function. For these reasons it is of paramount importance that the air arm of the Navy shall be developed and improved side by side with the gunnery arm, the torpedo arm, the submarine arm, and all the other arms which go to make up the efficiency of the Fleet.

We will now pass to another naval question which is exciting considerable interest and comment—Singapore. This project of developing Singapore, or I might say of putting Singapore in order so that it shall be of use to the Navy, has been attacked by many as if it was something new. This is far from the case; for many years it was a naval base, a base which was recognised by many of the most astute as being the best strategical position in the Far East; indeed, the gate of the East (quote Sir Stamford Raffles).

The western Pacific has always been a station for strong British forces.

The needs for this strength are surely as strong today as they were in the past. Our possessions are no less, and have become more valuable.

The Empire was founded on commercial enterprise. It was considered in the past necessary and desirable to protect that enterprise. The flag followed the trade and not the trade the flag, and our commitments in the Pacific are now greater than they were before.

Australia and New Zealand have increased in population and prosperity. They are portions of the Empire which require as much protection or more protection today than ever they did in the past. The wealth of the Crown Colonies has increased, and our trade in the Indian Ocean is more important.

If protection was required twenty years ago, how much more so is it required today. If those who are responsible for our destinies say that protection is not required, that we can afford to live on the good-will of others, then Singapore is not necessary; but if, on the other hand, we think it is desirable to safeguard our interests in that part of the world, then Singapore is necessary, for without it they cannot be secured.

5. *SPEECH BY ADMIRAL OF THE FLEET, EARL BEATTY, AT THE LORD MAYOR'S BANQUET, 9TH NOVEMBER, 1925*

It is a great privilege to respond to the toast of the Navy on this distinguished occasion.

In the process of recovering from a Great War, it is but natural that demands should be made to reduce those National forces on which the fate of the country depended in time of danger.

We do not need to probe history to realise that this phase has occurred after all our great wars of the past, and that history is but repeating itself.

It may be well, therefore, to recall the facts which demand the existence of an adequate British Navy today. It exists for the preservation of peace in the world and for the security of the British Commonwealth of Nations.

In the words of the Articles of War, which date from Elizabethan times, 'It is the Navy whereon, under the good Providence of God, the wealth, safety, and strength of the Kingdom chiefly depend'.

It exists, therefore, as a great potential factor in the development of the British Empire and in furtherance of closer relationships between the British peoples.

By the Washington Treaty the strength of the navies of the Great Powers was definitely laid down so far as capital ships and aircraft were concerned. Therefore, the policy of the Government as regards these ships is equality with the strongest naval power, the 'one-power standard'.

It was agreed at Washington that our peculiar situation as a scattered Empire admitted of special treatment in the matter of cruisers. Therefore, the policy of the Government in this respect is to provide an adequate number of cruisers for the protection of our territories over the seas and the sea communications of the Empire, on which the safety and existence of the various British peoples depend.

The Board of Admiralty are accordingly charged by the Government with responsibility for putting this policy into execution.

This duty necessitates tendering of advice to H.M. Ministers, which in present circumstances is unpalatable to the country. It is sometimes said that the Admiralty are going beyond their duty and are attempting to assert an undue influence on the policy of the country. This is a most profound misreading of the situation. Their duty is to *advise*, and the searching examination to which the latest Admiralty proposals have been subjected by the Government before receiving approval should satisfy any reasonable man that they have been accepted only because they represent bare necessities.

If and when the country adopts some other policy, the Admiralty will loyally advise in accordance with the new formula, whatever it may be.

That the present policy imposes a great strain on the finances of the country is undeniable, but what are the facts of the situation? The world-wide trade routes upon which we are dependent for our food and for the raw materials of our industries are no shorter or less complicated in their geographical disposition than they were in 1914. We are no less, in fact more, dependent upon their security. On the other hand, our means of ensuring the safety of these supplies are now far less than in 1914.

It will be said, indeed has been said, that the conditions have changed: in 1914 we were faced with a powerful potential maritime enemy; that menace has disappeared, and today there is no sign of danger to the Empire. This is true, and has been taken fully into consideration, and the naval policy has been formulated accordingly.

In 1914 we possessed 108 cruisers.

Today we have 59 afloat, under construction, and to be laid down this year.

In 1914 we possessed a very great advantage from our geographical position in being able to command the exits of enemy vessels destined for attack on our trade, yet still the number at our disposal was barely adequate. Such a favourable strategic position would not obtain in the unfortunate event of war with any other Power, and the demand for cruisers and the protection they provide will be far greater than in the Great War.

Therefore, the suggestion that this number is unduly large, is one which I personally, and I venture to say any Board of Admiralty, can never support.

The task of the Admiralty in carrying out their great responsibilities is not made any easier by a campaign of ill-informed criticism. Many of the statements made are so wide of the truth and so oblivious to the necessities of the Empire, that it can only be concluded that the object of the critics is political.

Fair criticism is always welcome, misrepresentation cannot be helpful.

The campaign is persistent and one-sided, in that the attacks are given prominence while the replies to the attacks are given obscurity, and the critic returns to the attack on the same ground.

I ask—is this fair play? I ask—is it patriotic to attempt to stir up in this great service dissatisfaction and want of confidence in administration for purely political or personal reasons?

The First Lord at Colwyn Bay, and the Parliamentary Secretary of the Admiralty at Harpenden, made very clear statements and replies to the allegations of reckless expenditure forced upon successive Governments, and have made plain the causes which have brought about increases in the cost of the Admiralty Office.

It is forgotten that 1914 was the end of a prolonged period of naval peace, which did not tend to the full development of the capabilities either of the personnel or of the material of the Fleet.

It is not the fault of the Admiralty that the impetus of war has added vastly to the complexity of the technique of naval warfare, that new weapons have been evolved, and the scope of existing weapons expanded beyond imagination. They were but natural and inevitable processes of science and psychology. To cope with this development and to keep pace with further progress, the organisation of the Admiralty as it was in 1914 was totally inadequate. This phenomenon was not peculiar to the Admiralty; for instance, the Government found it necessary to create a new Ministry and Service to meet the extension of war into the air.

The formation of new Technical Departments and new Divisions of the Naval Staff to deal with strategical, tactical, and material aspects of old and new weapons and contrivances was imperative if we were not to lag behind other countries in scientific attainment.

When it is remembered that the size and number of capital ships and the size of cruisers and aircraft carriers is now limited by International Convention, it will be realised that now, less than at any time in the past, can we afford not to utilise the fruits of progress to their fullest extent.

Apart from this side of the question, I ask if any industrial concern or business in the country finds that it can conduct its affairs with the same overhead charges as it incurred in 1914.

The proposal of the Board of Admiralty to effect substantial economies by limiting the activities of Rosyth and Pembroke Dockyards in time of peace has met, quite naturally, with a volume of opposition from the localities interested, and less reasonably from many people whose demands for economy are not the least clamorous.

As to whether these yards are necessary for naval purposes, the Admiralty is the only competent judge. As to whether they are necessary for political or social reasons is for the Government to decide. The fact is, that so far as the upkeep of the Fleet is concerned, they are entirely redundant.

Is it suggested that the Admiralty should not have brought this fact to the attention of the Government? And is it intended that the Naval Estimates should include the expenditure of money for social purposes extraneous to the maintenance of the Fleet?

Earnest amateur strategists have been prolific in advice to the Admiralty, pointing out the strategic advantages of Rosyth and Pembroke Dockyards over the Southern Yards. In the first place, the reduction of Rosyth and Pembroke to a state of Care and Maintenance does not render them any less available for use in emergency than their upkeep at their present standard. The suggestion that either of the Southern Yards should be closed and that Rosyth or Pembroke should take its place is one which is altogether out of the question from the financial point of view, apart from other important considerations.

To render Rosyth or Pembroke capable of dealing with the work which can be undertaken by one of the Southern Yards would entail cost which is beyond contemplation under present circumstances. The alternative is, in short, to keep Rosyth and Pembroke going in their present state in addition to the other Yards, or to cease keeping them in active operation, as has been proposed.

A much more reasonable line of criticism is to the effect that the Admiralty, having produced estimates this year for a sum which they considered to be the minimum necessary, have subsequently undertaken to produce further economies, and until the facts are examined there would seem to be reasonable grounds for criticism of this nature. The explanation is, however, perfectly plain and comprehensible.

The Admiralty have, during the past four or five years, advocated continually the adoption of a steady programme of replacement for Naval defence, but owing to the instability of the various Governments, who have never lasted more than a few months, no programme has been accepted, and therefore no programme adopted. Obviously, it is far more economical to have a steady programme than to do as we have had to do in the last five years.

The present Government, with its prospects of stability, has been able to accept a definite programme, and so, by stabilising expenditure on new construction, it has enabled the Admiralty to exercise economies which would not have been possible under the previous circumstances. The effects are far reaching, and include the demolition of many older ships now on the active list, with a corresponding reduction of expenditure on repairs, maintenance, and personnel.

A factor of still greater importance is that the Government, having taken into consideration the international outlook, have authorised some temporary relaxation of the immediate readiness of the Fleet for active service. This recent decision has opened up fields of economy hitherto closed to us, and the sacrifice of preparedness has already resulted in financial gain. To tamper with the traditional standard of the Fleet is a grave step which can only be justified by the most serious exigencies, and we know that the Government has reached its decision only after the most anxious consideration.

This step has rendered more important than ever the utmost efficiency in the Naval Staff.

Vigilance, foresight, and the study of problems in conjunction with the Military and Air Staffs become matters of even greater moment than before.

Such Naval disasters as occurred during the war were the direct result of the lack of a sufficient and efficient staff, and it would be criminal to lapse once more into such a state.

We paid very dearly for the experience which led to its formation, and nothing should interfere with its development.

The task of the Sea Lords during the last few years has at periods been carried through with personal feelings of bitter regret. It has been their duty to reduce the Fleet from a magnificent and incomparable force to the modest dimensions at which it now stands, and concurrently to deprive of their professional livelihood thousands of zealous, highly efficient, and loyal officers and men.

It has indeed been a painful duty, but it has been made easier by the unquestioning loyalty and resignation with which the blow has been accepted by individuals. All honour is due to these officers and men for the example they have set of subjugating their personal claims to public interest.

MEMORANDUM BY PRIME MINISTER INAUGURATING THE COMMITTEE OF CHIEFS OF STAFF

3RD AUGUST, 1926

TO

Admiral of the Fleet David, Earl Beatty, Knight Grand Cross of the Most Honourable Order of the Bath, Member of the Order of Merit, Knight Grand Cross of the Royal Victorian Order, Companion of the Distinguished Service Order, First Sea Lord and Chief of the Naval Staff,

General Sir George Francis Milne, Knight Grand Cross of the Most Distinguished Order of Saint Michael and Saint George, Knight Commander of the Most Honourable Order of the Bath, Companion of the Distinguished Service Order, Chief of the Imperial General Staff; and

Air Chief Marshal Sir Hugh Montague Trenchard, Baronet, Knight Grand Cross of the Most Honourable Order of the Bath, Companion of the Distinguished Service Order, Chief of the Air Staff

GREETING.

WHEREAS it has been found to be essential for the defence and safety of the realm that a permanent body should be created and charged with the duty of considering and investigating the question of Imperial Defence as a whole, of co-ordinating the functions and requirements of the Navy, Army, and Air Force, and of the Civil Administration in matters of Imperial Defence, and of advising His Majesty's Government on the matters of general policy arising therefrom;

AND WHEREAS the Committee of Imperial Defence has been appointed for the aforesaid purpose and charged with the aforesaid duties;

AND WHEREAS it is necessary for the due and efficient discharge of the aforesaid duties that the Committee of Imperial Defence should be furnished with expert advice and assistance in regard to the respective functions and requirements of the Navy, Army, and Air Force, and the best method of combining and co-ordinating their efforts for their common object of the defence of the Empire;

NOW THEREFORE I, the Right Honourable Stanley Baldwin, His Majesty's Prime Minister, one of the Commissioners for executing the office of Lord High Treasurer of the United Kingdom of Great Britain and Ireland, and Chairman of the Committee of Imperial Defence in consultation with the Secretary of State for War, the Secretary of State for Air, and the First Lord of the Admiralty, do by these presents constitute and appoint you the said

David, Earl Beatty, being First Sea Lord and Chief of the Naval Staff;
Sir George Francis Milne, being Chief of the Imperial General Staff;
and

Sir Hugh Montague Trenchard, being Chief of the Air Staff
to be a standing Sub-Committee of the Imperial Defence, under my
direction, to investigate and consider in common all such matters as may
from time to time be referred to you by the said Committee of Imperial
Defence, and to report thereon for the information of the said Committee
to the best of your knowledge and capacity.

AND YOU are to submit to the Chairman of the said Committee of
Imperial Defence, for the consideration of the said Committee, any
matter relating to Imperial defence on which, in your opinion, further
enquiry or investigation is necessary, and to forward copies of all Reports
and Minutes of your proceedings to me and to the Secretary of State for
War, the Secretary of State for Air, and the First Lord of the Admiralty.

AND YOU are expressly to take notice that in all matters in respect
of which you are so required jointly to investigate, consider, deliberate,
and advise, each of you is to keep always before his mind the object for
which the said Committee of Imperial Defence was created and exists,
that is to say, for the consideration of questions of defence as a whole and
for the co-ordination of the function of the several arms of His Majesty's
Forces, all considerations concerning a single Service being subordinated
to the main object of National and Imperial Defence which the three
Services have in common.

GIVEN under my hand at Downing Street, Westminster, this third
day of August, 1926.

(*signed*) STANLEY BALDWIN.

INDEX

Aberdour House, 207, 215, 284, 300
Aberlady Bay, 347
Aboukir, H.M.S., wears Beatty's flag, 115; torpedoed, 156
Abu Hamed, 26, 31
Abu Klea, gunboat, 18, 20, 36
Abyssinian crisis, 378
Action information, 202
Admiralty, Beatty's criticisms of, 91, 156, 205, 314, 318, see also Appendix VI; adverse to Beatty, 107; control operations, 142; tributes to Beatty, 155, 353; strategy, 157, 161, 181; allocate forces for operations, 165; intelligence from room 40, 165, 182, 184, 222, 225, 259, 297; anti-submarine division, 304, 335; air division, 379; naval staff, 473
Admiralty yacht, 110, 114, 399
Affectations, 122
Aircraft carrier as flagship, 360, 468
Air Ministry, 360, 379; differences with Admiralty, 380, 405, 426
Air operations, 182, 212, 228, 318
Alacrity, H.M.S., 62
Alexander-Sinclair, Admiral Sir E., 226, 275, 299, 303
Alexandra, H.M.S., 7, 11
Alexandria, 379
Alexieff, Russian admiral, 64
Alfonso, King, 416
Algerine, H.M.S., 50, 55
Allen, Lieutenant Charles, torpedoes *Moltke*, 310
Allied fleet in China, 46
Allied Naval Council, 335, 337
Ambuscade, H.M.S., 167
America, see United States
American Legion, 366
Amery, Rt. Hon. L. S., 370, 378, 394
Amethyst, H.M.S., 141, 150
Ammon, Rt. Hon. C. G., 394
Ammunition, shortage of, 211, 379
Anglo-Egyptian Army, 18
Anglo-Japanese Alliance, 369, 372
Annihilation, 307, 324, 329
Anti-submarine operations, 206, 294, 297, 302
Arbuthnot, Rear-Admiral Sir R., 251
Archduke Ferdinand of Austria, 130
Arethusa, H.M.S., 144, 191
Ariadne, German cruiser, sunk, 149
Arkansas, U.S.S., 300
Armistice, 329; Beatty protests, 330; addresses war Cabinet, 332; signed, 341
Armstrong, Sir George, 94

Armstrong, Lieutenant H. G. B. (R.M.L.I.), 51
Army, co-operation with, 32, 41; admiration for, 323, 342, 412
Army Council, Beatty appointed as Naval Adviser, 90
Army & Navy Stores, 306
Arrogant, H.M.S., 88
Ascot, 100, 408
Asquith, Rt. Hon. Herbert, 96, 112, 115, 393
Asquith, Miss Violet, 114
Atbara, 26; battle of, 32
Atlantic Fleet, 90
Attack, H.M.S., 191, 208
Attlee, Rt. Hon. Clement, 432
Audacious, H.M.S., sunk, 157
Aurora, H.M.S., 50, 184
Australia, 469; a friend in need, 375, 379
Australia, H.M.A.S., 211, 222, 410; in collision, 215

Bacon, Admiral Sir R., 94, 96, 101
Badger, H.M.S., at Jutland, 252
Bagot, Commander W. T., 343
Bailey, Admiral Sir Sidney, 211
'Balderdash', 205
Baldwin, Rt. Hon. Stanley, 380, 382, 383, 393, 394, 401, 430
Balfour, Rt. Hon. A. J., 161, 275, 389, 409
Ball at Kronstadt, 129
Banquet, Lord Mayor's, 466, 469; Beatty's prophecy, 360
Banquet to Beatty, by men of the fleet, 355; by Highland Society, 359; at New York, 367; by United States Navy, 368
Banquet to Jellicoe and Beatty, 408
Barfleur, H.M.S., Beatty commander of, 44; landing party from, 50–71
Barham, H.M.S., flagship of Admiral Evan Thomas at Jutland, 225–268
Barnby, Major A. C., Royal Marines, 379
Battenberg, Admiral of the Fleet Prince Louis of, 91, 99, 104, 112, 114, 124; keeps fleet mobilised, 131; resigns, 160
Battles: Hafir, 20; Atbara, 33; Omdurman, 36; Tientsin, 43; Heligoland, 142; Dogger Bank, 183; Jutland, 220; 17th November, 1917, 302
Battle cruisers, British, functions of, 120, 182; high speed, 131, 153, 280; save situation at Heligoland, 146; formed as fleet, 201; vulnerability of, 232, 234, 253

Battle cruisers, German, 173, 185, 229–271; toughness of, 253, 261, 310; fail to find convoy, 310

Battleships, use of, 361; Beatty's view on, 362

Bayly, Captain E. H., at Tientsin, 52, 62, 67, 69, 73

Bayly, Admiral Sir Lewis, 302

Beatty, David, of Borodale, M.F.H., grandfather, 1

—Mary Longfield, grandmother, 1

—David Longfield, father, 1, 2, 4, 13, 23, 82

—Kathleen Edith, mother, 1, 2, 3, 5, 6, 7, 23

—Charles, brother, 2, 3, 315

—William Vandeleur ('Vandy'), brother, 3

—George, brother, 3

—Kathleen ('Trot'), sister, 3, 5, 77, 392

—Ethel, Countess, wife: meets Beatty, 44; marries him, 83; social life, 100; visits Kronstadt, 129; lends yacht as hospital ship, 161; strain of war, 216; opens Jutland Fund, 323, 419; maintains Brooksby Hall as convalescent home, 418; illness, 385–418; dies at Dingley Hall, 418

—David Field, 2nd Earl, son, 90, 125, 132, 206, 289, 345, 394; member of parliament, 417; at father's death bed, 428

—Peter, Hon., son, 105, 111, 125, 318, 394, 397; wins Derby, 417

BEATTY, DAVID, Admiral of the Fleet, 1st Earl: birthplace, 2; parents' home, 3; school, 5; first ship, 7; friendship with Princess Marie, 9; selected for Nile expedition, 18; commands gunboat, 19; commands flotilla in battle of Hafir, 20; D.S.O., 23; diary, 24; lands with rocket detachment at battle of Atbara, 33; battle of Omdurman, 36; special promotion to commander, 41; more war service in China, 45; diary, 50–69; lands for defence of Tientsin, 51; severely wounded, but returns to duty, 61; specially promoted to captain, 73; fortune-teller accurately predicts career, 78; marriage, 83; commands *Juno*, *Arrogant* and *Suffolk* in Mediterranean Fleet, 85–90; Naval Adviser to Army Council, 90; commands battleship *Queen*, 91; leads march through London and speaks at Guildhall, 100; promoted by special order in council to flag rank, 104; refuses flag appointment, 107; selected by Mr. Churchill as Naval Secretary, 107; commands cruiser squadron

Beatty, David—*continued*.

in manœuvres, 115; selected to command battle cruiser squadron, 116; high speed tactics and gunnery, 120; meets Tsar of Russia at Kronstadt, 129; knighted, 131; proceeds to war station, 132; battle of Heligoland, 142; saves situation and achieves victory, 146; narrow escape off Scarborough, 156; defeat of Hipper at Dogger Bank, 181; achieves object at Jutland, 267 (see also under Jutland); succeeds Jellicoe as Commander-in-Chief, Grand Fleet, 274; meets flag officers, 275; revises battle orders, 280; proposes measures against enemy submarines, 294; starts a convoy system, 295; revises views on seeking fleet action, 304; moves Grand Fleet to Rosyth, 308; disagrees with Admiralty and Supreme War Council over armistice terms, 330; addresses war Cabinet, 332; reactions to victory, 341; acclaimed by Grand Fleet, 348; enforces surrender of German fleet, 349; presses for increase in naval pay, 350; stimulates public interest in sea power, 351; promoted by special order in council to Admiral of the Fleet, 354; entertained by lower deck, 355; takes office as First Sea Lord, 356; attitude to Harper Report on Jutland, 358; anxiety about home life, 365, 385; at Washington Conference, 365; successfully opposes Geddes Report on naval expenditure, 370; struggle for sea power, 372; offers to resign, 373; addresses M.P.s, 379, and Imperial Conference, 380; first chairman of Chiefs of Staff Committee, 380; leaves Admiralty after record term of office, 382; seeks no further public office, 415; addresses officers of the combined fleets at Gibraltar, 416; health undermined by series of accidents, 424; concern about Fleet Air Arm, last letter, 426; rises from sick bed to attend funerals of Earl Jellicoe and King George V, 427; last words, 428

Characteristics

attitude to Admiralty and Ministers, 289, 295, 313, 316, 402, 419, 420; see also Letters and Appendix VI

—to his staff, 194

bravery and fortitude, 20, 22, 25, 61, 66, 235, 425, 429

Beatty, David
Characteristics—continued.
capacity for taking pains, 364
caution, 22, 150, 158, 266
concern for officers and men, 122, 125,
137, 161, 217, 285, 308, 322, 353, 355
dislike of publicity, 123, 180, 431
horsemanship, 4, 5, 8, 12, 364, 424;
see also Hunting
leadership, 22, 27, 42, 71, 73, 150,
184, 209, 235, 275, 308, 432
literary taste, 93
love of the Navy, 91, 105, 121, 217,
389, 399, 407, 415
—family, 92, 117, 126, 206, 318, 401,
407, 414
—music, 320, 392
—sport, 5, 13, 30, 44, 207, 364, 402, 417
moral courage, 86, 107, 108, 118, 135,
200, 337, 373, 429
offensive spirit, 20, 33, 41, 65, 149,
214, 233, 235, 277, 279, 281, 349
parallel with Nelson, 32, 192, 205,
274, 348, 354, 401, 423, 424, 428, 433
prevision and foresight, 22, 93, 102,
121, 332, 337, 342
religion, 348, 413, 423
seamanship, 14, 41, 91, 280
speeches at Guildhall, 100, 466, 469
—to House of Lords, 374; see also
Appendix VII
—to ships' companies, 136, 208, 452
statesmanship, 311, 408, 410, 411,
412, 413, 415, 431
views on convoy and anti-submarine
measures, 294
—Admiralty, 91, 97, 161; see also
Letters
—gunnery, 87, 98, 119, 193, 211, 269,
277, 290, 316
—Jutland, 262, 316, 317, 393
—manœuvres, 88, 91; see also Letters
—senior officers, 91, 95, 99, 124; see
also Letters
—strategy, 42, 108, 112, 214, 293, 328
—tactics, 109, 119, 120, 277, 422
wounds and accidents: Nile, 25,
Tientsin, 61; motoring, 424; hunting, 425

Tributes from
Lord Kitchener, 22
Admiral Sir Walter Cowan, 26, 27
Admiral Sir F. Field, 44, 73
Captain C. C. Walcott, R.N., 48
Captain E. H. Bayly, 69
Admiral Sir E. Seymour, 71
Admiral Lord Keyes, 71, 208, 428
Commander B. Guy, V.C., 72
Prince Louis of Battenberg, 91, 104
Rt. Hon. Winston Churchill, 108, 401
Lord Chatfield, 116, 121
Admiralty, 155, 353

Beatty, David
Tributes from—continued.
Admiral Jellicoe, 195, 266
Admiral von Scheer, 250
Admiral Lord C. Beresford, 264
Commander von Hase, 267
Rev. J. L. Pastfield, 270
Admiral Alexander-Sinclair, 275
Admiral Hugh Rodman, U.S.N., 301
Admiral W. S. Sims, U.S.N., 301
Field Marshal Sir H. Wilson, 348
Admiral W. R. Hall, 349
Cities and city guilds, 351
Lord Long, 363
Lord Hankey, 381
Lord Baldwin, 383, 430
Lord Bridgeman, 384
Rt. Hon. C. Attlee, 432
Sir Archibald Sinclair, 432
House of Commons, 433
Beatty, Sir William, M.D., surgeon of
H.M.S. *Victory* at Trafalgar, 422
Belgians, King Albert of the, 327, 386,
391
Bellairs, Rear-Admiral Roger M., 280,
343
Bentinck, Admiral Sir R., 203, 276
Berber, 26, 31
Beresford, Admiral Lord Charles, 7, 85,
89, 94, 199, 348
Berkeley-Milne, Admiral Sir A., 176
Berlin, German minelayer, 157
Biarritz, 371, 391
Bingham, Commander Hon. E. B. S.,
236, 279
Birkenhead, Lord, 393, 410
Birmingham, H.M.S., 138, 141, 170
Bismarck, German battleship, 361
Black Prince, H.M.S., 247
Blanche, H.M.S., 166, 276
Blockade, distant, 134, 288; result of, 344
Blunt, Captain W. F., 144
Blücher, German battle cruiser, 173,
185; sunk, 191
Blue, Captain V. (U.S.N.), 300
Boadicea, H.M.S., 166
'Bois Roussel,' Derby winner, 417
Bonar Law, Rt. Hon. A., 382
Bond, Engineer E. E., 24, 40
Boredom, 112, 140, 306
Borodale, 1
Bosphorus, 377
Boxers, 45
Boxing, 12, 207, 321
Bradford, Admiral Sir E., 183
'Brain waves,' 204
Brand, Admiral Hon. Sir H., 276, 285,
308, 342
Brest, 126
Bridgeman, Admiral Sir F., 104
Bridgeman, Rt. Hon. W. C., 373, 401,
405, 409
British soldier, admiration for, 323, 342

Britannia, H.M.S., training ship, 5
Brock, Admiral Sir F., 105
Brock, Admiral of the Fleet Sir O. de
B., 276, 285, 296, 404
Brooksby Hall, 355, 386, 417
Browne, Midshipman G. C., 51
Browning, Admiral Sir M., 343
Bruce, Major, Wei-hai-wei Regiment, 65
Bruce, Rear-Admiral J., 44, 73
Bruce, Rt. Hon. S. M., 411
Brummer and *Bremse*, German cruisers, 247
Bryony, H.M.S., 407
Buchanan, Sir George, 129
Buckingham Palace, 390
Bullard, Captain W. (U.S.N.), 300
Burghersh, Sub-Lieutenant Lord, 129
Burke, Captain J. H. T., 51, 73
Burney, Admiral of the Fleet Sir Cecil, 275
Burney's Naval Academy, 5
Butterfield and Swire, Messrs., 52

Callaghan, Admiral Sir George, 73, 118, 120, 121, 124, 135
Calpe Hunt, 101
Cameron Highlanders, 38
Camperdown, H.M.S., 15, 16
Canada, Expeditionary Force, 3, 157;
Prime Minister of, 154
Canberra, H.M.A.S., 411
Canterbury, Archbishop of, 428
Capital ship, 362, 369; definition of, 467
Capua Palace, Malta, 114
Cardiff, H.M.S., leads German fleet, 347
Carlton Hotel, 364
Carmania, H.M.S., 176
Carson, Rt. Hon. Sir E., 284, 286, 289, 313, 446
Cataracts, Nile, 18, 24, 26
Cavalry Club, 13
Cecil, Lord Robert, 412
Centurion, H.M.S., 50
Champion, H.M.S., 222, 230
Chanak, 377
Chancellor of the Exchequer, 376, 380, 393, 394
Chart goes overboard, 242
Chatfield, Admiral of the Fleet Lord, 106, 116, 119, 121, 129, 150, 184, 203, 207, 211, 234, 276, 342, 356, 370, 453
Chelmsford, Lord, 394
'Chequers,' 404
Chester, H.M.S., 245
Chicago, 44, 368
Chief of Staff to Beatty, selection of, 203
Chiefs of Staff Committee, Beatty first
Chairman of, 380; inauguration of, 474
China, Boxer Campaign, 43–74; revolution, 408, 409; Beatty's views on policy towards, 413
Chocheprat, French admiral, 286

Christian, Rear-Admiral A. H., 141
Christmas, 285, 322
Churchill, Rt. Hon. Winston, eyewitness of Nile operations, 19, 24; selects Beatty as Naval Secretary, 107; at Admiralty, 107, 183; creates Naval War Staff, 109; in Admiralty yacht, 110; Beatty's opinion of, 111, 313; interest in Navy, 112, 124; relations with Lord Fisher, 114, 179; selects Beatty to command battle cruiser squadron, 116; supports Beatty, 371, 388; views on cruisers, 373; Chairman of Chiefs of Staff Committee, 381; Chancellor of the Exchequer, 401, 402
Churchill, Lady Gwendeline, 129
Cinderella, 129
Cleopatra, H.M.S., rams enemy destroyer, 213
Clynes, Rt. Hon. J. R., 395
Coaling ship, 88
Coast patrols, vigilance of, 223
'Coat trailing,' 140
Coates, Rt. Hon. J. G., 411
Collective security, 376, 378
Colonies, German, Beatty's view, 329, 469
Colville, Admiral Hon. Sir Stanley, 11, 12, 16, 18, 19, 20, 22, 24, 44, 61, 106
Combined operations, 296, 418
Commanding officers under Beatty at Jutland, list of, Appendix IV
Committee of Imperial Defence, 379, 380
Communications, sea, defence of, 360, 380
Communications, signal, see under Signal
Compton Verney, Warwickshire, the home of Mr. Tree, 44
Construction, naval, 271, 408
Continental military mind, 329, 337
Controversial points, 260, 265, 267, 268, 269, 271
Convoy, Beatty starts a system, 295, 312, 448; surface attacks on, 297; battleship escort for, 301; success of system, 305
Cook's Gorse, Beatty meets future wife, 80
Coolidge, Mr. Calvin (U.S.A.), 368
Co-operation with Naval Staff, 296, 449; between ministries, 449
Co-ordination of fighting services, 380, 381
Corbett, Sir Julian, account of Jutland, 357
Cordite flash, 232, 252, 273
Corfe, Rev. C. J., 11
Cornwallis, Admiral Lord, 281
Coronel, battle of, 161
Cotillion, dance, 409

Cottesmore Hunt, 371
Coué, Dr. E., 386
Courage, Mrs. M. F., 3, 5, 77
Courageous, H.M.S., 302
Court of Enquiry into loss of convoy, 298
Cousins, Mr. R. A., 52, 61
Cowan, Admiral Sir Walter, Bt., 2, 11, 13, 24, 26, 40, 77, 198, 291, 303, 418
Cradock, Rear-Admiral Sir Christopher, 48, 106, 161, 180
Craig, Midshipman A. W., 11, 12
Cressy, H.M.S., 156
Crewe, Lord, 96
Criticism, 325, 471
Cromarty, 108, 139, 166
Cromwell, 463
'Crossing the Bar,' 428
Cruisers, Beatty's views on tactical employment of, 272; Britain's need for, 369, 372, 470; Labour Government accepts Beatty's demand for, 373; Beatty offers to resign, 373, 404
Culme-Seymour, Admiral Sir Michael, 15
Cunningham, Admiral of the Fleet Viscount, 361
Curzon, Lord, of Kedleston, 314, 377, 393
Curzon-Howe, Admiral Hon. Sir Asshe-ton, 97
Cust, Captain Sir Charles, 11, 123
Custance, Admiral Sir R., 126
Cyril, Grand Duke, 291

Daily Telegraph, 394, 403, 426
Dal, Sirdar's steamer at Fashoda, 39
Dannreuther, Commander H. E., 252
Danzig, German cruiser, 146
Dardanelles, 296
Davies, Canon, 413
Day, Captain S. M. (R.N.R.), 290
de Robeck, Admiral Sir John, 275, 286, 296, 316
Dead reckoning ('D.R.'), 202
'Death ride,' 329
Decentralisation of command, 278
Defence, H.M.S., sunk at Jutland, 251, 272
Delaware, U.S.S., 300
Dengler, Dr., 386
Department of Scientific Research, 360
Depew, Mr. Chauncey, U.S.A., 367
Derby, The, 191, 389
Derfflinger, German battle cruiser, 173, 185, 229; sinks *Invincible*, 251; a wreck, 255
Dering, Sir Herbert, 400
Dervishes, 18–38
Desborough, Lord, 402
Despatches, extracts from: Kitchener on the Nile, 22, 40; Seymour in China, 71; Beatty at Heligoland, 148, at Jutland, 229, 234, 258;

Despatches—*continued*.
Jellicoe at Jutland, 249, 257, 266, 271
Destroyers, at Heligoland, 144; at Dogger Bank, 185; at Jutland, 233, 237, 254, 261; Beatty's views on, 277, 279
Dewar, Vice-Admiral K. G. B., 358
Dewar, Captain A. C., 358
Diaries, Nile, 24–27; China, 50–69
Digby-Bell, Surgeon-Commander K., 307
Dingley Hall, Lady Beatty dies at, 418
Divorce decree, A. M. Tree *v.* E. F. Tree, 82
Dockers' strike, 397
Dockland settlements, 423
Dogger Bank, battle of, 182–197; comment on, 195, 197, 403
Dogger Bank shoal, 169
Donaldson, Midshipman, killed at Tientsin, 51, 60, 64
Dongola, 20
Dorward, General R. F., 64, 68
Dover, 96
Drake, Sir Francis, 274
Drax, Admiral Hon. Sir Plunkett-Ernle-Erle, 120, 153, 179, 209, 276
Dreadnought, H.M.S., 91
Dress, 207, 209, 363
Dreyer, Admiral Sir F., 273, 276, 448
Duchess of York, H.R.H., 398
Dufferin, Lord, 397
Duke of Connaught, H.R.H., 399
Duke of Sutherland, 403
Duke of York, H.R.H., 392
Dunboyne Castle, home of Beatty's mother, 2
Duncan, Admiral, 430
Dundee, H.M.S., 290
Dunrobin Castle, 87

E42, British submarine, 310
Economy, 352, 360, 402, 410, 420
Edinburgh, Admiral H.R.H. Duke of, 7
Edinburgh City, 352
Edinburgh University, 351; Lord Rector's address, 454
Ednam, Viscountess, 398
Edward VII, H.M. King, meets Mrs. Beatty, 98
Egypt, 18
El Teb, gunboat, 18; capsizes, 24
Ellerton, Captain W., 358
Embarrassing incident, 151
Empire, importance of naval defence of, 352, 403, 457, 465
Enchantress, H.M.S., see Admiralty yacht
Engadine, H.M.S., seaplane carrier, 182, 224
'Engage the enemy more closely,' Nelson's signal not in signal book, 190

'Englishman's Home,' a play, 91
Enterprise, German lack of, 139, 154, 157, 175, 214, 236
Ersberger, Herr, 341
Esdaile, Midshipman F. S. D., 51; killed at Tientsin, 66
Evan-Thomas, Admiral Sir Hugh, 222; at Jutland, 225–251; Beatty's tribute to, 268
Expeditionary Force, British, 90, 138, 139, 160

Falkland Islands, battle of, 164
Falmouth, H.M.S., 141, 170, 229, 253; sunk, 274
Fame, H.M.S., 50
Fashoda incident, 38
Fate, 107, 317
Fateh, gunboat, 19, 31; Beatty takes command, 25; passes Fourth Cataract, 26; at Omdurman, 36; to Fashoda, 39
Fearless, H.M.S., 144
Field, Sir Frederick, Admiral of the Fleet, 44, 73
Field, Mr. Marshall, 44, 77, 81
Field, Mrs. Marshall, 409
Fifth battle squadron, 222–251; comment on, 268
Filson Young, 123, 179, 403
Firth of Forth, 211, 288
Fisher, Admiral of the Fleet Lord, 85, 94, 112, 114, 160, 179, 382; see also Letters
Fisher, Admiral Sir W. W., 335
Fitton, Captain H. G., 28
Fleet Air Arm, control of, 360; Beatty's concern for, 426
Florida, U.S.S., 300
Foch, Marshal, fails to appreciate naval war effort, 330; overruled by Supreme War Council, 340; in U.S.A., 367
Fog, 8, 98, 214, 272, 288, 309, 345
Frankfort, German cruiser, 245
Frauenlob, German cruiser, 144; sunk, 259
Frederick the Great, 177
Freedom of cities, 351
Freedom of the seas, 340
Fremantle, Admiral Sir S., 109
French, Field Marshal Lord, 126, 292
French Navy, 127
Frewen Lieutenant O., 146
Friday the thirteenth, 165
Fried eggs and bacon, 9
Frigates, Nelson's need for, 375
Fripp, Sir Alfred, 161, 315, 418
Fruits of victory at sea, 336

*G*38, German destroyer, 261
*G*39, German destroyer, embarks Admiral Hipper at Jutland, 252

Galatea, H.M.S., 226
Gardner, Major B. C. (R.M.), 277
Geddes, Sir Eric, 298, 362, 449; Report, 370
Geneva, 375, 400, 415
George V, H.M. King, 11, 315, 388, 402; meets Mrs. Beatty, 98; visits fleet, 111, 131, 295, 318, 397, 407; dines with Beatty, 414
German fighting qualities, 152; character, 411; see also under Enterprise
German Navy Act of 1900, 85
Gibbs, Midshipman V. F., 51
Gibraltar, Beatty's views on, 87, 113; hunting, 101; air defence of, 379
Glencross, Lieutenant J. B., scheme for destroying submarines, 204
Glorious, H.M.S., 302
Gneisenau, German cruiser, 198
'Gold Bridge,' famous racehorse, 425
Gompers, Mr. Samuel, 326
Goodenough, Admiral W. E., 142, 166, 171, 184; exemplary cruiser work, 186, 230, 237, 243, 253, 272; night encounter, 259; report on naval pay, 350
Good Hope, H.M.S., 180
Gordon, Major W. S. (R.E.), 24, 40
Gourko, S.S., 'the theatre ship,' 306
Grand Fleet, in war plan, 135; vulnerability in harbour, 139, 157; formation at sea, 140; at Jutland, 245–261; high morale, 274; battle orders, 277, 278, 280; readiness for battle, 294, 297, 305; reaction to victory, 341; escorts German fleet into Firth of Forth, 347
Grand Duchesses, 129
Grand National, 3, 352
Grantully Castle, 386, 417
Grasset, Admiral, 388
Green, Captain J. F. E., 269
Green, Engineer-Captain Sir Percy, 153
Greenwich Royal Naval College, 12
Grey, Rt. Hon. Sir Edward, 96
Grillions Club, 388, 393
Grint, Captain W., 427
Grosser Kurfurst, German battleship, 242
Grosvenor, Lady Henry, 178
Grosvenor Square, 386, 487
Guards, Brigade of, 411
Guest night, 129
Gunnery, 87, 98, 119, 163, 186, 193, 203, 211, 251, 269, 270, 290, 316
Guy, Midshipman B. J. D., 51, 72, 73, 79

Hafir, action, 20
Hafir, gunboat, 36
Haig, Field Marshal Lord, 325
Haldane, Lord, 96, 393
Hall Barn, 402
Hall, Rear-Admiral W. R., 153, 178

Halliday, Major L. S. T. (R.M.), 73
Hamilton, Lieutenant F. T., 11
Hampshire, H.M.S., 291
Hampton Roads, U.S.A., 295
Hankey, Lord, 381
Hanover Lodge, 111, 386; sold, 406
Hardy, H.M.S., 167
Harder, Captain von, of the *Lützow*, 261
Harper, Captain J. E., report on Jutland, 357
Hartlepool attacked, 169
Harvey, Major F. J. W. (R.M.L.I.), 232, 252
Harwich, advanced base, 135; German submarines interned at, 347
Hase, Commander von, 230, 236, 251
Hawke, H.M.S., 178
Heathfield Horse, 1
Heidelberg University, 1
Heligoland in armistice terms, 339
Heligoland Bight, battle of, 142; results, 151, 157
Hertzog, Rt. Hon., 411
High explosives, curious effect, 262
High frequency direction finding, 202
High Seas Fleet, remains in harbour, 140; restrictions on, 151, 174; increased activity, 218; at Jutland, 237–261; operates with submarines and Zeppelins, 273; influence on submarine war, 294, 297, 333; last sortie, 310; mutiny, 340; surrender and internment, 341–349
Hill, Surgeon-Rear-Admiral Sir Robert, 345
Hipper, Admiral von, 214; at Scarborough, 173; at Dogger Bank, 182; at Jutland, 228–261; in last sortie, 310; High Seas Fleet disobeys order to sail, 340; love of sport, 421; Beatty's tribute, 421
History, value of, 455
Hodges, Mr. Frank, 394
Hogue, H.M.S., 150, 156
Hong Kong, 372
Hong Kong Regiment, 67
Hood, Rear-Admiral Hon. Sir H., 24, 40, 222, 245, 249
Horne, Rt. Hon. Sir Robert, 362
Horns Reef, 139, 213; High Seas Fleet escapes by, 259
Horsemanship, 11, 107, 429
Horse-racing, 3, 4, 5, 85, 87, 425
Hoste, H.M.S., sunk in collision, 284
'Hostilities only' officers and men, 350
Houghton, Mr. (U.S.A.), 368
House of Commons, 373; questions re loss of convoy, 298; tribute to Beatty, 430
House of Lords, 374, 425
Howbeck Lodge, Beatty's birthplace, 2
Hoyer, Zeppelin base, 212

Hozier, Miss, 112
Hsi-Ku arsenal, relief of, 48, 63
Hughes, Captain C. F. (U.S.N.), 300
Humber, River, 141, 160, 168, 181
Hungarian Rhapsody, 306
Hunter, General Sir A., 28
Hunting, 1, 5, 22, 23, 44, 80, 85, 101, 387, 394, 398, 416
Hussar, H.M.S., 115
Hustle, 165
Hymn of Hate, 215

Imperial Conference, 380, 397, 466
Imperialism, 395
Indefatigable, H.M.S., 119; blows up, 233
Indomitable, H.M.S., 119; tows *Lion*, 188
Inflexible, H.M.S., 153, 162, 211
Ingenohl, Admiral von, 173, 182
Inglefield, Lieutenant F. S., 11
Initiative, 192, 278, 371
Inspector of Target Practice, 119
Intelligence, see Admiralty
Invasion, 91, 297
Invergordon, 125
Invincible, H.M.S., 117, 141, 162, 211; blows up, 251
Iron Duke, H.M.S., at Jutland, 245–261; Beatty hoists flag in, 275

Jackson, Admiral of the Fleet Sir Henry, 106, 293
Jade River, 149, 165, 225
Jardine, Mathieson, Messrs., 55
Jellicoe, Admiral of the Fleet Earl, in China, 46, 73; wounded, 48, 63; Third Sea Lord, 104; manœuvres, 125; Commander-in-Chief Grand Fleet, 135, 136, 137, 142, 153, 166, 211, 278; at Jutland, 245–261; criticism of, 266; views on Jutland, 271; First Sea Lord, 274, 296, 319; issues Grand Fleet battle orders, 278; establishes anti-submarine division, 304; guest of honour with Beatty, 408; reorganises naval staff, 449
Jerram, Admiral Sir T., 246, 254, 275
Joffre, Marshal, 287
Juno, H.M.S., 85
Jutland, battle of: authority for account, 220; events leading to, 221; Scheer's plan, 221; Jellicoe's plan, 223; Admiralty intelligence, 223; air reconnaissance, 224, 228; Beatty's dispositions, 225; Beatty's decision on receiving first report of enemy, 227; radio reports of enemy, 227; visibility, 228, 229, 230, 240, 241, 243, 255; Beatty v. Hipper, the gun duel, 229–250; narrow escape of *Lion*, 231; British destroyers attack, 233; Fifth battle squadron joins action, 233; loss of *Indefatigable*,

Jutland—*continued.*
233; loss of *Queen Mary*, 234; Hipper breaks off action, 236; Beatty sights High Seas Fleet, 237; Hipper re-engages, 237; Beatty prevents Hipper from sighting Grand Fleet, 245, 250; Jellicoe's point of view, 245–249; enemy reports at variance, 246; battle fleets in action, 249; criticism of Beatty, 249, 267, 268; tributes to Beatty's tactics, 250, 266, 267; desperate position of German battle fleet, 250; Beatty sights Grand Fleet and proceeds to the van, 251; loss of *Invincible*, 251; *Lutzow* and *von der Tann* out of action, 252; Hipper loses his flagship, 252; German massed destroyer attack, 254; Beatty requests that leading battleships should follow him, 255; Beatty closes the enemy and re-engages, 255; defeat of German battle cruisers, 255; dispositions for the night, 258; Scheer's final thrust for home, 259; criticism of Jellicoe, 265; controversial points, 265, 267, 268, 269, 271; successful results of Beatty's tactics, 267; analysis of hits, 269; Harper report on battle, 357

Kaiser, The, 174, 226
Kambly, Mlle., 390
Kansas City, 367
Karlsrühe, German cruiser, 164
Kattegat, 304
'Keep nearer to the enemy,' 266, 429
'Keep the home fires burning,' 308
Kelly, Admiral of the Fleet Sir John, 6
Kennedy, Captain F. W., 191
Keppel, Admiral Sir Colin, 11, 24, 37, 40
Keyes, Admiral of the Fleet Lord, 55, 71, 73, 141, 149, 208, 296, 309, 316, 364, 427
Keyes, Lieutenant-Colonel Geoffrey, V.C., 316
Khalifa, 18, 31, 35, 36
Khartoum, 18, 34
Kiel, 126; discontent at, 326; canal, 294
King George V, H.M.S., 246, 254
King's College Hospital, 425
Kipling, Rudyard, 402
Knighthood, 131
Kolberg, German cruiser, 181, 184
Köln, German cruiser, 145; sunk, 149
Königsberg, German cruiser, 341
Kosheh, 19
Kronstadt, 121

Labour Government, 396; supports Beatty, 373, 405
Ladies of the stage, 13

Lambart, Midshipman Hon. L. J., 14
Lambert, Admiral C. F., 317, 322
Lancashire Fusiliers, 35
Lang Fang station, 46
Larking, Captain Dennis, 388
Lascelles, Lord, 390
Lauder, Sir Harry, 208
Laurel, H.M.S., 150, 234
Lavery, Sir John, 342
League of Nations, 370, 378, 400, 414, 419
Leake, Captain Martin, 290
Leave, 125, 207
Lee, Lord, of Fareham, 370, 389
Lerwick, 297
Letters from Beatty: to his mother, 6; to his wife, before marriage, 75–83; to his wife, before war, 87–133; to his wife, on outbreak of war, 136; to his wife, from the *Lion*, 137–218; to his wife, from the Grand Fleet, 284–292, 312–327; to his wife, as First Sea Lord, 367, 371, 373, 386–414; to a friend, on the end of the war, 328; to a friend, describing his meeting with German envoys regarding surrender of their fleet, 343; to a friend, on leaving the Admiralty, 415; to Mr. Winston Churchill, 158; to Lord Fisher, 198; to Lord Jellicoe, 222, 269; to the Admiralty, 304; to Admiral Lord Wester Wemyss, 330–341; to Mr. Walter Long, 363; to Admiral Walter Cowan and the Duchess of Rutland on the death of Lady Beatty, 418, 419; to a religious society, 423; to the *Daily Telegraph*, 426; to Sir Edward Carson, 446; to Sir Eric Geddes, 449
Letters to Beatty: from Princess Marie, 10; from Captain E. H. Bayly, 69; from Prince Louis of Battenberg, 104; from Lord Fisher, 163, 196–200; from Lord Charles Beresford, 264, 348; from Admiral of the Fleet Sir H. Jackson, 293; from H.M. King George V, 296; from Admiral Lord Wester Wemyss, 330–341; from Admiral W. R. Hall, 349; from Admiralty, on leaving the Grand Fleet, 353; from Sir Maurice Hankey, on leaving the Admiralty, 381; from Mr. Stanley Baldwin, on leaving the Admiralty, 383; from Mr. W. C. Bridgeman, on leaving the Admiralty, 384; from Mr. Winston Churchill, 401; from Sir Edward Carson, 446; from Sir Eric Geddes, 449
'Levanter,' 379

Lhoyd-Owen, Midshipman J. H., 234
Light cruiser reconnaissance in low
  visibility, 253, 272
Lightfoot, H.M.S., 212
Lincoln Regiment, 33
Lion, H.M.S., Beatty's flagship, 116;
  at Kronstadt, 130; at Heligoland,
  141; at Dogger Bank, 188; towed
  to Rosyth, 191; at Jutland, 225;
  narrow escape of, 232; wireless shot
  away, 233, 260; burial service at
  sea, 262
Liverpool, H.M.S., 141, 152
Liverpool, city, 454
Lloyd George, Rt. Hon. David, 111,
  296, 314, 372, 387
Locarno Pact, 412
Loch Ewe, 139
Loch-na-Keal, 157
Loder-Symonds, Captain F. P., 213
Loftus-Jones, Commander W., 167;
  posthumous V.C., 289
London season, 99, 131
Londonderry House, 394
Long, Rt. Hon. Walter, 356, 362
'Long Forties,' 223
Longmore, Air Chief Marshal Sir
  Arthur, 124
Lough Swilly, 157
Lovat, Simon, 402
Lowestoft, H.M.S., 141
Lowestoft attacked, 218
Lowry, Admiral Sir R., 205
Luard, Lieutenant H. du C., 51
Luck, 322
Luke, Major E. V. (R.M.), 51, 56, 57, 58
Lurcher, H.M.S., 145
Lutzow, German battle cruiser, 198,
  229; a wreck, 252; sunk, 261
Lydall, Rev. C. W., killed at Jut land,
  262
Lynx, H.M.S., 167

MacDonald, Rt. Hon. Ramsay, 373,
  382, 393
Macdonald, Sir Claude, 45
Macdonald, General Sir Hector, 37
Mackenzie-King, Rt. Hon., 411
McCarthy, Able Seaman, 72
McKenna, Rt. Hon. Reginald, 94, 96,
  104, 107
McLennan, Mr., Canadian senator, 326
Madden, Admiral of the Fleet Sir
  Charles, 101, 275, 284, 303, 382, 392
Magazines, vulnerability of, 186, 193,
  271, 273
Mahan, Captain A. T., 422, 455
Mahdi, 37
Mahmud, Dervish leader, 26, 32, 34
Mainz, German cruiser, sunk, 145
Malaya, H.M.S., 241, 243
Mall House, 385
Malta, 8, 87, 114

Maori kilt, 269
Mar and Kelly, Countess of, 409
March through London, 100
Marchand, Major, 38
Marie, Queen of Roumania, 9, 399
Markgraf, German battleship, 242
Markham, Vice-Admiral H., 16
Marlborough, H.M.S., 246
Marriage, 75–86
Marsh, Sir Edward, 123
Marshall Hall, 402
Marten, Dr., 386
Mary Rose, H.M.S., 297
Masts and yards, 7, 15
May, Admiral Sir W. H., 92, 95
Medusa, H.M.S., 212
Melik, gunboat, 36
Memorial service for battle of Jutland,
  317
Merchant losses, 274, 292
Merchant Navy, 44, 111, 323, 456
'Merrie England,' 306
Metemmeh, fort, 28
Metemmeh, gunboat, 18, 20, 26, 36
Meurer, Rear-Admiral Hugo, accepts
  Beatty's terms, 341–347
Milford Haven, Commander Marquis
  of, 160
Milne, Field Marshal Lord, 475
Milner, Lord, 287
Minefields, in Heligoland Bight, 141,
  153, 302; off British coast, 157,
  164, 166, 312; against submarines,
  294, 297, 311; disclosure of, 331
Mine production, 294, 446
Minesweeping, 302
Mining policy, 446
Ministry of Defence, 382, 410
Ministry of Munitions, 294, 446
'Moat, The', the family home, 3
Mobilisation of the fleet, 131
Moltke, German battle cruiser, 173, 185,
  229, 257; torpedoed, 310
Monarch, H.M.S., 138
Monmouth, H.M.S., 180
Monteagle, Lord, 98
Monte Carlo, 116, 122, 407
Monument, 433
Moore, Rear-Admiral Sir Archibald,
  141, 182, 190
Mountbatten, Earl, 160, 306
Moscow, 131
Munro, Commander D. J., 158
Mussolini, 408
Mustapha Kemal, 377
Mutiny of High Seas Fleet, 274, 340

Napier, Rear-Admiral T., 228, 303
Napoleon, 324, 464
Narborough and *Opal*, destroyers, total
  loss, 322
Narrative of the Battle of Jutland, 359,
  400

INDEX

Narrow escape at Scarborough, 174
Nasir, gunboat, 19, 26, 36
Natal, H.M.S., 320
National Physical Laboratory, 360
National Playing Fields Association, 425
Naval Brigade, 178
Naval Review, 399
Naval Staff, 356, 471, 473
Negro, H.M.S., sunk in collision, 285
Nelson, Admiral Lord, 32, 96, 101, 190, 197, 270, 281, 324, 375, 422, 430
Nelson, H.M.S., 370
Nerissa, H.M.S., 236
Nestor, H.M.S., 236
'New Light on Jutland,' 270
New York, 367
New York, U.S.S., 300
New Zealand, 379, 469
New Zealand, H.M.S., 130, 141, 155, 185, 229, 269; in collision, 215
Newcombe, Lieutenant R. U. A. (R.E.), 24
Newmarket, 98, 425
Nicator, H.M.S., 236
Nicholson, Rear-Admiral W. C., 360
Nicolas, Grand Duke, 291
Nieh, Marshal, 53
Nile campaign, 18
Nomad, H.M.S., 236
Norddeutsch W/T station, 140
Norway, 309, 311
Nottingham, H.M.S., 141, 170; sunk, 274

Oak, H.M.S., 345
Obolensky, Prince, 406
O'Connor, T. P., 402
Offensive, the, 210, 236, 277, 283, 349
Oldfield, Captain H. (R.M.A.), 20
Oliver, Admiral of the Fleet Sir Henry, 183, 296, 410
Omdurman, battle of, 35
Operation on Beatty, 77
Opportunity, 17, 107, 313
Optical instruments, German superiority, 271
Orders in Council for Beatty's promotions, 104, 354
Orlando, H.M.S., 50
Osman Digna, Dervish leader, 34
Ostend, occupation of, 142; blocking of, 308
Overseas trade, defence of, 374

'Pack up your troubles,' 308
Pakenham, Admiral Sir W., 100, 166, 198, 276, 284, 303
Palma, Marjorca, 407
Parity, 369, 375
Partridge, H.M.S., sunk in defence of convoy, 297
Pastfield, Rev. J. L., 270
Patience, 289
Patrol, H.M.S., 168
Pay, 350

Peace, 336; at any price, 366; blessing of, 456
Pekin, threat to legations, 45; Seymour's attempt to relieve, 46
Pellew, H.M.S., 297
Pembroke dockyard, 472
Penarth, S.S., 45
Pentland Firth, 300, 318
Persius, Captain, German critic, 263
Phillimore, Admiral Sir R., 11, 51, 68, 303
Piccadilly, 13, 118, 322
Picnics, 9
Piggott, Captain W. A., 14
Pilgrims, the, 367, 389
Pillau, German cruiser, 245
Plotting enemy positions at sea, 202
Pohl, Admiral von, 193
Point to Point, 424
Poldhu, W/T station, 140, 176
Pollen, Lieutenant J. F., 358
Pollenza Bay, 407
Polo, 8, 30, 87, 424
Pompeii, 114,
Poole, Engineer, R.N., 24, 40
Portsmouth, 106; corporation records, 355
Posterity, 354
Pound, Admiral of the Fleet Sir Dudley, 400, 450
Powell, Lieutenant G. B., 52
Powlett, Midshipman A. T., 11, 77
Press, 318, 374; campaign against Jellicoe resented by Beatty, 321; against Beatty, 394, 409
Press-gang, 26
Prince George, 399
Prince of Wales, 387, 399
Princess Royal, 390
Princess Royal, H.M.S., 117, 141, 162, 164, 229, 240
Promotions, special, to commander, 23, 41; to captain, 73; rear-admiral, 104; admiral of the fleet, 354; see also Appendix II
Publicity, dislike of, 123, 180, 354, 431
Pyramid prophecies, 410
Pytchley Hunt, 4

Queen, H.M.S., 91
Queen Elizabeth, H.M.S., 275, 288, 299, 306, 342, 416, 453
Queen Mary, H.M.S., 119, 136, 141, 229; blows up, 234
Queen's Hall, 392
Queenstown, 93
Quorn, The, 398, 424, 428

Radar, 175, 201
Radio, method of reporting enemy, 201; liability to error, 201, 240, 242, 254; direction finding, 201, 225, 247, 310

Raiders, 290
Raleigh, Sir Walter, 455
Rangefinders, inaccuracy of, 120, 229
Ratapico, trawler, sinks submarine, 204
Record of services, 434
Regensburg, German cruiser, 236
Rehearsal of speeches, 131
Reigate Priory, 386, 392, 406
Relative positions of ships at sea, 201, 240, 248
Religion, 348, 413, 423
Repulse, H.M.S., 303
Resignation, 370; Beatty forces hand of Government, 373, 403, 409
Results of battle of Heligoland, 151, 157; of Dogger Bank, 193
Rewards and distinctions, 436
Richmond, Captain H. W., 324
Risks, 150, 278, 301, 432
Robertson, Field Marshal Sir W., 296, 323
Robinson, Mrs., forecasts Beatty's career, 79, 102
Robinson, Commander Hope, 18, 20
Rocket detachment, Beatty lands with, 33
Rodman, Admiral Hugh (U.S.N.), 326, 347; views on command, 299; tribute to, 452
Rodney, H.M.S., 370
Roon, German cruiser, 167
Rosebery, Earl of, 100, 394
'Roses of Picardy,' 308
Rosyth, 108; poorly defended, 139, 158, 285; becomes main base, 308; dockyard, 472
Rosyth Force at Jutland, list of commanding officers, 437
Royal Air Force, 379
Royal Marines, 51, 56, 59, 62, 64, 69, 231, 344, 412
Royal Marine Artillery, 40
Royal Marine band, 306
Royal Naval Staff College, 105, 209, 220, 358
Royal Navy, political value of, 378; national tradition, 425, 430; spirit of, 431
Ruby, H.M.S., 12, 14
Rugby, 4
Rugby football, 6, 398
Rum runners, 368
Russell, Sir Charles, 402
Russian ballet, 307
Russian characteristics, Beatty's view, 57, 94, 387
Russian colonel compliments British seamen, 59; proposes to evacuate Tientsin, 62
Russian hospitality, 128
Rutland, Lieutenant F. S., flies seaplane at Jutland, 228
Ryan, Captain C. P., 205, 313, 448

Sadleir, Nicholas, 2
'Sailors' and Workmen's' delegates, 342
St. Paul's Bay, Malta, 16
St. Paul's Cathedral, 392, 428
St. Petersburg, 129
'Salt of the earth,' 407, 416
San Antonio Palace, Malta, 9
Sandford, Lieutenant C. S., 252
Sargent, John, 100
Sassoon, Sir Philip, 386
Scales, Captain A. (U.S.N.), 300
Scapa Flow, 108, 183; poorly defended, 137, 158
Scarborough attacked, 168–175
Scharnhorst, German cruiser, 164; battleship, 361
Scheer, Admiral von, 212, 218; at Jutland, 220–261; sortie with Zeppelins and submarines, 273; last sortie, 309
Schleswig-Holstein, Major Prince Christian of, 40
Schwerdt, Lieutenant R., 118, 128
Scott, Admiral Sir Percy, 361
Sea Power, 334, 336, 352, 375, 414, 425, 455, 465
Sea time, 90, 104
Seamanship, 8, 14
Seaplane carriers, limitations of, 212, 225
Secretary, Admiral's, duties of, 210
Selbjörns Fiord, 309
Selbourne, Lord, 362
'Seven Bell Tea,' 262
Seydlitz, German battle cruiser, 173, 185, 229; a wreck, 252, 261
Seymour, Admiral of the Fleet Sir Edward, 45, 48
Seymour, Commander Ralph, 152, 190, 210, 320
Sforza, Count, 377
Shark, H.M.S., 167
Shebaliya Island action, 31
Sheelah, steam yacht, 129, 133, 355, 416; as hospital ship, 161
Sheikh, gunboat, 36
Shell, poor quality of British, 234, 269, 273, 276, 290, 304; new shell supplied, 329
Shendi, 31
Shields, Marmaduke, surgeon, 75, 418
Shirinski, Russian colonel, 48, 63
Shooting, 417
Signal communications, at Heligoland, 143, 150; at Scarborough, 170; at Dogger Bank, 190; at Jutland, 227, 239, 240, 255, 257, 260; with U.S. battle squadron, 300
Signal log, 421
Sims, Admiral W. S. (U.S.N.), 301
Singapore, 372, 379, 394, 397, 405, 468
Sinn Fein, 378
Sirdar, see Kitchener
Sitwell, Major, 31

Sixth battle squadron (U.S.A.), 300, 301, 305
Skagerrack, 215, 222, 297
Smith, Dr. Frank, 360
Smith-Dorrien, General Sir Horace, 36–39
Smoke, 185, 227, 272, 300
Snowden, Rt. Hon. Philip, 394, 396
Somerville, Admiral of the Fleet Sir James, 277
South, George, boatswain, 12
Southampton, H.M.S., 141; sinks *Mainz*, 146, 170, 184; reports High Seas Fleet, 237; sinks *Frauenlob*, 259
Southend, 100
Southwark Cathedral, 413
Sparks, Lieutenant J. B., 24, 40
Spee, Admiral von, 164
Speed, Beatty's views on, 119, 149, 185, 288; Fisher's views, 199; use of, 297
Spickernell, Sir Frank, 129, 131, 204, 210, 342, 364, 366, 368, 378, 386, 389, 425
Staff organisation, 210, 356; see also Naval Staff
Staff work, defects at Heligoland, 143, 145
Standardt, Russian imperial yacht, 131
Star, The, newspaper, 427
Startin, Lieutenant J., 11
Staveley, Lieutenant C. M., 24, 40
'Steam tactics,' 16
Stettin, *Stralsund* and *Strassburg*, German cruisers, 144, 145, 146
Stevenson, Lieutenant A. G. (R.E.), 24, 40
Stirling, Lieutenant A. J. B., 51
Stoner, Harry, 402
Strain of war, 154, 163, 176, 216, 289
Strategy, 32, 108, 112, 157, 162, 183, 202, 328
Strikes, 378, 397
Strongbow, H.M.S., 297
Strutt, Captain Hon. A., 242, 262, 276, 320
Stuart-Wortley, Major Hon. E., 28, 40
Sturdee, Admiral Sir Doveton, 101, 162, 275, 316, 320
Submarines, British, in war plan, 135; at Heligoland, 145; at Dogger Bank, 183; in anti-submarine operations, 204, 294; in Grand Fleet battle plan, 277; torpedo *Westfalen*, 274, and *Moltke*, 310
Submarines, German, first appearance, 138; early counter-measures, 139, 204, 294; sink three cruisers, 156; influence at battle of Dogger Bank, 189; indication of German fleet movements, 218, 273, 335; co-operate with High Seas Fleet, 274; unrestricted submarine warfare, 287, 293; counter-measures, 295, 335; defeat of, 311

Suffolk, H.M.S., 88
Sultan, gunboat, 36
Sunset, bugle call, 349
Superstition, 81, 126, 413
Supreme War Council, 335, 337, 420
Surrender of German fleet, 349
Sutherland, Duchess of, 137
Sylt, 212

Tactical school, 221
Tactics, 118, 185, 250, 278; results at Jutland, 267
Taku forts, captured, 55
Talbot, Captain H. F. G., 24, 35, 40, 317
Tamai, gunboat, 18, 20, 26, 28, 36; rescues Beatty, 25
Taranaki, trawler, sinks submarine, 204
Task of the Navy in war, 134
Tattenham corner, 191
Taylor, Engineer-Captain G. C., 196
Temperance, 319
'Ten-year rule,' 376
Terrible, H.M.S., 62
Terschelling, 139, 141
Texas, U.S.S., 300
Thanksgiving service for victory, 348
'Theatre ship,' 306
Thomas, Rt. Hon. J. H., 395
Thunderer, H.M.S., 392
Tientsin, Beatty lands for defence of, 48; siege, 46–69; capture of Native City, 69
Tiger, H.M.S., 162, 185, 188, 229, 234
Times, The, 105, 394
'Tip and run,' 298
Tipperary, 163
Tirpitz, German battleship, 361
Tirpitz, Grand Admiral von, 270
Titanic, disaster, 111
Togo, Admiral, 198
Tollemache, Henry, 23
Torpedo attack, 236, 280; 'turn away' from, 235, 254, 279
Tradition, 343
Trafalgar, battle of, 190, 288
Trafalgar, H.M.S., 15
Tree, A. Ronald, 82
Tree, Arthur M., 44, 78
Tree, Ethel, meets Beatty, 44; marries him, 83; see also Beatty
Trenchard, Marshal of the Air Force Lord, 475
Trewin, Paymaster G. S., 228
Tribute from the House of Commons, 430
Trondheim, Norway, 157
Troubridge, Rear-Admiral E. C. T., 176
Tryon, Admiral Sir George, 15
Tsar of Russia, 129, 291
Tsarina, 129, 291
Tsarskoye Selo, 129

Turf Club, 427
Turkey, 317
Tuscania, transport, torpedoed, 323
Tyne, river, 191
Typical letters from Beatty to First Lord, Appendix VI
Tyrwhitt, Admiral of the Fleet Sir R., 11, 135, 141, 165, 183, 212, 344; accepts surrender of German submarines, 347

Undaunted, H.M.S., in collision, 213
Unfortunate misunderstanding, 171
Union flag, 355, 428
United States, President of, 329, 365; cavalry, 367; hospitality, 367; unknown warrior, 367; policy, 369, 378
United States Navy, provide battle squadron, 299; easy co-operation with, 301; strengthen anti-submarine forces, 302; 'comrades of the Mist,' 368; tribute to, 452
Unpalatable truth, 276

V5, German destroyer, 189
V187, German destroyer, 145
Valiant, H.M.S., 312
Vanguard, H.M.S., blows up at anchor, 320
Vanity Fair, 2
Vaterland, German liner, 164
Vestal virgins, 368
Victoria, H.M. Queen, 2
Victoria and Albert, Royal yacht, 14, 111, 407, 417
Victoria Cross, 23, 72, 79, 367
Villeneuve, Admiral, 288
Vindex, H.M.S., seaplane carrier, 212
Visibility, 150, 170, 229, 230, 240, 243, 255; peculiar phenomenon in North Sea, 215
von der Tann, German battle cruiser, 173, 229; ineffective, 253
Vyl lightship, 212

Walcott, Captain C. C., 48
Wall Street, 367
Walsh, Rt. Hon. Stephen, 395
War, study of, 8, 32, 105, 108; plan, 134, 140; outbreak of, 135
War Cabinet, 304, 335
War course, 106
War plans, 108, 112, 134, 183
Warrender, Admiral Sir George, 111, 126, 166
Warrior, H.M.S., 272
Warspite, H.M.S., 199, 306
War Staff, 109, 110; see also Naval Staff
Warwickshire Hunt, 4
Warwickshire Regiment, 33

Washington, 367
Washington, Captain T. (U.S.N.), 300
Washington Conference, 365, 369, 466
Waterloo, 1
Watkins, Mrs., 90
Wealth, 83, 418
Webb, Admiral Sir Richard, 11
Wei-hai-wei Regiment, 64
Welch Regiment, 63
Welfare committee, 432
Wellington on Sea Power, 458
Welsh Fusiliers, 62, 67, 69
Welsh miners, 306
Wemyss, Admiral of the Fleet Lord Wester, 90, 98, 330–341, 353, 357, 450
Wemyss Castle, 87
West, William, Master, Merchant Navy, 45
Westfalen, German battleship, torpedoed, 274
Westmorland, 129
Westphalian Duelling Corps, 1
Wexford Hunt, 1
Whitby, 169
White House, 367
Whiting, H.M.S., 50
Wiesbaden, German cruiser, 245
Wiley, Captain H. (U.S.N.), 300
'Will to win,' 235, 271, 292, 324
Willoughby, Lieutenant Hon. Peter, 180
Wilson, Admiral of the Fleet Sir A. K., 16, 85, 109, 183
Wilson, Assistant Paymaster H. G., 51
Wilson, President Woodrow, 334
Wireless Telegraphy, introduction to fleet, 89
Wives, 161, 215
'Wobbly Eight,' 183
Wogack, Russian colonel, 57
Woodley, Mr., Admiral's steward, 130
Worcester Races, 4
Wright, Lieutenant P. N., 52, 58
Wyoming, U.S.S., 300

Yarrow, Messrs., 20
Y.M.C.A., 4, 8
Ymuiden, 274
York, Archbishop of, 393
York, Duchess of, 398
York, Duke of, 392
Ypres, 296

Zafir, gunboat, 19, 26
Zaki, Dervish leader, 34
'Zakuska,' 128
Zeebrugge, 296, 308, 309
Zeppelin airships, 192, 212, 224, 261, 274, 312
Zoo, 364
'ZZ,' the last operation, 440